Comments on Previous Editions

"There isn't another book that gives as full and accurate a portrait of reggae culture. This is a biography no serious pop fan should be without."

—J. D. CONSIDINE, *The Baltimore Sun*

"The strange island of Jamaica with its obeah spells, cosmic coincidences, and tragic fatalism is rendered with a gifted, accurate touch that recalls the best of García Marquez."

—CHRIS SALEWICZ, *The Face*

"Aloof, cagey, proud, funny, Marley has been made human in this book. He's no longer just a fierce-eyed legend who died too soon. . . . One of the most vivid portraits of a pop artist ever written."

—KEN TUCKER, *Knight-Ridder Newspapers*

"*Catch a Fire* should stand as the best available document on his life and work."

—MARC LEEPSON, *USA Today*

"The definitive book on Bob Marley."

—LISA ROBINSON, *The New York Post*

"Because of Mr. White's extensive research, this biography is not only informative but also absorbing."

—JON WEINER, *The New York Times Book Review*

"Superb . . . As fine and moving a biography as Marley could have wanted."

—*New Musical Express*

"Excellent . . . White has made *Catch a Fire* a journey into Jamaica, the land that created Bob Marley, and the sound of its people."

—THULANI DAVIS, *Essence*

"White has a deep appreciation for reggae's immediacy, hypnotic power and contradictions. . . . An exhaustively researched labor of love."

—DON McLEESE, *Chicago Sun-Times*

"Probably the finest biography ever written about a popular musician."

—*San Francisco Chronicle*

DAVID BURNETT (CONTACT)

Catch a Fire

The Life of Bob Marley

Revised and Enlarged

TIMOTHY WHITE

St. Martin's Griffin

New York

 For information, address St. Martin's Press, 175 Fifth Avenue, New York, N.Y. 10010.

www.stmartins.com

Due to limitations of space, permissions acknowledgments appear on pages 460–61.

Designed by Lucy Albanese

The Library of Congress has cataloged the Henry Holt edition as follows:

White, Timothy, 1952–2002

Catch a fire : the life of Bob Marley / Timothy White.—Newly rev. and enlarged.

p. cm.

Includes bibliographical references, discography, and index.

ISBN 978-0-8050-8086-5

1. Marley, Bob. 2. Singers—Jamaica—Biography. 3. Reggae musicians—Jamaica—Biography. I. Title.

ML420.M3313W5 1998

782.421646'092—dc21

[B]

98-6305

D 20

Contents

Photograph sections follow pages 103, 169, and 241.

Acknowledgments

First and foremost, my gratitude to Bob Marley. He made himself available for numerous interviews over the seven years before his death and always answered even my most trivial questions fully and honestly while at the same time preserving the ineffability of his character.

I would also like to thank the Marley, Malcolm, Willoughby and Brown families for their time and assistance, particularly Rita Marley, David Malcolm and Lurline Brown Malcolm. But most of all, thanks to Cedella Marley Booker. After three years of searching (Bob liked to tell people his mother lived in Africa), I found Mrs. Booker in Wilmington, Delaware, in the winter of 1977 and she granted me the first in-depth interview she had ever given. She sat for four subsequent interviews between 1977 and 1982 and tolerated no less than thirty often lengthy follow-up calls in the summer and fall of 1982. She is a woman of enormous charity and courage, and I am deeply grateful for her generous assistance and support.

Thanks also to the many others who allowed me to interview them repeatedly over the years, and who took me into their homes and their confidence, particularly Chris Blackwell, who was never less than a great sport. I am also indebted, of course, to Peter Tosh, Bunny Wailer, Aston Barrett (for the great interview in Harry J's Studio the night that Bob recorded "Jah Live"), Al Anderson (for all the ringing rock with Chuck B. in Jersey back when he played with the Red Bred, and for getting me *in* to the "Jah Live" session that hot Kingston evening) and to all the rest of the Wailers. Others who gave me their time over the years for interviews were: Glen Adams (thanks for hooking me up with the elusive Coxsone); Clement Dodd; Lee Perry; Lawrence "Jack Ruby" Lindo; Justin Hines; Ras Morris Fabian Clark of Clarendon; bush doctor Nernelly of St. Catherine; Burning Spear; Ernest Ranglin, the King of Ska Guitar; Roland Alphonso; Frederick "Toots" Hibbert and the Maytals; Tommy Cowan; Sonia Pottinger; Seeco Patterson; Jimmy Cliff; Ras Michael and the Sons of Negus; Big Youth; Aswad; Gilly; Lee Jaffe; Mikey Dread; Jah Malla; Duckie Simpson of Black Uhuru; Countryman; Dickie Jobson; Diane Jobson; Bird; Joe Higgs; Dream; Wayne Perkins, the White Wailer; Neville Garrick; Howard Bloom; and numerous others.

I want to extend a special thank-you to Jeff Walker, former publicity director of Island Records, a loyal, reliable friend and a valorous, principled man.

This book simply could not have been written without access to the extensive archives (historical data, tapes, articles, etc.) of Roger Steffens and Hank Holmes of "The Reggae Beat," the since cancelled weekend show on KCRW in Los Angeles—once the finest reggae radio show in America. Thanks to Hank and to Roger and his wife, Mary, for their warm hospitality and patient cooperation.

Peter Simon, the peerless reggae photographer who served as photo editor for this book, lent every kind of support a colleague could, through thick and thin. Bruce C. Fishelman, Esq., served as tail-gunner nonpareil.

A special thanks to David Steinberg, Bob and Rita's lawyer, for his cooperation and generous assistance.

Others who deserve special thanks: Mitchell Glazer, my best friend and a tireless booster who talked me into doing this book in the first place; Vivien Goldman, reggae soulmate of long standing; press agent Charles Comer, a consummate professional who helped smooth Bob Marley's path to superstardom; Charles M. Young, who guided the book through "customs"; George "Bo" Bryan, who rode shotgun; Robert Sabbag, who gave me the gift/shove of confidence; and research assistant Ken Braun, who never let me down.

I would also like to express my appreciation to Edward Seaga and Michael Manley; Olivia "Babsy" Grange, Director of Cultural Development for the Jamaican government; Jane Levenson, executive assistant to Prime Minister Edward Seaga; Anne Sabo of Sabo Associates, New York City; the Jamaican Institute; Hector Wynter and the Jamaican *Daily Gleaner* staff; the University of the West Indies, Mona Campus, Kingston; the Jamaican Consulate and the Jamaican Tourist

Board in New York City; the Research Institute for the Study of Man in New York City; the New York Public Library; Ellen Smith, head of publicity for Island Records.

Thanks to my reggae editors over the years: Harriet Fier, Barbara Downey, Paul Nelson, Peter Herbst, the folks at *Reggae News*, Terry McDonell, Susan Murcko, Alan Weitz, Jim Henke, Jane Karr, John Rockwell, Gene Sculatti, Joe Robinson, Mitchell Glazer, Greg Mitchell, Jon Pareles, John Swenson, Peter Knobler and Stephen Davis. Thanks to Vic Garbarini and Sam Holdsworth for support in the homestretch, and to Bob Merlis for being a Jah-guide from the old days.

More thanks to David Silver, Greg Scott, Dave Wilder, and to Chet Flippo and Martha Hume for kindly advice; Cameron Crowe and Bob Greenfield for cheering from the sidelines; to Chris Evans, Sam Zurich, David Susskind, Kate Simon, Adrian Boot, Jay Bergen, Rob Partridge, Perry Henzell, Denise Mills, R. B. Wilk, Gary Kenton, Maryanne Vollers, Joe Menell and Kim Gottlieb for general assistance over the years; and to Theodoros Bafaloukos, for creating *Rockers*, the finest reggae film ever made.

Thanks, as well, to all the writers who have informed, delighted and inspired me: Carl Gayle, Neil Spencer, Penny Reel, Vivien Goldman, Luke Erlich, Dr. Robert Hill, Garth White, Jon Bradshaw, Michael Thomas, Ian Fleming (on Jamaica), Lenny Kaye, Chris May, Rory Sanders, Randall Grass, Charles Shaar Murray, Idris Walters, Malu Halasa, Lester Bangs, Carol Cooper, Ed Ward, Robert Hilburn, Michael Goodwin, Adele Freedman, Ric Mentus, Ed McCormack, Rob Houghton, Ken Tucker, Courand Milloy, Milo Miles, Ray Coleman, Scotty Bennett, Michael Thelwell, Dick Hebdige, Leonard Barrett, John Milward, Robert Palmer, Kathy McKnight, John Tobler, Joseph Owens, Orlando Patterson, Steve Shapiro, Richard Cromelin, Fred Schruers, Rex Nettleford, V. S. Naipaul, Patrick Carr, Phillip Sherlock, Roz Reines, John Morthland, Crispin Cioe, Greil Marcus, Steve Morse, Tracy Nicholas, and so many more.

Deepest appreciation to Daniel Maffia for the cover painting.

Warmest thanks to my editor, Paul Bresnick, and to my agent, Erica Spellman, for the original edition. I am deeply grateful to Jim Stein, and most especially to John Macrae III for years of caring and energetic support.

Preface

This book gives itself over in an atmospheric fashion to the confluence of belief systems that informed Bob Marley. It posits that if everything soberly stated about Marley by those closest to him were true, the story would unfold as I have recorded it. However, there are no manufactured facts here. Besides my investigations of existing documents and records, which involved carefully thumbing through forty years of the Jamaican *Daily Gleaner* in the Institute of Jamaica in Kingston and the Research Institute for the Study of Man in New York City, as well as any article of consequence published in Jamaica, the United Kingdom or the United States on Jamaica, Bob Marley or reggae, the information distilled herein is based on the interviews I conducted with Bob (I spoke with him on some two dozen separate occasions) between 1975 and 1981, plus interviews I conducted over the years with other members of the Wailers, the band's producers, additional backup musicians, various other co-workers, record company executives, bodyguards and roadies, as well as family and friends. Other sources included prominent figures in the Jamaican recording industry, island politicians (who have made their own unique contributions to Jamaican music), Rasta elders, country soothsayers, backwoods preachers, social workers, sociologists, ghetto thugs and bush nannies.

There are more knotty problems confronting any journalist or biographer wading into Jamaica's history and the life of one of its sons: precise documentation is frequently hard to come by. For instance, the exact date of Bob Marley's birth may never truly be known. On his passport (No. 57778, first issued on March 6, 1964, but not used for travel purposes until February 11, 1966), Bob Marley's birthdate was listed as April 6, 1945. Cedella Marley Booker, Bob's mother, told me on several occasions that, *to the best of her recollection*, Bob was born two months earlier to the day. However, since she resided in a remote area at the time, it took her many weeks to get around to journeying to the nearest registrar to officially record the birth and, being a timid young woman, she "didn't wan' ta get in trouble wit' dem." (To this day, many poor Jamaican country and city folk are uncertain of when, where and to whom they were born.)

Several thorough searches by Jamaican archivists of all available records have yet to produce a birth certificate for Bob Marley—news his Rastafarian brethren greet with a sage nod, believing that Marley, like Emperor Haile Selassie I of Ethiopia, was never born and could not die. ("Him was de inheritor of Jah's legacy; him cyan't die. Rasta nuh fear death, because Rasta never live, an' never die.")

Similar difficulties arise when noting the release dates of most Jamaican 45 RPM and long-playing discs, since records were rarely, if ever, kept, and a 45 could be released in a number of preliminary stages before it actually reached the mainstream commercial marketplace. The release dates in this book, unless otherwise noted in the text, refer to the *Jamaican* release date, not the release date in the United Kingdom, where so many Jamaican hits are subsequently issued. This information was obtained—in most cases down to the month of release—by interviewing the record producer or the artist if possible, or both. (In the back of the book is a comprehensive discography of Wailers and their extended musical family.)

Jamaican patois is used extensively throughout the book, the rhythms of the dialect akin to that of a rubber ball bouncing down stairs and into a child's gentle grip. As for the spellings and definitions of most of the patois words threaded through the text, I am indebted to Cambridge University Press's *Dictionary of Jamaican English*, edited by F. G. Cassidy and R. B. LePage, without which I could never have transcribed many of my interviews. Other spellings employed in the replication of the island vernacular follow as closely as possible the slightly inconsistent style of the *Daily Gleaner*, Jamaica's 158-year-old newspaper.

Throughout the latter part of the book, mention is made of the widespread suspicions among Jamaica's Rastafarian brethren that during the 1970s and early 1980s the Central Intelligence Agency kept tabs on their activities in general and on the career of Bob Marley in particular. By means of requests made under the Freedom of Information Act (5 U.S.C. 552) in 1982–83, I received documentation from the CIA confirming that it and other United States Government agencies have indeed kept files on the Jamaican reggae scene, the Rastafarian movement and the activities of Bob Marley.

For the expanded and enlarged 1991 edition, I distilled research, fieldwork and notes accumulated over the course of nine years with a large number of new and supplemental interviews—some of which corrected long-held misconceptions. For instance, it has been widely published over the last two decades that Rod Stewart played the harried harmonica on the ska classic "My Boy Lollipop." According to Rod: "It wasn't me, mate! I believe that it was this guy [Peter Hogman] who replaced me in an early sixties R&B band, Jimmy Powell and the Five Dimensions. I couldn't play as well as him, but he did have the same fuckin' *haircut* as me—which I was more annoyed at than the rest." Also, several sources and archivists sought *me* out to offer new details or help amend a factoid or two. Yet Bob Marley's world was one in which opinion, memory, interpretation and belief were often held in higher esteem than mere fact, and the confluence of conflicting outlooks, exotic recollections, fiercely expounded doctrines and otherworldly belief systems interwoven herein are a major part of the book's philosophy and premise. In a way, there are three unique presences in this story: Bob Marley, Jamaica and the power of faith. Once the reader has digested the harsh truths and deep background of "Riddim Track," I invite him or her to enter the world of Bob Marley on the terms of those whose wondrous faith informs it.

Supernatural events and surreal coincidences are recounted in this book. In the chapter about Haile Selassie, the beliefs elucidated are those of the Ethiopian peasantry and their equally credulous leaders during Selassie's reign—though many of the heroic tales and supernatural abilities that surrounded Haile Selassie were reportedly concocted by the emperor himself and duly circulated by the central government and the Coptic priesthood. Further interpretations and details offered in the latter parts of the book are derived from the teachings, down through the years, of a host of exponents of Jamaican magic, folk healing and the black arts, as well as those of quasi-Rastafarian and Rastafarian leaders, among them Robert Athlyi Rogers, Leonard Percival Howell, B. L. Wilson, H. Archibald Dunkley and Claudius Henry—often as further filtered through the memories and personal catechisms of Bob Marley and his close relatives and friends.

Whether the reader wants to believe that such "supernatural" events are credible is his or her decision. My point in attempting to tell this story from the subjective viewpoint of its protagonists is to convey the fact that the people around Haile Selassie and Bob Marley, past and present, indeed believed in "magic" and lived their lives in accordance with these beliefs.

Just as the 1992 edition included a host of amendments, discography additions and fascinating new specifics (such as the fact that Marley's 1963 "One Cup of Coffee" single was actually a cover version of Texan Claude Gray's 1961 U.S. country hit, "I'll Just Have A Cup Of Coffee [Then I'll Go]"), the 1994 revision featured numerous new details, updates and insights. For instance, although Coxsone previously claimed the parenthetical notations of "Scorcher" on early Coxsone Wailers singles "just describe the beat," it also seems they describe the copyright too, with the producer recently revealing to *Billboard* that Scorcher was also his "nom de plume" with the U.K.'s Performing Rights Society and other copyright agencies. BMI, for instance, has Dodd registered as the writer of 141 songs, including "Simmer Down" and other Wailers tracks, despite the fact (see p. 20) that Bob Marley won an Opportunity Knocks talent show with a solo rendition of "Simmer Down" written some two years before he cut it for Dodd with the Wailers. "Who the hell is Scorcher?" commented Rita Marley in exasperation, saying she was aware Coxsone Dodd had claimed credit for some of her husband's ska standards: "Bob had a problem with it."

Half the fun of being a reggae and Wailers fan is the learning process as one explores this complex realm and its wide range of murky, clashing and compelling perspectives. That is why each of the dozens of printings of this book is different, always containing as much fresh information as I can find. The extensively revised and much expanded 1998 edition of *Catch a Fire: The Life of Bob Marley* is a dramatic reflection of my own constant interviews, inquiries and archival sleuthing during yet another decade of travel in the Caribbean Basin and in England, as well as breakthroughs in the cataloging of the Wailers' extensive recording activities by collectors and amateur historians in frequent touch with this author. There are surprising new insights herein concerning the Marley children and how they are confronting the future and their own intriguing place in it. Sadly, readers will also learn about sorrowful pitfalls and behind-the-scenes power struggles in the Marley and/or Wailers realms and the often startling manipulations of those covetous of the Marley legacy. Deep background and documentation regarding the ongoing reporting process can now be found in new appendices in the back of the book.

The work of updating and improving this text also took place during the realization of a longtime dream: the conception and introduction of *Billboard*'s first regularly scheduled Top Reggae Albums chart, which debuted in the issue dated Feb. 5, 1994—one day before Bob Marley's 49th birthday. (I wanted the chart to be up and running smoothly by Marley's 50th birthday the following year.) Seven months earlier, in a special *Billboard* supplement devoted to the genre and the announcement of the historic upcoming reggae chart feature, I stated, "A personal and professional goal when I came to *Billboard* as Editor-In-Chief at the start of 1991 was that the magazine would one day institute reggae charts. These charts are a testament to the massive sales volume reggae now enjoys at the mainstream retail level. We at *Billboard* are here to help reggae and all Caribbean music expand and prosper, chronicling its inroads and charting its commercial strides. As Bob Marley once sang, 'You think it's the end, but it's just the beginning!'"

—TIMOTHY WHITE

Notes on the New Edition

I loved the look on Tim's face when he would play me a tape of one of his interviews with Bob Marley. He would be grinning ear to ear, watching me expectantly, looking for my reaction to the musician's brilliant responses. What my husband saw on my face was something between a hopeful-but-puzzled gaze and a blank stare. I couldn't understand a word of it. Tim would then translate Bob's colorful patois sentence by sentence for me (in his slightly Irish brogue–tinged version of a Jamaican accent), so I could share in his joy. Bob Marley was Timothy White's hero.

Marley clearly got a kick out of this odd, preppily dressed (always dapper in his trademark white bucks, sometimes sporting a bow tie), New Jersey–raised, Irish/French-Canadian/American writer who managed to track him down in the seventies and knew an extraordinary amount about his music. When Tim was on one of his many fact-finding trips to Jamaica and entered a small village deep in the Blue Mountains, people came rushing from their houses because they thought he was Prince Charles. Tim might have seemed an unlikely candidate to become one of Marley's and reggae's biggest champions but his understanding, empathy, and passion for the music won people over. To their surprise, he never "smoked" (though he was capable of enjoying an estimable amount of beer) and never attempted to take on a Rasta style, yet because he was always very present—sincere, enthusiastic, engaged—he blended astonishingly well into Marley's world.

When Marley died, Tim was devastated. Having lost his father at a young age, Tim tended to look for father figures throughout his life, and although Marley was only seven years his senior he had become one, as well as a close, albeit professional, friend. Tim had just left *Rolling Stone* magazine, where, hired as a senior editor, he had for years also been a prolific writer, so he was already enduring much soul-searching. He went through some dark days, experiencing a minor crisis of the spirit, but it was major enough that when he came out of it his handwriting—even his signature—had completely changed. He also had a new mission: the writing of this book.

Broke, still a bit unsure of his new status as an independent author, no longer having a *Rolling Stone* credit card and unable to obtain one of his own (he was paying off school loans in slow motion . . . "soon come," as the Rastas say), Tim struggled through the arduous, occasionally dangerous process of researching, interviewing, and writing this book. He often ran out of money, even for food. Having been betrayed by a researcher during this time (forced to fight him in court, Tim won) only made the process longer and more psychologically straining. But there were also many fortuitous, one might say magical, happenings.

While walking down Charles Street near my Boston home, I saw in an antiques-store window a 1940s Marcus Garvey poster, of all things, which depicted the legendary, rasta-inspiring Jamaican as a giant statesman aboard a ship presumably headed back to Africa (see page 104). Tim saw this as a sign and decided, though he could not afford it, to purchase the rare artifact and give it to the Jamaican people. When he next returned to Jamaica on a research mission, he officially presented it to Prime Minister Edward Seaga for the country's historical archives. At the end of that trip, he found himself stranded at the Kingston airport, having not only missed his flight but also fifty dollars short of buying a new ticket. Another small miracle occurred. A Jamaican woman (Tim might have called her an angel), with her child, came up to him and said, "Timothy White?" She, a complete stranger, handed him the money he needed and took off. Tim was so relieved and grateful to get on that plane that it only hit him later how lucky and inexplicable the exchange had been.

My husband had a sudden heart attack and died on June 27, 2002, at the age of fifty. Tim has said that this book is about "personal destiny." He believed that you are never handed your destiny but that you have to chase it like a moving train; you run until your legs and lungs ache, and if you are extremely lucky you might *catch* it, thereby living the life intended for you. He loved and admired Marley for not only boarding that train but also becoming its engineer. In Tim's also short life, he managed to do this as well; he lived and worked with such intensity that he made a difference in countless peoples' lives, becoming a moral force in the music world, a fighter for artists' rights, and a tireless, trusted, eloquent chronicler of their stories. He was also the beloved father of our twins, Alexander and Christopher, and will always remain their hero and mine.

Tim has done something with *Catch a Fire: The Life of Bob Marley* that is arguably a first: he has kept it constantly and often dramatically changing, with the kind consent and assistance of his publishers, since it was first out in 1983. There have been well over thirty printings and each one has kept the book evolving, allowing it to retain its bible-like status in the reggae world. It is now more than two hundred pages longer than when he first wrote it, and it has been published around the world in at least seven languages. In addition to garnering prestigious awards, it has been heralded for significantly raising the world's expectations of music biography, especially in the genres of rock and popular music.

We are committed to maintaining the vitality of Tim's living monument to Marley and his legacy. For helping to bring about this new edition, I wish to thank in particular: Tim's friend and publisher Chris Charlesworth at Omnibus Press, Vanessa Mobley and Sadie Stein at Henry Holt and Company, Harry Hawke for his dedication to updating and accuracy, the multi-talented Jan Morris for her extraordinary efforts, William Whitworth for his valued advice, and Vivien Goldman for her generous support, expertise, and effervescent nature.

Until recently, Jamaica was like a close relative of Tim's whom I had heard much about but strangely never met. Though it took many years to get me to that place, when I found myself there it felt like all of a sudden. I never thought I would be standing in the tiny room where Bob Marley was entombed ("six feet above the ground," as was his wish). The truck ride to Nine Miles with Diane Jobson (Marley's friend and lawyer) had been more than bumpy. Annoyed by current U.S. actions in the Mideast, she harangued me mercilessly the entire way. She was spitting mad, and I mostly didn't blame her. The others—her son, my sons, and friends—got to ride in a comfortable van from Goldeneye, where we were staying thanks to the generosity of Chris Blackwell, its owner. It had been less than a year since Tim died, and my emotions were still extremely raw.

Already shaken by the intensity of the ride, I stood at the grave with tears rolling down my face. Seeing my distress, a local dread youth offered me some "weed," assuming, I'm sure, that I was weeping for the loss of Marley. I was, but I wept also for the loss of my husband, the loss of both of their strong presences in this troubled world where their voices could have made a difference right now. Since then, this sadness has been tempered by the fact that their voices not only *do* reverberate but often seem to be getting louder—Bob Marley's through the vast, growing reach and messages of his beautiful music, Timothy White's through the timeless eloquence and truth of his words.

Tim was always bumping into fans of the book, from U2's Bono to our mailman. It was a great day at our house when he heard that the book was on the Harvard reading list, but not as great as the day he received a dog-eared copy from a friend who had just returned from Jamaica. He had found it for sale at a rural roadside stand. The book was covered with signatures—over a hundred of them—presumably having been passed along and read by each of those who signed it. Nothing could have moved Tim more, because he knew that the story told inside might inspire; he believed, as much as anything, that in the accomplishments of anyone there is hope for everyone.

—Judy Garlan White
Boston, February 2006

Catch A Fire

1
Riddim Track
an introduction

"Facts? About Jamaica? Aha! I love when the country people say there are no facts in Jamaica. It sounds so poetic and spooky, but they're absolutely right, of course. Because there really aren't any, when you think of it. Not a one."

—CHRIS BLACKWELL, 1982

"Facts an' facts, an' t'ings an' t'ings: dem's all a lotta fockin' bullshit. Hear me! Dere is no truth but de one truth, an' that is de truth of Jah Rastafari."

—BOB MARLEY, 1978

"Some mon just deal wit' information. An' some mon, him deal wit' the concept of truth. An' den some mon deal wit' magic. Information flow aroun' ya, an' truth flow right at ya. But magic, it flow t'rough ya."

—NERNELLY, A JAMAICAN "BUSH DOCTOR," 1982

It was just before midnight, and the cheers from the distinguished audience were mingling with the shouts of the ragged crowd climbing over the walls surrounding the Rufaro Stadium in Salisbury, the capital city of Zimbabwe. The wind suddenly shifted, and billows of tear gas being used by police outside the arena to control the throng had blown across the grounds to inflame the eyes of the man performing on the small stage in the center of the arena. Momentarily disoriented, he darted about, eventually stumbling through an opening in the stinging fog. Soldiers brandishing M-16 rifles led him off to the side and down into a trailer, where he dabbed his eyes with a water-soaked cloth.

The concert, which had been in progress for about twenty minutes, was part of the official Independence Day ceremonies on April 18, 1980, for the new nation-state of Zimbabwe. The paying customers and dignitaries (among them Marxist Prime Minister Robert Mugabe and England's Prince Charles), who had assembled to celebrate the casting off of white colonial tyranny, were now witnessing a demonstration of another form of repression: thousands of adulatory peasants and rank-and-file members of the revolutionary army had amassed outside the arena hoping to see the performance of international reggae sovereign Bob Marley, hero of black freedom fighters everywhere and the most charismatic emissary of modern Pan-Africanism. Hearing the reggae rhythms pulsing within, wave upon wave of idolators attempted to storm the gates. Police responded with tear-gas grenades and rifle volleys over their heads, but the people would not be held back, and they surged over the walls.

Marley pushed the thick, ropy strands of his "dreadlocks" (long matted strands of hair) away from his swollen eyes, peering into the darkness beyond the blinding lights onstage. There were shouts, screams and the muffled thuds of police batons against bodies as what looked from a distance like a swirling tide of people was beaten back from the crest of the stadium's parapets. Rallying to rejoice over their deliverance from the yoke of white oppression, much of the black population of the city was now fighting for the simple right to hear reggae.

"Madness," Marley muttered. He felt the firm grip of a soldier's hand on his left arm, and was escorted to safety. Forty-five minutes later, order would be restored, and Marley would return to the stage to perform the battle hymn he had written the year before about this country's revolutionary struggle.

To divide and rule
Could only tear us apart
In everyman chest
There beats a heart
So soon we'll find out
Who is the real revolutionaries
And I don't want my people
To be tricked by mercenaries

Natty dread it in a Zimbabwe...
Africans a liberate Zimbabwe...

But Marley's singing lacked its customary snap and bite. The scene he had witnessed earlier had shattered the vision of black African solidarity he had brought with him to Zimbabwe.

Four years earlier, Bob Marley had slammed an open palm on a tabletop in the kitchen of his Kingston, Jamaica, home and explained why he and his Rasta brethren wanted to migrate out of Babylon—a land without borders in which men sin and suffer for it—and return to Mother Africa, to Ethiopia. "De higher people in Jamaican government should clean up de dumps an' slums an' feed my people, my childran!" Marley had said. "Me read da paper an' am ashamed. Dat's why me must leave dis place an' return ta Africa. If Jamaica was me home, den me love Jamaica, and me wouldn't feel like me feel: dat dis place is *not* me home. Me don' want ta fight da police who help start de riots wit' cruelty, but when me move ta go ta Africa, if dem say no, then me personally will have ta fight."

Yet when Marley finally did go to Africa for the first time in December 1978, he saw the same slums and hungry faces he'd left behind in Jamaica, the same corrupt, strong-arm governments towering over the misery. This Africa was the sole continent where virtually no modern political leader had ever been peacefully voted out of office. He entered war-torn Ethiopia from Kenya to discover that his beloved Haile Selassie, the man he worshipped as God, had died in disgrace and had been buried in an unmarked grave. The absence of any memorial to the man, coupled with the open contempt with which the Ethiopians recalled their former emperor, had left Marley severely shaken.

And now, in Zimbabwe, all his illusions were ebbing away. His ulcerated, nailless right toe ached horribly. He had repeatedly told the press that the bandages he wore concealed a soccer injury, but the throbbing pain was a constant reminder of what doctors had been telling him over the past two years: have the toe amputated or make his peace with life; if he wouldn't undergo radical treatment for this cancer, he would fly away home to his heavenly reward in Zion a lot sooner than he had planned.

"Rasta no abide amputation," he had spat back at them. "I and I [me and my brethren] don't allow a mon ta be *dismantled*. Jah, de living God, His Imperial Majesty Haile Selassie I, Ras Tafari, Conquering Lion of the Tribe of Judah, two hundred twenty-fifth ruler of the t'ree-t'ousand-year-old Ethiopian empire, Lord of Lords, King of Kings, Heir to the Throne of Solomon, He will heal me wit' de meditations of me ganja chalice, me cutchie [clay hookah pipe], or He will tek me as a son inta His Kingdom. No scalpel shall crease me flesh! Dem cyan't kill Jah, cyan't kill Rasta. Rastamon live out."

Twelve months before, he still might have been able to save himself. If he'd stopped calling doctors "samfai," the Jamaican patois term for a confidence man who cheats the gullible by pretending he has the power of "obeah" (witchcraft). If he'd submitted to chemotherapy or radiation treatment and faced up to the inevitable fact that his dreadlocked lion's mane would drop from his head in snaky clumps. If he hadn't believed the stoned-out sycophants hovering around him who kept insisting he was the "talawa [sturdy, fearless] Tuff Gong,"* one of the steely fingers of Jah's own mighty hand. (Marley earned the title Tuff Gong for his fierceness as a street fighter. Gong was also the nickname of the early Rastafarian leader Leonard Howell. The nickname's significance was further reinforced by the fact that in some Rasta settlements it is customary for a convert to strike a gong hanging at the entranceway to announce his first step into the fold.)

And now the malignant, deliberately unchecked cancer cells were running rampant, burrowing their way through Marley's spindly body like the ravenous tree-nesting Jamaican "stink ants" that scurry up into the ackee boughs and devour the ripe fruit from the inside out. He suspected he would have one more year of torment, maybe two at the most, before the end came. He wondered if he might die in the bosom of white America while on his upcoming tour there and considered the ironies inherent in such a scenario.

He had scored his biggest critical and commercial successes as a recording artist in America and Europe, where young whites became intrigued by the ethno-political thrust of his snarling reggae anthems, and mesmerized by the inside-out time signatures that kept them pulsating. In his native Jamaica, he was both rock star and folk hero, as famous for his ability to get white American and European audiences to pay rapt attention to his songs of black retribution as he was for inducing Jamaican creole culture to dance with pride to the heartbeat of its own sorrows and follies.

Later that night in Salisbury, he would be present as the Rho-

*After Bob's death, Bunny Wailer claimed the term had begun as "Tuff Gang," with Bunny as the gang's leader.

desian and British standards were lowered and the new flag of Zimbabwe raised, twenty-one cannons exploding in salute not sixty yards from where he stood. Yet the sun hadn't set on one official day of freedom before the people were turning against one another.

In Africa, he was beloved as an apostle of Pan-Africanism, a charismatic entertainer whose elemental passions were readily embraced on the continent that invented the talking drum. But watching from the stage as the crowd battled against itself, he saw that none of them had been listening to the music, to its message. And he sensed that perhaps no one anywhere was paying close enough attention to hear the mounting inner rumblings, the frightened tremors of someone trying to explain a religious concept he'd long ago embraced but only just this moment had begun to feel: that for all mortal men, there was no safe place.

The millenarian-messianic cult of Rastafarianism that Marley championed through his music draws some of its ideology from the teachings of back-to-Africa advocate Marcus Mosiah Garvey. Born on August 17, 1887, in the town of St. Ann's Bay in the Jamaican parish of St. Ann, Garvey (nicknamed "Mose") was one of eleven children sired by a once prosperous printer. He was descended from the Maroons, originally a band of fifteen hundred African slaves released by their Spanish masters in 1655, who fled to the impenetrable interior of Jamaica as Cromwell's forces invaded the island. (Maroon is a corruption of the Spanish word *cimarron*, meaning unruly.) Garvey moved to Kingston during his late teens and gained some experience as a labor organizer and orator during a major printers' strike in 1907.

After the dispute was settled (in favor of management, the union having collapsed after its treasurer made off with its funds), Garvey left Jamaica for an extended period of travel financed by pickup jobs. He landed first in Costa Rica, where he filed a protest with the British consul about the deplorable working conditions there for blacks. It was ignored. He went next to Bocas del Toro, Panama, where he started a short-lived newspaper called *La Prensa*. Moving on through Ecuador, Nicaragua, Honduras, Colombia and Venezuela, he took note of the exploitation of cheap muscle in the mines and tobacco fields, and debated labor issues with his fellow workers, basing his political outlook on the sorry lot of poor laborers in the white-dominated West.

In 1912, while on a visit to London, he struck up an acquaintance with Sudanese-Egyptian scholar Duse Mohammed Ali, author of the highly regarded book *In the Land of the Pharaohs*, and their discussions provided Garvey with insights into the historical and religious significance of the black diaspora. The writings of Booker T. Washington, particularly *Up From Slavery*, were also much on his mind. But the book that had the most profound effect on Garvey was probably *Ethiopia Unbound—Studies in Race Emancipation* by Casely Hayford, which was published in London in 1911 and became an instant classic among the small black intellectual community there. A work of fiction, *Ethiopia Unbound* told the story of a young African who left the Gold Coast for an education in England and then returned home to a career of political protest. The book's ideas about African race salvation were drawn from the work of missionary professor Edward Wilmot Blyden of Sierra Leone, the acknowledged "modern prophet" of black emancipation.

"The work of men like Booker T. Washington and W. E. Burghart Du Bois is exclusive and provincial," states the book's main character in a scene in a lecture hall. "The work of Edward Wilmot Blyden is universal, covering the entire race and the entire problem." The lecturer goes so far as to describe Blyden as "the greatest living exponent of the true spirit of African nationality and manhood."

His head swimming with such heroic ideas and the lofty reputations of those espousing them, Garvey boarded a steamer at Southampton early in the summer of 1914, setting foot on Jamaican soil again on July 15. Out of the country for roughly two years, he had been back in Kingston less than a week when he founded the Universal Negro Improvement and Conservation Association and African Communities League, an organization whose main goal was to institute a separate-but-equal collegiate educational system for Jamaican blacks, modeled on Booker T. Washington's Tuskegee Institute. The association's motto, apparently inspired by a line in a chapter of *Ethiopia Unbound*, was "One God! One aim! One destiny!"

The time-honored British tradition of identifying with "one's betters" had turned the island's predominately creole population into naïve strivers and pathetic social climbers longing to "pass for white." As Garvey later wrote: "Men and women as black as I and even more so, had believed themselves white under the West Indian order of society. I was simply an impossible man to use openly the term 'negro'; yet every one beneath his breath was calling the black man a 'nigger.' "

The majority of his own people would remain hostile to Garvey's ideas. Ironically his most enthusiastic supporters were the mayor of Kingston and the Roman Catholic bishop, both of whom were white.

By 1915 a disheartened Garvey was corresponding with Booker T. Washington as a prelude to a face-to-face meeting in Alabama they had been planning, but Washington died before it could take place. Fed up with Jamaican resistance to the concept of black pride, Garvey went to the United States in 1916 in search of disciples. After seeking a more responsive audience in approximately thirty-five states, he finally found one in Harlem, and the next year he announced the formation of the Universal Negro Improvement Association (UNIA) as a fraternal organization for local politicians, business leaders and ambitious, civic-minded blacks. Garvey was not content with the political clubhouse, however, and soon the association became his pulpit for the black repatriation program he saw as the solution to America's—and, indeed, the world's—problems with black-white racial friction.

Garvey was a genius at media manipulation, sponsoring a newspaper called *The Negro World*, a monthly magazine called *The Black Man*, as well as a shipping concern he christened the Black Star Line. He claimed a membership for the UNIA of two million and organized spectacular parades and rallies in Madison Square Garden, where he electrified his followers with his "Ethiopia, Land of Our Fathers!" rhetoric. Innovative in his determination to win respect for black people everywhere, he even sent a commission to a League of Nations conference in Geneva after World War I, asking that certain territories held by Germany be given to American blacks as a reward for their role in helping to win the war.

"We Negroes believe in the God of Ethiopia, the everlasting God—God of Gods, God the Holy Ghost, the one God of all ages!" he boomed. "This is the God in whom we believe, but we shall worship Him through the spectacles of Ethiopia"—a blessed land, generally considered by African peoples to be the cradle of civilization and celebrated in both the Coptic and King James Bibles in such passages as this one from Psalm 68: "Princes shall come out of Egypt; Ethiopia shall soon stretch out her hands unto God."

Garvey's most portentous prognostication, supposedly first delivered in his speeches to Jamaica's desperately poor blacks (the mulatto middle and upper classes having already rejected him), was the bold statement "Look to Africa, for the crowning of a Black King; He shall be the Redeemer."

When, in 1930, Ras Tafari Makonnen, great-grandson of King

Saheka Selassie of Shoa, was made Emperor of Ethiopia and proclaimed Negusa Negast (King of Kings), Jamaica's slum-dwellers and rural poor, for whom Garvey had been something of a gallant oracle, regarded this event as the fulfillment of a prophecy of deliverance. Indeed, Ethiopia had symbolized all of Africa for the slave-descended Jamaicans since as far back as 1784, when American Baptist minister George Liele founded the Ethiopian Baptist Church on the island. These "Garveyites" were awed by newspaper and newsreel accounts of the pomp of Selassie's coronation in Addis Ababa and took note of the symbolism in the choice of his formal title, Haile Selassie being an honorific meaning "Power of the Holy Trinity." Selassie, they knew, claimed to be directly descended from King Solomon, so they reasoned that he must be the long-awaited savior of the planet's far-flung African peoples.

Garvey's statement ("Look to Africa . . . ") is customarily cited as the spark that galvanized Garveyites into founding the sect that came to be known as Rastafarianism (so called because "Ras Tafari" was Selassie's given name). In the book *Reggae Bloodlines*, Stephen Davis states flatly: "Rasta starts with Marcus Garvey." However, according to recent research carried out by such historians as Robert A. Hill of UCLA, there is no evidence that Garvey ever made such a prophecy about a divine black African king in his entire life. And if he had, it would have been a highly unusual departure from his strictly political stance, for while he sometimes employed the reverent rhetoric of the church in his speeches, he presented himself neither as a preacher nor a prophet.

Moreover, he was highly critical of Selassie, viewing the successful invasion of Ethiopia by Mussolini in the mid-1930s as the nadir of the King of Kings' imperial ineptitude. Although Garvey's UNIA followers in Harlem had been allowed to march carrying posters of Garvey and Selassie in a now-famous street parade held with members of the Black Jews on Sunday, January 4, 1931, Garvey himself would later become an open opponent of those who proclaimed Selassie's divinity. Early in 1933, he adamantly refused to permit Rastafarian leader Leonard Percival Howell to distribute the emperor's picture in Garvey's Kingston headquarters in Edelweiss Park. And in his opening address at a session of the 1934 UNIA convention, "Mr. Garvey also referred to the Ras Tafari cult," according to the August 25 issue of the *Jamaica Times*, "speaking of them with contempt."

It appears that the stirring directive to "look to Africa..." was uttered instead by Rev. James Morris Webb, a clergyman/mystic from Chicago who was an associate of Garvey's and the author of a book published in the Midwest in 1919 entitled *A Black Man Will Be the Coming Universal King, Proven by Biblical History*. Webb spoke the fateful words at a UNIA convention in September 1924. And while Garvey, however inadvertently, did become the father of Rastafarianism in the minds of most believers, he was actually the inheritor of a tradition of messianic black mysticism that had been in full flower in Jamaica and elsewhere for some time.

The spiritual pioneer of the back-to-Africa movement was Alexander Bedward, a Jamaican healer and herbalist who was said to have performed miracles in Spanish Town in the early 1900s in anticipation of the day when the black man would reign supreme. Like so many of his controversial colleagues, he wound up in a mental hospital; he was admitted in 1921 and died there in 1933.

The true foundation of Rastafarianism is the Holy Piby, the "Black Man's Bible," compiled by one Robert Athlyi Rogers of Anguilla from 1913 to 1917. It was published, not coincidentally, in the same year Rev. Webb made his declaration—1924. A Barbadian minister named Rev. Charles F. Goodridge came upon the secret Bible in Colon, Panama. But at the same time large quantities were being printed in Newark, New Jersey, by other believers, and from there copies of the Piby were shipped to Kimberly, South Africa, where missionaries of black supremacy started a church for the diamond-field workers called the Afro-Athlican Constructive Church (AACC). Through these proselytizing efforts, Goodridge became associated with a woman named Grace Jenkins Garrison, and together they brought the doctrine of the Holy Piby to Jamaica in 1925, founding a branch of the AACC under the name the Hamatic Church.

Meeting immediately with much persecution from the Fundamentalist, Revivalist and more conventional Christian church leaders for their adherence to the occult Bible, Goodridge and Garrison fled into the bush country of the parish of St. Thomas, in Eastern Jamaica, and it was there that the seeds of Rastafarianism were implanted. Early Rasta leaders like Leonard P. Howell gravitated to the forbidden encampments to read the Holy Piby—purportedly the closest thing to the first Bible, which was said to have been written in Amharic (for centuries the official language of Ethiopia, and allegedly the original language of mankind). Goodridge and Garrison maintained that under the early popes white church scholars distorted the Amharic Bible in the translating and editing process to make God and His prophets Caucasian instead of black. Among the chapters in the Piby was one called "The Black Man's Map of Life," which spelled out his difficult but ultimately glorious destiny from Creation to Armageddon and beyond.

The earliest Rasta songs and chants, including the basic, traditional "Rasta Man Chant" which Bob Marley would record in the mid-seventies, were taken from the Piby, where they were set down in "glossolalia," an unintelligible "angelic language" that turned out to be quite similar to the ritualistic jargon used in the thirties and forties by the self-styled English sorcerer Aleister Crowley, the so-called "Great Beast," in his occult Golden Dawn ceremonies.

Among those who examined the Piby in St. Thomas was Rev. Fitz Balintine Pettersburgh, who in 1926 introduced an equally hallowed document into the secret brotherhood of the Piby. It was the *Royal Parchment Scroll of Black Supremacy*, which Pettersburgh called the "supreme book of royal rules for the Ethiopian Western Repository." It was in this book that Pettersburgh incorporated the prophecy of the Rev. James Webb, describing the coming of a new Ethiopian empire ruled by a black divinity. The *Royal Parchment Scroll* was taken to heart by devotees of the Pan-African "Ethiopianist" fraternal organizations springing up in Jamaica, such as the Ethiopian Guild and the Brotherhood Mission. The last piece in the theological puzzle was the Promised Key, also called the Rasta Bible, which was a plagiarism by Leonard P. Howell of the *Royal Parchment Scroll*. Being something of a charlatan, Howell tricked converts into thinking the book was an ancient tome that had originated in Accra, the Gold Coast, but it was actually published by him in Jamaica in 1935.

While all this was happening in Jamaica, a beleaguered Marcus Garvey, the most visible exponent of Pan-African hopes and yearnings, had been floundering in the United States on his mission of mass black repatriation. In 1922, he and three officers of the UNIA were arrested for mail fraud. Tried and convicted in 1923 for fraud and income-tax evasion (he claimed he was framed), Garvey languished, after failing in his appeals, in federal prison in Atlanta until President Calvin Coolidge commuted his sentence in 1927. In December of that year, he was deported to Jamaica by way of Panama, but he was nearly denied entry to his homeland. In March 1926, the acting governor of Jamaica had written to the British secretary of state for the colonies, warning: "My apprehensions are confirmed by two of the elected members of the Legislative Council, who state that there is already a small amount of anti-white propaganda by a religious body in at least one district which is likely to be fanned by Garvey."

The district referred to was St. Thomas, and the religious body was the brotherhood of the Piby. As for antiwhite propaganda, the brotherhood simply believed that the African race, once the most exalted on earth but now the most reviled and tormented, would one day regain its status as Jah's favorite.

On May 17, 1926, the *Daily Gleaner* published a sketchy report on the Piby. Two days later, the *Gleaner* offered a follow-up piece: "New doctrines contained in the Holy Piby, remarkable book printed and circulated in the United States. Credible religion of which Marcus Garvey is pronounced an apostle." The *Gleaner*, May 27: "Talk about a mass meeting called to denounce the Holy Piby."

On June 4, UNIA spokesmen were quoted as saying that Garvey's organization had nothing whatsoever to do with the Piby. But with Garvey due to return to Jamaica within the next few weeks, the staunchly upper-middle-class *Gleaner* would not be swayed from its ultimate objective, the discrediting of Garvey among the island's black religious establishment.

An editorial appeared in the *Gleaner* on June 6, headlined "A New Religion":

> We have received two publications of the new Ethiopian religion, to which we have alluded more than once recently. These books or pamphlets are complementary to the Holy Piby, the Bible of the Garveyites, which has replaced the Holy Bible and which proclaims that Elijah was the Messiah, a claim which would have horrified that stern and uncompromising old Hebrew. It is only fair to say that this religion seems to have made precious few converts anywhere. Some silly, credulous people may have been induced to invest their money in a Black Star Line, whose ships were never quite three in number and never could get from port to port without soliciting a contribution from friends to pay expenses. But these same people demurred when it came to taking over a religion with their unfortunate commercial enterprise. As to Jamaica, it is certain that this sort of thing will be laughed out of existence. There is only impudence in it. There is a sort of vulgarity about this that will disgust even the vulgar.

Thus was the homeward-bound Garvey set up as a huckster/felon turned heretic, an irresponsible, dishonest and blasphemous black leader worthy of the most venomous scorn. He tried to pick up the pieces of his movement with energetic visits to old UNIA headquarters in the West Indies and Central America but was met with indifference. In 1928, he spoke in London's cavernous Royal Albert Hall to a nearly empty house. His constituency scattered, his beloved Jamaica utterly hostile, Garvey resettled in England in 1935. "Leadership means everything—pain, blood, death" went his personal credo. By 1940, there was nothing else left for him and he was buried in British soil.

But the Rastafarian faith had taken root in his native land, slowly gaining ground primarily as a peasant squatter movement with religious underpinnings. As Howell would tell his flock, "That man in England [first George V, then Edward VIII] is not our king! Keep the land, pay no taxes, because our king, the king of all kings, has now been crowned in Ethiopia and all tribute is due to him!"

Howell and a host of other Rasta and quasi-Rasta leaders applied themselves to the task of fleshing out the tenets of the bold new religion. Among these theoreticians were H. Archibald Dunkley and Joseph Nathaniel Hibbert, both members of the ultra-secret Egyptian Masonic order known as the Great Ancient Brotherhood of Silence; Robert Hinds, a disciple of Bedward; David and Annie M. Harvey, founders in 1931 of the "Israelites" sect; and the self-proclaimed Prince Edward Emanuel, who claimed he had descended bodily from heaven to the parish of St. Elizabeth in 1915 and thus, like the biblical Melchizedek, he had no mortal parents. Other early Rasta leaders were Claudius Henry, Altamont Reed, Paul Ervington and Vernal Davis.

These self-appointed "prophets" formulated a set of dietary and hygienic laws to accompany the religious doctrine. They urged their flocks to shun the ingestion of alcohol, tobacco, all meat (especially pork), as well as shellfish, scaleless fish, snails, predatory and scavenger species of marine life, and many common seasonings like salt. In short, anything that was not "ital," a Rasta term meaning pure, natural or clean, was forbidden. They also outlawed the combing or cutting of hair, citing the holy directive in Leviticus 21:5: "They shall not make baldness upon their head, neither shall they shave off the corner of their beard, nor make any cuttings in their flesh." Their nappy tresses were allowed to mat and twine themselves into ropy dreadlocks, so called to mock non-believers' aversion to their appearance. (The noun "dread" has also since evolved into a word of praise.) The herb "ganja" (marijuana) was regarded as "wisdomweed," and the Rasta leaders urged that it be smoked as a religious rite, alleging that it was found growing on the grave of King Solomon and citing biblical passages, such as Psalms 104:14, to attest to its sacramental properties: "He causeth the grass to grow for the cattle, and herb for the service of man, that he may bring forth food out of the earth."

The cult decried as decadent the African-derived Pukumina religion of Jamaica, as well as all Christian churches. They also asserted that blacks were the superior race and that after Armageddon they would rule all creation as they had done in the beginning.

The Rastas denied allegations by other religious groups that they were antiwhite or antibrown (mulatto) and invited all to repent and accept Jah (a shortened form of Jehovah). They vowed that at a secret hour known only to a devout few, converts would return to Ethiopia by an undisclosed means, leaving behind the tropical steambath of Jamaica, which they considered to be literally Hell on Earth. Until that time, Rastas would refuse to take part in the machinations of daily life and commerce in "Babylon," the sphere of temporal captivity of the spirit.

The poor flocked to the Rastas' call, since the cult's creed lent a certain nobility to their alienated status. As Rastas, they could now await with dignity the Judgment Day, when the last shall be first and the first shall be last. By 1934, Rastafarianism had a strong following among the lower classes, particularly in the ghettos of Kingston.

A branch of the Ethiopian World Federation, Inc., a lobbying organization established to solicit sympathy and outside support for the Ethiopian struggle against Italian fascism, was established in Jamaica in 1938. The response from both Rastas and non-Rastas was enthusiastic, and in 1955, Selassie, who had been in exile during Mussolini's occupation (1936–1941) of his empire, announced that five hundred lush acres of his own personal landholdings were being offered to black settlers from the West who had supported Ethiopia's fight to preserve its freedom. Jamaican Rastas were thrilled by this invitation and began exhorting their countrymen, who had been migrating in great numbers to England in search of work: "Ethiopia, yes! England, no! Let my people go!"

In the meantime, Leonard Howell had led his band of followers from his Rasta mission in the hills of St. Catherine to a remote Spanish Town settlement called Pinnacle, an abandoned estate near Sligoville purchased in 1940, where they cultivated ganja while he occupied himself with his thirteen wives. One morning he announced it was *he* and not Selassie who was the Living Deity and asked the brethren to refer to him henceforth as Gangunguru Maragh (a concatenation of Hindi words that translates as "Teacher of Famous Wisdom, King of Kings"). While his followers were slightly confused, the constabulary was thoroughly exasperated and police raided his mountain cave in 1954. The local magistrate pronounced Howell mentally unbalanced and threw him in an institution for the criminally insane, while his displaced dreads wandered down into Kingston, loitering in large groups and generally outraging the populace with their unusual hairstyles and public consumption of illegal ganja.

By the end of the 1950s, other Rasta congregations, impatient for social justice as well as spiritual deliverance, began to grow more militant. One group attempted to capture Kingston's Victoria Park, and another seized Old King's House in Spanish Town in the name of Selassie. These uncharacteristically aggressive actions were denounced by the authorities as the logical consequence of the Rasta convention organized by Prince Emanuel in 1958, which drew hundreds of brethren to a site in the Back-o-Wall section of West Kingston. There were huge bonfires, much drumming, religious ceremonies and, claimed police officials, threats to decapitate members of the force as sacrifices to Jah.

For many onlookers, it was the most upsetting thing to hit the greater Kingston area since the Port Royal earthquake across the bay in 1692. But the Rastas were simply trying to establish a United Church of Rastafari. Their efforts had been stymied because none of the far-flung brethren could reach a consensus on where Selassie stood in the great scheme of things. Was he really God? A close relative? A prophet to succeed Abraham, Moses and Jesus?

Among those to receive a personal invitation from Prince Emanuel to this exotic convocation in Kingston was Rev. Claudius Henry, who dubbed himself "The Repairer of the Breach." Stirred by the elaborate rituals he witnessed, Henry hurriedly established the African Reformed Church in West Kingston and announced that October 5, 1959, was the "date of Emancipation." Leaflets issued by him stated that "no passport will be necessary for those returning to Africa." A ticket for passage to Ethiopia, illustrated with a picture of Selassie, sold for a shilling. Thousands were purchased, and on the appointed day, the streets surrounding Henry's church on Rosalie Avenue were jammed with expectant Rastas and their families, many of whom had sold off all their possessions. By day's end, however, no means of departure had appeared on the horizon and Henry was arrested.

Humiliated, Henry threatened revenge against the government after his release. He later landed in prison when a huge cache of weapons—including guns, machetes, dynamite and ammunition—was found in his church. His son Reynold took up the fight. A state of emergency was proclaimed in 1960 following a shoot-out in Kingston's Red Hills district between Rastas loyal to the Henrys and the Royal Hampshire Regiment. Three guerrillas and two soldiers died in that confrontation.

Hostilities brewed over the next two years as Rastas began calling themselves Niyamen, after a fiercely violent group known as the Niyabingi Order—supposedly sanctioned by Selassie—that appeared in Ethiopia in the thirties. The government had responded by dispatching the police to break up Niyabingi meetings, and more violence ensued. In 1963, a clash between Rastas and police on the North Coast, near Montego Bay, left several dead on both sides.

Even in the face of repression by the authorities, Rastafarianism continued to flourish in Jamaica, finally penetrating the middle class in the late sixties, when it began to attract numerous converts (largely males in their teens) following the mounting mainstream acclaim accorded Rasta painters, sculptors, poets, dancers and musicians. (Noted Rasta poet-politician Samuel Brown recently asserted that six out of every ten Jamaicans are Rastas.)

On April 21, 1966, Haile Selassie paid a state visit to Jamaica, and a crowd of Rastas estimated at 100,000 surrounded his plane on the tarmac. Selassie remained inside the plane for a half hour after landing, supposedly frightened by the unexpectedly lavish reception. It was not until Rasta leader Mortimo Planno (later a guru of Bob Marley's) calmed the assemblage that the emperor emerged.

During his visit, Selassie made no official comment on the sect's evaluation of his spiritual status, but a rumor quickly spread in Rasta circles that a secret communiqué had been passed by the emperor to some of the Rasta elders, instructing them to "liberate Jamaica *before* migrating to Ethiopia." The rumor had a tranquilizing influence on the restive Rasta community since the awesome responsibility of announcing the date of the ultimate exodus from Babylon was thus indefinitely deferred. But it was also viewed as a mandate for increased political action on the part of Rastas, much of it soon to be focused on demands for the legalization of ganja.

Called *kan* in the Amharic Bible, the ganja of India, i.e. Asian hemp, was brought to the New World by the Spanish around 1545. Britain offered colonial planters generous subsidies to encourage them to cultivate hemp and break the Russian monopoly on the crop, whose fibers were used mainly for rope. Today, an estimated 65 percent of Jamaican adults and 80 percent of the population under twenty-one have tried ganja. The rural poor and enterprising Rastas grow and sell the crop simply because it is a splendid source of income, its cultivation and harvest requiring far less exertion than toiling in the island's bauxite mines.

The police continue to harass Rastas, mostly for their flagrant use of ganja, which remains illegal in Jamaica, but also because of their strange appearance and their "subversive" political and religious beliefs. The authorities' principal targets tend to be Rasta reggae singers whose songs tell of Jah's wrath and the government's moral decay.

To be a Rasta takes enormous faith, say the brethren, for the veracity of Jah's vision and meditations is assailed at every turn, even in Africa. Yet Rastas point out that the Bible prophesies that there will be much confusion just before Babylon falls; many jackals will raise their voices in falsehood, directing truth-seekers into spiritual cul-de-sacs. So, they conclude, ridicule and repression are but ratifications of the Rasta gospel.

In time, the Rasta creed would be spread far beyond Jamaica, due primarily to the musical missionary work of Bob Marley and the Wailers. But the reggae that carried the message had taken several years to develop.

As far as Jamaican record-buyers are concerned, the word *reggae* was coined on a 1968 Beverley's dance single, "Do the Reggay [sic]," by Toots and the Maytals. Some believe the term is derived from Regga, the name of a Bantu-speaking tribe on Lake Tanganyika. Others say it is a corruption of "streggae," Kingston street slang for prostitute. Bob Marley claimed the word was Spanish in origin, meaning "the king's music." Veteran Jamaican studio musicians offer the simplest, and probably the most plausible, explanation. "It's a description of the beat itself," says Hux Brown, lead guitarist on Paul Simon's 1972 reggae-flavored hit, "Mother and Child Reunion," and the man widely credited with inventing the one-string quiver/trill that kicked off Simon's single as well as many of the top island hits of the preceding years. "It's just a fun, joke kinda word that means the ragged rhythm and the body feelin'. If it's got a greater meanin', it doesn't matter."

For decades, beginning in the 1920s, the dominant music in the Caribbean was Trinidad-based calypso. Island performers originally sang the lilting, topical and frequently risqué folk songs in an African-French patois but gradually switched to English as the music began to attract the interest of American record labels such as Decca and Bluebird. In Trinidad, the biggest calypsonians, who vied each year for the title of calypso king at the pre-Lenten Carnival festivities, were largely males: King Radio, Growling Tiger, Lord Beginner, William the Conqueror, Attila the Hun, Lord Executor. After the music was discovered by Americans and exploited as a novelty, calypsonians like Attila (Raymond Quevedo) and Lord Executor (Phillip Garcia) found themselves on live Stateside radio broadcasts with such stars as Bing Crosby and Rudy Vallee. While on a Caribbean U.S.O. tour during World War II, comic Morey Amsterdam heard a humorous song by Lord Invader ("Rum and Coca-Cola") about the cultural wrinkles caused by American servicemen stationed on Trinidad and passed it on to the Andrews Sisters.

The post–World War II years saw the emergence of various Caribbean music forms, notably the steel-pan music of Trinidad and Tobago, which was developed by Ellie Mannette (the first man to "sink" and then tune, in raised sections, the surface of an oil drum top), Winston "Spree" Simon and Neville Jules. Steel pan would eventually provide accompaniment to the more hectic, commercial calypso styles popularized by such artists as Aldwyn "Lord Kitchener" Roberts and Slinger "the Mighty Sparrow" Francisco. In the late 1940s and early 1950s, Jamaican musicians began combining the steel-pan and calypso strains with an indigenous mento folk beat (Harry Belafonte's "Jamaica Farewell" was originally a mento song), laying the groundwork for an aggressive amalgam that also contained South African elements and a percussive tack similar to the highlife music of Nigeria.

At roughly the same time (1950–1959), Jamaican youth was turning away from the American pop foisted on them by Radio Jamaica Rediffusion (RJR) and the Jamaica Broadcasting Corporation (JBC). Weather conditions permitting, they listened instead to the sinewy music being played on New Orleans stations or Miami's powerful WINZ, whose playlists included records by Amos Milburn, Roscoe Gordon and Louis Jordan. They could relate to the sound of Milburn moaning about "Bad, Bad Whiskey" or Fats Domino's lamenting "Walking Blues" a lot better than Mitch Miller's "Tzena, Tzena,

Tzena." As fond as Jamaicans were of American blues, they went wild when Fats Domino, Smiley Lewis, Huey Smith and the Clowns, Lloyd Price and other New Orleans artists took the sound a step further with a double shot of the Crescent City's unique rockin' rhythms. It was a strutting, half-stepping "second line" approach to R&B, the tempo incorporating the New Orleans-based dirges and jump-for-joy perambulations of jazz funerals; the Latin-tinged bass patterns of cathouse pianists like Jelly Roll Morton; rhumba, samba and the mambo of Perez Prado; the barrelhouse boogie-woogie of Kid Stormy Weather, Sullivan Rock, Robert Bertrand, Archibald, Champion Jack Dupree and Professor Longhair; and the chant-along exultations of the traditional black Mardi Gras fraternal societies (known as "Indian" tribes).

Jamaican bands began covering U.S. R&B hits, but the more adventurous took the nuts and bolts of the sound and melded them with energetic jazz conceits—particularly in the ever-present horn section—and emerged around 1956 with a hybrid concoction christened "ska." Ernest Ranglin, the stellar jazz-rooted Jamaican guitarist who backed up the Wailers on such ska classics as "Love and Affection" and "Cry to Me," says the word was coined by musicians "to talk about the *skat! skat! skat!* scratchin' guitar strum that goes behind."

Practically overnight, ska spawned a major Jamaican industry called the Sound System, whereby enterprising record shop disc jockeys with reliable American connections for 45s would load a pair of hefty PA speakers into a pickup truck and tour the island from hilltop to savanna, spinning the latest hits by the Fat Man and Joe Jones or tunes by local favorites like Kentrick "Lord Creator" Patrick and Stranger Cole. For added effect, the journeyman DJs gave themselves comic-book nom de plumes reminiscent of those of the early calypsonians: King Edwards, V-Rocket, Sir Coxsone Downbeat, Prince Buster. They would show up at the open-air dances dressed in gold lamé waistcoats, black leather Dracula capes, imitation ermine robes, Lone Ranger masks and rhinestone-studded crowns, waving a thumb-high stack of the island's most exclusive singles in one hand and an ornate pistol or night-searing machete in the other. The competition among DJs for the most current U.S. and Jamaican singles grew so heated that they covered the labels of the 45s with black paper or scratched them off altogether. Obviously it was a lot harder to keep up with rivals when you didn't know the name of the record or the artist causing the latest furor. Frustrated parties often settled their differences in a back alley or a lonely stretch of bush with pistols and ratchets (razor-sharp German switchblade knives).

The ska craze spread to London in the late 1950s and early 1960s, where an expanding West Indian population and curious Britons packed the "shebeens" (sleazy, unlicensed basement clubs) and Sound System dances to drink Long Life Lager, smoke ganja and revel in the tumult created by island recordings and visiting performers. In the United Kingdom, ska soon came to be called "bluebeat" in deference to Melodisc Records' Blue Beat label, which started releasing tunes by such Jamaican groups as Laurel Aitken and the Carib Beats, Basil Gabbidon's Mellow Larks, and Desmond Dekker and the Aces. Encouraged by Jamaican audiences, English organist Georgie Fame added selections from the latest Blue Beat releases to his sets at London's Flamingo Club. Fame went on to record several ska-based singles on the R&B Disc label, the best being "Orange Street" and "JA Blues." At the same time, the Jamaican musicians in London picked up on the funky jazz of organist Jimmy Smith and saxman Lou Donaldson and took it back home with them.

But this music probably would have remained a mere curiosity were it not for the efforts of a white Anglo-Jamaican of aristocratic lineage named Chris Blackwell. As a hobbylike business venture, he had set up a small-scale distribution network for ethnic records. But he had a vision about the potential appeal of Jamaica's oscillating answer to the blues.

In 1962, Blackwell took his tiny Blue Mountain/Island label to England, purchased master tapes produced in Kingston and released them in Britain on Black Swan, Jump Up, Sue and the parent label, Island. Among his initial artists were Jimmy Cliff, Lord Creator, Wilfred "Jackie" Edwards, the Blues Busters, Derrick Morgan, trombonist Don Drummond and the Skatalites, and Bob Marley, whose first singles on Island were issued under the name Robert Marley.

In England, Blackwell struck up a synergism with the fashion-conscious mod and skinhead teenage movements through his seminal Jamaican rock records. But the major breakthrough came when Millie Small, an adenoidal pixie he managed, scored a huge U.S. hit in 1964 with "My Boy Lollipop," which showcased the guitar of Skatalite Ernest Ranglin and an unsung harpist from Jimmy Powell and the Five Dimensions.

Back in Jamaica, "Stay and Ketch It Again!" was the rallying cry of Sound System ska. The man behind the turntable would thrill a yardful of hard-grindin' shuffle dancers with a flash of his polished cutlass and a whooping "Please a lady! Jump it up now!" as he introduced Don Drummond's "Jet Stream" or the Wailers' risqué "Jerk in Time." Soon, every "rude boy" (ghetto tough) and country orphan wanted to hear his own voice barreling out of a bass speaker.

The Wailers' first single, "Simmer Down,"* was a ska smash in Jamaica in late 1963–early 1964, the lyrics calling for the island's young hooligans to control their tempers and help put a stop to the gang wars and savage lawlessness that had reached epidemic proportions. Unfortunately the record and subsequent releases such as "Rude Boy" and "Jail House" lent the street punks a perverse celebrity.

The ska-bluebeat advance into what came to be known as "rock steady" occurred around 1966, when its pervasive trombones, trumpets and tenor saxes blended into the background, the electric bass took on a down-stroking prominence, the guitar asserted itself to punctuate the hiccupping cadence and solo vocals were featured more frequently. The archetypal tune of the era was Alton Ellis's "Rock Steady" dance hit. In general, the most significant aspect of ska's development into rock steady was that it coincided with the emergence of a new generation of Jamaican musical talent.

"Da guys who were in control robbed da older musicians up," Bob Marley said in a 1975 interview. "Dem get frustrated an' stop playin'. So de music changed from da older musicians ta de younger, hungrier ones. People like I, we love James Brown an' love your funky stuffs, an' we dig inta dat American bag. We didn't wan' ta stand around playin' dat slower ska beat anymore. De young musicians, deh had a different beat—dis was rock steady now! Eager ta go! Du-du-du-du-du . . . Rock steady goin' t'rough!"

Marley was on target when he linked James Brown with the transition, since R&B was to ska what soul was to rock steady. And when Jimi Hendrix and Sly Stone arose to inject some adrenaline into soul, the Wailers were prepared to do as much for rock steady.

By the 1970s, the U.S. Top 40 hosted several rock steady and early reggae hits—most notably Desmond Dekker and the Aces' anti-colonial diatribe, "Israelites" (1969), and Jimmy Cliff's joyful "Wonderful World, Beautiful People" (1970)—without record-buyers even realizing what these songs represented. But American and British artists attuned to the thematic and rhythmic assertiveness in the reggae

*Bob won an Opportunity Knocks talent contest at the Ward Theater with an earlier solo rendition.

of the early seventies heard a cash register ringing behind the unforgettable sound, and they began scoring with their own reggae interpretations. Paul Simon's 1971 sojourn at Byron Lee's Dynamic Studios in Kingston to cut "Mother and Child Reunion" helped spark a lively and lucrative musical cross-fertilization among prominent rock, R&B, punk, disco, funk and New Wave artists, including Stevie Wonder, Paul McCartney, Elvis Costello, Boney M, 10cc, the Rolling Stones, Orleans, Linda Ronstadt, ABBA, the Staple Singers and the Clash, among others. Eric Clapton reached the Number 1 spot in the United States and in much of Europe in 1974 with his version of Marley's anguished shantytown confessional, "I Shot the Sheriff." And an eclectic new sound was introduced in 1979–80 by interracial English groups like the Specials, Madness and the English Beat, which combined a ska revival with the antic energies of punk.

Bob Marley and the Wailers' mesmerizing and often incendiary songs were customarily steeped in images of Third World strife and underscored by the turbid tenets of the Rastafarian faith, as well as by symbols and maxims derived from Jamaican and African folklore. And, as the Wailers showed themselves to be much more than a mere Jamaican rock phenomenon, their music began to concern itself with social issues on the island, whether it was a sulfurous denunciation of police harassment of Rastas in "Rebel Music (3 O'clock Road Block)," or "Them Belly Full (But We Hungry)," in which the Democratic Socialist regime of Prime Minister Michael Manley was advised that the disenfranchised ghetto population was a volatile—and potent—political force.

But no one in Jamaica was prepared for the impact the music of Marley and company would eventually have worldwide. The Wailers had been quite successful commercially in the Caribbean during most of Jamaican rock's evolutionary phases. But after signing in 1972 with Island Records, the Wailers issued eleven well-received albums as a group on the internationally distributed Island label (both Peter Tosh and Bunny Wailer, who left the group in 1975, have released numerous solo albums). Delivered in lyrical patois like fervent incantations, the Wailers' songs were a global sensation, and Marley was hailed as a major musical *and* sociopolitical influence. From 1976 onward, Wailers concerts were invariably sellouts. And they appeared throughout the world: from the United States and Canada to France, the United Kingdom, Italy (where in 1980 they drew a crowd of 100,000 for a single concert), West Germany, Spain, Scandinavia,

Ireland, Holland, Belgium, Switzerland, Japan, Australia and New Zealand, the Ivory Coast and Gabon. To date, some $240 million worth of Wailers albums have been sold, with significant sales in countries in which the group never performed: Brazil, Senegal, Ghana, Nigeria, Taiwan and the Philippines. Marley himself became a hero of mythic proportions, mobbed during trips through South America, Africa, the United States, Europe and, of course, the Caribbean.

Considering his facility for holding masses of people in his grip with highly charged songs about Third World uprisings and social revolution, it is ironic that Marley's political alignment was never clearly identifiable. But that was perhaps the least perplexing aspect of a man who seemed to deliberately enhance an already elusive personality. There is much about Bob Marley that remains mysterious. He seemed to embody the magical qualities of Anancy, the impish spider of African folklore who has the ability to alter his physical form at will and who is cunning enough to sometimes deceive even the Supreme Being. (The Anancy stories were brought to Jamaica in the 1600s by slaves, the Akan people of the Gold Coast [now Ghana], and they were told and retold in the three Twi dialects—Ashanti, Fanti, Akwapim—that were by far the most important African sources of Jamaican patois.) Marley became a symbolic, larger-than-life figure for his people, in the same way that Anancy evolved in the slaves' minds from a character in folklore into a crucial symbol of courage embodying the concept that a supposedly lowly creature can outwit his formidable adversaries.

When, in the presence of one's oppressors, one told Anancy stories in patois, it was possible to bolster one's self-esteem by mocking the uncomprehending slaveowners. Such fables also served as a constant reminder of the rich cultural heritage from which the slaves had been cut off. The art of storytelling is highly regarded in Jamaican culture, where the skilled raconteur deftly obscures any distinctions between various twice-told tales and his own personal experiences. The best stories are an arabesque of supernatural menace and wry jesting.

In a land where so many people possess so little, personal mystique is a highly valued form of social currency—it can buy the enduring respect of others. A familiar figure about whom precious little can be discovered is a powerful presence indeed.

Bob Marley was such a man. Obsessed with privacy, he devoted considerable time and energy throughout his life to constructing an elaborate screen to protect his valuable mystique. He insisted for years, for instance, that he was born in Africa, and that his parents were, too. No one who was connected with Marley, no matter how closely, had a complete picture of the man. The network of restrictive confidences that Marley developed over the years was extensive, encompassing business arrangements, extramarital affairs, daily comings and goings, and songwriting collaborations. (In order to protect some of his publishing interests in later years, he reportedly made cunning arrangements to credit many of his songs to hangers-on and ghetto chums.)

His countrymen esteemed him for his inscrutable nature, for his unfathomable behavior. They marveled that he was able to rise from wretched poverty to become one of the most renowned figures ever to emerge from the Caribbean, and they were held spellbound by the graphic intensity of his brand of storytelling, as in the terrifying vision of "Burnin' and Lootin'," in which a man awakes to find that he is in the custody of anonymous armed officials, an innocent victim of martial law, while insurrection rages in the streets.

But perhaps what is most amazing about Marley's rise to fame is how little his fans around the globe needed to know about the thematic undercurrents in his music, the different levels on which his message was delivered, and the roles Rastafarianism and traditional Jamaican culture played in all of this. For example, one of his most vivid songs is "Small Axe," an almost buoyant bit of reggae sagacity. What seems like a simple allegory, in which a woodsman informs a large tree that it is about to be felled, is actually a fascinating three-pronged assertion that is readily understood by all Jamaicans but utterly obscure to almost anyone else. Not only is "Small Axe" intended as a warning to oppressors everywhere that the people of the Third World will one day cut them down to size, but it is also a bit of bravado that had a particular application to the Jamaican recording industry. When the song was originally written by Marley and noted Kingston producer Lee Perry, it referred to "the Big T'ree," the island's dictatorial record company triumvirate—Dynamic, Federal and Studio One. And the central image of tree-felling, accompanied by the excuse that it is being done according to the wishes of a superior, is a sober throwback to the old plantation-era pecking order, when slaves who were ordered to topple the island's gigantic silk-cotton trees, which they held sacred, would sprinkle some rum on the roots of the trunks and sing a woeful song. This was done to assure the spirits lurking within that this destruction was not the slaves' idea, but rather the will of their masters.

That so many around the world would adore Marley's records and revere him as a revolutionary Rasta firebrand while never entirely comprehending the complexity of his message made his people love and cherish him all the more. They understood the magnitude of his accomplishments, and they regarded his artifice as being quite mystical in origin. He was a shaman, a duly appointed apostle of Jah, scolding the sinful, threatening the pernicious and reaching out to the righteous with arcane language the untrained ear could not completely decipher.

The references to dried kernels being tossed to chickens in the song "Who the Cap Fit" are incomprehensible to the average non-Jamaican listener, who is unaware that the central phrase is actually a rural proverb. It evokes the image of a farmer silently scattering feed who is saying, in effect: "Don't call yourself a chicken just because you eat my feed; I never *said* I was endeavoring to feed chickens." That is, "You are who you show yourself to be, not who you might say you are."

In the tradition of Jamaican storytelling, such maxims and proverbs are rarely offered in casual conversation. Usually they are addressed by a parent to a child, by an older person to a younger one, by a teacher to a student, or by a storyteller to his audience. And in these folk expressions are the seeds of social protest, as when a slave would turn his analysis of the eternal enmity between tyrant and chattel into the canny advice, "Kick darg, him fren' you, feed him, him bite you." In other words, "Treat an underling poorly and he'll fear you, treat him well and he'll come to *demand* your respect."

The chief guardians of Jamaica's folk wisdom and lore have been the sorcerers, known as "obeahmen" (from the Twi *obayi*—meaning magic or sorcery) and "Myalmen" (related to the Hausa word *maye*, "wizard"). Obeah is the practice of exploiting the power of "duppies," or spirits of the dead, to harm or help people and influence events. A myalman, however, has the ability to thwart or neutralize the evil wrought by duppies. Under colonial domination, Jamaican slaves would align themselves in large numbers with obeahmen and myalmen (and women) in order to cast spells to defeat their captors.

The magicians also acted as behind-the-scenes military strategists, calling slaves to arms for major revolts like those in the parish of St.

Mary in 1760, 1765 and 1766, during which thousands of renegades fought the British tooth and nail. Significantly these were the first slave uprisings aimed at establishing a revolutionary future rather than restoring an African past.

Throughout the Third World, Bob Marley was viewed as a modern myalman who had the will and the means—literally and figuratively—to repel evil. He was, as he himself claimed, a "duppy conqueror." He recorded a song called "Duppy Conqueror" in the late 1960s, shortly after being released by the Kingston police following a minor ganja arrest, in which he paraphrased the traditional Jamaican street saw used when defying a bully: "If yuh bullbucker, me duppy conqueror."

The Akan people, from whom most black and brown Jamaicans are descended, believed that man has three souls: the Life-Soul, sent directly from the Supreme Being at birth; the Personality-Soul, which determines his destiny; and the Guardian/Shadow-Soul, which protects his conscience and remains behind, in the form of a duppy, after his body has gone into the ground and his life-soul has returned to God. There are both benign and malevolent duppies, but all are feared for their unpredictability and because they can be sent on grievous errands by the power of obeah.

After a person has been dead for three days, it is said that a stream of smoke can be seen rising from the burial plot. This vapor transmogrifies into his duppy, which is capable, not unlike Anancy the spider, of assuming a variety of forms, both human and animal. The duppy is capable of almost any sort of mischief. Possessing many of the powers of the living, it can speak, laugh, whistle, sing, smoke, cook and even ride a horse or a donkey, albeit with its head pointing backwards, the duppy grasping the animal's tail as a bridle. In order to see a duppy, one must take the liquid that drops from a dog's eyes, wipe it on one's own and look over one's left shoulder. Apart from basic misbehavior, a duppy "set" upon a person by an obeahman can strike him, cause grave or fatal illness or—worst of all—rob him of his own shadow.

It is the mission of the Rastaman to drive out such "odious superstition" and replace it with the Revelation of Jah Rastafari, His Imperial Majesty Haile Selassie, and to encourage the smoking of ganja "spliffs" (hand-rolled, cigar-sized joints) and herb-packed "chillums" (water pipes) among the people to "aid dere meditations on de truth," as Marley put it.

The Wailers' music used the language, lore and idioms of the humble country folk of Jamaica to explain the goals of Rastafari on earth—principally that of ascending to "iration," the highest form of Creation, a level of existence at which no false dogma holds sway, no evil exists, and there are no duppies, obeahmen or even Screwface himself, the name by which the Devil is commonly known in rural Jamaica. The Rastaman, the ultimate black pariah, explains that the bitter passage through time of the forcibly displaced black man—his captivity, his awakening with the aid of the proper religious teachings and his struggle to return to Africa—mirrors the spiritual pattern by which all men suffer and strive for deliverance. This journey replicates the mystic migration of the life-soul to earth and then back to Jah.

The problem is that superstition continually invades the dialogue between the Rastaman and his would-be brethren, who see him through veiled eyes and judge him to be akin to the "blackheart mon," the bogeyman about whom mothers in Jamaica still warn their children.

Some in Jamaica are joyful that Bob Marley has gone to his reward, his guardian-soul alive in the land to act as an instrument of good. Others feel his passing is a sign of the approach of Armageddon, a time when the best of men are removed from the earth and the Darkness descends for the Reckoning, wherein Jah will cast the Devil and his vassals into the Bottomless Pit.

In such a climate, many weak men make the wrong choices, follow the doomed path. Some country folk say the obeahmen have returned to the Jamaican cemeteries in force, throwing turpentine and pepper in front of tombstones to summon forth the duppies of dead relatives, so that the spirits might assist them in secret acts of mayhem and revenge.

But the Rastaman laughs and dismisses such talk as the cant of a "bloodclot" (heathen, the term of opprobrium derived from both menstruation, and the cloth with which slaves cleansed themselves after vicious beatings), reminding the heedful of the words of Bob Marley's "Redemption Song":

Old pirates yes them rob I
Sold I to the merchant ships
Minutes after they took I from the Bottomless Pit
By the hand of the Almighty
We forward in this generation, triumphantly
All I ever had is songs of freedom . . .
Won't you help me to sing these songs of freedom
'Cause all I ever had redemption songs . . .

Emancipate yourselves from mental slavery
None but ourselves can free our minds
Have no fear for atomic energy
'Cause none a them can stop the time
How long shall they kill our prophets
While we stand aside and look
Yes some say it's just a part of it
We've got to fulfill the book . . .

In April 1981, Bob Marley was awarded Jamaica's Order of Merit, one of its highest honors, in recognition of his contributions to the nation's culture. A month later, he was dead from brain, liver and lung cancer, his body lying in a bronze casket in the National Heroes Arena in Kingston. His gaunt, waxy face was clean-shaven; his dreadlocks, which had fallen out during the radiation treatments, had been sewn into a wig and set back in place. One hand held a Bible, open to the Twenty-third Psalm, the other lay upon his battered blond Gibson electric guitar.

When Marley went to Africa exactly a year before to perform at the special Zimbabwe concert, he found several cover versions of his recent single, "Survival," selling briskly from Nigeria to Senegal, the records cut by the continent's top singers and musicians out of respect, admiration and sales savvy. Fans turned out by the thousands to shower him with adulation and their smiles seemed to evince the essential communion with Africa that all Rastas yearn for. A similar, although more somber spectacle occurred at the public wake in the National Arena. Tens of thousands of mourners—Africans, Americans, Europeans, West Indians—filed past the bier, which was guarded by soldiers in white uniforms who held M-16 rifles, while various "tribute" singles rushed out by local stars crackled and droned in the streets.

At a state funeral presided over by His Eminence Abouna Yeshaq, passages from the Scriptures were read by Jamaica's governor general, Florizel Glasspole, and by the leader of the opposition party, Michael Manley. The Honorable Edward Seaga then eulogized the Honorable Robert Nesta Marley, O.M.

The Wailers played some of Marley's compositions as the I-Threes, the female vocal trio that includes his wife Rita Marley, backed them up. The Melody Makers, a group that consists of four of Bob and Rita Marley's children (while Marley had a legally recognized total of ten offspring by various women, some relatives estimate he fathered as many as twenty-two), also performed in his honor, and his mother Cedella sang one of the last songs he wrote, "Coming In from the Cold."

The coffin was placed upon a truck and slowly driven seventy-five miles to his hilltop birthplace in the Jamaica parish of St. Ann (Jamaica is divided into fourteen parishes) where Rastamen had hewn a sepulcher out of the living rock of the hillside.

For a man like Bob Marley, life and Jah were one and the same. Marley saw Jah as being the gift of existence; that is, he believed that he, Bob Marley, was in some way eternal, and that he would never be duplicated. He believed that the singularity of every man and woman is Jah's gift. What we struggle to make of it is our sole gift to Jah. He believed the process of that struggle becomes, in time, the truth.

Historically certain figures sometimes emerge from stagnant, despairing and/or disintegrating cultures to reinterpret old symbols and beliefs and invest them with new meaning. An individual's decision to play such a role may be purely unconscious, but it can sometimes evolve into an acute awareness that he may indeed have the gift/burden of prophecy. This realization may be followed by the public declaration on the part of such a person that he is merely an instrument of a new source of knowledge, a new direction and a new order.

For Jamaicans, and ultimately for much of the Third World, Bob Marley was such a messianic figure. He maintained that spectral emissaries invaded his sleep to enlist him as a seer. He was frightened by the responsibility, he said, but he had decided to assume it. "By and by," he explained, "Jah show every mon him hand, and Jah has shown I mine."

A man who looked like a skinny lion, moved like a spider and lived like a ghost, Bob Marley died trying to control the duppies within himself. This is a disturbing story about the thin ice that is mere information, the terrible onrush of truth and the ebb and flow of magic.

2
Kingdom Come

On July 23, 1892, a baby was born in Ejarsa Gora and was suckled in the fertile lands of Harage province, some eighteen miles from the city of Harar. On that first day a stern-faced nobleman kept a vigil outside a round house of dried earth and ash with a conical thatched roof of wattle-wood, listening for the child's first crackling cries for breath and life. He wore a black bombazine tunic, against which shone a smart sword in a silver sheath. Around his waist was a bandolier of cartridges, an ivory-handled pistol tucked in it at the belly, and upon his head was an Italian-made fedora of stiff black felt.

A gun bearer stood behind him, cradling the man's fine rifle in a scarlet cotton sheath, holding it high above the swirling dust. Farther back from the pair, fanned out in a wide half-circle upon the sloping hillock, was a large contingent of soldiers in ceremonial dress, each grasping a loaded carbine. And beyond this mass of men were tight clusters of peasants, prostrate and in prayer, the torrid breezes from the desert carrying their fervently chanted *zemas* (prayers) into the cool recesses of the house.

Inside, physicians and servants ministered to the mother under the watchful gaze of priests clutching long *malwamiyas* (prayer sticks). Keeping their heads bowed and their eyes averted, the servants fulfilled all requests quickly and quietly, but with extravagant care, knowing their very lives depended on their serving their mistress well on this momentous occasion. The mother was in the final stages of labor, and as they forced back impulses toward panic, the servants almost failed to hear the sputtering whimpers as the babe emerged from the womb, his tiny body steaming slightly.

The awful tension exploded with a shrill bawling from the tawny male infant, and all hands concentrated on preparing the child for inspection by his father. The servants' eyes blurred with tears of relief as they washed him, anointed him with fine oils and daubed his thin lips with melted, blessed butter, and their ears rang with the din of rifle reports as hundreds of guns saluted from every valley and hilltop the nativity of Tafari Makonnen, son of Governor Ras Makonnen of Harar under Emperor Menelik II and Makonnen's wife, Woyzaro Yashimabet.

This child was believed to be a direct descendant of the biblical King Solomon of Jerusalem and Queen Makeda of Sabo (Sheba), the southern lands of Ethiopia. Indeed, his bloodlines had been traced back to Solomon's grandfather, Jesse, the blackest Jew the world had ever known.

For several years, Ras Makonnen's chaplains and astrologers had been foretelling the infant's birth; Neptune and Pluto, they explained, had started slowly moving toward each other in the year 1399; both planets travelled along the Heliocentric Line, taking 493 years to intersect; the moment would come in July 1892, sparking off radiations from other zodiacal signs that would mystically influence the constellation Leo, which corresponded to the biblical House of Judah, Jacob's fourth son, who was born the same month, as recounted in Isaiah.

But before this birth, said the seers, there would be a great drought in Ethiopia, beginning in 1889, despite the fact that the country traditionally enjoyed two rainy seasons. The eventual return of the rains would confirm the identity and destiny of the child, as it was written in Isaiah 9:6: "For unto us a child is born, unto us a son is given; and the Government shall be upon his shoulders; and his name shall be called Wonderful Counsellor, The Mighty God, The Everlasting Father, The Prince of Peace."

When all was in readiness, a saddled mule was brought to carry Ras Makonnen the few yards from where he had been waiting to the front door of the house. He entered, beheld the luminescent baby, and offered a solemn prayer that, unlike all his previous offspring by Yashimabet, this son might survive his infancy. The priests made similar supplications to ward off demon spirits and *buda*—the human agents of the evil eye who transform themselves by night into predatory hyenas.

The customarily stiff and taciturn *ras* (prince) murmured a few words of comfort and praise to Yashimabet, who thanked him meekly. Then he departed on his mule, his retainers and soldiers following close behind him as he headed off in the direction of the walled city of Harar. At some point along the way he would partake of a celebratory meal of *wat*, a strongly spiced beef stew, traditionally eaten with the highly absorbent flat bread called *injera*, and washed down with sweet wine and *talla*, a robust beer.

As Ras Makonnen reached the main road leading to Harar, a few raindrops stained his tunic. A servant scurried up alongside his master, deftly covering him with a *barnos*, a black cloak of fine wool with a cowl for the head that was standard foul-weather equipment for the wealthy during the summer rainy season. Deep in contemplation, Makonnen scarcely noticed either the drizzle or the obsequious gesture.

He wondered if this child of his would live to manhood. For what reason had so many others perished in the cradle? Was his own seed cursed by a devil, a *zar*, dispatched by sorcerers to mock his ambition? Or had corrupt servants poisoned the infants with bad coffee? And if the boy thrived and grew strong, would he succeed where his father had not in securing the emperor's crown for the house of Makonnen? Or was it God's will that the son should rise as high as his father—but no higher—in order to teach this proud family the meaning of true humility?

Yet there was no guarantee that the boy would have the governorship; not even as the lineal descendant of Jesse and Solomon and the great-great grandson of King Sahela Selassie, regional sovereign of Shoa province, who had imposed his will upon the powerful Galla peoples, made treaties with foreign monarchs like Queen Victoria, and carried on the traditions, responsibilities and glories of the Solomonic dynasty, as set down in the holiest of Ethiopian books, the Kebra Nagast.

This was a land of treachery, deceit and low deeds in high places, Makonnen knew. While Menelik II might be his beloved cousin, a man to whom he pledged undying loyalty, the Empress Taitu was a scheming serpent who would stop at nothing to install one of her own line on the throne when the aging emperor died. If his son would endure, he would have to learn a great deal about the responsibilities of noble birth, obedience and the art of manipulation.

The rain intensified as the governor and his retinue crossed a lush field of *durra*, a sudden high wind knifing through the dense sorghum and scattering some guinea fowl that had been hiding among the shorter stalks by the road. The party pulled off into a mango grove to take shelter until the squall died down.

Still brooding, the prince absently pulled a ripe, rose-red mango from a low-hanging branch as his mule passed under it, causing his retainers to gape with shock. It was most uncommon for Ethiopian nobles to perform even the smallest tasks themselves, especially one so menial as picking fruit. Ras Makonnen bit deeply into the custard-soft flesh, warm juice spilling out of both corners of his mouth. He was about to gulp down the generous lump of pulp when he felt a strange quivering against his tongue. He spat and examined the fruit in his hand: the remaining half of a large gray worm wriggled out of the mango's creamy yellow center.

Makonnen slammed the rest of the fruit to the ground in revulsion and spat again, rubbing the inside of his mouth with his cloak. Just then a violent gust of wind and rain threw back the sheltering mango boughs, a thick bolt of lightning lit up the charcoal sky and in the ghostly flash it appeared to the prince as if the trees themselves were cowering in alarm, as their seasoned fruit was ripped from their limbs and flung a great distance by the furious blast of the storm.

The drought was over! Makonnen exulted to himself, but then the prince's mood darkened. Truly, mighty signs and portents were rapidly multiplying on this most curious and fateful birthday, but they were in conflict. The rains had come, the drought was at an end, but the spoiled fruit of the earth and the harsh, skeleton fingers of the sky were contrasting omens. Makonnen longed to trust completely in the fulfillment of the oracles, but he could not; instead he wanted to curse God aloud for His cruel uncertainties. Yet something in him made him hold his tongue.

The rain grew heavier, rendering the flimsy shelter of the trees worthless. So the party took to the road again and pressed on to Harar, each of the prince's retainers wearing the same uncertain expression as his master.

Makonnen decided that young Tafari would have the benefits of both a traditional and a European education. This was considered most unusual by the isolated, ethnocentric citizens of late-nineteenth-century Ethiopia. The nation's peoples, most of whose ancestors entered the country from Arabia, are divided into two main linguistic families,

Cushitic and Semitic. The Galla (Tafari's mother's people) were the most formidable of the Cushites, and the Amharic peoples of Shoa the most influential of the Semites, with the language, politics and religion (the autonomous Ethiopian Orthodox Christian, or Coptic, Church) of the latter becoming predominant as Tafari came of age.

A member of the Shoan-Amharic nobility, Tafari was brought up as befitted a young prince who was one day to be wedded to a worthy *woyzaro*, or titled lady. Makonnen, having made a number of trips to Europe on state business (including the coronation of Edward VII of England), shared Menelik's view that an awareness of European politics, commerce and culture was essential if Ethiopia was ever to awaken from its feudal doldrums and join the modern family of nations. So Makonnen hired a French tutor from Guadeloupe, Dr. Vitalen, and later invited Abba Samuel, an Ethiopian working in the French mission, to provide his son with a solid Western education.

But Makonnen also believed that a future *ras* must learn to accept and appreciate the unusual dignity and preeminence over his countrymen that his descent from the Solomonic dynasty afforded. The trembling of the peasants and tenant farmers whenever they found themselves in the presence of royalty was natural, respectful and appropriate, he felt, as well as a sign of favor from God. An Amharic aristocrat, endowed with vast, untaxed lands handed down from his ancestors and augmented with gifts from his emperor, should be able to impose with the confidence of Divine Right strict standards of administration for his properties, and to employ his soldiers (Makonnen had more than six thousand men in his private army) to protect his holdings and collect rent and taxes. The privileged must be vigilant in maintaining a social order based on loyalty and humble submission on the part of their inferiors, while showing the same respect and fealty to the imperial court. Makonnen had spent a lifetime learning a painful lesson: he who does not know how to identify and assess power, in oneself and others, will be deceived by it, and he who does not know how to wield the power he possesses will eventually be undone by it.

From the start, Tafari was aware of a queer dichotomy between his father's European enthusiasms—specifically, an admiration for the orderliness and social mobility of Western society—and the Shoan-Amharic traditions that his father nonetheless adhered to, maintaining a rigid, regal household. The objective, his son eventually came to realize, was to somehow overlap these contradictory elements in his world without one canceling out the other.

It soon became obvious that he would be left to his own devices in this matter. His mother, Yashimabet, had died two years after his birth, and his father, a loving but extremely reserved man, was traveling most of the time on official errands or serving as a judge in the civil court in Harar. Embittered by his near-complete isolation, Tafari loathed his mother for deserting him, but admired his distant father for his detachment from sentimental bonds and obligations. In several respects, Tafari was nothing if not his father's son: he amplified Makonnen's romantic notions about the edifying value of cultural links with the West; he shared his esteem and his thirst for power, as well as his cold, aloof temperament. At a very early age, Tafari had developed the personality of a thoroughgoing autocrat.

Taking notice of this, Makonnen appointed his thirteen-year-old son to the largely honorary post of Dejazmatch, or Keeper of the Door, for a section of Harage province. A year later, in 1906, the proud father was dead.

When the first tests of his mettle came, young Tafari confronted them with the unwavering conviction that all that had been accumulated—both materially and politically—by his late father should be inherited by him. Furthermore, his stored-up resentment of women prepared him to face his two chief adversaries: Empress Taitu and her daughter Zauditu.

Taitu was keen on having Yelma Makonnen, the late prince's son by his first wife, replace his father as governor. Tafari (son of Makonnen's second wife) was devastated and then furious that Yelma should be favored over him. But he understood the nepotism of Ethiopian politics well enough to see why this course was adopted: his father's first wife was a cousin of Taitu's, and with her aged husband in poor health and favorably disposed to Tafari, Taitu was anxious to secure her family's hold on the throne while there was still time to set such a precedent.

And so Yelma got the governorship of Harar, as well as the army that went with it, while Tafari was sidelined with a minor appointment as governor of Selale, a small and insignificant corner of the realm, located to the northwest of the imperial city of Addis Ababa. In an effort to neutralize him completely, Tafari was compelled by Taitu to rule the tiny area in absentia from within the confines of Menelik's palace.

Ironically, this confinement turned out to be quite beneficial for him. Forced to live in an atmosphere of unceasing intrigue as the skirmishes for control of the throne escalated, Tafari gained a great deal of valuable knowledge by observing the snakes in their own pit.

Menelik's frail health gradually worsened, and in 1908 he suffered a stroke. Cut off from the now-incapacitated emperor, his last ally, Tafari was exiled to the southern frontiers of Ethiopia to serve as governor of Sidamo province. But he got three thousand soldiers in the bargain, in addition to the cynical counsel of his maternal grandmother, Woyzaro Wallata Giyorgis, who was banished along with him. While Tafari was tranquilly growing accustomed to holding sway over his own outlying territory, Taitu was madly fending off endless plots in Addis Ababa.

The year before, Menelik had designated Lij Yasu, his headstrong twelve-year-old grandson, as his successor. Taitu, however, was pushing a more malleable candidate in Zauditu, one of Menelik's daughters. At this juncture, Tafari's half-brother Yelma died, and the governorship of Harar was left vacant. In 1910, with political muscle supplied by a loose confederation of other princes, Tafari regained his birthright, and then moved swiftly, in concert with his newfound comrades, to surround the imperial palace with troops. He then calmly but firmly informed Taitu that her duties at court would henceforth be confined to the nursing of the infirm Menelik, and that the torch of power would be handed over, for the time being, to a well-placed schemer sympathetic to Tafari, Ras Tasamma.

For a time, these audacious measures were effective, but in 1911 Tasamma died, and Lij Yasu once again began to make a determined bid for the throne. In 1913, Menelik finally succumbed, yet Lij Yasu went uncrowned because he had been impudent enough to convert to Islam, in direct defiance of the considerable authority of the Monophysite Ethiopian Orthodox Church. The church and the Shoan nobles fought long and hard to discredit Yasu, and in 1917 they decided to confirm Zauditu as empress.

While the puppet empress was left stranded in the vortex of a maelstrom, Muslims, led by the excommunicated Lij Yasu, sought to subvert the three-thousand-year-old Solomonic succession. But the twenty-five-year-old Tafari, who had since been named a *ras* by the church in recognition of his loyalty, prevailed upon the Zauditu regime to appoint him regent. Strikingly handsome, extraordinarily soft-spoken and deferential, he seemed an ideal second figurehead for the church and the Shoan faction, and he was granted his wish. He thus achieved through guile what he could never have gained by force of arms: ultimate proximity to the imperial scepter.

For the next thirteen years, Tafari maneuvered his way to a position of political indispensability. He assembled a staff of confidants and then installed them in government offices in Addis Ababa. He introduced a European-style bureaucracy and imported advisors and statecraft from the West. By 1923, he had ushered Ethiopia into the League of Nations. He traveled abroad extensively, accompanied by a retinue which included zebras and lions, and became the figure most closely identified with exotic, enigmatic Ethiopia on the international scene. And when he returned from such trips, he was chauffeured to the palace in a European limousine—as rare an item in Ethiopia as tame lions were in the West.

During these years, he ferreted out and punished his enemies. Renegade Lij Yasu was captured in 1921 and thrown into prison, where he remained bound in the golden chains Tafari had ordered to be cast for this purpose. Yasu was fed fine food, and was allowed to indulge himself with a host of concubines in whatever manner he wished; indeed, Yasu could have most anything he desired—except to be released from the dungeon. He would remain manacled there in strictly circumscribed luxury until his death twelve years later.

In 1926, Habte Giorgis, a war minister who had opposed Ras Tafari's rapid ascendance, expired of natural causes—or so it was claimed. Ras Tafari swiftly confiscated Giorgis's private lands and assumed command of his sixteen-thousand-man army, employing them to move against Empress Zauditu's last belligerent supporters. "He creeps like a mouse, but has the jaws of a lion," observed another *ras* that same year.

Ras Tafari had become the most formidable man in Ethiopia, and he insisted that Zauditu crown him *negus*, or king, vowing that he personally would drag her down from her throne if she dared refuse. In a final attempt to thwart him, Zauditu sent her husband's sizable army against Tafari's forces, but the army was immediately crushed and her husband killed. On April 2, 1930, two days after Ras Tafari's victory, Empress Zauditu was also dead, in circumstances that remain a mystery to this day.

But the Ethiopian people could be certain of this: against all odds, a thin, seemingly fragile man who stood but five feet four inches tall and had rarely been heard to raise his voice, a man who twenty-odd years before had no living parents and no powerful connections to pave his way politically, had somehow risen to challenge, outwit and finally vanquish the last of his opponents.

Rumors cropped up in Addis Ababa that even Ras Tafari's trusted personal counselors were terrified of him, reluctant to shake his hand or gaze directly upon his stark features, with its pointed nose, sparse beard and penetrating, almost black eyes, all framed by wild, bushy hair.

Many of his countrymen were reminded of the biblical prophecy that after the Last War is fought, a King of Kings out of Jesse's root would be crowned in the land of David, a man whose eyes are like flames of fire, whose hair is like wool and whose feet are black like burning brass, and that in due course that greatest of all kings would vanquish Death and proceed with the Last Judgment, toppling the thrones of Babylon, and throwing all pretenders to temporal power and their deluded followers into the Void.

Queer tales began to circulate about Tafari's boyhood, the most notable concerning his supposed ability to speak to animals. During his youth, it was claimed, he had on several occasions been seen conversing in the bush with leopards and lions, the fierce jungle beasts becoming docile at his feet, much as they had responded centuries before to the fabled Ethiopian hermit, Saint Abbo.

Further, it was said that as a young student Tafari was quite bright and competent at his lessons, but that he had truly astounded the priests with the depth of his knowledge concerning religious and mystical matters. Not only could he quote freely from the Kebra Negast, but also from the Book of Kufale, the Book of Enoch, the Shepherd of Hermas, Judith, Ecclesiasticus, Tobit, the Matshafa Berhan (Book of Light), the Sixth and Seventh Books of Moses, the Books of Eden (secretly deleted from Genesis during the Dark Ages), all thirty-one books of the Hebrew Bible, the twenty-one canonical books of the New Testament and numerous other apocryphal and pseudepigraphic works.

According to one story, a local priest in Harar had visited the young Tafari shortly after the death of his father and asked him where he had gained such vast knowledge. Tafari replied that much of it had come to him at the moment of his baptism, conducted according to tradition on the fortieth day of his life. The priest who presided at the ceremony had opened Tafari's eyes with the first touch of holy chrism, and everything that ensued was as comprehensible to the infant as if he had been an adult. The priest pronounced his surname, he remembered, and next his baptismal name, and then of course he blew softly in Tafari's face to drive off the evil spirits. At that instant,

Tafari claimed, he felt himself enveloped by a golden glow, and as the priest began to anoint him, water touching his forehead, breast, shoulders and all of the other thirty-seven prescribed places, he felt his knowledge increase, filling him up like a vessel and endowing him with a great sense of clarity about Creation and the final purpose of man.

However, in the weeks afterward, the knowledge and this special sense of lucidity seemed to ebb away.

When did it return? the priest inquired.

When the birds and the beasts and even the insects began to greet him and speak to him, reminding him of what he already knew, Tafari replied.

Which was the first creature to speak to him?

Tafari requested a sheet of paper and some pastels and began to draw, with extraordinary facility, a picture of a bird. It resembled a dove, but with exotic, multicolored plumage. The priest was about to ask Tafari what sort of bird it was when he was dumbfounded to see the bird fly off the page and out through the nearby window, disappearing into the sky.

Word of the late governor's strange boy spread rapidly but discreetly through the network of *liqe kahnat* (chief priests) in the provinces, and it is said that they arranged several secret meetings with him to question and perhaps catch him in what they supposed might be blasphemous mischief or pagan magic.

At one of these meetings the boy is said to have made it plain that he was well acquainted with the rare manuscripts of Abba Aragawi and the other Coptic monks known as the "Nine Saints," who entered Ethiopia in 480 A.D. and founded the first monasteries in Tigre province. He also revealed that he was acquainted with the occult applications of Urim and Thummim and the mezuzah, as well as the use of the magic words *gematria* and *notarikon* in Egyptian necromancy and also of the magical names Adonay, El and Elohe. He exhibited familiarity with the cabalistic doctrines, the writings of Gilgamesh, the pagan rituals surrounding the worship of Isis, of the serpent Arwe, and of the Abyssinian gods of Earth (Meder), Sea (Beher) and War (Mahrem), as well as the arcana of astrology and numerology. But most importantly, Tafari exhibited to the priests his understanding of the central messages in the Egyptian Book of the Dead and the Egyptian Book of Two Ways.

In the ancient Egyptian, or Coptic, language, the word for magician meant "scribe of the House of Life." Men so styled were known as kindly wise men, not evil tricksters, and the requests for spells to ward off malevolence that people sought from them were a facet of everyday existence. However, there were several formal rituals that were reserved for ceremonies of the utmost seriousness, among them the Heb-Sed Festival, in which, after he had reigned for thirty years, the pharaoh would travel to Sakkarah, some thirty miles from the Great Pyramid. There, in a holy place flanked by immense monuments, the aged pharaoh would run, jump, wrestle, dance and become miraculously rejuvenated, newly endowed with the vigor of an adolescent. There was also the ritual known as the "Breaking of the Red Jars," in which red clay bowls from Thebes and human figurines fashioned in Sakkarah were smashed in meticulous sequence to repel or destroy the ruler's enemies.

These rituals were performed under the supervision of senior Coptic magicians, the very same order of men who were once bidden by the pharaoh to match their sorcery with Moses and Aaron in a contest of enchantment, to determine whether or not they were actually speaking with the authority of God's Word in demanding that the Egyptians let the Israelites go free. For the Egyptians believed that with the proper sequence of rites and incantations performed in the House of Life, there was no limit to the magical possibilities.

At the core of this conjury was the Word. To say or write the proper word was to make it so. Names, of course, were of the utmost significance in ancient Egypt. All Egyptians had many different names, only one of which was their real name—and, if possible, this was never revealed to anyone. Spells could only be effective, no matter how artfully crafted, if they were cast against a person under his true name. It was said of a man as powerful as the pharaoh that "even his mother does not know his name."

No one, Tafari told the priests, knew his true name.

At one point, an old *abmnet* (abbot) allegedly asked to examine Tafari's palms. He saw that there were stigmata there, and that the lifeline circled back upon itself in an emblem of infinity. Tafari whispered a word in the abbot's ear, and all color drained from the old man's face. He left the room, apparently in shock, refusing to return or to speak with his colleagues.

Tafari concluded his final session with these scholars and holy men by recounting, as vividly as if he had witnessed the events himself, the story of how King Solomon of Jerusalem had come to know and woo Queen Makeda of Sheba. For uncounted hours, or so it is maintained, the holy men listened with rapt attention, astounded by the young boy's intimate familiarity with these ancient events, without the slightest interruption on their part.

The boy spoke slowly, careful not to skip over any detail, whether it concerned the aspect of a sunrise on a given day and the weather that followed, the architecture and interior design of the palaces and the squalor of slaves' hovels, the stinging, chafing dust in the city streets and the heat waves shimmering up from the vast desert basins in the late afternoon, or the dress, speech, manner and even diet of one of the venerable figures who appeared in his narrative. Descriptions of emotions were handled with particular respect, the complexities of various key events were unhurriedly unraveled, and all of it was deftly woven into a tapestry of utterly arresting discourse.

Tafari explained that the ravishing and wealthy Queen Makeda had learned of the great King Solomon from the Ethiopian merchant prince Tamrin, who owned almost four hundred ships and caravans numbering five hundred camels. After returning from a trading voyage to Jerusalem, where he had delivered large quantities of ebony, red gold and sapphires to the Hebrew king, Tamrin told Makeda of his majestic temple and palace, and of his goodness and righteousness as a judge over his subjects.

Enthralled, Makeda decided she must visit this great king and set out, Tamrin acting as her captain, with a caravan of eight hundred camels, innumerable attendants and a massive baggage train. Upon her arrival in Jerusalem, she was welcomed into the palace by Solomon, who overwhelmed her with his hospitality and enlightened her with his wisdom. Solomon persuaded her to turn away from the worship of the sun and Makeda became a follower of the one true God, the God of Israel, He Whose Name Should Not Be Spoken.

At length, the virgin queen announced her desire to take all that she had learned back to her own people, but Solomon, feeling amorous toward Makeda, persuaded her to linger another season to "complete her instruction in wisdom." On her last night in the palace, there was a farewell banquet of unprecedented splendor, after which Solomon requested to lie with her. She declined, entreating that he swear not to take her by force. He complied, on the stipulation that she take nothing more from him on that night. She agreed, and so Solomon satisfied himself with her slave. But during the night, she arose to get a drink of water from the cistern in the sleeping chamber, and Solomon, who had been feigning sleep in order to observe her, insisted she had broken her oath by taking such a precious substance in so dry a land. Thus, she had no choice but to submit to his lust.

The following morning, Solomon gave her a ring upon which was engraved the seal of the Lion of Judah, instructing her to give it to her firstborn male child, and then to send the boy to him for his education when he came of age. During the long journey back to Ethiopia, Makeda gave birth to a boy she named Ebna Hakim, meaning "son of the wise man."

Growing up in Sheba, Ebna was continually teased by his companions because of his illegitimate birth. By the time he reached his teens he could endure no more ridicule and mortification. Angry and confused, he summoned the courage he had previously lacked and questioned his mother about his unknown father. Pleased, she told him of Solomon, producing the ring for him.

Elegant in its bold simplicity, it was unlike any that Ebna had ever seen. Initially he resisted when Makeda sought to slip it on his finger, but he eventually accepted the ring and put it on. Its effect on him was unsettling, as if a surge of jagged, burning energy were suddenly coursing through him. Embarrassed that his mother should see him so discomfited, he tried to curb his anxiety, but the turmoil in his spirit would not be assuaged, and his hand was shaking furiously as he fumbled to pull off the ring. Light-headed and perspiring heavily, he held it out to Makeda, but she refused to take it back. It is a man's ring and a king's gift, she told her son, and then she sent him to his father to study.

When Ebna presented himself before the king, he was rebuffed at first, much to his chagrin and astonishment, since Solomon believed him to be an impostor. "I will know my son," he thundered, "by the ring he wears!" Ashamed, Ebna produced the ring, and his father's anger gave way to sorrow. "You are fearful of its power," said Solomon, "yet its power comes from you. You must learn to embrace your destiny."

Ebna spent many happy years in Solomon's court but eventually decided to return to "the mountains of his mother's land." The king, disappointed that he would not be his successor (since Solomon's eldest son, Rehoboam, was rather frivolous-minded), permitted him to go on the condition that he take with him the most erudite sons of his personal counselors to teach the Hebrew Law in Ethiopia. Ebna was agreeable to this, but the counselors and their sons objected, believing they would be beyond the reach of God's special grace and protection if they left Israel.

Enraged by their impudence, Solomon placed the counselors' sons under a sacred ban. They capitulated but plotted vengeance. Azarias (also known as Eleazar), son of the high priest Zadok, hatched a plot to steal the Ark of the Covenant and take it to Ethiopia.

When Solomon realized what had taken place, he sent his cavalry to overtake the caravan, but Jehovah, displeased with Solomon's debauchery and his vanities, befuddled the king's horsemen and caused the travelers to move so swiftly that they arrived at their destination months ahead of schedule.

Thus, the Ark found a new, permanent home in Ethiopia, with Jehovah's blessing, Tafari explained to the priests at the close of his monologue, and Ebna, wearing Solomon's ring upon his finger, became emperor, taking the name Menelik.

At first humbled by the force and beauty of Tafari's recital, the priests gradually grew jealous and greatly suspicious of the wealth of uncanny detail with which the youth had embellished the biblical stories. They demanded to know the sources of his information.

Instead of replying to the question, Tafari addressed a monk who had served in the Cathedral of Axum, where the Ark is kept.* Tafari described to him in hushed tones the *kedusta kedussan*, the Holy of Holies or inner sanctum where the *tabbot*—the Ark—is kept, and then recited various inscriptions written upon it. Close to fainting with the shock of what Tafari was disclosing, the monk is said to have covered his ears to shut out these blasphemous revelations, and he and the rest of the priests hurriedly dispersed.

Later, they made a solemn pact among themselves to do everything within their means to keep the young Tafari from ever gaining power in the land. He was too dangerous, dangerous beyond belief.

The stories about Tafari's boyhood encounters with the priests and his occult wisdom and uncanny powers were spreading like a runaway brushfire throughout Ethiopia in 1930 as the country prepared to carry

*As Axum monks reaffirmed in a *New York Times* cover story on January 27, 1998.

out Ras Tafari's vow that his coronation in November would be the grandest and most solemn that Africa had ever known.

It was the law of the land that any lion slain within its borders was the property of the emperor, the Conquering Lion of the Tribe of Judah. Months before the coronation, a bale of lion skins was shipped to London, to be transformed into ceremonial garments by a Bond Street tailor. One million dollars' worth of gold and jewels were acquired in Europe by Tafari's envoys and likewise dispatched to England, where they would be fashioned into two imperial crowns incorporating Solomon's seal and the Lion of Judah crest. (The crowns had to be completed and hand-delivered to Addis Ababa in time to permit Coptic priests to pray over them for the required twenty-one days prior to the coronation.) Also, the state coach of Kaiser Wilhelm II of Germany was purchased to transport the emperor and empress, along with a team of snow-white Hapsburg stallions, and an Austrian coachman formerly employed by the Emperor Franz Josef was hired to drive it.

Throughout Addis Ababa, new roads were built, existing ones widened and a host of new buildings, monuments, archways and statues erected to commemorate the occasion, scheduled for the second of November. Invitations went out to dignitaries around the world, and the guests began arriving in mid-October, by steamship at the port of Djibouti on the Gulf of Aden in what was then French Somaliland, and making their way into the mountainous interior of Ethiopia on railways specially refurbished for the 780-mile trip. Among those who had arrived by the end of the month were Isaburo Yoshida of Japan, Marshal Franchet d'Esperey of France, Rear Admiral Prince Udine of Italy, Greek Count P. Metaxas, Baron H.K.C. Bildt of Sweden, Muhammad Tawfiq Nasim Pasha of Egypt and Great Britain's Duke of Gloucester, who came bearing a one-ton coronation cake. German President von Hindenburg sent five hundred bottles of fine Rhine wine, and the French government dispatched a private airplane. But it was Special Envoy Herman Murray Jacoby, appointed by Herbert Hoover to represent the United States, who was entrusted with the greatest largess. Besides an autographed and handsomely framed photograph of the President, he was accompanied by an inventory of unofficial, privately purchased presents that included an electric refrigerator, a red typewriter emblazoned with the royal coat of arms, a radio-phonograph console, one hundred records of "distinctly American music," five hundred rosebushes, including several dozen of the so-called President Hoover variety, a new strain of amaryllis developed by the U.S. Department of Agriculture, a bound set of the *National Geographic*, a bound report of the Chicago Field Museum's expedition to Abyssinia and prints of three motion pictures: *Ben Hur, King of Kings*, and *With Byrd at the South Pole*.

Among the events of the days preceding the coronation were the unveiling of a statue of Menelik II in front of the Cathedral of St. George and an all-night service in the cathedral on the eve of the coronation ceremonies. The Negus Ras Tafari and his wife Woyzaro Menen prayed in unison with richly costumed priests and deacons, who danced, chanted and beat drums and prayer sticks in time with the music of harps, lyres, tambourines, cymbals and the one-stringed *masanko*. Periodically the incense-clouded sanctuary vibrated with the impassioned singing of the female choir and the rhythmic hand-clapping which accompanied the hymns. Outside, on the steps of the cathedral, nobles and diplomats stood holding lighted candles.

Sunday, November 2, 1930, dawned clear and balmy, and by 7:00 A.M. most of the seven hundred official guests had taken their places in the luxuriously draped hall at the west side of the cathedral, lion-maned feudal chieftains seated side-by-side with uniformed foreign dignitaries. Shortly after 7:30 A.M., the great doors of the Holy of Holies opened ponderously and hundreds of chanting priests filed out, followed by the negus, dressed in white silk communion robes, who stepped to a gold-posted canopy near the center of the nave and settled lightly onto his red and gold throne. The Amharic liturgy was celebrated by the Abuna Kyril, Archbishop of the Ethiopian Orthodox Church, assisted by a representative of the Alexandrian Coptic Patriarch.

His Majesty rose to pledge his loyalty to the church and to the state and promised to put the welfare of his subjects above all personal concerns. As each declaration and blessing was made, he received the symbols of his imperial office: the royal insignia, the gold-embroidered scarlet robes, the jewel-encrusted saber, the scepter and the orb, the ring of Solomon, two diamond rings and two gold lances. The Abuna came forward and, repeating a rite that dated back to the consecration of David by Samuel and Solomon by Nathan and Zadok, he anointed Tafari's brow with oil and crowned him Haile Selassie I, Power of the Holy Trinity, Two Hundred Twenty-fifth Emperor of the Solomonic Dynasty, Elect of God, Lord of Lords, King of Kings, Conquering Lion of the Tribe of Judah. The Abuna sealed the moment with the benediction "That God may make this crown a crown of sanctity and glory. That by the grace and blessings which we have given you may have an unshaken faith and a pure heart, in order that you may inherit the crown eternal. So be it."

As Selassie's eldest son, Crown Prince Asfa Wossen, knelt before the emperor in a gesture of the most profound respect, 101 cannons thundered a salute outside the cathedral. For days, the celebrations and rejoicing went on throughout Addis Ababa and the rest of the empire, even among the peasants and townspeople, who were barred from the coronation festivities and the immediate precincts of the cathedral. Correspondents from the international press filed glowing accounts of all that had occurred.

In Africa, Selassie was hailed as the greatest of modern monarchs and a symbol of the continent's vast potential. In the United States, residents of Harlem jammed movie houses to watch the newsreel footage of the event. And in the Caribbean, as elsewhere in the West, the advent of Selassie's reign was taken as shining proof for all downtrodden people of color that, as the back-to-Africa Garveyites and the firebrands of the syncretistic Rastafarian cult had foretold, the day of Deliverance was at hand.

To the Garveyites, Haile Selassie I was a hero without peer. To the Rastafarians he was the Living God of Abraham and Isaac, He Whose Name Should Not Be Spoken.

Soon after Selassie assumed the throne, he launched a campaign to introduce democratic institutions and in general to lead Ethiopia out of its feudal past. The new constitution, adopted in 1931, changed the status of Ethiopia's 26 million people from the chattels of the nobility to citizens of the empire.

In an effort to nudge the poor, illiterate and largely rural population into the twentieth century, a primary and secondary school system was created. The antiquated system of land tenure was reformed and slavery was outlawed. The civil service was streamlined, more roads built and other public works projects initiated. But progress was slow in a country of 455,000 square miles, whose tribal population spoke more than two thousand different languages and dialects.

The long shadow of fascism that was spreading across Europe in the 1930s suddenly darted in the direction of Ethiopia in 1934, when

Benito Mussolini attempted to expand Italy's colonial interests in Africa beyond Eritrea and Italian Somaliland. Selassie looked to the League of Nations for support, but he was ignored. Ethiopia was invaded in October 1935, Addis Ababa fell shortly afterward and Selassie went into exile in 1936, going first to Jerusalem to pray and then to Britain. In June of that year, he addressed the League of Nations in Geneva, shaming the delegates for their cowardice in an extraordinarily dignified and impassioned speech on behalf of self-determination. "God and history will remember your judgment," he told them. "It is us today. It will be you tomorrow."

Winston Churchill rescued him from his tribulations in May 1940, when Italy formally entered World War II as an enemy of the United Kingdom. Smuggled into Khartoum by the British, Selassie organized an army in the deserts of the Sudan. The triumphant emperor reentered Addis Ababa on May 5, 1941, five years to the day after the city had been taken by Italian forces. Pressing forward with his work of reform and modernization, he built two hundred new schools and also set about reviving the stagnant economy, obtaining a vital coastal port on the Red Sea.

Selassie issued a new constitution in 1955 that granted universal suffrage and equal rights under the law for all his subjects, but the document contained a crucial caveat: "By virtue of His Imperial Blood as well as by the anointing which He has received, the person of the Emperor is sacred. His dignity is inviolable and His Power indisputable."

Five years later, while Selassie was on a state visit to Brazil, there was a palace-based coup attempt sanctioned by his son, Crown Prince Asfa Wossen. The emperor returned to crush the mutiny and hang the ringleader, who was the commander of the imperial bodyguard. The prince was spared, a gesture of leniency that recalled the emperor's kindly treatment of defeated Italian troops in 1942. But Selassie had sensed a chilling shift in the political winds that were sweeping across his realm.

The stated objectives of the coup were to install a new regime that would promote speedier social and economic advancement. Selassie began to give periodic radio addresses in which he kept his countrymen apprised of his latest programs and policies. But many of the people felt this was too little, too late. A tiny faction of Ethiopia's intellectual elite began to throw its weight around in the early 1970s, a time when the so-called Horn of Africa was beginning to emerge as one of the most strategically important, and politically volatile, regions of the world. With the United States sending military aid to upgrade the Ethiopian army, the Soviet Union moved to arm the country's age-old enemy Somalia and backed the ongoing revolutionary-secessionist struggle in the region of Eritrea.

Meanwhile, discontent was spreading among the general population, who were angry with extremely low standards of living and soaring prices. When a 1973 drought in two northern provinces resulted in approximately 100,000 deaths, discontent and outrage at government ineptitude was mounting. The peasant-based army demanded a pay raise, furious at the spectacle of an emperor who lived in opulence in the midst of dire poverty and was reputed to have stowed away billions of dollars in Swiss bank accounts (although such charges were never substantiated).

The dissident forces organized, and they came for the emperor in the cold rain, on Thursday, September 12, 1974. This was after a solid week of bleak, wet weather, broken up for him only by television news reports of the arrests of his ministers and friends. A few relatives escaped the revolutionaries' dragnet, and Crown Prince Asfa Wossen was recovering from a stroke in a hospital in Switzerland, but most of the House of Makonnen and its inner circle were imprisoned or executed.

At the appointed hour, the emperor confronted a contingent of troops in the vestibule of his office in the Jubilee Palace. He stood before a decorative map of Ethiopia, resplendent in full dress uniform. He was driven to an army barracks as roadside crowds screamed "Thief!" then taken into a grimy barred cubicle and left there, bundled in his woolen cape, a tin plate of cold food with cockroaches scampering over it at his feet. He knelt and prayed.

Months later, eighty-two-year-old Haile Selassie I was returned to the Jubilee Palace, where he was confined to his small bedroom apartment for whatever remained of his stay on this earth.

The clock struck seven on the morning of August 27, 1975, as a servant stood weeping at the bedside of the Lion of Judah—according to government reports. In London, Crown Prince Asfa Wossen issued a written statement demanding that "independent doctors and the International Red Cross be allowed to carry out an autopsy to ascertain the cause of death of Ethiopia's and Africa's father."

No *tezkar*, or memorial service, was held in the Cathedral of St. George or anywhere else in the country.

In the years that followed, despite extensive sleuthing by outsiders, the burial site of Haile Selassie I was never located.* And no one could find the sacred ring of Solomon.

In the Caribbean, on the island of Jamaica, devout brethren of the Rastafarian cult flashed strange, unfettered smiles.

"You nuh cyan bury Jah," the Rastas said.

*It was quietly revealed in the mid-1990s, several years following the 1991 overthrow of Marxist military dictator Lieutenant Colonel Mengistu Haile Mariam, that Selassie's reported remains had been recovered, sealed, and discreetly placed behind glass in the closet of a crypt of the Bhata Church in Addis Ababa near the marble tomb of Selassie's ancestor, Emperor Menelik II. As late as January 1996, however, the new government of Ethiopian Prime Minister Meles Zenawi refused to acknowledge Selassie's presence with an official resting place or imperial funeral and declined followers' requests for a nationwide day of mourning.

3
Misty Morning

The front page of the *Daily Gleaner* on Tuesday, February 6, 1945, was dominated by news of the world at war. The Red Army of Marshal Zhukov was within thirty-five miles of the Reich capital and Patton's tanks were boring deeper through the Siegfried Line while, on the other side of the planet, planes from the British carrier *Indefatigable* were bombing Japanese strongholds in Sumatra and General Douglas MacArthur's forces had returned to Manila.

In the local news, there were continued reports of a slump in Jamaican citrus production for the war effort (blamed on the hazards of the shipping routes to Britain), as well as shortages of beef, petrol and matchsticks. Farm workers had just been airlifted from Montego Bay to Florida to help harvest crops there. The day before, the Bishop of Kingston opened the annual Anglican Synod by hosting a cricket match in Sabina Park between the clergy and the police. Later that afternoon, Lady Huggins was honored at the nearby Jamaica Turf Club and Mrs. McWhinnie gave a tea.

There was no mention in the *Gleaner*, however, of an event which took place during the early hours of the morning in the rural parish of St. Ann. Nineteen-year-old Cedella Marley had given birth to her first child. The moonfaced Cedella—or Ciddy, as she was called—had had a difficult pregnancy and had suffered greatly from morning sickness. When she went into labor on Sunday evening, she was taken to the house of her father, Omeriah* Malcolm—a black man. She remained in labor through all of Monday; at 2:30 the

*Also spelled Omariah.

following morning Robert Nesta was finally delivered: a fawn-colored boy with the thin lips and the slender pointed nose of his father, Captain Norval Sinclair Marley—a white man.

Just after sunrise, the afterbirth was wrapped carefully in a page from the *Gleaner* that contained a story describing the arrest in Kingston the day before of a young rude boy who had stolen £35 from a Chinaman. The hooligan's alias was "Pearl Harbor."

The afterbirth was buried at the foot of a young coconut sapling that would from that day forth be Robert Nesta Marley's "fren' tree": it would grow as tall and as strong as he wished it to, its health and height reflecting his care; it would bend with the passage of time in the same direction as its cultivator.

Ciddy was fed mint tea and arrowroot while Omeriah placed the child on a rusty vegetable scale taken from his roadside produce stand: Robert weighed exactly six and a half pounds. Swaddled in a blue and white nightgown made by Ciddy from muslin Omeriah had ordered from a wholesaler in Kingston, he was then laid in a crib beside his mother's bed that was cushioned with pillows.

As Ciddy and child had slept soundly under Omeriah's roof, a group of young "kidren" playing outside sang a "ring song" (a traditional ditty that accompanied games played in a circle) that ricocheted through the hills:

Dere's a black boy in de ring, tra la la la la,
Dere's a black boy in de ring, tra la la la la,
Him like sugar, I like plum, tra la la la la
Him cyan't be my lover nuh, tra la la la . . .

"De Devil 'im want dat lickle bwai [little boy]."

Omeriah Malcolm was shaken to hear himself whispering this ghoulish assertion and no less surprised by the fear and the weariness in his own voice. "Somebody science 'im," he muttered to himself, "put duppy on 'im bwai."

His four-month-old grandson had suddenly been taken ill, and Omeriah was certain that malevolent forces were responsible. Only that morning, Ciddy had been tending her son in the usual way, breast-feeding him and then placing him on a rubber sheet in her one-room hilltop shack while she did her share of the family sewing—mending the clothes of her five brothers and three sisters. Sensing that all was well and feeling a trifle peckish, she had double-checked the child around noontime and then hurried down the hill to buy a sweet at the grocery shop. Upon her return not ten minutes later, she found him lying on his stomach quivering, water dripping from his nose. He was making short coughing noises.

She lifted him up and stroked his brow, thinking he had not digested the milk. His stomach tightened and he threw up. Then his neck went limp and his eyes rolled back.

Ciddy screamed for help, and her sister Enid, who had been washing clothes outside, ran to get Omeriah and Yaya, the young girls' grandmother, both of whom lived within walking distance.

Omeriah examined the child gravely and decided that an evil spirit had touched him during Ciddy's absence. Yaya concurred, and the father and grandmother discussed possible remedies. At length, it was decided that he would mix a potion of susumba bush, garden bitters, cotton leaves, black joint, baby-gripe, hug-me-close and sweet-cup, while she fetched a medicinal love charm to protect the child from further demonic assaults. These things accomplished, the boy was consigned to a trio of around-the-clock monitors, consisting of Ciddy, Enid and Auntie Beatrice Wilby, the elderly cousin who had served as Ciddy's midwife. There was little to do but wait and pray for the shadow to pass from him.

As dusk approached, the boy began to breathe more freely and his nurses reacted with exclamations of relief.

"Yahso! What a way 'im revive!" said Enid.

"De potion an' amulet favor me pickney!" said Cedella, her eyes wet and swollen.

"You cyan't block de powers of de Almighty," said Beatrice. "T'anks and honor fe de Holiest One, whose name is Goodness and Love, fe de helpless chile and him pickney mumma!"

But Omeriah, hearing the exultations from across the rise, was not so quick to celebrate or to dismiss the significance of the incident. Every illness, he knew, was a visitation of either Satan or the Almighty. For what reason, he asked himself, would a suckling become the target of a duppy? "Sure as God mek water a-cool an' fire a-burn," he thought, "dat bwai been in de firs' grasp of Nookoo, Mother Death 'erself. And, give t'anks and bow de head, was only de swiftness of de retaliation dat expelled de demon."

Omeriah was standing by himself on the veranda of the one-story dwelling known as "Big House" in the village of Nine Miles. It was a handsome, though steadily deteriorating house built fifty years before by the Malcolm family matriarch Yaya (Katherine Malcolm) in the style of an English planter's residence. The project was financed with the profits yielded by her bountiful farmlands. With two full-sized bedrooms (usually reserved for boarders), a dining room, living room, large kitchen and a proper parlor, as well as several cottages built off the main house, it was easily the most imposing complex within running distance. Situated all alone near the top of a stepped glen that was the natural focal point of Nine Miles, Big House was a source of pride for all who lived within sight of it.

Omeriah removed his sweat-stained field cap and rubbed his rough palms on the knees of the heavy, gray cotton work pants of British manufacture that he was wearing (commonly called "ol' ironcloth"). He took a short swig from a long-necked bottle of Appleton Rum, then sprinkled just as much as he had swallowed on the ground to " 'member" the benign and watchful spirits of his ancestors. A cock crowed into the amber glow filtering through the palm forest in the western hills, announcing the sunset. Malcolm set his head back for a more generous gulp of liquor, then put the bottle down on a rickety bench and sat on the sagging wooden railing, gazing out over the family homestead and the village of Nine Miles.

Before him was a teeming, impossibly tangled network of clumpish knolls, steep spindletop hills and intersecting ravines, thick with groves of palms, bamboo, mango, coco and ackee, and interspersed with stands of cedar, mahoe and mahogany. Clinging to the high ground were the huts and sheds of the population, some constructed of woven withies with thatched roofs, the sturdier ones built of "Spanish walling" (masonry fill inside a wooden frame) and topped with patchwork arrangements of corrugated zinc sheets. They had dirt floors and no more than two tiny rooms—one a closet for storing utensils and foodstuffs and the other for sleeping. Each hut had a low outdoor fireplace and a small pen for young livestock. There was always an apron of rock-hard ground in front, the rust-colored clay pounded solid by the bare feet of cousins and cousins of cousins. Fat-bellied goats, gray with black undersides, munching and worrying pockets of trash and table scraps that swarmed with gnatlike tropical pests called sour flies, were tethered in the labyrinth of bark-stripped tree trunks surrounding the huts.

This was the domain of the Malcolms, Willoughbys, Lemoniouses, Lewises, Davises and a dozen other closely related families who had been farming in this region since two hundred years before the abolition of slavery in 1838. During the era of the great plantations that began in the early 1700s the wide, arching belt of sugar estates that stretched along the north coast from St. Ann's Bay through Montego Bay to Savanna-la-Mar made their absentee proprietors fabulously wealthy. While the flatlands that stretched to the sea were given over to sugar cane, the tenant slaves were allowed to cultivate "provision ground" in the mountain lands, and to sell or barter what produce the estates did not require in the towns and cities.

The Malcolms were among the most prosperous of their descendants, and Omeriah had become Nine Miles' most respected citizen, the custos. (*Custos* was originally a Jamaican title for the colonial magistrate; the meaning had been expanded over the years to include the principal landowners and local figures esteemed for their outstanding wealth, prudence and diplomatic capabilities.)

A powerfully built man in his mid-fifties, with a large globular head, strong squarish chin, wide nose and warm caramel eyes, Omeriah had a gentle, ageless quality about him that made him popular with children and with women. Besides the nine children with his wife, Alberta, he'd had a dozen others with various ladies in the district, most of these liaisons occurring after the death of his lawful spouse in 1935, the same year that his sister Rittenella had passed on. Still, Alberta Malcolm had accepted her husband's early meanderings without complaint and even a hint of pride. After all, it was obvious to her that he was no mere sportin' man; he had honorably and discreetly helped to provide for each of his illegitimate offspring.

As ambitious and industrious as he was amorous, Omeriah deftly cultivated a sizeable piece of prime cropland in a sector called Smith, a fertile valley lying between Eight Miles and the village of Rhoden Hall in the district of Stepney. He also ran a bakery, a grocery store and a loosely organized dry goods concern that sold English cloth for making dresses, suits and trousers and offered other services, such as cobbling shoes and repairing machinery. In addition, he owned a modest but profitable coffee factory. His wife, the former Alberta Willoughby, had been equally well off by rural standards; her parents had title to considerable acreage that was densely planted with coffee, bananas, oranges and tangerines.

But the respect accorded Omeriah by his neighbors was inspired by none of these material assets (nor his burgeoning brood) so much as by his reputation as an accomplished herbalist and "myalman"—a person who possessed the knowledge and the power to deflect or defuse the machinations of obeah and to heal with folk medicine.

Omeriah had been schooled in the ancient myalist arts by his father, Robert "Uncle Day" Malcolm, who was descended from the Cromanty slaves shipped to Jamaica from the Gold Coast in the late seventeenth and early eighteenth centuries. The Cromanty were an especially fierce Akan tribe that was never tamed by the slave bosses and the colonial overlords, and Cromanty leaders Tackey and Cudjoe were the instigators of two of the most savage slave uprisings of the plantation era. Not even the indomitable Maroons, who had escaped early on into the impenetrable Cockpit country in the interior of Jamaica and who were bound by the provisions of their treaty with the British to cooperate in the suppression of other renegades, ever succeeded in diminishing the Cromanty's appetite for freedom at any price. Indeed, the Maroons eventually adopted the Cromanty dialect as their secret language, and learned the healing qualities of such island herbs as kema weed, lion's tail and hundreds of others.

Jamaica boasts more shrubs, fruit trees, quirky vegetables and peculiar spices and roots than most countries many, many times its size, and it is a fitting irony that many different species, now thoroughly crossbred in even greater horticultural multiplicity, had originally been brought to these shores by the Royal Navy at the behest of the British planter class, so they could feed their slaves without the additional expense of importing food. But the Africans culled saplings and seedlings from the flourishing crops and ran off with their brethren to found independent settlements in remote pockets of the bush.

The runaway slaves steadily grew more cunning and vengeful, few more intensely so than the Maroons, who paid the Cromanty another compliment by learning and applying with chilling regularity the ancient Cromanty Curse, through which the hand of the oppressor is caused to turn upon its owner. The Akan fervently believed that it was sorcery that had brought them to the West Indies in the first place, so turnabout seemed fair play: many a cruel slave boss committed suicide shortly after the curse had been cast upon him.

Although schooled in the myalistic Cromanty arts since adolescence, Omeriah had never had the occasion nor the inclination to pronounce such a sentence as the Curse on any person. On the contrary, he was appalled by such practices and had devoted himself to thwarting what he saw as abuses of spiritual powers. Yet Omeriah was also aware that the medicine man and the diviner must know how to do in order to undo, and thus Omeriah had had to acquaint himself with obeah, the Dark Sciences, guzu-guzu and the hierarchies of the sorcerer's otherworldly confederates, chief among them the so-called Fallen Angels: Lucifer, the heinous bargainer; Rutibel, otherwise known as Gabriel, the angel of wrath who carries a drawn sword in his right hand; the more peaceable Zanz and Zangiel, who were said to have stood at Jesus's head inside his tomb when he arose from the dead; and the moody, unpredictable Saints Michael, Saschael and Raphael, who were also part of the angelic honor guard present at Christ's Resurrection.

But beware, Omeriah was cautioned by his father, for the spirits who are summoned forth by obeahmen in Jamaica are not divine messengers but celestial scavengers. In these Last Days they proffer knowledge at the threshold of Hell, and they should be prayed for and pitied rather than invoked.

Uncle Day explained to Omeriah that those who answer the vocation to "rise up fe healing" should only seek an understanding based on faith and entreat the Lord Most High to grant them an affinity with the richness of the earth and its therapeutic plants, herbs and spices, so that they might acquire the skills necessary to do the "upful" work of remedying, curing, mending and human restoration that dates back to the scribes in the House of Life, to Jacob and Moses, to John the Baptist and the Nazarene Himself, the Word Made Man.

In Africa, Omeriah's father had explained, the use of magic was a routine practice in the service of succor and protection, its practitioners functioning as priests and philosophers. But in Jamaica, it gradually evolved from a buffer against injustice in slavery days into another weapon in the unending modern guerrilla warfare of necromancy. In such an environment, no man could guess what fate held in store for him. And few could expect a life untouched by the vagaries of hoodoo and wizardry.

"**W**hen de Lawd summon me, ago deh yah," said Omeriah quietly as he shifted position on the porch rail, the rum enhancing the reverence with which he intoned to himself the Jamaican variation of the African prayer of acceptance of God's will. Omeriah's dark thoughts were interrupted by a sudden cloudburst and a downpour, rippling sheets of rain winding and stabbing their way into the nooks and crannies of the Nine Miles settlement.

For Omeriah, and for rural Jamaicans in general, the island's erratic rainstorms were accompanied by many pleasant complications. A downpour soothed tempers agitated by the otherwise incessant heat, temporarily lowering the temperature and turning the sticky, stupefying wind into a sweat-cooling balm. And the rain served as a botanical catalyst, releasing dormant or otherwise sun-deadened fragrances from the tropical plants, flowers, fruits and scrubs that coat the landscape. But the Jamaican downpours could also be unsettling, the mist lingering in the still air like a veil, shrouding the scene with a casual solemnity that masked the cruelty and capriciousness of the elements. For Jamaicans like Omeriah, the showers could turn an empty field into a duppy dancing ground or a bleak, hollow cul-de-sac into a demon-filled quarry, and transform the benign countryside into an ominous wilderness. And the rain carried a message: Jamaica is an unknowable place with eternal rhythms and undercurrents that flow around—and often through—its human guests with exquisite authority.

More than anything else, the spooky aftereffects of rural rainstorms caused men like Omeriah Malcolm to think of his country as the Land of Look Behind: a repository of magic and spells and spirits and enigmas where no one could walk his plot of ground in a straight line, either literally or figuratively, due to the countless queer, invisible obstacles lying between him and the completion of the most mundane errand. Omeriah believed that, given the circumstances, the best course was a casual zigzag which would confuse the duppies that might be lurking about. And Omeriah advised those who were so unfortunate as to be accosted by a duppy to stop and quickly make an X in the soil: a duppy can only count to nine, so he would be detained at that spot, attempting in vain to count to ten, until the rain or wind washed the X away.

Imagine! Even a young child, laying helpless in a shack, cannot avoid bumping into nameless misfortunes! thought Omeriah as he gazed out on the dripping scene in front of the porch, still in the grip of the rain's spell.

Yet, such early intrusions upon the life-soul of Ciddy's child could possibly have been prevented. The boy's mother had not even been baptized until she discovered that she was pregnant. The foolish, woeful girl had to be taken down to the Shiloh Church of the Lord Jesus Christ of the Apostolic Faith in the village of Alva amidst a flurry of "susu" (local gossip), to be immersed and christened in the baptismal pool under the hasteful guidance of Elder Thomas.

"And what a rude, stupid mumu business dis yar pickney-mumma daughter o' mine bring pon 'erself!" Omeriah barked, low and gravelly, sucking down another mouthful of rum. She had been seduced by that old "bockra" (white-skinned) "busha" (overseer) in red tunic, canvas leggings and shin boots, "Captain" Marley. This Marley fellow was a pipe-puffing superintendent for the crown lands, born in the parish of Clarendon, who came riding into Nine Miles almost two years ago on a fine government-bought horse trying to induce poor country people to sow crops or even resettle in the deepest sections of the "John Williams" jungle, the largely uninhabited "bridle lands" beyond the point where the crudest roads quit.

Those were his activities during the day. At night, while a tenant in Big House, the short, soft-spoken man had been fornicating with Malcolm's seventeen-year-old Ciddy! The silly girl lying with a white man at least two or three years her father's senior! At least Marley had had the decency to marry her many months later, but it had been the Devil's play-play from the start. A dumb, "bungo-bessy" (an adjective for unseemly conduct by a rural female) relationship carried on in trite secrecy, nourished on illicit assignations, instigated by a British Jamaican with money and position who had lured an innocent black girl to his bed with a boldness that recalled the license of plantation owners in slavery days.

And then into the world comes a creole pickney, named Robert after Marley's brother—*not* Omeriah's father—but, regardless, still a "slave name." (Robert Malcolm was believed by the family to have originally been a plantation owner's surname, which he then bestowed on Uncle Day.) And where is Captain Marley now that his son suffers? Gone-a Kingston in shame, under a mantle of disgrace from his own family for being so idiotic as to legally wed a "foo-foo" (foolish) country waif naïve enough to believe his "fuck-a-bush" (backwoods seduction) talk of love!

At the very least the boy, the product of this regrettable union, could have been named from the Bible, bonding him to Africa and the folk culture of his people, like Omeriah and his brothers, James, Nemiah, Ramses and Isaac.

"Ya mon! Leas' a lickle bit a caution in dos names," Omeriah spat out with rancor, sucking the last finger of rum from the bottle and then tossing it into an ash pail by the front door.

Now the baby was stranded by his bloodlines, and beset by every other cultural tribulation, right in the center of nowhere. In Jamaica, the African folk traditions of the slaves and their descendants and the European traditions of the white rulers are constantly at odds. But even among blacks, the values of whites and mulattoes are openly preferred to their own natural Akan–West Indian ethos. Omeriah did not share the widespread opinion that it was better to be brown than black, fair than brown. And for status-conscious Jamaican blacks to go around wearing heavy English boots and dark Manchester serge suits in the hot tropical sun while trying, as so many did, to talk like Oxford graduates struck him as madness.

The boy will have plenty of time to sort out the sorrows of his heritage, Omeriah thought. And what's the difference? The worse things got, the better things got, the more they remained the same. Omeriah remembered something his own father used to say: "Changey fe changey, black daag fe monkey." It was a maxim steeped in self-hatred and resignation. The monkey symbolized the colored man and the dog the full-blooded black. The message: there was no gain in the exchange; one is as badly off afterward as before.

Thoroughly disgusted, and troubled by the evils that had cropped up in their midst during the day, Omeriah went out behind the pig poke in the gathering darkness to relieve himself. The last traces of twilight hovered above the treetops as he went to bed, where he slept fitfully. Last evening he had dreamt of death, a sure sign of impending birth in the family. Tonight he dreamt of copper and of animal feces, both good omens. And then deep in the night he dreamt of fire, which signifies confusion, and of snakes, a sign that enemies were plotting the destruction of a loved one.

Rising at 3:00 A.M., he dressed and made his way over to Grandma Yaya's. It was her custom to retire each evening at six or seven P.M., in the coolness of the early evening, and then to get up around midnight to cook in the kitchen of Big House. Like many Jamaican countryfolk, Omeriah feared the night and disliked traveling even the shortest distances by himself after sundown, but the goat path to Yaya's was clear and well worn. Often as not she would be expecting him and would proudly serve up a hearty "wash-mouth" (breakfast) consisting of ackee soup, the codfish fritters known as "stamp-and-go," baked pawpaw, yams and "bammy," this last being a muffin made of cassava flour.

They would sit in the glow of the stone fireplace by the kitchen until dawn, eating and sipping black coffee or angelica-root gin from her demijohn, discussing the farming life, the weather, local occurrences and their relative significance, family squabbles, the meanings of recent dreams and the shielding of the clan from the forces of darkness. (Yaya was herself well versed in mysticism.)

On this night, as croaking lizards, shrill cicadas and screeching "patu" (owls) answered each other in the still air, Omeriah and Yaya could speak of little else but Ciddy and the events of the last year. Neither of them could conceal their anxiety concerning the spiritual and physical well-being of the child and his mother. Assailed by demons and abandoned by Captain Marley, their fortunes seemed precarious at best.

Two months later, something occurred that reinforced Omeriah's and Yaya's worst apprehensions. On the very morning that Ciddy had moved herself and the child out of Omeriah's house and into her own shack, she had undressed the baby in his new home, carefully removed Yaya's love amulet, and bathed him in her white enamel wash basin, using a new cake of store-bought brown soap. A fresh change of clothes laid out next to the child, she had begun powdering him when she realized the amulet was nowhere in sight. She began searching for it, going over every tabletop, sifting through the discarded clothing on the floor, crouching down and peering into every niche, crack and corner. Again and again and again. And as her anxiety approached its peak, a sudden, freezing breeze blew over her, covering her entire body with a rigid pebblework of clammy goose bumps.

Sinking to her knees, burying her face in her trembling, powder-caked hands, she burst into tears. She knew that she was not going to find the talisman.

"Nesta! Nesta! Where 'ave ya gone to dis yar day?" called Ciddy Marley, striding out of her shack and into the late afternoon heat. Blinded by the low sun's glare, she shielded her eyes with one hand

and squinted around the grounds, looking for her errant four-year-old son.

"Roslyn!" she hollered, addressing Nesta's godmother, Roslyn Downs, who was sauntering along a lower trail that bisected the one leading to Ciddy's place. A huge basket of "coco" (taro) tubers was balanced on her turbaned head.

" 'Ave ya seen me Nesta? Him gone and me don' know wheres!"

"Ah mus' say no fe sure Missah Marley," Roslyn replied, with the affectionate deference of an older mother sharing the concern of a younger one. They were in the midst of discussing the matter when the tot appeared in the distance, holding fast to the thick neck of David Malcolm as Ciddy's portly brother pedaled a heavy steel bicycle up the hill toward them.

"Cho!" Ciddy raged, for the benefit of Auntie Roslyn. "Mercy, my Gawd! Dat bwai an' 'im foolishness gwan mek me heart pop out me chest!"

Actually, Ciddy had momentarily forgotten that David had come by earlier to take Nesta—she much preferred to call him by his middle name—along on a trip to the post office for Omeriah, so overwhelmed was she by the chores of the morning: cooking, cleaning, chopping wood, feeding the animals. Her feigned anger did not fool Roslyn, she knew, but it helped chase the sadness she felt welling up inside her as she watched her skinny little boy, grinning with glee as he hugged the broad back of his jolly twenty-three-year-old uncle.

One of the first times she had ever seen Captain Marley, he was giving David a ride on the gleaming back of his sweat-drenched horse as he guided it to Yaya's house to inquire about a room. Norval had been working in the area for some time, living first in the nearby district of Sterling with a family named Morris, then with some other people in a village called Ballantine, and then in the house of a man named Luther Flynn in Stepney. Norval was well liked by the local children, always sending them off to buy him pipe tobacco and rewarding them with two shillings, and when his favorites would be making trips with their parents to the surrounding towns, he'd also give them spending money. David was one of his favorites.

And it was David who had become especially upset when she began stealing off to Yaya's at night to see Norval, fearful that Daddy Omeriah would beat her and banish the captain from the district. That would have made a lot of children, and many of their parents, unhappy. Most people liked the overseer, were charmed by his courtly manners and the kindly way he tipped his hat and greeted them in the quasi-British accent of a well-born Anglo-Jamaican.

Watching as the battered, overburdened bicycle approached, Ciddy's face clouded over and she fell silent. Roslyn saw the change in Ciddy's mood and moved on as the girl offered a distant "Walk safe now, Auntie" in farewell.

Ciddy was remembering the first night she had stayed with Norval in his room at Yaya's—the rum and tobacco on his breath, the sandpaper sensation of her face held hard against the stiff white whiskers that covered his jaws, and the rough-skinned hands that slid up under her chemise and caressed her buttocks as he pressed her back onto the firm mattress of his bed. It was the finest bed she had ever slept in.

Naked together in the moonlit room, he spoke to her of marriage and children, of sharing the quiet last years of his life and the wealth of his fine family. And she believed him, nuzzling against his hairy chest, pulling his long arms, firm as fenceposts, around her small frame.

He said he liked her musical laugh, and when they went for walks in the bridal lands, he would ask her to sing. Beaming, she'd give a fervent rendition of "I'm Going to Lay My Sins Down by the Riverside," projecting her resonant alto as she had that Easter morning in Rhoden Hall's Bible school when she'd won the hymn contest, beating out her sister Gloria. (At the school picnic the following day, she received as her prize a home-baked gingerbread "bun"—an oblong, honey-glazed holiday cake traditionally eaten with slices of cheese.)

"Ya mek a fine songstress, chile," the teacher had told her before the entire class. "It please Gawd ta 'ear memory verse, golden text and holy musical praise fe His handiwork!"

Pleasing God, pleasing her family and friends, pleasing Captain Marley, pleasing herself—it had all seemed so easy. When she sang, all of these demands on her spirit seemed to dovetail neatly into a joyful unity. But that budding sense of completeness was soon to burst at its tender seams.

She and the captain were wed on a breezeless Friday, June 9, 1944, in a stiff, perfunctory rite that represented an ending rather than a beginning. Prior to the ceremony, Norval had revealed to his pregnant bride that he was leaving Nine Miles the next day for Kingston, and that he had no intention of returning.

Ciddy's slow-blinking eyes burned and blurred with bitter tears as he explained that he had informed his family of his relationship with her, and that they had reacted by denouncing the union and disinheriting him. He was feeling old and tired, he said. No longer willing to gallop around in the wilderness as he had done for so many years, he was returning to the city to take another government post that involved less physical strain (and prestige) than his present one. Having been cut off by his family, he could barely afford to support himself, much less a wife and child. He would legitimize their union for the sake of the child, and then he'd be gone.

The vows were exchanged at Yaya's house, with Ivy, another of Ciddy's sisters, serving as bridesmaid. Hubert Davis, a close friend and neighbor of Omeriah's, was the best man. Ciddy wore a plain white dress with three-quarter-length sleeves made for her by Ivy. The captain wore a dark suit. Afterward, the wedding party and a few close friends chatted quietly, sipping punch and breaking off pieces of a long, wide loaf of banquet bread; Norval had not wanted the fuss of a fancy iced cake. It was one month before Ciddy's nineteenth birthday.

Riding off on his horse the next morning, complaining of an inflamed back, Norval promised to return every weekend until the child arrived. But over the course of Ciddy's pregnancy, he paid only two brief visits. Ciddy wrote to the captain following Nesta's birth, and he took a week off from his new job as a foreman on a bridge-building project in Kingston to come and see his son. After that, there were a few letters exchanged, and then no further word from Norval. Ciddy's notes to him came back unopened; her husband had moved, leaving no forwarding address. Ciddy knew nothing of his family background, except that he had once mentioned that his mother's name was Edith.

Heartbroken, she sought counsel from Omeriah, who told her to put aside her grief and learn from her indiscretions. Her first responsibility, he proclaimed, was to her son, not to her husband, and he advised her to build a decent life for them both in the district. He helped her start a tiny grocery shop in Alva, in which she sold produce from his fields and her own small plot. Her sister Enid pitched in to care for Nesta; Enid's son, Slegger, and Nesta grew up as brothers. The rest of the clan was supportive, and everyone seemed to adore her boy. While Omeriah made no attempt to disguise the fact that Nesta was his pet, Ciddy thought it a pity that David, her father's best hand in the fields, had elected to move to Maryland in 1945 to work as a laborer for the War Food Administration. Industrious, good-natured, optimistic—but a bit restless—he was an almost ideal role model for Nesta, and as it was the boy insisted on shadowing his every move during his visits.

"Cho!" Ciddy exclaimed again with mock scorn as David brought the bicycle to a halt before her. "Where ya tek me pickney? Nesta! Where ya uncle tek ya seh?" Peeking over David's massive shoulder, he answered his mother meekly, but the expression in his deep, dun-colored eyes startled her. Something about the boy's direct gaze had always made her feel slightly skittish and intimidated. There was an intelligence in his eyes that belied his tender years. The boy had proven sufficiently precocious by his fourth birthday to move Ciddy to enroll him at Stepney School nearly a year ahead of schedule. Miss Isaacs, the teacher, immediately confirmed that it was the right thing to do, noting that Nesta seemed as smart as a child twice his age. But still his mother found that she felt most comfortable in her parental role when she avoided those cool stares of his. The piercing effect of Nesta's gaze seemed to transcend mere schoolboy precocity.

"Faddah, me t'ink me bwai got a preachar's fire in him eye," she had blurted out to Omeriah one evening some months before, needing to know if anyone else had noticed this in her son. "Somet'ing mannish an' bullyrige [menacing] dere dat me don' nevar recognize. It mek me lickle 'fraid sometime."

Her father had looked at her with harsh scrutiny and then, to her surprise, nodded. "Fe true," he murmured. "An' mebbe, praise Gawd, it help keep bullbucker, bugaboo and Old Hige from 'im," he added, referring to common bullies, country hobgoblins, and witch hags, respectively. (Old Higes are crones who divest themselves of their wrinkled skins at night and go abroad in a ball of fire to suck the blood from sleeping youngsters.)

"Is de chile obedient?" he asked with a rhetorically imperious air, knowing full well that Nesta was more prone to mysterious silences and cryptic moods than to mischief, but wanting to ease the tension. Ciddy did not follow his lead.

"Oh, yes, sah. Bot' him an' Slegger are good 'elpers, well behaved. But Nesta go off by hisself a lot fe lickle walks in de bush. Me come upon 'im an' find 'im sittin' dere doin' nutin' much, jus' t'inkin'. An' when me ask wha' he been doin', him show me a smile so blue-swee."

Omeriah bristled at the term. "Blue-swee" meant cunning, difficult to catch, elusive. It was the sort of phrase one would normally use to describe a charlatan, an obeahman, or Anancy, the spider trickster of African folk legend.

"Min' yar tongue, Ciddy," he cautioned sternly. "Nuh man want facety [impudent] woman, an' nuh chile need foolish muddah. Me don' want ta 'ear 'bout 'orse dead an' cow fat [irrelevant details]. Set an example fe de bwai an' get a blessin' from Gawd. As de twig is bent, so de tree incline."

Fe true, she thought now, as she beheld the boy lying peaceful against David's back, sucking his thumb drowsily. Lawd surely must know she loved the child. So spindly, shy and sweet-natured, with never a "kass-kass" (a piece of contentious backtalk) or a quarrel. He feeds the fowls, learns the cultivation, respects his elders. And he plays so nicely with Slegger—the boys build little forts together in the coconut and jackfruit groves or pretend they're Captain Bligh's sailors, carrying rum and treasure and the "otaheitie" (Malay apple) to Jamaica aboard the great ship *Providence*, or listen to Omeriah's tales, making believe they are West African kings. And doesn't Nesta sometimes ride to Smith on Nimble, his pet donkey, to bring lickle refreshment from Yaya to the field hands?

Fe true, fe true, she sighed to herself, a "kin teet' " (grin) growing on her lips as she leaned forward to kiss the boy's little head and take him into her arms. 'Im a good, good pickney, yeh.

"Well, I mus' say dat yuh are in dem ackee," she chided David with a giggle. She meant that David appeared well fed and happy, i.e., well provided with ackee, the podlike, large-seeded fruit of West African origin that is a Jamaican staple.

David rubbed his barrel-sized belly and laughed with a rolling wheeze, telling his sister that he had been doing well in Maryland and eating rich American fare as a consequence, but that it would be good to have home-cooked food fresh from Omeriah's farmlands again. Her brother's visit coincided with the tail end of a harvest, and tonight there was to be a dusk-to-dawn shelling session at Omeriah's house to celebrate a good corn crop.

By custom, everyone in the clan was expected to toil in Omeriah and Yaya's fields, and since the age of five Ciddy had done her share, sometimes attending school only three days a week, reserving the rest for the group efforts of clearing and burning away the old "top 'n lop," plowing, harrowing, fertilizing, planting, weeding, reaping. It was an exhausting but somehow exhilarating cycle, the loamy aroma of the soft soil and the slow-building excitement with the progress of each sowing giving participants a stimulating sense of oneness with the land, its colorful heritage and its inhabitants.

Sometimes the tasks along the way were tedious, particularly when everyone kept to themselves as they worked. But Ciddy was uplifted when the men joined together in diggin' songs, chanting like militia on the march as their pickaxes fell to loosen the dirt for corn, gungu peas, cassava, callaloo, or to make the hundreds of foot-high mounds of dirt, called "yam-hills," in which the root of the tuber would be replanted. Freely passing the rum bottle with wet smiles and bloodshot winks, one man would "raise" a tune, calling out a series of lines, and the others would respond with the "bobbin," the brief refrain that set the pace for the task at hand:

Toa-dy, Toady, min' yar self!
(Toa-dy! Toa-dy!)
Min' yar self mek I plant me corn!
(Toa-dy! Toa-dy!)
Plant me corn fe go plant me yam!
(Toa-dy! Toa-dy!)
Plant me yam fe go court me gal!
(Toa-dy! Toa-dy!)
Court me gal fe show me mumma!
(Toa-dy! Toa-dy!)
Mumma de one a go tell me yes!
(Toa-dy! Toa-dy!)
Poppa de one a go tell me nuh!
(Toa-dy! Toa-dy!)

In the last year, Nesta had begun to accompany his mother to the fields at Smith, where he carried a water pail and messages back and forth between his relatives, and was made to listen carefully as they took time out to instruct him in various techniques of tillage. Thus initiated into bush agriculture, he was also made to feel included in the many successes of the time-honored procedures. The shelling matches were the final and most enjoyable stage of the work cycle, and Ciddy took a special delight in seeing how Nesta was mesmerized by the community spectacle.

"Nesta, is ya too weary fe go a shellin' match dis yere night at Grandpapa Omeriah's?" she teased, as she bade David good-bye and moved toward the shack.

"Seh nuh, Mumma!" he pleaded with flailing arms, bursting with exaggerated energy. "Seh nuh, Mumma!"

Both David and Ciddy exploded in laughter at this earnest display, and she bounced him in her arms reassuringly, then set him down.

"Den run fe fetch da washbasin so I cyan tidy yuh up nicely so!" she ordered, sending him scurrying to the cooking shed, as David rode down toward Omeriah's house to assist in the preparations for that night.

All day long, since first light, men and women in starkly sun-bleached frocks and work clothes had been bringing the silky ears of unshelled corn from Smith, heaped in huge "cutacoos" (baskets with hemp shoulder straps), brimming over in donkey carts and piled high in the canvas aprons gripped at their corners to form bulging pouches. Nesta had watched them arriving from the shack window at dawn, the procession moving noiselessly into the heart of Nine Miles, heads bobbing in and out of the wisps and spirals of dewy fog. Awakened by the braying of a stubborn jackass, he had peered over the sill and abruptly ducked back down again, uncertain whether he was witnessing a scene from this world or the next. Grandpapa talked a lot about how the Bible said that Jacob fell asleep on a rock and dreamt of the dead ascending difficult mountainsides and sheer ladders into Heaven, weighed down by all their worldly possessions and the wages of sin, and how the greediest would lose their footing or tire and swoon because of their onerous burdens, tumbling down into the Pit of Fire.

Warily, Nesta had rubbed the "sandmon dust" from his eyes and stolen another peek. No, it was no duppy business. He could make out Auntie Enid and other relatives, all very much alive, but cloaked in a spectral gray mist. Looking, mebbe, the way they would on Judgment Day.

Impressed by the sobriety of the procession, the size of the groups and the scope of their activities, Nesta had kept a vigil, conscientiously counting the glinting tusk-shaped blades of the men's "boar machetes" as they swung from their belts, until Mumma had found him slumped over on top of the "kick-and-buck," the big clay water jar that took its name from the mallet blows that formed it. His head was lying upon the sill, tucked in the crook of his numb elbow.

"Mercy me! Wha' dis yere?!"

He'd looked up, disoriented by the flood of morning light and the *cluk-cluk-cluk* of the guinea fowl around his ankles as Mumma's bemused face popped up before him, his jaw cupped in her fleshy hands. Had he been dreaming?

"Goodness! Is me pickney tryin' ta get ta de shellin' before de res' a de district?" Ciddy had said with a tender chuckle as she wiped the last remnants of sleep from his diamond-shaped face. "Well now, for de wise mon ta find de right road 'im shud keep him eyes open! Right seh?"

Now, as he rushed inside the shack, fetching the washbasin that was leaning against the kick-and-buck and then hopping in place to snatch down his best pair of overalls, which hung from the highest nail above the straw bed, he reviewed the recurring mental images of the last twelve hours. Reflexively he looked out the window again into the rapidly descending dusk, puzzling over the secrets of morning before the sun and of night before the moon.

In palm-obscured pockets all over the far hills, dinner stoves could be seen glowing ever brighter, the distant orange-red cores of their fires flickering like lightning bugs. Nesta turned to find himself hoisted to the table top by Mumma, who stripped him naked, set him back down and scrubbed him sore with a coarse white rag tangy with soap. The dunking of his head in the basin—almost before he could think to shut his mouth and eyes—signaled the end of the "tidy-nice." With the day's dust and stickiness washed away, he felt more relaxed, his stomach less fluttery in anticipation of the festivities to come. Then, through the window, he saw the torches in the valley. Floating alone in the inky twilight, clustering in corners of the farthermost ravines and then spilling onto the sloping trails leading into Nine Miles, they appeared to Nesta as long, swaying rivulets of flame. The sound of vigorous voices grew louder, and the air thickened with the scent of burning rubber as the thin streams of light snaked nearer—the men holding stick-skewered hunks of burning tires (which doubled as an insect repellent) and talking "boasty" like barking dogs, the women berating them or chattering among themselves, the children squealing and romping in and out of the light shed by the trembling, smelly torches.

Nesta was so excited by such sights that he immediately wet his overalls, and had to endure a dimly felt spanking by Mumma before he could thread his way through the crowd of people that surrounded Omeriah's massive bonfire, his head swimming with the kinetic shadow play of a full-tilt "jamma," a raucous country night picnic.

It was almost too much to take in. Dozens of buxom women in

bright print dresses hunkered close together in susu sessions at one end of the blaze as they systematically tore open the corn husks. The bare ears were passed along to the opposite side, where sinewy male hands stripped the raw, hard kernels from the cobs with a crunching corkscrew motion, the kernels spilling into crocus bags between their knees. Amid all this furious activity, everyone somehow found a way to conduct lively conversations, to consume copious amounts of white rum, and to empty huge tin platters heaped with roasted breadfruit, cho-cho squash sopping with butter, curried goat, fried grunt fish, peppery jerk pork sizzling with the fumes of allspice and charcoal, and a fruit salad of starapples, oranges, grapefruit and sweetened milk called "matrimony."

As the night deepened and the manic intensity of the work subsided to a dogged tempo, the clamoring and feasting gave way to songs, riddles, Anancy stories and tales of Africa. This was the part of the evening Nesta loved most, and he found a good spot on the trunk of a felled apple tree next to Neville Livingston, nicknamed Bunny, a companion from Stepney School. Seated behind them were Ciddy and Bunny's father, lantern-jawed Thaddius "Toddy" Livingston, an itinerant carpenter, mason and Nine Miles shopowner well liked by the Malcolms (and said to be quite fond of Ciddy).

All ears were pricked for the words of an elderly cousin of Yaya's who was relating the saga of Prester John, the legendary Nestorian Christian king of Asia Minor. From his gigantic realm, the old man assured his listeners, Prester John had subdued the pagan Mongols and the Muslim infidel who had very nearly vanquished the European knights in the Crusades of the twelfth century. Revered throughout Christendom as the living emblem of God's dominion on earth, Prester John held Pope Alexander III spellbound with his holy strength, as he did Frederick Barbarossa, the Holy Roman Emperor, Louis VII of France, and all of the Byzantine potentates. Prester John's patronage gave the Crusaders hope in their most hapless hours and rescued them from potentially humiliating defeat. But no white man, pageboy or prince, was ever granted the privilege of seeing his ethereal ebony face.

"Fe not a one white on eart' worthy of de radiant sight!" the hollow-eyed cousin boomed at the conclusion of his exotic tale of bloody battles, unwavering faith and the majesty of a black monarch who had eclipsed King Arthur in the annals of medieval chivalry. And at the conclusion of his account, scores of rum bottles were raised to toast the merits of the cousin's storycraft.

Another man leapt up to tell of the glory of the black race in "de modern age," rhapsodizing with considerable eloquence about the grandeur of the reign of His Majesty Haile Selassie I of Ethiopia, two hundred twenty-fifth heir to the Solomonic throne, who had routed Mussolini and his Fascist invaders in 1941, some eight years before. It was one of the first glorious victories of the Second World War, the man recounted, awed at how merciful Selassie had been toward the vanquished Italians and how generous he was to his own brave forces.

Sensing he had captured his audience, the new storyteller continued. On one occasion, after Selassie had personally dispensed gifts to a multitude of Ethiopian soldiers, a lowly corporal known to few of the rank and file approached His Majesty and complained that he had been excluded from the emperor's benevolent expressions of gratitude and largess.

"You *lie!*" thundered Selassie, citing the precise place, day, hour and amount of the soldier's reward. The corporal dropped to the ground and hid his face in terror and shame, crawling away from the emperor's magnificent presence. But Selassie demanded that the man rise to his feet again and repent of his falsehood. Weeping and wailing, the corporal did so, and as His Majesty turned to go, he took pity on the soldier and tossed him a roll of banknotes.

Everyone around the bonfire was breathless at the wonder of the tale, but its teller was not finished. Just prior to His Majesty's coronation in 1930—the portentous event having been foretold by Marcus Garvey, an enlightened and courageous son of Jamaica—the Duke of Gloucester had been granted an audience with Selassie, during which he returned the golden scepter of the House of Judah, stolen from Ethiopia in antiquity by Julius Caesar, who had made use of it to build the Roman Empire. Following the imperial coronation, the duke became intoxicated and wandered into the bush, where he ate a magical strain of brush weed that removed his mortal disguise and allowed the emperor, with the help of his golden scepter, to recognize the duke's true identity: the reincarnation of Nebuchadnezzar, the infernal last king of Babylon.

Hatching a plan that hastened the fulfillment of the biblical prophecy, Selassie tricked the duke into returning to England with an intricate medal for King George V that actually was a mystic seal of avengement. When the British monarch saw the seal, his body froze like unto Lot's wife, and he perished soon afterward. The duke assumed the throne and then renounced it in favor of George VI, secure in his ultimate aim: to be reincarnated as the final sovereign of Eviltude in the dreadful Last Days.

"Praise de teachar! Prophecy fulfilled!" whooped the rum-inflamed guests huddled around Omeriah's crackling embers. Then a strange quivering shot through the group, followed by a sudden silence. It felt as if the entire congregation was engaged in grave inner meditations on their own individual degrees of righteousness, the order of their spiritual houses.

"Dere be a jing-bang [noisy] balmyard [where the myalman ministers to his flock] and a crowded church dis Sabbath," Omeriah mused to himself, drawing deeply from his "fronto" (tobacco) pipe.

The air was electric with tension. Surveying the group with hooded eyes, one of the young men, a cobbler from the village of Endeavor, finally made a diffident joke about the blackheart man, and everyone responded with grateful guffaws. A woman had just begun offering a riddle when she was interrupted by an outburst from Nesta.

"Mumma! Mumma seh! Wha' de blackheart mon?"

"Hush, me pickney! Hold yar tongue or tek yar rest!"

"Nuh, Ciddy," said the cobbler with a rascal's twinkle, "de bwai mus' know fe blackheart mon if 'e shud meet 'im by da moon."

Before Cedella could protest, the cobbler had launched into a description of the blackheart man that had Nesta's eyes as wide as johnnycakes and every other child clutching his or her parents' skirts and pantlegs.

The blackheart mon lives in perpetual darkness, he began. He carries night with him like a robe draped about his head. And such a head! Flowing from it are tangled snake-finger locks, coiled about like the hissing, viperous mane of Medusa. The blackheart mon has no friends, no home, no family. A stranger to all, he lives in the "gullies" (open drains) of the city and the lonely hollows of the country, enticing with candies and fair words all children who dare to stray from their mothers or who stay out alone past sundown. He takes them away, never to see their kin again. He consumes them, limb by limb, or presents them to Satan as slaves, doomed to work forever at brimstone-stoked furnaces on the charred banks of the River Styx—the lifeless watercourse that encircles Hell.

"Tikya [take care] de blackheart mon, childran, me seh don' go near 'im," the cobbler admonished. "Tikya de blackheart mon, fe evan lions fear 'im!"

"Nuh, Mumma! Nuh wan' see de blackheart mon!" Nesta yelped.

"Hush, chile! An' shame on yuh, mon!" seethed Ciddy. "Scare me pickney so! Dere is nuh such a mon as de blackheart mon, chile!"

"Ahhh, but dere *is*," shouted another cousin in the crowd. "'Im de cursed Rastamon. Lazy, shif'less, dangerous madmon, dem, who wan' mosh up de nation. Dey spit in de face of de Almighty, dem trash!"

De Rastamon. Nesta was too stunned to speak. Several weeks ago he had seen a willowy man with long ropy hair—hair like a serpent's nest. The man came strolling out of the woods near Stepney School, toting a "bankra" (basket) of yams. Seeing him, several of the other children had abandoned their roadside game, hurrying toward the schoolhouse in a fuss, and Miss Isaacs had summoned the rest indoors, standing watch until the man was gone.

Just as the door was being shut behind him, Nesta had glanced back to see the Rastamon smiling, his teeth as white as a tiger's, his shiny, bulging eyes fixed directly on him. . . .

"Nuh, Mumma! Nuh, Mumma! Me nuh wan' ta see de blackheart mon!"

Ciddy shook the boy awake. Through his tears, he saw he was home again, safe in his straw bed in the hilltop shack. His mother had carried him back in her arms, just before first light.

"Hush, me love. Yuh jus' dream bad. Sleep nice."

Exhausted, the young woman groped her way back to her dry grass pallet and stretched herself out upon it, drifting into a blank slumber.

Propping himself up on his own brittle mattress, Nesta peeked through the weather-warped shutters into the eddied realm of mist beyond the shack—and he screamed.

Maybe he saw something. Maybe he didn't. But he flew into his mother's bed and hid his eyes under his sleeping gown, shivering, until sleep claimed him once more.

4

Bad Card

Nesta's favorite meal was laid out on the table, deliberately prepared as a preface to Ciddy's fateful announcement.

He sat before her in the shack, his legs dangling from a teetery tubular steel kitchen chair upholstered with remnants of red and yellow vinyl, as he gobbled a plate of macaroni and cheese with boiled callaloo, a leafy vegetable akin to spinach. Occasionally he paused to gulp from a cup filled with brown Albion sugar (originating on the sugar estate in St. Thomas parish where modern processed sugar was first made in the 1870s) mixed with warm water. The drink was a special treat in the bush, referred to as "coolie-foot sugar sippa," because it was originally made with sugar spilled and stepped on by the East Indian contract laborers who bagged it in backwoods factories; swept up afterward, it was sold to poor people for a fraction of the normal price. For dessert there was a bowl of rich, golden corn meal pudding.

"Nuh eat suh quickish!" a nervous Ciddy warned. "Craven [craving, gluttony] a go choke puppy!"

It was July 1950. Five-year-old Nesta had just completed his first year at Stepney School. For him, the eleven months had been happy ones, but for Ciddy they had been worrisome, clouded by the unexpected letter received in September 1949 from Captain Marley, the first in some time. He announced that he thought it might be best for the boy if he were to be adopted by one of Norval's nephews, a son of his brother Robert (recently deceased), who, Norval explained, was a well-to-do Kingston businessman and chief operating officer of Marley & Plant, Ltd., a construction and civil engineering firm with offices at 48 Riverton Road, between Spanish Town Road and the Duhaney River in the southwest part of town. The letter had sparked a weekend of lively deliberation on the part of Omeriah, Yaya, Enid and Ciddy, culminating in the unanimous decision that it was out of the question, particularly since Norval seemed to be implying that the boy's mother would never see Nesta again.

There the matter had rested until several days ago, when Norval wrote again to say that if young Robert would not be permitted to become the ward of his wealthy nephew in the city, he should at least be allowed to live there so he could take advantage of the superior facilities of the Kingston public school system. This seemed reasonable to Omeriah, who felt the quality of the child's education should not suffer because of his parents' estrangement. Plans were made to send Nesta to the city, where he would live in the captain's custody for a trial period, with the provision that Ciddy would have unrestricted visitation rights.

Now the hour was nearly at hand, and Nesta had yet to be told. But his mother half-wondered if he already knew.

Ciddy had been in her grocery shop in Alva around noontime one day in the preceding spring, when Mrs. Hanson, a regular customer, had come in, fairly flustered.

"Auntie Ciddy," she had exclaimed. "Nevuh yuh guess wha' happen! Nevuh!"

Collecting herself as best she could, Mrs. Hanson began to tell how she had seen Nesta the previous morning on the road to Smith and that he offered to read her palm. She was stunned to hear the child recount the intimate details of numerous events in her life, and to then foretell several more, some of which had just come to pass.

Ciddy burst out laughing, but Mrs. Hanson hotly insisted, "Nuh! It fe true!"

Ciddy dismissed Mrs. Hanson's talk . . . but later that spring she was forced to give more credence to the various accounts of her son's prescience. The local constable, known for his level-headed, skeptical attitude toward the supernatural, showed up at the shop raving about Nesta's fortune-telling prowess.

"Everyt'ing dat bwai tell me was amazin'!" he assured her.

"Mebbe 'im see more in 'is innocence," she replied, "den we see as growed people."

"Well, yes and nuh," said the policeman, " 'cause de boy see wha' near but also wha' is far in da future. Is a spiritual gif' fe certain."

By the time Captain Marley's second letter had arrived, his mother had begun to believe she was not entirely equipped to teach a "special" child like Nesta all the things he might need to know. Or to shield him from the things he didn't.

Reviewing the problem, Omeriah had put it another, more direct way: "De finger of de Lawd is upon de bwai. Him a man chile wit' powers that may grow or may fade. But 'im mus' be out in the world ta discover dat fe hisself."

Ciddy knew from experience that Jamaica was a place where people grew up in a hurry or not at all. And Kingston was a place where anything could happen to anyone at any time. Elder Thomas liked to say that it could swallow a grown man like a whale and spit him out again like the big fish in the Bible did with Jonah, or choose *not* to spit him out at all.

She had arisen early on the morning of his intended departure and paid a visit to the local balmyard to get a blessing for the boy from the mistress in attendance. Afterward she'd lit a candle in the tabernacle for his safety and then returned home to fix wash-mouth for him. She let him eat his fill before seating herself across from him.

Haltingly Ciddy broke the news to the child. She described it to him as an exciting surprise journey, an adventure she could only marvel at. Nesta responded with a barrage of questions. But when it became apparent that his mother was not to accompany him, he jumped down to the dirt floor and ran over to her. Throwing his arms around her waist, he erupted into shrieking sobs coupled with the heart-wrenching question, repeated over and over, "Yuh nuh love me, Mumma? Yuh nuh love me, Mumma?" He held on to her with all his might.

Overcome with grief and guilt, Ciddy also wept, mother and child hugging each other tightly until Nesta fell asleep in her lap and she herself dozed off as well. But when the nap was over, it was time to go.

Nesta was dressed in his good overalls and a crisp new cotton jersey and brought into town in the afternoon to be packed off to Kingston on the next "bungo-bungo" (country bumpkin) bus. He would be met at the station by Captain Marley, who would take him to a bungalow at 15 Hillcrest Road that was owned by Yaya and inhabited by relatives. The captain was going to rent a room there to be close to the boy, but Nesta would still be under the wing of the Malcolm clan.

For the trip, Nesta was temporarily placed in the care of an elderly female cousin who was a "higgler," one of the itinerant produce peddlers who serve as the critical link between the rural farmer and the urban marketplace. Like most higglers she was making weekly runs into Kingston: arriving Thursday night and bedding down in the marketplace, selling all day Friday and Saturday, and returning Sunday night. Some male higglers "go a market" to sell water coconuts and to butcher meat, but female higglers predominate. The cousin, a gawky, hatchet-faced woman of sixty, wore the uniform of her profession: a drab pinafore with separate patch-pockets for "coppers," "silvers" and banknotes, worn over a detergent-dulled shift, and topped with a "tie-head" (tightly wound scarf). She was shouldering a large crocus sack filled with okra, thyme and peppers.

When they encountered her at the bus stop, the higgler had confirmed with a casual "Howdy do" and a soberly self-confident "Tek me 'surance, Missah" to see the child safely to the end of the line. As the battered blue-green bus lumbered through the winding mountain pass into the center of Rhoden Hall, it occurred to Ciddy that the boy had never seen a motor vehicle before.

"Mercy me!" she said enthusiastically, hoping he would respond in kind. "Lookit dat dere bangajang machine!"

He examined the vintage conveyance with detached curiosity as it screeched and wheezed to a halt, the overload of luggage and crates tied to its roof shifting dangerously. Any additional inspection of this bizarre contraption was cut short by the driver, a chubby man wearing sea-green sunglasses and a slouch cap.

"Wha' de fock yuh staring at!" he shouted through the broken accordion door, which was tied open with a length of wire cable wound through its shattered glass panes. "Get in, little mon! Get in, people! Yuh all waitin' fe a fockin' royal liv'ry mon wit a coach an' four?"

Ciddy came back with a vulgar riposte of her own, such exchanges being typical between drivers of bungo-bungo buses and "de backward" clientele they openly disdained. But the argument was halted when he let up on the brake and allowed the bus to lurch ahead a few feet.

"Me gone now, an' ya can kiss me raas!" the driver roared. "Me gone now, ya fockin' bloody pussy clot!"

The people who had been waiting on line behind Ciddy, Nesta

and the higgler cousin at the bus stop suddenly shoved their way past them and scrambled aboard to the din of the horn and jeering curses from the passengers.

"Wait!" Ciddy yelled with alarm as she chased the boy and his aged cousin to the bus door. "My Lawd, what a mout' on him driver! Wait!" The good-bye was short but boisterous—at least on Ciddy's part. The boy seemed by his aloof manner to have already left her.

Stepping onto the grossly overcrowded vehicle, nudged along toward the end of the bundle- and crate-crammed aisle by the higgler, Nesta immediately became the target of some self-conscious scorn and sly signifying on the part of the other passengers.

"*Jus' so*," said a sharply dressed, scowling young man to the pretty young woman seated next to him as he pointed to Nesta. "Look fe poppy show [ridiculous exhibition] comin' dis way. Another bungo in 'im bes' work regjegs [ragged clothes], headed fe hu-mil-i-ation in de city. My Gawd, if I laugh I gon' drop an' die!"

"Nuh min' de fool," murmured Nesta's aged chaperone as they passed by. "Ev'ry spoil a style." (Every kind of attire has its own particular brand of dignity.)

Seeing an unsettled expression flash across the faces of the smart aleck and his beau, the higgler smiled to herself with satisfaction. But the couple hadn't heard her remarks. They were reacting to the malevolent look that the little boy had shot their way. In Nesta's eyes they had seen the cool appraising look of a wild animal examining his potential prey.

The incident had not gone entirely unobserved by the rest of the passengers. Two other higglers, settled in with their wares one seat farther up on the opposite side of the bus, had been watching. Once the old woman and the child had pushed past them to the back, they began a whispered conference, the one telling the other about "de lickle bwai wit de wolf eyes." He had lately been volunteering to read palms in the district, said one of the women, and a certain lady from Eight Miles had approached him with a request to examine hers. With the boy's mother looking on, he'd taken one fleeting glance at her upturned hand and declined.

"Me cyan't," he told the lady. "Yar palm is full of crosses." Two days later, the woman's heart stopped beating.

"Cho!" hissed one higgler to the other. "Yuh mek a bad joke!" Her companion shook her head.

"Nice," said the first higgler with grim sarcasm. "Me mus' ride all de way ta Kingston wid me back ta a devilish damned jumby bwai ["jumby man" means obeahman]. Jus' great."

The engine howled into gear. "Rhoden Hall, ta fockin' *raas!*" hooted the driver with lunatic gusto as the bus hurtled into the center of the road, raising dust and gravel as it sped along the long circuit of towns and tiny villages that led to the city.

Although the ride was filled with constant pitches, bumps, rude stops and starts, and hairpin turns that caused the passengers to scream with distress, Nesta somehow managed to sleep for most of the trip. The bus had hurried down through Brown's Town and Orange Valley, passing terraced farms and savannas cleared for makeshift cricket pitches, and the occasional gas-station-and-rum-parlor complex, a dozen or so men loitering around a domino game. The sharp *swack* of palmed dominoes being slammed down upon metal tabletops cut through the rumbling drone of the bus, the sound followed by the drunken exhortations of the players.

Reaching the sea at Runaway Bay, the bus roared along the coastal road, rocking back and forth during an annoying zigzag through the dingy midtown labyrinth of the town of St. Ann's Bay, capital of the parish, and passing very close to the site of the first capital city of the island, Sevilla Nueva, founded in 1509 by Juan de Esquivel, first Spanish governor. Farther on, there was a dizzying series of tire-singing twists and bends, and then they were ripping past a long stretch of highway lined with elegant, trellised signs indicating the entrances to the fine tourist hotels on Turtle Beach and Dunn's River Beach. Lunging into a lush tropical glen, they could smell the spray from the mighty, many-tiered Dunn's River Falls as a creaky wooden bridge was hastily crossed. Acrid black smoke spewing from the tailpipe, the bus mounted a hilly section of road, the engine coughing hard with the effort, and moved into the whitewashed splendor of Ocho Rios, tourist jewel of the North Coast.

Nesta awoke to the sounds of horns honking in counterpoint and saw that the progress of the bus had been slowed by a pileup of small, pastel-colored compacts driven by red-faced white people wearing bright clothes and sunglasses. Judging from the "warify" (fighting) words being exchanged outside, several of the white people had been having difficulty remembering to drive on the left side of the road, and some of the little cars had locked bumpers.

"Stupid white devils! Gwan back 'ome, Yankee slave dri-vars!" the bus driver ranted, to the frowning disapproval of most of his passengers, who were God-fearing Pentecostal and revivalist churchgoers who believed in the brotherhood of man. One middle-aged gentleman seated behind him had pointed out the error of the driver's ways to a little girl. Overheard, both were treated to a hail of blasphemous scorn.

"Ah, yes!" barked the driver. "Me hear ya bot' susu 'pon me. But will Gawd come dow' from Heaven, git dese white trash outta me way, and steer dis yere bus ta Kingston on time? Nuh, suh!"

As the roadway was cleared, most of the bus riders muttered their disapproval of such sacrilegious talk, and a few crossed themselves in genuine fear that the Lord, so challenged, might yet take a hand in the matter.

Nesta watched the white tourists as they got back into their autos, their discomfort and incompatibility with everything about the sultry climate acutely obvious. Strange, foolish people, he thought to himself. He had seen so few of them before—and those were mostly British Jamaicans, who were reserved and poised. These whites were from America; they had noisy mouths—Mumma would punish him severely if he behaved as they did—and they looked so bewildered, their sunburns blotchy and unattractive, their hair matted with perspiration. Why did they come to this island at all?

Then the bus was moving once more, heading away from the ocean, which was just a thin azure line in the distance, and back into the mountainous interior. It slipped down through Fern Gully, a high-walled chasm so overgrown with feathery green fronds that the sunny afternoon nearly became night, and then out into undulating farm and grazing lands.

Nesta slept as he rode through Walker's Wood and Moneague, but he stirred at a place called Schwallenberg as gaggling voices remarked about the "blood lake." The bus was nearing the top of Mount Diablo and far below the steep road a smooth, flat expanse of redness, still and gleaming, could be seen.

Nesta asked his cousin if it really was blood. She laughed and explained that it was the runoff from the bauxite mines in the area, which had contaminated the entire body of water. He dozed again as they glided through the hamlet of Mount Rosser and past the sugar refineries and Alcan alumina mines scattered around the sweeping gorges outside Ewarton.

The signs of the towns began to crop up more quickly—Linstead, with its tumultuous country market, Bog Walk, site of a hulking cinderblock structure housing a pineapple canning factory, Kent Village, Raby's Corner, Angels. A quadrangle of jalousied pink stucco government buildings signaled that the bus had reached the seedy elegance of Spanish Town's Admiral Rodney Square, the old headquarters of the Supreme Court, the House of Assembly and the Jamaica Archives. Formerly known as Santiago de la Vega, Spanish Town had been the capital of Jamaica for three hundred years, until the seat of government shifted to Kingston in 1872.

The bus paused before one of these imposing, clay-shingled Georgian edifices to refill the sizzling radiator with water, and they could hear the sound of adult voices raised in song inside an upstairs office on the courtyard, and the closing strains of a patriotic colonial anthem drifted toward them on the lazy gusts of southwesterly wind.

To thee belongs the rural reign;
Thy cities shall with commerce shine;
All thine shall be the subject main,
And every shore it circles, thine.
The Muses, still with Freedom found,
Shall to thy happy coast repair:
Blest Isle! with matchless beauty crowned,
And manly hearts to guard the fair.
Rule, Britannia, rule the waves,
Britons never will be slaves!

Roused, Nesta was told by his cousin that Kingston was near, yet he saw only furrowed fields of tobacco and asparagus as they left Spanish Town—and the occasional "ceiba" (silk-cotton) tree, its giant grayish-white trunk believed to be the gloomy dwelling-place of duppies. The higgler told him that Spanish Town also was known as the home of Sasabonsam, the most loathsome of evil island deities. How dreadful, thought Nesta, to be lost in these unfamiliar fields at night, with Sasabonsam the duppy so near!

A glen dotted with small concrete houses became, at the next upturn in the road, a mere outcropping of a fantastic network of similar houses. Some were small, some as large as Yaya's, and many so big—with two stories!—that Nesta couldn't imagine how their inhabitants could make use of all the space inside them. Ironically each was enclosed with suffocating exactitude by neat rectangles and squares of fencing, further subdivided for goat and pig pens and gardens.

Nesta thought of Nine Miles, once the most imposing community he could envision, now reduced to a village in a coffee cup when compared to what was sprawled out before him.

The afternoon sun was past its peak as the bus swung onto Half Way Tree Road in upper Kingston and began the agonizingly slow crawl through the narrow, congested streets. It was heading for the bus terminal, located far downtown in the oldest section of the city, a decaying gridwork of streets advancing from the harbor that had been laid out in the 1690s.

Making progress was so difficult that Nesta, now wide awake, had an opportunity to investigate the city from an almost static vantage point just above the heads of the passing throng. It was a welter of black and brown faces, lightly speckled with yellow and the odd pink dot. They moved by any means available and with no sense of unity whatever, ambling on foot, leading sulking, fly-encircled donkeys, balancing uncertainly on bicycles festooned with random accessories (broken rearview mirrors, rows of rusty reflectors and globular lights, photos, decals, flags and religious gimcracks), pushing bulky, inefficient clapboard handcarts mounted on coconut-sized wheels and piloted with large iron steering wheels.

Intermittent gaps in the pandemonium revealed a curb-level landscape of garbage and filth: smashed bottles, flattened tin cans, animal and human waste, yellowed newspapers, fish and fowl bones and oily rags intermingled with all manner of vegetable husks, crushed grocery cartons, shattered household articles and dismembered domestic conveniences, the latter ranging from the scorched spinal column of a dressmaker's dummy to the shell of a radio set and the rusty rib cage of a tattered trundle bed.

Abandoned automobiles, stripped clean of anything remotely desirable, formed a broken line parallel to the bumper-to-bumper rows of whole, humming cars that were attempting in vain to escape this glutted graveyard. There was just no way to proceed, and apparently nowhere in particular to go to. Nesta was accustomed to seeing ancient but doggedly maintained structures in the country, but most of these cast-concrete hovels were sinister bunkers into which no light intruded, and the eyes that blinked from their dusky doorways were anything but inviting.

Nesta spontaneously burst into tears, disoriented by the chaotic ugliness. It was half an hour before his cousin could soothe him—with the help of a pear and a piece of guava cheese provided by a pillowy matron in the seat in front of them.

The depot, at the corner of Beckford and West streets, was a simple tin shed. It stood a few blocks south of the Parade, a small park around which were several churches dating back to the heyday of the colonial planters, and the Ward Theater, legendary home to plays, calypso concerts, talent contests and holiday variety shows presented on Christmas and Easter mornings. In the other direction was Coronation Market, destination of all hopeful higglers, and Victoria Pier, where poor naked boys from West Kingston ghettos like Trench Town would dive into the deep water for starfish, then try to sell them to wealthy tourists drifting by in their yachts. If the youths didn't drown after the initial plunge, they frequently did as they searched too frantically for the coins flicked overboard as payment. Desperation hung in the air, wedded to the heat and the clamor and the floury soot stamped up from the earth. As the passengers alighted from the bus, they seemed to be instantly transformed—snappish, deliberately obstructive and full of loud recriminations.

The slickly attired young man who had derided Nesta back in Rhoden Hall disappeared in a flash with his girlfriend, as did every other familiar personage. It was oppressively humid and the air was sour. Scanning the wall of people who pressed and jostled against him, Nesta could find no friendly face except his cousin's. She held fast to the child's hand, pulling him briskly along a course he could not anticipate.

Before he realized it, her hand had released his, replaced by the coarser, hairier hand of someone else. He squinted upward.

It was a white man! A stumpy, craggy old white man whom he had never seen before, dressed in a soldier's uniform. His hair was the color of goat's milk, and his teeth were bared in a nasty smirk. And he wouldn't release his hold! *Was he a duppy?*

"Nuh! Nuh!" Nesta shrieked. "Mumma! Mumma! Where yuh? Where yuh?! Nuh! Nuh! Nuh! Mum-maaaa!!"

Nesta fainted, falling to the ground.

"Oh, come now! You little fool! I'm your bloody father, Robert," Norval grumbled, the little boy dangling limply in his grasp. He scooped him up, carrying him over to a broad donkey cart and setting him down on top of two plump sacks of rice.

Climbing onto the dray, Captain Marley gave the beast a taste of the whip, and they rode off, not towards Yaya's house on Hillcrest Road, which skirted the base of Wareika Hill on the easternmost tip of Kingston, but in the opposite direction, toward a decrepit cottage one block from the Parade, on Heywood Street.

It was several weeks before Ciddy realized that Nesta was missing. There had been no reports on him from relatives at Yaya's house in Kingston, no letters from Norval, no word from anyone at all about the child's well-being. Deepening concern turned to alarm when Ciddy's cousins at Hillcrest Road finally wrote to ask why the child had not arrived on schedule, but two more letters were exchanged between the parties before it transpired that no one had the slightest idea what had become of the boy—and that Captain Marley's whereabouts were also unknown.

The news had a devastating effect on Ciddy, who grew so overwrought with guilt and worry that she fell ill and was unable to perform the simplest chores. Worst of all, there seemed to be no place to look for either the father or the son. Assuming they actually were in Kingston, the city proper was an impossibly complex jumble of teeming business districts and ghetto "towns," human beehives which were subdivided into government or privately managed "yards" of eight or more houses in which as many as twenty-four families might be living. The crime-plagued "lanes," or footpaths, running through these areas rarely had names, and were perilous enough for locals, let alone strangers who appear to be searching for someone or something. Uptown Kingston, with its orderly middle- and upper-class suburban neighborhoods, was even more impenetrable terrain for an outsider, unschooled in the niceties of "making inquiries." And the idea of asking a policeman or government official to assist in the search was unthinkable—such people investigate crimes, not family misunderstandings and private sorrows.

And so Ciddy had little to do but weep, pine and wait for developments, occasionally consulting with Yaya about spells and potions that might unlock the secret or entreating Elder Thomas after Sunday services for prayerful support in her petitions to the Lord for Nesta's safe and speedy return.

The first and only breakthrough in the mystery came more than a year later. And only by pure chance. Ciddy was leaving her shop late one day in August 1951, her heart heavy, her arms wrapped around a bankra containing a pile of ripe, season's-end Bombay and

St. Julien mangoes, when she saw her best friend, Maggie James, a higgler, running toward her.

"Auntie Ciddy!" she called as she drew near. "Auntie! Guess me who I saw yesterday?"

"Who?"

"Nesta! Me saw Nesta!"

Ciddy's firm hold on the bankra gave way, the light burden turning leaden as it slipped through her fingers.

"My Gawd!" she cried, trembling with joyful tears as her mangoes tumbled and rolled on the dirt at her feet. "Where, Maggie? Where was dis yere?"

Maggie explained with short-winded jubilation that she and her niece Merle had seen the boy the previous day on Spanish Town Road. They'd been hurrying along with their unsold produce, eager to catch their bus back to Rhoden Hall, when they heard a child's voice raised behind them. Whirling around, they saw it was Nesta. He looked a lot chubbier than he'd been in Nine Miles, but it *was* him, no doubt of that. "Nesta!" Maggie had said. "What are ya doin' here?"

To this, he had simply replied, "Why me mumma nuh come look fe me?" The six-year-old child then explained that he had been sent to buy coal at the market by "Miss Grey." Asked who that was, he pointed in the direction of the Parade and gave an address.

"What address? Where?" Ciddy shouted.

Maggie James fell silent, eyes downcast. Ciddy shook her frantically, her face streaming with tears.

"Maggie! Tell me seh! Where me pickney?"

"Me don' remember," she groaned. "Merle and me, we was so happy, and I forget de address."

Ciddy was on the verge of hysteria, but Maggie hugged her hard and reassured her, saying, "Merle will remember! Me swear it! We gon' write her tonight fe de address!"

They did so, and the reply was prompt. Merle reported that the child had said he lived on Heywood Street, although she couldn't recall the number. But she added that the street was a short one, and if Ciddy would come to the city, they could walk along it together and inquire until they located the house. This proposal was agreed to, albeit with some skepticism on Ciddy's part, and she set off the next day on the Claremont bus to Kingston, an experience no less exotic for her than it had been for her little boy.

The astonishingly narrow mountainside roads and the cocky

abandon of the bus driver as he negotiated them kept the young woman's imagination locked in high gear for the first half of the trip, Ciddy convinced a gruesome collision lay around the next hairpin turn. Finally won over by the driver's supreme self-confidence, she allowed herself to relax and contemplate the grandeur of the scenery. The limestone-imbued ridgelands of St. Ann climbed in a nearly vertical palisade against the sea, while the high ground unfurled beyond them could be the plains of Kenya or the depths of Windsor Great Park. Handsome Hereford cattle and Santa Gertrudis imported from Texas meandered around luxuriant tracts dotted with fine old planters' houses that squatted amid copses of guango, logwood, fusti and blue-green bamboo. And the plains were subdivided by low, meticulously constructed stone walls.

Some 134 rivers formed a silvery web in the interior of the island, which is why the bygone Arawak Indians called it Xaymaca, or Jamaica, "Land of Springs," but as verdant as St. Ann was, relatively few course through its valleys and gorges, and the climate was among the driest on the island. Since the days of the Spaniards, the sparsely populated parish had been a center of "pen-keeping," as cattle raising was called, and the indentured servants who tended the herds for the English ranchers were better treated than most, much in the manner of tenant grangers in the British Midlands.

The character of St. Ann had changed drastically after World War II, when Jamaican businessman Sir Alfred d'Costa had samples of the parish's characteristic red dirt analyzed and found them to be full of alumina ore, though of a type that required special attention in the refining process. After British and Canadian firms passed on the challenge, one R.S. Reynolds, head of the American Reynolds Metals Company, which had graduated in 1940 from manufacturing aluminum foil to mining bauxite, moved in to help feed the American war effort. Afterward, Reynolds purchased the formerly subsidized plants, which then were standing idle, and converted them to peacetime production. This was a consequential act of capitalistic enterprise and initiative comparable to, though less sinister than, the free hand granted Cecil Rhodes's British South Africa Company by Queen Victoria in 1889, or the monopoly the United Fruit Company gained over Jamaica's banana crop.

There was a saying, Ciddy knew, that all Jamaica is run by the Twenty-one Families: the Chungs, Manleys, Shearers, Lindos, Desnoes, Sealys, Bustamantes, Clarkes, Spauldings, Ashenheims, Abrahams, Mansfields, Footes, d'Costas, Geddes, Henriqueses, Goldings, de Cordovas, Jarretts, Mitchells, Issas. Considering just their visible political clout and material and industrial wealth, this belief appeared quite plausible, and most of these fine folk had their baronial mansions and leisure hideaways on the beaches and moors of St. Ann. The Garden Parish was their playground.

The ordinary citizens of St. Ann's, surrounded as they are by gentleman farmers, retired officers and the descendants of planters who had "fallen in love" with the countryside, are believed by other Jamaicans to be the most heavily tainted by colonial creole pride, usually arriving in the city "poppin' dem style an' huff," putting on the haughtiest airs. But Ciddy had a vague sense as she rode onward that she and her compatriots were simply the most misunderstood, living so close to the political and cultural upheavals of the capital yet immersed in a life so completely removed from it. The culture shock experienced in the city was extreme because it was reciprocal.

Descending to the grasslands of St. Catherine, she became intrigued with the conversation buzzing around her on the bus, most of it concerning the aftermath of the hurricane that had swept Jamaica earlier that month, reputed to be the Caribbean's most severe in seventy years. In the countryside, damage was fairly light. Torrential downpours had transformed low-lying sections of Nine Miles into ponds and swamps, but the water had receded rapidly into the porous earth, and the heavily wooded hills had shielded the inhabitants of the Rhoden Hall region and their homes from the full bluster of the gale-force winds.

Judging from the buzz on the bus, the coastal rim had not fared as well: Morant Bay was hard hit, portions of Kingston were practically leveled and Port Royal was completely destroyed. One of the most effective means of alerting the urban populace to the danger, and thus sparing many lives, was said to have been the broadcasts of the island's first commercial station, Radio Jamaica Rediffusion. Prior to the hurricane, the American pop music that was piped into the homes or shops which could afford their own receivers was the rage of the island. Now citizens had begun to comprehend the practical necessity of such a modern convenience.

"Cyan't stop progress, but cyan't stop Jamaica neither," was the reverent assessment of one swarthy black gentleman in a sweat-yellowed white seaman's cap, obviously a retired sailor, who was seated near Ciddy. "De wind cyan blow and de rain fall tough, but dis lickle island is still anchored 'ere in de sun, seventeen degrees and forty-t'ree minutes from de Equator."

"Cooya!" scoffed a young man brashly, in a voice so loud that all could hear, "de stupid ol' fishermon t'ink we gwine a Kingston inna canoe!" The bus shook with laughter.

"Wha' dat you sayin', bwai?" the sailor hissed threateningly, pushing his rolled sleeves back to reveal a powerful set of forearms.

"Is not you, sah," the young man answered shakily, realizing he had gone too far too fast and with the wrong adversary. "I jus' t'rowing words at the moon, sah," referring to the Jamaican custom of addressing one's most insulting observations about a person to the moon while actually within that person's hearing, thus not being deemed guilty of slander.

The obsequious apology was greeted with even louder, more derisive laughter by the other passengers, reaching a crescendo as the sailor dismissed him with the wry admonishment, "Next time ya kass-kass, no curse alligator till you cross de ribber!"

Ciddy was well accustomed to the cantankerous give-and-take of impromptu conversation in Jamaica, but not with the hard edge that underlined this one and many of the others that she overheard during the ride. For there was no quarter given, no conciliatory gesture made, as if to back down in the slightest or show any signs of fear or weakness would bring drastic consequences. Moreover, everyone seemed to be a potential opponent, siding with you one moment against another, and then turning on you when you became the next target in the round robin of mockery.

This was what Ciddy had always heard about city people, though she had never taken the time to imagine what it would be like to be stuck in their company. "City folk play rough," Omeriah liked to say, "cause dem never learn ta play at all." Yet what was most disturbing was the sight and sound of the country people aboard who were steadily hardening and coarsening themselves right before her eyes in preparation for the place where they were headed. In some cases, they seemed determined to out-Kingston the Kingstonians.

As they reached the outskirts of the city, she shut her ears to the bickering and back-biting going on around her, concentrating on memories of her son, and on her prospects of finding him.

Arriving at her destination, it was only the thought of regaining Nesta that spurred her into stepping off the bus into the thicket of confusion and general "bangarang" of the bus station. Merle, whom she knew casually, was there to meet her, and the two immediately set off on their mission. But as they headed down Beckford Street toward the Parade, Ciddy felt herself being swallowed up by the unruly mobs pouring through every alley and thoroughfare the eye could discern. Peering around her, she wondered how anyone could retain his or her identity here and she choked back tears as she quickly realized how easily a small defenseless child could drown in such a place.

Cleanup after the hurricane was well under way, but much of the city was without running water. In the main square, buckets of both fresh and brackish water were guarded judiciously, some of them by hollow-eyed men with pistols stuck in their belts who were selling a small cup of it for three shillings. Strewn everywhere was masonry debris garnished with splintered palm and cassia trees, the yellow flowers of the latter trampled to brown by the impatient crowds. The sturdy roofs of many of the city's older buildings had been ripped off, their slate shingles shattered like glass and piled in the caved-in wreckage of motor cars. The zinc sheets that had sheltered flimsier dwellings had been flung as far as a half mile, some of them with such force that they cut through tree trunks or were partially imbedded in concrete walls, where they remained floating and quivering in the harbor breezes. The center of town might have been shelled by bombers, so deep were the piles of refuse and flotsam. And the people could not have seemed more indifferent to the consequences of the calamity as they swarmed over and past the wreckage like insects.

Beginning at the intersection of North Parade, Orange and Heywood, Ciddy and Merle began to explore the street. Evening had come to the commercial district and the human congestion was thinning out; gangly higglers and wizened cart men with hair the color of driftwood were heading off to their shacks and resting places for the night. All of the shops were closed. Heywood, which was lined mainly with warehouses, seemed particularly deserted. After a few blocks, Ciddy was dismayed.

"Dis place don' look like nobody live here," she said softly to Merle.

"Let's go a lickle further," Merle pressed sweetly, taking her hand.

The first private house they encountered was a run-down little bungalow on the left, with an old man in dusty canvas pants and a flannel shirt sitting on the curb in front of it.

"Good afternoon," said Ciddy as they approached.

"Good afternoon," he replied, rising to his feet with a polite nod.

"Do ya know a lickle bwai livin' anywheres aroun' 'ere by de name a Marley?" she asked.

"Who da ya mean?" said the old man. "Robert?" He glanced over his shoulder and then turned to survey the immediate area. " 'E was jus' 'ere playin' a while ago . . ."

Ciddy's heart was beating so hard her whole torso had started to shake and her tongue was as dry as sandstone. "Where? Where?" she heard herself pleading in the meekest tone. The old man continued to gaze one way and then the other.

"See dere!" he stated decisively, pointing. Ciddy looked over and saw a portly urchin in tattered shorts and T-shirt kicking a rag ball around in the lane next to the house, along with another, much skinnier child.

"Nesta! Nesta!" she yelled, afraid to approach him for fear of being mistaken.

The child looked up, his piercing eyes leaping out of the shadows to meet hers.

"Mumma!" he bleated, running to her. "Mumma!" He reached up and clutched her around the hips, sobbing. "Why yuh nuh come look fe me? Why yuh nuh come?"

"Me didn't know where ya was, chile! Nobody 'im know!"

The boy drew back slightly and looked up at her. "Seh, Mumma, you fatty?"

Ciddy erupted with a volcanic "Haw! Haw! Haw!", swaying with amusement. "Yes, me fatty! Mumma put on bit a pound since yuh go from me! An'," she added, tickling his belly, "me don' miss dat it's de same fe yuh, me pickney."

Nesta jumped away giggling and then pulled her over toward the house. "Yuh mus' see Miss Grey!"

"Oh? Who is dis yere Miss Grey?"

The two entered the house while Merle stayed behind chatting with the old man. The place was dilapidated but orderly; just a few rooms furnished, city-style, with upholstered chairs set in various corners, each badly in need of repair. There were some thin rugs underfoot, and several water-stained pictures of a handsome, porcelain-skinned Christ hung crookedly on the walls. In the dim, dun-colored light of the back room, an elderly, heavyset black woman clung to a cane chair, her head almost bald, her skin scaly and her eyes glazed. She was frail and sick.

"Miss Grey, see me mumma 'ere!"

The woman lifted her head. "Is yuh maddah dat?" she said, indicating Ciddy.

"Yes! Yes!" said Nesta.

Ciddy introduced herself and shook Miss Grey's shriveled hand, thanking her for caring for Nesta all these months.

"So yuh is Robert's maddah." Miss Grey sighed. "Well, I don' know wha' happened, but from de day 'is faddah bring him bwai here, I nevah behold 'is faddah again. He nevah give me anyt'ing fe de bwai. An' I often ask Robert where is him maddah. 'E say, 'She in de country.' An' I wonder why you nevah come ta see 'im."

Nesta's now-twenty-five-year-old mother explained everything that had happened, beginning with the tremulous statement that "Captain Marley *stole* the chile from me" and concluding by thanking her again, saying that she, Ciddy, was to blame for it all. "You'll get a blessin' fe sure, for yar kindness ta me son," she offered by way of farewell.

Once outside, Nesta insisted on saying good-bye to his city friends, and Ciddy, Merle and the boy paid a visit to some yards nearby to find his companions and then to the local drugstore, where the proprietor gave him a stick of sugarcane and the people there wished him well. Merle left for home with a hug and kiss, and the child and his mother walked on through the steamy, vacant streets to her brother Solomon's place on Second Street in the Trench Town section of the slums.

Within the sagging checkerboard pattern of butterscotch-hued windows rising up before them, the inhabitants of the ghetto could be seen boiling clothes, fixing dinner, gurgling rum, washing up, slapping down dominoes, necking and feuding and howling and singing hymns. Smudge fires of withered palm leaves and trash, lit to ward off mosquitoes and flies, flickered in the foreground. Mother and son trudged down the center of Spanish Town Road, which shone blue-black under the three-quarter moon.

The next day Nesta went to the barber for a "shear-cut," and Ciddy bought the uncomfortably bald boy a brown suit, discarding his shabby clothes. "Yuh look so sharp!" she told him as they caught the bus home. "So cute!" He grinned, chewed the remains of his cane from the druggist and then slept all the way to Nine Miles.

Nesta awoke the next morning in Omeriah's house, and everyone in the family took turns handling him until he finally refused any more affection. Down at Ciddy's store that afternoon, Mrs. Hanson stopped in and asked Nesta if he would read her palm once more. He said he didn't read palms any longer because he was a singer now. Taking two sticks, he began to tap on the lip of a vegetable bin as he sang a song he'd learned in Kingston:

Please, mister, won't ya touch me tomato!
Touch me yam, me pumpkin an' potato!
All ya do is feel up, feel up!
Ain't ya tired of squeeze up, squeeze up?

Delighted, Mrs. Hanson gave him tuppence as a reward, and he continued to sing the little songs he'd learned.

The Malcolm clan and the people of the villages in the vicinity were extremely pleased the boy had been located and brought back. The matter had been a widespread source of both empathetic and pessimistic speculation since news of his disappearance had first been circulated. The whole unfortunate "botheration" had been universally blamed on the city and its attendant evils, and his wholly unexpected return was viewed as proof positive of the power of prayer—plus a measure of well-aimed obeah. A fresh spate of warnings were issued to all young folk who might dare to contemplate venturing out to where Nesta had nearly lost his mother and probably his immortal soul as well.

"Stay home an' tend de cultivation!" their elders clamored. "Why reap de sin, iniquity an' depravation of de city when ya cyan reap the abundance of the earth 'ere in tranquility!"

Only Miss Isaacs, the outspoken mistress of Stepney School, struck a somewhat discordant note. She fretted, as expected, that the estrangement had been "most unhealt'y" for Nesta. And while she expressed her confidence that his intellect was "hardy" enough to catch up, she wondered what havoc the return to the country had wrought on the boy's physical condition.

"Mrs. Marley," she asked one day, "how is it dat when he was wit' strangers in Kingston he was so robust, and now dat he's home he's so t'in?"

It was true. Within weeks of his return, he had become so thin that his kneecaps stuck out like doorknobs. And the same thing—perhaps a sympathetic response to his companion—had happened to Enid's son, Slegger.

"Me don' know why," said Ciddy. "He eats de same amount as always!"

As a remedy, Miss Isaacs prescribed goat's milk instead of cow's milk (this was, ironically, one of the few suggestions Captain Marley had made for the rearing of the boy), and so Ciddy resumed her postnatal habit of obtaining it fresh every morning from a local goatherd, James Day.

"Nesta 'as struck a change," Ciddy told Omeriah. "'E's filled out just a little more, and Slegger too, but Slegger gettin' tall while Nesta stayin' small. Nest be slim wit' a lickle bottom an' take de shape of a boy-man. The Lawd mus' be carvin' him into de way Him want, cause nuh food or anyt'ing change 'im appearance."

God also showed Nesta the face of Death, and implanted a lasting mark upon him to remind him of this disclosure. Shortly after his seventh birthday, Nesta had been playing along the road between Stepney and Nine Miles at the end of the school day. He and his classmates were engrossed in a rough game of tag when he clambered up the porch and through the entrance of what he had judged to be a vacant house to elude his pursuer. There, in the center of the vacant parlor, was an open coffin containing the ashen body of a farmer who had passed away on the previous evening. Nesta had never seen a corpse before, and the queer atmosphere that surrounded this macabre tableau told him he was not a welcome guest.

He was just about to go when a frigid wind howled down upon him from a spot directly above his head. Simultaneously the streaks of light and shadow that were fanned out over the casket seemed suddenly to be pulled out of their natural alignment by some unseen force and to take on an almost solid form, like ribbony patches rent from fabric. They leapt at him in unison, seizing the boy in their icy network and flinging him through the doorway and off the porch in a high arc, slamming him down upon a sharp rock that suddenly jutted up from the front pathway.

His shocked companions saw that it was duppy business and scrambled away as swiftly as their rubbery legs could carry them, the skin on their shoulders and backs tingling with horror. Nesta lay on the ground, the large gash on his right knee bleeding profusely, and as he tried to get to his feet, the door of the house slammed shut with a resounding *crack*!

Neighbors found him blacked out on the pebbled path, the wound in the knee gaping. Yet there was no sharp surface around him that could have inflicted so nasty a cut. No matter, he was lying before the house of a dead man, and that was all the explanation anyone required.

He was carried to the clinic in Rhoden Hall for stitches and released. Omeriah cast spells that night to protect the boy's soul-spirit from additional reprisals, and everyone hoped that the incident had run its course.

As near as Omeriah could figure it, someone had lit a "bad lamp" on Nesta. "Wha' happen is dat an obeahman tek pin an' tek candle," he explained to the family, "and 'im stick de pin in de candle and him light de candle on 'im victim. De candle burn an' 'im burn an' 'im burn. An' yuh waste an' yuh waste an' yuh waste. Yer healt', luck an' life dwindle away. An' when de flame touch pin—yuh die."

So why, everyone asked, had the boy survived?

"Because him young an' strong, an' because Gawd blow out the candle when the pin tek heat. Dat way, de bwai get a sip of da pain a death, but Gawd spare 'im ta *know* it."

And what, Ciddy wanted to know, was the reason for the continual troubles that had been visited upon her boy since birth?

Omeriah had no firm answer for that. Maybe it was because his father and his father's people had rejected Nesta at birth, or because Norval preferred him to be brought up as an orphan, separated from the fortifying love of his kin. Clearly the child had enemies, and they were determined.

There were dark clouds hovering over the British Empire in the winter of 1952. King George VI was dead. The king had been ailing for some time, and his convalescence after a serious operation had been slow and fraught with setbacks. He was succeeded by Princess Elizabeth, who ascended the throne as Queen Elizabeth II.

In Jamaica, the most momentous local tidings centered on the opening of a cement plant in Rockfort, four miles from Kingston, by the Caribbean Cement Company. It was to be the first of many such plants to be established on the island, a lucrative business opportunity in which many of the wealthier families would invest, among them the Marleys.

Back in Nine Miles, the routine was virtually unchanging, the cock crowing according to his own unalterable clock, the citrus ripening in October, naseberries and soursops maturing by March, the

Malcolms and their cousins and friends faithfully dividing their time between fieldwork, churchgoing and childcare.

It was a modestly self-sufficient sphere in which the goat's kids took care of taxes, citrus and yams bought new shoes and schoolbooks, the fruit of the pimento tree bought a sheet of zinc "fe de intendin' house" of a young couple, and whatever food was left over was served at home with rum and local port—and perhaps some codfish bought from the Chinese shopkeeper in exchange for a large bankra of cassava. For those born to the farming and pen-keeping life, Nine Miles offered a demanding but reasonably satisfying trade-off. Companionship was an important prerequisite for contentment in this austere existence, and on February 16, 1952, Omeriah was remarried in a simple ceremony to the former Lurline Brown, a dressmaker from Lucky Hill, St. Mary's, who had moved to Stepney in the early 1940s to live with her sister Rosa Davies. It was Rosa who had introduced them. Lurline was in her early thirties; Omeriah was in his mid-sixties.

For Ciddy, the "peckishness" of which she often complained, the sensation that great events were passing her by, had become stronger since her retrieval of Nesta. She'd been loathe to mention it to Omeriah at first, knowing he'd block any avenue of discussion that led to relocation in Kingston, but she'd discussed it with Toddy Livingston, father of Nesta's friend Bunny, with whom he'd been keeping company. He approved, asserting that a woman has to see her share of the world while she's "still fit to enjoy it ta de fullest." Buoyed up by his support, she went to Omeriah one afternoon to tell him she'd decided, out of a combination of boredom and ambition, to stay in the city with her aunt Ivy on Beckford Street as a first step toward building an independent life for herself and her son. The idea of living in Kingston was not especially pleasant, but she viewed it as temporary, a springboard to somewhere else, possibly the States or England.

Omeriah later objected, saying she was being unrealistic, insisting it would be a burden on their relatives for her to move in with them. But she had rehearsed her reasoning. Solomon, a divorcé with a good job driving an omnibus in Kingston, had secured a house in a government "yard" in Trench Town, she explained. He was planning to move to England once rid of his ex-wife, Ruth—give or take the few additional months that any Jamaican's "soon come" relationship with clocks and calendars inevitably imposed—and he'd suggested she eventually take over his lodgings rather than pay the high rents prevailing elsewhere in Kingston. The dwelling's address was 19 Second Street.

"One t'ing 'dough," Solomon had cautioned. "Ya mus' move in wit' me before I go. Ya cyan't come in after me, or de government will give da place ta somebody else. Ya mus' step in over me luggage."

All of this was recounted to her father, along with the declaration "Me a big young lady and me wan' more excitement in me life!"

One of the few factors in her favor was that Omeriah wanted far less excitement in his. He'd gone through this tug-of-war half a dozen times with other children, each of whom had won out. Since the Malcolms now had a sizeable stake in Kingston, it was pointless to attempt to "stem de tide after it gon' out," as he phrased it. Ciddy was granted his approval, and something more: her father suggested that Bob be allowed to stay in Nine Miles for a while longer to continue his schooling and get to know his kinfolk better—because when the time came, Omeriah was going to leave his house to the boy, and he wanted him to feel comfortable enough in Nine Miles to cherish the gift.

Ciddy was touched by her father's generosity. She'd always known that Nesta was his favorite, and she recognized how many other offspring were being passed over with this gesture, but most of all she saw how the years had whittled away at Omeriah. Still the most formidable man in the district—somehow able to dig a ditch, break a horse, strip a field, bed a woman, empty a rum bottle and drive out a demon with less effort and more alacrity than contenders half his sixty years—he had quietly shrunk in his own estimation.

In his dulled eyes was regret, brought on by the business that he was certain would now go unfinished, a private agenda it would be impertinent and cruel to question him about. She'd seen resignation creep up on other, less capable and less respected men. She would protest hotly when the matrons of Nine Miles would sit about and cackle that "a country mon go dead inna de gaze, an' den go dead inna de grave." Not her father! she'd insist. Not that way! Never!

Once, after a bevy of gossipers had moved on, a middle-aged aunt had lingered behind to quell her temper.

"Young miss," she had told her, in a tone as gentle as it was unyielding, "dat's how ev'ry country mon in Jamaica tek him final aging. In de city, 'im burn out quicker. In country, him have time ta hear 'im slave ancestors wail and cry out in de night wind. Who feels it, knows it; who knows it, shows it. After a while him mus' listen. An' den 'im mus' go."

Ciddy had shuddered. While grateful for Omeriah's permission, she was grieved to accept the fact their paths were so grimly divergent. But she was still young enough that bright promise could win out over pathos. The creole culture in Jamaica equates geographic mobility with social mobility, such advancements usually being made on one's own, just as slaves had once escaped singly rather than as families.

For the venturesome outlander, all roads lead to Kingston, and for the nonwhite, the initial bivouac is the "yard." The city's yards date back to the mid-1700s, when such housing schemes were favored by substantial slaveowners. A 1770 law stipulated that where there were four slave huts on the same piece of urban land, they had to be enclosed by a wall at least seven feet high and provided with only one means of entry—a directive that adequately described Kingston's modern yards, although the huts were more likely to be attached sheds or cast-concrete cottages, twice as many in number and supervised by a landlord. Migrants from rural Jamaica looking to hire out their labor in Kingston in the late 1800s tended to congregate in such yards and sleep there for a paltry fee. As higglers and cartmen sought out such shelter on a half-weekly basis, the enclosures were further institutionalized.

By the turn of the century, yards were a formalized residential arrangement for lower-income groups—mostly creole women and Chinese and East Indian servant families (descendants of indentured laborers imported after slavery was abolished) who were intermittently engaged in commerce in Kingston. The yard's ground plan resembled that of an eighteenth-century courtyard with its outbuildings for servants and horses. The inhabitants usually shared a single standpipe—the source of water for cooking, bathing, etc. Overall, conditions were miserable even in the "penny lodging" units constructed by the Salvation Army for itinerant peasants in the first decade of this century. By the 1930s two kinds of yards had become a fixture of the Kingston landscape: tenant yards and government yards.

The tenant yard consisted of a sloppy half-circle of one-room shacks, enclosed by a wall or fence and usually lorded over by a middle-class owner who occupied the larger, more substantial house standing at the entrance. It duplicated the old colonial arrangement in which the master's house stood before the front gate and the dwellings of slaves and indentured tradesmen squatted along the lanes behind it.

The government yard was an imitative innovation that cropped up in the wake of the hurricanes of 1944 and 1951, when adequate housing was in desperately short supply. The enclosed rows of semi-detached and terrace-type single-room buildings built in Southwest Kingston after these disasters were immediately regarded as the next step up for migrants from the rural parishes. They were sturdier and had more domestic conveniences (kitchen and indoor lavatory), but were also cheaper due to strict rent regulation. What they lacked, however, was the enriching sense of community of the tenant yards, where people were united against the landlord and steadfast in their regard for each other's comfort, stability and protection from outside assailants. An alienating amenity like an indoor kitchen said it all. The wealthy Kingstonians for whom the people of the tenant yard cooked and cleaned had indoor kitchens; they were a European contrivance. Jamaicans traditionally cooked outdoors, where a full pot on the coals was a cheery symbol of good fortune and an invitation to those less blessed.

Economic advancement in the ghetto can be excruciatingly slow, if it occurs at all, and it is tied to the traditional cycle, according to which the migrant goes straight from the bush to a tenement yard. Later, after years of saving and scheming, an opportunity may arise to rent an apartment in a government yard. If that chance ever comes, the lucky party had better be lucky enough to gain entrée into a more prosperous and independent social circle to complement his new accommodations, because he can never include or reclaim his former friends. Trench Town is a world too forlorn to be flexible and generous toward transients.

The plan was for Ciddy and Toddy Livingston to live together, Ciddy helping to pay the rent by working in a rum bar. (But he kept his own lodgings, too.) Nesta and Bunny would stay behind with separate relatives. The £1.20 a month that Ciddy agreed to pay (after Solomon left) for the government-yard quarters on Second Street in Trench Town seemed well worth it, and as she packed her few things to go, she glowed with self-confidence.

But Ciddy, paid £2.10 weekly as a barmaid, would never find her place in the boiling melting pot that was West Kingston. For her son, whom she was not intending to take in with her until he was much older, it would be quite another matter entirely. Nesta had already been embraced by Shantytown, and he would fit in far too well.

5

Pass It On

The services of the Kingston-based Shiloh Apostolic Church (Ciddy's worship with the city/country denomination dated from her status at 14 as a star chorister), were typical of most Pentecostal sects in Jamaica at the time. Led by the elder of the small ghetto church, services got underway at approximately 9:00 P.M. The congregation was made up of women of all ages and a smattering of men, most of them middle-aged. The women were dressed entirely in white, with white turbans or headdresses, and the men wore black slacks, short-sleeved white cotton shirts and thin black ties.

Things began rather stiltedly, with the "shepherd" of the congregation (usually a charismatic young man in his twenties) stalking back and forth before an altar decorated with effigies of saints, portraits of Jesus tormented by his crown of thorns and fiery Sacred Heart, and yellowed photos of pastors past and present. At the base of the altar sat tin basins filled with water, grapefruit halves and mint leaves, for use in "soul healin'" ceremonies. With one hand holding an open Bible and the other free to gesticulate, the shepherd would read and vociferously interpret chapter and verse in an improvised variation on the weekly lesson, as the elder of the church sat directly behind him, hands upon his knees, staring straight ahead. Sometimes there would be a guest elder from the Toronto chapter seated next to him, a middle-aged man who specialized in healing by the laying on of hands. At one side crouched two teenaged acolytes who would later fill in as musical accompanists. On the other side of the altar was an organist, seated at an inexpensive electric console.

From time to time, the shepherd would beckon to the congregation, seated on rows of rickety wooden chairs. Prompted, exhorted, guided and/or reprimanded by the middle-aged church mistress walking among them, they would answer the preacher in the traditional call-and-response mode:

Shall we praise Jesus Christ?
(Praise Jesus Christ!)
Shall we praise His Holy Name?
(Praise His Holy Name!)

The Gospel readings would last for approximately two hours, several lengthy hymns being sandwiched in between, and then the elder would take over to offer a sulfurous sermon that mingled his own commentary on local issues and current events with the Word of God.

The length of the sermon was determined by the degree of vanity, covetousness, sloth, debauchery and other trespasses against the Commandments with which the elder assessed the community or the congregation to currently be tainted. He dared not cease nor slacken in his admonishments and censure, he explained, until every heart, every mind, every soul in his care had been purged of the ministrations of Satan, and tears of remorse and repentance and relief gleamed on every face on both sides of the altar rail. At this point, he would call for a thunderous hymn of thanksgiving underscored by percussion, organ and his own athletic tambourine, which he would snap against his hip on a spot where the fabric of his trousers was shiny and almost worn through, the skin underneath bruised and callused.

And when the spiritual cups of all the worshipers were overflowing with grace and emotional abandon, the shepherd would step in and start the procedure over again.

By the third go-round or so, when the temperature in the church was well above a hundred degrees and everyone was dabbing themselves with ivory handkerchiefs gone gray with perspiration, the liturgy would abruptly be transformed into a ritualistic rumpus more pagan than Christian. This was the spontaneous onset of what could be described as a West African seance. The acolytes would play a martial *thrum-a-dum* beat on calabash drums, the congregation supplying a counterpoint of precise hand-clapping, hoots and shrieks as they "travailed," stepping sideways in a great clockwise circle, chanting, "Yes,

I know, yes, I know . . ." until the tabernacle was vibrating with the delirious discord. Individuals would break out of the circle, bending and dipping almost to the floor, then spinning backward, gurgling in glossolalia, uttering garbled prophecies and eventually collapsing entirely, their bodies shaking spasmodically. Once the "possession by de spirit"—a state also referred to as "pocomania" (literally, "little madness")—had subsided, the congregant would be pulled to his or her feet and refreshed with fruit juice and some night air. The duration of the last stage of the service was entirely up to the congregation, often continuing until first light.

Many such Jamaican liturgies in which the Deity is accessible to direct persuasion incorporate New World syncretism and African religious practices like the Kumina ancestor-communicating dances of the Twi. (The word *kumina* is a combination of *akom*—to be possessed—and *ana*—an ancestor.) Pentecostal, Seventh-day Adventist, Shouter, Pocomania, Vodun, Revival, Revival Zion, Convince and other Afro-Christian rites popular on the island all culminate in similar magical seizures and paroxysms. Likewise, the balmyard obeah and myalistic rituals. Missing from obeah rites, however, are the lessons from the Bible, which is supplanted by L. W. De Laurence's *Great Book of Magical Arts, Hindu Magic and East Indian Occultism, Now Combined with the Book of Secret Hindu, Ceremonial and Talismanic Magic,* published in Chicago in 1915, along with *Albertus Magnus* and the *Sixth and Seventh Books of Moses*.

In rural and urban Jamaica, attendance at such churches is limited to working-class creoles, while the middle class and the elite are aligned principally with the Methodist, Baptist, Presbyterian and Roman Catholic denominations. The elite, however, attend church infrequently, and then usually with the intention of affirming their civic status rather than out of any sense of religious obligation.

For Ciddy, the church ceremonies were devout diversions from the cares of the week. She had found employment as a cook at various restaurants in Kingston and as a housekeeper and laundress for well-to-do families uptown. She worked evenings mostly and would walk home alone, her wages tucked in the small vinyl purse she clutched tightly. (By week's end, her earnings amounted to about thirty shillings.) Despite the destitution of the area, she was never robbed or accosted. On weekends, she would go back to Nine Miles (with less and less frequency) or stop in on relatives in the city. Sundays were set aside for church.

In the city, she especially enjoyed the church outings to the Hope River, which runs between Dallas Mountain and Long Mountain outside of August Town in Eastern Kingston. On the banks of the island's urban equivalent of the River Jordan, the faithful would conduct Bible-reading sessions, prayer flags fluttering overhead, and they would participate in total-immersion baptisms in the shallows.

On these excursions, as in church, singers were invited to praise God with solos. Ciddy's were particularly plaintive and uplifting, and a hearty city diet that had increased her girth had also helped anchor and deepen her voice. If memories of afternoons spent serenading Captain Marley in the bush ever compromised her devotional intentions, the emotional authenticity of her delivery did not suffer for it. Listeners could hear the pain of living in her voice as it gave texture and confirmation to the fervor of the moment; the particulars were unimportant. Who feels it, knows it.

Still, Ciddy felt the Kingston services lacked the elemental warmth and color of worship in the country chapels, where the congregation would thank the Lord every season by tying fresh produce and tethering live fowl to the altar rail as gifts. The very scents in the air at various harvest times were reminders of what those gifts would be, especially in the early winter months of each new year, when the rum-redolent sweetness of ripe sugarcane fairly assaulted the nostrils as the congregation intoned a hymn of thanksgiving.

We plow the fields and scatter, Father,
The good seed on the land!

In Nine Miles, Nesta and his cousin Slegger were carrying on in a less pious fashion. Since his exposure to Kingston, Nesta had shown himself to be a more independent—and mischievous—boy, frequently enlisting Slegger as a confederate. While Nesta could do almost no wrong in Omeriah's eyes, it became increasingly apparent that he required more attention than either his grandfather or Yaya felt equipped to provide.

Ciddy's sister Amy, who lived about eight miles outside Ocho

Rios in the village of Alderton, was known for her strictness toward her own brood, and she soon found herself delegated to the discipline two more charges, Slegger and Nesta. That arrangement was initially pleasing to Amy, providing her with two more strong backs to work the land, and in the household, Bob was appointed cook and was responsible for trekking twice a week to Pearo, a place five miles away, for firewood, while Slegger did the cleaning and cared for the livestock.

The reins appeared well in hand and impressively tight until, during a Sunday visit to Nine Miles many months later, Amy went off to church, leaving Bob and Slegger with the assignment of preparing a large quantity of rice and peas (as kidney beans are called in Jamaica) for the afternoon meal. (Being relatively inexpensive, rice is considered "city food" because it is never consumed without the luxury of costly red beans being mixed in; although rice and peas is acknowledged to be the national dish, it is hardly eaten daily, especially by country folk. Cooked with coconut milk, the dish is a delicacy to reward an industrious family on the Sabbath, and fortunate adult males in some households receive the additional treat of a large portion topped with a chunk of salt pork called "de watchmon.")

Amy's decision to allow the boys to prepare the meal unsupervised was a two-way compliment meant to illustrate their trustworthiness and show off her facility as an effective taskmaster. Unfortunately Nesta and Slegger elected to eat half of the meal themselves and then run off to Omeriah's with the rest, leaving not a grain or a pea for Auntie Amy and company. Mortified and spitting-mad, she promptly washed her hands of the two of them, once again leaving them in the custody of their grandfather and Slegger's mother, Enid. To Omeriah, the only solution seemed to be to split the culprits up, and Nesta landed back in Kingston with his mother.

Ciddy watched the bus arrive as she waited at the Parade terminus depot, and Nesta's reentry into Kingston was eased by the presence of Bunny, whom Toddy had decided to bring in from Stepney, where he had been living with his mother, the former Margaret Freckleton. Toddy had seven sons by Margaret and nine daughters by her and other women, but Bunny, who was born in Kingston on April 10, 1947, was the only one of his children with whom he had established a close relationship.

Forming a sympathetic alliance, the four of them became a companionable, improvised family. Toddy ran his rum bar and did some masonry contracting on the side. Ciddy put whatever money she could after all the bills were paid toward Nesta's education. Because of the unsavory reputations of large ghetto schools like Boy's Town and St. Aloysius, said to be breeding grounds for young hoodlums or unsuccessful reformatories for the same, Nesta was enrolled in a lesser-known private institution, the Model Private School, off Hanover Street.

Nesta had by now "busted 'im double figures" (reached the age of ten) and thus fallen prey to the personal apprehensions, prejudices of color and parental perturbations that afflict many adolescent Jamaicans, giving them often acute anxiety problems and even ulcers. Documentation of this had begun to surface in the reports of social scientists dispatched from places like Liverpool University, who were canvassing children in the slum schools of Kingston to discover the sources of their marked symptoms of stress. "I am black and I wish I could be born again and become a little clearer [lighter-skinned]," the children scrawled in pencil on the questionnaires, or "The thing I would like to do is to be born over, and have tall [long] hair, blue eyes, and to be white."

They wanted to have aquiline noses, thin lips and straight or wavy blond hair. If their skin was black, they wanted it brown, if brown, they wanted it fairer; they wanted to be spared the disdain their own race felt for their appearance. They also begged for the abolition of corporal punishment—chiefly flamboyantly public scoldings and flogging with a cane—that they constantly received for the most trifling infractions. Pubescent girls were unable to sort out the queer standards by which they were denied any form of sex education and systematically harassed, harangued and/or barred from any social involvements with boys that could lead to intimacy and pregnancy. And yet, if they had not had a child by the time they were seventeen as proof of fertility, they were ostracized as "mules"—barren, worthless women.

As for the boys, particularly those who migrated from the country to the city, every one of them was regarded as a potential street hoodlum of the most violent description, a type epitomized by Vincent "Ivanhoe" Martin, the twenty-four-year-old Kingston gunman who came to be known as "Rhyging," patois for "angry," "wild," "foolhardy." Arriving in the city from St. Catherine at fourteen as a stowaway in the back of a produce van, he was a five-foot-three black dandy who wore elevator shoes, two side pistols and a permanent scowl. He became a ghetto folk hero after escaping from the General Penitentiary in April 1948. Several sensational shooting matches in West Kingston ensued, and Rhyging, who soon had numerous notches in his pistol, vowed he would never be taken alive. A massive six-week manhunt led to the raffish murderer's demise in a hail of police bullets on Lime Cay Beach.

Parents and preachers pointed with a self-righteous severity to the story, headlined "DOWN THE CROOKED ROAD TO DOOM," on the front page of the October 9 special edition of the *Daily Gleaner*. Positioned next to a large photo of Rhyging's bullet-ridden remains, it read:

> If you asked his mother who lives in Lower St. Andrew she would tell you that Rhyging was just an ordinary boy. He grew like that too. There was no indication that in his adolescence he would begin to show a tendency for crimes and blood and explosive death.

It was further reaffirmation of what "de bettar people" had always known: "dat a colored mon cyan go either way." It was considered a victory for lower-class parents if a boy could be kept out of "gaol" until his fifteenth birthday, at which time his actions were deemed beyond the blame of his guardians.

The attitude was perhaps a subtler part of the legacy of slavery days, when people of color, both young and old, were considered lazy, shiftless, amoral, quick to defy the law and tameable only through repressive discipline. Between the poverty and the parents and the pulpit and the police, Trench Town and its sister slums were tropical ovens of negative expectations and the jobless, sun-drunk youth cracked with predictable regularity under the pressure.

When the outbursts came, they frequently took the form of ratchet fights triggered by some real or imagined slight. There was a catch phrase called out with regularity to one's opponent that set forth the ground rules for confrontation: "If a fire, mek it burn, if a blood, mek it run." Which meant, "We fight like a raging fire, and if blood is drawn, let it flow freely. This is a battle without quarter."

Nesta would grow up seeing his playmates slowly transformed into bitter "rude boys," vicious teenage toughs contemptuous of all authority who would, say, rob a liquor shop at knife point and then trip down to the Odeon to catch a triple feature of "Nigger Charley," "Johnny Tough" and "Jaws of Death." Three hours later, they'd be

MARCUS GARVEY (1887-1940) THE STATESMAN

ORGANIZER AND PRESIDENT GENERAL OF THE UNIVERSAL NEGRO IMPROVEMENT ASSOCIATION AND AFRICAN COMMUNITIES LEAGUE; FIRST PROVISIONAL PRESIDENT OF AFRICA, JOURNALIST, ORATOR, PHILOSOPHER, IDEALIST, PATRIOT, LEADER AND MARTYR.

HE AND HIS ORGANIZATION EMBRACE ALL PEOPLE WITH AFRICAN BLOOD; ADVOCATE REDEEMING THE RACE BY UNITY; BY POLITICAL AND ECONOMIC FREEDOM OF AFRICA; AND BY LEADING THE RACE TO ITS CUSTOMARY POSITION OF DIGNITY AND REVERENCE.

GARVEY IGNORED ALL THREATS TO CEASE ACTIVITIES. SHOT AND WOUNDED, HE KEPT HIS COURSE. FRAMED AND IMPRISONED IN U. S. A.—YET STUCK TO HIS GUN. DEPORTED TO WEST INDIES THEN EXILED IN ENGLAND, WITH BACK TO THE BRITISH WALL DYING, BUT FIGHTING ON.

To their honor and integrity, he left to have, to hold and carry on his

ACCOMPLISHMENTS

a) A Flag—Red, Black, Green; their own—symbol of Hope and Unity.

b) A National Anthem—that cuts across all climes, boundaries and nationalities: *"Africa, the land of our fathers, The land where the Gods love to be, As storm clouds of nights sudden gathers, Our armies come rushing to Thee..."*

c) Organized an *"African Legion, an African Royal Guard, Black Cross Nurses, etc."*

d) Organized *"The Black Star Line Shipping Co.* with the ships *"S. S. Shadyside, Orion, Yarmouth* and *Phylis Wheatley* also *"The Black Cross Navigation & Trading Co.* with the *S. S. Booker T. Washington."* for Commercial and Industrial Development of his people. Beside the *Negro Factories Corporation.*

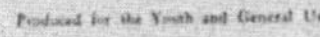

e) The Document *"African Fundamentalism"* a creed guiding the future, written and published while in prison. Published *"Negro Times,"* daily newspaper; *"Negro World,"* weekly; *"The Blackman,"* monthly magazine; *"Philosophy and Opinion of Marcus Garvey, vol. 1 and 2,"* books, etc.

f) Organized *"The African Redemption Fund."*

g) Perfected an *"African Colonization Plan."*

h) Sent *Commission to League of Nations at Geneva,* demanding territories held by Germany as black man's share for fighting in war 1914-18.

i) Opened the *Liberty University* at Jamestown, Virginia; first slave landing 1619.

j) Organized a *Political Union* for proper representation.

GARVEY ADVOCATED

a) *Africa* for the *African* at home and abroad.

b) *Black be deified* as the symbol of *Beauty, Dominance* and *Perfection.*

c) Seeing Heavenly *Beings* through African eyes, etc.

Produced for the Youth and General Use — By African Picture & Information Service. — 8 West 117th Street, New York 26, N. Y. Copyright 1947

Marcus Garvey commemorative poster, Harlem, 1947.

Ras Tafari Makonnen (later known as Emperor Haile Selassie I), after being appointed *negus* (king) of Ethiopia in 1928. PETER SIMON COLLECTION

Jamaican tourism ad, circa 1937. COURTESY OF WALLY FRIEDOPFER

Street scene in Trench Town ghetto of Kingston. Note small sign at the corner, affixed to the Miracles and Wonders Church of Christ the Redeemer Zion Healing Temple, and the People's National Party (PNP) graffito below it. PETER SIMON

A tenement yard in Trench Town, Kingston. PETER SIMON

Cedella Marley's one-room hilltop shack, Bob's first home. PETER SIMON

The village of Nine Miles, St. Ann. PETER SIMON

Opposite: Omeriah Malcolm, Bob Marley's maternal grandfather, standing before the house in which Bob was born in the village of Nine Miles, St. Ann. COURTESY OF CEDELLA BOOKER

Producer Duke Reid (left, in white cap) and Fats Domino (right, seated) at a Kingston stage show in the late 1950s.

Bob Marley with his mother and half sister, Pearl Livingston, in Kingston, circa 1966. COURTESY OF CEDELLA BOOKER

Bob Marley on his wedding day, February 10, 1966. COURTESY OF CEDELLA BOOKER

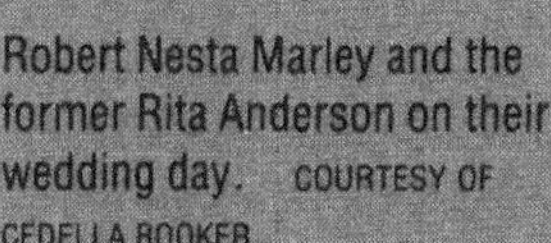

Robert Nesta Marley and the former Rita Anderson on their wedding day. COURTESY OF CEDELLA BOOKER

back on the street, drunk as donkeys on Dragon stout and so wired from all that simulated violence that the sap would start bubbling, someone would start talking carelessly about "pushin' up" someone's sister, and then one bwai's ring fingers were suddenly missing and another was a shrieking siren of agony as a ratchet blade was ripped straight up from his groin to his rib cage.

Sometimes Trench Town was a picture of defeat in which almost nothing occurred unless by detonation.

Ciddy shot out of her home one Saturday just before noon, rocketing past Mr. Livingston, who was playing draughts with a customer on a barrel outside of his bar, and Bob and Bunny, who were booting around the secondhand soccer ball Toddy had presented them with a few days earlier.

"Ciddy!" Toddy called out as she strode past in a crisply pressed housedress, without a sideward glance, obviously in a furious huff. "Wha' de beef, woman?! Yuh face favor bullfrog."

No answer. No obligatory retort. No change in her expression. Toddy pondered the matter as he watched her proceed for a block and turn left, disappearing into the crowd at the corner of Queen Street and Spanish Town Road. Recently returned from a visit home to Nine Miles, Ciddy had been in a foul mood last night; something having to do with correspondence between one of her sisters and Aunt Ivy Malcolm about the long-missing Captain Marley. But she'd been cheery enough this morning, preparing a batch of cassava tubers for the first meal, squeezing the juice out of the grated cassava and drying the starchy meal for "bammy" pancakes, using the juice for spicy cassareep stew, and even deciding to turn the excess cassava into a tasty tapioca, humming as she went.

Whatever was up, Toddy was fairly sure he couldn't be implicated in it. He made a mental note to see about fixing the rotted floorboards in the bedroom, which she had been nagging him about, and went back to his game, jumping two of his opponent's checkers to reach the other end of the board. He demanded with a flourish that he be crowned.

He shot a final glance down West Street. Ciddy didn't get riled often, but she was one fockin' hornet's nest when the mood took hold, he thought. He broke a knuckle-sized plug of tobacco off a twisted and balled-up length of "jackass rope," crumpling the aromatic coil of dried leaves and poking them into his pipe. Catching the concern in his friend's face, he nodded after Ciddy as he lit the tobacco with a glowing twig from a trash fire in a nearby oil drum.

"Coward man keep sound bone," he said with a wink, and his companion laughed heartily.

Ciddy's sandled feet hit the soft, heat-bubbled tar in a staccato rhythm, her heels leaving faint indentations as she marched between Greenwich Town and Denham Town, threading her way through the jagged corridors that opened up in the throngs of urchins, merchants and mendicants along the route, occasionally hopping sideways to avoid the asthmatic white "chi-chi" buses, the fancy hydraulic inner-city variety that were treacherous for pedestrians and murderous competition for the bungo-bungo bus. There had been a flash shower around 9:00 A.M., and billows of damp mist still drifted over the hills in the distant outskirts of town, casting broad shadows on the sloping suburbs of Meadowbrook, Havendale and Constant Spring.

On her left, between the highway and the sea, was the May Pen Cemetery, the grounds choked with thorny acacia trees which were themselves being strangled by the orange-red filaments of the parasitic "love weed." Ciddy ruefully recalled the superstition that if a young girl rubs her body, especially the back of her neck, with the weed, and then claps her hands and holds them out palms up as her hoped-for-lover approaches, reciting "By Saint Peter, James and Paul," his heart will forever be bound and true.

Beyond the cemetery rose the Dungle, a piazza of flattened refuse ringed by cardboard huts behind which rose mounds of garbage. The Dungle did double duty as a municipal garbage dump and a derelict community erected on a platform of filth, human waste and the jetsam of the more discerning scavengers. The people who skittered crablike over its stinking, gull-and-rat-infested ridges were absolutely the lowest human creatures in the Caribbean caste system. These nameless scavengers were shunned by all as worse ghouls than the mythical God-cursed "gwine-gog" hogs and hideous "gorgon" devils who had snakes instead of eyes. Unwelcome even in the humble hierarchy of the ghetto, the inhabitants of the Dungle were not spoken of by anyone, their very existence acknowledged only by an assiduous avoidance of the precinct.

Something between the death-in-life of the Dungle and exquisite malignancy of the love bush would be Captain Marley's just fate, Ciddy thought as she continued on, stomping off the road, bearing right and heading straight up Waltham Park Road into the middle of Whitfield Town.

It was drippin' hot, as always. Life was awesomely unfair, as always. The slightest comforts seemed fleeting, as always. She began to cry and immediately hated herself for wavering from the real purpose of her errand—which only made her feel worse.

"No, *suh*!" she spat out loud, forcibly flooding her thoughts with fortifying images of church and the stoutness of her family tree. She threw her shoulders back and walked on, her sense of self-worth nearly restored.

Just two days earlier she had learned from a visiting relative that her long-estranged husband—lordly white Captain Norval Sinclair Marley, deceiver, heartbreaker and reptile—had now added bigamy to his many sins, getting married under her very nose to a light-skinned woman who had installed herself at his residence. It was a bitter pill to down, and while she had no idea what she would say or do to him, she could not forestall the confrontation even for a day. She had to shame him with the fact of *her*, to denounce the loathsome falsehood face to face, to crush his pretense of respectability. As she approached his bungalow at 56 Waltham Park Road she swallowed with difficulty, her throat so dry the muscles seemed to crackle.

She swung the rickety gate wide and walked to the small, broom-cleaned veranda. A fair-complexioned, middle-aged mulatto woman stepped out of the doorway to meet her. She was dressed in a print shift, her nappy hair pulled back tightly.

"How do you do, Mrs. Marley," said Ciddy, her voice refusing to remain steady.

"Hello," the woman said evenly.

Ciddy's heart shriveled, or something inside it that had long been forgotten seemed to have withered and died in the space of an instant. She regarded the woman, studying her weary, supple features. But she was conscious of nothing but the moment, the authority of her perspective, the frame she was imposing around the frame. The day began again, the air cleared, lost its haziness. Everything seemed new, not quite pristine, but fresh and crisp and one-of-a-kind. The next, physical step forward for Ciddy would cancel out all that lay behind her, and she crossed it with conviction and poise.

Her sandals lightly scraped the concrete walk as she ascended the bungalow steps.

"Can I speak wit' Mr. Marley, please?" she asked with patient clarity. It pleased her that she had no desire to break into a nervous, triumphant smirk.

"Who are you?" said the woman.

"Me name is Davis," Ciddy replied firmly. "I want ta speak wit' him for a brief moment."

The woman planted her feet, as if to bar Ciddy's way, then hesitated, relented. Turning on her heel, she called out to the garage. "Captain," Ciddy heard her say, "a young lady named Davis is out here to see—"

The familiar, queerly quaint voice cut her off.

"Who is it?" he said hoarsely. "Ciddy?"

Captain Marley shuffled out into the walkway. Puffy-eyed, bloated, his thin hair mussed and matted, he was clearly an invalid. He began to sob. Ciddy noted the shiny pinpoint of a tear staining the toe of one of his slippers. She searched herself for remorse and pity, and found none.

He composed himself. "How is Robert?" he asked.

"Him fine," she said blandly. "Mebbe me bring him come look fe yuh."

"All right," he said quietly. "Awright."

The woman wanted to know who Ciddy was. The captain explained that he had a son, and the woman's hand went to her open mouth. He began to cry again.

If Ciddy said good-bye, she couldn't recall. All she knew was that she was suddenly a block away from the house, and then six blocks. She could smell the rum on Toddy's breath before she realized she was home. The familiar surroundings looked solid but unreal, so that everything seemed to be jumping out at her. She realized she was sweating and rubbed her moist forearms. The slightest breath of a breeze crept up and chilled her. Next day, she brought Nesta for a brief visit.

Shortly afterward, she went to the Alexandria police station and swore out a complaint against Norval. The hearing was set for several weeks later at the courthouse.

Ciddy and Nesta waited in line all morning outside the courtroom for the judge to hear the case. She was dressed in an itchy blue twill dress. Two uncles who'd attended the 1944 wedding accompanied Ciddy, who cast a baleful glance at the second, light-skinned Mrs. Marley and the Captain, who looked "maaga" (wretched thin). The guard crooked a finger and escorted them inside. The spotless, high-ceilinged courtroom smelled of varnish, and the dark wooden floors shone from being scrubbed with a "coconut brush" (half an unripe coconut, dried and coarsened). They approached the bench, where Norval's portly nephew, Cecil, a lawyer, was waiting with the captain. Ignoring Ciddy, who had no legal counsel, the judge asked Norval how many times he had been married.

"Once, Your Honor," he replied softly, "and I have one son."

Minutes later, the court officer motioned for Ciddy to move to the rear of the courtroom. She nodded and obeyed.

"Wha mus' me do now?" she asked the guard at the entrance.

"It's done," he said. "Don' yuh know dis case is closed now? Why fe yuh nuh come wit a solicitor?"

"Why, w-w-why, me don' know," Ciddy stammered. "Guess me didn't wan' t'ings to go any further den did yere. Me jus' wan ta know dat the faddah is ta himself an' I am ta meself an' we are free from each other. Dat's all me needed, suh."

Later, she fretted to herself as she walked through the streets with a bewildered Nesta.

"Dat was me faddah den?" he said as they crossed against the traffic, referring to his short visit in the garage with Norval.

"True," Ciddy replied shortly. "Sad an' true."

Nesta considered this for several blocks, and then took his mother's hand.

"Mama," he said coolly, "we nuh need dat mon."

She stole a look at Nesta as they walked along. He's almost a man himself, she thought, a man-child with a cloaked heart and a resolve like iron. He had got neither trait from his father, God knows, and both are assets. All the boy can thank the captain for is the white blood in his veins and a certain cast to his features. But there was something else about her son, she thought—a quality, an aura, something. . . .

"Yes, suh!" she agreed. "We don' require anyt'ing of dat rascal! Come!"

She stepped into a small shop, a red rag hanging from a pole outside the door identifying the owner as an ice vendor. She bought two cups of crushed ice coated with a thick sweet-sour cherry syrup, and gave one to the boy. They enjoyed the treat on the trek home, neither speaking another word.

A few months later, on May 20, 1955, word reached Ciddy that Captain Marley had died of a heart attack following a bout with pneumonia. He'd once had malaria and had never completely recovered from it. There were also unconfirmed rumors that he had had cancer. As for Ciddy, she felt nothing.

That Saturday evening she was returning from some shopping on St. Joseph's Road in Whitfield Town when she bumped into Norval's woman.

Muttered pleasantries were exchanged, and then Ciddy lost her temper.

"Tell me now," she demanded, slapping the back of one hand against the palm of the other in a gesture of impatience. "Aren't ya givin' me anyt'ing fe de captain's lickle bwai out of what he left?"

"Lady," the woman retorted, very nervous and jumpy, "I have to be workin' plenty, plenty hard fe me bread an' butter."

"Very well," said Ciddy. "Go on yar way. Gawd will provide fe de bwai."

The woman turned to leave and suddenly started shrieking. "I am bleedin'!" She yelped like a wounded animal. "I am bleedin'!"

Ciddy saw that she had blood running down her hands. "Goodness!" she said to her. "Yuh got ta have a pin somewheres in yuh dress dat stuck you!"

The woman protested that she had no pins anywhere and began to hurry away, stumbling and almost falling down in her haste. There was horror in her eyes.

Then Ciddy realized the woman thought Ciddy had set obeah on her. But where had the blood come from?

Two days later a letter arrived from the woman's lawyer stating that if Ciddy ever molested her on the street again she would file a formal complaint with the police. Ciddy showed the letter to Toddy.

"Look at dese cry-cry people," she said. "I'm a woman who fight fe somet'ing fair and ignore de rest. Look what dem doin' to me because I am a black woman! Me never touch dat woman, not even ta shake her hand!"

Toddy asked her to tell him again about the woman's bleeding, and he shook his head as she recounted the bizarre incident.

"Somet'ing goin' on 'ere we cyan see," he concluded. "Sometime spirits tek action even when yuh nuh summon dem. Somet'ing science dat woman, an' it wasn't yuh neither."

He spied Nesta skipping down the street, soccer ball underfoot, and shook his head again.

6

Small Axe

"Cub-*bena*!" Toddy hollered, summoning Nesta by the Twi word (Kwabena) for a child born on a Tuesday, Toddy's melodic inflection making the ancient pet name sound particularly affectionate.

Nesta popped up from behind some logwood bushes, where he had used stones and clay to corral a lizard.

"Cubbena, come suh!" Toddy beckoned, tilting his head in the direction of the morning sun. "De eyes of the day 'm plenty clean. Now we gwan live in government yard!"

Nesta knew. His mother had been chattering about little else for the last several weeks after her brother, after nearly two years of threatening to do so, had finally packed his "leaving trunk" for England. Solomon and Ciddy had sat up the previous night by the dim light of a burning kerosene-soaked rag stuck in a bottle, him extolling the virtues of "de Continent" and her heaping thanks upon her brother for his beneficence in turning over his two-room tenement flat to her and her "menfolk." Around them spread the gaiety of a "moulood," or "dinner yard" (a drinking and dancing party, once a ceremony conducted by Muslim and Hindu Indo-Jamaicans as an austere prayer meeting of thanksgiving but transformed through years of ghetto influence into a lowdown inner-city blowout). Judging from all the drunken fuss, an outsider might have deduced that Ciddy and company were en route to a palace, all worldly cares henceforth cast to the winds.

The hangovers of the next day notwithstanding, it had taken only the dawn hours for Ciddy, Toddy, Bunny and Nesta to load a donkey cart with their possessions and relocate to Second Street in Trench Town. And for all the brouhaha that had preceded the move, their new quarters were at best a rather modest step up from what they had left behind in the last few months as they shuttled from Toddy's place to temporary quarters on Oxford Street and then on Regent Street while waiting for Solomon to clear out.

Sitting behind a seven-foot concrete and zinc wall, their new home was located in a two-storied stucco unit of twelve apartments in the center of a horseshoe-shaped settlement, hemmed in on all sides by a welter of squatters' shacks constructed of squashed petrol tins and termite-perforated cast-off lumber. Each apartment housed as many as eight people, with a total of seventy currently living on the grounds.

The apartment was not much bigger than Toddy's, although cooler and less ramshackle, the thick concrete walls and tile floor a big improvement over the splintered plank construction of his place. There were two double beds (one for children, one for adults), a pine china cabinet, a lacquer vanity and two cane chairs, all the furniture battered but serviceable. The kitchen (shared with the adjoining flat) had a hearth for coal pots and a boxy, faucetless drainage sink. Just outside the front door sat another of the shallow, three-legged braziers upon which poor city folk cooked their meals. The common toilet and sanitary facilities on the premises consisted of four water closets (two of them had been out of order for months), four showers (one defective) and two standpipes.

Scrawny chickens skittered around in the barren yard, and strangers were sprawled in the slivers of shade created by the encircling wall, giving the newcomers a comprehensive "eye pass." The feeling of spaciousness they'd enjoyed at Toddy's place, with its windows overlooking the bustling street, was absent here. Between one paved official thoroughfare and another in Trench Town ran a network of extremely narrow unpaved footpaths; their yard was located at the confluence of a number of these bewildering dirt tracks. There were few trees and no grass anywhere, the only thriving vegetation being prickly cacti and acacia. Walking around, one quickly became accustomed to the constant crunch under one's soles of the dead cockroaches, waterbugs and "chinks" (bedbugs) embedded in the soil. Only the very poorest people went barefoot in the yards because of the danger of contracting "jiggers," a disease caused by the minute chigoe, an insect which burrows under the skin to lay its eggs, which often results in hideous disfigurements.

Few electric lines were strung through Trench Town or the adjacent ghettos of Ackee Walk, Concrete Jungle, Lizard City and Boy's Town, the darkness challenged only by the meek glow of kerosene lamps and crude lanterns. Running water was likewise nearly unavailable. One trickling standpipe might serve as many as two thousand people, only a few of whom would be fortunate enough to have the spouted clay cisterns that country folk used to keep their stored water fresh.

Outside the gate, the coop-sized "tattoo" hovels with cardboard roofs that were perched at the edges of the concrete gullies sheltered as many as a dozen or more wretches apiece. While the government yard and tenant yards almost all had water closets or private outhouses, the rest of the citizens of Trench Town had to relieve themselves in common pit latrines, or among the barbed shrubs. The latter method provided food for roving pigs and goats, who moved along the lanes with a presence and self-assurance greater than that of their owners. Men and women who could afford the luxury of a belt-length strand of jackass rope smoked it constantly to screen out the loathsome, gagging odors hanging in the atmosphere. Come sundown, anything combustible that could be spared was tossed onto bonfires built for the same purpose, and slum dwellers would awaken in the morning covered with a thin layer of soot.

Why, Nesta asked, had his mother and Toddy brought them to this awful place?

"Fe cheaper rent," she snapped, "suh me cyan feed four mout' an' send yuh ta school an' save fe better conditions!"

Nesta found that the daily routine of the government yard was more monotonous than any he had known before. Adults and children dispersed around 7:00 A.M., heading off to jobs and school, while the elderly tidied up behind them. Women and schoolchildren returned in force around 3:00 P.M. and milled about discussing the day's events and playing until 5:00 P.M., when daughters combed their mothers' hair and vice versa and they both used the showers; the children were scrubbed afterward in tin tubs. At 6:00 P.M. charcoal fires were lit for supper and the men arrived around 7:00 P.M., not washing up themselves—assuming the standpipes or showers still had enough water to accommodate them—until after their repast. By 10:30 P.M., all but the "sportin' " and the disreputable were asleep in their beds or hammocks.

The schedule changed only on a Sunday, when breakfast came as late as 8:00 A.M. The women, pressed for time before the 11:00 A.M. tabernacle services, did not partake of it themselves so that they could start grating the coconut for the modest Sunday dinner of rice and peas.

Outside the wall, there was no routine to speak of, and the only meal of any given day might be no more than gruel or banana slops. Even among the very poor there were sharp subdivisions. The great social equalizers were the political gangs, loyal to either the Jamaica Labour Party or the People's National Party, who extorted protection money in exchange for the privilege of having a domicile in a particular district, and the poker-faced police of the Denham Town Police Station, who kept the lid on the despair of West Kingston, their high-powered rifles loaded with Mark 7 bullets capable of punching a hole the size of a quarter in the toughest human flesh.

During the period when ghetto gunman Rhyging was a symbol of reckless rebellion for the downtrodden, killing three policemen and wounding two as he tried in vain to escape them, contempt for the shantytown militia surfaced with unprecedented boldness. Fans of the renegade scrawled the snide message "*Rhyging was here, but him just disappear*" on walls all over town—from the police station to the government buildings uptown. When the fallen outlaw's body, reduced by trained marksmen to a dun-colored sponge, was taken to the Kingston morgue, more salvos were fired by police to restore order among the thousands of mourners and unruly rubbernecks. The bullets soared harmlessly skyward, but though no one realized it at the time, this was the start of an undeclared war between the police and the poor.

In his first weeks in Trench Town, Nesta made few friends; he and Bunny kept to themselves as they explored the area. Their first acquaintance was a bearded man in his sixties who had an around-the-clock card game going in one corner of the yard. He had presented them each with a small piece of salt fish one evening as they stood watching the gambling and since that time had given them a friendly wave whenever they passed by, casually introducing them in time to most of the other residents.

One night they were watching the low-stakes hands being dealt out on a weather-warped door propped up on sawhorses when one of the older boys in the yard ambled into view.

"Hey, Winston!" the old man called out, not looking up from his cards. "You do da t'ing fe me?"

"Which t'ing dat?" said Winston.

"Give back de ol' woman to her mon!"

At that instant, the entire yard seemed to unite in laughter, from the card sharks to the bone-weary laborers lolling outside their rooms. It even infected Ciddy, who was sitting on the stoop stirring a concoction of tomato and mackerel called "run down," a stuffing for breadfruit that she was preparing for Toddy to thank him for having whitewashed the interior of the flat.

While Ciddy was slightly embarrassed by her own laughter at the naughty jibe, Nesta was captivated by the reflexive solidarity of his neighbors and felt drawn to them. He had wandered gingerly through ghetto yards on occasion during his earlier days in Kingston but always as an interloper, chased away by other children or adults who bade him "gwan back ya own strikin' plot!" Now he actually had his own yard, and despite the decrepit state of it, he reveled in the sense of belonging.

Ciddy made it plain she had little interest in finding acceptance in the settlement, forever telling the few women she was friendly with about her intentions of moving onward soon, and eventually as far as Wilmington, Delaware, where she had some family and friends. But Nesta dove into the social "runnings" of the ghetto as if they were a pool of bright water, eager to learn everything about the population of Trench Town, about its habits, rules and secrets.

Surveying the city and its attractions from the vantage point of Second Street, he could not believe it was the same place in which he had been marooned as a small boy, and it quickly became apparent how sheltered he'd been during his stay at West and Beckford streets. Or was it just that he hadn't been paying attention? From his new playmates he learned to play cards and dominoes, and was taught how to use a ratchet (one popular trick with the sinister, finger-long blade was to peel an orange, using only one hand, in a perfect spiral so that the globular peel could stand alone, intact, "like 'im buccaneer skull"). He was instructed in tactics for fightin' to win, and he learned to boot a soccer ball like a wizard. He acquired a facility at "t'rowing partner" (swearing fluently), especially at other boys fresh from the country: "Yuh t'ink yuh cyan cuss like me? Me is Kingstonian! Go back a yuh mountain bush, jegge [fool]! Fe me duma an' dundu [thrash and razor] yuh!"

And then there was the art of dealing with girls. While young boys were permitted by unspoken communal custom to have free time for conversing around the yard gate and chewing on cane "wit dere breddahs," girls from twelve years upward were expected to help their mothers and not congregate with others their own age or older, lest "deh teach each other t'ings before dem time." The wisdom of early sex education was often strenuously endorsed in public discussions among their parents, outbreaks of VD in the yards being charted with the same concern and enthusiasm accorded politics and fast horses at Kingston's Caymanas Park race track, but actual instruction remained rare. A boy was not considered a man until he had entered the job market—usually at the age of fifteen, after a stint at primary school—but another prerequisite was carnal familiarity with girls his own age or older. And there was little or no shame attached to impregnating one or more of the "pickney stuckadees" (attractive young virgins) in the process.

A girl was said to ascend to womanhood on her eighteenth birthday, but the dividing line was largely an idealized one, since it was accepted that any young female "big" with child had automatically earned adult status; it was common in shantytown for girls who had not conceived by their mid-teens to grow openly mortified with the prospect of being branded a mule. As a result, teenagers of both sexes were eager for sexual experience, and the practice of stowing spare clothes and personal effects in other yards was widespread, as was the precaution of securing, for a modest fee, a place to have sex and sometimes even "cotch" (sleep) for the evening.

The chief legitimate rendezvous for adolescents were the "blues dances" periodically held in outdoor settings around Trench Town, Denham Town and Jones Town. In 1957, the most renowned of these were sponsored by the great Sound System boss Sir Coxsone Downbeat on Love Lane and on Beeston Street. All of Kingston was abuzz with runnings about Coxsone's mighty "control tower," a heap of hefty turntables and glowing gizmos studded with silver, black and gold knobs, all wired up to several columns of bass speakers, booming out murderously overamplified songs by Fats Domino, Amos Milburn or "Louis Jordan an' de Tympani Five on da tekin'-nuh-prisonar attack!" as the "toaster" (DJ) would announce it.

Swarmed inside the premises would be slit-eyed, "stoshus" (sharply dressed) young bloods moving in a stuporous waltz to the treble-soaked R&B, their "stuckies" (girlfriends) joined to them just below the waist, the young ladies eventually leaning up against a tree, the speaker column or a fence while their fellas would "tek 'im free grind ticket" and rub up against them, knee to crotch, "greasin' da crease" in a rowing, bend-down-low gyration. After the record had been spun several times by "scientifical" Sir Coxsone, whose job it was to gauge the sexual frenzy of the dancers and "supply da beat ta feed da heat," he would turn the microphone over to feature toasters like Count Machuki, King Sporty and King Stitt, who would shout out syncopated political harangues and social commentary over the speakers' bombastic menu of "blues, ta *raas*."

In the late 1950s, Nesta and Bunny found themselves growing up in an era of considerable political unrest as the Jamaican lower and middle classes began demanding to play a role in deciding the island's destiny—a development heralded by the radio, or more specifically, a deluge of cheap portable transistors shipped in from Miami. The transistor was the rage among young adults who could afford one, and the high visibility (and audibility) of the noisy gadget had a trickle-down effect on the way many Jamaicans perceived themselves, accelerating the final stages of some great changes that had been brewing for two decades or more.

In 1938, a succession of bitter, bloody strikes, job actions and labor riots by sugar plantation workers, banana grove workers, dock hands and the unemployed left 8 dead and 171 wounded, 32 by gunfire; all the casualties were black—not one white planter, policeman or politician had been harmed. The workers, who had assembled in groups as large as fifteen thousand, demanded better wages (many earned a shilling a day, or less, for sunup-to-sundown shifts cutting cane in the fields), better housing (it was not uncommon to find the entire work force on a sugar estate sleeping under trees or in makeshift hammocks in grossly overcrowded barracks), and improved organizational and hiring policies on the part of employers.

The unrest led to the formation of the first Jamaican labor union to be officially recognized by the government, and the flowering of two rival political parties, the conservative Jamaican Labour Party (JLP) and the Democratic Socialist People's National Party (PNP). Since 1936, various native splinter groups had been advocating self-government for Jamaica, but the consolidated strength of the two political parties struck a death blow to the obstructionist policies of the crown-supported plantocracy. For, in spite of Emancipation in the 1830s, the British had continued to treat Jamaica as a possession to be exploited at every level, its black population kept subservient, excluded from the mainstream of politics, commerce and social intercourse.

British attitudes and those of their wealthy white foreign guests had been summed up in the year before the labor riots by full-page rotogravure ads in *Town & Country* magazine—interspersed among the international social notes and articles like "The Newport Idea"—that celebrated Jamaica as "the re-discovered Garden of Eden," and "the rendezvous of Old and New World aristocracy," offering "traditional English hospitality," the "sporty golf links" and polo fields just a luxurious sail away on a United Fruit, Colombian or Standard Fruit liner or a short hop in a Pan American Airways seaplane.

But while the British proprietors of the fabulous, whites-only Hotel Casa Blanca and Constant Spring Hotel expected the black staff to dutifully keep the grass tennis and croquet courts manicured, the silver polished and the scones warm, Jamaican emigrés, who had been forced by job discrimination into years-long sojourns in Latin America (and, in some cases, the States and England), were then returning home with a fresh sense of their own disenfranchisement. They carried with them the doctrines of Marcus Garvey and the Holy Piby and Ethiopianism, they had seen something of politics—and political repression—in the world outside, and they were inclined to put more stock in race consciousness and trade unionism than in the smug paternalism of the Kingston government and the Colonial Office in London.

With the pugnacious goading of the high-minded PNP and JLP, somnolent Jamaica had been shaken awake in the 1940s and chided by the newly enlightened black lower classes for its ignorance of contemporary race consciousness, self-determination and revolutionary politics, and by the creole middle class for its lack of interest in the ambitious cultural and economic self-help programs of the rest of the "modern West Indies." An Anglo-American Caribbean Commission was formed to coordinate agricultural research and planning in the region; a conference was held at Montego Bay in 1948 to consider the possibility of uniting the British West Indies (Jamaica, Trinidad, Barbados, the Windward Islands, the Leeward Islands, British Guiana, British Honduras) under a single federal government; the University College of the West Indies was founded in 1948; the outmoded Jamaican tramway system was replaced by new buses; the novels of John O'Hara, Pearl S. Buck and Raymond Chandler were readily available in downtown Kingston.

Thus roused, the first step by the average, untraveled, moderately literate Jamaican into the global village and its materialistic embrace—a brazen bearhug of Shick Eversharp Injector Blades, Players and Fatima cigarettes, Cheeze-It Crackers, Smarties sugar-coated chocolate candies, Parker Flaminaire cigarette lighters, Scripto pens, Tabcin cold tablets and Groucho Marx pitching the smooth no-shift ride of De Soto–Plymouth on "You Bet Your Life"—was brought about with the help of the "rediffusion box," a small, rented speaker, permanently tuned to the one radio frequency available on the island.

The groundwork for all this had been laid during the labor struggles of the 1930s, when a venturesome fellow by the name of Frank Lyons began experimenting with offshore broadcasts from his boat. In 1939, a local ham operator named John Grinan had turned his first-rate amateur facilities over to the government, and Radio ZQI was put into commission with donated hardware to advertise the Allies' cause. When peace came, an English firm, Rediffusion, Ltd., bought out this patriotic enterprise and debuted in 1950 with a low-cost cable radio service with the call letters RJR (for Radio Jamaica Rediffusion, Ltd.). While the mostly musical fare ran to Patti Page and Frank Sinatra, the records being introduced by aloof British announcers, the general public's attention was nonetheless captured.

In September 1959, the newly formed Jamaica Broadcasting Corporation (JBC) went on the air to meet the mounting demand for more diversity, and it expanded the frontiers of acceptable programming by playing a smattering of records by local talent as well as sponsoring live talent shows.

For Nesta and Bunny, hovering around a book-sized black and gold Sylvania transistor radio hanging from a clothesline in the government yard (the prized possession of an auto mechanic neighbor), the R&B oozing forth was an ongoing epiphany. They would spend whole evenings listening to the blues and R&B beamed across the ocean from WINZ and WGBS in Miami, imagining they were on stage harmonizing on songs by the Moonglows and the Tams. Now that tunes recorded by young Kingstonians were emanating from jukeboxes like the one in the Fats Domino Beer Garden near the corner of Retirement Road and Half Way Tree Road, blending with the hot breezes blowing across Union Square, and local amateurs could have the opportunity to publicly follow their lead, the universal goal of rising above the stink and degradation of shantytown—to stardom, no less!—had at least become a semirealistic dream. Prior to the advent of the radio and record industries in Jamaica, the only avenues to riches and fame for the underprivileged were cricket, soccer and violent crime—the last route offered the greatest chances for success.

In the late 1950s, while the teenage Nesta was living in the yard off Second Street, Jamaica became a member of the West Indies Federation with the approval of the British Crown and was granted full internal autonomy, with a parliamentary system modeled on that of the United Kingdom. Bauxite exports rose sharply at this juncture, and the island's citizens began their own dramatic exodus, approximately ninety thousand of them migrating to the United Kingdom between 1956 and 1959 in search of jobs. Many of them departed from the new Montego Bay International Air Terminal or from the freshly laid 7600-foot runway at Kingston's Palisadoes Airport.

The PNP, led by the lordly and aloof former labor leader Norman Manley, was in power, opposed in the House of Representatives and in the lawless streets of the ghetto by the goon squads of the blustery, pistol-packing Alexander Bustamante. "Busta," as he was called, was a cousin of Manley's who claimed to have been adopted at the age of five by a Spanish mariner (hence his name change from William Alexander Clarke), who took him to Spain, educated him and turned him loose in his twenties to engage in military escapades in Morocco. Few observers believed that side of the story, well aware that both Manley and Bustamante were blood heirs to the economic privilege and political hegemony of the Clarke strain of the Jamaican plantocracy. Either man could almost pass for white due to his creole heritage, and whether one claimed to have been the ward of a Spanish seaman while the other flaunted his years of schooling in the best British institutions, they both understood the uses of inflammatory rhetoric backed up by a gun barrel.

To the Jamaican ruling class, politicians like these were always considered the fortunate few among the upper-echelon functionaries, much like the head butler in a great house. Such men sought power for the honor of doing the bidding of the silent aristocracy and whatever powerful new business interests might have quietly surfaced to keep the country's infrastructure barely functional while stripping the country of its meager wealth.

In such a sinister political climate, virtually the entire population was regarded as rabble, utterly useless in a post-slavery creole society because they were too bitter, contrary, divisive and headstrong to be united in the service of dynamic group goals. So the slave boss was replaced by political leaders of a certain stripe: fair and biscuit-skinned men who resembled the planters of yore in physical appearance and bearing, but who could bark out their platforms with machine-gun bravado and were willing to use actual firepower to punctuate their sternest dicta.

Intimidation was the order of the day, because talk of independence for Jamaica was in the air, and when and if the glory day arrived, Manley, Bustamante and their constituents knew full well that there could be only one top dog in the service of his masters.

Fourteen-year-old Nesta was meanwhile getting his own unique education, in and out of Model Private School (he had also briefly attended Wesley, Ebenezer and St. Aloysius). Model Private School, a small junior secondary institution, strived with limited resources to approximate the curriculum of the better government-subsidized secondary schools in the Kingston suburbs. It usually took boys at the age of twelve, grilled them to ensure they had not forgotten the basics hammered into them in primary school and released the lot three years later to fend for themselves. This usually meant joining the distended ranks of the semiskilled, a work force faced with extremely circumscribed job opportunities, after they had learned to add and subtract and to read about the salaries they would never earn, the Kelvinator refrigerators they could never afford, the single-family split-level housing schemes to which they would never gain access.

History was Nesta's favorite subject, and he listened intently in the large, louvered classroom building as the young instructor talked about Christopher Columbus's discovery of Jamaica on May 4, 1494. The explorer anchored in Discovery Bay in St. Ann's and found that the island was inhabited by the Taina, or Arawak, Indians, a peaceful tribe that had migrated there from the Guianas around 700 A.D. Principally farmers, the Arawaks grew sweet potatoes, corn and tobacco. (The word "tobacco" is derived from the Arawak word for the two-pronged nostril pipes they used. The brain-deadening smoke from these pipes induced stupors and insensibility.) Still reeling from an unsuccessful but violent attack by the cannibalistic Carib Indians, the Arawaks were indisposed to attempt any large-scale resistance when the Spaniards appeared on shore. Soon enslaved by the gold-mad conquistadors, those Indians who did not perish while toiling in the depths of profitless speculative mines, or who did not commit suicide, were subjected to some of the most perverse and despicable tortures their Spanish conquerors could devise.

In 1624, the English began to colonize the Caribbean, beginning with St. Kitts. They invaded Jamaica thirty years later. After two more decades of war in the West Indies, Spain officially ceded the island to England in 1670. During their century-and-a-half-long reign over Jamaica, the Spanish had systematically eradicated their Arawak hosts, but they did introduce bananas, lemons and oranges, which were helpful in nourishing the English and warding off scurvy among the pirate bands who made their living emptying the holds of Spanish galleons returning from Panama. Installing themselves on the peninsula opposite Kingston, in the town of Port Royal, buccaneers like Sir Henry Morgan presided over a Caribbean version of Sodom and Gomorrah, encouraging levels of debauchery and lawlessness which no application of the lash or the ducking stool could quell.

Nesta marveled at the story of the earthquake that plunged the sin-drenched city into the ocean in the summer of 1692. It was a pointed Act of God that seemed like a dress rehearsal for the Last Judgment, right down to the hundreds of worm-eaten corpses thrown up from the submerged graveyards that floated amid the splashing survivors and the dismembered casualties.

The teenage boy was also much taken with the exploits of the Maroons. They had been fighting the British since they came ashore in 1655 (which was why their Spanish masters had released them in the first place) and were never enslaved again, although those captured in the Second Maroon War in the 1770s were deported to Nova Scotia and Sierra Leone. Masters of the art of ambush, they vanquished virtually all the militia detachments that were sent against them. Fierce Indians shipped in from the Mosquito Coast of Central America expressly to conquer the Maroons were neatly disposed of; two full regiments of redcoats marched into Cockpit country and vanished without a trace; word spread among the other slaves that the Maroons could hide and strike by melting in and out of solid rock, and that the trees themselves would bend their branches to conceal them. A mighty African people, they were everything their white tormentors, the pirates and the colonialists, were not: brave, wise, proud. However, the whites had whittled away at these virtues during their campaigns against them—for example, the notorious slavecatching clause of the treaty of 1738.

To Nesta, conditions in the Jamaica of the 1950s, when compared with his history lessons, appeared to have changed very little since the early days. The white and the fair-skinned still held sway over the brown and the black, and the former continued to find ways to play the latter two against each other to further the aims of the whites. The police and the political goon squads were the modern successors to the misguided Maroons.

In slavery days, Britain never put any effort into actually colonizing Jamaica. They sought only to ensure that it was the most cost-efficient sugar-making machine imaginable. The island was considered a private greenhouse for the production of a cash crop which had not even originated there, having been discovered in the South Pacific and brought to Europe from India. The European climate was unsuitable for its cultivation, however, and Jamaica was deemed ideal. In the seventeenth and eighteenth centuries, sugar revolutionized the profoundly bland European diet; the profits to be derived from filling the demand for the substance were similar to those possible in the Far East opium trade or today's world cocaine market.

The sugar trade dwindled rapidly with the abolition of slavery—only the poorest of the unskilled had any desire to continue toiling at the abhorrent task of harvesting cane—and so did England's interest in the Caribbean outpost that supplied it. In 1850, the island had five hundred sugar plantations. By 1929, there were less than seventy. If Jamaica hadn't found other outsiders willing to tout the banana as a novelty in the West, it would have reverted to the Stone Age economically. Later, the discovery of bauxite barely averted disaster, but the story always had the same sad ending: most of the profits were banked and spent elsewhere.

Increased tourism and invitations to foreign investors were constantly pushed for, but former slaves make poor servants for well-to-do white visitors, and so do the sons and daughters of former slaves. Tourists have trouble relaxing in a country that erects billboards emblazoned with appeals to the natives to be civil to outsiders, and businessmen from overseas can hardly be expected to build auto plants in the country after seeing the full-page ads placed by the government in the *Daily Gleaner* deriding the populace for its sloth and lassitude.

But it was not as if the people themselves weren't humiliated and angered by such public put-downs by their own officials. In the Sunday *Gleaner* of April 2, 1961, on a page all by itself, there appeared an open letter from a student at the University of the West Indies:

> The black people of Jamaica has [*sic*] served and slaved for people of other races for many a decade. Our newest masters are the Chinese who are doing a good job of treating Negroes the way white people do. In spite of all they have suffered the black man still likes to serve and honour the white man in preference to his own brethren. . . .
>
> Chinese shops are going up all around us every day all over Jamaica and good shops they are too. But the Chinese shopkeeper with the quickness of his race has learned to snob [*sic*] the Negro customer when there are white or fair people around. . . .
>
> It can't be by accident that in a country in which 75 per cent of the people are Negroes that in almost every bank in Kingston the staff is composed entirely of people of every other race except the Negro race. (The coloured girls in the banks would be offended if you called them Negroes.) It is an insult to the Negro race. . . .
>
> Today the black man, unless he has an education, is still a "black boy." In the civil service respectable men with families are called "Caleb" and "Williams" just like that because they happen to be on the subordinate staff. If anybody thinks the black man is satisfied with the status quo, he is mistaken. He wants a change in this social structure geared to help a few and hinder the many; he wants respect and recognition for his status. He may be deciding that if he is not respected he won't respect anyone. Above all he wants money and economic stability as a race. The saying, "The black man has no money" which is true now must not be true in the next thirty years. If a change cannot be effected by social evolution then it will become necessary to use the methods the white man has used so successfully in so many countries. Either way we are going to get what we want. . . .

Sitting on a stoop outside a jerk pork stand on Central Road in Trench Town, the greasy aroma of the smoked meat and fried potatoes making his empty belly ache, Nesta finished reading this manifesto and then folded the newspaper into a tight square, scaling it at a nettlesome billygoat. The projectile struck the animal hard in the head, and it bleated and lowered its horns menacingly, but something made the goat freeze in mid-motion and then draw back. The boy, who had paid the goat no mind, sat and brooded as it dashed away. Come July, his schooling would end. His head was bursting with an awareness of all the things he hadn't learned and the jobs he wouldn't get, and it nagged him as much as his empty stomach.

Toddy and Ciddy had discussed Nesta's being apprenticed over the summer to a welder Toddy knew who had a workshop on Hagley Park Road; he did repair work and made iron latticework for the terraces and piazzas of fine homes "up on de high."

The idea did not please the boy. It was dirty, dangerous work and didn't pay well. Nesta didn't see himself going through his life as a "penny ketcha," a lowly buffoon willing to toil for a pittance.

A welder. He would do it to please his mother, who would insist he try, even though she knew how much he hated the idea, knew what he really wanted for himself, even though he'd never told her in words. She had seen him and Bunny playing and singing in the yard, Bunny strumming on a makeshift guitar he had created out of a large restaurant-size sardine can, a bamboo staff and some copper electrical wires, while they crooned Sam Cooke hits, a version of "Jim Dandy ta da Res-cue" and a little song Nesta himself had thought up—his first attempt at lyrics—called "My Fantasy":

Hey lickle girl
Wit' dos fancy lickle curls
Yuh know yuh better treat me right!

She knew his heart without his having to speak it out loud. Talk was just talk, and he didn't have much patience with conversation. Too frustrating. He was a watcher. And he liked being a watcher.

Weldin'. Dere would be some fockin' donkey dung sass-mouth an' jestering an' fights fe draw blood over dis yar business, yes, suh, he decided, since "welder" was also street slang for a cocksman, a stud. He could already hear the taunts from the neighborhood youths: "Yahso, Nesta! Who fix dat job fe yuh, Nesta? Yuh, Mumma? Cold-choke [cold food, i.e. an unappetizing situation] hard fe swallow, eh, suh? Haw! Haw!"

He'd cut de firs' breddah who susu pon 'im, fe certain. Wha' was it da Rastas seh? "If a egg, natty in de red!" The reference was to a fertilized egg; the red pinpoint in the yolk epitomized the Rasta, the wise man in the center of things, in the know, making no wrong moves. Where you see him is the place to be; what he does is the thing to do.

The Rastas were a breed apart, staunchly uncompromising in their rejection of the material world, decrying the "sufferation" of shantytown and condemning the police who protected "Babylon." Nesta recalled that he'd been terrified of Rastas when he was a child. Even now, they were regarded as blackheart men by the ghetto children. But every rude boy in Trench Town mimicked their quirky expressions. To use the Rasta jargon was "de joint"—the hippest possible behavior.

"I cut de face a de mon wha' jester me," Nesta hissed to himself. "*So Jah seh!*" ("So help me God!")

Though barely five feet tall, Nesta already had a reputation as a good street fighter; he could throw his hands and take a stiff punch, his muscle-knit abdomen sculpted like a turtle's underbelly. He had quick, footballer's feet that could jab a groin "ta de raas," and thin, dexterous fingers that could produce a blade on a blink's notice. Bigger bwai knock him down, and he get right back up again, plenty, plenty fast, seizing more of his opponent's ground with each rebound.

"One blue-swee bwai, 'im Bob Marley," said the respectful young rudies in Rema, otherwise known as Wilton Gardens—the surliest section of Trench Town, which extended from First to Seventh streets along Central Road. "Yuh never tek popgun a stop alligator. Same wit' Bob."

"Nesta, why yuh keep company wit dem bad bwai, wit dem rude people?" his mother would ask him, flustered and vexing. "Kanana? [Do you hear me?] People judge yuh by company ya keep, and dem lot is rhyging!"

"Me tell *dem* wha' ta do. None a dem tell me," he would calmly reply.

It was the truth. He knew his own mind and wasn't very interested in the thoughts and actions of others. Not disinterested or scornful, just preoccupied.

He rose, dusted off the khaki school uniform and shambled off in the direction of Clement Dodd's new record store, Coxsone's Musik City, down on the corner of East Queen and Duke streets. Deep in thought, he was oblivious to the commotion at the corner of Sixth Street, where a billygoat lay dead, its skull crushed after it had been struck and slammed against the side wall of a tiny storefront tabernacle by a speeding lorry. Several shopkeepers recognized the poor dumb beast as belonging to the coolie man who ran the jerk pork concession two blocks away.

The fact that JBC had its own one-track studio and that any yardboy with a decent voice and a tune to match could conceivably get himself recorded there was the talk of Trench Town. Add to that the news that JBC was instituting its own charts beginning in August to gauge the sales of American *and* Jamaican records on the island, and lines of anxious singers with guitars under their arms began to form outside the radio station.

The same thing was happening over at RJR, where the Vere Johns Opportunity Hour, a popular talent show broadcast live every Saturday night, took on more importance in the minds of aspiring local vocalists and instrumentalists than the £10 given as the top prize. The program was an outgrowth of the weekly talent shows held downtown at the Majestic, Palace and Ambassador theaters. As the host of the radio show, Vere Johns, a journalist, offered overnight celebrity to the winners, who were selected by the audience. Although you could never reenter the contest once you had won, Johns had a habit of inviting the favorites back again and again as "special guests," giving them a chance to showcase their latest unrecorded material for every producer and studio owner in Jamaica.

The range of material performed by the tenacious young talents that elbowed and finessed their way into the cramped and poorly equipped radio studios was staggering, with far more different musical styles and themes represented than the straitlaced middle-class entrepreneurs were interested in hearing, able to grasp or willing to foist on their listeners. The practice of airing local record releases on Jamaican stations was to remain a conservative, cautious and highly restrictive one; there were many more performers with original material than the station managers were ready to handle. It would be a long time before any show that was exclusively devoted to contemporary Jamaican artists would be slotted into a station's broadcast schedule. Yet the immature and inflexible medium of Jamaican radio found itself to be an irresistible magnet. The awesome pressure of a thousand years of repressed musical gestation, much of it heavily African in its underpinnings, was too great to be contained any longer. Something had to give.

Isolated for centuries, Jamaica rejoiced to find itself linked, however tenuously, to the rest of the music world. The populace was overwhelmed by an unconscious drive to announce its own cultural identity. The natives—especially the youths—wanted to talk back to the static-cracklin', pastel-plastic transistors.

In the course of Jamaican history, there had been no shortage of musical activity from which to draw fresh inspiration. The Arawak Indians fashioned drums and tambourines from the trunks and stumps of trumpet trees and covered them with the supple skins of aquatic mammals like the seven-foot manatee, or sea cow. Primitive woodwinds were carved out of tree limbs and bones. The instruments were played by tribal chieftains at ceremonies celebrating a good harvest or bemoaning the burial of slain warriors. The West African slaves who had endured the Middle Passage brought with them a musical tradition based on the dialogue of "burru" drums. The Ashanti used them in groups of three, the high-pitched "atumpan" acting as the free-form lead, accompanied by alto and bass drums called "apentemma" and "petia," respectively. Pounded in concert with rattles, rhumba boxes, shakers, "saxas" (bottle saxophones, whose mouths were covered with a membrane), the burru drums often greeted a slave returning home after incarceration or the victim of a whipping whose wounds had healed.

(In the 1930s, the early Rastafarians adapted if not outright adopted the burru tack in their sacred "akete" or "repeater" [lead], "fundeh" [rhythm] and bass drum ensembles, burru odes to the latest triumphs over the evils of captivity being supplanted by the traditional Rasta prayer chant derived from Coptic mysticism.)

As the slaves began to receive regular permission to congregate for periods of recreation, they resumed the ethnomusical customs of their past, playing and dancing in public—expressing and interpreting through song and dance what had happened to them and how they perceived the days to come. The African-rooted Jonkonnu celebrations held each December (dubbed "Pickaninny Christmas" by whites) were re-creations of West African yam harvest feasts dominated by a male masquerader who pranced to the furious rhythms of the "gombayers," who struck their square and barrel-shaped drums with one short stick while scraping another along a notched strip of wood affixed to the side. Just as the "John Canoe" dancer included steps from the English Merry-Andrew and Morris dances, so the drummers merged their antiphonal mode of singing and their articulate drum improvisations with the chanties, folk and drinking songs of the seamen in port, and the European dance tempos they overheard at the lavish plantation balls, particularly British reels and the French quadrille. These interminglings would later be the bases for the slaves' and free peasants' praise songs, ring tunes, digging songs and "sankeys" (revivalist hymns, named after singing evangelist and composer Ira David Sankey, who published the widely used hymnal *Sacred Songs and Solos* in 1873).

Separated from their enslaved brethren by their hide-and-seek guerrilla life-style, the Maroons preserved African ways in the plaintive signal codes of their multitonal "abeng" cow horns, an instrument of warning similar to the Akan *abertia*. To divulge the code to a non-Maroon meant death by obeah most baleful.

Jamaican migrant workers in Central America and Trinidad and Tobago in the early 1900s were introduced to the tango, the merengue, the rhumba, pasco and samba by their fellow field hands, plus the saucy/topical calypso. This monumental hodgepodge of influences culminated in Jamaican mento, a syncopated rhumba-shaded rhythm with a European chord structure. Mento bands became the nucleus of any country fair or rural get-together and in the years between the two world wars, mento bands thoroughly dominated the music scene in urban Jamaica.

In the late 1940s, the tourist industry tried to revive the dwindling fraternity of active mento musicians by marketing mento as an offbeat alternative to the calypso craze. Mento stars like Hubert Porter, Lord Flea, Joseph "Lord Tanamo" Gordon, Lord La Rue, and Count Lasher were invited to make records of some of their spicier and more amusing songs for export. Oddly enough, the sound nose-dived overseas but clicked anew with a young native audience unaccustomed to encountering it on the radio. It inspired them, in fact, to take up their instruments and play. When friends and relatives returned home with their savings after months laboring in the Canal Zone, the Dominican Republic, or the cane fields of Georgia and the citrus groves of South Florida during World War II, they brought along copies of Latin swing and American R&B record albums, whose crisp, propulsive arrangements the green young musicians ached to imitate.

What resulted was an amalgam of mento and R&B called ska, a twelve-bar blues shuffle with accents on the second and fourth beats, badgered benignly by an afterbeat—an impish little lick—on piano or a percussive rhythm guitar. Everybody and his auntie wanted to write a tune to fit the framework, and when it came to lyrics they shrugged and threw in the kitchen sink: a plethora of hoary bush-parish adages and proverbs, distilled revivalist sermons, biblical verses, soap-flakes jingles and motor-mouth appliance pitches, ad copy from movie posters and cereal boxes, headlines off the sports pages, vintage obeah oaths and recipes for folk medicine, snatches of political speeches and Rasta screeds. Nothing was off limits, so long as it was entertaining and customized to conform to the beat.

The problem was that once the lyrics were penciled on butcher paper and taught to a few yardboys to approximate an arrangement, there was nowhere to go with your song. The lines of the hopefuls at the radio stations trailed around the block, and the clubs were not receptive to rank amateurs.

The solution lay in the Sound Systems. But the owners were so busy going on off-island spending sprees to obtain the most exclusive or superbly obscure dance singles from the States that they hadn't noticed that much of the black music being made there had grown too pop-oriented and mushy to appeal to Jamaicans. The islanders had responded to the grittiness and bawdiness of the Golden Age of R&B (1945-1960). Now the songs on the Hit Parade and the Top 40 had become saccharine, self-conscious and precious—too slick to excite. Sound System tunes had to be raw and spacious to allow the DJs some shouting room.

What Jamaicans wanted, first and foremost, was *the beat* that had hooked them from the start: the hard, jam-down, come-and-get-me, click-clack, catch-a-fire clincher in the clutch of the kind that would put young rude bwais in the mood to "play fe chicken" by jumping on and off the backs of screaming chi-chi buses, and make the "la-la" (sexually indiscriminate) girls at blues dances want to wriggle half-senseless for hours at the short end of a "joy bwai." Then, at the moment when they least expected it but needed it most, the crowd wanted to hear the selector manipulate the dials in the control tower so that the bass note, so bullyrige that it was a force of nature, would drop with the ringing resolution of libido blitzkrieg. Just to remind everyone in attendance that no dance with the right Sound System crew was ever simply a *dance*.

"It don' mean a t'ing," whooped King Stitt over Sir Coxsone's mountainous equipment, "if it don' got dat scorchin' sting!"

So the selectors began to create their own scorchers. From out of the pack of Sound System leaders gaining ground during the legendary West Kingston Sound System wars of the mid-1950s—V-Rocket, Skyrocket, King Edwards, Count Nicks, Bells, Tom the Great Sebastian, Count John, Count Boysie, Count P, Duke Reid, Coxsone Dodd—the last two, Reid and Dodd, had emerged as titans. The battleground had been Forrester's Hall on North Street, the Union Hall downtown and the various outdoor locations in Trench Town and Jones Town where the "Sounds" held their jump-ups. Each of the Sounds had spies who would attend rival dances to learn, if possible, the names of the records and artists getting the strongest reactions from the dancers. This practice escalated to include "dance crashers," whose job it was to loudly criticize the song selections, ridicule the DJs and violently disrupt the evening's entertainment in order to discredit the presiding Sound by giving it a reputation for staging disorderly affairs. Whenever two systems were foolhardy enough to share a bill, the police would invariably wind up arresting a score of the spectators for possession of deadly weapons and inciting a riot. At least one rudie per jump-up would have to be hospitalized after having his chest ripped open or an ear bitten off.

Reid, a tall, stocky man who owned a liquor store, Treasure Isle Liquors, in downtown Kingston, was a mean cuss said to have connections with the black underworld in New York and Miami, and he ruled by a mixture of Mafioso swagger and the assurance of swift retribution for those who dared cross him. Reid was a flashy but erratically parsimonious fellow (he would spend a fortune on a sharkskin suit and then wear it with a pair of "Hitler boots," the slippers made from old automobile tires that appeared in Jamaica in the 1940s), and while he had a smart, tightly knit organization, he liked to handle most of the details himself, including doing his own DJing at the turntable. He'd make a grand entrance wearing a shiny coronet and carrying a shotgun, bandoliers crisscrossing his broad chest and a well-oiled .45 in a cowboy holster on his right hip. He'd have his henchmen hoist him onto their shoulders and carry him over to the turntable, the crowd closing in as he waved to them in the torchlight, the flames catching the gold rings he wore on all ten fingers—gangster-type ostentation, *ta raass*.

Dodd was a more low-key, complex figure. The Kingston-born son of small-time building contractor Benjamin Dodd and the former Doris Darlington, Clement Seymour Dodd received the whimsical title of Sir Coxsone while playing for the cricket team at the All Saints School. Coxsone was the name of a star batsman for Yorkshire in the early 1950s, and because Clement himself was a standout batsman and good all-around cricketer for the "English" side in All Saints' intramural matches, he was given the complimentary nickname, and it stuck.

Dodd was making a meager living as a cabinetmaker in the mid-fifties when he answered an open call for short-contract cane cutters in the American South. While attending rent parties and outdoor dances organized by the locals, he was able to observe at first hand the popular furor R&B was inciting among rural and urban blacks. Reasoning that there might be sizeable side money in staging such events back home, he sank most of his wages into a PA system, turntable and receiver, and shipped it back to Kingston along with a box of records. Sure enough, the response to his Sound System jump-ups was so enthusiastic that he had to hire security guards to turn crowds away at the gate.

While Dodd's was not the first Sound System (variations of the portable discos having been around since the late 1940s), his was the bellwether, featuring the most rib-rumbling speakers, the "ring-down" (first-class) discs, a theme song (American saxophonist Willis "Gatortail" Jackson's "Later for Gator," which fans renamed "Coxsone's Hop") and the top DJs, King Sporty and King Stitt, looking strictly "spree-boy" (dressed to kill) and toutin' up a typhoon: *"Nuh matter wha a people say, dese sounds lead da way! It's da order a da day from yar boss dj! I King Sporty! I King Stitt! Up to de top fe de very last drop!"*

To help oversee the business he hired a handsome young amateur boxer who called himself Prince Buster to find new singles and monitor the Kingston scene for recordable talent, and he appointed one Lee "Little" Perry, a feisty fireplug of a fellow, as his selector. When fights broke out—which was frequently, thanks to Duke Reid—these two also had the responsibility of fending off rude boys intent on "moshing up" the equipment while the gun-shy (quite literally, although he later bought one of his own) Dodd carried the evening's take to safety. On one such evening, Buster found himself also protecting Perry, who had been knocked unconscious by thugs determined to stomp him and the hardware into the dust. Buster lived up to his name, dropping four of the bruisers before help arrived. Meantime, Dodd had reached home and was sipping a rum and Coke, counting the receipts.

Not fond of personal risk, Sir Coxsone was just as diffident when it came to expanding the business. In the 1950s, the modest resources of the Jamaican record industry were attuned to mento and calypso, most of it recorded at the radio stations or, a bit more professionally, at the one- and (later) two-track Federal Studios built by Ken Khouri in September 1954. Because Khouri had pressing facilities under the same roof, producers were spared the expense of mastering and obtaining their acetates in Miami, and Federal became a haven for all the comers in the business of promoting ska.

The innovative ska beat was keyed to a dance of the same name, a tricky two-step in which the stiff upper body bows forward in time while the knees are bent and the arms are fanned out and crisscrossed. Showboating steps included a knee-to-crotch rowing motion and then a slow head-to-head or "riddim" (buttocks)-to-riddim roll to cool off. Once this torrid tropical variant on the fox trot caught on, records calculated to cater to it began to pop up.

The normally wily Dodd had reacted with zest to the concept of recording his own Sound System acetates of new material by Kingston artists (because it defrayed the cost of questing after U.S. hits), but he didn't believe the sides could have any value in the marketplace. When he was asked to turn over some tracks for commercial pressing, he agreed but scoffed at the notion. When the inaugural batch of several hundred sold out in an afternoon, he waved off the middleman and appointed himself president of a new record company, World Disc. He cut his first record at Federal Studios, a calypso called "Shuffling Jug" that featured his old friend Cluette Johnson, who had a small combo. Coxsone christened the group Clue J and the Blues Blasters. The virgin acetate went to the Sound System, where it was spun with pompous solemnity to titillate the hipsters. Days later a limited pressing would be knocked out for salivating DJs in satellite outfits, and in the coming weeks a slightly less limited edition was sold, with no label affixed, to avid fans. At the end of the month, the finished product hit the open market. It was an eccentric but ingenious four-tiered method of consumer enticement, which ensured SRO turnouts at dances and a five-figure sales volume per single—quite impressive in slums where the price of a record equaled a day's pay.

The chances of the records—made by rising artists like Owen Gray, Danny Ray, Laurel Aitken, Wilfred "Jackie" Edwards, the Maytals, Basil Gabbidon and the Mellowlarks, Derrick Morgan, trumpeter Baba Brooks—getting any airplay remained dubious, but the Sound Systems built them into blockbusters and made it possible for some of the singers and bands to fill Kingston's nightclubs, the hottest spots being Johnson's Drive-In, Club Parascene, the Glass Bucket and the Silver Slipper. One bright morning JBC made the announcement that

Laurel Aitken's "Boogie in My Bones" was Number 1, and the whole country was astounded.

This was a time when migration from the country to the city was on the increase and the median age of the newcomers began to drop into the teens. These were ambitious kids drawn by ska, the sound of the city. The youth of Western Kingston were spending their adolescence in lanes that throbbed with electric anthems of redemption, but the rustic cadences of their former bush environments were still vivid in their memories. Colliding with each other in the ghetto, the tempos of the old country life got confused with the rhythms of the city; the youth had to adjust to a pace that seemed to have been set by a drunken metronome. Then the radio literally took over for any clock, and ska became its spring-wound heartbeat.

Coxsone's Musik City, which opened at the end of 1959, was the rallying point for would-be "star bwais," and Nesta spent several hours there each day over the next two years, listening to songs stabbing out of a speaker hung over the doorway. In the autumn of 1961, he secretly wrote three songs that he planned to present to Mr. Dodd, visions of radio and Sound System glory vibrating behind his eyes. Urged on by a neighborhood boy named Desmond Dekker, who had made a recording at Federal under the tutelage of Count Boysie, Nesta went over to the company office at nine-thirty one morning early in 1962 in search of Mr. Dodd. Federal was located in a vacant lot on Marcus Garvey Drive, the shore road on Kingston harbor. Dodd wasn't there yet, but another producer named Leslie Kong was.

Kong, a Chinese Jamaican who ran a combination restaurant, ice cream parlor and record shop called Beverley's in partnership with his three brothers, had just entered the music business on the production end. He was working with a fourteen-year-old tailor's son from Somerton, St. James parish, named James Chambers. Chambers had come past his shop with a guitar several days before to play him a song he'd composed and named after the business, "Dearest Beverley." Kong's brothers had chuckled derisively, but Kong pulled some money out of the cash register and told Chambers to follow him. They recorded the song and a topical number inspired by Hurricane Hattie, which had ripped through South America that year. Both songs were released under the name Jimmy Cliff.

Nesta bumped into Cliff and Kong outside the Federal building while he was looking for the man he believed to be the only viable alternative to Coxsone—Count Boysie. Cliff was warning the boy that he had done a session for Boysie for which he had never been paid when Kong, a pudgy, pushy twenty-nine-year-old, spoke up.

"Yuh 'ave a tune, bwai?" he said, flinging back the stringy black hair clinging to his broad forehead.

"Yes, suh."

"Sing de tune fe me."

"Me need musician ta play it," said Nesta softly, resenting the man's aggressive tone.

"Musician!" said Kong, sneering. "Wha' musician? A wey me tell yuh! Dem cost plenty money, pickney bwai! Dere time is money an' so is mine! Sing de strikin' damned tune!"

"Me don have guitar! Nuttin' fe sweeten da words!"

"Why yuh mus' raise a kite [cause a fuss], bwai?! Me is businessman! Yuh seh yuh is singer wit' song! If it please me ears, me pay da money an' yuh mek a record. So me seh stop da shoolah [loafing] an' sing de tune!"

Hurt and angry, but too nervous to back down, Nesta shifted his stance in the already broiling morning sun, and gazing away toward the hills of St. Andrew, he sang the verses he'd composed, interspersed with a refrain taken from a recurrent childhood admonishment from Grandpa Omeriah: "Judge not, before you judge yourself."

Halfway through the performance, Kong cut him off. "Is fair tune," he said. "Fair ta feeble. Come!"

Before Nesta could object, he was ushered in the front door, down a dank hallway past a grimacing Ken Khouri, who sat behind a desk flanked by several tough-looking men in their twenties wearing tight jerseys that accentuated their well-developed chests and arms. One of the men gripped a shiny hook-and-bay (cutlass).

"Now, suh!" shouted Khouri as Kong moved pass the desk. "Yuh know de rules! Pay me now! How many demo yuh want?"

"One," said the suddenly timid Kong. "Jus' one!"

"Tr'ee pound," said Khouri, slamming his palm down on the desk top, the rings on his hand hitting the wood with an ugly *crack!*

Kong gave him the money, and Khouri tucked it into a kind of bib with pockets he wore around his neck, nodding to the men to let "da Chinee" and Nesta pass.

They stepped into a poorly lit room filled with recording equipment and a single mike. In one corner of the room sat a blank-faced combo of pianist, drummer, horn player and guitarist. Coached by Kong, who prodded a petrified Nesta, the musicians succeeded within twenty minutes in mastering the melody line of the song. An hour later "Judge Not" and another of Nesta's songs, "Do You Still Love Me?", had been recorded.

Kong came out of a little glass booth he'd been sitting in with the engineer, a man named Dowling, and handed the boy a sheet of paper.

Nesta squinted at it. "Wha dat?"

"Release form!" said Kong. "Yuh sign, I give yuh twenty pound fe da tunes and two acetates."

"Acee-tate?"

"Discs! Vinyl copy of da tunes!"

"Jus' twenty-pound? Wha' if it a hit?"

"A hit! Coo pon [look at] dis bungo boy!" said Kong to the grinning musicians. "Him try ta rax up [louse up] me investment! Lissun, bwai, me tek da risk, me pay fe session. Sign de paper or forget de deal."

Rattled, Nesta signed his name, his hand trembling so badly it came out an illegible scrawl.

Six hours later he was out on Marcus Garvey Drive, headed back to Trench Town clutching two black vinyl platters in thick gray cardboard sleeves, with two ten-pound notes pushed deep into the pockets of his baggy trousers. Every hundred yards or so, he pulled the gleaming platters halfway out of their sleeves and giggled as the afternoon sun reflected off the sides. Each time he looked at the records the sight of them made him quicken his pace. He broke stride when he got to the May Pen Cemetery and began running up Industrial Terrace to Spanish Town Road.

He was at the corner of First Street and Central Road when it hit him: he didn't know a soul who owned a phonograph.

7

Who Feels It, Knows It

Nesta cursed and spat. It was suffocatingly hot inside the welder's shed, and the air itself seemed thick and syrupy; he almost expected the dense gob of saliva that he had expelled from his mouth to linger in the still air, drifting slowly downward to the dirt like a pebble sinking through a pudding. Now employed by a master welder at South Camp and Emerald Roads, he was trying to concentrate on the bicycle frame he was repairing, aiming the tapered blue-white flame of the acetylene torch at a blackened joint to soften it for the hammer blows, but his thoughts kept straying to the British-made Emaphone jukebox in the rum shop just down from the Ward Theater, to the third selection in the second column of the scrawled record directory: JUDGE NOT, BY BOB MORLEY. No matter that Leslie Kong had misspelled his proper name on the disc, or that a lot of people thought it was a different boy. It was his tune! Just pump sixpence into the squat machine for a two-and-a-half-minute play, and the reedy, high-pitched voice you heard was unmistakably Robert Nesta Marley's.

But just to make sure others knew, Nesta had spent most of his wages over the past three weeks punching up the tune, again and again, standing out in front of the shop to survey the unbiased reactions of passing strangers when they heard the music. If some youths stopped to listen, he suckered them into asking who the singer was.

"Yuh like de tune?" he asked. If they nodded, he leaned back against the doorway, his arms folded across his chest, and stated evenly, "Is me recordin'," enjoying the envy on their faces. The shop-owner finally moaned that the record, which featured tin whistle effects, was giving him "a fockin' head complaint," and removed it from the box, telling Nesta not to come around anymore.

A neighbor had alerted Nesta's mother to a big talent show at the other end of the island, in a hotel in Montego Bay, and he and Ciddy had taken the bus there together, just so he could get up on stage once, clammy and shaking, and sing his song—and hear the applause! His somewhat inflated recollection of the show still intoxicated him, the image of himself being showered with adulation continuously replaying in his head. The feeling it gave him was so pleasurable he almost felt guilty. Yaya used to warn the children of Nine Miles about the dangers of pride: "Too much praise dim a mon's sunsum' [spirit]."

Still, he thought to himself as he worked, me love all da clapping of de crowd fe true. . . . I not gon' be stuck in dis yere shed for long. Nuh, suh! One day soon I gonna quail [quit] dis business and be one quality scorchin' singer—"*Aw, shit! Oh, me Christ! Me eye! Me eye!*"

He was shrieking, jolted from his daydream by the scalding, stabbing sensation of a hot sliver of metal that had shot into his right eye. He dropped the live torch in alarm, and it fell against his foot, the vicious blue flame searing his bare ankle. Yowling in pain, he tumbled back against the wall of the shed, knocking over the flimsy workbench and toppling shelves of tools and equipment. The older workers, who had been outside repairing a carriage frame, heard the boy's screams and came running.

"Yahso! Turn off de damned torch!" hollered one of them as they burst into the shed. "See it dere! By de oil can! Turn it off before de whole place blaze up!"

"Aw, fe mercy's sakes!" said another, trying to pry Nesta's hand away from his eye. " 'Im bwai got a steel splinter stuck solid in 'im yeye! Why dese quashie [foolish boys] don' wear da damn strikin' goggles hangin' 'round dere strikin' necks is something I don' neva know!"

Nesta felt the men's strong arms lifting him from the dirt as he pressed his palm against his injured eye, his fingers fiercely clutching at his skull while his other hand pawed at his foot. He was sobbing uncontrollably, begging for relief from the excruciating pain.

"Stop crying, bwai!" shouted the burly boss man of the shed. "Stop yar weeping, son, 'cause it only mek dat yeye hurt worse!"

The boss man must have shouted this a dozen times before the words penetrated the headsplitting haze Nesta now swam in. In shock, the boy seized upon the suggestion as if it were a miracle remedy, frantic to clear his mind enough to respond to it. But there was no keeping back the tears; they poured out freely as his body twisted grotesquely. He bawled and bellowed and begged for his mother and prayed to God that the pain would cease, that he would lose consciousness, that he would die if that was what it would take to banish the unbearable pain. But the furious, piercing sensation grew. And grew. He vomited once, twice, the half-digested mango he'd eaten for breakfast clinging to his pants and shirt, the stink filling his nostrils.

"Alla time me tell dese bungoes ta wear de God-cursed goggles!" roared the boss man. "All de strikin' time!"

Helped to his feet, Nesta was slowly walked the many blocks to Second Street. A gaggle of labrishers (gossiping idlers) joined them as they passed, offering loud expressions of sympathy. But as the crowd grew, some on the outskirts who could not get a clear view of the weeping, quivering boy began to murmur that he was "trumping and laboring," meaning that he was possessed by spirits, so that by the time Nesta reached his yard the opinions held by the hangers-on concerning the cause of Nesta's suffering were evenly split between the actual injury and workings of obeah.

He was guided to his bed as one of the other women in the yard ran to fetch Ciddy. She arrived a half-hour later, flustered and haggard. The gawkers were chased away and women friends marshaled to prepare hot and cold compresses to see which worked best, but neither seemed to soothe the boy. He told his mother that the light aggravated the suffering from the now badly swollen eye, and she hurriedly hung blankets over the windows and doorway. A branch of "strong-man's weed" was brought and the leaves of the herb, whose aroma resembled garlic, were rubbed against and then tied to Nesta's forehead, while the roots were boiled with white rum to make a broth for him to sip.

All night the boy moaned, the torment unrelenting and the folk medicine having little effect. In the morning, Ciddy took Nesta to Kingston Public Hospital on North Street. After waiting three hours in the jammed emergency room, Nesta was admitted as an outpatient, and a physician spent another three hours trying to remove, without anesthesia, the tiny steel shards embedded in the white of Nesta's eye. The boy's screams were audible from the sidewalk outside.

Afterward, a large cheesecloth patch was affixed over his eye to shield it from the light. That night the pain was still unabated, and Ciddy took Nesta back to the hospital the next day, where she was told that some metal still remained in the eye near the lower rim of the socket. After two more hours of delicate digging, he was released with a fresh eye patch.

Ciddy had pleaded with the physicians in the poorly equipped ghetto hospital for some pain-killers and was eventually given several codeine tablets, which later provided the boy with his first uninterrupted sleep since the accident. The following morning, as Ciddy dabbed his brow with a handkerchief dipped in cool water, her blindfolded son made her promise that she would not force him to return to the welder's shed. He told her that he had been writing songs with Bunny and that they had made friends with another boy named Peter McIntosh who lived several blocks up on West Road. They'd formed a vocal trio and wanted to make records. He wanted to be a musician and singer—full-time—like former welding trainee chum Desmond Dekker.

Ciddy's heart sank as she listened to her son's foolish plans, repelled by the crude street slang in which he expressed them. Somehow she had never noticed it before, but he had completely adopted the coarse and cocky vernacular of the ghetto and he drawled it out with the same arrogance she'd observed in the idle young toughs who hung around outside of the Carib Theater on Slipe Road. The boasty kids would act out scenes from *Blackboard Jungle*, *Jailhouse Rock*, *The Guns of Navarone*, and most particularly *The Magnificent Seven*—one lad calling himself Steve McQueen, another dubbing himself Yul Brynner, a third announcing he was "James Coburn *ta rass*." They were buffoons in a cowboy poppy show, but the pantomimes were death dances, feigned executions by ratchet and gun. Ciddy was disgusted to see the young girls acting impressed by such shameful play-play. In so many cases, this new fascination with street violence and death in West Kingston, generously fed by the picture shows, wound up being reenacted in jealous eruptions between the youths. Had no one learned a lesson from Rhyging? Apparently not, because the rude boys' smart-ass pantomimes, where they "put mout' on" (cursed out each other) to win the attentions of some stupid girls, were often dress rehearsals for their own sad demises.

Without Ciddy noticing, had her own pickney grown into a rude bwai? A future Rhyging? She remembered the articles in the *Daily Gleaner* after the criminal's death, alluding to how he had started out in an honorable profession—blacksmithing—and quickly descended into a life of thieving, "rieling" (having intercourse) with tramp women, drinking sweet wines like Puerto Pruno, and getting his way with "rushings" (browbeating) backed up by drawn guns. Soon as Rhyging had gotten his picture in the *Gleaner*, the slum youths had made him into a hero and tried to "pawn" (imitate) his style.

Although Nesta's speech was slow, dulled, as he described his new career plans, Ciddy caught the impertinence in the boy's self-absorbed tone, watched as he clapped one hand down into the palm of the other to drive home a point, frowned at the pompous delight he derived from carrying on like a full-grown man with a well-earned right to be so flamboyantly enraged at the world. It was an improvised cant, raffish and reckless. Her son was bantering like the rude bwais outside the movie house, like the ones that cussed her back on the chi-chi buses, badgered higglers in the produce stalls on Half Way Tree Road and tried to steal "shuks" (kisses) and more from the schoolgirls they cornered in lonely lanes near Calvary Cemetery.

Ever since Nesta had come home with those recordings of his, she reasoned, he had been acting a bit too damned mannish for his own good. She wanted to slap her son's face, to give him a beating he would never forget, but he was already drunk with pain. And she hadn't dared to strike him in years.

Her mood clouded, and a deep melancholy crept over her; she was grieved to see her son suffering so, and she was stricken with a foreboding that her only child might end up leading the criminal life. Slouched at his bedside in the gloom of the darkened room, she brooded, unspeaking, one woe steadily feeding the other. The boy suddenly surprised her by speaking a few words of reassurance and consolation. His tone of voice had softened, and Ciddy felt even sadder than before, knowing that her son remained a near-total stranger to her and that she was powerless to influence his personal course. She had little choice but to trust in the Almighty.

"Nuh cry, mumma," he whispered, "me be awright."

"I know, me luv," she said, kissing him on the forehead, " 'cause dat's da prayer of me very life."

In both the streets and the studios of West Kingston, the scene was heating up in 1961. The JLP and the PNP were battling over two issues: Jamaica's continued membership in the West Indies Federation, which it had joined in 1958 (a move championed by the PNP, with Norman Manley hoping to become the Federation's prime minister), and Jamaican independence, accompanied by admission into the British Commonwealth as a dominion (which the JLP endorsed, fanning the nationalistic/chauvinistic flames and pandering to the suspicion and even outright contempt many Jamaicans harbored for the rest of the Caribbean, which they considered poorer, more backward and a potential drain on their own limited resources).

Bustamante was still smarting from the tactical victory Norman Manley had scored in 1956, when he called a state of emergency during a JLP-sponsored strike on the Kingston waterfront, ordering soldiers to unload ships carrying flour, codfish and other staples (as well as Jamaican stamps and currency). Before Manley took action, the country seemed poised for outright civil war. This time, Bustamante wanted to rout his cousin from the political arena or, short of that, to permanently cripple his career.

The tension this struggle had created spilled out of the halls of the legislature and into the ghetto neighborhoods of Kingston, where the desperately poor were made to feel that the enactment of either measure would mean the difference between poverty and prosperity for the Jamaican underclass. Violence of all kinds became the order of the day.

Over the preceding two years, a number of local singers had built up a sizeable following in the West Kingston–based music community by covering American R&B hits or releasing original material with an R&B groove. Chief among these musicians were Lascal Perkins, Derrick Morgan, Jimmy Tucker and Noel Simms. Others, like Wilfred "Jackie" Edwards and Laurel Aitken, were making a nice living doing ska- and mento-shaded imitations of Nat King Cole and Louis Jordan, respectively. The leading vocal groups were the mento-based Gaylads, who had made big impressions on the local charts with suggestive records like "Lady in a Red Dress" and "Rub It Down," and the Jivin' Juniors, whose "Lollipop Girl" was a staple at Sound System jump-ups.

But the savviest young stars were creating something all their own, scaling the heights of the JBC and RJR charts with singles born and bred in the ghetto's concrete gullies (the largest of which were discovered to be good echo chambers for harmonizers and fledgling guitarists). Jimmy Cliff was having much success with "Miss Jamaica," a Leslie Kong release on the Beverley's label, and Owen Gray was flying high with "Darling Patricia," also produced by Kong.

However, other producers had appeared to dispute the hegemony of Kong, Coxsone Dodd and Duke Reid. One such entrepreneur was Edward Seaga, a Boston-born, Harvard-trained anthropologist from a prominent Jamaican-Lebanese family. After receiving his degree in 1952, Seaga had been drawn into the business while conducting a scholarly study of Kumina, Pocomania and obeah practices in the island's hills; he went to supervise the sessions of a 1955 album of cult music for the New York City–based Ethnic Folkways label. Moving into more commercial territory, he began conducting sessions at JBC and Federal, signing the Trench Town singing duo of (Joe) Higgs and (Roy) Wilson to a management and recording contract with his outfit, West Indies Recording Limited (WIRL). The duo had been formed in 1958 at the behest of the promoter of a talent show audition at the Ward Theater. They'd both been selected for the bill, but when the judges realized they had exceeded the eight-act maximum for the program, Joe and Roy were urged to team up, since their voices sounded as if they might be compatible. Seaga tested the waters for Higgs and Wilson in 1959 with a ska track cut at JBC called "Manny-O." Released on the WIRL label, it sold an astronomical thirty thousand copies. But what was perhaps most shocking was the way he treated Higgs and Wilson: they were handsomely remunerated for their hit! Seaga had other acts under contract, including Slim Smith and Byron Lee (who had a hit on the WIRL label with his debut single, "Dumplings"), but Higgs and Wilson were the standout, constantly acing out the rival Blues Busters at the talent shows and dance hall contests.

Joe was the brains (i.e. the songwriter) of the duo. A handsome, sweet-natured young man born in Allman Town and raised in the Rema section of Trench Town, Higgs was well known in the area as one of the first musically prominent Rastas to have been subjected to police brutality, being beaten and imprisoned by police during the political riots in Trench Town in May 1959. His neighbors were proud of the way he retained his dignity without giving in to bitterness after a trumped-up ganja bust that led to a stretch in jail. A slim but powerfully built man, he returned to the streets as hopeful and even-tempered as before, discouraging with stern but soothing language the hotheaded calls for vengeance from the rude boys.

"Life too brief fe de foolish sufferah," he proclaimed. "The sufferah mus' put dat retaliation t'ing behind himself because dat's a confrontation dat only lead to death. Wise mon don' deal wit' petty gun fussin'. Wise mon put 'is energy into making a contribution to Jah's Creation!"

The yardboys and ghetto punks were unaccustomed to hearing a street-wise fellow like Higgs spout the homilies of the customarily retiring Rastas. Higgs wasn't a hermit or a pariah like most Rastas; he was a public figure of some stature in West Kingston, a forceful presence to be reckoned with. His Rasta integrity made the meanest rudies scratch their heads in bewilderment.

Once Higgs recognized he had the attention of the youth of Rema, he set about keeping it by using his success as a performer to help motivate them. He started a free music clinic at his home on Third Street, schooling green singers in harmony techniques, breath control and music theory. Well versed in jazz, calypso and the dynamics of American blues, R&B and pop, he used the work of Major Lance, Nat Cole, Lord Kitchener and Billy Eckstine to illustrate his points, but he insisted that his pupils write their own material. There were constant jam sessions, with as many as fifteen young singers and musicians participating, and Higgs was famous for halting even the most informal improvisation to correct mistakes and scold anyone who was off-key.

Nesta was among those drawn to these get-togethers, bringing along Bunny, Peter Tosh (he had since shortened his surname from McIntosh for stage purposes) and a kid from First Street named Winston "Pipe" Matthews, who had cut some singles under Prince Buster's sponsorship. Higgs was much taken with the haunting reediness of Nesta's voice and gave him special encouragement—to the mild consternation of Pipe, whose voice was strikingly similar but lacked Nesta's power and subtlety.

Buoyed by the interest of a big shot like Higgs, who continued to cut popular records with Roy Wilson for Seaga, Nesta—who now preferred to be called by his more "adult" first name—cajoled Bunny and Peter into trying to make their little group more professional. Having no guitar of their own, they had been using an ancient acoustic at the Ebenezer Church in Trench Town, practicing with it in the church hall. The nervy Peter went to the rectory and persuaded the minister to loan him the guitar on a long-term basis. Tosh refurbished the instrument, sanding it, polishing it and working at odd jobs to earn the money for a new set of strings.

Tall and swaggering, Peter Tosh liked to brag that he was the leader of the group. Born in Church Lincoln, Westmoreland, on October 19, 1944, Tosh was an only child whose father, James McIntosh, left Peter when he was an infant and whose young mother, the former Alvira Coke, had turned him over to an aunt to raise because she was unwilling to accept the responsibility. Tosh was taken as a small child to the coastal town of Savanna-la-Mar and then to the Denham Town section of Kingston in 1956. After his aunt died, he had moved in with an uncle on West Road in Trench Town. Lacking a trade, or a guardian to help him settle on one, Tosh saw music as a way out of a lonely, dead-end existence. But while Bob and Bunny took the group seriously, Peter took it *too* seriously, expecting it to immediately transform his life and put him securely on top of the fierce adolescent pecking order in Rema.

But nothing could alter the fact that, of the three members of the group, Bob was the only one who had any practical experience and a professional track record, having cut five more songs for Leslie Kong; two of them, "Terror"* and "One Cup of Coffee," had attracted some notice. Moreover, Bob gradually began to exude a confidence that transcended ambition and made others believe there was a sense of mission in the calm, careful maneuvering that silenced or at least scattered most opposition. It was a quality he exercised in both his musical and business dealings.

It was well known in Trench Town that Bob had broken off his relationship with Kong when the producer failed to pay him for the last two songs he'd done for him. The story circulated in shantytown that one morning Bob had gone over to a Chinese restaurant which the prosperous Kong had recently purchased from a former employer, Charles Moo. Kong was running the place as a front for a "peaka-peow bank," an illegal Chinese numbers lottery. (A peaka-peow sheet has two hundred numbers on it. A player circles eight of these, and thirty winning numbers are selected by throwing dice—if any of these are circled on the player's card, he wins.)

Bob demanded to see Kong, who soon appeared in the doorway, flanked by his brothers. Bob asked for his money; Kong replied that he owed the ignorant bungo nothing while his brothers guffawed. Bob pointed at Kong and made a queer prediction, telling him that they would work together again some day, and that the association would bring Kong much more money than anything he had promoted thus far—but that Kong would never get any enjoyment from the money.

Kong began reviling Bob, telling him to beat it before he thrashed him or called the police. As Bob was walking away, he glanced over his shoulder at the producer and Kong's face suddenly turned ashen. He fled into the restaurant, followed by his brothers, who asked what the matter was. Kong, petrified, would not answer them.

Bob wanted the group, first called the Teenagers, then the Wailers, to have a full New Orleans–style vocal sound, so he asked two

**Its formal release, if it occurred, was severely limited.*

Rema girls, Beverly Kelso and Cherry Green, to sing backup. Another big-voiced boy, Junior Braithwaite, was added to share lead vocals with Bob. Urged on by Bob's pal Desmond Dekker, the six practiced for several weeks in Bob's Second Street yard, working out a proper presentation for Higgs. Hearing the results, Joe was impressed by the tenacity of the group and began to coach them in earnest, taking particular care to teach Peter and Bunny how to mesh their resonant baritones with Bob and Junior's quirky, untamed tenors. Higgs knew that Braithwaite's voice was more mature than Marley's but he felt that Bob's showed more personality and promise. He told Bob to sing constantly—in the lanes, at the beach, along with records at the Sound System dances—to strengthen and deepen his voice. As for the girls, they were shrill but added interesting coloration when they weren't trying to be belters, so Higgs helped to ensure their role would be a secondary one by restricting their contributions in songs he helped arrange to the choruses.

Higgs also worked with a group that Pipe had assembled called the Schoolboys, drilling them in the kitchen of Pipe's quarters on First Street. When Edward Seaga decided in 1959 to devote less time to the record business and more time to politics, he handed his burgeoning interests over to associates of his father for supervision and eventual sale. Higgs (minus Roy Wilson, who had left Jamaica) went over to Coxsone's camp, and the first group he recommended to the producer as a ripe property was not Pipe's Schoolboys but the Wailers.

Meanwhile, Seaga had been named to the Legislative Council (upper house) of the Jamaican Parliament by Alexander Bustamante. Seaga chose to build his constituency in West Kingston—hotbed of the recording scene, but no man's land on the Jamaican political landscape since the 1920s. Rema was to be the center of Seaga's power base, but not even Bustamante had ever been able to hold his seat in such a snake pit, pulling out after a single term to take up service in the rural parish of Clarendon.

A brilliant, cunning (some said ruthless) politician—the Rastas claimed he had been recruited by the CIA while he was at Harvard—Seaga was the first to openly make use of two potent political weapons that had hitherto been confined to the murkier undercurrent of political life in Kingston: these were the gun and obeah. His rallies and political convocations exploited the style and symbols of Kumina rites, and gangs of "enforcers" were organized to carry out orchestrated violence against PNP organizers and wayward or contrary JLP members, with the strong implication that these gunmen had the added muscle of black magic on their side.

In the early spring of 1961, Seaga gave a blistering speech before the Legislative Council, claiming that the PNP's support of continued membership in the federation was a ploy by the haves at the expense of the have-nots, as typified by his constituency in Rema. Drawing selectively from available statistics for the years 1958–1959, he alleged that Jamaica's economic growth rate had seriously faltered, and that 93 percent of the population could be considered underprivileged, earning less than US$300 a year. "The Government is mobilizing the resources of the country to the disadvantage of the underprivileged . . . This is a clear and personal indictment!" he seethed, adding that membership in the federation held out no prospects for improvement of the situation.

An early date for a nationwide referendum on whether to remain with or quit the federation was called for, and Bustamante whipped his supporters into a fever pitch with a follow-up tirade, describing Jamaica as being "on the edge of a volcano," with conditions intolerable and revolt inevitable if the island's woes were permitted to be exacerbated by its ties to the federation. With this distinction between the "haves" and "have-nots" thus firmly fixed in everyone's mind, the age-old problems of class and color in the creole society resurfaced, and rioting in the ghetto erupted in deadly earnest. There were many bloody skirmishes between the police and poor people, the greatest brutality being reserved for the Rastafarians, who declined to pay any attention to the political issues involved and were thus regarded as impertinent by people on all sides.

Since many of the prominent singers and musicians on the ska scene were Rastas, their careers and physical well-being were in jeopardy. Naturally, many of them took to the barricades—meaning the airwaves—with records that explained and celebrated the Rasta world view, with its emphasis on tolerance, brotherhood, moral rectitude and defiance of all forms of oppression. Many of the producers were adamantly opposed to releasing overt Rasta material. It was one thing to issue an ambiguous track like "Time to Pray (Alleluia)" by the gospel-rooted Basil Gabbidon and the Mellow Larks, but quite another to issue downright spiritual, dogma-filled singles like Laurel Aitken's "Judgement Day."

Prince Buster was one of the boldest of the young producers, daring to actually make the first move in approaching devout Rasta percussionist Count Ossie in 1960. Ossie was taken aback, thinking that Buster was insincere or insulting him, anticipating the outcry that would come from the traditional church establishment. Buster persevered, however, and Count Ossie brought his four drummers in from his Adastra Road settlement in the Springfield section of Kingston, plus musicians from Brother Issie Boat's Rasta camp in the Wareika Hills. Time was booked at JBC, but at the last minute an outraged Duke Reid tried to foil the date by extending another booking already in effect. Undiscouraged, Buster improvised facilities in another room down the hall and several tracks were recorded with Owen Gray lending piano support.

Radio stations refused outright to play the "blasphemous" Count Ossie tunes, but they started moving in record shops, and Coxsone, as always, took notice. He'd had his own problems trying to dissuade Don Drummond, the gifted jazz trombonist who was the linchpin of his roster of local sessions musicians, from recording Rasta-oriented material. Now, with Joe Higgs lobbying for the practice, Prince Buster making money on these side projects, and other employees like Lee Perry, who was virtually running the Downbeat Sound System, supporting the trend, Coxsone softened his hard line against Rasta music, but emphasized that he wanted to restrict such releases to instrumentals for the time being.

"Sweet vocal groups de t'ing," he ruled. "De Sound Systems wan' a sweet beat."

By the summer of 1962, Dodd had five thriving labels—World Disc, Coxsone, Musik City, Studio One and D. Darling, the last named for his mother. And in the first week in August he put out a record by Kentrick Patrick that roared almost nonstop out of every available speaker on the island for two solid months: "Independent Jamaica."

At the stroke of midnight on August 5, the Union Jack was lowered throughout the island and the green, gold and black standard of Jamaica was hoisted. Jamaica had become a free and independent nation within the British Commonwealth.

Three months earlier, the JLP had won a twenty-six-seat majority in Parliament and taken over the reins of government with Bustamante as prime minister. The West Indies Federation was summarily dissolved (Jamaican voters having decided by a narrow margin to secede some six months earlier), and the Royal Hampshire Regiment, the last British troops stationed in Jamaica, had departed, closing the book on an era of colonial domination that had begun with the first British garrisons on the island in 1665.

Ceremonies commemorating the sweeping change were held at the newly constructed National Heroes Stadium, built on the site of what had once been George VI Memorial Park. Marcus Mosiah Garvey and antislavery advocates Paul Bogle and George William Gordon, who had been architects of the 1865 Morant Bay Rebellion, were among the national heroes commemorated there (two years later Seaga would have Garvey's body brought back from England and interred there). Dignitaries attending the ceremonies at the stadium, which held a capacity crowd of thirty-five thousand, included Her Royal Highness Princess Margaret (representing Her Majesty Queen Elizabeth II); her husband, the Earl of Snowdon; Sir Alexander Bustamante; Norman Manley; and Lyndon Baines Johnson, Vice President of the United States.

There followed two days of rejoicing throughout the island; all the parish capitals were decorated with bunting and lights, and rum flowed freely. On August 7, the first session of Jamaica's new Parliament was convened at Gordon House in Kingston, and on August 11, the ninth Central American and Caribbean Games were held at the National Stadium, Jamaica winning gold, silver and bronze medals in events conducted in gagging heat. On September 11, Jamaica was admitted to the United Nations.

There was a feeling everywhere of great impatience, expectations of immediate prosperity and social reform. But the only sector of society that was responding swiftly enough to appease popular appetites and desires was the record industry. Accordingly, Leslie Kong released Jimmy Cliff's "Miss Jamaica," Cliff assuring his sweetheart that while she was not "in such a good shape" as Miss World contestant Carol Joan Crawford, he was "crowning yuh myself."

Coxsone had been doing well in both the Sound System and record businesses and had decided to use some of his profits to build (with the assistance of his cousin Sid Bucknor, an electronics whiz) his own one-track studio at 13 Brentford Road (once a club called The End) near the Carib Theater and the business district known as Crossroads, where Half Way Tree Road and Old Hope Road joined to form

Slipe Road. The new enterprise was called the Jamaica Recording and Publishing Studio, Ltd.

Local percussionist Alvin Patterson heard the Wailers sing for Higgs, and he arranged for Bob and the Wailers to audition for Dodd on a December morning shortly before the Christmas holidays, and they sang in the just-completed structure, surrounded by loose wiring, the dank, dull smell of drying concrete in the air, closing with "Simmer Down."

Pleased but not overly impressed, Dodd offered the Wailers a contract that gave him exclusive rights to release their records and to act as their manager; he would pay them a flat twenty pounds for each side they recorded. He conducted the first session the next day, using local studio musicians. Coxsone was hoping to get four or five songs out of the get-together, but the Wailers were too nervous and inexperienced. The three ska tunes they wrapped up were "Simmer Down," "I Am Going Home" and "Do You Remember," with Peter Tosh adding occasional lead guitar and Beverly Kelso singing backup on the first single, "Simmer Down."

Horns clamored and pumped throughout the session, "I Am Going Home," having much of the same hectic tempo and squalling mood, the female backing especially shrill on the latter track and the wavery male support vocals lending an unsteady mood to the melodramatic plaints.

Bob's singing wasn't much better, and he milked the lyric for every hapless ounce of melodrama, standing so close to the boom mike as he crooned that Dodd was wondering if he was going to swallow it.

As primitive as the tracks were, they did have a little bit of the energy found in the lesser New Orleans love laments. Jah Jerry Haines played a rambling lead guitar, and Lloyd Knibbs and Lloyd Brevett provided workmanlike support on drums and bass, respectively. Dodd debated which track to issue as a trial balloon, deciding to push the less ponderous "Simmer Down" as a Sound System single. He got three hundred copies of the tune pressed up and had Prince Buster, Lee Perry and keyboardist Jackie Mittoo, his right-hand arranger in the studio, see to it that they were circulated, sold and touted. Several days later, he scheduled another Wailers session after the word reached him that "Simmer Down" was catching on with the crowds at dances. This time Bob, Peter and Bunny showed up without Beverly in tow. The top track from the second session was "Mr. Talkative," a rambling song about the lethal effects of gossip, with Bob's vocal patterns similar to "Simmer Down."

Miffed, Dodd told Higgs that the group needed to be better organized, with a readily identifiable leader. There was opposition to this within the group, since all three young men had songs of their own that they wanted to sing lead on, but after some deliberations it was decided that Bob would be the lead singer on the initial singles, especially since the hit song he'd brought to the sessions, a piece of advice for rude boys called "Simmer Down," was Dodd's favorite. Bob had composed the tune in response to his mother's concern that he was keeping company with young thugs and ruffians; his intensity as he sang the lyric sprang as much from his irritation with (and his desire to prove himself to) his parent as from any particular desire to offer a warning to the island's jaunty juvenile delinquents.

For these and subsequent sessions, Dodd brought in a full contingent of his best ska session men, many of whom had been making reputations for themselves doing live mento and calypso dates with singer Joseph "Lord Tanamo" Gordon. The chief arrangers were keyboardist Jackie Mittoo, when the emphasis was on piano-based New Orleans–style boogie-woogie, and trombonist Don Drummond, when the feel called for something more jazzlike, with bright, athletic-sounding charts for the horns. Other members of the loosely organized band were Rico Rodriguez and Rupert Dillon, trombone, Roland Alphonso, Gaynair and Tommy McCook on tenor sax, Raymond Harper, Johnny "Dizzy" Moore and Baba Brooks on trumpet, Karl Bryan, Hedley Bennett and Lester Sterling on alto sax, Theophilus Beckford and Gladstone Anderson on keyboards, Ernest Ranglin and Jah Jerry on guitars, Cluette Johnson on bass, Drumbago (Arkland Parks) and Hugh Malcolm on drums, with Lord Tanamo and Tony DaCosta providing occasional vocals.

These men saw themselves primarily as jazz musicians, inheriting the mantle of prominent Jamaican artists before them: Bertie King (clarinet and alto sax), who had made his mark in England in the 1930s, Harold McNair (alto and tenor sax) and Dizzy Reece (trumpet). But early in 1963, the group decided to give itself a formal name and Lord Tanamo thought that "the Satellites" would be a hot name, considering the space race between the United States and the Russians. Tommy McCook laughed and suggested "the Skatalites." The rest of the musicians took it for a joke, but the name stuck.

The stellar Ernest Ranglin led the Skatalites for the "Simmer Down" sessions. The Wailers were only dimly aware of the honor being paid them. Hailing from the remote village of Harry Watch in Manchester parish, Ranglin came from a family of gifted guitarists, and at sixteen he was a featured player in top mento bands run by

Val Bennett and Eric Dean. By then Ranglin had become a respected jazz guitarist and arranger who had worked with Owen Gray and Jackie Edwards. Dodd was hardly surprised when "Simmer Down" wound up a runaway smash, since it had a tight, raw arrangement and dealt with the currently raging issue of teenage crime. The producer himself had taken to carrying a gun to protect himself from the stardom-"squally" (hungry) rude boys who hung around the studio. When they failed to respond to his orders to "back weh! [back off]," he had no qualms about pulling out his pistol and waving it about to disperse them.

The militant rudies got bolder as "Simmer Down" got bigger, however, and while Dodd was moving a thousand copies of the single a week, he was also paying for extra muscle around the premises. When "Simmer Down" hit Number 1 in February 1964, Dodd faced a dilemma: should he steer the Wailers in the direction he'd hoped they'd go—as a slick R&B unit similar to the Moonglows, the Louisville, Kentucky, group that Bob Marley idolized—or should he let them record more of their ghetto songs? During the height of the mento era, there had been plenty of mildly controversial records available, most of them offering calypso-style commentary on current events or lewd observations about social mores, but "Simmer Down" was something quite new: music of the *sufferah*, a crude, spontaneous volley from the psychic depths of the Dungle underclass. The people who ordinarily had no voice in creole society, who were not spoken of in polite circles, depicted on billboards, quoted in newspapers or singled out in any fashion beyond the briefest mention of crimes they'd committed outside their ghetto enclaves, were now a force in the local arena of ideas.

Most significant of all, the shanty-dwellers were addressing their own kind. That they were telling them to watch their step on pain of the most dire reprisals from the police and courts was perhaps laudatory, but the language used was the "jargon of the gutter," as the white and fair-skinned matrons of St. Andrew might have described it at Sunday afternoon tea. It was like having some half-naked old cartman projecting his lowly mutterings over the garden wall—with a public address system! And equally dismaying was the difficulty of deciphering the lyrics. As the songs gained notoriety, the well-to-do began to eavesdrop on conversations between their housemaids to try and make sense out of this gibberish.

Reaction in the gutter itself was roughly akin to what might attend a hail of thunderbolts: a communal shock of self-recognition severe enough, in the words of the street-corner sages, "to knock dem bamboo [penis] inna dem backpocket."

Sufferah on the phonograph! Sufferah on the radio! There had been no comparable event in the whole sorry saga of the Jamaican poor. But this initial jubilation, especially on the part of the youth, was immediately replaced by a new state of rage inspired by the miserable truths in the music.

Assessing the ugly doings in the streets of West Kingston, which the Wailers were glamorizing even as they decried its heroes—and monitoring vocalist Junior Braithwaite's rising popularity on a safe 1964 ballad like "It Hurts to Be Alone"—Dodd decided to hedge his bets. He released "It Hurts to Be Alone" as a *slow*-groove sequel to "Simmer Down," and he gave the Wailers an advance against royalties to pay for snazzy stage suits he'd ordered—gold lamé collarless suits and checkered tab-collar shirts, a matching sequined dress for Beverly and pairs of pointy black shoes for each of the guys. They were given a weekly salary of three pounds apiece (also advanced against royalties), and Coxsone arranged for the group to debut at the All Champion Night talent show at the Majestic Theater in Kingston (later moved to the Ward Theater), singing songs like the Moonglows' 1958 hit "The Ten Commandments of Love," "Play Boy" (which was a reworking of the Contours' 1962 Motown single, "Do You Love Me") and "It Hurts to Be Alone" (without Braithwaite, who'd moved to Chicago), but featuring their "slum records" like "Simmer Down." The show was a huge success, winning over those who liked the romantic R&B covers as well as those who admired the ghetto realities in their more incendiary songs. And it somehow didn't hurt matters any when, after the Wailers lost the contest to the slicker Uniques by a narrow margin, Bob got into an all-out brawl with the cocky winners.

"Wailers de best fockin' harmony group a Kingston!" he raged, as he punched and kicked them around in the wings until the police arrived. The word quickly spread through Rema that, on or off stage, the Wailers were not a group to be trifled with.

Dodd smiled nervously. He realized he could make a lot of money with the Wailers—provided he could control them. He and the rest of the producers had enough malcontents grumbling on the outskirts of the business; no one intended to tolerate any more on the inside.

8

People Get Ready

Bob was standing in front of the mirror, sizing himself up in his gold jacket. It was a cheap garment, made of thin material and sewn with rice thread, a theatrical costume. But it looked splendid onstage when it was bathed in the footlights. He liked to look down at his arms as his hands gripped the microphone stand, the red and blue lights bouncing off the metallic fabric.

Coxsone had had a publicity still taken of the group in their outfits, and Bob looked the least comfortable, the most preoccupied, as if his mind were thousands of miles away. Bob's appearance in subsequent photos was exactly the same, which began to mystify the producer. Watching him onstage, Dodd began to see that Bob didn't really project to the audience at all; rather, a certain distracted sort of magnetism drew their attention to him.

Ciddy saw a slightly different side of Bob at home when he habitually lingered around the looking glass dressed in his stage clothes. Striking poses, he seemed to be titillated by what he viewed, yet curiously wistful, as if he were seeing an image of himself that he had glimpsed long ago, one he now had the power to freeze in time so that he could examine it more carefully.

"Me always look good dis yere way," he'd whisper to himself, almost sentimentally. But then he might giggle and pretend he was introducing himself to a capacity crowd at the Ward Theater.

"Check fe Bob Marley, people! Spree bwai *ta raas!* Me one singer dat cut yanga [dresses stylishly]! Quality star! Next stop, television!"

The Jamaica Broadcasting Company had introduced television to the island in August 1963, and while few but the wealthiest natives could afford to buy a set, it was the ambition of virtually every man, woman and child to *appear* on TV—the latter concept somehow seeming more plausible than the former one.

Leslie Kong had taken Jackie Opel, noted Barbadian singer and occasional substitute bassist for Lloyd Brevett of the Skatalites, into the studio to cut a song Opel had written called "TV in Jamaica." Like most topical Jamaican records, it quickly caught the public's fancy.

Prancing back and forth before his reflection, Bob patted his nappy little halo of hair, trimmed "jus' like a Sam Cooke!" as he liked to brag after visits to the barber, and began to sing with the studied diction of a well-spoken Barbadian:

Just like in America, we have TV in Jamaica . . .
No more to wonder: "What's happening in studio?"
Same time you hear the words, same time you see the show!

Just then Ciddy came into the house, cradling the infant Claudette Livingston, Ciddy's child by Toddy, in her arms. Crossing the threshold, she paused, regarding her grown son's display of vanity. He gave his hair and clothes as much attention as she did her baby, she mused, almost repeating the observation out loud. But she stopped herself, and the moment of petulance passed. Uncertain of what to make of the transformation that had come over Bob—he'd informed her, politely but firmly, that he now preferred to be called Bob, especially in the presence of his friends—she realized that in the last several months she had been virtually ignoring him. Not that he complained, being so recessive to begin with. She used to fuss over and spoil him so! But then she had the well-being of her unborn child to think of.

Pregnant at thirty-seven, Ciddy had carried the baby with a minimum of physical discomfort but had grown fearful as the delivery date approached. She was getting rather old for childbearing, of course, and relatives had advised her to take special precautions and get the best prenatal care she could find. Too many years had passed for her to even consider returning to the country and placing herself in the hands of an experienced midwife. She was citified now, and so she'd gone up to the University College Hospital in Mona Heights, just off the campus of the University of the West Indies, to see about the possibility of having the child there when the hour came. But she was turned away by an official when she revealed her Trench Town address.

"Yuh mus' go to a facility in yuh area," said the female administrator in a clipped tone. "Either de Jubilee or Kingston Public 'Ospital."

A young nurse had taken Ciddy aside as she was leaving the admissions office and told her she should have given a false address, or that of a relative or friend who lived, say, in the better neighborhoods like Liguanea, Camper Down and Barbican.

"Me cyan't fake an' play lie," said Ciddy, hurt and irate, remembering how, because she was a black peasant, she had been treated with utter indifference during Norval's bigamy hearing. "Me cyan't lie, anymore den me could say is not me child! I jus' wan' de best fe de pickney, like any maddah!"

The young nurse shrugged and walked away.

That was two months ago. Pearl—as Ciddy liked to call Claudette—had been born four weeks later. Since that time her mother had been doing a lot of thinking. Kingston scared her; the political violence and teenage hooliganism were spreading unchecked. Hearing Bob singing about television, she thought of the crowds outside the appliance stores on Half Way Tree Road who stood for hours, watching the blue-gray TV screens blinking in the windows. Most of the programming was news of Hurricane Flora, which had rammed the North Coast en route to Cuba, as well as the latest reports on the crime wave. In addition, Seaga had charged the police were little more than hired guns for the PNP and that they habitually framed poor Kingstonians on ganja raps. This led to increased verbal clashes with Michael Manley, son of the leader of the PNP and a graduate of the London School of Economics, a former journalist who had started organizing among the sugar workers and had achieved growing political prominence. Seaga succeeded in getting the Denham Town police on his side, however, and several of them had actually beaten Manley up during the 1962 election campaign. For most of the following year, the whole country seemed divided against itself along party lines.

After writing nearly every two weeks for the last two years to her relatives and friends in Wilmington, Delaware, Ciddy elected to go on a quick look-see visit in 1962, shortly after she found out she was pregnant. She liked what she saw. While a bit run-down, the neighborhoods her friends lived in had none of the ramshackle confusion and grotesque ugliness of Trench Town. The cold weather was a definite drawback but also a novelty. Returning home, her mind was made up that, with Bob now seventeen years old and able to fend for himself, she was going to use what little savings she had accumulated to move to the States. The idea of raising another child in a tropical ghetto was too much for her, particularly since Thaddius had shown little interest in parenthood. Although the decision had been thrust upon her by Pearl's unexpected arrival, Ciddy knew this was the moment she had been scrimping for. Independence notwithstanding, she had much more faith in her own future than that of her country.

She had reviewed her decision with Thaddius who, unflappable as ever, had encouraged her to acquaint herself with American life the same way he had endorsed her original move to the city. Ciddy wrote to Omeriah and told him of her plans, and he likewise approved, feeling that anyplace had to be better than Kingston. As for Bob, he greeted the news with a spooky remoteness, not unlike his reaction when he was placed on the omnibus in Rhoden Hall for his first trip to the city.

Everything seemed to have come full circle, in Ciddy's estimation, and a new cycle was beginning precisely where the previous one had left off. The sense of déjà vu unnerved her, in light of the traumas of the last go-around, but once she had gotten the idea of leaving Kingston fixed in her mind, she felt as good as gone, right up to the winter day in 1962 when she took a taxi with Thaddius, Bunny, Pearl and Bob to Palisadoes Airport to catch the flight to Philadelphia, where her married sister, Ivy Brown, from Wilmington would be meeting her.

Somehow, after all the wishing and waiting, the abrupt move felt too easy. Her only regret was her inability to comprehend her son's strange attachment to the ghetto. She understood that he was wrapped up in his music and wanted to stay with his friends, but there was something more in his quietly resolute manner than mere dedication to his career. The perils of street life seemed to fire his imagination, to give him something to rub up against, to challenge and outwit. He was a fighter, but not reckless like his companions. He was shrewd, but not a promoter of petty scams, like the other young men in Rema. Even Bunny sometimes seemed to have things up his sleeve, riddles in reserve, perhaps even more so than the average Jamaican male, for whom this was standard behavior. But Bob seemed to have his every thought stowed in a secret place. There was nothing troublesome or forbidding about his mysteriousness, though—just the fact of it.

"When the root is strong," Yaya liked to say, "the fruit is sweet." Mindful of Bob's enduring ties to Omeriah, to whom he continued to write, Ciddy wanted her grandmother to be right.

Her bags loaded on board, she kissed everyone good-bye, shedding confused tears when she got to Bob.

"Walk safe, me Nesta," she said. "'Member seh yuh visit me next year."

Then Ciddy hurried across the tarmac to the plane, balancing Pearl in one arm and two "ti-tai" (twine)-bound cardboard cartons containing three dozen spicy beef patties in the other, a house present for her kin.

"Bull horn nebber too heavy fe bull head," said Thaddius, as he watched Ciddy ascend the ramp, turning back twice to wave. "Dat woman a bullcow fe sure, an' she tek her burden wit' a will."

"Me maddah abbly [able] missis," said Bob quietly, the unabashed admiration in his voice causing Bunny and his father to eye him with surprise.

Coxsone kept the Wailers busy throughout 1964, doing live dates and recording numerous songs ("Habits," "Go Jimmy Go," "Teenager In Love," "I Need You," "Lonesome Feelings" and "There She Goes," the last two with Kelso aided by singer Cherry Green.

New recording studios sprouted up in Kingston as the demand increased. The West Indies Recording Studio went up on Bell Road, Duke Reid installed his own Treasure Isle facilities, and Dodd upgraded his to two tracks.

Byron Lee, who headed a lackluster calypso-ska tourist-hotel band called, by turns, the Ska Kings or the Dragonaires, opened an agency named Lee Enterprises Limited to promote concerts around the island and book package shows at the Carib and Regal Theaters, both of which could hold approximately fifteen hundred people. Foreign acts were also brought in, and leading Jamaican stars found themselves opening for the likes of the Drifters, Jimmy Clanton, Fats Domino, Chuck Berry and Sam Cooke.

No fool when it came to ferreting out commercial possibilities and lucrative tie-ins, Lee turned 1964 into a busy year for boosterism. He got friendly with Seaga and would end up buying his WIRL setup, renaming it Dynamic Sounds Recording, Inc. Then he built up a new distribution network and worked out a deal with Atlantic Records to issue a dance record (complete with photo charts on the jacket showing a fair-skinned couple demonstrating seven basic steps) in the States, *Jamaican Ska*. "Recorded in Kingston with the Greatest Jamaican ska groups" read the jacket copy of the LP; top billing was accorded Byron Lee and the Ska Kings. He got the rights from Ahmet Ertegun to distribute Atlantic's R&B catalogue in the West Indies and also mapped out promotion deals with the powerful Martin's Jamaican travel agency.

Lee's timing was so inspired it might have been scientific (in the obeah sense). The time was ideal to invite the world—the music world, at any rate—to investigate Jamaica, if only because of the immense curiosity engendered by the ska novelty single called "My Boy Lollipop," by Millie (Small), which came out in London in March 1964 and became an international hit. Formerly half of a Jamaican duo, Roy and Millie, the fifteen-year-old girl with the calliope singing voice had been brought to England in early 1963 by Anglo-Jamaican record producer Chris Blackwell to cut the song for his Island label (so named in tribute to Alec Waugh's 1956 novel, *Island in the Sun*).

Blackwell was a one-time accountant from a prominent white Jamaican family, who had turned to professional gambling in Britain and then come back to Jamaica in 1958 to work as an aide for the governor, Sir Hugh Foot. After stints selling real estate, renting motor scooters and teaching water-skiing at the Half Moon Hotel (owned by his cousins) in Montego Bay, he'd discovered American jazz, met Miles Davis on a trip to America and then started Island Records in London. While muddling through a series of flop releases, he'd run a club on Spanish Town Road, the Ferry Inn, managed sixty-three jukeboxes in the rum bars of the bush, and kept his ear to the ground for acts of his own. He'd picked up "Independent Jamaica" for release in England, providing a U.K. outlet for leading Jamaican 45s that would be warmly received in the West Indian record shops in Brixton, Shepherd's Bush and Lewisham. He had also reissued two songs by one Robert Marley in London in '63: "Judge Not" (backed by "Do You Still Love Me") and "One Cup of Coffee," with an Ernest Ranglin instrumental on the flip side.

The first and last real revenue he'd seen prior to Millie's fluke fame was when Laurel Aitken gave him a Number 1 hit in Jamaica in 1960 with "Little Sheila," but that windfall was a washout compared to "My Boy Lollipop." Leased to Phillips records worldwide, it sold some six million copies in 1964.

Edward Seaga, who had recently ascended to the post of Minister of Development and Welfare, saw ska as ideal for exploitation as a drawing card for tourism promotions and made arrangements to take a ska delegation to the 1964 World's Fair in New York City's Flushing Meadows Park. He made Millie the star of the troupe, the other invited performers being Roy "Prince Buster" Campbell, Roy Willis, Eric Morris and Jimmy Cliff. The backup band, of course, was Byron Lee's Dragonaires.

The Skatalites were not asked because many of them were Rastas and smoked ganja. Also excluded were the younger groups like the heavily religious Maytals and the Wailers—who, in their first few months of active recording, had already been labeled a rude boy band, and therefore undesirable as representatives of Jamaica abroad. Prior to the World's Fair engagement, Seaga arranged a two-day tour in New York to promote ska, the music and the dance. The performers did a show at Shepheard's nightclub in Manhattan in April at which Prince Buster sang "Tongue Will Tell" and "Wash Wash," Eric Morris did "Sammy Dead," and Jimmy Cliff did "King of Kings," its Rasta theme undetected by Jamaican Tourist Board officials or by the club's patrons.

Shapely Carol Joan Crawford, who had taken the 1963 Miss World title (the first time a Jamaican had won, which gladdened the hearts of Jamaica's middle classes), demonstrated the ska steps while Byron Lee lumbered on. Renowned American dance instructor Arthur Murray commented afterward to the New York press that the ska was "an interesting dance which everyone could learn easily."

Returning from the trip, Seaga told the *Daily Gleaner* that Dorothy Kilgallen and Earl Wilson had mentioned the music in their columns, that *Life* magazine had run a photo of the dancers at Shepheard's, that disco DJs in New York, New Jersey, Philadelphia and some West Coast cities had given ska records some exposure, and that the *Clay Cole Show*, an *American Bandstand* imitator on New York's WPIX-TV, had shown a special film clip on ska. For the rest of the year, the most prominent headlines on the front page of the *Daily Gleaner* concerned Alexander Bustamante's hospitalization and recuperation from an eye ailment, youth gang disturbances, the arrival of Ginger Rogers and Ray Milland on the island for the location shooting of the film *The Confession* and endless variations on a May story headlined SKA BOOM IN U.S. SEEN.

The Wailers were the undisputed stars of the major 1964 stage shows of the spring (especially on Easter morning) and summer, at which thousands had to be turned away. Under Dodd's tutelage they recorded a string of 45s, which were well received but (considering the political mood of the islands) regrettably flippant.

The civil rights movement in the United States and the racial strife that accompanied it were the principal topics of discussion from Guadeloupe to Belize, and disenfranchised Jamaican black youths strongly identified with the increasing militancy on the part of their American counterparts, particularly in the South. Coxsone, however, was anxious to steer the Wailers away from songs that explored such burning issues, mainly because he believed they could spell trouble at the Sound System dances, which were being policed more closely than ever.

In Lee Perry's hands, the Downbeat Sound System had become the biggest on the island, and Perry kept it on the road constantly for jump-ups held five nights a week: Monday, Wednesday and Friday in the country, Saturday and Sunday in the greater Kingston area, with Sunday being the biggest day. Setting up the equipment on Gunboat Beach on the Palisadoes peninsula or (far more frequently) on a remote beach on outlying Hellshire Point near old Fort Clarence, Coxsone would sponsor all-day, all-night picnics called "Gold Coasts." The huge speaker cabinets would be positioned on the shore to face the water. Powered by creaky portable generators, their thick black power cables buried in the sand, the speakers shook with whimsical selections from the current charts, played without comment, as the crowds romped in the surf: "Run Joe" by Stranger Cole, "Dick Tracy" and "Dr. Kildare" by the Skatalites, "John and James" by the Maytals, and the lewd "Penny Reel-O" by Eric Morris. This last was a tune about a girl who been avoiding a guy to whom she owed "lickle money"; the guy suggested she let him "rub out" and "push up" the money—in other words, erase the debt with a good screw.

Come twilight, Lee Perry would take over from the daytime selector and open the show with a few of his own records (Perry being one of the first selectors to put out his own, fairly filthy singles) as he strutted in place, bringing his arm down like a whip as the bass dropped a "bomb" note: "Open Up," "Roast Duck," "Old for New." As the sun went down and the moon climbed over the sea, the dancers would slap down shillings for bottles of Red Stripe beer sold out of the backs of pickup trucks, and feast on goatfish, bammy and fried bread cooked on "patas" (barbecue grills set on stones) while "Scratch" Perry spun his signature single, "The Chicken Scratch."

When everyone was nicely tanked up, the rudies assigned to ward off interlopers and uninvited toughs would slip off to the outskirts of the festivities with a few "streggaes" (whores), carbines slung over their bare shoulders —sometimes loaded, sometimes not—as they rieled in the dunes.

Back at center of the action, dreadlocked Rasta fishermen from settlements in the Hellshire Hills and along Manatee Bay would come in on the twinkling tide, the red, green and gold paint jobs on their rowboats visible in the moonlight. A child might ask what the colors represented as the brethren, toting little crocus satchels of ganja, would hop out to a warm welcome, and a wizened old gray-locked dread would bellow: "Red, fe de bloodshed inflicted on de sufferah since slavery deys! Gold, fe de wealth stolen from de sufferah since Solomon's temple was laid low! Green, fe de blessed land in Africa dat awaits de black mon's return!"

After a few spins of "Coxsone's Hop," delivered with a barrage of Mad Hatter chatter, Dodd himself would introduce the featured records for the evening "shakefoot" (dance), usually half a dozen hip R&B singles from abroad and the latest pre-release selections by the Skatalites (who, if the shakefoot was at Gunboat Beach, could often be heard holding forth, live, from the terrace of the Bournemouth Beach Club on the other side of Kingston harbor), the Clarendonians, Derrick Morgan, Clancy Eccles, the Heptones and the Wailers.

The Wailers wound up their summertime domination of the local scene with a ska treatment of the playful calypso standard "Shame and Scandal," a wickedly satiric comment on the crumble-prone family structure in the Caribbean:

In Trinidad there was a family
And much confusion, as you will see
It was a mama and a papa and a boy who was grown
And he wanted to marry and have a wife of his own
He found a young girl who suited him nice
And went to his papa to ask his advice
His papa said, "Son, I have to say no.
The girl is your sister but your mama don't know."

He weep and he cry and the summer came down
And soon the best cook in the islands he found
He went to his papa to name the day
His papa shook his head and to him he did say,
"You can't marry that girl. I have to say no
The girl is your sister but your mama don't know."

Haile Selassie and acting Prime Minister Donald Sangster (center) during Selassie's April 1966 visit to Jamaica. GRATH MORGAN/JAMAICAN INFORMATION SERVICE

Left to right: Peter Tosh, Rita Marley, Bob Marley, Kingston, 1966. COURTESY OF CEDELLA BOOKER

The Wailers—left to right: Peter Tosh, Bob Marley, Bunny Livingston—as they appeared on the rock-steady compilation issued by producer Leslie Kong.

The Wailers, circa 1965. Left to right: Bunny Livingston, Bob Marley, Peter Tosh. PETER SIMON COLLECTION

The Wailers, circa 1964, wearing their gold lamé stage costumes. Left to right: Bob Marley, Peter Tosh, Beverley Kelso, Bunny Livingston.

Clement Seymour Dodd, Jamaica Recording Studio, 13 Brentford Road, Kingston, 1976. PETER SIMON

Joe Higgs, noted Jamaican singer who was the vocal coach of the early Wailers. PETER SIMON

Ernest Ranglin, the King of Ska Guitar, Kingston, 1980. PETER SIMON

Peter Tosh on Hellshire Beach, outside Kingston. ADRIAN BOOT

Bunny Wailer. ADRIAN BOOT

Island House, 56 Hope Road, Kingston. Bob Marley's home as it appeared in 1976, with Bob's BMW parked out front. PETER SIMON

Chris Blackwell, head of Island Records. © LYNN GOLDSMITH

Bob Marley in Kingston, 1972. © CHUCK KRALL

Cedella Booker and Rita Marley, Miami, 1982. PETER SIMON

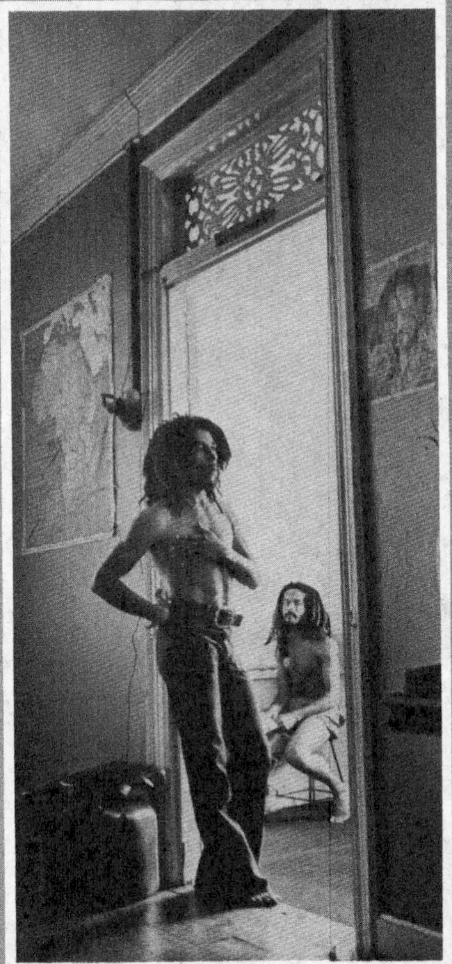

Left: Bob Marley and Alan Cole upstairs in Island House, 1975. © KIM GOTTLIEB
Below: Bob and Rita, circa 1972, with (standing, left to right) Sharon, David ("Ziggy"), Cedella and (in carriage) Stephanie. COURTESY OF CEDELLA BOOKER

Opposite: Rita Marley, 1981. ADRIAN BOOT

Bob Marley in concert, 1976, before a massive scrim of Haile Selassie I. PETER SIMON

Left: Judy Mowatt COURTESY SHANACHIE RECORDS
Right: Marcia Griffiths DAVID VANCE, COURTESY MANGO RECORDS

He went to his mama, these thoughts in his head
And told his mama what his papa had said
His mama she laughed, she said, "Go, man, go!
Your daddy ain't your daddy but your daddy don't know!"

Several weeks after the "Shame and Scandal" sessions, Bob, Peter, Bunny and Bob's friend Alvin "Seeco" Patterson, a tall, rawboned St. Ann's lad in his twenties who had played percussion with Lord Flea, were walking up Greenwich Park Road. En route from Trench Town to Coxsone's studio (where they had been rehearsing some lightweight material, like a cover of Dion and the Belmonts' 1959 success, "Teenager in Love"), the four were absorbed in a debate concerning the quality of their recent releases, the Wailers asking Seeco if he felt their sound was getting too "soft." With competition on the ska scene increasing in both quantity and in sophistication, such perceptions on the part of the islanders could be ruinous to the Wailers' musical reputation as well as their street image in Rema.

They were jealous of the quality of recordings by vocal and instrumental groups currently crowding the top ten: the Blues Busters, one of their stronger rivals for bookings at showcases like the Majestic, Ambassador, Carib and Ward Theaters, had been doing well with "Soon You'll Be Gone," a single that had an intricate harmony arrangement; the sprightly "Yeah Yeah," by the Riots, featured a hotly miked tambourine, wordless vocal histrionics and a cuffed guitar riff that resembled a spasmodic rattlesnake; "I'm in the Mood for Ska," by Lord Tanamo, had the old master carrying on like a banshee. But the hands-down scorcher on the Sound Systems circuit was "Man in the Street," a "Tequila"-derived dance instrumental by Don Drummond that served as a soundtrack for the ever more insistent demands for racial and economic equality emanating from the ghetto.

Named by George Shearing as one of the top five trombonists in the world, Don Drummond's preeminence among his international peers reflected on all of Jamaica's shantytown musicians, since Drummond had for years been a part-time music teacher at Alpha School, an all-boys Catholic school situated on South Camp Road, across the street from Sabina Park. A kind of reform school, Alpha subjected its students to severe beatings for such minor infractions as talking out of turn. Considerable emphasis was placed on participation in the school band, with the prelude to admission being rigorous instruction in theory and the classics. Drummond went from being a star member of the senior band to one of its top instructors, and in his classes sat future greats like Rico Rodriguez. Drummond's chief influences were American trombonists Kai Winding and J. J. Johnson, and he in turn helped shape the styles of Rico, Rupie Anderson, Vernon Muller, Carlos Malcolm, Carl Masters and other superior Jamaican trombonists.

The discipline Drummond and the other instructors demanded of their underprivileged pupils paid off. The Alpha School turned out a virtual roll call of the leading lights in the West Kingston studios: Tommy McCook, Eric Clarke, Vincent Gordon, Joe Harriot, Bobby Ellis. The list grew longer with each graduating class.

As for Drummond, he was in demand from the inception of the Jamaican recording scene, working with all the top producers and artists like Laurel Aitken, Theophilus Beckford and Derek Harriot, before Dodd signed him to an exclusive contract with Studio One as a solo artist and session player, and appointed him as the Skatalites' titular leader. (Drummond would continue to stray into Duke Reid's camp for pickup jobs, however, much to Dodd's dismay.) His first solo single was "Don Cosmic" (Dodd's nickname for him), and his output was to be prodigious: "Confuscious [*sic*]," "Ringo," "Treasure Isle" (for Duke Reid), "Eastern Standard Time," "Heavenless," "Occupation," "Meloncolly [*sic*] Baby," "Snowboy," "Elevation Rock," "Schooling the Duke," "Valley Princess." And his commitment to the Rasta creed was far more pronounced than most: "The Reburial of Marcus Garvey," "Addis Ababa," "Far East," "African Beat."

Dodd first saw Drummond perform at a show at the Majestic Theater in 1960. Coxsone was still specializing in calypso sessions with performers like Lord Tanamo, but he'd already put out a few solo singles spotlighting certain rising jazz musicians—the first being "Shuffling Jug," cut by Dodd's studio buddy, bassist "Clue J" Johnson. Drummond, who had a history of mental problems, had just concluded a three-month stay in a mental institution (he'd committed himself) when Dodd caught his live act. While Dodd had heard stories about the good-looking, mustachioed hornplayer's brittle, erratic personality, he was struck by the consistency of his playing. Lively and vivid melodically, Drummond was also precise in his phrasing and his original material had a darkly emotional undertow.

Dodd was astounded to learn that Drummond didn't possess a trombone of his own (he rented or borrowed others'), and Coxsone expressed his confidence in his new artist by purchasing a brand-new one for him (charged against his royalties, naturally).

The Wailers decided as they approached the studio that, since they were just as intimately involved with Dodd as the famed trombonist was, they wanted to strengthen their ties to Drummond and the Skatalites—the combination being potentially "invincible," in Bob's words. Everyone nodded in agreement.

While taking their customary shortcut to Coxsone's—a lane that ran alongside Calvary Cemetery—the Wailers and Seeco were stopped by a pretty teenage girl in a nurse's uniform who pointed to her house nearby and introduced herself as Rita Anderson.

"Ev'ry day me watch yuh pass on de way ta studio!" she said, giggling coquettishly. "Me know yuh is Wailers!"

Peter flirted with her as she accompanied them for a stretch, but Bob and Bunny paid her no mind and she finally said good-bye.

Over the next two months, the young nurse was usually lingering outside her house, ready with a well-timed hello whenever the tough-looking trio of singers sidled by. Eventually, due entirely to her low-key persistence, a friendship developed between Rita and the Wailers.

The daughter of Leroy Anderson, a carpenter by trade but a musician (stand-up bass, tenor sax, woodwinds, congas) by preference, and his Cuban wife, the former Cynthia "Bada" Jarrett, Rita was born in Cuba and was brought to Jamaica when she was three months old. Since the late 1950s, when her parents migrated to England in search of work (Rita was eight when they left), she and her five brothers and four sisters had been living with various relatives, Rita sharing the house with her Auntie Britton "Viola" Anderson and several other cousins. The last anyone had heard of Cynthia and Roy, they had split up, Roy going on to Sweden with a mento-jazz band and settling in Stockholm, his wife remaining behind in London for a spell and then moving on to Toronto.

Auntie Viola was strict, insisting that Rita help run the household and act as a "goddie" (godmother) to the younger children; she was also expected to attend church regularly and to sing in the choir, since she had been in the school choir at Central Branch School on Slipe Pen Road. The evening practice sessions for the church choir had become one of Rita's few outlets, since Viola forbade dating. Rita had become pregnant a year before by a man she scarcely knew, and now had a year-old child, Sharon, to care for. Viola, who had agreed to shelter seventeen-year-old Rita until her twenty-first birthday, wanted no repetition of that deplorable incident—there were already too many mouths to feed in the cramped little house, and Rita and the baby had to share a small room with another girl.

Rita had left Dunrobin High School in Kingston after Sharon's birth and taken the nurse's job to help make ends meet, but her real ambition, like too many ghetto teenagers, was to make it as a ska singer. She'd formed a group called the Soulettes with her first cousin, Constantine "Dream" Walker (son of Viola's sister, Vesta Anderson), and a mutual friend, Marlene "Precious" Gifford. Independent of Rita, thirteen-year-old Dream had also gotten friendly with the Wailers, asking them questions about harmonies and discussing Marcus Garvey with them, since Dream's mother was a devout Garveyite.

Through Dream, a formal meeting was arranged between Coxsone and the Soulettes, and when the group showed up at Brentford Road, Bob recognized Rita as the "naggy nurse."

"Yuh singer too?" he asked bluntly.

"Yes, mon," Rita answered, defensive. "From five years old. Me first stage appearance was de Lannaman's Children Hour talent show at de Carib Theater. Me was so small me sang standin' on box so dem could see me!"

She laughed, but Bob just nodded mechanically, unsmiling.

The Soulettes' talk with Coxsone led to an audition, and he put the green vocal group in Bob's hands, asking him to develop material for them. As they became regulars around the studio, Rita's flirtations with Peter continued, although she was wary of his reputation as a "Lash LaRue" (oversexed playboy). Bunny ignored the group altogether, which was fine with them, since he was known around Rema as a powder keg with a short fuse; phrase something the wrong way to the man and you were apt to lose a few teeth. Bob was constantly cross and irritable around the Soulettes, rehearsing them with unrelenting strictness and showing less patience than Joe Higgs when it came to sour notes and ragged timing. The group grew to dislike him intensely.

When Bunny strode up to Rita one afternoon with a note from Bob, she assumed it was the latest list of directives and harsh criticisms. Reading it, she was disturbed to see that it was a love note.

"Dis bwai an' yuh mek fun?" she snapped at Bunny.

"Back weh, sista! Yuh brabo [quick to anger]!" he barked in retort, angry at being cast in the role of go-between. "Me don' dip [meddle] in nuhbody's business, sista! De message in de note, me nuh have anyt'ing to tek from it, an' nut'ing ta add."

Disturbed, Rita stuffed the note into the pocket of her dress and departed.

The sweet, scribbled messages kept coming, but Bob remained the disciplinarian in the studio, arranging the Soulettes' first single, "I Love You Baby." The single clicked on the charts and would be followed by "Opportunity," "Pied Piper" (a cover of the U.S. hit), and "A Time to Turn" (a remake of the Byrds' "Turn, Turn, Turn").

Wanting to clarify the situation, Rita confronted him one evening in the little room off the studio that he used as an office and sleeping quarters. Since Cedella's move to Delaware, Coxsone had all but adopted Bob, making him chief rehearsal manager for his artist roster and offering him the room to live in. Crammed into the tiny space were a small wooden table, piled high with letters, an acoustic guitar and a "jam-a-corner" (crude bed) consisting of a wooden door balanced on cement blocks and covered with a mattress made of three crocus bags stuffed with straw. On wire hangers dangling from a nail above the bed hung two spare shirts, a second pair of jeans and, protected by a dry cleaner's plastic sleeve, his gold suit and a black, collarless suit of similar cut. Under the table was a brown paper sack containing his pointy black shoes. Tacked on the wall over the bed was a *Playboy* foldout of a naked blonde, Melba Ogle, Miss July 1964.

Rita asked him who was sending him all the mail.

"Me maddah," he mumbled. "She 'fraid fe me."

"Huh? Wha' she 'fraid of?"

He shrugged. Rita noticed they were from the States, with a Delaware postmark.

"Yuh maddah live in Delaware?"

He didn't answer.

"Now lissun 'ere, Bob Marley!" said Rita. "Yuh mus' explain yurself ta me. Me nuh cyan read yuh feelings."

She began to weep, explaining her confusion about his tender notes in private and the iron hand he displayed in public. He told her not to cry and made room for her on the bed. They sat and talked for two hours, and he told her that his mother kept writing to him, asking him to come to Delaware, but that he hadn't replied to any of her letters.

"Not one?"

He shook his head.

"Yuh maddah be sick wit' travail!"

"Me too taken up wit' de music," he said softly. "Would yuh answer dese letters fe me?"

Rita readily agreed, thinking it would be a rare opportunity to learn something about her elusive mentor. He collected them in a neat stack and handed them to her, a thin, crooked smile rising, then quickly receding. Rita wasn't positive it had been there at all, but she took the letters.

"Me mus' go now," she said, and he nodded. On her way out he mumbled something.

"What yuh say?"

"Secretary," he answered, not looking up. "Yuh me secretary."

Rita wrote Cedella the next day, explaining who she was and answering all of her basic questions.

The following evening she stopped by Bob's room again to show him the letter before posting it, but he waved it away, saying he was sure it was fine. Then he started telling her about the horrible nightmares he'd been having over the last few weeks, dreams in which malevolent duppies were trying to gain control of his body, and then his mind.

"Ev'ry midnight, dis black puss dat hang 'round de lanes 'ere come upon me, an' him start mek queer noises dat mell [trouble] me suh much. Den somet'ing wan' pull me off a de bed, put me in blue maaga [serious trouble], an' me feel is a macca [very strong] duppy wan' steal me shedda [shadow] an' tek me fe his servant! Ev'ry night it go dis yere way. Me really wonder if it science."

Bob explained that if it were a duppy invading his dreams and it indeed wanted his shadow, he must not be alone at night anymore. The duppy could be repelled if he had witnesses. But if the evil spirit succeeded in its mission, Bob would either have to go back to the country to have his shadow restored or face the consequences of being manipulated by an unseen hand.

"Bob, me nuh believe in duppy business," said Rita. "Yuh know me live 'cross from Calvary, right? Well, de Soulettes rehearse our singin' dere, sometime jus' sittin' on gravestone and play-play wit' harmonies. We overpower dem spirit—"

Bob cut her off, saying that no graveyard was dangerous in and of itself, especially if well-intentioned people were entertaining the spirits with music. He believed he was possibly under siege by obeah-directed demonic forces and might soon need a "shedda-catcher" (shadow-catcher, a myalman).

Omeriah, who had performed such services for others, had often told Bob that, in the country, when someone believed he had lost his shadow, meaning his temporal soul-force, he was dressed entirely in white, his head covered with a white bandanna, and taken to the silk-cotton tree nearest his birthplace—which is where his shadow would most likely have been taken. After trusted neighbors and friends had tied the victim to the tree, the myalman would stalk back and forth before it, a white cloth upon his left shoulder, shouting to God to witness the evil taking place on the very doorstep of Eternity. Fresh eggs would be thrown at the roots, the head of a live chicken would be wrung off and its quivering body thrown down in the same spot. Led by the myalman, the crowd would then raise a prayerful commotion, so great that it could be heard in the depths of the earth, so that every demon in Hell would have to hold his burning hands over his ears. If there were signs that the tree was ready to relinquish the shadow, the myalman would hold a basin of clear water beside the trunk. If the water splashed, he would take the cloth from his shoulder and cover the basin with it. The victim would then be untied and told to run home as swiftly as possible, without looking back or to either side. The procession of people would follow after him, the myalman carrying the basin, cautious not to spill any of the water. When he got home, the man would lie down on his bed until the myalman brought the water-soaked cloth, which he would lay upon his forehead, restoring his soul-unity. Omeriah was customarily paid eight shillings for such services. "Jus' breeze fe bollo [a small price for help in an emergency]," the old man had remarked.

Rita continued to protest that she didn't believe in such things, but seeing Bob's increasing distress, she stopped arguing the point and asked how she could help.

"Jus' stay here wit' me tonight," he said. "Stay an' check de t'ing fe yuhself."

Come sundown, Rita stayed away from home for the first time in her life, sharing Bob's bed. Neither initiated any sexual advances; while drawn to each other physically, the anxiety engendered by the darkness and uncertainty of the moonless night ruined their appetites for "shegging" (intercourse). They lay close together for several hours, talking low, he naked to the waist, she dressed in a loose-fitting "sacka" (dressing gown). Eventually their eyelids began to droop and they snuggled close, drifting into sleep.

Rita awoke to the sound of a cat hissing—harshly. Her head shot up with a start. She blinked, listened, peered in the direction of the sound. No more than four feet away, in the doorway, two lime-green eyes hovered in the blackness. She blinked again, wiped away the sleep. They were cat's eyes, but they seemed so enormous! Shivering, she shook her head to make sure she was awake and noticed that Bob was still sound asleep.

There was a tickle at the back of her neck. She snapped her head around. Nothing behind her. Sweat ran down to the small of her back. She was about to nudge Bob when the hiss came again, growing louder, higher in pitch, filling the room, reverberating in her ears. Something commanded her to look back at the doorway. Her mind twisted against itself, half of it refusing, half of it longing to surrender.

The bed felt cold and hard. When she touched her hand to it, she thought it had the texture of a tombstone. She realized she wasn't on the bed any longer. She was crouching on the concrete floor! Bob was in bed, now several feet away. Asleep.

She screamed. There was no sound. Screamed again. The silence seemed to shove itself down into her throat. She tried to stand and could not. Something was forcing her back, pressing irresistibly on her shoulders. She swooned, braced herself with her hands and, using all her strength, managed to rock forward, to force herself into a squatting position. She felt like she was underwater, incredible pressure against her head and shoulders keeping her down. Something was grinning. Grinning. A beast was grinning. There were teeth. Long, grinning teeth. She couldn't speak. Couldn't make a sound of any kind.

This is real, she kept telling herself. This is a fight and I must win. This must be what Bob fights. She tried to pray, first out loud—no sound—and then to herself. She could feel her sacka draped against her knees, soaking wet, impossibly heavy. *This is real. This is a fight. Sweet Jesus. Help. This is a fight.*

Her thoughts were becoming too cumbersome. Hard to hold on to. The room swam around her, yet the darkness took on a crystal clarity. She was beginning to panic. *This is real. Sweet Jesus. This is real. Help me. Help.*

She was amazed to realize she was now on her feet, though bent over from the pressure. She inched toward Bob, trying to touch him, sensing the cat was still there in the doorway. She was unable to get her head up high enough to glimpse either of them. She pushed forward, a half-inch at a time, growing dizzier. *Real. This is real. Jesus.*

She could not lift her arms to touch Bob. They hung uselessly at her sides. Something was pulling them down, yanking them out of their sockets. *Je-sus.* She begged for energy, her chest aching, the pain in her shoulder joints so excruciating that she almost blacked out.

Mute, the pressure crushing, she tried in the name of God to lean—to lunge forward. She fell against the edge of the bed; now seeing it flush against the side of her face, feeling nothing.

"*Rrreeeeeeeeeooowwww!*"

The demonic caterwaul tore into her ears, the sudden return of audible sound sending her senses spinning—down, down, rolling, tumbling, clanging about like stones in an oil drum.

"Bob!" she heard herself sobbing. "*Bob!*"

He was standing over her as she retched. She recoiled, palpitating, and retched again, the vomit splashing across the floor like paint.

Locking his arms around her waist, he lifted her up and half-carried her out to the standpipe behind the studio. The night was dead calm, the air heavy. They kneeled together in the dust. She retched again, dryly.

Easing her head under the spout, he washed her face and hair, gently pressing his thumbs into the nape of her neck, massaging her temples with his fingertips.

"Bob," she said, coughing hard, ". . . s-s-sickenin'. How . . . tek . . . ev'ry night?"

"Don' talk," he said soothingly. "Keep yeye shut, stucky. Feel de water. Cool. Nice. Nuh speak."

He knew what she had gone through. Last night, he'd been out here at around the same hour. So weak he had to crawl.

"Yuh ketch science meant fe me," he whispered. "Ketch Big 'Fraid, fe certain. Duppy, ta raas. So Jah seh."

Bob needed a temporary place to live or, at the very least, to sleep at night, since he spent most of his waking hours working at Coxsone's studio. With Cedella gone, Toddy Livingston had no longer been able to afford the place on Second Street and had relocated; Bob had to find a place for himself.

Rita suggested that he stay with her, at least for the first few nights following the ordeal in Coxsone's back room. Accommodations were cramped; he would have to sleep in the same bed with Rita and her cousin and contend with the nocturnal bawling of Sharon, who slept in a crib next to the bed. Also, he would have to sneak in through the window once Rita's cousin was asleep, and leave before first light.

Faced with the choice between this elaborate ruse or the hazards of the streets, Bob agreed to accept Rita's offer. It was about ten o'clock when Rita opened the window and beckoned her boyfriend inside. Lithe and guarded in his movements, he slipped in quietly and took his place on the edge of the bed, with Rita in the middle.

They had been asleep barely thirty minutes when Sharon began yowling—she was hungry and ready to be changed. The light flashed on before anyone had time to do more than react, and Auntie Viola was looming over the spectacle of the overcrowded bed, her eyes wide and her shrill expostulations drowning out the baby's screeches.

"Box [strike] me soul, dear Gawd! What vileness do me see *in me very house!*"

Bob was back out the window before the pandemonium was in full swing, but even then he had no recourse but to stand outside and listen to Rita catch the full brunt of Viola's wrath. He hated her, hated the humiliation he felt, hated his own vulnerability. It wasn't long before Rita was heading out the same window, and the two wound up staying up the entire night, hunched in the shadows outside the house, trying in vain to come up with some alternative to the whole hopeless mess.

Come sunrise, Bob trekked out to Coxsone's studio feeling dejected, forlorn. Rita went back to Viola's and had it out with her auntie, telling her she was making a bad situation worse, that she had to respect the fact that Bob was her boyfriend, that they had not been fornicating, merely sleeping, that she and Bob needed understanding and assistance, not condemnation. Rita also told Viola that she and Bob were in love, and that he could very well end up as Sharon's father. It was no longer a matter of sheltering a girl and her illegitimate child; Auntie might be hurting a family's chances of getting started.

Viola's rage subsided as Rita's reasoning took hold. The young woman was as quick-witted as she was well spoken, and plainly sincere. Reluctantly, Viola agreed to allow the young couple to take over the shed behind the house and convert it into their living quarters.

Rita was happy to have reached a compromise she could bear, but Bob never forgot Viola's self-righteous outburst. Where, he seethed, did that woman come off behaving that way in the ghetto? The baleful looks he gave her filled her with such stomach-churning apprehension that she felt she must have a reptile in her belly.

9

Natural Mystic

Bob rededicated himself to the task of making the Wailers a first-class act, and Rita set about making a home for Bob and Sharon, of whom he was extremely fond.

On the political front, the JLP stoked the furnace of Jamaican nationalism and earned the gratitude of Rastafarian brethren when Edward Seaga announced in the autumn of 1964 that the body of Marcus Garvey would be brought back to Jamaica. The news also temporarily diverted the population's attention from severe beef shortages, the disclosure that the government could not fulfill previous pledges of cash grants to farmers who had sustained damage from last fall's Hurricane Flora, and slowdowns in the campaign to introduce electricity to rural areas.

Alexander Bustamante's failing eyesight had impelled him to relinquish his day-to-day duties as prime minister to Donald Sangster, the deputy prime minister and minister of finance. Sangster was appointed acting prime minister, but major policy decisions were still made by Bustamante, his cabinet under orders to consult him at his home on Tucker Avenue, halfway up in the Wareika Hills. None of his ministers dared to defy or circumvent the authority of Bustamante, who also remained president of the JLP. Bad eyes or not, the eighty-year-old labor boss was still said to be quite capable of aiming his side pistol toward the sound of a man's heartbeat and finding his mark.

On September 10, 1964, Bob Marley awoke at second cockcrow (1:00 A.M.) with sharp chest pains. He had been dreaming of Nine Miles and a new house that was being built on the plot where Omeriah's now stood. There was a wedding taking place at the site, but he could not identify the groom, whose face was silhouetted against a freakishly glaring sun, nor the bride, whose face was hidden behind a veil.

Rising from his place on the "box 'n' boards" (a crude peasant's bed) beside Rita, he stepped outdoors to drink from the standpipe. Just as he was about to take a sip he heard the mournful howl of a dog coming from the direction of Calvary Cemetery and was stunned to see a large, wintry-white partridge fly into the yard. His skin became clammy as a cool wind licked his naked body, and he shuddered, knowing now that all the signs spelled death.

Two days later, a report reached him that merely confirmed what he had already guessed: Omeriah Malcolm was gone.

The immediate family who were still in Jamaica journeyed to Nine Miles for a traditional "nine-night" ritual, commencing with the "set-up" or "keep company"—the wake that preceded the funeral and the nine nights and eight more days of mourning. Among the Malcolms who attended were two of Ciddy's sisters, Imogene (nicknamed Amy) and Enid, and three of her brothers, John, Gibson and Solomon; Yaya had gone to her reward in 1956. Of Lurline and Omeriah's four children, only Roy, Rose and Dawn attended, infant daughter Joy having passed away in the mid-1950s after having lived for only a year and ten months.

Born in the 1880s, Omeriah had endured as the most important figure in his native village for more than half a century before succumbing to cancer. The customary preliminaries had been taken care of within hours of his death. Shortly before he drew his last breath, a little water was poured into his mouth to aid him on his passage into the next world. Two family members washed the body—one starting at his toes, the other at the top of his head, both of them finishing together. The water used to wash the corpse was set aside to be poured out just as he was carried out to the burial ground.

Since he died in his own bed, the position of Omeriah's body was reversed for the company-keeping—the head laid at the foot of the bed to confuse any evil spirits lurking about. All mirrors in the house were turned to the wall, lest the image of the corpse be reflected in any of them, causing further deaths in the family. Lurline, a woman of enormous poise and dignity, spent the day greeting the vast numbers of mourners who arrived from surrounding villages, offering them hot food and the best rum available in the district.

As the body was removed late in the afternoon, dressed in a dark burial suit and laid in a simple wooden coffin, the house was methodically swept out with a crisp new straw broom and his bed was taken outdoors to remain there for the next nine days and nights.

The burden shouldered by the pallbearers was deemed to be a light one on the way to the burial ground, thus indicating that none of Omeriah's enemies were helping to carry it. At the gravesite, all young children in the immediate family were hoisted up and passed over the coffin, the deceased's name being called out each time to protect them from retaliations by duppies.

As night came, all were expected to return to Omeriah's house for the "watch-dead" or "silence wake," a requiem that was anything but silent as people sang and performed Kumina possession dances, while local elders who shared Omeriah's "fo-yeyed" (four-eyed) ability to track the progress of spirits as well as the shadow-souls of duppies of the recently deceased gave testimony. Speaking before a bonfire as Omeriah himself had spoken for so many others in the past, they recalled all the high points of his life, his courageous deeds and many kindnesses. And they also caught glimpses of his duppy as it began to retrace his steps in this world, passing through the various rooms of the house, looming up behind loved ones and friends to bid them good-bye and—God forbid—perhaps extending a spectral finger to indicate those who might have sought to undo him.

During the course of the remaining days and nights of the convocation, everything that Omeriah had owned was polished, ironed, folded, mended, weeded, watered, pruned and bathed. There were ring dances by the children of the clan, Anancy stories told and retold, games and musical instruments played, potions prepared and a series of intricate spells cast to pay homage to the ancestral dead, to nurture and shield those surviving and to lend order to all agendas on both sides of the threshold to Eternity.

These rituals led up to the all-important Nine Night, when all remained vigilant until first light, their every thought and action at the house of the deceased intended to welcome and entertain the duppy of Omeriah during his last circuit before retiring to the grave. As dawn approached, the riddles became more and more tricky, the laughter louder, the hymns the most heartfelt.

Jamaican country people's anxieties about the unseen world seldom are more pronounced than at the moment of a patriarch's passing, but Omeriah's death caused more consternation than most. A bush doctor who had knowledge of the phantom forces that can fell a man, he had said he felt he was passing before his time. Troubled in mind before his body began to fail, he fretted about unspecified misfortunes that he believed were in the offing for his only grandson, and in his final hours, he let it be known among the clan that he wished his farmland in Smith to be at the disposal of Nesta and his descendants.

As the new day broke, and it was once again proper—and prudent—to mull over such questions of destiny, obeah and inheritance, most of those gathered there still could do little but express to each other how ignorant they were of the inner thoughts and motivations of Omeriah Malcolm and Bob Marley. As Omeriah's bed was carried back into the house and his worldly goods were distributed to those who were thought to be worthy of them, many found the principal legacy of the deceased to be inexplicable. They were astonished at how little they actually could piece together about Daddy Malcolm, who had ruled the family for as long as any one of them could remember.

And then there was the matter of Bob, another human conundrum who seemed to be holding out the answers to questions which they could only guess at; for one not yet out of his teens, he was a most mysterious character.

Bob had accepted the land bequeathed by Omeriah in silence, his expression betraying nothing. None of the Malcolms who still lived in Jamaica were especially close to the intense nineteen-year-old, but all were struck by the strong aura of solitude surrounding him. If he had been virtually alone in the world before, he was even more so now, having lost the most formidable friend and ally he was ever likely to find. Yet he showed no sadness for the present or trepidation about the future. Little was known about the depth of Bob's relationship with his grandfather since Bob had taken up permanent residence in Kingston, and there was no small amount of speculation over the trove of knowledge the older man might have handed down to the younger.

In any case, Bob showed no desire to be his grandfather's successor as head of the clan. On the contrary, he made it plain by his very silence that he was committed to another path entirely, a path much more recondite than any the rest of the family aspired to. He was a public figure of increasing power and presence, said to be a gang leader in the most sinister sector of West Kingston as well as one of the island's most promising young entertainers. He was also rumored to be drawn to the mystic arts, but not necessarily in the same fashion that Omeriah had been.

His relatives couldn't reconcile his reputation with his appearance. Like many Jamaican males, he appeared distracted, his head constantly cocked to hear things they could not even pretend to be tuned into. He would sometimes murmur like an absentminded philosopher-poet about the music of raindrops on the rooftops. But there was always a razor-sharp ratchet poking out of his back pocket, and he had scars and a faint sneer to show he had squared off with street punks similarly armed. Word was, he commanded the respect of the most unsavory elements of the Dungle, yet he was scarcely the spitting image of a goon, bully or reckless rudie.

But there was one thing of which everyone was certain: Bob Marley did not share the rest of the clan's commitment to middle-class ambitions and eventual emigration to the States. He had no interest in inching up the splintery sufferah's ladder out of ignominy—though he didn't exactly scorn it either. Quite the opposite, in fact. But he personally had no interest.

As far as his relatives could ascertain, Bob's place in society was no place they knew of, yet he came off as being much less restless. He was more at ease, *at home* in Limbo than they could hope to be in Heaven.

Most of Bob's family was content to respect him from a comfortable distance. He was part of the ancient contradictory essence of Jamaica, an organic product of its motley, murky ecology—much like the cabbagelike calaloo plant, a safe-as-milk staple once it's boiled in a pot, but a psychedelic poison until it's undergone that simple procedure. Who had figured that trick out, and at what cost? Nobody in Jamaica has a clue, but everyone has managed to embrace the mystery.

Like the Jamaican creole culture, which focuses on all aspects of its factionalism to the total exclusion of the untenable whole, skinny young Bob Marley was a paradox that exemplified the tensile strength of snarled roots firmly embedded in . . . mist.

But even mist has a claim to substance, as Ranford Willoughby, one of the late Alberta Malcolm's nephews, observed late one afternoon when Bob was not around. A Garveyite and Coptic Freemason, Ranford pointed out that the grandfather of Omeriah's first wife was an Egyptian. A murmur of surprise went around the circle of people eating and drinking on the porch of Yaya's house.

"Egyptian, yuh seh? Yuh tek me fe precky [foolish]?" said Roslyn Downs, Bob's errant godmother. Called "kriss-miss" (a pretentious, pompous girl) behind her back by locals, she was a skeptical, argumentative woman who was disliked by the Malcolms because she had never assumed her responsibilities toward the boy. "Wha' yuh bringle [irritate] me wit'? Dis' serious t'ing?"

The family was aghast at her arrogant, sacrilegious prattle. But Willoughby brushed her off with a scalding, "Hush ya nettle [meddlesome fuss] nung-nung [right now], woman! Forget yuh bru-bru [lowly affairs] and learn some of wha' Omeriah know about Africa an' its childran.

"Now me seh," he continued, as the sun began to dip behind the hills and fires were lit against "brown" (first) dusk, "dat Nesta have 'im some macca fam'ly tree! Him grandmaddah descended from de Egyptian people. Yes, fe true! An' grandfaddah was Cromanty of de Gold Coast, de slave people what possess some of de secret language of Egypt, knowledge of de power of de Word. Power to kill, like dem Cromanty Curse, an' power to heal too, like bush doctor.

"How de Bible begin, how go de firs' passage in St. John's book, de one 'bout Genesis? Who know dem Scripture?

"Chile," Ranford called out, addressing one of the children drawn to the family huddle by the magnetism of his trebly voice. "Fetch me Yaya's Bible, bless her sweet departed soul."

The adolescent girl ran inside, emerging a few moments later with the late Katherine Malcolm's ancient Bible. The man turned to John 1:1 and read the first verse aloud: " 'In de beginning was de Word, and de Word was wit' God, and de Word was God.' "

He snapped the book shut and scanned his rapt audience.

"Now, wha' dat mean? Seh dat mean dat ta know the Word was ta know God, to be wi' God, ta manifest God. To know the Word and speak it was to mek de Word of God occur. An' where belief dat come from? Ancient Egypt! Yah, mon! Pharaoh's time!

"Hear me! Moses was a black Egyptian, him name comin' from de word *mose*—dat Egyptian fe 'child.' Ya, mon! When Pharaoh daughter pick up de t'ree-year-old child who dem find in a bankra in de reeds, Moses tek de crown from Pharaoh head an' place it on him own head! Moses know Pharaoh name an' Pharaoh shake an' vex, and summond him magicians! But lickle Moses science too mighty ta defeat! Moses grow ta be warrior an' have him an Ethiopian wife.

"When Moses lead de Exodus, unitin' de tribes of Israel ta trod outta bondage, Moses carried wit' him the religion of the husband of Nefertiti, Amenhotep, a renegade Pharaoh who changed him name ta Akhnaton, which mean, 'God is satisfied'!

"Yes, mon! Akhnaton, de only enlightened black Pharaoh, him seh dere is but one God, omnipotent, terrible an' swift in Him Judgement. An' Akhnaton, him permit no graven image ta be made of God. Un de Eighteenth Dynasty, Akhnaton outlaw all spells and prayers ta bogies, djins, monsters, witches, demigods an' servants of serpents, including Osiris and all him Court of de Underworld. Akhnaton banish de mythmakers an' priests, smash de idols, erase hieroglyphics and picture language dat praise many gods instead of one God, an' shut all de temples—for seventeen years!

"Akhnaton mek an' alphabet ta replace dat pagan picture language, and him compose de first Psalms, by God's Almighty inspiration, as a model fe de prophets. But in 1358, Akhnaton's enemies ambush him, an' tek him life in cold blood! Yes, mon! An' den dem mek Tutankhaton, Akhnaton's son-in-law, restore de pagan ways!"

The family shifted in their places and settled in as Willoughby built up steam in his tale-telling, a few of the eldest nodding slightly to themselves, dimly recalling hearing fragments of these legends from Omeriah's own lips.

"De Mos' High call upon Moses an' charge him ta teach the true faith ta de Levites, an' lead dem out of bondage an' into Canaan! Da new Pharaoh nuh wan' dem go, so him test Moses knowledge of the Word. Pharaoh call him own magicians, Jannes an' Mambres, to duplicate all da wonders Moses perform. Dere was real sorcery on bot' sides! But because Moses known Pharaoh's true name, him cyan conjure wit' de full force of de Word, all obstacles removed. An' Moses sorcery, from de Plagues ta de summoning of de Angel of Death, was as great as da Ta, da gift of knowledge symbolized by de ageless Great Pyramid! [There is only one geometric symbol in hieroglyphics that is a pyramid; called *Ta*, it translates as "gift."]

"One night, Moses ask God wha' Canaan gon' be like, and God mus' tell Moses dat he will lead de tribes to the Promised Land, but dat Moses will never enter it 'imself. An' prophecy is fulfilled, because Moses ambushed an' murdered mos' brutally by dem who 'e rescued! Yes mon, it de ancient trut'! Jealous Levites slay Moses!

"Ta dis day, dem have tablets in museums around de world, Egyptian manuscripts an' tablets an' t'ings wit' de Psalms written on dem in Aramaic—even in hieroglyphics!—wha' dem found in Thebes an' Tell-el-Amarna an' Jerusalem. An' dem scholars and professors don' know why!

"But in de ancient world, in de House of King David, David have Ebjatar, da Coptic scholar, set down de wisdom, de visions an' de psalms of Akhnaton, fe spread dem ta Ethiopia, all Africa! Ya, mon! When de Nazarene Himself disappear for a time in early manhood, Him study de teachings of Akhnaton in India an' in Abyssinia! An' Him read the Book of Raziel, King Solomon's guidance manual an' de same book revealed ta Adam an' Eve after de Fall ta help dem survive an' strive toward de Coptic Revelation.

"So, wha' dis have ta do wit' Nesta?" he declaimed, his tone almost one of chastisement. "Well, breddah an' sistah, when Omeriah see Nesta, him see a son who carry four strong winds in him chest. Nesta come from de white man, from de black man, from bondage, an' from de banks of de Nile, where de Word shone down upon de Great Pyramid an' de ruins of Tell-el-Amarna!

"Not one other mon in dis yere family carry dem winds in him breast. Not a strikin' one! Dat's why Bob was Omeriah's favorite. Him see the burden de baby carry, and him at least have a guess why dem ancient duppy return ta mek war on de lickle bwai!"

When the learned and well-spoken Willoughby had finished, there was a respectful silence. Coptic Freemasonry was prevalent in certain quarters of Jamaica, particularly in the parish of Clarendon, and it was considered a privilege by most non-members of the fraternity to hear its beliefs and philosophies articulated—notwithstanding the implications of Willoughby's analysis, which were thoroughly bizarre.

But Roslyn rudely kissed her teeth and broke the thoughtful stillness with a scoff. "Me is churchwoman," she leered. "I nuh tek fe Gospel dis talk. Yuh tek dat bwai, me godson, who read palm as a yout' an' have yeyes like wild animal, who mek ska record fe praise de sinner, and yuh seh him favor bush prophet. If I laugh, I die."

The group gasped. To make such a remark at such a moment! Enid Malcolm, who had been listening to Roslyn's slurs in mute rage, barely able to contain herself, leapt up and threw words at the moon, stating that Roslyn Downs had never been a fit godparent to Bob, either before or after Ciddy's departure, and was totally unworthy to judge him or anyone else. There are more things in heaven and earth, Enid cautioned gravely, than any of God's creatures know of.

"Judge not, before yuh judge yuhself," Willoughby warned, with a sly, savvy nod to a certain recent ska record voicing the same view. "Like mammy [a balmyard mistress] always seh, 'De last shall be firs' an' de firs' shall be last.' "

With that, everyone rose and torches were lit to guide them to their beds. Rosyln Downs had to make her way alone, no one wanting to "company" her home, lest Omeriah's duppy should disapprove and take action. There was bad energy in the crackling night breeze, and the moonlight knifed through the trees, dividing the lonely roads and goatpaths into livid pits connected by thin platforms of light.

By the evening of the tenth day, most of the clan had scattered, Bob traveling back to Kingston to pick up exactly where he had left off, saying nothing to his musician friends about his personal loss.

Shortly before the Christmas holidays, Bob received a manila envelope from Wilmington. Inside was a long letter from Cedella, who was worried about her son, now that his closest kin, besides her, were all buried. She had gotten married again in October 1963, to Edward Booker, a civil servant in Delaware who was involved with soil and water conservation, and they'd found a home for themselves and Pearl on Twenty-fifth Street, in Wilmington. Bob's mother wanted him to come to America to build a new life for himself with them, and she had enclosed a plane ticket and the necessary papers in the envelope to admit Bob for an extended stay: Mr. Booker had some pull and helped arrange everything.

Bob waited a week before showing Rita the letter and ticket, saying that he was reluctant to make the trip and asking her to write out a formal refusal.

"Nuh, suh!" Rita said. "Out of respect fe ya maddah, yuh de only one cyan explain dat ta her!"

He could not protest. But, apart from his correspondence with Omeriah, it would be the only letter he had ever written. Poking out of the shack one morning before he was due to leave for a rehearsal with the Skatalites, he hunkered down on the stoop with a piece of note paper and began to scrawl his thoughts:

> Mom, here I enclose this money. I just send it to you as a token of love. It is not much, but I worked hard for it and I want you to be proud of me. Now I am singing. You remember when you are singing and you go on the stage singing with feeling so you touch the people? Well, that's the same way I feel. There is something in me, and when I am singing with everything in me I feel it.

He wrapped the note around some money and took it to the Jones Town post office on Byrnes Street, sending it off to Wilmington by registered mail. When his mother received it she wept over every word. She told Edward: "I t'ink he is goin' ta mek it in music."

10

Stir It Up

The 1964 Christmas morning show the Wailers gave at the Ward Theater was the hottest ticket in Kingston, and fights broke out on the Parade between police and rude boys trying to gain entrance by any means necessary. Several people were slashed in the melee, and the Wailers were on the verge of being barred from performing in the city's important halls because of the "criminal element" they attracted. Vitriolic letters to the editor appeared in the *Daily Gleaner*. Disapproving statements were issued by prominent church and civil leaders, calculated to single out the Wailers as whipping boys for the rising middle-class backlash against Edward Seaga's public relations campaign to push ska as the greatest Jamaican export "since rum and bananas."

"Rum can intoxicate the intemperate, and bananas can easily rot without proper precautions being taken," said one white vicar in a sermon during Christmas week, "and this is the effect we are witnessing the ska having on our young people."

The Wailers might have greeted the New Year as outcasts, had not the grisly exploits of a more serious malefactor captured the front pages on January 2. The banner headline in the *Gleaner* teased the stunned reader and the avid ska fan: RHUMBA DANCER STABBED TO DEATH; TROMBONIST HELD ON MURDER CHARGE. Don Drummond was in custody for the killing.

It was one of the most sensational crimes since the heyday of Rhyging, and it sent shockwaves through the Jamaican record industry. The artists in Coxsone's stable were dumbstruck, few so much as Bob, who had begun working closely with Dodd on what he believed would be benchmark arrangements for some Wailers material.

The Skatalites promptly disbanded, the band members badly shaken by the incident and forced to contend with considerable scorn and mistrust on the part of the general public—a certain degree of which would never completely subside—who wondered whether all ghetto musicians were murderously maniacal Rastas who smoked too much ganja at studio sessions and then arrived home at night with drawn ratchets, to viciously slice up their girlfriends.

Twenty-three-year-old Margarita, Jamaica's leading exotic dancer, had returned to the apartment she shared with Drummond on 9 Rusden Road in the Johnson Town section of Eastern Kingston at approximately 3:30 A.M. after an engagement at the Baby Grand Club in Cross Roads. Margarita, born Anita Mahfood, had made her debut as a dancer at the age of twelve, appearing on a Vere Johns "Opportunity Hour" bill at the Palace Theater. The mother of two small children by her former husband, British Honduran boxer Rudolph Bent, Mahfood had been living with Drummond since obtaining a decree nisi from Bent. The petition, heard in the divorce court in Kingston, was granted on grounds of cruelty.

Neighbors, among them dressmaker Enid Hibbert who lived in the same yard, testified at an inquiry at Kingston's Sutton Street courthouse that at 3:30 they had heard a car door slam twice outside the gate, followed by footsteps going up the stairway to Drummond's apartment. They heard Mahfood's voice calling, "Junie [her pet name for Drummond], please open de door fe me." Drummond, who was inside the apartment, replied, "Nuh, it is not locked." Mahfood knocked on the door twice more before Drummond answered it.

Shortly afterward, Miss Hibbert, an insomniac who had stayed up reading from the Gospel of St. John in accordance with the scriptural exhortation to "watch and pray," heard an argument between Mahfood and Drummond. She recounted it for the judge.

MAHFOOD: Imagine I tekin' a five-minute nap an' when I wake up I see yuh sittin' beside me very serious. Wha' happen, mon?

DRUMMOND: Yuh don' wan' ta sleep. Go an' sleep nuh, mon. Ain't yuh just come in?

MAHFOOD: Ah cyan't sleep under dese conditions fe yuh have a knife wrap in a chamois between yuh feet!

Hibbert told the court that Drummond replied that the knife was in his pants behind the door.

> MAHFOOD: Nuh, de knife is not in yuh pants pocket, it is wrapped in a chamois between yuh feet.
> DRUMMOND: Nuh!
> MAHFOOD: Nuh, Junie, nuh, Junie, nuh, Junie—help! Murder!

Miss Hibbert told the court that she didn't take the shouting seriously "because whenever they have a fuss she would bawl out fe murder."

According to Constable Aston Pennycooke of the Rockfort police station, Don Drummond had walked into the station and approached the duty desk at around 4:30 A.M. on January 2. Pennycooke said that Drummond told him, "Ah woman in a de yard stab herself with a knife and ah would like de police to come and see her."

Pennycooke dispatched Constable Horace Reid and another officer to 9 Rusden Road, requesting that Drummond accompany them. On their arrival, Drummond directed him to a front room leading from the veranda. Inside, on one of two single beds, lay the body of Anita Mahfood. She was on her back, her head hanging over the edge of the bed. Drummond pointed to a chamois cloth which was draped over the woman's left breast, and said, "Dis is de cloth which she held the knife with and stabbed herself." Reid lifted the chamois and saw a ratchet knife protruding from the woman's breast. She was dead. Reid looked around, and noticed Drummond's trombone case open on the floor beside the bed. The dead woman's hand was stuck into the bell of the instrument.

On the morning of Tuesday, February 9, 1965, the Sutton Street courtroom was jammed with spectators. Others crowded in the corridors and blocked doors and windows; traffic in the vicinity was snarled. Twenty-nine-year-old Drummond, bearded and wearing a light green jersey and brown trousers, sat expressionless as Harrihar Pershadsingh, the government medical examiner for Kingston, described the postmortem examination of Mahfood's body.

The *Gleaner* reported all the particulars the next day. Peter Tosh and several Skatalites were clustered around the paper Bob held in Coxsone's studio, and read the coroner's report with with morbid fascination:

Externally, he found (1) an oblique incised wound on the left side of the chest, half an inch long and three inches from the midline, and there was a bruised area on the outer end of the wound; (2) an oblique incised wound on the upper half of the front fold of the armpit; the outer end of the wound was bruised; (3) an oblique incised wound on the edge of the left breast coinciding with 10 o'clock on the face of a clock; and (4) an incised wound along the same areola of the left breast coinciding with 4 o'clock on the face of a clock.

Internally, deponent said wound (1) extended inwards and backwards just above the left lung for a distance of three and a half inches; wound (2) extended through the chest wall inwards, downwards and backwards into the lung for two and a half inches; and wound (3) extended through the chest wall inwards and backwards into the lung for two and a half inches; and wound (4) extended through the chest wall inwards and backwards into the lung for two and a half inches.

The last wound, he said, almost severed the gristle of the fourth rib and there was evidence that it had been twisted out, causing a hole with a diameter of a half-inch; and surrounding the diameter was a bruise with a diameter of two inches. "All four wounds had penetrated the chest wall," the doctor said.

Deponent further gave the opinion that death was due to massive hemorrhage and clots in the left chest cavity from the stab wounds described. A knife like one shown to him in court could have caused the wounds, he said. The wounds were produced by four separate stabs and all four were inflicted with considerable force. The implement, he said, was driven to the hilt and each wound was serious. Any one of the wounds could have caused death.

THE COURT: In your opinion, doctor, do you think these four wounds could have been self-inflicted?

DEPONENT: No, they could not have been.

Dr. Pershadsingh also said he had examined Drummond on January 2, at the Rockfort Police Station and found fresh scratches on his wrist-joints, which could have been inflicted by a finger nail.

Not long after the hearing, Drummond was adjudged to be legally insane, and was sent to the mental ward of Bellevue Hospital on Windward Road. He died a raving madman.

The Skatalites had recorded tirelessly with Drummond and had a hefty backlog of tracks in the can; Coxsone placed their instrumental singles in the top ten for the next eighteen months. Dodd organized a new studio band under the guidance of saxman Roland Alphonso and called them the Soul Brothers. Backing up the Wailers for all subsequent recordings on Dodd's labels, the Soul Brothers became the ensemble that Bob Marley had dreamt of enlisting in the cause. When the Soul Brothers weren't supporting the Wailers, they went by a shopping list of aliases denoting different producers or the featured performer: Tommy McCook's Supersonics, Drumbago's All-Stars, Roland Alphonso's Alley Cats, Sir Cavalier's Combo, Buster's All-Stars, Baba Brooks Band.

If there had been any lingering shreds of innocence on the Jamaican recording scene, they were done away with in the pitiful drama of Don Drummond's denouement. Sure, he killed the woman, brutally. But the poor didn't see the case as being so open-and-shut. The musicians railed on about how Don Drummond's soul had been eaten away a little bit each day, each month and year: one of the best jazz instrumentalists in the entire world, he had steadily been ignored, year after year, and that had slowly sapped his heart and broke his spirit. Drummond's actions were the grotesque consequences of well-earned despair, a metaphor for the hopelessness that was served every sufferah on a soiled platter. And now, at last, Drummond had gained international recognition: "JAMAICAN JAZZ MAN SLAUGHTERS LOVER," "GHETTO FANATIC TRADES HORN FOR KNIFE."

The ghetto saw its dirty laundry strung across the front pages for all the world to see and be properly revolted by. Henceforth, survival in shantytown was spoken of in belligerent terms. Even among the Rastas, who had begun to gain converts in considerable numbers, the dogma of passive resistance put the stress on *resistance*—to the police, to the politicians, to the people on the hill and the stiff-collared preacher who susu 'pon de sufferah from a polished mahogany pulpit, to the Twenty-one Families, to the JLP and the PNP and the trade unions and the bauxite interests and the banana growers, to the Mafia and the CIA and the tourists and, of course, everyone in the Jamaican record business, who were the modern-day equivalents of Morgan the Pirate and his band of buccaneers.

The choice was between equal rights or the madness that is inescapable when one can no longer stand one's own stink. Deep in the ghetto, the switch was thrown, the current on full, and it was never to be turned off again.

The Wailers' "Rude Boy" was issued as a single in June 1965, just a few weeks before U.S. civil rights leader Rev. Dr. Martin Luther King arrived on the island to deliver the commencement address at the University of the West Indies. Discontent among poor young people was at a fever pitch and the combination of Dr. King's eloquent rhetoric and Drummond's imprisonment helped create intense hostility in West Kingston in response to oppressive measures by the civil authorities. As waves of ninety-degree heat rippled over the reeking squalor of shantytown, Dr. King was handed the key to the city by uptown coeds while the Wailers expressed the bitter sense of futility felt by downtown adolescents. The police had branded all of the youth in Trench Town and environs as rudies and malcontents; and in reaction, hordes of kids elected to assume the role, *ta raas*. What little semblance of stability in the area was strained to the point of collapse as shops were looted, bus drivers slashed, power lines cut, sporting events and public ceremonies disrupted, and guerrillalike squads of teenagers made raids on uptown neighborhoods under cover of darkness.

The upper and middle classes called for shoot-to-kill measures against all young criminals and their confederates, blaming the widespread unrest on the paganism and godlessness of the Kumina and Rastafarian religious cults in West Kingston and on the mental abnormality and moral turpitude of those who chose to live in such astonishing filth. One of very few prominent Jamaicans to offer another perspective on the roots of the insurrection was Mrs. Amy Jacques Garvey, widow of Marcus Garvey.

Speaking to more than fifteen hundred people in a courtyard in the large farming town of May Pen, Clarendon, she had warned that Jamaica was not taking advantage of its independence in the right way; for unless money was used for the improvement of the people in the gutter, the slum and the backyard, Jamaica would not be able to combat hooliganism. She said that many of the wayward young boys and girls of the nation had become delinquent because they lacked vocational training; boys who could get no work resorted to hooliganism, girls to prostitution.

When the third annual independence celebration culminated in August 1965 with a lavish parade in Kingston, an army of six hundred heavily armed policemen was called out to maintain order. The upper classes were totally bewildered when no significant disorder ensued. It wasn't until weeks later that ghetto politicians spelled out the obvious: the procession had been dominated—though not through any particular calculation or foresight on the part of the organizers—by the music of the Sound Systems and the slum studios. The Skatalites, under the direction of Tommy McCook and Roland Alphonso, had been asked to play on the Cable and Wireless Float; the National Symbols Costumed Group Float featured Duke Reid's regal hardware; the Systems of Sir Mike, the Musical Dragon and Lloyd the Matador each got space on flatbed lorries; Prince Buster and the Western Kingston Juveniles Band (largely Alpha School instrumentalists) brought up the rear. Even the Granville Williams Orchestra had the crowds jumping to an effervescent tune the parade organizers failed to recognize as the subversive ska hit, "Gun Fever." Notwithstanding the presence of the Dry Cleaners Float, the Hardware and Lumber Float, the Sugar Industry Labour Welfare Board Float, the Jamaican Library Service Float, the Agricultural Marketing Corporation Float, Joe's Sno-Kones Float and other more prosaic attractions, the entire affair had been rightly perceived by the swirling masses as a sufferah's jamboree.

One of the biggest crowd reactions was reserved for a pre-release Wailers single blasting out of Prince Buster's speakers called "Jail House." The lyrics at first seemed to paint a bleak picture of the future of rude boys should their misdeeds go unchecked. But by the end of the song it was obvious to ghetto ears that the confrontation between the rudies and police was being glorified by casting it in a biblical, David-and-Goliath light:

Jail house keeps empty
Rudie gets healthy
Baton sticks get shorter
Rudie gets taller

Can't fight against the youth
('Cause it's wrong)
Can't fight against the youth, now
('Cause it's strong)

Prediction: Them people a-going wild
Dem a rude, rude people . . .
The message: we gonna rule this land!

One could hardly hear the rest of the lyrics for the cheering, as lusty and uproarious as any heard emanating from the cheap seats at Caymanas Park race track that day.

Another long letter from Cedella arrived in the autumn of 1965, asking Bob to come to Delaware for a visit in February of the following year. Taking the matter up again with Rita, they agreed he should go, but Bob insisted that get they married before he left. That way, if he found life in Delaware to his liking, it would be easier for him to sponsor Rita's immigration. At the very least, it would facilitate their being together in the States should Bob decide to stay on longer than a few months.

He was determined to earn at least enough money while there to finance his own record label. He had grown weary of Coxsone's notions of shrewd career moves and surefire "scorcher" songs. In the Wailers' most recent session, they had cut, at Dodd's insistence, a cover of the theme song from the Peter Sellers–Woody Allen comedy *What's New, Pussycat?*—not exactly the sort of tough Jamaican ska that had been created as a reaction against unctuous American pop.

"Cho, Bob! We cyan't marry now," said Rita. "Yuh mom not know me, an' my mom and dad are not here to give approval. I don' think Auntie would accept de responsibility, an' what if she say nuh?"

After much emotional haggling, Bob agreed to declare his intentions to the loathsome Auntie Viola in a respectful manner, but he left open the question of whether he would abide by her ruling.

Dressed in dark slacks and a crisp white shirt that Rita had ironed, Bob appeared at the front door of Viola's house carrying a bottle of wine. She accepted the present gingerly and offered him a seat. Bob tried not to be too "short-hearted" (hasty-tempered) as he asked for her blessing.

Viola behaved as expected, trying to minimize her responsibility and plead helplessness in the absense of the Andersons. Bob was insistent, saying he loved Rita, that they planned to have children regardless and that he might proceed with or without anyone's blessing in arranging the wedding ceremony. Hearing this, Auntie did an abrupt about-face and said that since she was powerless to prevent the match, she might as well lend her reluctant approval. Bob was initially surprised by her permissive stance—until he realized that such a position left her free to nudge Rita out of her nest ahead of schedule, and reclaim Bob and Rita's living quarters. This was a decision made by a conniving landlady, not a loving guardian.

The rest happened so fast that Rita was still giggling and telling girlfriends "it all sounds like a page from a fairy book," right up until a few days before she was confronted with the ring Bob had bought and the plane ticket his mother had sent them.

The sun rose at 6:37 A.M. on the morning of February 10, 1966, the "doctor wind" blowing in from the ocean with a salty savoriness, taking over from the "undertaker's wind," whose interminable nightly duty it was to rush down from the hills and push the previous day's stale air out to sea. It was a day when the island was abuzz with the news that millionaire showman Billy Rose, a major stockholder in AT&T, onetime spouse of Fanny Brice and composer of songs like "That Old Gang of Mine," had died of pneumonia in his winter home in Unity Hall, near Montego Bay.

The topic accorded second-place status among the labrishers chattering between Mo Bay, Port Maria and Kingston that balmy morning was the latest episode of *The Fugitive*, the most popular TV show in Jamaica (*The Beverly Hillbillies* being a close runner-up), in which actor David Janssen had not only bumped into his one-armed nemesis but had also come within a whisker of being caught. Of lesser moment on the island was the news that Lunokhod 9, the unmanned Soviet space craft which had made the first soft landing on the moon, had sent back proof that the moon's soil could bear the weight of moving men.

At approximately 11:00 A.M. in the neat but spare Trench Town home of a friend of the Andersons, Robert Nesta Marley was wed to Alpharita Constantia Anderson. A local justice of the peace named Jim Russell officiated at the simple ceremony. Bob had gotten a close-cropped razor cut for the occasion and wore the black stage suit and fancy shoes Coxsone had gotten for him. Rita was radiant in a ruffled white party dress cut just below the knee, a mother-of-pearl tiara, and a short lace veil. Bob had just turned twenty-one and Rita was nineteen—the same age as Ciddy when she was married. Rita had something else in common with her mother-in-law: her husband also left her the day after the wedding. Bob boarded a plane for Philadelphia the following morning, with the ska strains of "Put It On" (a Wailers' song enjoying Sound System popularity, which had been repeatedly spun at the wedding party) still resounding in his head.

11
Rat Race

It was a mistake. He felt it from the first.

"Everything too fast, too noisy, too rush-rush in Delaware," he told his mother within days of his arrival. "Why dem run so?"

"Dat's America, Nesta," Ciddy replied. "Ev'rybody gettin' ahead doing different t'ing, seeking out opportunity."

The whole city seemed like a kind of factory, a stark, paved-over marketplace, with no human frailty or dimension. There was no place to hang out, to reason with one's brethren, to hide. If you weren't running around working, screaming into telephones, hurrying into elevators, unloading trucks or shuffling papers, you looked foolish, a fish out of water. You could get arrested for loitering!

Bob held a variety of jobs: waiter, lab assistant for DuPont, forklift driver on the night shift in a warehouse, assembly-line worker in a Chrysler plant. He used the pseudonym Donald Marley, since he had no work permit. He spent most of his free time in the house on Twenty-fifth Street, keeping very much to himself, picking out tunes on an acoustic guitar and writing lyrics in the archetypal schoolboy's ledger—a Colonial composition book. Scrawled in block letters on the black and white marbled cover were the words EXERCISE BOOK; it became a combination diary and musical sketchbook which he guarded zealously.

He broke the news of his marriage in stages, first telling Cedella that he was "madly, madly" in love with Rita, and taking pains to describe her. "Mama, she walk an' roll [is knock-kneed] but me feel strong 'bout her!" He beat everyone to the mailbox each day to check for letters from her—even though he wrote very few in return. If Rita was due to telephone, he wouldn't leave the house until she did, regardless of the circumstances. Ciddy suspected she was more than a girlfriend when local girls began to phone and he refused to speak with them.

"Bob," she said one day while she was fixing dinner in the kitchen, "me seh dis yere girl got yuh in a crazy way! It nuh healthy. Yuh nuh eat well, and yuh looking shekrey [thin, run-down]. Why yuh nuh go ta a dance? Have a lickle fun an' t'ing? Dere be plenty occasion fe seriousness an' when de time come fe marriage."

"Mumma, dat time past gone. Me an' Rita is 'usband and wife."

"What!" Ciddy bellowed, cutting herself with her paring knife.

The details came pouring out, along with Bob's dislike of Delaware and his dream of amassing enough money to get his own record company going. He told Ciddy how he had watched Coxsone's records being pressed in the plant. He saw how the workmen squirted a "lickle turd" of soft vinyl on a press and how the silver stamp of the record matrix was slammed down on the vinyl, making an imprint. Same thing on the other side, the labels being glued on simultaneously, the excess vinyl then trimmed off the disc with a linoleum knife. A good pressman could make five hundred records in a day! It was an easy business to get into, the major overhead being the vinyl, and since he also sang and wrote the tunes, Bob could be "him own boss an' numba'-one-quality star!"

Cedella listened with a mixture of disappointment, incredulity and awe. He really did seem to know what he was talking about, and the fact that he had put all this together himself and was sufficiently motivated to save all his wages impressed her and made her proud. Maybe there was something to this record business, after all. If that was to be his direction in life, he was at least thinking past the next stage costume and the kick of catching his own jingles on the jukebox. But what a shame it was that he was committed to returning to the ghetto, to his wife and his life there. Much as she tried, she couldn't understand why he would choose such a rathole to live in; she eventually stopped trying to puzzle it out.

Back in Jamaica, Bob's backlog of work with the Wailers had continued to click with the fans: "Love and Affection," "Put It On," "I'm Still Waiting," "And I Love Her" (the Beatles song), "Cry to Me,"

"Where Will I Find." Rita continued to record with the Soulettes, having a hit with her version of the current U.S. pop hit, "Pied Piper." But her cousin Dream was spending more and more time filling in for Bob with the renascent Wailers, who, after having shut down for several months after Bob's departure, were now doing live appearances again, sometimes with Rita singing backup instead of Beverly Kelso, who was losing interest. With a basic lineup of Bunny singing lead, Peter second lead and Dream on harmony, they worked up new material and performed it at the State Theater, where they were booked to open shows for visiting American R&B singers Betty Everett ("The Shoop Shoop Song [It's in His Kiss]") and sometime Drifter Ben E. King ("Spanish Harlem").

Coxsone liked the new stuff, cut it and released it as "Wailers" material: "Let Him go (Rude Boy Get Bail)," "Dancing Shoes," "Who Feels It Knows It," "What Am I Supposed to Do," "When the Well Runs Dry," "Sinner Man," "Hoot Nanny Hoot," "Dream Land," "Rolling Stone," "Can't You See." Most listeners at the Sound system jump-ups were blissfully unaware that Bob was not on the records. But while the public was largely in the dark, Bob wasn't. The group kept him abreast of their activities in his absence through Rita and occasional phone calls. Of the moves they'd made that he felt ambivalent about, the one that bothered him the most was the release of "Let Him Go," an overtly pro–rude boy record. Bob told Bunny, "Yuh better watch out dem police don' shoot ya fockin' dead."

Of the two other original Wailers, the haughty Peter missed Bob the least and his compositions suffered the most from the lack of editorial judgment Bob often exercised over them. "Hoot Nanny Hoot" was as asinine a single as the group would ever put their name to. Bunny, who felt forlorn without the company of his childhood sidekick, turned out haunting songs like "Who Feels It Knows It," as well as "Dancing Shoes," the effervescent ska stomper that became the signature song for the ultra-hip new "skank" dance step the rude boys had devised.

We're goin' skankin' all night long
Just as long as they play our song
And the sound you can't refuse
'Cause we got on our dancing shoes!

Having inexorably entwined the Wailers with the latest craze, Bunny sealed the connection with Bob's "Jerk in Time," a follow-up skank record that opened with a drum roll right out of "Caravan" and built against a hard rhythm guitar riff peppered by Jackie Mittoo's organ. Meanwhile, the singer wryly contrasted his mounting dance-floor lust with the throbbing of his sore feet.

Restive Jamaicans were urged by the government to be on their best behavior in March, when Her Majesty Queen Elizabeth II, accompanied by His Royal Highness Prince Philip, Duke of Edinburgh, arrived for a four-day visit, her first in thirteen years. The upper and middle classes primped and preened and pranced about like peacocks, acting with greater deference toward the monarchy than when the island was still held by the Crown. The police were under orders to prevent the poor from getting within squinting distance of the queen and vice versa.

The sufferahs had their own glory day a month later, when the Jamaican government, learning that His Imperial Majesty Haile Selassie was planning to visit Trinidad and Tobago at the invitation of Prime Minister Dr. Eric Williams, asked Selassie to include Jamaica in his itinerary.

When Selassie's Ethiopian airliner, emblazoned with a roaring Lion of Judah insignia and trimmed in stripes of red, green and gold, touched down at Palisadoes airport at 1:30 P.M. on Thursday afternoon, April 21, 1966, there were more than 100,000 people there to greet him, most of them Rastas or members of Afro-Jamaican societies. The crowds had begun streaming toward the airport since early Wednesday morning, traveling by bicycle, dray, bus, donkey cart and on foot, clogging roads leading from the Wareika Hills, Cockpit country, the John Crow Mountains of Portland, Guy's Hill and Mount Diablo in St. Catherine, Dolphin's Head in Hanover, Munro College in St. Elizabeth, the cool, lush recesses of Mandeville, and the seaside villages of Negril, Savanna-la-Mar, Oracabessa, Manchioneal and Morant Bay. From an economic perspective, attendance was dominated by the sufferah, with nearly every "wappen-bappen" (one-room hut constructed of miscellaneous scraps) in West Kingston emptied out as residents rushed to find prime vantage points for the epochal event.

It had been a queer morning, weather-wise: overcast and forbidding, lightning bolts leaping out from roiling clouds, dark rain pummeling the island. Shortly before the droning engines of the imperial plane were heard in the heavens, the sky brightened, and seven white clouds resembling gigantic dogs surged out of the mass of low-hanging overcast. As the rear wheels of the aircraft alighted on the runway, blinding sunlight sprang from the firmament and countless jaws dropped in unison. Most of the assemblage sank to their knees.

As the door of the plane swung open and Selassie stepped out, a deafening tumult went up from the masses, who beat on calabash drums, lit firecrackers, waved bunting, shook banners and signs that read: "Human Rights Now," "Behold the Lamb of God," and "Lay Not Thine Hand on the Lord's Anointed." They shouted exhorations like "Hail the Man!" and sounded the huge Abeng bullhorns of the Maroons, whose echoing call was unchanged since they were used in antiquity to marshal African fighters during the Ashanti wars.

Protocol was ignored in the passion of the spectacle. All prearranged introductions and presentations were discarded as police batons and army bayonets were thrust aside and the faithful pressed forward, trampling on the red carpet that had been rolled out. Standing at the top of the portable steps, Selassie raised a trembling hand, either to wave hello or call for order—it was impossible to interpret the gesture. Then he began to weep, tears rolling down his gaunt face. The crowd cried with him, many Rastas remembering the biblical passage which said that Christ wept when he beheld the multitudes.

Selassie went back into the plane, and did not reemerge until Rasta elder Mortimo Planno ascended the steps at the request of the authorities to address the zealots, telling them to make way so the emperor could get to Governor-General Clifford Campbell's limousine for the ride through Kingston to King's House. Hurriedly escorted down the steps, Selassie declined to walk on the red carpet en route to the waiting car, a move that puzzled the journalists on the scene.

Rita, who had had her hair conked and styled for the occasion, was wearing her best dress as she and her friends walked from Trench Town to the airport. They had progressed no farther than the Rockfort Cement Factory on Windward Road when people began screaming, "He's coming! The motorcade!"

She searched the windows of the state cars as they sped by, seeking out someone stocky and imposing. Her gaze found a small man in a medal-festooned khaki uniform, wearing an officer's cap that nearly obscured his features. For the last several weeks, the Rasta musicians at Coxsone's studio had been assuring her that Selassie's palms had the holy stigmata—nail prints just like those of the risen

Christ—and as she realized the man whose limousine had paused before her was none other than Selassie himself, her mind raced. "Could it really be?" she wondered. "Could he be the King of Kings?!"

As the car began to pull away, His Majesty's gaze met hers and he raised his hand in farewell. There, in the center of his palm, was the deeply recessed black-brown scar of the crucifixion nail. Rita began sputtering unintelligible exclamations of astonishment. Inside her head, the cries took on form and substance and she heard herself asking, "Could it be? Are you the True God?" Selassie's eyes burned into hers and he nodded, slowly, solemnly. Then he was gone.

Dazed and nearly incoherent, Rita was taken back to Greenwich Park Road by her friends. She wrote to Bob that very night about what she had witnessed and said that she was being "penetrated" by the doctrines of the Rastafarians and that she was very close to embracing their religion.

The next evening, rumors swirled around Selassie's visit. The Rastas alleged that during a pre-dinner reception at the governor-general's house, Donald Sangster, the acting prime minister, had had the audacity to stamp his foot at Selassie's pet lapdog and that the dog had responded with a roar not unlike that of a lion. After dinner, Selassie reportedly distributed gifts among the government officials and guests. The Rasta leaders who attended received gold medals bearing the Ethiopian seal, while certain politicians, including Sangster, received cigarette cases—from the nonsmoking Selassie—that resembled miniature coffins.

After three days of state functions, during which Selassie addressed members of both houses of the Jamaican Parliament and was given an honorary Doctor of Laws degree by the University of the West Indies, the emperor departed. Considering the reciprocal respect Selassie had shown the Rastas, the various factions of the sect expected some form of official recognition from the Jamaican government. Three months later, on July 12 at precisely 9:00 A.M., the Rastas received a formal acknowledgment of their current clout and socio-religious worth in the form of 250 police armed with rifles and fixed bayonets, cudgels and pistols, who advanced from the Denham Town station ahead of a phalanx of bulldozers. Overrunning the Back-o-Wall section of the Dungle, a Rasta-dominated wappen-bappen' village located off Fourshore Road, the police scattered the squatters and demolished every single hut. Over the next three days, the entire neighborhood was leveled, with the Rastafarian Movement Center of

Sam Brown and the African Congress of Prince Edward Emanuel given a conspicuously brutal bulldoze-and-burn treatment. Hundreds of the destitute and now homeless Dungle dwellers had no choice but to sleep on sidewalks or take refuge in the tombs of the May Pen Cemetery, a lucky few finding temporary lodging in the Spanish Town Roman Catholic Church.

During the siege, a distraught Rasta woman was reported to have watched from a piece of crushed pavement as she chanted, "Since we are squatters in Jamaica/Send us back to Ethiopia/We will be citizens there."

In early August 1966, Rita flew to Delaware with Sharon to see Bob and meet his family. Ciddy fixed a big supper and everyone got acquainted. Rita and Bob's mom got on nicely, and Edward Booker made a positive impression on Rita because of his affection for children. Ciddy told Rita stories about her childhood in St. Ann, and Rita reciprocated with the startling news that when she had stopped in at a dry cleaner's in downtown Kingston, a counter girl who looked to be in her mid-teens had noticed the surname on Rita's receipt and asked if she was any relation to singer Bob Marley. Told that she was, the girl introduced herself as Constance Marley, a child of the captain by another black woman! She begged Rita to pass the word along to the rest of Bob's family with the suggestion that they should try to get together some time. Unfortunately when Rita returned to the cleaners a few weeks later, she found the girl had left her job and moved on.

Bob was greatly distressed by the incident, but Ciddy took it stoically, telling Bob, "Yuh faddah de cause of plenty-plenty grief an' travail." It had been a typically Jamaican chance encounter, of a piece with the tragicomic "Shame and Scandal."

Dream had gone up earlier to stay with friends in Brooklyn and took the train down to Wilmington a few times while Rita was there. Sitting down in the basement of Ciddy's house one day, Bob and Dream jammed on acoustic guitars, Bob showing him the bare-bones framework of some of the songs he'd been working on: "Misty Morning," "Sun Is Shining" and one called "It's Alright," which described has ass-backwards work schedule at the Newark, Delaware auto plant, the song opening with a quote from Psalms 121:6: "The sun shall not smite thee by day, Nor the moon by night."

Dream was struck by the craftsmanship as well as the confessional quality of the material. On his next trip to Delaware, he brought Bob a copy of the Beatles' *Revolver* album, telling him he had a song he wanted him to hear. Taking Bob and Rita down to the basement, Dream put the album on the phonograph, lifting the tone arm over to the second track on the first side. "Eleanor Rigby" issued from the phonograph's little speaker. Rita started to say something, but Bob yelled, "Pipe down!" and turned the volume up. Rita's jaw dropped; Bob had never raised his voice to her before.

Murmuring that he understood how the character in the song felt, Bob played the song over and over, slipping into a trance, ignoring Rita and Dream, mesmerized by the melancholy narrative, with its themes of loneliness, death, loss and the failure of the Christian church to offer comfort to the afflicted.

Bob brooded about death and loss for several days after Dream and Rita had departed (he back to up to Brookyn, where he was enrolled in high school in Canarsie; she and Sharon back to Viola's in Kingston). His mother noted his depression and asked what was troubling him, but he begged off discussing the matter.

Ciddy came home from domestic work one evening in July and asked Bob if he wanted to go along with her for some grocery shopping. He said no, saying he was expecting a phone call about his work assignment at the Chrysler plant.

"From mornin' yuh been in de house," said Ciddy. "Come ride wit' me an' tek a lickle breeze." He shook his head.

While she was gone he fell asleep on the sofa, and when his mother returned, he told her that he'd had a disturbing dream. There'd been a short man dressed in khaki and an old felt fedora who came through the front door of the house and stood next to the sofa as he dozed. The man had dug his hand into his jacket pocket and produced a ring, set with a black jewel embossed with some sort of insignia. He took Bob's hand and pushed it onto his forefinger, saying, "This is all I have to give you."

"Wha' you mek a dat?" Bob asked his mother.

Ciddy said to hold on a minute and went upstairs to the bureau in her bedroom, where Edward Booker had a teddy bear on whose tail he kept his and Ciddy's assorted rings. There was one on the tail with a plain black stone, a small delicate ring she thought she'd gotten from Norval—although she wasn't certain—and she brought it downstairs to show Bob.

"Yahso! Dat like de ring in de dream!" he exclaimed, and Ciddy slipped it on his fourth finger.

"Me t'ink dat dream might be a blessin' from ya faddah," she said. "Norval was a short mon, jus' like yuh, an' him dress in dat same fashion. He never give yuh anyt'ing when him alive, suh maybe him want ya ta have a blessin' now."

Bob didn't like the ring and took it off at the end of the week, telling his mother it made him feel uncomfortable, as if he were being tested about his attachment to material things. He tried to give it back, but Ciddy said to hold on to it, since it must have some symbolic significance in light of his dream.

"Cyan't be pure coincidence," she observed.

After being laid off from his job at the auto plant, Bob applied for welfare, and in October he received a notice from the Selective Service Bureau telling him to register for the draft. Exasperated, Bob packed up his things and caught the next flight back to Kingston. But before he left, his mother begged him to take the ring along whether he wore it or not.

"Yuh been given a sign," she said. "De ring might help yuh ta ketch de meaning of it."

12

Coming In from the Cold

One of the first things Bob did when he got back to Trench Town was roll a big spliff—a conical joint of ganja the size of a stogie. Something about the smoke as it twisted around his head, the perfume of the top-of-the-stalk Blue Mountain leaf as it burned and the potency of the draw gave him a sense of expansive control that had been unattainable in Delaware. The Rastas said they achieved great religious insights from their steady herb smoking, but Bob had never given much consideration to ganja's effects, other than to enjoy the tingling buffer zone it created for him, the tangible ring of tranquility that kept suffering and adversity at arm's length.

He'd been a moderate smoker since his early teens; mostly spliffs, the chillum only sporadically—that was more of a Rasta apparatus. Smoking ganja was as commonplace among the youth in the ghetto as steering a soccer ball or playing "puddung gollang" (put-down-go-along). Referred to as "pee-gee" for short, this is a game of ritualized larceny in which adolescent participants, usually two at a time, must be constantly on guard not to carry valuable articles in full view when going or coming from school unless the little finger is crossed over the fourth finger. Thus made vulnerable when spied by your opponent, who shouts out "Pee-gee!", you must show the proper hand sign before he shows his, or you forfeit your possessions. Such battles of wits and reflexes, entered into by locking fingers with one opponent and having a witness knock them apart with a chop of the hand, usually last for a week.

Bob had been good at pee-gee, probably because he liked the sport of it more than its possibilities for exploitation as a form of bullying, which was more common. Similarly, deft soccer-ball handling was, for Bob, a metaphor for handling one's enemies with aplomb, whereas for many Jamaican ghetto youths, a soccer game was considered a prelude to a gang fight. Bob was proud of his soccer prowess, as well as his street-fighting skills. His emphasis on the finer aspects of playing football, fleecing the unwary in pee-gee, and kicking ass on the streets was much admired by those around him. He set standards for cool, calculating deportment in the slums that were envied and imitated by those outside his circle. As he liked to tell potential adversaries, "Me got de handle, focker, *yuh* gon' get de blade."

Nonetheless, there was concern among the expanding roster of performers down at Coxsone's that Bob might be less effective in the studio than he'd been before, that he might get lost in the competitive new shuffle. Coxsone had made a series of canny talent acquisitions, and his stable now included the Maytals, who had been virtual slaves to Leslie Kong; Burning Spear, a Rasta vocal trio named after Jomo Kenyatta that Kingston producers had belittled—until they started scoring hits with lead singer Winston Rodney's echo-y bottom-of-the-well baritone and bush themes; Johnny Osbourne; Joseph Hill; Marcia Griffiths; the Gladiators; and Dennis Brown. Rita and the Soulettes had another hit moving up the charts with "You Lied," and the Wailing Souls, Pipe Matthews's new group, were doing well with Coxsone, Pipe's voice still a near-ringer for Bob's.

Moreover, Dodd had become better acquainted with the two-track equipment he had obtained from England. The capability to isolate a vocal or solo instrumental break and rehearse it thoroughly before adding it to the finished product had multiplied the possibilities for exciting and innovative end results. This modest technological advance generally inspired all concerned to forge highly individual new modes of expression.

The disintegration of the Skatalites had also established its now freelance membership as the elder statesmen of a bygone era. Along with canonization came neutralization, however, as younger inheritors familiar with their forerunners' strongpoints and seminal contributions streamed into the studios. The ska beat had been slowed down, with the rhythm cut in half and the bass and drum asserting themselves in a downright threatening manner. The new music had the sassy tension of the emerging Bossa Nova sound, plus the athletic confidence of American soul, which had eclipsed the tired repetitiveness of sixties R&B. Alton Ellis had given the trend a defining label with an elastic Duke Reid dance single called "Rock Steady," but others provided the punch, expounding on social themes that were the Jamaican parallel of the injustices exposed in Stateside soul.

In the wake of independence, Jamaicans had swarmed in record numbers to the city in the belief that bountiful new opportunities lay there. Their relocation translated into little more than crisis-level overcrowding of the ghetto. Bob Andy's "I've Got to Go Back Home" said it all. In a brawny, searing rock-steady tempo, the admittedly suicidal character in the song states that the urban haven he had traveled so far to find now seems more distant with each ghetto block he walks.

The energetic experimentation ushered in by the advent of rock steady and the upgrading of technical facilities created a certain cockiness among the younger artists (such as Trinidadian guitarist Lyn Taitt and trombonist Vin Gordon, whom his cohorts called "Don Drummond, Jr."). It never occurred to them that Bob Marley might have undergone a transformation of his own, one just as individual and possibly more distinctive.

Shambling around Studio One, Bob was initially cagey about getting down to some actual playing and singing. Cajoled by Peter and encouraged by Bunny, who had heard through Dream that he'd been woodshedding, Bob confessed that he had done a lot of writing and began to explain the framework of a new tune, "Bend Down Low." Warming to the subject as well as his old stomping grounds, he opened his notebook and set it on a stool, leaning over it with a guitar pressed to his ribs.

Bopping on the balls of his feet, Bob began to strum. Then he began to wail, singing a prickly mid-tempo testament to the individual's timeless need for freedom, delivered as if murmured into everyman's ear.

Gradually the musicians joined in, picking up on the beat. It was peppy like ska, which made it sound a trifle passé, but then the narrative toughened, berating those who believed that sinful pleasures could be a springboard to spiritual ones.

As Bob unveiled, day by day, the seductive contents of his "exercise book," the appeal of the songs, notwithstanding their somewhat dated rhythmic base, became explicit. These songs were intensely *personal*, yet they managed to be universal at the same time. They were not linked to current events or fads; they did not capitalize on voguish shantytown catchphrases; they did not sway in synch with the prevailing political winds. "It's Alright," with its consideration of the importance of one man's finding inner dignity at a job characterized by a numbing sameness, somehow had more urgency than ten singles advising rude boys to put up, shut up or simmer down. The swaggering, rakish aspect of the Kingston record scene was supplanted by intimacy and vulnerabilty.

When he heard some of the tunes, once they had been streamlined and adapted slightly to the rhythmic attitude of rock steady, Dodd removed his porkpie hat, scratched his balding head and told Dream with undisguised admiration, "Bob in 'im ackee now seh. Dat bwai past de pack, clear [entirely]."

Due to his hasty exit from America, Bob had not been able to accumulate the money he needed to establish his independence on the music scene. There was barely enough (approximately U.S. $700), even considering the highly favorable exchange rate, to get a running start. With the help of the Wailers, Rita, Dream and even Viola ("Dat ol' woman drive a nail like a mon!" he told Dream), he built his first record store—a four-walled stall with a counter window—in front of Auntie's house on Greenwich Park Road. He sold Coxsone's records on consignment, plus a very few releases on his own label, which he christened Wail 'N' Soul 'M, since its first two acts were the Soulettes and the Wailers. The inaugural Wail 'N' Soul 'M single was "Bend Down Low," with "Mellow Mood" on the flip side, both produced by rising young West Kingston producer Clancy Eccles at Dynamic Studios. Next came a duet by Rita and Bob called "Hold On to This Feeling," the blithe lyric reaffirming a commitment made six months earlier.

Both records were well received but Bob lacked the ready cash to keep up with the demand, so distribution flagged and airplay was restricted. (Coxsone offered intermittent distribution during 1967–68.)

The Wailers issued a few more singles on the Coxsone label, mostly open letters to rudies, but their output was reduced to a trickle as they slowly made the transition to rock steady. Knowing they were just treading water, Coxsone backed off and channeled his resources into promoting the Gaylads and the Heptones, two top rock-steady vocal trios, and his leading light, Alton Ellis.

A graduate of Boy's Town School, located in a treacherous West Kingston neighborhood, Ellis had gotten his break winning a dance contest on the Vere Johns Opportunity Hour and had his first big singles in the early 1960s with "Muriel" and "Girl, I've Got a Date" (the latter also found favor in England). Not long after "Rocky Steady" sank from the top ten, Dodd had Ellis doing cover versions of songs ruling the U.S. Hot 100 in 1967, like the Bee Gees' "Massachusetts" and Procol Harum's "A Whiter Shade of Pale." Shortly thereafter, Ellis's once-loyal local audience abandoned him.

Watching from the sidelines, Bob figured that the extended hiatus in Coxsone's now predictable career guidance was for the best. "Why play pee-gee wit' an easy mark dat continually tote de same merchandise?" he reasoned. Instead, he concentrated on his songwriting. By the spring of 1967, however, Wail 'N' Soul 'M was hurting for investment capital, and Bob was hurting for subsistence capital, so he packed up Rita and Sharon and invited Dream, who was back from Brooklyn, to move with them to St. Ann, where they took up residence on Omeriah's property and began to cultivate the land in Smith.

Bob's pet donkey, Nimble, was still being cared for by relatives but was too old to help with the chores, his belly hanging close to the ground. So Bob and company restricted their farming to a portion of the plot, living on what they grew and trading rather than selling their surplus for other basic needs. Keeping to a strict budget, they hung on in Smith for six months, with Rita making periodic trips back to the city for additional provisions.

Bob started writing in earnest during this sojourn in the country, often working up material with Rita's help. Moving the family back to Kingston, shuttling back and forth from the residences of various friends and relatives, Bob spent what little money he could scrape together to cut two Wailers singles (with Clancy Eccles producing again) at Dynamic studios in the autumn of 1967: "Thank You Lord"/"Nice Time" and "Hypocrites"/"Pound Get a Blow." First he attempted to distribute them himself by taking the records around to the Kingston outlets by bicycle, then abandoned the scheme after being sideswiped by a bus in the heart of the downtown area. His injuries were minor, but his pride was seriously bruised. He muddled on, though, and he got the Wailers together once again to cut another single for Wail 'N' Soul 'M called "Pyaka," street slang for "muddy" or "a mess." The title was something of a commentary on the group's unrewarding relationship with Coxsone.

Also in need of money and studio time, Bunny and Peter still maintained relationships, however strained, with Dodd. The producer issued a Peter Tosh solo single (Bunny singing harmony) called "I'm the Toughest" that turned out to be Peter's swan song with Coxsone. The bitter end came one afternoon when Dodd, short a session player, asked Tosh to contribute keyboards to another artist's session. Peter refused, told Bunny of the "insult" and the two confronted Dodd in the control room, railing that their "blood and sweat" had made the Jamaican Recording Studio what it was. A shouting match erupted, Dodd telling them to leave and never come back. Bunny taunted Coxsone, daring him to draw his fabled "anti–rude bwai" side gun. The police were called and responded from the Denham Town station, whereupon more commotion ensued, and Bunny segued into a scathingly eloquent denunciation of the constabulary.

From that point on, Livingston was a prime target for police harassment in West Kingston. Early in 1967, Bunny was busted on a street corner in Rema along with two Trench Town musicians, the charge being possession of ganja. Despite the fact that he had no weed on his person, he was the only one convicted, after the officers testified that he had stashed the herb in a nearby barrel. He served one year and two months in jail, first at the General Penitentiary on Tower Street near Kingston harbor and then cutting sugarcane on Richmond Prison Farm before being released in September 1968.

While Bunny was in prison, Bob, who had come back from St. Ann with the intention of staying, was also busted on a trumped-up traffic offense. He spent forty-eight hours in jail. Upon his release, he went straight back to Nine Miles. Word in the ghetto was that the Kingston police wanted all the Wailers behind bars. Peter ignored the rumors, only to find himself in stir in early 1968 after he and Prince Buster were collared while participating in an anti-Rhodesia demonstration.

When Bunny was released from Richmond Farm Prison, Bob returned to town, leaving Rita and Sharon back in Nine Miles, and the broke and bust-weary Wailers approached the last producer who would have them, Leslie Kong. Bob and Peter had set aside their distaste for the herky-jerky rock-steady sound and written a dozen songs between them, the best being Peter's wryly vitriolic "Soon Come" and Bob's "Do It Twice" and "Caution," the latter of which recounted the tale of his nighttime arrest for riding in an unlicensed car on a rainy night in Kingston.

Bob also declared a truce with the Chinese-Jamaican producer. One of Kong's brothers advised Leslie against dealing with the Wailers, reminding him of Marley's ominous prediction of some years before that he would one day record again for Kong, but that Kong would come to regret their association.

Despite the fact that the Wailers were down on their luck and a financial risk, Kong brushed off the naysayers in his camp and cut a series of singles with the group, getting a middling return on his investment. The Wailers and the producer parted company afterward without hostility, and Kong held this fairly uneventful collaboration over his brother's head as an object lesson in the foolishness of superstition.

The Wailers' atypical approach to rock steady was characterized by a visceral, feisty flamboyance fighting a tugging backbeat. Their philosophy was "Give the drummer some!" (as soul giant James Brown liked to shout), but be sneaky about it. They had mastered the beat, but the lyrics tended to be flaccid and lame, lacking the naughty, calypso-anchored cleverness of Alton Ellis's best performances.

"Can't You See," cut with Leslie Kong, was indicative of their muscular but uncomprehending posture, with its overwrought rhythm section and tepid refrain, in which the lady in question is blind to the emotional chains with which she has bound her beau. The tremulous arrangement of "Caution" fared a bit better, propelled by an agitated lead guitar line and Marley's irate wisecracks to the cops, swearing at them as if they were his backup band.

"Soon Come" and "Do It Twice" captured with precision the snide/sassy vivacity of rock steady. The first was a droll denunciation of a fickle girlfriend whose guy chose to mock her capriciousness with Jamaica's irksome old folk maxim of reassurance and guarantee, "soon come."

In "Do It Twice," the song's young lover uses the palpitating rhythm as a waggish vehicle for a pledge of devotion. After making love, he confesses to his partner that he has found her so delightful that he would like to start all over again.

Despite their occasional sparks and flashes, the songs that came out of the Kong sessions sold poorly, and the Wailers found that their cozy relationship with the local record charts had disintegrated. Alienated from Dodd, their raw sound ill suited to a polished rock-steady environment, they were outcasts.

Happily, so was Lee "Scratch" Perry. A quarrelsome, unpredictable fellow who liked to get smashed on Tia Maria, he felt that Dodd was holding him back as a maker of records and had elected to release two vengeful singles directed at his old employer, "Run for Cover" and "The Upsetter," both of which were best-sellers. At the age of twenty-seven, Perry was a successful maverick who had pulled off the quintessential Jamaican hat trick: he had three simultaneous nicknames—"Little," "Scratch" and "the Upsetter." Before anyone could make a bid for his crown, he released a loping single called "People Funny, Boy" that was a last dig at Dodd, and which presaged the rock-inspired beat that would soon come to be known as reggae. The single was a smash and his fans hailed him as Lee "King" Perry.

The Maytals tagged the latest tempo transition on their 1968 dance single, "Do the Reggay," which showcased the typically tireless two-chord reggae pattern, its throbbing bass and the timbale-like double takes on the snare drum offset by crisp strumming on the teasingly tardy off beat. The lead vocal was chanted, the answering harmonies darted in and out and an electric organ provided additional counterpoint. Everything was in a hurry but the beat itself. Reggae was unbearably addictive, the aural equivalent of a slow-motion taffy pull in the midst of a street brawl.

Perry had gotten in on the ground floor of what promised to be the beat that would overrun rock steady; he and his crack session men began celebrating their reggae prescience by tripping down to the Odeon or the Bijou to catch the latest Clint Eastwood and Lee Van Cleef horse operas, retreating into a fantasy world increasingly frequented by many poor Jamaicans who were frustrated by the stagnant fortunes of independence. Galvanized by the gory spaghetti westerns, the Upsetters cut violent instrumental 45s ("Clint Eastwood," "Return of Django") that increased "de presshar" mounting in shantytown.

The backbone of Perry's Upsetters studio band was the two-brother team that comprised the rhythm section. Bassist Aston Francis Barrett, then twenty-two, and drummer Carlton Lloyd Barrett, eighteen, were the Kingston-born offspring of Wilfred Barrett and the former Violet Marshall. Both Barretts earned a skimpy wage as welders, but they had been moonlighting by doing session work as either the Soul Mates or Rhythm Force. Later they formed the Hippy Boys with singer Max Romeo and cut a hit in 1967 called "Dr. No Go."

The remainder of the Upsetters consisted of former Heptone keyboardist-singer Glen Adams, a sometime tailor who had recorded with Coxsone back in 1961 ("Wonder Thirst") and who had solo hits in 1967 ("I Remember," "Silent Lover," "Grab a Girl," with producer Bunny Lee), and guitarist Alva Lewis, well known for his aggressive riffing.

When "Return of Django" rocketed up the British charts in 1969 holding the Number 5 spot for four straight weeks, Perry took the group there for a six-week tour, the first of its kind for a Jamaican instrumental act. They were a sensation.

After returning to Jamaica and grousing about the paltry fees Perry had paid them for their roadwork, the Upsetters were approached by the Wailers, who asked them to support them on a song Bob had written called "My Cup." Rehearsing together, bitching and moaning about the dirty deals of the recent past, the two groups became friendly and one song led to another, Bob turning them out as fast as the Upsetters could master them: "Duppy Conqueror," "Man to Man (Who the Cap Fit)," "Soul Almighty," as well as the material Bob had written in Delaware and Nine Miles.

Bob pumped the Upsetters for stories about their English tour, amazed that a Jamaican act could get the kind of reception usually reserved for Motown soul revues and white rock stars. He talked the Upsetters into quitting Perry and joining the Wailers, and they unanimously agreed.

Perry was understandably furious when he learned that his lucrative band had been stolen out from under him. He actually threatened to kill Bob. The two held a summit conference in Rema that most expected to culminate in bloodshed. Instead, they emerged hours later with a new song they'd collaborated on called "Small Axe," another "cockaty" (boastful) Perry salvo that warned the Big T'ree Jamaican studios that Upsetter Records' new band, the Wailers, was prepared to decimate the competition. The Jamaican reggae supergroup's exclusive producer was to be, of course, Lee Perry.

Bob was slow in warming to the Rasta way of knowledge. He heard about it constantly from Rita, who never tired of describing Selassie's visit in 1966, her glimpse of His Majesty in the limousine, the eye contact, the nod, the frozen moment. The intensity of Rita's emotional involvement with Rastafarianism made Bob uncomfortable, scraped against his nerve endings. But her sudden conversion (in which she took the new name of Ganette Mander, signifying "Paradise") gave him pause, since she had previously been a dedicated Christian and a Sunday School teacher.

When he returned from Delaware, Bob noticed that increasing numbers of ghetto youths were growing their hair, allowing it to twine into long nappy tresses. Their heads looked spiky, like Alfalfa's in the Little Rascals, he once joked. He had sported locks briefly once before, just to see how they would look on him. Later, he huddled with Joe Higgs and began to "reason" about Rasta more seriously, because he felt Higgs was calm and collected about Jah, not a proselytizer. Their conversations led in due course to Bob "checking fe" (seeking out) the one dread on the island who had actually stood shoulder to shoulder with Selassie, Mortimo Planno. It was Planno, a Rasta affiliated with the Divine Theocratic Temple of Rastafari in Kingston, who had ascended the steps leading to Selassie's plane, bowed to the emperor and then turned around to call for order from the brethren, the wind catching his flowing white "kinte" robes, the camera hanging around his neck making him look like a tourist at the Sermon on the Mount.

Marley and Planno met in Trench Town, hung out, reasoned together. Planno took Bob up to Rasta settlements deep in the interior of Jamaica, hallowed places like Castle Kelly, which does not appear on any map. Beginning in 1968, Bob sat in on the Grounation ceremonies that had been conducted every April 21 since Selassie's visit—all-night convocations in which hundreds participated, feasting in the afternoons on coconut meat, rice and peas, passing the nights intoning the traditional "Bongo Man," "Lumba" and Niyabingi chants, drummers setting the stupefying pace on the percussion trio of repeater, funde and bass. Dreads would sit on their haunches in tight circles, passing the chillum pipe, a clay hookah with an "unskanked" (unbent, hence the name of the dance step) six-inch tube. The chillum would be packed tight with ganja; a marble or round stone at the base of the bowl permitted the smoke to pass through but prevented hot ash and fiber from doing likewise.

The women were usually segregated from the men, particularly if they were menstruating, which the Rastas regarded to be an unclean state. Women's role in Rasta life is clearly a restricted one—they are childbearers, fire-builders, cooks and honored servants. They may wear no makeup but the beaded gleam on their brows and the dust on their necks, their only fragrance that of perspiration; they are not permitted to join in discussions of consequence, nor may they draw from the chillum. Their dress must be modest, as dictated by Deuteronomy 22:5: "The woman shall not wear that which pertaineth unto a man, neither shall a man put on a woman's garment: for all that do so are abomination unto the Lord thy God." Rasta women's heads must be covered, as called for in I Corinthians 11:5–6: "For every woman that prayeth or prophesieth with her head uncovered dishonoureth her head: for that is even all one as if she were shaven. For if the woman be not covered, let her also be shorn: but if it be a shame for a woman to be shorn or shaven, let her be covered."

From Planno, Bob learned the Rasta dietary laws, which forbade all meats, predatory species of fish and lowly crustaceans, all dairy products, white-flour breads, alcohol, sweets and sugar-based beverages, anything containing salt.

He told Planno of the strange dream he had had in Delaware about the old man and the ring. Planno said he was being picked for a task of some sort, and that the emissary, whoever he was, might be the first of many. He also told him not to be afraid of science and obeah. "Who Jah bless," he said, "nuh mon curse."

Bob told about his overwhelming desire to write songs, *new* kinds of songs that blended his own day-to-day thoughts and observations with the folk wisdom of the hills—the adages Yaya had repeated to him as a child and the lessons he had learned from Omeriah. Planno told him, "King David seh, 'A song is a sign.' "

They spoke of Egypt, and Planno explained that the Great Pyramid at Giza had been built under the direction of an Ethiopian-born pharaoh named Khufu, and that the pharaohs used to smoke the black herb that grew in the valley of Gojam in Ethiopia, the most powerful ganja on the planet, the strain from which Solomon cut a stalk which he sowed inside the Temple. He told Bob that in their mystic, ganja-assisted reveries, the pharaohs came to comprehend the one truth in the journey of life, the Alpha and the Omega of this passage: "word-sound is power." Jah created the earth by speaking the words, by naming the sacred names. Only the most enlighted men know their own names.

Before we are born, Planno explained, we have a name, and when we enter this world, we get a new name. In each man is a separate genesis joined to that name, and most men learn their name only at the hour of their death. A very few, however, learn it beforehand, along with the knowledge of their own end.

Planno recounted the story of Selassie's visit. He told how Count Ossie and the Mystic Revelations of Rastafari band had played "Haile Selassie Is the King of Kings" for the emperor at a reception that also included Kumina dancing and a school choir singing "Shine Eye Gal." He confirmed that in the weeks after Acting Prime Minister Donald Sangster had stamped his foot at Lulu, Selassie's pet chihuahua. Sangster's health had steadily deteriorated; indeed, Sangster eventually lost his mind and died of a brain hemorrhage in April 1967. Moreover, a member of his cabinet who had chuckled at the incident and was one of those to receive the miniature "coffins" also died, breaking his neck after falling off a balcony while sleepwalking. Planno also told Bob how he had shaken Selassie's hand at the airport and how, ever since, he had occasionally felt an uncomfortable burning sensation in his right hand.

He gave Bob a warning, telling him that his dream was a "laigz" (which can mean either an opportunity or a wily trick). Bob would either grow in spirituality through such experiences, or he would "ketch a fire" (catch Hell).

In 1968, Bob had once more begun to grow locks; when Bob came back to Delaware for a brief spell, Cedella strongly disapproved, being a Christian woman, and he clipped them in the bud. But he continued to chant Selassie's title in Amharic: *Girmawi-ya-Girmawi* (Lord of Lords), *Negus Negesti* (King of Kings), *Madhane Alam* (Savior of the World). And he continued to reason with Planno.

Through Planno, he met another singer, Johnny Nash. Born in Houston, Texas, in 1940, Nash graduated from choirboy to television personality at the age of thirteen, becoming a regular on KPRC-TV's *Matinee*. Discovered by the Arthur Godfrey *Talent Scouts* show, he made frequent appearances on Godfrey's TV and radio programs. Signed to ABC records in 1957, he had a moderate hit that year with "A Very Special Love." In 1967, he signed with JAD records, an outfit he had formed with entrepreneur Danny Sims and producer Arthur Jenkins, and had a top-ten success in the States in 1968 with "Hold Me Tight," which he cut at Federal Studios in Jamaica under Jenkins's direction. Marley showed Nash and Sims his material, and Sims suggested he put his energies into songwriting and forget performing.

"Him seh me voice nuh good enough, but me songs are," Bob told Dream.

Sims signed Marley to a contract with JAD and Cayman Music, Sims's publishing company, and beginning in 1968, Bob, Bunny, Peter and Rita recorded a slew of Bob's songs, with Arthur Jenkins manning the board. The repertoire ranged from the familiar ("It Hurts to Be Alone") to the freakish, like "Milk Shake and Potato Chips," a puerile novelty song about a girl who pays more attention to junk food than to her fiancé.

Throughout the late 1960s and early 1970s Bob kept two trains running on the same track, recording with the Wailers for Lee Perry and making himself and his cohorts available to Sims and Nash for whatever U.S. or British singing or writing deal JAD might strike.

Working with the Wailers, Perry developed them into a heavily rock-slanted unit that typified the *best* in early reggae exploration. It was Scratch who redirected the group musically and vocally. He urged Bob to tighten up his lazy singing, and Marley's leads suddenly became compelling, plaintive, unencumbered by the silly, high-pitched vocal gymnastics that had sometimes marred the Wailers' ska and rock-steady 45s.

Lee advised the group to minimize their hackneyed falsetto harmonies and work on unobtrusive backing vocals that would serve as a cushion for sharp, assertive leads. Peter had a wandering baritone he'd long tried to discipline, and both Bob's and Bunny's tenors were fluid but untempered and sloppy. It didn't matter, Scratch told them. The important thing was to be genuine and go for the gut. And Perry wasn't obsessed with horns like so many other Jamaican producers; he preferred a flinty rhythm guitar that was cuffed in sharp stabs and wound around the bass line, which he allowed to belly up to the foreground. Carly Barrett was a genius at the "one drop" style of reggae drumming, the bass drum finding the basement on two and four, and he had a rapid-sticking high-hat accent that sounded like the first savage rattle in a snake pit.

The tempo was thud-heavy, volatile, insistent as a nagging child. "Dis is how reggae should sound!" Perry insisted.

The Wailers spent the better part of 1969 recording at Randy's Studio 17 on North Parade. These tracks included "My Cup," "Soul Almighty," "Mr. Brown," "It's Alright," and "Duppy Conqueror," which was the group's first local single in 1970. Glen Adams* mixed over two dozen tracks for Scratch, and the crafty producer put Adams and the master tapes on a plane to England to seal a bargain with Trojan Records. For the tacky-lewd album jacket art, one of the girlfriends of a Trojan staffer found herself costumed in fatigues and lured out to a studio in Surrey for a photo session with a dummy machine gun. The company preferred a shot with the lady's shirt wide open (although it airbrushed her nipples out of the picture). The finished portrait of a "soul rebel" was superimposed on a Jamaican Tourist Board photo on Dunn's Rivers Falls, with a fuzzy picture (taken by

*Lyricist for "Mr. Brown"

Winston Barnes, a friend) of the Wailers in the mountains slapped on the back. *Soul Rebels*, Bob Marley and the Wailers' first album (from which "Duppy Conqueror" was missing), reached stores in Jamaica and England by the summer of 1970 and met with a resoundingly positive reception in the roots community, which had all but discounted the group as has-beens. Sales were brisk in West Indian ghetto outlets on both sides of the Atlantic, but the album, whose singles had already topped and then faded from the Jamaican radio charts, never got much radio play in Britain.

Bob took his share of the profits, bought a brown and beige Hillman automobile and made long-postponed improvements on his place on Greenwich Park Road in Newland Town, which had fallen into disrepair during his family's extended absence. It was an expanded home for an expanding family, now housing, in addition to Rita and Sharon, two-year-old David "Ziggy" Marley and the infant Cedella. Rita was increasingly left to look after the flock as Bob's star ascended, her own recording career was deliberately curtailed, but she issued the odd single under the names Esete and Ganette.

The Wailers were working on a follow-up album when an urban development project was set in motion in the Greenwich Park Road precinct. Much of Newland Town and neighboring Arnett Gardens was razed, and what came to be known as "Concrete Jungle" was constructed. Bob wrote a few lines in his ledger for a future tune about having to relocate, and they evolved into a song of the same name.

"Duppy Conqueror" finally surfaced on the Wailers' second LP, *Soul Revolution*, a 1971 release on Perry's Jamaican Maroon label. The album also featured versions of "Keep On Moving" (about a gunman wanted by the law), "Put It On," and "Kaya," the last title being a street appellation for good ganja, although kaya is actually a native herb, similar to strong-back, that is used by bush doctors for healing. Glen Adams took the photos for the album jacket with an Instamatic camera, posing Peter, Bunny and Bob on the front lawn of Perry's house off Cardiff Crescent in Washington Gardens as they brandished toy guns belonging to Lee's children.

During 1970 and 1971, a jumble of Wailers singles were fed to the Jamaican audience, backed by "dub" and "version" mixes of the A side. Osbourne "King Tubby" Ruddock was one of the originators of dub music. He devised this novel wrinkle in the recording game while working as a selector for Duke Reid's Sound System and Treasure Isle studio. Tubby was fond of using a dub machine to eliminate the vocals from test cuts of a two-track single, getting a private charge out of the way the rhythms—in the space of a microsecond—seemed to snap, crackle and then pop like a champagne cork when they had no vocal track to soften them. Equally exciting to him was the abrupt reintroduction of the complete mix—"Jus' like a volcano in yuh head!" Tubby would say.

Springing the effect on a crowded dance hall one evening to blow a few minds (and possibly some speakers—since he liked the prankish ploy to be *loud*), the "dub-out" stunt was received like a revelation from on high. It soon became an essential novelty at the larger jump-ups and then a standard fixture. Everyone began to examine the dub versions closely, to determine whether Kingston rhythm sections held their own when stripped naked. Tubby added echo and reverb at ever more erratic intervals to enhance the "haunted house" effect of the stark trompings and backbeats going bump in the tropical night.

By late 1971, Kingstonians' appetites had been whetted for all-dub LPs, and Perry provided a remixed dub of *Soul Revolution*, called *Soul Revolution II*. When that sold out (which didn't take long), he began selling the original LP in surplus *Soul Revolution II* jackets (he didn't bother to press more copies of the dub LP), and the mixup never got sorted out.

Perry eventually got so hooked on dub that he began layering sound effects (train whistles, running water, animal noises) on just about every old track he had in his possession. Since musicians were customarily paid only once for their services, the dub LPs Perry hustled out represented pure profit.

Leslie Kong also saw dollar signs in reconstructions of past Wailers sessions for the overseas markets and announced that he was going to repackage his trove of the Wailers' rock-steady meanderings. But Kong made what turned out to be a fatal error when he titled the substandard collection *The Best of the Wailers*. Bunny got wind of the scheme and cornered him in his record shop.

"Don' do it, mon," he said to Kong. "It cannot be de best of de Wailers, 'cause our best is yet ta come. When yuh seh dat de best of someone has gone, den dat person is already dead or soon dyin', so we don' wan' dat."

Kong protested, and Bunny cut him off, seething, "If yuh do dis t'ing I prophesize dat it is *yuh* who will die."

The altercation had drawn a good-sized crowd, and Kong, feeling his ghetto reputation among the sufferahs was at stake, called Bunny's bluff and hollered that the deed was done, the album was already at the pressing plant.

Kong's brothers thought it was a bad business, recalling the dire prediction Bob Marley had made years earlier when Kong refused to pay him the money he owed him for his fledgling solo sessions. What had been the gist of Marley's prophecy? the Kongs fretted. Wasn't it something about Leslie one day working with Bob again, but never enjoying the considerable profits the producer would reap from the project?

Several weeks after *The Best of the Wailers* was pressed, packaged and burning up the marketplace, Kong's accountant popped into Beverly's record shop to inform Leslie that, based on the latest bookkeeping figures, the conniving Chinese-Jamaican was now officially a millionaire. Later that same day, Kong went home early, complaining in a whisper that he didn't feel well. Within hours he was dead at thirty-eight of a sudden heart attack. The coroner was puzzled by the case; Kong had no history of heart trouble. The young producer's untimely demise made no medical sense.

13

Crisis

JAD Records was still accumulating Wailers studio and demo tapes, as well as the publishing rights to much of Bob's best reggae output—some seventy-two songs—when Danny Sims came to Bob late in 1970 with a ground-breaking proposition. Sims had lined up a film deal which was essentially a vehicle for Johnny Nash. The movie, *Want So Much to Believe*,* was being shot in Sweden, and Danny needed a soundtrack score. Sims suggested that Marley might collaborate with Nash on the score, and Bob readily agreed.

Bob went to Sweden to begin working and found that, despite the relatively chilly temperatures, he loved Scandinavian cities. The following year, Bob landed in London, where his work was well known and there were lots of shebeens to welcome him as a celebrity and "bredren." Both Johnny Nash and Bob had been signed to CBS International via Sims and JAD Records, and Bob went into the studio with Nash's own group—known as Rabbit and the Jungles on records and the Sons of the Jungle when touring—to cut material for Johnny. The leader of the band was keyboardist-arranger John "Rabbit" Bundrick.

As it turned out, no Marley songs for *Want So Much to Believe* soundtrack ever materialized. But Bob's extended presence in Europe induced Sims, who was acting as Bob's manager, to ask Peter, Bunny and the Barrett brothers to come to England to join him for a speculative Wailers tour. Sims felt that this might stimulate some interest in the group on the part of a major label.

**Vill Så Gärna Tro*

They came, but their tour wound up being an unorthodox series of stints at British secondary schools in the Midlands, interspersed with a few dates at London-area clubs like the Speakeasy and Mr. Bee's. Afterward, the Wailers were coaxed into the studio to help lay down more tracks with Rabbit for Johnny Nash. Nash's Epic LP, *I Can See Clearly Now*, contained three Marley compositions: "Stir It Up," "Guava Jelly," and "Comma Comma," plus a collaboration with Nash, "You Poured Sugar on Me." "Stir It Up" went to Number 12 on the British surveys in 1972 (and a notch higher in the United States the following year, preceded by the LP's title track, which hit the U.S. top five).

A full-fledged Wailers tour kept being promised but was continually postponed. CBS put out a limited edition of a Marley solo single, "Reggae on Broadway"/"Oh, Lord, I Got to Get There," which sank like a stone. At this point, the Wailers were spending their days rehearsing (mostly to keep warm) in a cellar in Surrey, and their nights first in a cheap hotel in London's West End and then in a cold-water flat on Bayswater. They woke up one morning to discover that Nash and Sims had left to develop new projects amid the sunshine-and-citrus pleasures of Miami, Florida.

Penniless and stranded in a cold, damp country that couldn't have been more alien to their Caribbean temperaments, the Wailers turned to freelance promotion man Brent Clarke (who had been enlisted by Sims to pitch "Reggae on Broadway" in Greater London) to see if anything could be salvaged from the wreckage of their abortive grand tour of the Continent. Clarke sought out Chris Blackwell of Island Records, who had spoken highly of the group in the past and had leased more than a dozen of their Jamaican 45s for U.K. distribution. Blackwell had heard that Bob and his boys were a contrary crew at best, but he listened to Clarke's terms, which boiled down to an advance of approximately £8000 to do their own album. Clarke got his commission and lent the group money for the plane fare home, but the Wailers ultimately decided against signing a management deal with the man who had saved their freezing asses.

Back in the altogether warmer atmosphere of their home island, the Wailers bought studio time at Dynamic and, with Bob supervising, worked quickly and enthusiastically to deliver a serviceable album to Island by year's end.

Bob flew back to England in the winter of 1972 with the masters, walking straight into a legal fray. Sims claimed to retain control of

Bob's destiny. Moreover, CBS insisted Bob was *their* property. A deal was finally struck whereby Sims was reportedly paid £5000 for Marley's release. CBS got $9000 and a 2-percent override on his first six albums. The way was thus cleared, and the Wailers' debut album for Island Records, *Catch a Fire,* was readied for release.

Although they were not credited anywhere on either of the two versions of the record's jacket, the finished product benefited from the creative contributions of a small army of instrumentalists besides Bob, Peter, Bunny and the Barrett brothers.

Famed Muscle Shoals lead guitarist Wayne Perkins was upstairs at Island's Basing Street studios in the spring of 1972, working on a second Smith, Perkins & Smith album with brothers Tim and Steve Smith. Blackwell stepped in and asked the twenty-one-year-old Perkins, "Want to take some time out to do some overdubs in the downstairs studio?"

"Sure," said Perkins. "What kind of stuff is it?"

"Reggae."

"Huh?"

"Reggae. From Jamaica. Bob Marley and the Wailers. You never heard of reggae?"

"Chris, I'm a Birmingham, Alabama, boy. I've never been to Jamaica, man!"

"No problem. I just want some rock-and-roll guitar on three tracks. You'll like the tunes."

Perkins went into the lower studio, and was introduced to an intense black fellow with wild hair named Bob Marley. Perkins couldn't understand anything Marley said, but nodded obligingly as he spoke. Then he put on headphones, and "Concrete Jungle" assaulted his ears. Perkins noodled around as he listened, trying in vain to get a fix on the wiggly beat.

"Don't worry about that," Blackwell shouted from the control room. "Check out the bass line. It plays its own melody and catches up for the upbeat. Just play straight through the breaks."

Perkins nodded and improvised a sinuous, meticulously phrased lead in one take, tagging the track with a flowing dose of feedback that smoothly spanned three octaves. Blackwell was very impressed. Bob went into the studio as the track faded and shook Perkins's hand, thanking him. Perkins was still unable to understand what Bob was saying.

"Listen," Perkins told him, a bit intimidated by the fearsome-looking young dread. "I'm from the South, you're from the islands. But when the tape rolls, we're communicating."

Perkins went on to dub the lead guitar on "Stir It Up" and "Baby, We've Got a Date" and then went back upstairs to finish his album.

Rabbit Bundrick's keyboards, from synthesizer to clavinet, were prominent throughout the nine tracks. Robbie Shakespeare handled the bass on "Concrete Jungle," and Tyrone Downie played organ on that tune and "Stir It Up." Chris Karen, Francisco Willie Pep and Winston Wright all contributed percussion. Female backing vocals were by Rita Marley and her girlfriend Marcia Griffiths, who was a solo star in Jamaica and had done albums and singles with her husband, Bob Andy. Chris Blackwell disentangled, revised and otherwise restructured Bob's primitive mixes and sometimes stiff arrangements.

The original album jacket for *Catch a Fire* was an outsized two-piece cardboard depiction of a stainless steel cigarette lighter, designed by Rod Dyer and Bob Weiner. It had a button hinge, and when you opened it up, you saw a huge cutout of a flaming wick, the record looming behind it. The package got a lot of attention in the music press in Britain—almost as much as the LP itself.

In its April 12, 1973, edition, the white, middle-class American rock journal *Rolling Stone* handed down its verdict on *Catch a Fire*, sandwiched between reviews of *The Best of the James Gang* and the second album by a group called Wild Turkey: "A mature, fully realized sound with a beautiful lyric sensibility that turns well known stylistics into fresh vibrant music. The reggae beat has the capacity to lend direction to the Wailers' music and force limits on their sound. But it is not a mere gimmick, although it could develop into one should it become a rage."

Whether or not such vexatious pitfalls could be sidestepped and the Wailers' mainstream promise reach fulfillment, only time would tell. Sales of *Catch a Fire* initially reached a level (fourteen thousand units) far below the James Gang's album and well above that of Wild Turkey.

Chris Blackwell knew that he needed a sequel to *Catch a Fire* quickly to take advantage of the press interest the album had generated. Publicity and critical acclaim would be essential in making the Wailers' music comprehensible to the outside world.

He also knew he was going to have to get to know Marley better: determine what he wanted from his relationship with Island, explore his feelings about the direction of his career, find out what new songs he had in his head. Although they had worked together getting *Catch a Fire* into shape, they were still practically strangers, and Bob spooked Chris as much as he did just about everyone else he came into contact with. But Blackwell sensed a bond between them: they both had Jamaica in their blood. Blackwell felt that something extraordinary was bound to develop from that first day in 1972 when Marley turned up in his office with the *Catch a Fire* tapes, fresh from the sound boards of Dynamic, Randy's and Harry J's.

Marley had recently resumed growing his locks, and at that stage his hairstyle was not quite an Afro, not quite "natty dread." Brushed back from his forehead, the thick, nappy wave of rust-colored frizzles resembled a disheveled turban. He mumbled a greeting and made some remarks in his squeaky sandpaper tenor about his long plane flight.

"Yuh release me firs' record, yuh nuh," he said evenly.

Blackwell nodded. " 'Judge Not.' I remember. The catalogue number was 88. When we got up to around number 120 or so, I stopped being active in the Jamaican area of Island for a long time and concentrated on pop music."

"Yuh," Bob said absently.

Dressed in the heavy winter clothes that West Indians wear in England irrespective of the season (a yellow and black-checked woolen lumber jacket with a broken zipper, two layers of dark pullover sweaters, jeans, heavy work shoes), Bob appeared as an embodiment of the nicknames that had preceded him: Five Foot Four, Mess, Skipper, Tuff Gong.

He had a lazy stance—a half-slouch to the left, his taut chest thrust forward and his squarish pectoral muscles visible because his sweaters were two sizes too small. His arms hung confidently at his sides, his hands half-closed as if he were just about to lift a set of large suitcases. His legs were springy and slightly bowed, the calves slender with bunchy muscles just below the fisted knees and the thighs uncommonly thick for a man his size. He moved with a bobbing gait, childlike in its earnestness; the pensive face, with the two deep creases stamped above the handsomely sloping nose, didn't seem to jibe with the coltish strut. Apart from a few freckle-sized acne scars in the hollows of his high-boned cheeks, his skin was smooth and lustrous. He had hooded eyes, shellac-brown and shiny, but with black pupils so hard and focused that they sometimes made those in their path feel as if they might be capable of implanting crude puncture marks like a cobbler's awl.

A musty smell clung to him. Some days it was pleasantly piquant, like decaying palm leaves; others it was bland and whiffy, like a shuttered, airless country bungalow suddenly thrown open to the breeze. The uncouth "smuttiness" (aroma) was a consequence of uncounted hours of ganja smoking. So were the two burn scars on his lower lip—one a thin, crescent nick near the center, the other a pinkish notch in the right corner. His long, oval mouth was framed by a delicate mustache that flowed into a wispy jawline beard which all but concealed a prominent Adam's apple. Someone raised in Jamaica, accustomed to grappling with its incorporeal essence and unsettling superstitions, might wonder if Anancy could indeed assume human form.

The Wailers had recently released a single called "Screw Face" on their new Tuff Gong label, headquartered at 127 King Street in Kingston. It was available in England on the Punch label, and it could be heard pulsing incessantly from the shebeens in Stoke Newington, Ladbroke Grove, Notting Hill and Brixton. Dreader than dread, it was a direct challenge to the forces of darkness, to Screwface (Satan) himself, to try and pry Bob away from the militant Rasta gospel he had chosen to adopt. The West Indian selectors in the dank basement clubs liked to spin the song a few times and then leave the dub-wise flip side, "Faceman," on the turntable for hours while the patrons got pixilated on Long Life Lager and seedless "sinsemilla" weed. One locksman after another would take turns chanting Marley's portentous lyrics, which often rang out in the London night like an incantation from the crypt.

The meaning of the song was threefold, referring to Screwface's propensity for scaring those most susceptible to his wiles, to the custom of grimacing fiercely in order to unsettle nighttime bushwhackers who preyed on those caught alone in shantytown's trash-carpeted back alleys, and to the increasingly popular practice among ghetto gangsters of punishing their victims by slicing up their features with a "well-sharp" ratchet.

The song's advice—to have courage in the presence of Screwface—was easier dispensed than taken, and a multileveled menace permeated the inner sanctum of Chris Blackwell's office in St. Peter's Square as Marley slid down to chair level to confer with the white executive who ran Island Records—Bob's own visage now grotesquely contorted to maximum effect.

Easily a head taller than Marley and graced with the reddish-blond hair, bright blue eyes, ruddy complexion and soft-spoken self-assurance of the Anglo-Jamaican planter class, Blackwell felt that Marley was coiled to strike but holding back, like a good street scrapper does before letting fly with his sucker punch. But once they became immersed in conversation about the matters at hand, Bob's hard look melted and the force field emanating from him vanished with a suddenness that almost made Blackwell's ears pop. Chris was not unaccustomed to the sensation of abrupt decompression when dealing with ghetto Rastas, having confronted their customarily pugnacious opening gambit many times before.

Chris had had close contacts with dreadlocked sufferahs since he was in his twenties. On a sunny afternoon back in 1958, while enjoying a morning of motorboating with a buddy and his girlfriend out past Bush Reef, near the Hellshire beaches, they had developed engine trouble. They drifted into the razory teeth of a coral reef and then managed to ditch the gnashed-up boat on a sandbar before swimming to shore. Chris's buddy volunteered to go for help and spent six fruitless hours plowing through scrub brush and prickly reeds looking for a road out of the remote swampy region. He returned to the beach; it was Blackwell's turn.

Chris took a piss into the steamy shallows and then began to walk the endless beach, following the shoreline, the afternoon sun snarling down on his bare back, the flies ravenous. He was dehydrated, badly sunburned and nearly exhausted when he came upon a low-lying hut inhabited by a Rasta fisherman, who offered him a cup of fresh water. Motioning Blackwell into his home, he indicated his pallet and the young white man laid down and dropped into a deep sleep. When he awoke, it was night, and there were seven other Rasta fishermen and a small child scattered around him in the shack, their ebony faces burnished by the firelight, horns of matted hair jutting from their temples, much longer clumps draped over their shoulders and trailing in the sand.

Blackwell was petrified, having always been led to believe that Rastas were racist lunatics and murderers. But this group behaved most cordially when they saw him stir, welcoming him with a buzz of concordant greetings, offering roast silver shad on a gray piece of plank, and chatting colorfully about the Bible. He had been in the village about twelve hours when they escorted him to one of their dugouts and paddled him the five miles to Port Royal, where he got help in retrieving the disabled boat and his companions.

The experience had left an indelible impression on the well-to-do Britisher. He learned something else about the Rastas the following year while he was running a business renting motor scooters in Kingston: the Rastas were the only ones who puttered by regularly to pay up. So when he entered the Jamaican record business in 1959, he made a point of investigating the Rastas' ideological and social influences on ska, rock steady and reggae, believing the heroic, principled passivity of the sect to be the source of many of the music's more appealing permutations. Like the rest of the island's institutions, Jamaican music seemed to be ceaselessly reinventing itself in order to retain the prerogative of remaining essentially the same. It was "a sound dat stand him ground!" in Prince Buster's words, and Rasta had slowly become the mortar in the foundation.

Although based in London, Chris kept abreast of the island runnings, making frequent trips to Kingston to find out who was in the vanguard of reggae's crackling evolution, and he had learned that—after various commercial ups and downs, coupled with some queer goings-on in obeah quarters—the Wailers were back on top. "Dem de joint in Jamdung," as Kingston radio DJ Don Topping put it.

But the Wailers were something more than a rejuvenated hit factory, once more pleasing the bad boys who liked to jerk in time and sheg their stuckies to the motion of the cuckie skank down in the Dungle's cockroach-ridden bedrooms. These breddahs were bringing about the first glimmerings of a fundamental change in the Jamaican attitude toward their music. Led by Marley, they were reaching out in an organic sense, aiming their undiluted dreadrock at the outside world, defiant in their crazy belief that Rasta reggae was not parochial, not just shantytown sankeys for pariahs—that it was music that could interpret, explain and beat back the planet's moral turpitude and racial oppression. There was a single, wailful, searing sufferah's voice inside their sound, and it was being raised to serve notice on all those who knew nothing of Trench Town and rude boys, chillum pipes and chuckie-fockin' that reggae was the overture to the Apocalypse. *Well-sharp.*

The concept was more than a little bit outlandish, thought Blackwell at the time, but it was certainly something new under the sun. For his part, Blackwell believed that Marley was the only figure in Jamaica remotely capable of having a lasting impact on mainstream popular music, the only one with the charisma to back up his atypical talent. As for the weird, preternatural Rasta message threaded through the riddim, it would have to take care of itself—just as it always had.

Only a Jamaican would be eccentric enough to conceive of such a campaign. Only an Englishman would be arrogant enough to try to execute it. Only a unreconstructed misfit with cash to bash would have the free time to bother. Blackwell filled the bill. Like Marley, he was his own brand of eerie hybrid.

And he had a healthy respect for native mysticism. In 1961, confused about his future, he had consulted a Kingston myalwoman. She read his palm, judged the signs and told Blackwell to stick with the record business. He didn't dare ignore her advice.

Born on June 22, 1937, in London, Blackwell was descended from moneyed merchant stock. His Irish father, Joseph Blackwell, had circuitous blood ties to the Crosse & Blackwell foodstuffs and tinned-goods fortune. The ancestral wealth was too distant to bank, but near enough to trade on, and his mother's side of the family took advantage of the proximity.

Blanche Lindo was a descendant of Sephardic Jews who, fleeing the Portuguese chapter of the Inquisition, had settled in Jamaica in 1743. The Lindos bartered coconuts for cattle, tea and spices for land and hard currency, but it was the decision to traffic in rum in the eighteenth century that solidified the fortunes of the family.

So much so that by the time Omeriah Malcolm, for example, was old enough to freely refresh himself with the stomach-scalding beverage, he was drinking their brand. This was not some passable-in-a-pinch potable like Private Vat, a Planter's Punch elixir like Myer's or a high grade of bellywash like Charley's Old Jamaican Rum. This was none other than the island's rum of choice: Appleton—Appleton Reserve, Appleton Special, Appleton White, Appleton Punch, Appleton 151. The Lindos' liquor concession was the Caribbean equivalent of the passkey to King Solomon's Mines.

The descendants of the distilleries' founders had dispersed in various directions by the 1930s, each taking a parcel of the ongoing enterprise with them, but the center held. And so it happened that when Christopher Blackwell was brought to Jamaica at six months of age, he was carried by his parents into the luxurious confines of the Terra Nova, a mansion in an affluent Kingston suburb, where he was looked after by butlers, maids and nannies as only a rich child can be (much as Cecil Vernor Lindo had raised Blanche in Devon House).

After nine and a half years of genteel opulence, undercut by bouts with acute bronchial asthma, he was dispatched to Catholic St.

Peter's Preparatory, Broadstairs, and then to Harrow, a distinguished "public" (a typically British inversion of the term) school. He quit in 1955, bouncing from a flirtation with accounting to the gambler's life to the record business, with a notable side trip into the world of cinema. Ian Fleming, a friend of Blanche Blackwell, recommended twenty-four-year-old Chris for a job working as a go-fer for producer Harry Saltzman on the location set for *Dr. No*. After the movie was wrapped, Saltzman offered Chris a more permanent position in his production company, then scheduled to transform Fleming's entire James Bond series into feature films. It was at this juncture that Blackwell went to the fortune-teller for a consultation.

In May 1962, Blackwell collected $5300 from backers and established Island Records, Ltd., as a licensing agent and U.K. distribution outlet for leading Jamaican records. This put him in competition with the Melodisc label (founded in 1946 to import American jazz, and moving into R&B and ska in the late 1950s), Sonny Roberts's Planetone Records and the small but important Pama label. In Island's first year it netted $8000, distributing its records from the back seat of Chris's blue Mini-Cooper. Chris made lots of contacts, and almost as many mistakes (his first few Maytals releases were mislabeled "The Vikings," so they had to perform under that name when they did some club dates in London), but he worked hard enough to drive Planetone, which had office space in the same building on Cambridge Road in Kilburn, London, out of business.

In 1968, Blackwell merged his business with B&C Records, another licensing firm run by East Indian accountant Lee Goptal; they called the new company Trojan Records. They handled virtually all the releases generated by the leading Jamaican labels and/or their producers: Upsetter, Duke Reid, Harry J, Joe, Clandisc, Treasure Isle, Rio, Doctor Bird, Leslie Kong, Coxsone Dodd—a total of more than fifty.

But as Trojan prospered, it grew unwieldy, its own managerial difficulties complicated by the internecine practices of Jamaican producers. They were continually slipping into London to sign additional deals with smaller labels, or making deals with labels already under contract to Trojan for non-Trojan licensing that would nonetheless be distributed by Trojan, or B&C, or Island, etc.

No one could figure out who was selling, licensing, distributing what, and Trojan Records eventually toppled of its own weight. (It would later be revived under new management.) Blackwell had quietly

The Wailers, June 1980. Top row, left to right: Tyrone Downie, Junior Marvin, Earl "Wire" Lindo, Alvin "Seeco" Patterson. Bottom row, left to right: Carlton "Carly" Barrett, Bob Marley, Al Anderson, Aston "Family Man" Barrett. ADRIAN BOOT

Bob Marley, performing at the "One Love" Peace Concert, April 22, 1978. PETER SIMON

Bob Marley singing "Redemption Song" on the last tour, 1980. PETER SIMON

The Commodores with Bob Marley, Madison Square Garden, 1980.
CHUCK PULIN/STARFILE

Left to right: Rita Marley, Chris Blackwell, Cedella Marley celebrate 10 million unit sales of *Legend*, the most popular reggae album in history, 1994. CHUCK PULIN/STARFILE

Some of the Marley children, at Cedella Booker's house in Miami, 1982. Clockwise from top left: David ("Ziggy"), Sharon, Stephanie, Cedella, Jah Nesta, Julian, Karen, Ky-mani. PETER SIMON

Bob's children by Rita Marley, on the front steps of Tuff Gong Records (formerly Island House), 1980. Clockwise from top: Cedella, David ("Ziggy"), Stephanie and Stephen. PETER SIMON

Bob Marley talking with police on the morning of the "One Love" Peace Concert, April 22, 1978. ADRIAN BOOT

Bob Marley induces Prime Minister Michael Manley (far left) and Jamaican Labour Party leader Edward Seaga (far right) to shake hands at the "One Love" Peace Concert, April 22, 1978. CHUCK PULIN/STARFILE

Bob Marley and Claudie Massop, several days before the "One Love" Peace Concert. ADRIAN BOOT

Poster for the "One Love" Peace Concert. PETER SIMON

Opposite: Bob Marley, wearing Haile Selassie's ring. ADRIAN BOOT

Bob Marley, September 1980, the evening after he collapsed in Central Park. STEVE BERMAN

Bob Marley, his dreadlocks gone due to radiation treatments, at the Bavarian clinic of Dr. Josef Issels, March 1981.
TRANSWORLD/LONDON DAILY MAIL

withdrawn from this byzantine superstructure of soon-come Babylon samfai men just before the end came, and he had significant rock-and-roll involvements to fall back on. After he had agreed to manage the Spencer Davis Group during the heyday (1964) of the British Invasion, they had charged up the international pop charts and generated the seed money for other auspicious signings, most of them of so-called progressive Anglo rock acts: Free, Traffic (when Steve Winwood left Spencer Davis), Jethro Tull, John Martyn, Fairport Convention, Spooky Tooth, King Crimson, Emerson, Lake and Palmer, Cat Stevens, Richard and Linda Thompson, Roxy Music. From 1969 to 1972, Island devoted itself almost exclusively to rock, with Jimmy Cliff being one of the few reggae artists to command its full attention.

In 1971, Blackwell had finally gotten his feet wet in the film business by investing in director Perry Henzell's *The Harder They Come* (originally titled *You Can Get It If You Really Want*), a movie about the life and death of Rhyging, the immortal Kingston outlaw. Actually Blackwell put up only $3000 of the approximately $200,000 required to make the picture. His contribution was getting Jimmy Cliff the leading role. Cliff bowed out of his contract with Island when the title song of the film, the single from the soundtrack album, did poorly in 1972. If it hadn't been Bob Marley's luck to get stuck in London without two shillings to rub together, Island Records might have withdrawn permanently from the reggae arena.

"Why," Blackwell asked Bob, "did you name the group the Wailers?"

" 'Cause as yout's we begin like dem people inna de Bible, wha' gwan de Exodus."

"I don't understand," said Blackwell.

"We call ourselves de Wailers," said Marley, his keen eyes luminous, "because we started out cryin'."

Before *Catch a Fire*, all ska, rock steady and reggae albums were semiannual compendiums of a hot artist's singles, or samplers of a leading Kingston studio's most successful songs, assembled by the producers out of garden-variety avarice and the most transparent vanity. Just to get Coxsone Dodd's goat, Duke Reid would knock out a "Burning Hot Hits" repackaging with a cover featuring a color photo of a stark-naked white girl wriggling inside a blazing furnace. Dodd, who blushed red as ripe ackee at such immodesties, would retaliate with "Hot Shot Ska," or "Alton Ellis Sings Rock and Soul," with jacket art as boring as Reid's was ribald.

When *Catch a Fire* appeared, Kingston artists were beside themselves with envy that a group should get such exalted treatment. In Britain, rattled West Indian immigrants swore off ganja for a week, convinced they had somehow spaced out and missed a year of Wailers 45s.

The Wailers toured England and the States in 1973 to support *Catch a Fire*, and Cedella, husband Edward Booker, Pearl, and their two boys, Richard, six, and Anthony, three, all came up from Wilmington to New York City in the summer to hear the group play at Max's Kansas City on Park Avenue South. The Wailers did three half-hour sets, sharing the bill with a band led by some guy from South Jersey named Springsteen. After the last show, there was a party in Brooklyn, and Ciddy and Edward got to meet Rita's dad, Papa Roy Anderson, who was in from Stockholm. Everybody was in a grand mood, in-laws chuckling because little Richard couldn't pronounce his stepbrother's name ("Nester! Nester! Me sing yuh songs in me firs' grade class at George Grey Elementary School!").

As the erratically booked tour progressed, the Wailers did one date in an ice rink in Las Vegas in October 1973, opening for the Atlee Yeager Band, with Sly and the Family Stone headlining. Much of the audience thought the Wailers were the old Tacoma, Washington, instrumental surfing band that had a hit in 1959 with "Tall Cool One." But the jaws of those well-scrubbed Nevada teens dropped down below the bleachers when Bob and the boys came out and tore into "Concrete Jungle," drums and bass riding on the one-drop, while the chicka-chicka rhythm guitar fed the Slinky-toy tempo, slipping down for the upstroke, and this skinny black Medusa stepped up to the mike and whooped about how the tables were being turned on the modern slavedrivers of the world—they were going to catch Jah's fire!

"Holy shit! What country are those guys *from*?" the drummer for Atlee Yeager asked the drummer in Sly's band. "They look like they're something out of the Old Testament!"

After this date (one of five with Sly), the Wailers were thrown off the tour; they had made far too big an impression on the crowd for a warm-up act. "Sly don't dig that," said the Family Stone's manager.

Joe Higgs was called in to replace Bunny on vocals and percussion when Livingston decided he couldn't take the cold north winds, but not before the Wailers had appeared on *The Old Grey Whistle Test* TV program in London. Bunny was resplendent in a red, green and gold sweater, his locks topped by a foppish maroon fez, as he played congas and percussion on "Concrete Jungle" and "Stir It Up."

It was the only Wailers roadtrip Bunny would ever make. The group was just gaining some recognition outside of Jamaica, but already a tight boyhood alliance was beginning to blister at the seams. Peter attributed it to Chris Blackwell (he sneeringly called him "Chris Whiteworst"), saying Chris had in mind from the start that he was signing not "the Wailers" but rather "*Bob Marley* and the Wailers."

"Who mek dat distinction, suh?!" Peter would shout backstage after shows, but never to Bob's face. "Who set one mon apart from Wailers an' mek one t'ing become two separate t'ing? Ta fockin' raas wit' dis bullrush, pussy clot double-billin'!"

In truth, it was Lee Perry who began the practice of releasing records with the "Bob Marley and . . ." designation, since the group had reorganized in 1969 around Marley's material. Yet when Perry authorized Trojan to reissue *Soul Rebels* and *Soul Revolution I* in 1974 as *Rasta Revolution* and *African Herbsman*, it was Perry himself who was credited as the author of "Duppy Conqueror," "Keep On Moving," "Don't Rock the Boat," "Kaya," "Stand Alone," "Fussing and Fighting," "Put It On," "Brain Washing," "All in One." This indiscretion would never be repeated. Six months after the albums' release in England, Bob walked into a record store on Kingston's Half Way Tree Road, spied an oddly familiar illustration on a jacket sitting in a bin, picked it up, and yelled, *"Shit! Dat motherfocker!"*

Bob went directly to Perry's house and had it out with him, the two wiry men screaming at each other in front of the framed pictures of Yul Brynner in *The Magnificent Seven* that hung over the china cabinet in Lee's living room, while his wife and kids cowered in the back bedroom. There was something predictably manic about Perry that charmed Marley, however; and his eccentric habit of planting his latest records in the gardens around his house, surrounding them with hand-painted plants, seemed to confirm the deep commitment, however unorthodox, he felt toward his artists. Even though Bob left Washington Gardens with money clenched in his fist and shattered crockery in his wake, the two were as blood brothers by the next day, hugging and laughing and slapping each other on the back as they outlined new songs to "mosh up de nation."

But Peter Tosh refused to settle his differences with Bob, and

Bob was openly hurt by all that he knew Peter was thinking and feeling. The awkwardness and unexpressed bitterness accumulated.

It got particularly awkward because Bob would forget all about the smoldering tension between them as he became more and more absorbed in his writing, only to be confronted at jagged moments by a sulfurous jealousy. Bob was just beginning to find solace in Rasta, and Rasta didn't dip and kass-kass. Bunny loved them both and didn't want to be in the middle; being a Wailer had grown chilly enough for him as it was.

In the early 1970s, Chris Blackwell bought a run-down great house at 56 Hope Road in uptown Kingston. It was a two-story jalousied building set back from the road behind rusty iron gates. In back of the main building were several acres of propery bisected by a rambling succession of shacks, sheds and decrepit carriage houses.

The palatially shabby complex was just down the street from both the prime minister's residence and Devon House, a showpiece of colonial architecture built in 1881 by a millionaire who had made his bucks in South America. Now an official landmark, Devon House was the preferred site for fashion shows and "ethnic dance concerts" sponsored by the society ladies of St. Andrew.

Blackwell's new address, renamed Island House, was the command post for his expanding reggae interests in Kingston. It was also an attempt to put down some new roots of his own in Jamaica. When the Terra Nova had been sold in 1960, his mother retreated to Bolt House, a North Coast mansion built on a sweeping lawn overlooking the sea in Port Maria. Blanche Blackwell had also let go of the family's summer retreat in the Blue Mountains—a large hilltop cottage in an area called Greenwich, not far from Newcastle, an old cliffside fort high in the mists where the Jamaica Defense forces trained, and Red Light, the village where the off-duty soldiers did their whoring.

Although the record business had been good to him, Chris was in need of personal renewal, having been through an unsuccessful marriage with Josephine Heimann, the wealthy ex-wife of one of his best friends, David Heimann. And then there had been an extended affair with Esther Anderson, a beautiful mulatto Jamaican film actress from the village of Esher, St. Marys. The daughter of an East Indian mother and a prominent white Jamaican architect, Esther had starred in such British films as *The Touchables* (1968), and had just completed shooting on *A Warm December*, playing opposite Sidney Poitier, who also directed the film.

Besides being prime real estate, Island House was a sentimental choice for a new base in uptown Kingston, since it was just a five-minute drive from the Terra Nova. And to compensate for the loss of the beloved retreat in Greenwich, Chris had Strawberry Hill, a rambling estate in the Blue Mountains which was perched on a knoll midway between Irish Town (where the retired Bustamante lived) and Newcastle. From the back porch of the run-down planter's house in the center of the grounds, he could glimpse the old cottage through the slow-drifting cloud cover.

Bob had begun to frequent Island House late in 1972 and was plainly covetous of the place. Surprisingly, Blackwell seemed to enjoy this. By the time *Catch a Fire* was released, he had made a deal with Blackwell whereby he would eventually take over the property so that he would have a proper address at which to meet and greet the press. He moved in with several dread brethren and Lee Jaffe, a white American musician-filmmaker who had met Bob in New York City through Jim Capaldi of Traffic. Lee and Bob had hit it off immediately and traveled down to Carnival in Trinidad on a chartered DC-3 with Chris Blackwell, Esther and Capaldi. Bob and Lee wrote a nonsense song together called "Trinidad, We Don't Like Your Carnival," when they discovered the scarcity of ganja during the rum-drenched celebration. Esther was amused by Lee and rather taken with Bob, and eventually joined them at Hope Road.

Word spread around Trench Town that the Tuff Gong had moved to a big white house uptown, but nobody would believe it. A contingent of dreads went up to check for themselves one morning, and when they saw Bob sitting on the veranda strumming his guitar, some white woman massaging his shoulders, they got "bringly" (irritated) *ta raas* and commenced vexing something fierce. Bob had to go down to Rema and explain himself. He got a fairly cool reception when he told the gang that his house was theirs too, and that they were free to come and go as they pleased. But the brethren didn't especially feature walking four miles just to "rest I head" in the courtyard of some long-dead slave driver's old digs. And if they did make the trek, they often found that all the shady places on the grounds were already taken by Bob's new friends. No one could puzzle out how he had made so many new acquaintances so swiftly. But there they were—fancy-looking women in designer jeans and silk blouses, white guys with British accents and gold cigarette lighters, brown dudes poppin' style in aviator shades and forty-dollar slacks that they couldn't possibly have purchased in Kingston. Bob explained that they all worked for the record company and most of them split at the end of the day. The Rema crowd figured that was cool—sorta.

Bob and Rita were raising a family. Cedella had been born in 1967, David in 1968. Bob said he wanted to " 'ave as many child as dere were shells on de beach." (The beach they went to nowadays was the one at Bull Bay, located about six miles outside of Kingston.)

Bob was a quality Rastaman now, committed to good health and an ital life-style that stressed a daily regime of exercise. He liked to rise before the sun, asking his ghetto buddy Antonio "Gilly" Gilbert, who was also his resident ital cook, to fix him a cup of bush tea, either mint or cerasee (a seeded vine that when boiled produces a bitter tea said to be good for clearing the blood). After that he'd roll a sleek spliff, take up his guitar and put out a nice vibe, and then begin "ta work fe stamina."

His many companions in these activities, besides Lee, Esther and Gilly, included Bunny and a new breddah named Alan "Skill" Cole. Gilly was a respected local soccer player, often called "General G'wan" or "Stonewall Jackson" because of his no-nonsense ball handling. Alan, on the other hand, was a professional footballer and coach of international renown—on a par, some said, with Pelé—and the only dread on the heavyweight soccer circuit when Bob first checked fe him.

A close, even symbiotic relationship had existed between Jamaican footballers, musicians and gunmen for as far back as the ghetto brethren could recall. But there had never been so prestigious and powerful a combination as Skilly Cole and Bob Marley, and the gunmen involved in the violent political tug-of-war between the JLP and the PNP that was being called "Heavy Manners" and the "Final Battle for Jamaica" completed an awesome, unholy trinity. There is a sphinx in Egyptian mythology from which the Greeks fashioned the composite beast they called Chimera. The ghastly creature had a lion's head, a goat's body and a serpent's tail. Bob was the lion in the Jamaican Chimera, Skilly the kicking goat, the gunmen the nested snakes.

Family Man Barrett went to see Bob at Island House one afternoon with a fragment of a song he was working up for the band that went "Now you get/What you want/Do you want more?" Bob was intrigued; several days later, Family Man had another couplet: "You think it's the end/But it's just the beginning." Sitting on the veranda, Bob suggested putting the lyrics together in the same song. Family Man smiled.

"Who the cap fit," said Bob, surveying the grounds of his uptown estate, "let dem wear it."

The house at 56 Hope Road was destined to be the spot where all curses and spells, all follies and dreams, all hopes and hungers, all hatreds and horrors would reach their apotheosis for Robert Nesta Marley. It was the hour of the Dark Sphinx—the Chimera. Prophecy would be fulfilled.

14

Who the Cap Fit

The routine was always the same: everybody would try to get up in the morning before Bob, but no one ever did. Some would attempt to outlast him the night before, but that never worked, either. It was uncanny; Bob was always the last to take to his little mattress in his upstairs bedroom (bare except for a portrait of Selassie hanging on the wall) and the first to awake. If everybody passed out around 3:00 A.M., Bob was asleep at 3:15; if one of the dreads lasted until first light, Bob did too. If Bob had to miss his sleep entirely to maintain the upper hand, he did and seemed none the worse for wear.

From 1973 on, the elite dread crew around Hope Road consisted of Bunny; Alan "Skilly" Cole; Antonio "Gilly" Gilbert; Neville Garrick, a graduate of the UCLA College of Fine Arts (and disciple of Angela Davis) who had returned to Jamaica in 1973 to be an art director for the *Jamaica Daily News*, but met Bob and became Tuff Gong Records' resident designer; Bird, a soft-spoken ghetto breddah of Bob's; the Wailers band. Others included Lee Jaffe, Alvin "Seeco" Patterson and keyboard player Earl "Wire" Lindo, another Kingstonian; Rita and the kids; Diane Jobson, Bob's lawyer and confidante; ravishing model Cindy Breakspeare; Virginia Burke, who was a friend of Cindy's from London; Esther Anderson; guitarist Ben "Sticko" Mitchell, Bob's informal male secretary; Lips, his sometime bodyguard; assorted dreads from shantytown just passing through to draw on the chillum, plus a steady trickle of attractive young women, most of whom were known only by their first names, but a few, like Lucien Pounder and Yvette Morris-Anderson (no relation to Rita or Esther), were treated with greater deference because of their closeness to Bob.

Peter visited occasionally with his girlfriend, Evonne. Chris Blackwell was constantly in and out, sometimes with his second wife, the former Marilyn Richards, or with his best friend, Dickie Jobson (Diane's brother), who was the sometime manager of the Wailers. Increasingly, Chris either stayed at one of the two hotels (the Kingston Sheraton and the Pegasus) in the fenced-in, guard dog-patrolled New Kingston tourist compound or at remote Strawberry Hill.

Regardless of the previous night's activities (which always centered on smoking herb, singing songs and discussing Selassie), Bob, Bunny, Skilly, Sticko, Lips, Gilly and Bird would be ready at sunrise for a jog, usually on the sprawling Jamaica House grounds near the police officers' club or at the field site of the Water Commission near Hope Road. But this was merely an "open-yeyes" sprint. If Bob was in the mood "fe discipline in stamina," then everybody would follow as he led the way along Hope Road and down Mountain View Avenue onto Windward Road, heading in the direction of the airport. At the traffic circle, the group would hook a right, and move out, running abreast along the Palisadoes peninsula, for as long as anyone could stand it.

On Sundays, the jogging entourage might go the whole eighteen-odd miles to Port Royal Point, their lengthening locks dancing in the wind. If they hadn't arranged for a car to pick them up, they'd hike back and pile into Bob's car for a drive to Bull Bay, where they'd wash themselves in the Cane River Falls, scrubbing each other's locks, and then position themselves in the roaring falls so that the torrents pounded against their chests and backs. Next they'd ride to Papine Market, and Gilly would select the day's produce: calaloo, pop-chow (a Chinese vegetable akin to Swiss chard), okra, yams, mangoes, citrus, bananas, plantains, gungo peas, rice, sweet potatoes, guava, pawpaw (papaya), cassava, breadfruit, ackee, arrowroot, avocado. Gilly would also purchase some snapper, kingfish, goatfish and doctor fish. For juices, Bob himself would choose the carrots, soursop and Irish moss, a type of seaweed used for making a sweet, gelatinous drink believed to encourage the libido. ("It mek yuh cum taste sweet, yahso!" according to Bob.) Everything would be stuffed into the car and taken back to Hope Road, where Gilly would prepare for a communal "ninyam" (meal). If they were feeling "ninyam-surrey" (hungry enough to devour the whole county of Surrey), he'd prepare an ital feast, the consumption of which would take up most of the rest of the day.

If the band wasn't recording or rehearsing, everyone just milled around the Hope Road complex until Bob organized the afternoon soccer game. If there weren't enough breddahs on hand for two full teams, the game took place informally on the front lawn at Hope Road. Conventional eleven-against-eleven matches were played on the Boy's Town field or on the police depot grounds in Rae Town. Bob played inside right and was a strong darter and dribbler who preferred passing over shooting; he left the scoring to Alan, whom he idolized. Cole was a native of East Kingston who had left his roots there years before to play for the Boy's Town team in West Kingston—a very controversial move in a city that takes both neighborhood loyalties and football quite seriously. In the early 1970s he had gone to Brazil to play, and then returned to lead the Jamaica Santos team. When he and Bob got chummy, the entire country took notice, their "football friendship" imitated by many boys in the ghetto, who referred to their own best buddies (a la Mutt and Jeff) as "Gong" or "Skilly."

The early Hope Road scene could be described as a non-dogmatic religious hippie commune, with an abundance of food, herb, children, music and casual sex. Jamaica being a country with a small but obsessively ambitious middle class, the American hippie movement did not arrive on the island for quite some time. It was not until well-to-do, hardcore hippie vagabonds who had survived the late 1960s began to make their way to ready-made paradises like Maui, St. Martin, St. Bart's and other tropical islands in the early 1970s that they discovered Jamaica. These tanned young haves who masqueraded as have-nots established beachheads and campsites between Port Maria and Port Antonio on the North Coast, and in the Chicken Lavish area of Negril, which was adjacent to Bloody Bay and Long Bay on the South Coast.

There seemed to be a superficial affinity between rich hippies and Rastas, the former having inherited the means to turn their backs on much of society, the latter having inherited the conviction. The Rastaman knew he had no choice; the hippies, full of themselves, said the same thing as they sat half-naked on the patio at Rick's Café and sipped rum punch. Young middle- and upper-class Jamaicans were drawn to these hot spots and happenings, and they began to mimic the appearance of Rastas—but they completely disregarded the strict dietary rules, the religious beliefs and the humility of the authentic dreads. Rude boys did likewise. Eventually, these two groups of quasi-dreads began to trip on acid, share the rum bottle, sprinkle opium into their spliffs and cruise the hippie strongholds in search of various kinds of action.

Jamaica had been trying to shake off the Caribbean malaise and establish itself in the world community since the days of Norman Manley and Bustamante. To this end, the government had undertaken a highly aggressive tourist campaign in the late 1960s, hoping to lure businessmen who would want to hold sales conferences at the island's hotels, purchase land along its coasts, and invite other investors and real estate speculators to help develop a poor but beautiful island that was not plagued with the population density and dictatorial oppression of other island nations in the area.

But these promotional campaigns succeeded mostly in attracting American hippies, who in turn were discovering and celebrating the *last* aspect of Jamaican culture the government wanted to promote: the Rastafarians—a murky, mystical cult composed of sufferahs who were praying every day for the whole island to sink into the sea in a hail of fire and brimstone, while the rest of the population was praying for Tappan ranges, color TV and young doctors and lawyers who would marry their sons and daughters.

In 1974, an event occurred that was to shake the tiny island to its foundations like a second Hurricane Hattie. Bob Marley and the Wailers had gone back into Harry J's studio in the summer of 1973 and emerged by year's end with a new LP, entitled *Burnin'*. Shipped to America and Europe, it was the first completely unique musical offering to arrive in record stores since the Beatles' *Sgt. Pepper's Lonely Hearts Club Band*. The Beatles album had generated considerable outrage in the straight world because of its apparent LSD boosterism ("Lucy in the Sky with Diamonds"). But that was a mild snit compared to the underground furor set off by the release of *Burnin'*. On the back cover of the LP was a photo of Bob, dreadlocks *ta raas*, drawing on a spliff as big as an ice cream cone. Inside were color photos of shantytown street life, of men and boys of all ages who also sported locks, of good-looking Bob Marley and his trim and fit band members wearing red, green and gold tams and passing joints in front of their King Street record shop. The record itself was filled with dangerous, wailing Black Power songs like "I Shot the Sheriff," "Burnin' and Lootin'," and the real sizzler, "Get Up, Stand Up."

A lot of people believed that a Mau Mau–inspired cult of demonic antiwhite murderers had been uncovered in the Caribbean. The music conjured up images of white tourists being hacked to death on the fringes of tropical golf courses.

Soon everyone (not unlike the two drummers on the Sly Stone tour) began demanding to know who the hell these snake-haired specimens from the Gone World *were*. Paul McCartney himself popped up in a British newspaper to nonchalantly explain that the Wailers were a reggae group that played "tighten-up music," as the British kids called it. McCartney added that reggae was "where it's at!"

Not only that, noted another British tabloid, but when Mick Jagger married Bianca, he had a reggae band (the Greyhounds) play at the reception. And even America's own Paul Simon had headed down to Kingston to do some recording.

The American press, which had been napping when *Catch a Fire* appeared, now began running long, detailed pieces on this Jamaican cult that salaamed in front of icons of an Ethiopian despot and smoked more pot than the populations of Haight-Ashbury and Greenwich Village combined. It was a good story, writers and editors agreed—irresistibly screwy, but falling right in line with the rest of the cult stories they'd been uncovering: the Manson family, the Lyman family, the Children of God, the acid churches, the suburban witch covens. Only this story was set on a nicely exotic island, and lent itself to eye-popping graphics. Pillars of communities from Manchester to Memphis were lining up to express their outrage, and the Wailers were in the eye of the gathering storm, which was rolling back toward Jamaica, building strength with every league.

But the grim realities behind the media blitz remained long after the silliness had evaporated and the ambulance chasers of the Fourth Estate had moved on to exploit the rumors about snuff movies and the pestilence of punk rock. A delicate balance on the highly explosive Caribbean island had been tipped in a lethal direction.

Jamaican society unfolded the *Gleaner* (or *The New York Times* and the Miami *Herald*, flown in from Florida) one morning to realize that a Rastafarian had suddenly become one of the best-known figures in the Third World. He was quoted like a poet, heralded as the Mick

Jagger of reggae, the West Indian Bob Dylan, even the Jamaican Jomo Kenyatta. Yet he was not a politician, not a statesman, not a business executive, not a scholar. He was a sufferah. A guitar-strummin' street urchin. The product of the dalliance of a horny white captain in the West India Regiment and a bungo-bessy from the bush.

And this Rasta's brethren, who refused to lift a finger for their country, who declined to hold a job or use birth control or honor any civilized institution within its borders, who wanted little more than a zinc sheet over their heads, a keen-edged cutlass, a dugout that didn't leak and a full pipe of "collie weed" (ganja)—*they* had been rewarded with international recognition, as poets and philosophers! And their own Bob Marley was being called a "black prince"! "We work and sweat for generations to pull this misbegotten slave depot out of the stone age!" Jamaica's leaders howled. "We knock ourselves out to gain respect as an emerging nation raised on hopes and dreams and blessed with skills and diligence, and these fuck-a-bush ghetto rats crawl out of their outhouses and hillside lean-tos to hum a few bars of some gully ditty, and they get sainted, turned into royalty, *lionized*!"

If the church leaders had ever longed to damn every rope-tressed pagan peasant to a Hell on earth; if the politicians had ever begged for permission to bulldoze and flatten every ghetto shanty, inhabitants included; if the police, who detested the poor (the Rasta poor, above all others), had ever schemed to send a Mark 7 bullet through the skull of every God-cursed man, woman and child who clung to the Rasta's bungle-in-the-jungle creed—these upholders of Jamaican "dignity" most certainly joined together now with one shrieking accord.

But the situation was far worse than that, because the Rastas had been drawn into the political arena and had become a significant political force. That outrage had been orchestrated by none other than Michael Manley, the fair-skinned pretty-boy son of Norman Manley. To Michael's mind, Bustamante and his henchmen had broken his father's heart and sent him to the grave regretting that he had not been allowed to serve as Jamaica's first prime minister when independence, which he had done so much to bring about, was finally granted. Employing demagoguery, inflammatory rhetoric and cheap show-biz charisma on a scale that made Bustamante himself envious, the junior Manley, brash standard-bearer of the opposition party, had conspired to take back the government from the JLP. And he did it by manipulating the growing Rastafarian population.

In plotting his retribution, Michael had taken a page out of Edward Seaga's political handbook. He organized in the ghetto, winning the hearts and minds of Seaga's natural constituency: the Rasta slum musicians whose records Edward had once produced. Manley had wrangled an invitation to visit Jah Selassie I in Ethiopia and returned with an elaborate miniature walking stick the emperor had given him as a token of his esteem. In Trench Town, that was the only imprimatur Manley required, but he went much further than that.

Christening the staff the "Rod of Correction," Manley had taken it into the hills, out on the savannas and into the lowliest lanes of the Dungle, where even the goats didn't graze. The superstitious peasants and Rasta sufferahs turned out by the thousands to kneel and *kiss* the relic, tearfully thanking Michael as if he were Joshua reincarnated. There were scenes of adulation among the working-class population that were wholly unprecedented in Jamaican political history. The PNP, out of touch with the grass roots since the mid-1950s, was mounting a comeback of truly Mosaic proportions.

Seaga, the JLP's minister of finance and economic "miracle worker," had waited his entire life for the day that "Busta" would bow out and his successor, Hugh Shearer, would pave the way for his own entry to Jamaica House. Despite disclosures of corruption in his low-level government, the incumbent Shearer could boast of an admirable record of achievement, not the least of which was the consolidation, in concert with Seaga, of Jamaica's financial and administrative infrastructure. They had established a food-processing industry, instituted massive public works projects, attracted important manufacturing interests, directed major tax reform to curb rampant corporate and upper-class income tax evasion and taken significant steps toward modernizing the economy. The country was in the hands of a distinguished statesman who deserved reelection, and Seaga had earned the right to be next in line.

Nonetheless, Manley was a virtual shoo-in, due to his canny adoption of the Rod of Correction as a symbol of the moral rearmament he supposedly wished to bring to Jamaican society. He had vowed to stamp out the rude boys' reign of terror and dismantle the underground gambling network in the island, from peaka-peow games to the national lottery the JLP had introduced. He also aligned himself with the religious hierarchy in calling for a new commitment to the ideals of peace and brotherhood and a wholesale rejection by government of ghetto tribalism and union goon squads. Behind the scenes,

Manley had the same kind of support among organized partisan roughnecks as Seaga, but he had also stolen a tactic from Bustamante and played to the pietism of the peasantry. He even used a reggae single by Delroy Wilson, "Bettah Must Come," as his theme song.

Shearer and Seaga were set up to be routed by a West Indian Elmer Gantry and his tent show. In the pressure-cooker of the campaign, the driven, chagrined Edward Seaga developed a nervous tic—a rightward rolling of the eyes at eight-second intervals—that he would carry with him for the rest of his political life. As the general elections of 1972 approached, the JLP was so desperate that in the final days of the campaign it seized upon a pamphlet printed up by the Reverend Claudius Henry, the renowned "Repairer of the Breach," which described Henry, Selassie and Manley as the "Trinity of the Godhead." In a land that has a certain admiration for slick political pool, the exploitation by the JLP of an idiotic slum screed handed out by a card-carrying ninny like Henry was too much for even the church establishment to stomach. In one of the most remarkably unlikely turnabouts any Jamaican expected to see in his lifetime, the mighty heads of the principal religious denominations published a full-page statement in the *Daily Gleaner*, the text of which can now be found in the history books of country schoolchildren:

> We consider that the use of the "Henry Pamphlet" to attack the leader of the PNP and his party represents a departure from our standards by being an example of personal abuse and deplorable dragging of the name of God into the election fight for party advantage. In the light of the repudiation of this pamphlet by the PNP leadership [by letter to the various church leaders and by public broadcast] we condemn the use made of this pamphlet in JLP advertisements and call upon those concerned with it to stop using it.

No God-fearing Jamaican citizen was going to contest such a fiat, and Manley carried the day.

He was no sooner in office than he took as a bride Miss Beverly Anderson, twenty-seven-year-old radio and television personality. (Seaga shared Manley's predilection for well-known island beauties. He himself had previously married a former Miss Jamaica, Mitsy Constantine.) And since he was practically next door to a Rasta superstar like Bob, he and his bride started dropping in on his noted neighbor. Indeed, Manley surreptitiously passed entire evenings at Hope Road on several occasions.

Bob and Alan were making their own rounds, frequenting the hippest and the toughest nightclubs in Kingston. Dressing up stoshus in expensive threads brought in special from Miami, they would stroll into discos not far from Hope Road, like the Genesis and the Epiphany and the too-rude Turntable on Red Hills Road in St. Andrew, and the ladies and bad boys would "check dem strong," especially because they were two of the first well-known dreads to display their locks socially rather than tucking them away beneath their tams to placate the cops. Soon enough, they were being given "de mightiest" herb by rude dudes like Earl "Tek-Life" Wadley and Earl "Frowser" Bright, and powwowing vigorously with political kingpins like Aston Thompson (alias Bucky Marshall) of the PNP and Claudie Massop of the JLP. These were the kinds of breddahs who could open doors in solid concrete walls and deliver tire traction in quicksand; they were connected *ta raas*. It was not that anybody was concocting any funny runnings with anybody else; it was just the idea of *knowing* the main men. And the main men themselves simply wanted to be damned certain they could put their arms around the nicest stucky in Kingston, wave to "uptown top-ranking" cats like Skilly and Gong and get a hearty "Yes I!" back. But nothing was entirely simple and straightforward in Bob Marley's Kingston—where the most casual slight can be avenged with a gunshot or a "steppin' razor."

Everyone in town with an axe to grind was monitoring the King of Reggae and his crowd to see what his friendship with Manley might add up to. Some felt they got an inkling of the answer when the Wailers released *Natty Dread* in 1974, the dreadest LP yet, with a painting of Bob on the cover that looked like the Rasta equivalent of the Shroud of Turin. On the back cover his fist was raised, his locks licked his shoulders, and he looked much like an urban guerrilla—one who was gonna tek nuh prisoners. In short, it seemed that Bob was becoming a self-styled revolutionary, a Jamaican José Martí, perhaps. Maybe Marley, like Manley, was too full of himself and his radical visions.

In the musical community, observers noted that there had been heavy personnel changes in the Wailers. Bunny and Peter had left the group, and the rumor mill was working overtime to sift out the truth. How could so much be happening so quickly in the life of a Jamaican, let alone a Rastaman? It was an open question.

On the musical front, Peter had been very worried he and Bunny were going to get left behind, considering what he regarded as Blackwell's divisive tactics. Bunny stayed cool, but Blackwell antagonized him by insisting he had to tour with the group or "nobody" would understand, and by adding that Bunny himself would remain a "nobody." Bunny reflected on this and interpreted the word "nobody" as a serious insult, "body" being a Rasta term for "dead man." Bunny was a Rasta who refused to acknowledge death in any way, shape or form. He told Blackwell he would not tour—ever.

Peter's disagreements with Chris boiled down to finances, the carving up of the pie. They could never reach an accommodation, and at one point, according to Hope Road brethren, Peter had actually threatened Chris with a machete.

When the Wailers did a show in Kingston in 1973 with the Jackson Five, the tension within the group was unbearable—everybody tasting in his own way the amazing fame that was at their fingertips and wondering who, within or without, might try and pull the plug.

It was around this time that Don Taylor entered the picture. A Jamaican born in Franklyn Town in Eastern Kingston, Taylor had hustled on the waterfront as a youth. Hanging around the Kingston theaters, he got to know the American black performers who came down to Kingston in the 1950s for shows and wangled temporary jobs with them as a valet and chauffeur. Moving to the States in the late 1950s, he got in touch with many of them again and landed a job as Chuck Jackson's man Friday, and when Jackson jumped from the Scepter label to Motown, Taylor went along. When Jackson didn't require Taylor's services any longer, Don signed on as valet for Anthony Gourdine of Little Anthony and the Imperials; he wound up managing them for nine years following their back-to-back hits "Goin' Out of My Head" and "Hurt So Bad." Taylor was able to book them into places like the Empire Room of the Waldorf-Astoria, despite the fact that they hadn't had a hit record in years; people took notice when he built them into a Vegas draw.

Taylor had returned home in 1973 with Marvin Gaye, who was doing a benefit concert organized by Anthony Spaulding of the PNP, then the minister of housing. Spaulding filled him in on Marley, and Taylor made his approach: he went up to Island House, sauntered into Bob's bedroom and woke him out of a sound sleep. This was something Bob's own brethren wouldn't dare pull.

Bob admired Taylor's moxie and within a half hour they had a deal. Taylor vowed to renegotiate Bob's contract with Island, since he was the primary force in the group. Meanwhile, Tosh had begun work on a solo album, asking Blackwell if Island would pick it up. Chris replied that it would put Peter at cross-purposes with the Wailers, who were still putting together their musical identity. Tosh balked and quit the band.

Tosh set about completing his solo record with the help of Lee Jaffe. Lee knew Eric Clapton, who had recently covered "I Shot the Sheriff," and introduced him to Tosh. Clapton was down in Kingston at Dynamic Studios, working on the follow-up LP to *461 Ocean Boulevard* (on which "Sheriff" had appeared), and he expressed interest in Tosh's own songs, among them "Burial." Jaffe helped Tosh get financing for studio time from Clapton's bassist, Carl Radle, and then pointed Peter in the direction of Gary Kurfirst, who was managing Toots and the Maytals. Kurfirst got Tosh a deal with CBS, and the ex-Wailer went to Manhattan to work on some of his tapes at CBS Studios in Manhattan.

Meanwhile, Jaffe, who had played harmonica on *Natty Dread* and also on Peter's new tracks, was still in Kingston hanging out with Clapton. Driving home from Dynamic Studios with Seeco Patterson one night around 3:00 A.M., coming from Clapton's "Burial" session (the track never made it onto *There's One in Every Crowd*, released in 1975), he was snared in a police roadblock. Jaffe, who was wearing a Wailers tour jacket when he stepped from his rental car, had a chillum in his possession and was promptly busted. Although Seeco had no ganja on him, he was pulled in as well. In the confusion at the crowded stationhouse, Seeco slipped out the door, but Lee landed in a cell with none other than PNP strongman Bucky Marshall. For eight days, Lee passed the time chatting with Marshall, who was behind bars for felonious assault. Rita brought ital food to the jail every afternoon, and she, Skilly Cole and Perry (*The Harder They Come*) Henzell appeared in court for Jaffe as character witnesses. He got off. (His illustrious cellmate was transferred to Spanish Town Penitentiary and later released.)

The rest of the Wailers had been much relieved by Tosh's decision to withdraw from the group, since it meant an ending to shouting matches at rehearsals and greater concentration on the music. And with Peter too busy cutting solo singles and developing his own Intel-Diplo H.I.M. label (short for Intelligent Diplomat for His Imperial Majesty) to find much time to frequent Island House, the overall vibes there also improved. Bunny still hung out at Hope Road, his exit from the Wailers having been more a generally accepted fade-out than a final flare-up, but he too was developing his own projects and his own label, Solomonic. Bob took on Tyrone Downie to handle all keyboards. While on a routine business trip to Island Records in England, Bob met a black American guitarist named Al Anderson who was working on an album project with Chris Wood, formerly of Traffic. Anderson, a native of Montclair, New Jersey, who had never been in a major group before, got talked into joining the Wailers and accompanied Bob back to Kingston to help with his next album, *Natty Dread*.

One of the songs on the new album disturbed some members of the JLP considerably. They interpreted it as a possible sign that Manley, whose Democratic Socialist regime was courting Castro, was indeed doing some heavy-duty huddling with the Gong. The track, called "Revolution," had lyrics that were as incendiary as any contained on a reggae record, declaring that there was no meaningful political change without revolutionary struggle.

Cats like Claudie Massop didn't know how to take that kind of talk. Neither, unfortunately, did Bucky Marshall and the PNP thugs. The police, who had their own perspective on things, decided they didn't like it at all.

"If yuh cyan't ketch quashie," goes the saying, "den ketch him shirt." In order words: If you can't hurt a bwai, hurt his friends.

During much of 1975, the Wailers were off touring in the United States and Europe behind *Natty Dread*, while the homebound Tosh earned petty police harassment intended for the band. It was for him a mild replay of mayhem in the summer of 1972, during a jump-up at his Cockburn Gardens flat on Solitaire Road. He'd been in the corner of his parlor, sucking on a spliff and writing a song called "Mark of the Beast," when the police kicked down the door. Peter was struck in the forehead with a rifle butt and knocked senseless. When he came to, he was lying on the floor in Kingston Public Hospital on North Street. Several of his ribs had been dislocated; his abdomen looked like someone had moshed it with a dock piling. There were police standing over him, one of them with his boot on Peter's chest. Peter pleaded with passing nurses to come and attend to him; they wouldn't even look in his direction. He was held down for hours without treatment. The intention was clearly to make an example of him: anyone passing by could see through the main door that Peter Tosh was helpless. Wailers or no Wailers, he was bleeding like a lowly cartman. The ghetto got the message. So did the Wailers.

As soon as Tosh recovered, he released three solo singles in quick succession; one was a song deriding his tormentors called "Whatcha Gonna Do," another was a pro-rudie tune entitled "Can't Blame the Youth," and the third song, about herb, was called "Legalize It." Each of these records was banned from the radio, and each one sold out. "Legalize It," in fact, was one of the top-selling singles in the island's history.

While the brethren were being beaten and busted in Kingston, the reconstituted Wailers were completing their successful European tour. They did a live LP at the Lyceum in London on July 18, 1975. At first it was released only in Europe, but the strong U.S. sales of the import and pressure from bootleggers forced Island to release it in the States. It was a biting, soaring document with an arena-sized sound that combined the ritualistic fervor of a Grounation meeting with the abandon of a rock concert. The Wailers began to get heavy FM airplay on the white progressive rock stations. Bob Marley was a full-fledged rock star, and an international audience was waiting impatiently for the next studio album. Everybody was thrilled, glowing. Expectant.

One month later, the *Daily Gleaner* was claiming Jah was dead.

Bob's reedy form was scarcely visible in the dim, bare-bulbed light of Harry J's Recording Studio at 10 Roosevelt Avenue in Kingston. Dressed in a brown cotton shirt, dungarees and expensive calfskin boots, he was standing with his arms akimbo in the middle of the cluttered, high-ceilinged studio. A wispy ribbon of smoke drifted up from a bulbous spliff in his hand, encircling his bowed, dreadlocked head as he concentrated. A clock overhead read 10:30 P.M. on a September night in 1975.

The sessions for the Wailers' *Rastaman Vibration* album had been temporarily set aside to allow for a special, emergency project. Engineer Sylvan Morris, a burly, solemn black, sat hunched over the sixteen-track board on the other side of the soiled glass window that separated the grimy control booth from the studio proper; he sipped from a bottle of Dragon stout and waited for some signal to start the tape. There was no sound, except Sylvan's labored swallowing, followed by a stifled burp.

Perhaps two minutes passed before Bob raised his Medusa's mane. He clamped on a set of headphones, took a cheek-hollowing tug on the spliff and nodded slowly. An instrumental track the Wailers had laid down during the afternoon began to pour from the giant monitors hanging above the mixing board.

There was a lock-step drum pattern, a numbing bass piloting the drums into the one-drop, and muted rhythm guitar. Bob stepped quickly to the boom mike and paralyzed the ten people gathering in the cramped engineer's booth as he began to sing:

Selassie lives! Jah-Jah lives, childran!
Jah lives! Jah-Jah lives!
Fools sayin' in dere heart,
Rasta yar God is dead
But I&I know ever more
Dreaded shall be dreaded and dread . . .

The faces of Family Man and Carly were frozen in a wide, beatific smile they shared with the others present: Al Anderson; Lee Perry and his wife; Rita; Marcia Griffiths and her friend Judy Mowatt, former lead singer with the Gaylets and the third member of a recently formed trio called the I-Threes—the Wailers' new backup vocal group; and two recent additions to the Wailers, organist Bernard "Touter" Harvey and rhythm guitarist Earl "Chinna" Smith. Nobody moved, their eyes riveted on the skinny man beyond the glass. His narrow teardrop head was thrown back and billowy garlands of thick white smoke were streaming from his flared nostrils as he pledged timeless devotion to Jah Rastafari.

As he sang, the crisp, sparse mesh of music grew louder and louder, spiraling upward, higher and higher in a dizzying cycle of tension-and-release, tension-and-release, until its psychic grip became unbearable. Beads of sweat spread across the wide brow of Family Man's round, bearded face, his massive grin growing manic, almost grotesque.

Without warning, Marley suddenly whirled about and exploded into a raspy, primal exultation that rumbled through the building like a tidal wave. The umber statues on the other side of the glass leapt to life; they began bucking and winging with furious abandon and then started to mambo back and forth from an anteroom as Marley shifted his coarse tenor into highest gear:

The truth is an offense but not a sin!
Is he laugh last, is he who win!

Is a foolish dog barks at a flying bird!
One sheep must learn to respect the shepherd!
Jah lives! Selassie lives, chill-drannn!
Jah lives! Jah-Jah lives!

Within a week, "Jah Live" was in every record store in Kingston. A fellow from the *Daily Gleaner* came past Harry J's to ask Marley about the instant single, and Bob gave him a look that nearly stopped the reporter's heart in midbeat.

"Yuh cyan't kill God," he whispered.

15

Redemption Song

Hope Road was attracting a faster crowd, and the life-styles of the regulars were accelerating apace. Bob was having a passionate affair with Esther Anderson, the two of them frequently slipping off in a red Renault to a fishing village beyond Negril that was a favorite hideaway. But Bob was also showing increased interest in Cindy Breakspeare, now twenty-one, who had done a lot of growing up in the last few years; at five foot five and three quarters, she was a trifle tall for Bob, but he loved the fact that the 35-24-36½ woman was a physical education teacher—"She spry seh, she one strikin' spry stucky!"

The older dreads at Island House joked wistfully about the way it was back in 1972, when Bob didn't insist on having first pick, and the breddahs use to sleep outside at night, stretched out around the long, wide veranda. That was the context in which the brethren said Bob came to know a woman named Patricia Williams, who had a child by him named Robbie. She had approached Bob as he stood naked in the moonlight finishing a piece of breadfruit. The next day he wrote a song on the back of the Kingston telephone book about their encounter. It was called "Midnight Ravers," and it was cut for *Catch a Fire.*

On Sunday evening, September 30, 1975, a few days after the "Jah Live" sessions, Alan Cole led the Santos team, National Craven "A" League champions of Jamaica, to a 1–0 win over the New York Cosmos at the National Stadium, a record crowd of forty-five thousand jamming the stands to check fe Skilly as his game completely overshadowed that of Pelé, who seemed to be playing at half-pace for most of the match. The Cosmos apparently hadn't expected much competition.

Seeing that New York was taking a low-energy attitude toward the home team, the fans turned ugly, beating sticks, rocks and shoe leather against any hard surface in the bleachers and calling for Cosmo blood. Bob, who was in the stands with a contingent from Hope Road, joined in the war chant. ("Sometime me t'ink da Skipper love football more 'im love music," Gilly later joked; the day before, Bob's right toe was gashed by a rusty nail on the Boy's Town field during unusually forceful playing by him.) On the playing field, Skilly responded to the crowd by seizing the ball; he whirled about to chip it to outside right Errol Reid, who scored in the twenty-fifth minute of the first half. Adrenalized by a deafening thunderclap of maleficent joy from the throng, a flying wedge of rudies hit the iron gate at the Mountain View side of the stadium and sailed inside, several thousand sufferahs quickly trampling over them. They were all just in time to witness Santos back four defender Billy Perkins's brutal second-half tackle of Pelé, who had to be helped from the field by two Cosmos coaches.

Skilly had been hoping to get an offer to sign with the Cosmos, but the next day's *Gleaner* carried a story under the headline FURTHER SCRUTINY FOR COLE that seemed to vitiate that dream:

> Chances of Jamaica's ball artist Alan Cole getting a soccer contract with the New York Cosmos are not very bright, if full weight is to be given to the opinion of Clive Toye, the president of the Cosmos, in a departure interview with the *Gleaner* at the Norman Manley International Airport last night.
>
> Toye, the man who will decide if Cole plays for Santos had "doubts about Cole's application even though I was extremely impressed with his ball sense and thought he played very well, though in spurts, against us on Sunday night."

The story went on to describe a scene in the airport's transit lounge in which Pelé came up to Toye complaining of the rough play during the game and indicating a pain in his chest, just above his heart, which he said had resulted from an elbow blow in the game against Santos. He insisted on a chest X ray when the Cosmos arrived in San Juan, their next stop.

The Rasta community maintained that the Cosmos management

were a bunch of "pussy clot maaga dogs" who were down on Skilly because he was the leader of a "tuff" team like Santos. The *Gleaner* ran a sidebar reaction story on the long-awaited game, and everyone from a King Street shopper to a Harbour Street bank clerk said Pelé was a "disappointment," a "joke" and that it was "just Skilly alone" that made the match worth watching. But the disappointment the fans felt ran a good deal deeper than that.

With Bob becoming a Rasta rock star in America, everyone up at Hope Road (and around the island, for that matter) was expecting Skilly to follow in his footsteps as the first Rasta soccer star in America. When the Cosmos passed on Alan, it had a deflating effect on the scene at Island House, one that made some of the regulars feel that they had to prove themselves to outsiders in bold new ways to, well, compensate for the setback. There was a collective ego being forged in the uptown encampment, a belief that *everything* had to be righter than right, dreader than dread and badder than bad.

Meanwhile, Skilly found some solace in his longtime breddah Bob's taking him to Rae Town to check fe Sebrant "Buddah" Davis, a wise locksman in his forties, who was one of Kingston's brightest dread leaders. It was customary for the ranking younger dreads to pay homage to Buddah whenever they left the island, returned from a trip overseas or had a problem or a vex. Buddah, an exceptionally intelligent and good-natured ghetto custos, made his living as a fisherman, but he was also an able soccer player, had a wide-ranging knowledge of world affairs and African history and knew his bush medicine. He would usually serve up a vivifying bottle of roots wine made from boiled chainey bark, sarsaparilla and turnaround root, combining that with some no-bullrush talk an' t'ing that put I-man back in a better head. Both Bob and Skilly had an ineffable love for Buddah and always enjoyed their reasonings with him.

Unfortunately, the trip back to Hope Road could bring on a case of the bends. Pulling onto the Island House grounds in the silver BMW ("Lettars stand fe Bob Marley an' Wailars") Bob had recently purchased, they would often be met by ghetto leaders like the famous Baya, the fellow who kept things sizzling down in Tivoli Gardens, the urban housing development in West Kingston that had been Seaga's pet project for years. Sooner or later, either Claudie Massop or Bucky Marshall would also show up, and the atmosphere would thicken to the point where everyone moved and spoke in slow motion, trying to keep a step ahead of the dangerous camaraderie going down, wanting to duck the flash point if and when it came.

Earlier in the summer, the Wailers and the I-Threes had done a hot U.S. tour, with sold-out shows at the Boarding House in San Francisco and the Schaeffer Music Festival in New York's Central Park. They had gotten considerable attention in the national press, and shortly after the tour Bob was approached by none other than Stevie Wonder.

A Wailers-Wonder "dream show" arranged by Don Taylor and noted New York–based promoter Karen Baxter was scheduled in Kingston for Saturday, October 11, 1975, with much of the proceeds earmarked to benefit the Salvation Army School for the Blind on Manning Hill Road. Harold Melvin and the Blue Notes, who were supposed to open the show at the National Arena, never showed, and the Third World band filled in.

The Wailers followed, with Peter back in the fold for a last flamboyant "scorcher" or two, and after some equipment problems, they locked into a set that included "Rasta Man Chant," "Legalize It" and "Battering Down Sentence," a song Bunny had written about his 1967–68, 14-month prison term. It was a powerful show, especially considering that the majority of the audience was made up of middle- and upper-class Jamaicans who had turned up to see Stevie Wonder.

When Wonder, backed by his Wonderlove band, segued from his recent hits into "Boogie On, Reggae Woman" and then invited the Wailers to come out and jam with him, the significance of the intermingling of the best of reggae and American R&B was lost on no one. As the police shifted uneasily on the outskirts of the crowd, the Wailers launched into "I Shot the Sheriff," Wonder playing piano in enthusiastic support.

The *Gleaner* hailed the concert the next day as one of the best arena shows ever held on the island, devoting considerable space to its coverage. The significance of the concert was inescapable: it had been an inadvertent display of power on the Wailers' part, demonstrating that they could attract the biggest musical star in the Third World simply because he admired what *they* were about—from Rasta reverence to antipolice diatribes and calls for the decriminalization of herb. The Wailers-Wonder show marked the last time the original Wailers would ever perform together, and it heralded a turning point in Bob's fortunes. Several months later, in 1976, *Rastaman Vibration* was released, and Bob Marley replaced Stevie Wonder as the biggest musical superstar in the Third World. He was also, as it turned out, the Third World's most vulnerable music superstar. For one thing, the soccer injury of last September had, strangely enough, only just healed. For another, he simply didn't know how to screen all those who suddenly craved access to him, or how to weigh the demands they made on his time and his spirit. As the hungry new faces came at him in increasing numbers, he looked to the old friends he had begun to feel he had outgrown for psychic support. He was unprepared for the inevitable isolation that such circumstances were creating.

Bob's strained bonds with the past, both symbolic and actual, finally exceeded the breaking point on a night at Hope Road when, ironically, the mood had started out magnificently mellow. Gilly, Bob, Bunny and Skilly were in Bob's upstairs bedroom reasoning when Peter blew in, catching them all completely off guard with his good humor and a lavish gift: a sizeable stash of aromatic top-of-the-stalk sinsemilla. Many spliffs later, Bob, Bunny and Peter were lying on their stomachs on the floor, talking soulfully, their arms around each other, and Skilly and Gilly were leaning against the back wall, admiring the unity among the childhood breddahs.

Tosh eventually rose and groped his way out, bidding everyone a good night, and left for home with his woman, Evonne. Whipping onto the Spanish Town overpass in his VW Beetle, the car was struck head-on by another that was speeding down the wrong side of the road. Evonne was in a coma for three weeks, her body entirely crushed; Lee Jaffe drove Tosh to visit her every day. Peter's own facial injuries were so severe that fans and even close friends did not recognize him. Throughout the time Evonne was in intensive care, Tosh stayed away from Hope Road. "Peter superstitious," Gilly told Bob. "Him don' feel right comin' 'round jus' now." When his woman died, Tosh buried his ties to the Wailers with her, and he turned his back on the Island House scene for good.

Island Records had just begun to send small press junkets to Kingston. These groups were largely composed of white journalists—who seemed the most interested—but a few black writers came as well. The blacks were put off by the haughtiness of middle-class Kingstonians, and they could not unravel the patois. Neither, of course, could most of the whites, but the blacks were at least willing to go outside the hotel compound to try. Most of the white writers stepped off the plane expecting a manicured landscape like Bermuda's, with a lot of courtly black policemen attired in white duck and pith helmets, directing traffic with a meticulous flourish from quaint little traffic gazebos.

What they saw on the taxi ride along the Palisadoes, past the cement factory and the Rockfort Mineral Baths and into the heart of West Kingston turned their pale faces alabaster: goats grazing in the front yards of tumbledown stucco hovels, every wall that was still standing half-painted in pathetic shades of some soiled excuse for a pastel; cart people screaming and sufferahs vexing and breddahs sleeping on gully banks; gnarled foliage lifting up the teeter-totter sidewalks and hovering over the rum sheds in the heart of the madness as if to serve notice that the jungle wasn't going to be held back another damned minute.

Arriving at their hotels, the writers would encounter barbed wire and guard dogs at the entrance. They would be accosted just outside the fence by three or four toothless sport boys who twirled some sort of tickety-tickety contraptions in the fingers of one hand that looked, through the blur, like praying mantises, but on closer scrutiny proved to be switchblade knives. At which point the writers would hurry up to their rooms and book a safety's-sake seat on the next flight off the island. Many correspondents never actually left the Kingston Sheraton or the Pegasus, insisting on staying by the pool, as close as possible to the few reassuringly Germanic types who were in town selling watches and—yes—ratchets in bulk.

When the sun went down and no moon came out and they had to listen to the *quee-quee* of pigs grazing over in the vacant lot across the street, they found themselves nearly jumping out of their skins every time they heard a piece of lawn furniture scrape against the concrete porches outside the guest cottages. The Englishmen drank double shots of Appleton's Special and caught that 7:20 A.M. flight to Miami the next morning. Some of the Americans left in such haste that they forgot their tape recorders and failed to notify the press officer from Island.

Those who went on up to Hope Road and were fortunate enough to find Bob on the premises then had to learn in a big hurry how to *talk* with the man. This didn't take any special talent; you simply had to figure out what he'd said by the time he had finished saying it and not allow yourself to be eased into an anxiety attack by the one-eyed dread with the shiny machete who was leaning hard against your shoulder, listening in.

In the beginning, Bob didn't mind reporters because most of the important interviews were conducted down in Kingston and the few writers who showed up were genuinely enthusiastic. He talked slowly, and tried to tone down the slanging and the patois. Peter, who was still willing to do interviews about the past (and to promote his own album, *Legalize It*, which had taken two years to complete), was easy to understand; he was an articulate, witty raconteur—when he wasn't swingin' a blade, trying to scare the living shit out of some correspondent for the kick of it. Bunny was the most elusive; it was difficult to figure out when and if he would be disposed to talk, what he had to say, where he could be found. Some of the press complained, especially about Bunny. They said that they were told that everything had been set up, yet they found themselves waiting for four hours in some squalid yard, and Bunny never showed.

Blackwell had to laugh. He himself had just gone through the unnerving ordeal of signing Bunny to a contract for his forthcoming solo LP, *Blackheart Man*. After days and days of hanging out and waiting around and checking fe him here in the bush and there in the ghetto, Chris was sitting in a rental car, ready to turn the key, start the engine and split for good, when he decided that maybe he ought to stop pushing so hard and just behave like a bloody Jamaican—i.e., adopt a soon-come approach. So he smiled, exhaled, glanced casually to one side and saw that Bunny was sitting in the seat next to him; the car door on the passenger side was still locked.

"B-B-Bunny! I've been looking everywhere for you!"

Bunny shrugged. "Lissun," he said. "When de right time come, *me* call for *you* and"—he grinned eerily—" 'ere you are suh, seen?"

Even the breddahs in Rema said that as Bunny had grown up—calm, collected, self-absorbed—he'd acquired a "guzu-guzu" (natural mystic) capability. Living out by himself in Bull Bay, not needing to be in touch for the sake of being in touch, he had tapped into an elemental force that he had bent to his will. Moreover, he was Bob's closest friend. And it was not a friendship predicated on proximity. There was never a moment when they didn't wish each other "irie" (the absolute, spiritual and temporal best) and each had always stated—out of earshot—that the other was his favorite singer.

It was a relationship of transcendent good will that Chris Blackwell might have envied, particularly after Bunny, in a highly uncharacteristic departure from his aversion to death-related issues, requested that Blackwell insert a "death clause" in Bunny's solo contract so that if anything should happen to Chris, he would be free of all obligations.

Blackwell thought about it and said, "Well, I don't know, really, about that. . . . But . . . . okay. I suppose we could do it." Chris wondered if maybe Bunny was needling him about their earlier contretemps about "nobody."

"Good," said Bunny. "That means I can get out of my contract *at any time*."

While all the reporters from the States, England and elsewhere were trying to get an audience with a Wailer and a grasp of Jah, there was a big change occurring in the Rasta orthodoxy as it was observed at the Hope Road house, and many felt it was another manifestation of the power that Bob Marley had accumulated and the interest others had in being close to it, having a share in it—or in destroying it.

There were new Rasta doctrines being preached in the ghetto, the most influential, mystical—and divisive—being that of the emerging Twelve Tribes of Israel sect, which had been founded in Trench Town in 1968 by a man named Vernon Carrington. Originally a juice man who had a pushcart and sold cowfoot—a medicinal drink made from the juice of the cowfoot leaf—Carrington had read the Bible devoutly and claimed to have been blessed with a vision. He called upon his followers to prepare themselves by mystical means for repatriation, when they would migrate to an area in Ethiopia's Goba Valley called Shashamani. The principal dogma they had to embrace beforehand proclaimed that the human race was divided into twelve scattered tribes, each named for one of Jacob's sons, whom Jah sent down into Egypt. Each tribe was associated with a certain month of the year, symbolized by a certain color and endowed with a secret blessing. Starting with the month of April, which was the first month of the ancient Egyptian calendar before it was corrupted by the Romans, the canon was: April—Reuben, silver; May—Simeon, gold; June—Levi, purple; July—Judah, brown; August—Issachar, yellow; September—Zebulun, pink; October—Dan, blue; November—Gad, red; December—Asher, gray; January—Naphtali, green; February—Joseph, white; March—Benjamin, black. Lastly, there was the matter of Jacob's daughter Dinah, to whom no month was assigned; a neutral presence, her colors were those of the entire spectrum.

Since Carrington was born in November, he became known as Prophet Gad or Gadmon. In promulgating their beliefs, the Twelve Tribes of Israel made use of a book called *Hebrewisms of West Africa—From Nile to Niger with the Jews*, by Joseph J. Williams, S.J., published in 1930. A dense, abundantly documented study by a Jesuit historian (ironic, since the Twelve Tribes had no use for Christianity, particularly as practiced by the Ethiopian Orthodox Church), the book describes the proliferation of Judaism and Jewish culture through Africa. Using the Bible and other religious texts, as well as previous histories, journals, studies and his own observations, Williams argues that Judaism was prevalent in Egypt, Ethiopia, the Sahara and West Africa, offering scholarly confirmation of the belief (generally accepted among Rastas) that they are actually black Hebrews.

The Twelve Tribes of Israel had the reputation among the Rasta brethren in Jamaica of being the most highly organized sect, with a ruling council and a group of alternates consisting of twelve men and twelve women plus one—a pyramidal structure. And it was precisely because of this strict hierarchy that Rasta leaders like Mortimo Planno disapproved of the Twelve Tribes. He felt the new group signaled a move away from the democratic traditions of Rasta. The concept of a Rasta elite (would-be converts could be turned down, and it was believed that only 144,000 would be saved come Judgment Day), the emphasis on conversion, the various rigid dicta, and, most significant of all, the secret rites—all of this traditionally had been anathema to Rasta. To make matters worse, in the eyes of other Rastas, the Twelve Tribes were collecting money; believers were asked to pay twenty cents a week into a fund for repatriation.

Nevertheless, Prophet Gad had had much success in converting uptown youths in the early 1970s, along with prominent singers like Dennis Brown, Freddie McGregor and Judy Mowatt, and athletes like star quarter-miler Ruppert Hoilett and Bob's buddy, Alan Cole. Alan, in turn, put a lot of energy into converting Bob.

Bunny, on the other hand, believed that no Rastaman should come on heavy or apply the slightest pressure on anyone to become a believer. Granted, some solidarity seemed to be in order of late; police had recently seen fit to forcibly shear more than eighty Kingston dreads of their locks, spontaneously prompting an island-wide Grounation reasoning out of which was formed a Jah Rastafari Holy Theocratic Government. A thirteen-member delegation from the Theocracy, as it was called, had a series of meetings with Michael Manley to improve communications "between both governments." When the Theocracy established a settlement in Bull Bay, led by Bongo Shafan and Bongo Gabby—who were friendly with Bob—Bunny was cordial toward them but ultimately standoffish. Same with the Bubbo Dreads of the Ethiopian African International Congress. Why, he reasoned, must he join something he already belonged to: Jah's Kingdom. More importantly, for Bunny, the concepts of converting and believing were contradictory. (The Twelve Tribes made much of the fact that they had several white members; traditional Rastas countered that *anyone* was welcome into the faith.)

"Nuh one cyan tell a mon where him head rest," said Bunny. "Him rest wit' Jah." But Bunny tired of the argument itself. "Yuh don' *argue* Rasta; yuh reason it, yuh celebrate it, yuh fin' yuh own path into da Oneness."

The fact that Bob chose to join the Twelve Tribes of Israel is perhaps not nearly as significant as the consequences: an intensive power stuggle developed at Hope Road between believers and non-believers. Inevitably, it was the traditional *downtown* Rastas versus the *uptown* Twelve Tribes Rastas, with the former eventually bowing out of the scene.

Bunny issued his own statement on the place of the Rastaman in this world on his *Blackheart Man* album, released the same year as Marley's *Rastaman Vibration.* He saw the lot of the Rasta as of a piece with that of the mythical bogeymen he and Bob were so terrified of when their relatives spoke of such beings during shelling contests in Nine Miles. And so he sang, in plain poetic language, of the superstitious fears that had plagued him during his childhood. He explained that as he'd grown and gathered more experience, his Jah-given curiosity about life had been rewarded with the blessing of common sense. The Bible noted that wisdom is often found in the simplest of places, and he'd come to the conclusion that everything was equal under the sun, since it had all been fashioned by Jah's mighty hand. It was therefore the duty of all men to recognize the suffering they shared—for how could the world go free, and let Jah bear the cross alone? The Rastamon should be modest, for he now trods the same road of afflictions as the Blackheart Mon, getting his share of humiliations just like the Blackheart Mon. But the hotter the battle, Bunny reasoned, the sweeter the victory, and Jah—and *only* Jah—will one day make the meekest and most forebearing of the brethren the wonders of the city!

Having offered his perspective on what was occurring in Hope Road and what he foresaw for the future, Bunny withdrew to Bull Bay and generally kept out of sight. He and Neville Garrick had been staying in a little two-bedroom shack on the Island House grounds which they had rigged up nicely, but they cleared out. As preparations for the 1976 tour were being made, Bob asked Gilly to come along as his cook again but Gilly had to tell him, "Skip, me t'ink it too heavy wit' de Tribes," and he stayed behind, being replaced by Michael "Mikey Dan" White—a member of the Twelve Tribes.

For Rita's part, she accepted Bob's conversion as she accepted his casual affairs with other women, and the children they bore him; it was all a part of life in Jamaica for the sufferah. She did her best to remain as neutral as possible and keep the children (including little Stevie, born in 1974) shielded and protected.

The *Rastaman Vibration* album was distinguished by four notable features. The first two were relatively innocuous: its brand of reggae was closer to hard rock than that of any previous reggae LP; it had an embossed, burlap-patterned jacket which, as was pointed out in the inside liner notes, made the cardboard surface "great for cleaning herb."

The third exceptional feature was the "Blessing of Joseph" on the back cover, announcing in formal, albeit cryptic terms, Bob's entrance into the Twelve Tribes of Israel. Having been born in February, he was assigned to the tribe of Joseph; his color was white; his blessing, culled from Genesis 49:22–24 and Deuteronomy 33:16, was: "Joseph is a fruitful bough, even a fruitful bough by a well; whose branches run over the wall. The archers have sorely grieved him, and shot at him, and hated him; but his bow abode in strength, and the arms of his hands were made strong by the hands of the mighty God of Jacob . . . let the blessing come upon the head of Joseph, and upon the head of Joseph, and upon the top of the head of him that was separated from his brethren."

The final extraordinary element on the album had to do with the *other* power struggle being waged at Island House: who was top dog among the top dogs in Kingston—the bad men or the ranking reggae Rastamen? One of the tracks on the new album was a heartbreaking reggae ballad called "Johnny Was":

Woman hold her head and cry
Cause her son has been
Shot down in the street
And died
From a stray bullet . . .

Woman hold her head and cry
Comforting her was a passerby
She complained, then she cry
Johnny was a good man
Never did a thing wrong

Every dread and gunman in Kingston recognized the "Johnny" in the tune as Trevor "Bat Man" Wilson, one of shantytown's famed hoodlums. An authority figure among the youths in Trench Town, Bat Man was a kind of Johnny Too Bad with a blackheart of gold. Being a hard-liner on protecting the people of the ghetto, he had a habit of walking into rude boy hangouts and even into the center of rudie confrontations-in-progress, two pistols drawn. Moving quickly, he would disarm both sides, taking their guns, smashing them up, and tossing them into Kingston harbor.

Since the presence of loaded guns among the sufferahs in Jamaica had reached epidemic proportions, maybe Bat Man was trying to spare the poor and save the youth from mandatory life sentences imposed by the Gun Court for possession. (The sentence had been indefinite detention until Britain's Privy Council ruled indefinite detention to be illegal in the Commonwealth.) Whatever his motives, Bat Man's actions were not universally appreciated. Since virtually every violent man in the ghetto had some political affiliation, Wilson's double-barreled Samaritanism annoyed certain factions who had need of their firepower. So they set Bat Man Wilson up one night. A pretty la-la girl with round hips and a grindy walk was dispatched "to mek him tek her a rum bar." Once they had Trevor where they wanted him, the rudies aimed to fill him so full of holes that his belly wouldn't be able to hold a thimbleful of Appleton's. They nearly succeeded. Diving for cover, Bat Man took slugs in the shoulder and the abdomen; several innocent bystanders were also wounded, at least one young boy seriously. Seeing him sprawled face down in a puddle of his own blood, his assailants left Bat Man for dead. (Rumor had it he crawled from the scene once the coast was clear, hiding out until the heat was off and then managing to escape to Brooklyn.)

When Bob put "Johnny Was" on the same album on which he had announced his allegiance to the Twelve Tribes, it meant something important to friends like Claudie Massop, Bucky Marshall, Tek Life Wadley, Frowser Bright and another top-ranking PNP man Rita was friendly with named Tony Welch. Bob was choosing sides; Bob was, in one way or another, showing his hand.

If there was one thing that Anancy had been trying to teach the sufferah since slavery days it was never to establish a position that can be clearly identified, never to assume one form to the exclusion of others. In the ghetto, people who become too visible, too easily categorized, are good for only one strikin' thing—target practice.

Baya and his JLP boys had their hands full down in Tivoli Gardens over the Christmas holidays. A press release was dropped off at the *Gleaner* offices on the morning of Tuesday, December 30, 1975: "The Leader of the Opposition, Mr. Edward Seaga, has written to the Commissioner of Police charging him with sending sporting missions into Tivoli Gardens shooting recklessly like drunken cowboys, discharging tear gas bombs like pirates sacking a city."

The most recent incident had taken place the previous day, Seaga charged, when police riding in two jeeps—license numbers NC6907 and NB2213—drove into Tivoli; a female officer in one of the vehicles fired at a woman hanging out clothes in her yard, while another shot six-year-old Wayne Christie in the face. The police charged that residents of the area were the aggressors, attacking their patrols with stones, bottles and gunfire; furthermore, they reported, the day before a young civilian driving along Bustamante Highway from Allman Town to Lizard Town had been stopped by a gang and beaten. The people of Tivoli countercharged that they had handed the young man over to police after discovering guns and money in his automobile.

It was the same in every neighborhood in shantytown. An election year was approaching, and the gunmen were getting a head start on the campaign. Things were so nasty in the Dungle that the tribalist practice among ghetto landlords of demanding to know someone's political affiliation before they even moved into so much as a refrigerator box had been escalated, and people too impoverished to merit eviction were literally getting their clothes stolen and burned so they had no choice but to sleep naked in the lanes as warnings to those who tried to buck tribalism.

There was one more significant feature on the *Rastaman Vibration* album: Alan Cole had gotten the idea of setting one of Selassie's most stirring speeches (an address His Majesty had given in California in February 1968*) to music and putting it on the LP. Marley and Alan called the song "War," and Selassie's urgent plea for human rights now had the refrain "And until that day, everywhere is war/ War in the East/War in the West/War uptown/War downtown."

And so it certainly was in Kingston at the start of 1976.

It was a time of dying. Edward Booker had passed away in February 1976, but not before Bob had flown up to Wilmington to see him in

*Some scholars dispute the *Rastaman* liner date, saying Selassie's speech was October 6, 1963, at the U.N.

the big house Bob had bought for his parents on Tatnall Street. Lying in the upstairs bedroom, which overlooked a small park in which young boys played basketball and soccer, Edward made Bob promise to take care of Ciddy and the children.

"Pearl, Richard, Anthony, me Ciddy, dem love yuh fe true, Nesta," he said weakly. "Watch dem fe both of us, seh."

Bob gripped his hand. "Me promise."

Bob had also purchased the house next door to Ciddy's. Now, with Edward gone, he began to spend a bit more time in Delaware, bringing brethren up with him to hang out and stay in the second house. Ciddy had been running a record shop on Market Street called Roots that Bob had set up for her, but after the latest in a series of burglaries, he insisted she give it up. He also began making plans to move her and the kids down to Miami. "It not warm enuf here fe yuh, Maddah," he told her.

In Kingston, it was hot. The random violence leading up to the election was intense and widespread. The managers of two downtown movie theaters whose patrons continually riddled the screens with bullets decided to erect whitewashed cement walls on which to project the films. At noon on June 19, 1976, Governor-General Florizel Glasspole declared a state of emergency, putting Jamaica under martial law. Michael Manley stated that the police and security forces had been battling what they believed to be calculated unrest orchestrated by Edward Seaga, leader of the JLP, who was in league with the CIA to discredit the present government. Down in Trench Town, students taking their high school examinations had to be transferred to the Lyndhurst Methodist Church Hall because of snipers. There were so many bullet holes in the blackboards at Trench Town Primary School that they were written off as useless by school officials. Parents removed all but 600 of the area's 2100 students from school until after the election.

Shortly before the Wailers took off on the *Rastaman Vibration* tour, Skilly Cole, who had a job as a soccer coach at the National Stadium—a PNP patronage job in the eyes of ghetto residents—had become suspiciously friendly, in some bad men's minds, with JLP heavy Claudie Massop. That is to say, Skilly wasn't merely being sociable at the Turntable Club, hanging tight with him. Then Massop invited Skilly and Bob out to Caymanas Park track, where he enjoyed considerable social cachet, and they made the mistake of accepting, although Bob declined to bet on anything. As a result, word traveled that Bob and Skilly were playing it both ways in case Manley couldn't get past Seaga in the next election. The politicians were not pleased. And in Kingston, when politicians express displeasure, it's often because their gunmen have come to them in a blind rage.

To further complicate matters, some bad men from Concrete Jungle had made a deal while they were hanging out at Island House to fix the Double Event (Daily Double) at Caymanas Park; a leading jockey was then kidnapped and made to understand that he was to throw the first two races. The jockey did as he was told, and then left for Canada as planned. The fixers made a fortune, with no one else the wiser.

Unfortunately some of the gunmen had skipped to Miami with the money, neglecting to pay off the rest of the syndicate. Knowing the deal had gone down in the front yard of Island House, dudes from Concrete Jungle paid a visit to Hope Road to urge Bob to pay his "breddah's" debts. Bob was on tour, Skilly with him. After the tour, Marley went back to Kingston, while Skilly went on a pilgrimage to Ethiopia with some members of the Twelve Tribes. Down on Hope Road, the bad men were waiting impatiently.

They took Bob out to Hellshire Beach and told him that they wanted $2000 a day in two daily pickups until the money, plus interest, was paid. Bob, who knew nothing about any fixed-race runnings, expressed mixed emotions about such an arrangement. The bad men were jumpy. A few drew guns.

Now this was indeed a crazy move, the surest imaginable indication that all of Kingston had gone completely mad. It had long been an incontrovertible fact: nobody pulled a gun on the Tuff Gong. Not even in the scuffling days down in Rema would anyone have considered such a stunt.

Bob was staring at the men who were pointing pistols at him, their grips growing unsteady. He stared at them a long time, and they knew they were marked. A Concrete Jungle heavyweight named Donkey Collar stepped in and tried to cool everybody out. The pistols went back into their holsters and waistbands, but the men who had drawn them were wavering on their feet, perspiring freely, their minds muddled. These men were *vexed*. The group dispersed. The collections began shortly thereafter, the bad men's courier showing up twice a day, like clockwork. Regular assignations such as this do not go unnoticed in the sluggish atmosphere of Kingston.

In October, a contingent of PNP bad men showed up at Island House, and Bob escorted them to his small upstairs office. Closing the door behind them, they opened the discussion by asking a few casual questions about his career, but it soon became clear that they were there to conduct an interrogation. They wanted to know whether he saw himself as a "hip dread capitalist" in a Democratic Socialist country.

At length, they got to the point: would Bob be willing to do a free outdoor "Smile Jamaica" concert on December 5 at the National Heroes Circle, to be sponsored by the Jamaican Ministry of Culture. No politics, they said, just music to "keep de lid on till de election on December 16."

"Yah, mon," he said quietly. "Me do da concert."

The show was originally scheduled to be held on the grounds of Jamaica House, but was shifted to the National Heroes Circle to make it look less partisan. Dread brethren came to Bob and told him to wait until after the election. "Nuh," he said. "Me mus' do it now."

The courier from Concrete Jungle continued to arrive twice daily for his money; the receipts, signed by Bob, had begun popping up in the possession of select Jungle toughs, who treated them like "rankin' souvenir t'ings." Bob knew he was trapped, right out in the wide open.

On Friday, November 19, Cindy Breakspeare, reigning Miss Jamaica Bikini and Miss Universe Bikini, phoned Bob at Hope Road from London to tell him that she had been crowned Miss World the previous night. She also told him she couldn't wait to see him again.

In the early hours of the morning of November 25, Bob awoke, sopping with sweat. He had been dreaming of gunfire; there were no images in the nightmare, just shadows, but the sounds, sparks and smells of discharged bullets were streaming from them.

By the end of November, many of the Wailers were getting too tense to rehearse. Marcia Griffiths of the I-Threes came to Bob and told him the show's timing was a mistake. He said, "Nuh, nuh. It cool." Marcia got on a plane and left Jamaica.

Starting on Monday of the week before the "Smile Jamaica" Festival, scheduled for the following Sunday, an armed cadre of PNP vigilantes calling themselves the "Echo Squad" mounted a twenty-four-hour guard at Hope Road. Brandishing automatic rifles, they allowed virtually no one but members of the band either on or off the property without permission.

Monday morning, the courier from Concrete Jungle arrived, describing himself as a "bredren" of Bob's, but was turned away; the same thing happened in the afternoon. The routine was repeated on Tuesday, Wednesday and Thursday. On Friday, the courier never showed.

At 7:00 P.M. that night, Chris Blackwell and Dickie Jobson arrived at the Kingston Sheraton Hotel from Strawberry Hill to meet with Jeff Walker, head of publicity for Island Records, and Don Taylor, Bob's personal manager. Also on hand were director David Silver, there to film the concert, and colleague Perry Henzell, as well as several dreads. Taylor left to go to Hope Road. Blackwell was in a so-so mood after having decided to fire Agnes, the Strawberry Hill housekeeper, for practicing obeah on the property and scaring the other staff with duppy business.

At 8:30, the pregnant Judy Mowatt, tired from rehearsal and feeling nauseated, vomited in the bathroom at Island House. Neville Garrick drove her home after clearing it at the front gate with the guards from the Echo Squad.

At 8:45, Seeco Patterson chanced to glance out through the jalousies on the front porch of Island House and noticed, as the sun was setting, that there were no longer any members of the Echo Squad on the grounds out front.

The torpor of the quiet tropical night was interrupted by a queer noise that was not quite like a firecracker. Bob was in the kitchen at the rear of the house swallowing a sweet-sour segment of grapefruit when a dull *crack* caused him to drop the fruit. That was when Don Taylor, who had been walking toward Bob and chatting, felt the bullets entering the backs of his legs.

Taylor was thrown forward by the force of the bullets' impact. He went down but remained conscious, hearing a lot of gunfire around him from what sounded like automatic weapons. Then Don blacked out.

It was 9:12 P.M. when a rifle-wielding assailant jumped back through the kitchen pantry into which he had nervously, then recklessly, fired.

"Did you get him?" shouted an armed confederate, his voice darting out of the darkness, as the rifleman ran out.

"Yeah!" he said. "I shot him!"

Don Taylor lay in a heap on the kitchen floor, bleeding internally and externally from four slugs lodged in his upper thighs and another at the base of his spine. He was unaware that because of his casual proximity to his employer he had shielded him with his body and thus saved Bob Marley's life.

Only moments before, six or so members of the Wailers had been assembled, along with the Zap Pow Horns, on the side porch of the house, rehearsing. A short break had just been called when Taylor, detained by the business meeting at the Kingston Sheraton, had driven onto the Island House grounds and begun searching for Bob.

Unbeknownst to Taylor, two white Datsuns with at least seven Concrete Jungle gunmen had been following his car. While he strode into the house, they slipped through the rusty gates at the bottom of the driveway, one car blocking the exit while the other swiftly approached the building. In an instant, the two cars had emptied and the gunmen were peppering the house with a barrage of rifle and pistol fire, shattering windows and splintering plaster and woodwork on the first floor. Four of the gunmen surrounded the house, while two others guarded the front yard.

Rita was shot by one of the two men in the front yard as she ran out of the house with the five Marley children and a reporter from the *Jamaican Daily News*. The bullet caught her in the head, lifting her off her feet as it burrowed between the scalp and skull.

It was at that point that the second gunman, a kid of no more than sixteen, pushed through a door facing Hope Road. Keyboardist Tyrone Downie's girlfriend was standing right behind the boy—he never even noticed her—as he pointed a pistol around the corner into the rehearsal arena, shut his eyes, and proceeded to empty his gun, bullets striking the organ and the ceiling.

Meanwhile, a man with an automatic rifle had burst through the back door off the kitchen pantry, pushing past a fleeing Seeco Patterson to aim beyond Don Taylor at Bob Marley, who made no attempt to dodge his assailant. When he saw the barrel of the automatic bobbing into the room, he assumed that it was the Echo Squad or the police making a spot check. Then Bob realized the rifle was *raised*.

The gunman got off eight shots. One bullet hit a counter, another buried itself in the sagging ceiling, and five tore into Don Taylor. The last creased Marley's breast below his heart and drilled deep inside his arm.

American lead guitarist Donald Kinsey, the newest addition to the Wailers, had been standing down the hall from Taylor and Marley when the rifleman stormed through the pantry. Kinsey ducked into the next room and took cover behind an equipment case, cowering. He had no idea what was happening. It was Kinsey's first time in Kingston.

Miraculously no one was killed in the nighttime raid. A passing police car happened on the scene at the height of the pandemonium, frightening the would-be assassins into a high-speed retreat. If the night riders had sought to murder Marley and his family and friends, they had failed. But Don Taylor was critically injured; Bob's friend Lewis Griffith needed immediate medical attention for his stomach wounds; Rita was bleeding profusely. Bob stumbled about in a daze, huge blotchy bloodstains spreading over his khaki outfit at his chest and thighs. The post-melee mood was one of defeat and static terror.

Ambulances arrived and took the injured to University College Hospital, since Marley's was an uptown address. Michael Manley met the motorcade at the entrance. Taylor and Griffith were placed on the critical list. Rita underwent surgery for removal of the bullet lodged in her scalp, and Bob was treated and, after a hasty conference with Manley, was released.

Marley was hustled away under police escort to a secluded encampment high in the Blue Mountains above Kingston, accompanied by various dreads. Heavy protection by soldiers in mufti stationed around the retreat was supplemented by contingents of machete-toting Rastas, who kept a constant vigil, some hiding in the surrounding trees. Chris Blackwell and Dickie Jobson hastily chartered a private jet and left the island.

Jeff Walker, Island's press chief, was one of the very few who knew Marley's whereabouts. The evening after the shooting, Jeff joined Bob and his brethren in the mountains for a conference. During the discussion, it was respectfully pointed out by several of the Rasta elders on hand that if the gunmen had been trying to stop the music, they would still have accomplished what they had set out to do if Bob did not play the next night. After a reasoning of several hours duration, the question of the Wailers' appearance at the "Smile Jamaica" Festival was left up in the air.

Spirits at the hideout lifted a bit on Sunday morning with the news that Don Taylor's condition had improved, although plans were being made to fly him to Miami's Cedars of Lebanon Hospital for removal of the bullet lodged against his spinal cord. If complications arose during the delicate operation, Taylor might never walk again.

There was also considerable concern over the fact that the gunmen had not yet been apprehended. One of the getaway cars had been found abandoned in Trench Town, but the police announced that the identities of its passengers remained a mystery.

As the day wore on, conversation about the festival was minimal, but the camp kept abreast of developments at the site. Rita was released from the hospital and brought to the camp, along with the kids. Singer Roberta Flack, who had flown down to Jamaica to see the show, arrived later in the afternoon, driven up by intimates of Bob; her private talk with him boosted his spirits considerably. One of the "Smile Jamaica" film crew had also found his way up to the camp—minus his camera. The Rastas had no inkling of it, but the cameraman was Carl Colby, son of CIA director William Colby.

Manning the walkie-talkie at the Hero's Circle as dusk fell were Ibo and Cat, keyboardist and lead guitarist respectively of the Third World band, which was expected to open the show in the absence of Bunny Wailer, Peter Tosh and Burning Spear, none of whom had shown up for their scheduled sets. Despite the slim chances of the Wailers' appearing, the early turnout at the site was a staggering fifty thousand. Their vibes were buoyant and positive.

Both Ibo and Cat spoke with Bob, telling him they had decided to go on. He was able to hear the audience's reaction to Third World's set over the walkie-talkie, which was being held up to the PA system by a roadie. He then listened to a warm tribute to himself and the Wailers, which the female MC addressed to the crowd.

Bob requested that someone be sent down to Hope Road to round up the band members. Don Kinsey, Tyrone Downie and Carly Barrett were located and taken to the arena, where they talked to Bob over the walkie-talkie. Family Man could not be found, so Cat volunteered to fill in on bass.

With Marley still wavering, PNP cabinet minister Tony Spaulding arrived and delivered a pep talk. Bob was finally convinced, and he and his bodyguards were hustled into a red Volvo that was waiting behind an idling police car. As the impromptu motorcade made its way down the narrow mountain roads, Jeff Walker, who was riding in a car behind Marley's, informed the contingent at the arena by walkie-talkie that the Wailers were on their way down. An announcement was made to the throng to that effect, and the exultant roar could be heard over the walkie-talkie's tiny receiver.

Speeding into the center of the city, the motorcade shot past a JLP rally that was dispersing. Seeing Marley, the people lining the roadsides began cheering. Attendance at the thoroughly garrisoned festival site had swelled to eighty thousand, yet the approach to the stage was remarkably clear. Bounding out of the Volvo, Marley was met at the microphone by Michael Manley, who hugged him with emotion and then stepped to the sidelines, where he stood, for the duration of the show, on the roof of a Volkswagen van, fully exposed, like Marley, to any gunmen.

Shaking his dreadlocked mane in exhilaration, Bob offered a diffident tribute to the sea of faces: "When me decided ta do dis yere concert two anna 'alf months ago, me was told dere was no politics. I jus' wanted ta play fe da love of da people."

Unable to strum his familar brown solid-body Gibson guitar because of his arm injury, Marley murmured that he would sing "one song." He thereupon launched into what became a ninety-minute tour de force opening with "War":

What life has taught me
I would like to share with
Those who want to learn . . .
That until the basic human rights
Are equally guaranteed to all . . .
Everywhere is war.

The proceedings were further electrified by the presence of Rita Marley, who was dressed in a nightgown and duster with a scarf covering her bandaged head—the decision to perform had been made so hurriedly that she had not had time to change clothes. At the close of his performance, Bob began a ritualistic dance, acting out aspects of the ambush that had almost taken his life. In Ethiopia, from Solomon's time to Selassie's, whenever a brave hunter killed a lion, he was summoned before the emperor to reenact his feat before receiving the pelt as a badge of his courage. Jamaica was witnessing the Rastafarian version of this dance in and out of the path of Death. Swaying slowly and half-steppin' to the beat, Bob opened his shirt and rolled up his left sleeve to show his wounds to the crowd.

The last thing they saw before the reigning King of Reggae disappeared back into the hills was the image of the man mimicking the two-pistoled fast draw of a frontier gunslinger, his locks thrown back in triumphant laughter.

16

Exodus

Michael Manley swept to victory in the December 16 election, the PNP capturing forty-seven out of sixty seats in the House of Representatives.

Those involved in both the race track scam and the ambush had begun to turn up. In the former case, Tek Life was found viciously murdered in Jamaica; Frowser was tracked down in New York City by anonymous avengers and shot through the head. In the latter matter, those of the unrepentant ambushers whose remains were discovered in the ghetto had died by the gun; the bodies of those who had fled to the hills had had their throats neatly slit, like the bushman does with his goats at slaughtering time. The last two assailants had confessed their involvement in the attack, begging their Rasta contacts for help in reaching the Tuff Gong in order to ask his forgiveness. Impossible, they were told. No one knew the Gong's whereabouts. He was, according to the brethren, "in seclusion."

When these men were last seen alive, they were wandering aimlessly through Trench Town and Rae Town, respectively, behaving like demented zombies. They stammered about a strange salivalike substance that would splash against their faces in the night, and of duppies cloaked in blue flame that came to them just before sunrise and slapped and punched them as they tried helplessly to fend off the phantom blows. They screamed about snakes in their heads that were trying to eat their way out of their skulls through their eye sockets. One of the men was found hanging from a tree in a field in St. Catherine; the other has never been found.

Bob had indeed disappeared. Three days after the "Smile Jamaica" concert, he met his mother briefly in Nassau, then left the island and laid low for a full month. He never told anyone where he went.

When he resurfaced, he spent a period of convalescence in Miami, New York and Delaware, dividing his time between his mother, step-sisters and brothers, Rita and the kids, and Cindy Breakspeare. It was three months after "Smile Jamaica" when he traveled secretly to England to begin working on his next album. (His Oakley Street address was learned after a £50 fine on two counts of cannabis possession.)

While in London with Lee Perry, he heard the Clash for the first time. He admired their spunky courage and anger in the face of England's social stratification and class-based economic oppression. He also admired the help that the Clash and other punk rockers were giving to East and West Indians (especially dreads, in the latter case) who were being hunted in the streets by disciples of the neo-fascist National Front and victimized by the bobbies' brutally racist application of the "sus laws"—edicts dating back to the Napoleonic Wars that allowed police to strip search and harass anyone judged to be "loitering with intent."

Bob went into the Basing Street studios with members of the Anglo-Jamaican reggae group Aswad and cut a song he had tossed together on the spot entitled "Punky Reggae Party." (Additional parts were later dubbed in by some members of the Wailers back in Kingston.) The song was released on the Tuff Gong label in Jamaica and in England as a twelve-inch single, with an incendiary Lee Perry dub on the B side.

"Rejected by society," Bob sang of Rastas and punk rockers, "mistreated with impunity. . . ."

Meanwhile, some of the ranking Rastas in London put him in touch with officials of the Ethiopian Orthodox Church. In the course of meeting with a number of Ethiopian exiles, he was granted an audience in London with Crown Prince Asfa Wossen.

It was a private audience, the two men speaking for almost two hours. Wossen talked about His Majesty Haile Selassie—his life, his betrayal by his own officers in 1974. Wossen went on to describe the situation in Ethiopia since the coup. The Provisional Military Council had taken over the government, promising a civilian democracy and, eventually, a new constitution. Fifty-one-year-old war hero Lieutenant General Aman Andom had arisen as chairman of the council. The military had said it planned to recall Wossen from Geneva, where he was then convalescing after an operation, to be crowned King (which was to be a purely ceremonial post). It was just a ploy; no invitation ever came. The government that emerged from the Ethiopian revolution proved to be Marxist, headed by Mengistu Haile Mariam. Prince Wossen regretted that the International Red Cross had not been more forceful in following through on his request to carry out an independent inquiry into His Majesty's death.

As Marley was leaving, the crown prince said he had something for him. "This belonged to His Majesty," he said, "you are the one who should wear it." He showed the Rasta a ring.

Bob was dumbstruck. It was the ring he had seen in his dream in Delaware—a black stone bearing the figure of the Lion of Judah. Wossen slipped it onto Bob's forefinger, just as the man in the dream had done. It fit perfectly.

Noticing the odd mixture of terror and joy in Bob's expression, the crown prince asked if something was wrong. Bob told him that a riddle he had lived with for a long time had finally been solved.

The Wailers' next LP, released in 1977, was titled *Exodus* and subtitled *Movement of Jah People.* The title track, the first single that would receive widespread airplay on black stations in the United States, concerned a final journey—of Damnation for some, of Resurrection for others. The central message, though, was a vision of a glorious end to the suffering of all Jah's people:

Men and women will fight you down
When ya see Jah light
Let me tell you, if you're not wrong
Everything is all right
Walk, through the roads of creation
We're the generation
Who trod through great tribulation

Exodus, movement of Jah people. . . .

Open your eyes and look within
Are you satisfied with the life you're living
We know where we're going
We know where we're from
We're leaving Babylon
We're going to our Father's land . . .

Island threw lavish parties for Bob and the Wailers in both Los Angeles and Paris, and photos appeared in the European and American papers of Bob dancing with pretty women in an LA disco and in the Club Elysée Matignon.

In Paris, Bianca Jagger ran up and kissed him. "Who wha dat?" he asked bemusedly. In Los Angeles, a bunch of white limousines had been rented to take the band to an exclusive party attended by stars like Diana Ross and by the heads of every major record company in the States. All the Wailers arrived on time, most (like Kingston-born Donald Hanson Marvin Kerr, Jr., aka Junior Marvin, the dapper new lead guitarist) wearing tailored tuxedos. But there was no sign of Bob, until about two hours later, when a dingy, dented panel truck pulled up to the club and he clambered out the back and made his grand entrance dressed in droopy jeans and a half-buttoned shirt. (He had been having dinner with brethren at an Ethiopian restaurant.) He danced—sparingly—and even sipped some champagne as he chatted with guests like Ahmet Ertegun but, as in Paris, his mind seemed to be elsewhere.

While playing soccer in Paris with a top French team in May 1977, during the European leg of the *Exodus* tour, he had injured his right toe again during a bad tackle. The toenail was torn off. Again, it seemed minor at first. This time, however, the lesion did not heal. But he pressed on through the Scandinavian concert dates. Worries among Bob's inner circle of dreads concerning his physical well-being quietly mounted.

As it was, 1977 was deemed a most ominous year by all devout Rasta brethren, especially the elder dreads. Culture, a group led by dread poet Joseph Hill, had earlier released a song called "Two Sevens Clash," foretelling that 1977 was to be a pivotal year for the West and Jamaica in particular. Allusions were made to the Book of Revelation, wherein St. John the Divine had described the onset of the Apocalypse. In his vision, John saw the throne of God, with seven lamps of fire before it—the seven spirits of God. And the one who sat upon it held a book sealed with seven seals. The Lamb of God, who had seven horns and seven eyes, took the book and he split each of the seven seals, and when he split the last, seven angels appeared before God, and each was given a trumpet. And as each in turn sounded a trumpet, another aspect of the Apocalypse unfolded. Then the seven angels initiated the seven final plagues, pouring seven golden vials of God's wrath down upon the earth.

Throughout Jamaica, Grounation reasonings focused on the implications of the numerical signs currently converging, drawing from the teachings of the African ancients, principally those of Egypt. The Coptic mystics of the distant past believed the number seven to symbolize two things: perfection and eternity. The gabled, so-called Queen's Chamber of the Great Pyramid, characterized in the Egyptian *Book of the Dead* as the Chamber of the Moon (also referred to as the Chamber of Rebirth), is a seven-sided room of remarkably sophisticated ventilation. It lies off the Grand Gallery below the so-called King's Chamber, in whose coffer the Ark of the Covenant would find a perfect fit. Unlike all other ancient buildings in Egypt, the Great Pyramid was not built for its own time; neither tomb nor temple, adorned with no hieroglyphic inscriptions or adornments of any kind, no use has ever been made of it.

The Rastas noted in their discussions that the Great Pyramid is spoken of with reverence in the Old Testament, particularly in Job 38:4–7, where God answered the patriarch out of the whirlwind: "Where wast thou when I laid the foundations of the earth? declare, if thou hast understanding. Whereupon are the foundations thereof fastened? or who laid the corner stone thereof; When the morning stars sang together, and all the sons of God shouted for joy?"

In Matthew 21:42, the brethren knew, the apostle had quoted the Nazarene as having said about himself, "The stone which the builders rejected, the same is become the head of the corner," or "headstone in the corner," according to an alternate translation. Indeed, Bunny Wailer had quoted the passage in "Blackheart Man."

Since 1865, archeologists have been aware that each of the lower four cornerstones of the Great Pyramid is fitted into a massive hollow or socket, thus bringing its entire construction into superb mathematical alignment. Any structure can have a cornerstone, of course, but only one can have a headstone in the corner, a fifth cornerstone that completes it: a pyramid. The Great Pyramid has awaited for uncounted millennia the capstone that will be its finishing feature.

On July 7, 1977, the Defense Force was on maximum alert in Jamaica and the streets were deserted. Despite official government bulletins that all was well, the majority of the citizenry declined to leave their homes, so potent had been the suggestive power of Culture's record.

At the seventh second of the seventh minute of the seventh hour of July 7, 1977, when seven sevens silently clashed, all righteous Rasta brethren fervently believed that Jah's final plan, as yet unrevealed, had begun to unfold. At 7:00 P.M., as five sevens clashed, Michael Manley introduced the new Jamaican constitution to wild applause from party members assembled at a PNP summit at Morant Bay. He was proclaimed in the town where Jamaica had seen some of its worse slave revolts as the country's "savior." But the Rastas had already decided this modern Joshua was a false prophet.

Thousands of miles away, on the same day, Denise Mills, executive assistant to Chris Blackwell and the chief Island Records official accompanying the *Exodus* tour, took a limping Bob Marley to see a physician, who told Bob his wound looked disturbingly bad. It got so bad, in fact, that London doctors ultimately prescribed amputation of the right toe. Bob refused, in accordance with Rasta proscriptions against such surgery. He was flown to Miami from London, where Dr. William Bacon, a black orthopedic surgeon, performed a skin graft on the toe. Bacon called the operation "a success."

Back in Delaware, Bob sat with Cedella in the kitchen of the house on Tatnall Street one evening after dinner and explained that it was His Majesty who had come to him in his dream years before. He talked about all he had seen and learned since Selassie had visited Jamaica, telling her about Rita's experiences; about his dreams, visions and nightmares; about Mortimo Planno; about Brother Gad.

"Wha' hidden from de wise an' prudent," he stated, quoting from the Scriptures, "is revealed ta de babes and sucklin'."

He told her everything he knew about Jah, Egypt, Solomon and the rest. He tried to tell her everything he thought she ought to know, but he purposely withheld the one thing she should not know: that he now knew his name.

Ciddy went off to visit her brother Gibson, and Bob spent some time with two of his Delaware friends, one called Ibis Pitts and the other Dion Wilson. They were sitting in a tree one day, and Bob started to talk about Christ. He said that Christ's mission began at age thirty-three.

"Me gwan die at t'irty-six," he said quietly, "jus' like Christ."

"Stop it, Bob!" said Dion, who had been his first buddy in Wilmington when he arrived from Kingston in 1966. "What are you talkin' about? You got a good career, you makin' good money. Why you want to die that young?"

"Next year 1978," Bob continued, speaking somberly. "Me be t'irty-t'ree in February. From dat month, t'ings tek dere course from den."

"Come on, Bob, knock it off," said Ibis, and the moment passed. Both Dion and Ibis told Ciddy about it later. They were disturbed by this kind of talk, but they convinced themselves it was just a temporary fit of depression associated with the troublesome soccer injury.

On February 26, 1978, twenty days after his birthday, an Air Jamaica flight carrying Bob Marley touched down a few minutes before 5:00 P.M. at Norman Manley Airport in Kingston. The plane was met by approximately two thousand people, who broke through police barricades and streamed across the tarmac. It was the first time Marley had been in Jamaica since the shooting. That night, at the close of an informal chant session led by Bob at the National Heroes Circle Stadium and attended by several thousand people, Kingston felt the tremors of two earthquakes, each of about twenty seconds' duration, the second stronger than the first.

Marley had been approached outside of Jamaica (in London and Miami) by Bucky Marshall (PNP) and Claudie Massop (JLP)—the two bad men meeting him, *together*, to ask him to return home to appear at what was being called the "One Love Peace Concert" on April 22, jointly organized by Massop and Marshall under the auspices of the Twelve Tribes of Israel. The concert's purpose was twofold, they said. First, it was intended to raise money to provide much-needed sanitary facilities and housing for the sufferahs in the West Kingston neighborhoods controlled by the rival parties, to wit: Tivoli Gardens and Denham Town (JLP), *as well as* Hannah Town and Arnett Gardens (PNP), would receive financial aid. But more importantly, the hope was that the concert might save the country from civil war and/or a military coup in the aftermath of the Green Bay Massacre. This was a 1978 security forces "action" in which an entire cadre of PNP bad men who had not been cooperating with their own party's radical new strong-arm ghetto programs were set up and ruthlessly purged. The men were told to go to a beach outside Kingston between Lazaretto and Fort Clarence to pick up guns for an anti-JLP raid. The army was then "tipped" they were guerrillas and moved in, mowing down the virtually defenseless men. A few escaped, however, to tell the tale. The judicial inquiry that ensued denounced the killings as wholesale murder. The army had been used, their integrity as a military force was grotesquely compromised and the party in power had thus lost control of the military. Jamaica was indeed moving toward civil war and a possible coup attempt. Only a situation that dire would send Marshall and Massop into each other's political embrace.

Under Manley, the economy was in a sorry state. Official government statistics showed unemployment at 35 percent, a conservative estimate. With virtually no money remaining in its coffers, the treasury had actually been bouncing checks. Imports had to be curtailed, and a gallon of gasoline sold for US$3.00. Soap, cigarettes and, of all things, guitar strings could only be had on the black market—the last being an exquisite irony under the regime of a prime minister who had issued a reggae-backed LP of his own speeches in 1976.

On January 9, 1978, Bucky Marshall was released from jail for the umpteenth time, having spent his imprisonment in the same cell with some JLP thugs. They had talked, trying to make sense out of their bitter rivalry, and hours after Marshall was free he contacted Claudie Massop. That evening, they held an all-night candlelight vigil in the streets of West Kingston, announcing a truce at daybreak. Two new songs hit the sound systems to herald the news, "The Peace Treaty Special" by Jacob Miller (sung to the tune of "When Johnny Comes Marching Home Again") and a track called "The War Is Over," the latter jumping to the Number 4 spot on the Kingston charts. The Jamaican Peace Movement was born, and sixteen of the island's most prominent reggae acts, including Jacob Miller and Inner Circle, Dennis Brown, Culture, Big Youth, Peter Tosh and Ras Michael and the Sons of Negus consented to appear at the One Love concert.

Ticket prices were kept extremely modest: two dollars for the "Togetherness" section, five dollars for the "Love" section and eight dollars for the "Peace" area directly in front of the stage; they were selling briskly.

All was well until April 17, five days before the concert. A peaceful demonstration in West Kingston, mounted to protest the truly horrible sanitary conditions in some neighborhoods, was broken up by renegade government security police, who shot and killed three demonstrators. Rising to the defense of his men, Minister of Security Dudley Thompson stated with arrogance and menace, "If one policeman is killed this year, the people who did it will be shot down like dogs."

To everyone's astonishment, the One Love concert actually came off, with a new Wailers' LP called *Kaya*—made up entirely of love songs—issued to roughly coincide with the event.

Peter Tosh, who had lately taken to demanding that he be addressed by his Ethiopian name—"Wolde Semayat"—preceded the Wailers on the bill. Dressed entirely in black, he seized the opportunity to lecture Michael Manley and Edward Seaga for their failure to support the legalization of ganja, after both had made veiled promises to do so during the last election campaign. Lighting up a spliff, he denounced the "shitstem" the two politicians fostered, one in which docile smokers of wisdom weed are continually tormented by corrupt police.

"Me don' wan' peace," Tosh hissed, "me want equality! I am not a politician. I jus' suffah de consequences." Both political leaders bristled but kept their seats and their cool. During the Wailers' set, Bob pointed to the moon and cried out, "Da Lion of Judah will break ev'ry chain an' give us da victory again an' again!" Then, during a nerve-tingling rendition of "Jamming," he somehow induced Manley and Seaga to come up and lock hands together with his as the crowd of thirty thousand watched—initially in stunned silence, but eventually snapping out of the spell of the unlikely tableau onstage to cheer—as the two political archrivals showed frozen grins.

That September, just five months after the concert, Peter Tosh was stopped by two Kingston policemen as he was coming out of the Skateland dance hall on Half Way Tree Road. Tosh, who was smoking a spliff at the time, suffered a broken right hand, lacerations to the head and a severely bruised right foot.

Nine months after the Peace Concert, Claudie Massop and two other JLP stalwarts, Trevor Tinson and Lloyd Nolan, were killed execution-style after a taxi in which they had been riding was stopped at the corner of Industrial Terrace and Marcus Garvey Drive in Denham Town. The police ordered them out and searched the car and then the men (Massop was carrying a .38 pistol). While the three men held their hands up, the officer in charge shouted, "Kill!"

After the execution, a police motorcade rode into town and circled around the offices of the Ministry of Security, the policemen blowing their horns and laughing derisively.

Bucky Marshall was shot to death in May 1980 while attending a Saturday night reggae jump-up on Church Avenue in Brooklyn, New York.

The Wailers embarked on a world tour in 1978 that took them across the United States (including an appearance in Hawaii and a sold-out show at Madison Square Garden), Canada and Europe, and then on to Australia and Japan—where non-English-speaking audiences sang along in perfect unison with "No Woman, No Cry."

In the winter of 1978, Island released a live two-record set called *Babylon by Bus* that documented the Wailers' June 1978 dates at the Pavillon in Paris. (The liner notes erroneously claimed that the two LPs also featured performances culled from the shows in Copenhagen, London and Amsterdam.)

In 1979, the Melody Makers, a group consisting of four of Rita and Bob's children (Sharon, fourteen, Cedella, twelve, David "Ziggy," eleven, Stephen, five) released a song by Bob and Rita that he had first written out and then recited on the front lawn of Island House in September 1975. He said he was saving it for, as he put it at the time, "when me childran are ol' enough ta sing it." Originally titled "Children of the Ghetto," it was released on Tuff Gong as "Children Playing in the Streets." All proceeds from the single went to the U.N. Children's Fund—1979 being the International Year of the Child.

On the sun-splashed autumn afternoon back in 1975 when Bob first introduced the song, he had been talking with several brethren and some visitors about small children: how close he felt to them, how their presence always strengthened him and how blessed he was by his own brood. Someone mentioned a story that appeared in the *Jamaican Daily News* just that morning about the plight of youngsters in the Dungle who forage in the gigantic trash heaps on Causeway Road outside Kingston for food and clothing. Slumped against the great, gnarled tree beside his house, Bob listened, nodding slowly, and then began to talk-sing the lyrics of his tune:

Childran playin' in da streets
In broken bottles an' rubbish heap
Ain't got nothin' to eat
Only sweets dat rot dere teet'
Sittin' in da darkness
Searchin' for da light. . . .
Mumma scream, "Watch dat car!"
But hit-and-run mon has gone too far . . .

When he had finished, Bob turned away to watch Rita and Robbie, his son by Patricia Williams, cavorting happily on the lawn, and he slipped into a trance. He picked up a stick, rolled it in his palms; his arms tensed suddenly, and he broke the stick in half with a loud snap.

"Ah, Jamaica," he signed. "Where cyan yar people go? Me wondar if it anyplace on dis earth."

The Wailers held a benefit concert in the National Heroes Arena for Rasta children on September 24, 1979. Bob previewed two songs from his forthcoming *Survival* album during the show. The first, he said, was called "Ambush in the Night," and the audience was stunned as he sang of those, now dead, who had tried to prematurely end his life and his work:

See them fighting for power
But they know not the hour
So they bribing with
Their guns, spare parts and money
Trying to belittle our integrity
They say what we know
Is just what they teach us
We're so ignorant
Everytime they can reach us
Through political strategy
They keep us hungry
When you gonna get some food
Your brother got to be your enemy

Ambush in the night, all guns aiming at me
Ambush in the night, they opened fire on me
Ambush in the night, protected by His Majesty . . .

He waved off the wildly enthusiastic applause at the close of the song, the spotlights catching the shiny, black-jeweled ring on his finger, and introduced the next offering—"Zimbabwe."

If those two songs were any indication, it was plain to the people of Jamaica that Bob was going for broke, openly lending his strenuous support to the struggle for a truly free and independent Jamaica—a struggle which could very well end with the installation of a black, Marxist government in a country that had long been dominated by right-wing colonialist white regimes.

In 1976, before the ambush, Bob had taken on the CIA in a song called "Rat Race," which stated in no uncertain terms: "Rasta don't work fe nuh CIA!" Now, with the October 1980 elections looming and people already being slaughtered as the last, all-out battle for Jamaica was commencing, Marley was already denouncing both sides, revealing pro-Marxist sympathies that powerful U.S. interests in the Caribbean basin considered inexcusable.

"Now Bob Marley got nuh friends *but* de sufferahs," observed one Rasta elder in Rema, and the rumor was that CIA operatives had threatened Bob's life if he dared come home before the election was over. By the time he appeared at the April 18, 1980, Independence Day ceremonies in Zimbabwe, Bob Marley knew he was doomed, but he wanted to keep it secret for as long as was humanly possible.

When Bob returned from Africa, a meeting was held in May 1980 at the midtown Manhattan offices of Inner City Broadcasting (ICB), the powerful communications company that controlled WLIB and WBLS, the two most important black stations in the New York metropolitan area and programming trend-setters for black stations nationwide. Seated around the long table in the conference room were Chris Blackwell, Danny Sims, star WBLS DJ Frankie Crocker, prominent press and public relations man Howard Bloom, and a dozen other top executives from various parts of the radio and record industries. The purpose of the summit was to discuss how best to break the Wailers' new LP, *Uprising*, in the black American radio and record market, where reggae had traditionally been a tough sell. At the head of the table was ICB head Percy Sutton, who began the meeting by gazing at Bob, who was slumped back in his chair, looking almost apoplectic.

"I'm happy to be working with you, Bob," said Sutton in an expansive tone, "because you've just come back from Europe and Africa, where you're bigger than Christ and Muhammad combined. We want to promote shows in most major U.S. cities! Get you three nights headlining at Madison Square Garden!"

There was no reaction whatsoever from Bob, but the rest of those assembled filled in for him with loud expressions of enthusiasm. Howard Bloom spoke up, saying that he thought such a move would be ill-advised and possibly very damaging because the booking of Wailers tours in the States had always been so erratic that no true arena audience had been built up. He suggested putting Bob in venues in the three-thousand-seat range for successive nights, thus guaranteeing sellouts and publicity-provoking crowds lined up outside the halls. The meeting grew heated, one person after another offering his theories of why Bob hadn't penetrated white and black AM radio, R&B stations and album-oriented FM formats. The only person who was not participating was Bob himself. He never said a word.

Afterward, Marley left for Florida, and Bloom and Blackwell shared a cab back to Island's Madison Avenue offices. During the course of the ride, Chris Blackwell hired the Howard Bloom Organization to handle the album and tour, which ICB would promote. Howard, eager to get to know Bob, whom he had never met before, arranged to fly down to Miami to confer with him, hoping to find out why he had acted so lethargic in the presence of all those high-powered boosters and hucksters.

"Anything you need, professionally," the effervescent Bloom told Bob, "I'll try and get it for you."

Bob stared at him for a moment, as if he hadn't heard anything Bloom had said, and then replied, "Okay suh. See if yuh cyan find pictures fe me a His Majesty Haile Selassie from his visit ta America in 1931."

He said that was all he needed. Then he told Bloom how, in the last two years, so many of the people around him had been hunted down and killed.

"Me be someplace wit dem an' a voice tell me ta leave. An' ev'ry time I go police an' bad men show up an' cut dem down wit gun shot. Me jus' knew it was nuh me time."

Bloom was struck by the same profoundly sapient aura about Bob that had jarred Junior Marvin and the rest of the Wailers during the sessions for *Uprising*. Working down in Dynamic Studios one afternoon, Bob had been leading the band through a preliminary take of "Could You Be Loved" when Junior Marvin, deciding there was enough lead guitar being supplied by Al Anderson to suit the track, unplugged his own guitar from his amplifier. He started to leave the studio to run some errands.

"Don' leave!" Bob told him, in a voice filled with a cool, knowing urgency. "Me don' 'ave much time!"

Almost involuntarily, Marvin was drawn back to the amplifier and plugged his guitar back in. There seemed to be both a sadness and a dread magnetism in Marley that had never been there before; he had never seemed more imposing, or more distant.

In the Rasta community, the ruling hierarchy of the Twelve

Tribes had begun to criticize Bob for his independent behavior, his disinterest in dogma and his decision to send his children to conventional schools like Alpha Academy and Vaz Prep, while also allowing Rita to have them baptized into the Ethiopian Orthodox Church—where Ziggy served as a deacon.

Gad was especially displeased when Bob accepted the Ashanti title of Osahene, meaning "redeemer," from one Kofi John Jantauh at the Progressive Arts Center in Chicago in November 1979, despite the fact that this was a traditional African ceremony of brotherly fellowship and respect without religious connotations.

What rankled the increasingly backbiting retinue of functionaries around Marley most was how disinterested he seemed to be in the enduringly petty pee-gee attitudes they had grown to take so seriously. And while ignoring their concerns, he was working with an unassuming will that was lifting him to the peak of his powers. Just when they thought he was becoming one of them, he had eluded them completely and inspired their fiercest envy.

When Chris Blackwell first heard the tapes for *Uprising*, which included a haunting song called "Come We Go Burn Down Babylon (One More Time)," he stunned the band by telling Bob he felt he had something more to give to the album. Marley smiled, uncomplaining, and returned the next day with two new compositions, "Coming In from The Cold" and "Redemption Song." The first song was among the most entrancingly melodic odes to hope among the sufferahs in the face of the hopelessness that he had ever unveiled. The second song was a plaintive, almost Dylanesque acoustic spiritual, devoid of any trace of reggae. When he sang it, he wore the expression of a playful child, but his voice bore the authority of a Biblical patriarch.

Attorney and confidante Diane Jobson commented to him one day that he had not been sleeping more than three hours a night for months upon months.

"Sleep is an escape for fools," he said gently, sweetly. "I mus' be about me Faddah's business."

On Sunday morning, September 21, 1980, Bob and Skilly had gone jogging in Central Park to get Bob "energized," as Cole put it. The night after the second show of his Madison Square Garden concert series with the Commodores, Bob had awoken in a daze; he had trouble remembering the show, even the fact that he had almost passed out during the performance.

Both after the concert and that morning he had been offered cocaine and freebase by some very heavy dread hustlers from Brooklyn. They had attached themselves to the Wailers entourage since the Wailers arrived in town fresh from European dates in support of *Uprising*.

In the course of the last twelve months, Bob had watched the Rasta scene in Jamaica deteriorate. A sinister cocaine, freebase and heroin trafficking network had spread from Negril into Kingston since Seaga had been elected.

The reasons behind Seaga's victory were clear: he was the darling of right-wing American corporate powers—the same people who were even then ushering Ronald Reagan into office. Seaga would clearly be Reagan's man, pledged to keep Jamaica free of left-wing adventurers and ideologues, and at the disposal of American corporate interests for whatever purposes Reagan, David Rockefeller and the other architects of the Caribbean Basin Initiative might envision. Reagan wanted the island cleaned up, and one of the things he insisted on was that the ganja trade be taken out of the hands of the poor and eliminated as a "cash crop." This would force them to look for other sources of income and make themselves more available for "constructive" employment in the private sector.

What had happened instead was that the ganja dealers had turned, starving, to the cocaine and heroin trade to earn a living. There *were* no employment opportunities in the private sector, the public sector or any subsector in between. But the hard drug trade doesn't offer profits for the poor because the market gets taken over by "professionals" who don't like to spread their profits around too freely. Many of the seven hundred people shot in the streets during the 1980 election had been fighting for control of the new, far more dangerous drug market that had been created by the banishment of the old.

All of which is why the still-devout older Rastas who had retreated to the remote interior of Jamaica had taken the time to count the number of letters in Ronald Wilson Reagan's name (6-6-6) and believed he was the Antichrist. As for the younger dreads who were "dabbling" in the faith, they liked the hard drugs and were beginning to think that Rasta was an awfully difficult road to travel and still manage to survive in this world.

As Bob was running around the pond near Central Park South

that Sunday morning, he felt his body freezing up on him. He turned to tell Skilly something was wrong, but his neck suddenly became rigid; he couldn't speak. He was unable to move his head as he fell forward.

Skilly got Bob back to their hotel, the Essex House. Bob gradually revived, but he was severely shaken. Nevertheless the decision was made to go on to Pittsburgh the following day for a Tuesday night show. No one had told Rita that Bob had collapsed in the park. The dreads around Bob had insisted she stay with the rest of the women in the Gramercy Park Hotel much further downtown, rather than in the Essex House.

There was no precedent for this, Rasta sexism notwithstanding. On past tours, even when Bob was keeping company with another woman, Rita had traditionally stayed in the same hotel, serving as a confidante, looking after his personal needs as he so desired, caring for any of the children who might be along, serving as a liaison between Bob and the rest of his family and acting on many occasions as his private secretary. Rita tried to call Bob at the Essex House but was unable to get through; finally she gave up and located Danny Sims. "Why such a drastic change?" she asked, furious. "What's going on?" Sims said it had been Alan Cole's idea. Alan would not accept Rita's phone calls, so she took a taxi up to the Essex House and confronted him. He put her off, saying she was imagining things. When she asked to see Bob, she was told he was resting and didn't want to be disturbed before the show. Rita noticed, however, that there were more hangers-on at the hotel than usual, and that there was a sleazy, macho vibe about the scene.

She wasn't the only one who was disturbed about the atmosphere at the Essex House. Other dreads from the old guard who stopped to check fe Skipper that weekend left murmuring in disgust about the goings-on at the hotel, alleging that Bob was being isolated from the genuine friends he had built up in New York over the years by a swarm of hustlers and hoods from Kingston and Brooklyn. These new "friends" were running up incredible bills around town in Bob's name and bringing hookers, liquor and hard drugs into the hotel for lavish parties. Some freebasing dreads had dared to adopt the sacrilegious practice of bestowing upon the glass pipe and the blow torch the Rasta blessing traditionally given to the chillum or cutchie before lighting it. The scene was so ugly that no one on the outside who had managed to penetrate the "security" net to witness it firsthand wanted to accept that it was actually happening.

On Sunday afternoon, the cash receipts from the previous night's concert had arrived. Bob was stretched out on his bed, the door closed, while dozens of anonymous dreads and fast-talking hustlers milled about his suite. The money was brought to him, and he lifted himself off the pillow, trembling slightly, looking hollow-cheeked and burnt out. He stared pensively at the crisp stack of bills as if studying an old gimcrack to see if it still held meaning for him or should be discarded. He absently passed the money to a band member.

Bob kept murmuring that he wanted to sleep, that all he wanted was peace and quiet, but the crowd that had taken over the rest of his suite declined to clear out, partying harder as the bedroom door was again ordered closed to shut out the din.

Arriving in Pittsburgh Monday night, Rita discovered Bob had not checked into the hotel. Troubled, she called New York and was told he had been taken to a doctor after "having a stroke."

Rita shrieked. "What? Be careful, yuh people! If anyt'ing happen to Bob yuh *all* gonna feel it!" She cursed furiously into the phone, demanded more information, but no one in New York would fill her in on the details of Bob's illness. That night in Pittsburgh, she had a dream in which Bob appeared wearing a hospital gown, his locks gone. She was talking to him through a fence.

"Wha' happen, Bob?" she asked.

"Me sick," he replied.

"I'm coming around ta tek yuh out a dis place 'cause nothin' wrong wit' yuh!"

She woke up and burst into tears. Phoning Judy Mowatt and Marcia Griffiths in their rooms, she asked them to come to her suite and told them all she knew—and didn't know.

Tuesday morning, Bob arrived at the hotel with Skilly and company, and Rita hardly recognized him, he looked so ancient and drawn.

"Wha' has happened ta you?" she asked, sobbing uncontrollably.

"Doctor seh brain tumor black me out," he replied, his voice so weak Rita had to restrain her weeping to hear what he was saying.

"Let's stop de tour," she said.

"Dem seh nuh," he said, meaning Alan, Danny Sims and the booking agency.

"Impossible!" Rita cried. "*Impossible!*"

As Bob was checked in, Rita phoned Ciddy and told her and Bob's personal lawyer, Diane Jobson, what was happening. "*Dis is not right!*" she hollered, nearly hysterical.

Bob went on and did the Tuesday night show, barely lasting the performance. Skilly went to Rita and said, "It meks nuh sense ta stop da tour. If dey stop da tour, Bob is gwan die anyway." This was the first time Rita had heard anything about the possibility that Bob might actually die—soon.

She got on the phone and summoned all available family members and legal advisors, including Diane Jobson, Don Taylor, Chris Blackwell and Bob's business lawyer, David Steinberg, all of whom had been in the dark about the state of Bob's health. The tour was immediately canceled, the pertinent contracts discreetly voided. The Howard Bloom Organization, the company contracted to publicize the tour—they had gotten Marley coverage in all major black publications for the first time in his career—was now asked to do everything in its power to see that no one in the press discovered that Bob might well be dead in a few months.

Bob was secretly admitted to Manhattan's Memorial Sloan-Kettering Cancer Center and underwent radium treatments that caused the locks around his forehead and temples to drop off. After two days, word leaked out that he was there. Although he was scheduled to be in the hospital for at least two weeks, when he learned the rumor had been announced on WNEW-FM and published in the New York papers, he immediately checked out, ignoring doctors' warnings that without proper, intensive treatment, he might not live another ten weeks. Based on tests taken thus far, cancer tissue was detected in his liver, lungs and brain, and there was evidence that the disease was spreading to other vital organs.

After several weeks as an errant outpatient (while staying at Danny Sims's apartment) Bob became demoralized by persistent local reports of his illness, refused to listen to anyone at Sloan-Kettering and left town, going first to Cedars of Lebanon Hospital in Miami, then to the cancer clinic in Mexico where actor Steve McQueen had been treated in an unsuccessful attempt to save his life, then back to Sloan-Kettering. Every doctor he saw told him the same thing: his chances of living out the year were very slight. Unbeknownst to the Twelve Tribes, Rita had Bob baptized in the Ethiopian Orthodox Church on November 4, 1980. Taking the name Berhane Selassie, he had become a Christian Rasta.

A Jamaican physician, Dr. Carl Fraser, a favorite of Twelve Tribes Rastas who called him "Pee Wee," suggested that Bob seek treatment from Dr. Josef Issels, a seventy-two-year-old German doctor who specialized in helping those with so-called hopeless, untreatable or terminal cancer. By November, Bob was scheduled to move to Issels's clinic in Rottach-Egern, a tiny town in the Bavarian foothills near the Austrian border.

Rita asked Howard Bloom to circulate the story that Bob was convalescing from "exhaustion" in Shashamanna, Ethiopia. Bloom had never been faced with such a bizarre and tragic ethical question. In the last few weeks he had been one of the few people in constant contact with Bob by phone. Every time he told Bob about another story announcing his impending death, the singer's depression deepened. Finally, Bloom agreed to go along with the Ethiopia ruse, and Bob was flown to Bavaria, accompanied by Diane Jobson, Rita, Cedella, his old Trench Town friend Bird, Skilly and Dr. Carl "Pee Wee" Fraser.

Riding up the white gravel driveway to the chaletlike Ringberg Clinic, Bob's spirits lifted a bit. It was a very cheerful but chilly environment, the terraced three-story hospital sitting in the center of the gently sloping, snow-covered hillocks of the Tegernsee Valley at the southern tip of the lake of the same name. Surveying the area from certain vantage points, the weary Rasta, a knitted skullcap covering his bald head, murmured that it looked a little like Nine Miles.

His deep depression returned with full force, however, when he entered the elegant, well-appointed reception hall and saw the large, gruesome crucifix hanging in the alcove above the main staircase.

Issels appeared in the hall and welcomed Bob warmly. The tall, broad-shouldered doctor, with deep-set eyes and swept-back wavy silver hair that crept over his collar, looked into Bob's eyes and said simply, "We can make it work."

Go Climb a Mountain, a 1970 BBC television documentary about Issels's highly controversial theories, had summed up his approach in this way:

> The Issels concept is that a healthy body cannot develop cancer. Therefore, he believes the entire metabolism of the body must be treated. Cancer cells which may lay dormant in everybody become active only when the body is no longer capable of destroying them. Conventional treatment is not enough. He says that often surgery and radiation only stop the cancer temporarily. It can return later as secondary tumors. To him cancer is a local symptom of a general body deficiency, a sort of red alert that the whole body is in danger.

The British medical community did everything in its power to prevent the documentary from being produced and, when it was completed despite their protests, attempted to bar it from being aired. After one broadcast on November 3, 1970, which was watched by a record fourteen million Britons, the film was never shown again; the Harley Street establishment had finally prevailed.

There had been four investigations of the unorthodox Issels *Ganzheitstheorie* (or "whole body theory") therapy since 1951, when Issels's clinic was founded. The first was conducted by Dr. Arie Aulier of Leiden University, Holland, between 1953 and 1958, who concluded that Issels's success with terminal cancer patients was unsurpassed in the world. A follow-up study by Dr. John Anderson of Kings College Hospital in London between 1967 and 1969 ended with the statement: "He is undoubtedly producing clinical remission in patients who have been regarded as hopeless." Another report by British cancer experts in 1967 was favorable, but a team of experts from the Coordinating Committee for Cancer Research, an association representing three British groups, stated in their 1970 study that while Issels "believes implicitly" in his treatment and did a "great deal" to help his patients, he was "misguided in his beliefs" and his clinic was "ineffective."

Whatever the judgment of the medical community, Issels managed to keep Bob Marley alive more than six months longer than any other doctor would dare even to project. Issels himself never made any predictions; he merely vowed to try his best. Bob was fed whole grains and fibers, supplemented by enzymes and special bacterial preparations; he was given yogurt to aid in removing unwanted bacilli, herb tea to help rid his body of toxic wastes from the tumors, trace minerals and selected vitamins. Areas of chronic infection, such as inflamed tonsils and decayed or devitalized teeth, were removed because they hampered the natural efficiency of the body's immune system. Most of the food that any Rasta would not deem ital had, coincidentally, also long been taboo in Issels's nutritional program. Issels's approach also included aspects of holistic medicine and psychology. Exercise was recommended to increase oxygen intake, and Diane took Bob out for strolls whenever he felt up to it. Oxygen and ozone were injected, by transfusions of oxygenated blood, in the belief that these gases could weaken cancer cells. Bob also received a host of controversial vaccines, some of which (including one substance called both CH-23 and F-26) have been banned by the FDA. Ciddy and Rita supplemented Issels's treatments with their own bush medicines in an effort to somehow delay the inevitable.

On February 6, 1981, Junior Marvin, Seeco Patterson and Tyrone Downie hosted a little birthday party for Bob in his quarters at the Ringberg Clinic. They sat together watching a TV show about the World Cup that featured highlights of Pelé's performances over the years in the championship matches. Bob seemed strong, alert and in good spirits.

But as spring arrived in the Tegernsee Valley, the day finally came when Issels announced he could do no more. Bob was flown back to Miami. In a phone call to David Steinberg, he made his attorney promise that he would not rest until the publishing rights to all of Bob's songs were retrieved and turned over to his family. "Maddah, don' cry," he said afterward to Ciddy as she stood at his bedside, clutching his hand, "I'll be all right. I'm gwan ta prepare a place." He died just before noon on May 11, 1981, only forty hours after he left Germany.

At that moment, back in Kingston, Judy Mowatt was sitting on the veranda of her home on the outskirts of the Liguanea section of Kingston when a great burst of thunder shook the firmament and a bolt of lightning hurtled through her open window, glancing off the framed photograph of Bob on her mantlepiece. Frightened, her children began to cry; after calming them, Judy turned on the radio and heard the JBC bulletin that Bob was gone.

Prophet Gad had let it be known that when Bob Marley died he wanted Selassie's ring, said to be a precious relic containing actual fragments of Solomon's own ring.

From the moment Bob died until the final minutes before he was sealed in his coffin and placed in the hilltop mausoleum in Nine Miles, Gad's campaign to obtain the mystical gift was unrelenting. But it was conducted with such secrecy and cunning that the overwhelming majority of the people closest to Bob never even guessed the significance of the ring. They never knew where it had come from, or thought to inquire about what, if anything, might become of it.

Unbeknownst to those who made their overtures on behalf of Prophet Gad—from Skilly Cole and Pee Wee Fraser to virtually all of the sect's ruling council (including many prominent Jamaicans who revealed their membership in the Tribes to the Marley family solely for the purpose of helping to obtain the ring)—Bob had taken it off just before leaving Germany and given it to Diane for safekeeping. At first he had mulled over the notion of entrusting it to her against the day it might be given to his son Ziggy, but then he decided he had no right to give it to anyone under any circumstances. (Besides Bob's other three children by Rita—Cedella, Stevie, the infant Stephanie—he had seven others, each by a different woman, who were legally acknowledged: girls Karen and Makeda Jahnesta, boys Rohan, Robbie, Ky-mani, Julian and Damian, the last being his infant son by Cindy Breakspeare. Also, he adopted Rita's Sharon.)

Cedella recalled a visit that Selassie's granddaughter and nephew had paid Bob more than a year before. The meeting took place in the Miami home in which Bob had recently installed Cedella, his half-brothers and half-sisters. Bob, Cedella and Selassie's kin were sitting in the living room talking when Bob indicated the ring, which he never removed.

"Dis indeed was His Majesty's ring?" he asked.

The Ethiopians nodded, saying that it was the very ring the emperor had worn throughout his life.

Bob was silent for a few moments and then, softly, matter-of-factly, but, in a voice that trembled in a way Cedella had never thought possible, he said, "Ya know, sometimes dis ring, it burn my finger, like *fire*."

The ring was on his finger when Robert Nesta Marley, O.M., lay in state in Jamaica, and once the coffin was sealed in a closed-door ceremony, the question of its whereabouts was likewise sealed. As the interment of Bob Marley's remains approached, Prophet Gad was rumored to be in a righteous rage beyond describing.

Finally, when Bob Marley was buried and all Jamaica had bade him farewell, top-ranking members of the Twelve Tribes of Israel presented Diane Jobson with a bill for three thousand dollars, telling her it was for ceremonial services rendered by the sect during the funeral services. She was appalled. "Yuh nuh get yar t'irty pieces a silver from me, Judases!" she spat back.

The delegation of Twelve Tribesmen next confronted Cedella Marley Booker and demanded to know what had become of Bob's mystical Solomonic legacy.

At first, she didn't quite comprehend what they were getting at. A recent convert to Rasta herself, she discussed the Scriptures, principally the book of Revelation, and she talked about how Daniel, who was a prophet held captive in Babylon in the sixth century B.C., had predicted woeful events that were to occur between 1948 and the end of the twentieth century, as preludes to the Apocalypse. She also fretted that Bob's godmother, Roslyn Downs, who had never stood by him, had actually had the nerve to phone, saying, "But, Ciddy, me nevar know Nesta was a prophet!" Cedella said she pitied the woman, and then quoted aloud from Matthew 25:13. "Watch, therefore, for ye know neither the day nor the hour."

The Twelve Tribes leaders were becoming impatient with these musings. Where had the ring gone?

"De ring gwan back ta where it come from, same as Bob," said Ciddy, still contemplative, her head bowed.

Where? they asked. Where was that? Tell us! Yahso! Exactly where was Solomon's ring to be found?

Cedella looked up, her eyes narrowing as she scrutinized her interrogators. Then her expression relaxed, a smile playing on her lips. She realized that these people, who called themselves Rastas, actually did *not* know the whereabouts of the ring.

"De ring gwan back from whence it come," she repeated, her voice quiet but firm. "It back on His Majesty's mighty hand. And *yuh*," she added, still more quietly, "know neither de day nor de hour."

17

Time Will Tell

a hereafterword

"A wicked and adulterous generation seeketh after a sign; and there shall be no sign given unto it, but the sign of the prophet Jonah."

—MATTHEW 16:4

"We are told how, in ancient times, Yahweh had commanded the prophet Jonah to go to Nineveh, the capitol of Assyria, and prophesy catastrophe for its people because of their evil behavior."

—MICHAEL GRANT, *The History of Ancient Israel*, 1984

"After this I looked, and there before my eyes was a door opened in heaven; and the voice that I heard speaking to me like a trumpet said, 'Come up here, and I will show you what must happen hereafter.' "

—THE REVELATION OF ST. JOHN THE DIVINE 4:1

As the veils of grief, guile and fear fell away, all figures around the departed Bob Marley displayed bold and disquieting new faces. Mourning gave way to manipulation, virtue to vanity, myth to menace. In April of 1981, a few weeks prior to Marley's death, recently elected prime minister Edward Seaga announced that the stricken singer had been awarded the Jamaican Order of Merit, officially designating him a national hero. Since Marley was still critically ill in Dr. Issels's Bavarian clinic in Rottach-Egern, Seaga arranged for Marley's eldest son, Ziggy, to accept the honor in Kingston. In the ghetto, the move was celebrated as a gesture of acquiescence to the desperate agenda of the sufferah—especially since it coincided with a Seaga-urged announcement early that year by Ronald Reagan of a U.S.-backed Caribbean Basin Initiative. (Speaking before the Organization of American States, Reagan said the Initiative was, among other things, designed to eliminate tariffs on virtually all Caribbean goods entering the United States. The concept, as described by the American president, was for the impoverished countries of the region to "make use of the magic of the marketplace" in developing their economies.)

However, a confidential CIA airgram dispatched to the State Department from the American embassy in Kingston on April 28, 1981—about four months after Ronald Reagan's inauguration—revealed the cynical motive behind Seaga's oddly timed bestowal of the Order of Merit: to depict as disreputably unpatriotic Opposition leader Michael Manley's People's National Party.

As the classified communiqué carefully explained:

> Jamaica's Governor General, Florizel Glasspole, was knighted by Queen Elizabeth II on April 17, four weeks after Prime Minister Edward Seaga had announced the Government of Jamaica's decision to allow Jamaicans to accept foreign honors. . . . (The Governor General received 150 congratulatory messages and cables on the first day after the announcement and many more on subsequent days.) Government members in the House of Representatives paid tribute to and congratulated the Governor General when the House met on April 22.
>
> At the same time that Jamaica House released the news of the Governor General's knighthood, it was announced that Jamaican reggae superstar Bob Marley, who is being treated for cancer in the Federal Republic of Germany, had been awarded the Order of Merit, Jamaica's third highest honor. In responding to the government's tribute to the Governor General, the Opposition moved to congratulate Marley at the same time and allowed itself to be maneuvered into a position of not paying tribute to the popular Governor General.

Thus, in one stroke, Seaga had both humiliated Manley's democratic socialists and defused the explosive legacy of the Third World's most renowned rabble-rouser. Once it might have been unseemly for Seaga's Reagan-steered regime to have celebrated a musician who actively endorsed black leftist struggles for freedom and self-determination in Zimbabwe, Angola, Mozambique and South Africa. But Marley's terminal illness and Seaga's election mandate of October 30,

1980, had allowed the canny new prime minister to cloak the courage of the reggae firebrand's convictions with a cultural garland that smacked of a gratuity.

The *Daily Gleaner*, which had facilitated Seaga's election victory through lurid coverage of campaign violence and sensationalist warnings of a possible Cuban takeover, fawned over Seaga's award for the reggae superstar. The *Gleaner* had grown increasingly right-wing ever since 1976, when managing director Oliver Clarke joined the board of directors of the mighty CIA-influenced Inter-American Press Association. With Seaga exploiting reggae culture just as he had once misused the grass-roots Kumina religion, the Twenty-one Families dominating the *Gleaner*'s own board hoped for a fresh popular credibility by means of the Marley magic. The surest way for a society to subdue an outlaw is to make him a laureate.

The cruel irony in Marley's Order of Merit decoration was that its odious subtext had been mirrored in a song called "Buffalo Soldier," one of the last tracks the singer had recorded before he took sick. The song recounted the true story of four post–Civil War regiments of the U.S. Army—the 9th and 10th Cavalry and the 24th and 25th Infantry. These units were composed of black privates and noncommissioned officers, under the command of white brass, who fought for a quarter century against the Cheyenne, Comanche, Kiowa, Apache, Ute and Sioux. In the end, fourteen key black campaigners, whom the Indians had dubbed "buffalo soldiers," were awarded the Medal of Honor as part of a public relations move to justify and glorify the genocide of Native Americans, underlining the U.S. government's policy of manifest destiny. Such were the ploys that, then as now, comprised the politics of neutralization.

Once Bob Marley was safely interred, the Jamaican government put the finishing touches on his new respectability by issuing a limited edition series of postage stamps bearing his image, each of the various miniature color photos superimposed on sheet music of his best-known compositions. The melody to "Exodus" graced the 2¢ stamp, "Coming In from the Cold" heralded the 15¢ issue, "Could You Be Loved" adorned the $3.00 stamp, and the impression on the $5.25 stamp was a moody charcoal portrait surrounded by pen-and-ink sketches of ten of his Island album jackets. However briefly, the image of Bob Marley was empowered to carry postcards, parcels and letters from Jamaica to the four corners of the globe.

Closer to home, Rita Marley, Jamaican attorney George Desnoes and Louis Byles, managing director of the Royal Bank Trust Company, Ltd. of Jamaica (later known as the Mutual Security Merchant Bank and Trust) began application proceedings in the Kingston court of one Justice Harris for a grant of letters of administration for control of the estate of Bob Marley, valued at $30 million in the States. As Bob's widow, Rita was entitled under Jamaican law to 10 percent of the estate, all personal possessions, and 50 percent of the monies generated by the estate during her lifetime, with the rest distributed to Bob's eleven legally recognized children by eight women. (After Rita's death, all monies would go to the offspring.)

However, Rita produced documents dated June 6, 1978, and witnessed by Philadelphia attorney David Steinberg, that showed transfer of 98 percent of Bob Marley's three chief publishing, recording and licensing companies—Bob Marley Music, Media Aids and Tuff Gong—to Rita's personal holdings. These holdings were being handled by Steinberg and Rita's New York accountant, Marvin Zolt—both of whom had worked for Bob in the years just prior to his death. Consequently, the lion's share of her husband's wealth went directly to his widow. As for the meager remainder of the estates accounts, co-administrators Byles, Desnoes and Rita Marley supervised monthly payments to his offspring that largely ranged from $75 to $90.

Overnight, Rita, who had never lived extravagantly in the past, transformed her spare existence into that of a hedonistic Caribbean heiress. The long-untidy Hope Road compound was lavishly overhauled, its outbuildings acquiring shopping center–like stucco facades, the main house and surrounding buildings daubed with red, green and gold enamel and redecorated to favor a museum cum tourist trap. When not ensconced in an upstairs chamber, artfully dealing with two phones while she simultaneously signed autographs, she could be found in one of her country residences—usually her retreat on the Milk River—trying on an array of expensive sports clothes, evening gowns and stage costumes flown in from Miami, Los Angeles and London.

Rita's normally demure manner gradually gave way to the indecorous giddiness of a debutante. This sense of good fortune also fueled Rita's rekindled recording career. She scored a smash JA success late in 1981 with "One Draw," a playful send-up of newly assertive ganja use amongst Rasta feminists. The clever single clicked in dance halls, Sound Systems, and even on the JBC, which adopted an attitude of tolerance to the pro-herb ditty, since it was, after all, being sung by the spouse of a national hero. "One Draw" originally appeared on two separate versions of a 1980–81 Rita solo album briefly issued on the Tuff Gong and entitled *Who Feels It Knows It* (after Bunny Livingston's ska-era Wailers classic of the same name).

By mid-1981, *Who Feels It Knows It* had been released in slightly different form in the States on the prestigious ethnic/progressive Shanachie label. Rita's debut American LP succeeded not only because of its crossover retooling of roots reggae but also for the disarmingly lighthearted self-assurance of the singer. Sexy, sagacious and occasionally stern in tone, she served up Rasta religious dictums with a sparkling directness that recalled the lusty verve of Phyllis Hyman or Linda Clifford, as well as the girlish sweetness of Angela Bofill and Minnie Riperton.

Part of the credit for the generous range of arrangements belonged to the instrumental support, which included Wailers Earl "Chinna" Smith and Junior Marvin on guitars, the Barrett brothers' rhythm section, and keyboardists Tyrone Downie and Earl "Wire" Lindo, plus stellar JA sidemen like bassist Robbie Shakespeare, percussionist Leroy "Horsemouth" Wallace, and the cream of Don Drummond's old Alpha School horn classes: Bobby Ellis, Tommy McCook, Vincent Gordon.

As a consequence of the sessions' warm family vibes—as well as material tailored to her girlishly silky voice—Rita shone on sophisticated dance fare like "That's the Way," "Easy Sailing" and the Motown-influenced "Jah Jah Don't Want," as well as remakes of the ska-period Wailers' title track and "I'm Still Waiting." The LP's gem, though, remained the exultant "One Draw," this ballad to the joys of sinsemilla swirling to intoxicating heights as Rita intoned, "I want to get high! *Soooo* high!" *Who Feels It Knows It* earned deservedly enthusiastic reviews from such mainstream popular music journals as *Rolling Stone* and *Billboard* magazine.

Now Rita was an international star too, her twelve-inch pressing of "One Draw" exciting ballroom skankers in Scandinavia, the United Kingdom and Europe. Several of the toniest night spots in Hong Kong, Singapore and Tokyo also featured the track. In demand for television interviews, she soon shifted her on-camera discourse from somber soliloquies about Bob's enduring message to imperious self-assessments. Several of these TV appearances, particularly a widely syndicated American newsmagazine broadcast, showed her seated in a thronelike tropical setting, crisply describing herself as a "queen."

By 1982, when the slick and vastly inferior *Harambe* ("*Working Together for Freedom*") album surfaced in Jamaica and the States, it was under the new publishing banner of Rita Marley Music. She openly insisted on being treated and even addressed as the "Queen of Reggae."

"Bob was the king, and as his queen I must carry on," she pointedly told one reporter, and many interviews had the deliberate air of royal audiences. Public relations veteran Charles Comer, a former Island Records press chief who played a pivotal role in guiding the reggae careers of Bob Marley, Peter Tosh and Judy Mowatt, privately found Rita's outlandish attitudes unseemly. Several times he declined to renew his handling of her account, only to have Rita come to him personally to plead ("Charlie, yuh de only one who tell me wha' yuh really t'ink of my actions!") for another chance.

To Rita's mind, her career had become a matter of divine right, and her tone of mystical entitlement extended even to the quasi-biblical inscription decorating the back cover of *Harambe*: " 'The race is not for the swift nor the battle for the strong, but for those who have endured.' This time is the time of Armageddon. And also the time of love. Whoever endureth shall overcome pests and pestilence, plagues like protons, neutrons, atoms gone astray. But as warriors all, no matter how hot or how cold, Rita Marley and the Crew fire us through the patient kindness of His Imperial Majesty Haile Selassie I."

In truth, there was little in the former Alpharita Constantia Anderson's background to equip her for the attention and responsibilities she'd inherited. A product of a broken home, impregnated and then abandoned while still in her teens, she'd gravitated to Sunday school teaching and the nursing profession in order to make a structured life for herself and baby Sharon. Life in the ghetto was either puritan or profligate, yet the increasingly Rasta-influenced recording industry seemed to offer a compromise. Her relationship with Bob Marley represented yet another midcourse adjustment, but her essentially shy nature was in synch with it. Her supporting role as an I-Three generated risk-free recognition, and her burdens as wife and mother were best shouldered in privacy. As Bob acquired a roster of kept women and "baby mothers," he had periodically treated Rita as a servant, sometimes even in the presence of his mistresses. Rita's hurt and embarrassment had been considerable. Hardworking, a good mother, and attentive to her husband's professional and personal needs—although she increasingly sought outside male companionship of her own during Bob's last years—she openly viewed the windfalls attendant to Bob's passing as payback.

Others seeking some form of remuneration were the ranks of the Wailers band, a close-knit fraternity that had cooked, cleaned, played and prayed for Bob's achievements until these were sometimes—if only to them—indistinguishable from their own. Now they were disgruntled, because the royalty portions they'd seen with so-so regularity had stopped coming since Rita became bursar. Stung, this group found their back o' yard vexing blossoming into public kass-kass.

In December 1982 attorney David Steinberg invited drummer Carlton Barrett, guitarists Al Anderson and Junior Marvin, keyboardist Earl Lindo and percussionist Seeco Patterson to his offices in Philadelphia's elegant Widener Building for a powwow. "I have something for you people," said the handsome salt-and-pepper-haired Steinberg, producing a fan of checks. These were dispensed with crisp sixteen-page contracts, and the assembled were permitted to ponder the amounts and particulars unique to each folio. Those who signed the deals got the dough. Those who didn't would depart as broke as most of them had arrived. Al Anderson, a footloose latercomer to the squad, saw his check was for $18,000. Carly Barrett, peerless master of the one-drop, was being offered $42,000. Others were dealt a lesser figure somewhere in between. (Family Man and Tyrone Downie's disbursals were done separately.) They protested that Bob had always split his pie down the middle with them. Steinberg said this was the final settlement. As they mulled over the proposition, the manager of the Warwick Hotel phoned wanting to know when they would pay their bills. Thus hectored, they all signed and split.

Ciddy, a proud and headstrong woman, had her own perspective on Bob's beneficiaries, feeling that she was the first amongst blood equals. Quick to remind everyone that Bob had inherited his vocal talent from her, she pressed on after his death with a project that he had heartily endorsed: the recording of a full-length gospel/reggae album. Ciddy had been cutting demos of gospel standards and original reggae homilies since 1977, when Bob had invited her into the studio during the assembling of the heavily biblical *Exodus* album. Early in 1982 she entered Tuff Gong studios to cut a fervent single of her own composing, "Stay Alive," which featured the stark refrain " 'E put a song in my mouth ta sing / Praises to de King / Stay alive Jah Jah children / Don't cry." The single's B–side was an informal medley of Marley songs ("Redemption Song," "Coming In from the Cold," "Could You Be Loved," "Forever Loving Jah") that Ciddy titled "Redemption Song" and published under her own name, C. Booker.

Once the single hit the Kingston record stalls, Ciddy underwent her own transformation. Having let go of the two homes she and the late Edward Booker had owned on Tatnall Street in Wilmington, Delaware, she settled permanently in the South Miami house she had frequently shared with Bob and/or Rita both during Bob's convalescence from the 1976 assassination attempt and at various stages of his illness prior to treatment in Bavaria. Although the deed of the rambling two-story Miami ranch house—which had a large swimming pool and was located on roughly three acres of land—was in Bob's name, Ciddy claimed that Bob had purchased it for her.

Under Jamaica's law of intestacy Ciddy herself was not entitled to any share of the estate, but as the adoptive parent of Bob's ten-year-old son Rohan she was empowered to pursue the boy's interests. However, she prevailed upon Rita to provide her with funds to maintain the Miami house and honor the family ties that bound them. Ciddy eventually received sums Rita's New York attorney Peter Herbert estimated (and reaffirmed by Marley estate counsels William Thomas and Robert Brundige) as "almost five hundred thousand dollars."

While sales of Ciddy's "Stay Alive" single were small, the press response was sizeable, and she swiftly lost some forty-five pounds in a physical revitalization that she described to friends and associates as "Miraculous!" (At the same point, circa 1980, that her son was adding ancient African mysticism to his Rasta creed, seeking out the counsel of Ghanaian occultist/healer Akonidi Hini—for whom Jimi Hendrix had purportedly penned the song "Voodoo Chile"—Ciddy began openly repudiating her Christian faith as her recent Rasta conversion took hold.) Smoking herb on a daily basis and reasoning with every Rasta philosopher she met, she ultimately proclaimed that "His Majesty has given me a new life an' a new chance. He has worked a miracle upon me body and spirit!"

Indeed, she showed a striking new vitality: her worry- and work-hardened features had smoothed out somewhat, and she looked almost ten years younger. Less attractive was her desire to be regarded—in the words of one writer—as the "Queen Mother of Reggae." To this end, Mother B. (as her nickname became) shed her conventional dresses and shifts in favor of flowing ceremonial gowns and quasi-African headdresses in various shades of scarlet and gold. She initiated an annual memorial concert at Bob's birthplace in Nine Miles, building a permanent outdoor stage on the hillside where a platform had been hastily erected for the speakers at Marley's funeral, and presented herself and Pearl Livingston, her daughter by Bunny's father, as the ceremonies' main draws.

The Melody Makers, the group consisting of four of Rita and Bob's children (Sharon, Cedella, Ziggy, Stephen), also did guest shots at the Nine Miles shows held on Bob's birthday of February 6, usually singing their 1979-80 Tuff Gong singles—"Children Playing in the Streets," "Sugar Pie," "Trodding" or the big hit they released in JA in 1982 on the Rita Marley Music label, "What a Plot." The frequency of Rita's own appearances depended on how she was getting along with Mother B., since the two women were increasingly locked in ego-aggravated feuds over Tuff Gong policies, the Marley estate, or financial support for the children outside of Rita's household. Neither woman had much practical knowledge of the record industry, the intricacies of music publishing (where much of the money actually resides), or the management of anything beyond a household. Sadly, their well-founded anxieties about the pitfalls surrounding them would drive them apart more often than it would unite them—not that there weren't many factions eager to exploit the tiniest rift.

For Mother B.'s part, her sensitivities were also the consequence of five decades of struggle, disappointment and disenfranchisement. Rejected by Bob's father, spurned by Norval's family, forced to grope for equilibrium in a hellish Kingston landscape and then to start all over again in an alien Stateside city, she had adopted her own fiercely independent stance. Once resettled in Wilmington, she had opened her heart and home to Bob's wife, children, band members, paramours and fellow travelers, asking little more than "mannersly" (polite) conduct in return. The stream of guests was constant, the additional tasks they necessitated nearly overwhelming, and as these connections drew her deeper into Bob's career, she came to feel that the luster of his reflected glow was her birthright. Once the tireless caretaker of the inner circle's needs, she resolved to be matriarch of his entire tattered clan.

Like Rita, Mother B. felt Bob's adoring public had magically decreed her boy to be royalty. "The last shall be first!" went Rita and Mother B.'s justification. But no one in either Rita or Mother B.'s sphere paused to point out that such Scriptural passages referred to the afterlife, the existence following the Last Judgment, rather than any temporal state. Moreover, it was never mentioned that, throughout his own career, Bob had uniformly and often angrily rejected any proffered titles or trite mantles, stating, "Dere is nuh king but His Imperial Majesty. Nuh king but Jah!"

In the ghetto, when a Sound System DJ or a toasting selector crowned himself Duke or Count or King, it was meant to be a jocular boast, a brazen joke in which the beleaguered community could share. But the moment anybody anywhere took titles of any stripe too seriously, Bob characterized such actions as works of the Devil—evil delusions creating a "separation t'ing" between one mortal and another, while making a mockery of the downtrodden souls his music championed.

Most of all, quarreling over hierarchies and material goods led to wars—"war uptown, war downtown." And so it would be in the 1980s, as the battle over Bob Marley's unspoken last will and testament raged parallel with the onrush of Armageddon.

As far as the Caribbean was concerned, modern war games had commenced in its midst in December 1981, when for the first time President Reagan placed the Key West–headquartered U.S. military forces for the entire Caribbean basin (including the Gulf of Mexico and Pacific regions abutting Central America) under the unified command of Rear Admiral Robert P. McKenzie. Reagan had been disturbed by the mounting influence of Cuba and Nicaragua's revolutionary leftist governments on Jamaica under Michael Manley and especially on Grenada, where Prime Minister Maurice Bishop's revolutionary New Jewel Movement installed a Cuba-supported government in 1979.

For twenty years prior, Grenada had suffered under the corrupt and erratic rule of autocrat Eric Gairy, a near-balmy UFO buff who ran the country's agrarian economy into the dust while turning local hotels and nightclubs into his own booming brothels. In contrast, Bishop's rhetoric-choked regime was naive and internally volatile, but four of its accomplishments during its five-year life were significant: an effective popular education program that embraced rural literacy, secondary school expansion and adult education; a restructured health care system that allowed private care while extending free, quality treatment to the peasantry; revitalized trade unionism through a mandatory union recognition law; and decentralized rule through the institution of New England–style zonal and parish councils. Even critics agreed that these innovations were models for the entire Caribbean.

Yet, since World War II, the communism-loathing U.S. government has usually preferred even a stooge polity within its span of influence to an ambitious one given to opportunistic alliances. The war had seen the U.S. forge novel agreements with Britain's fractured empire in which it traded some fifty warships to Her Majesty's navy in exchange for ninety-nine-year leases on military bases in Jamaica, Trinidad, St. Lucia, Antigua and Guyana. As Britain gradually withdrew from the region, the United States put into effect a bold new plan, begun in Puerto Rico in 1947, for corporate Caribbean investment in sectors ranging from tourism to mineral mining and manufacturing. What seemed like a benign new economic day, however, was actually a laissez-faire refurbishment of old-fangled colonialism, because the Caribbean was really being turned into a massive cheap-labor factory for whatever new products the neighboring industrialized power desired. Capital, technology and management were shipped into the tropical basin by multinationals anxious to avoid minimum-wage laws and healthy American trade unions, and the products and profits poured out, with the islands themselves seeing little benefit. Rather, since the islands were forced to compete for such dubious attentions, a country such as the Jamaica of 1966–76 saw incoming investment far *exceeded* by outgoing profits. And once their decade-long tax holidays were over, the corporations tended to say farewell to the swaying palms.

Because the Caribbean had become a prime audience for leftist arguments, raw might had to reinforce economic fealty. During August–October 1981, Rear Admiral McKenzie's Caribbean Command participated in the regional phases of Operation Ocean Venture '81–82, the largest peacetime maneuvers by the military of the Western alliances since World War II. America played host in the Caribbean to 120,000 troops, 1,000 aircraft and 240 warships from its own arsenals and those of thirteen friendly nations. One facet of the maneuvers was the staged invasion of "Amber," a nonexistent island seat of "anti-democratic revolutionary activities" for which the Grenada-like Puerto Rican islet of Vieques was the stand-in. Units of the 75th Ranger Division took part in the mock assault, whose elaborate official scenario encompassed air and amphibious support for a predawn attack of 300 paratroopers rescuing fictitious American hostages; plus troops left in place until new elections resulted in leadership "favorable"—

according to 1981 press briefings by Rear Admiral McKenzie—"to the way of life we espouse."

Throughout 1981–83, the Puerto Rican contingent of the American National Guard had trained troops of the Jamaica Defense Force, the Barbados Defense Force and the army of the Dominican Republic. Thus the U.S. invasion of Grenada on October 25, 1983, after a split in Grenada's ruling party had led to the assassination of Prime Minister Maurice Bishop, was well rehearsed; Reagan would term it a command performance.

Over 1,900 U.S. troops (including units of the 75th Ranger Division) were deployed in the invasion, which had ostensibly occurred at the request of five members of the Organization of Eastern Caribbean States, and a small military contingent from Jamaica, Barbados, Dominica, St. Lucia and St. Vincent assisted. The U.S. troops evacuated most of the 1,000 American citizens on Grenada. Within a year, a centrist coalition led by native lawyer Herbert A. Blaize won fourteen out of fifteen seats in an election carefully monitored by the States, and Blaize became prime minister. (The insecure PM soon set up a commission to vet the island's politically satiric calypsos.)

Dovetailing with this shrewd socio-militarism was the subterfuge of Reagan's Caribbean Basin Initiative (CBI). Seaga and Barbadian prime minister Tom Adams had approached Reagan immediately after his inauguration with their scheme for a "mini-Marshall Plan," and by the spring of 1982 Reagan had put his version of the concept before Congress. Reagan's widely touted CBI package (contrived with support from multinationals in the basin like the Chase Manhattan Bank, Alcoa and Inter-Continental Hotels) consisted of a cosmetic twelve-year duty-free agreement for Caribbean imports (87 percent were *already* duty-free) except footwear, textiles, rum and sugar—although five-eighths of a cent per pound was lifted on the last item; a 10 percent tax credit for U.S. investment; and an aid appropriation of $350 million to be divided amongst Reagan-designated islands.

By 1983, the administration had killed the Congress-opposed investor tax credits feature of the bill. The trade incentives measure wasn't passed until August 1983, and in a much-diluted form. Lastly, the $350 million in aid, which Congress had quickly okayed, proved to be a paltry handout for a region that officially sanctioned studies determined in need of $580 million in emergency funds for 1982 alone, as well as a minimum of $4.7 billion in external financing for just the early eighties.

The only relief of any consequence had been *military* subsidies, with Jamaica, Barbados and several eastern Caribbean islands around Grenada being the recipients. The entire CBI campaign had been a bribe to induce Jamaica and the rest of the Caribbean to accredit the armed confrontation in Grenada. It also provided a cover for $75 million in additional combat funding for the war in El Salvador.

What Jamaica got for its support was more misery. Seaga's decision to allow foreign imports into Jamaica killed the Jamaican economy, local markets soon being flooded with outside produce that included even the traditional Jamaican food, red beans. Smaller Jamaican businesses closed their doors, resulting in many layoffs. By early 1983, the Jamaican economy was in such bad shape that it could not pass the International Monetary Fund's performance tests on its vast loans. After Jamaica failed the March 1983 test, a waiver was granted that came with a series of crushing austerity measures. Prices for all necessities (gasoline, medicine, farm tools, schoolbooks, soap) skyrocketed, and thousands more public-sector employees were laid off. The only bright areas of the island economy were tourism and the starving peasantry's cultivation of ganja, which Reagan still demanded Seaga stamp out.

Jamaica was losing on all economic, social and humanitarian fronts, yet Seaga was still beholden to the United States and the IMF, so during the period of uproar over the Grenada invasion, Seaga imposed a 43 percent devaluation of the Jamaican dollar while also calling for instant elections on the basis of an outdated list of voters. The PNP boycotted these elections in protest, and before the public could absorb this latest sellout to foreign interests, it had reelected Seaga with a new five-year mandate. Moreover, Jamaica had become a de facto one-party system, locked into the dead-end role of client state for the U.S.

The other Caribbean confrontation of 1983 was the posthumous Bob Marley album of the same name. It wasn't generally known even in Kingston circles, but Marley had always planned *Confrontation* (he had named the LP in October 1980) as the last part of a trilogy that began in 1979 with *Survival* (at first entitled *Black Survival*, to underscore the urgency of African unity, but shortened to avoid misperceptions of the LP's theme), followed by *Uprising* in 1980. The first album was to be a laying out of the agenda for the apocalyptic battle between his brethren and Babylon, and it had all the incendiary might of a don't-look-back manifesto. Whether exhorting the faithful to "Rise yeh mighty people!" in "Wake Up and Live," or supporting revolutionary Third World struggles in "Zimbabwe," or asserting that "The preaching and talking is done!" in the title track, *Survival* was a fierce call to arms.

Uprising was an inspirational work, intended to offer support to the assembled multitudes as they hastened to set their spiritual houses in order. The song titles said it all: "Coming In from the Cold," "We and Dem," "Real Situation," "Work," "Zion Train" and "Redemption Song," each a solemn acknowledgment that the campaign would be a long and grief-laden one.

The serenity of so many of the selections on *Confrontation* came as something of a surprise to many close to Bob. The quiet passion so apparent in the studio proved even stronger on record as its deeper purpose was revealed: songs like "I Know" owe their magnetism to the honesty of the self-doubt revealed, Bob confronting the presence of good and evil inside his own soul.

On most of the tracks, the rhythm section was spare, precise, occasionally even delicate in a focused fashion. There was little, for instance, of lead guitarist Junior Marvin's customary grandstanding, and the I-Threes' organlike vocals and Earl Lindo's articulate keyboards were so intertwined as to be indistinguishable. In short, little jumped out of the fabric of the compositions. Yet if listeners sought out the quiet place within themselves that Bob was apparently gravitating toward on each of the tracks, the bridge burnings and soul yearnings that informed the collection roused the spirit in a way the Nyabinghi bombshells of yore did not.

On the cover of *Confrontation*, Bob was depicted as an Ethiopian horseman (complete with the traditional thong stirrup, a reference by art director Neville Garrick to the deadly cancer that began in Marley's toe) who's been transformed into St. George slaying the dragon. The legend of St. George had its roots in Christian Ethiopia, where the walls of a church in ancient Lalabella, Axum (now Tigre), built circa 600 A. D. for St. Gregorias, were adorned with renderings of the saint slaying the fire-breathing demon. The colorful drawing on the record jacket showed an encounter between good and evil, Marley wielding his lance, eyes wide and a satisfied smile on his face, aglow with faith in the rightness of his quest.

Garrick had once considered putting an illustration of Saint George on the back of the *Kaya* jacket, and in the original full-color draft of the *Confrontation* cover the dragon had a miter, a liturgical headdress worn by the Pope, on its head. Chris Blackwell vetoed that allegorical detail, fearing it might alienate the Catholics among Bob's admirers.

Had the image of the papacy as slain Satan been allowed to prevail as album art, it would have struck a dread chord in devout Rasta precincts, since settlements throughout Jamaica had been abuzz since 1981 with the sinister Vatican-related events making global headlines. The four-party coalition government of Italian prime minister Arnaldo Forlani had been toppled after June 1981 by disclosures that 953 respected members of the Italian establishment—including several in Forlani's cabinet—were members of the ultrasecret Masonic lodge known as P2. The scandal centered on the charge that these Masons were involved in an intricate plot to undo the country's parliamentary system and form "a state within a state." Since 1947, Italian civil servants have been forbidden to belong to any secret society, yet many of the P2 figures were linked to evil doings in the Vatican Bank that included alleged diversion of the Church's funds to the CIA and Mafia by Sicilian financier Michele Sindona—a man who served simultaneously as P2's financier and the Vatican's investment counselor.

Learned Rasta elders regarded Ancient and Accepted Rite Freemasons (of the thirty-three degrees unknown to common members) as fierce pagans whose occult gospel stems from their belief that Solomon drew his powers not from God but from Hiram Abiff, the murdered master builder of the Temple of Jerusalem, who was said to have renounced the Almighty in favor of a Dark Trinity centered on Baal, deity of the Semites. In many Rastas' eyes, it was Hiram Abiff's arrogant conjury, rather than any sin of Solomon's, that caused God to destroy the Temple, just as He once toppled the Masons-erected Tower of Babel. And it was the Masonry-infested papacy—which dared condone Mussolini's invasion of Ethiopia!—that would eventually self-destruct due to the skulduggery of P2. Such modern-day developments revealed the Vatican to be the horrible "name with the secret meaning" or "Babylon the great . . . a haunt for every unclean spirit, for every vile and loathsome bird," as foretold in Revelation 18:1–24.

Since the papacy of Pope Clement XII in 1738, the Church had tried to eradicate the High Masons, issuing papal edicts (ten between 1821 and 1902 alone) ordering the excommunication of any Catholic who entered the society. But Rastas felt the upper-degree or High

Masons had prevailed, corrupting the bishops of Rome. This was how, in the Rastas' view, Pope Pius XII had been induced to turn his back on Nazi genocide of the Jews and then to help the CIA hide Nazis in South America and the States after World War II. Following the death in 1963 of Pius's saintly successor, Pope John XXIII, the papal miter was passed to Paul VI, formerly Giovanni Montini, archbishop of Milan. During his wartime span as a monsignor, Montini was one of four section leaders of Vatican intelligence. Through Montini, General William Donovan of the Office of Strategic Services, or OSS (the forerunner of the CIA), established permanent ties with the Vatican.

Therefore, the Rastas felt, the first Holy Father with a modern espionage background allowed the Throne of Peter to become a tool of the CIA and then of P2, through the ministrations of Michele Sindona and the secret lodge's Grand Master, Licio Gelli (at whose home Italian police ultimately found the list of 953 plotting Masons). Once Rome had surrendered its moral authority, its sole source of power became money. So effective was the rape of the Vatican avowed by the Masons ("It will fall," said one nineteenth-century Grand Master, "beneath our vivifying Mallet!") that the Church was entering the 1990s facing the specter of bankruptcy.

Yes, the Rastas raged, the Vatican is the doomed latter-day Babylon decried in Revelation, where it is said John Paul I was poisoned in 1978 when he threatened to expose its iniquity, and where *L'Osservatore Romano*, Vatican City's own newspaper, now urges a mellowing of sacred anti-Masonry canons! "For her sins are piled high as heaven," warned Revelation 18, "and God has not forgotten her crimes. . . . The traders . . . who gained their wealth from her will stand at a distance for horror at her torment, weeping and mourning and saying, 'Alas, alas for the great city, that was clothed in fine linen and purple and scarlet, bedizened with gold and jewels and pearls! Alas that in one hour so much wealth should be laid waste!' "

In Jamaica over the last two decades there evolved a virtual black market for xeroxed articles perceived by Rastas as harbingers of the Last Days. The reading list at Grounations and other Rasta convocations ranged from *Time* and *Commonweal* excerpts to clippings from *Caribbean Contact* and the tiny Workers Party of Jamaica's *Struggle* newsletter, as well as extracts from journals reinterpreting such ancient mystic tomes as *Sepher Yetsirah* ("Book of Creation"), the *Fama Fraternatis, Book T, Book M, The Pimander, The Asclepius*, plus the Holy

Piby, the Kachina creed of the Hopi Indians, and the supernatural Ndemwau Ithatu ("Oath of Unity") underlying Jomo Kenyatta's Mau Mau–conceived Kenyan African Union.

During the late seventies and early eighties, much such material was brought to Bob Marley and his Hope Road companions by various Rasta holy men or ambitious partisans (Twelve Tribes leaders, etc.) for scrutiny and discussion. Condensed aspects of these mystic and political tracts found their way—sometimes quite naively—into the astrological and quasi-biblical columns published in each issue of *Survival*, the Tuff Gong newsletter.

As it was, such cabalistic material had been grist for the Jamaica music scene since Toots and the Maytals (under the name the Mighty Vikings) hit the ska jackpot in 1963 with "Six and Seven Books of Moses." And when one million Irish schoolchildren assembled in Dublin in 1980 to sing their interpretation of the Melodians' "Rivers of Babylon" to Pope John Paul II, it was one more piece of the sufferah's revenge falling into place. The pontiff was unaware that the lovely 1970 rock-steady ballad foretold the imminent demise of the religious principality he ruled, located near the juncture of the Aniene and Tiber rivers.

Being a fervent Rasta, Bob Marley firmly believed the Vatican to be Babylon—the one place on earth that in its activities had, as Revelation put it, "deceived all the nations." Yet he became neither dogmatist nor demagogue. He felt that Rome would sink under its own corruption and left it at that; he supported the struggles of freedom fighters in Africa not because of some Marxist or socialist analysis he had done but rather because he felt Africans obviously deserved self-determination, and because he believed Jah would one day return that continent—the true Promised Land—to its exalted place in His kingdom.

Ultimately Bob preferred to hear all sides on such subjects and then keep his own counsel, his outlook being revealed in his music. Like many of Bob's records of the late 1970s, *Confrontation* contained songs that had reached maturity in an utterly casual creative atmosphere. The material was culled from a wealth of unreleased work, and was freshly mixed with scrupulous care by Chris Blackwell, engineer Errol Brown and Wailers bassist Aston Barrett.

A track-by-track breakdown reveals much about the writer's modus operandi. On Side One, "Chant Down Babylon" was concocted in a Sheraton hotel room in Brussels during the 1979–80 *Sur-*

vival era. Seated on his bed, Bob began jamming on guitar with Earl Lindo on percussion, and at that juncture the song was called "I Believe in Reggae Music." It was eventually recorded during the 1979–80 sessions for *Uprising*.

Always a history buff, Bob had begun working on "Buffalo Soldier" in 1978 after reading about the black American soldiers decorated in the late 1800s. He cut an explosive demo version of the song with a band led by co-writer N. G. Williams, aka King Sporty, before settling on the more thoughtful treatment done with the Wailers.

"Jump Nyabinghi," a personal favorite of Marley's, was composed in 1979 while he was also writing an unreleased tune called "Jungle Fever." The title of the latter track was a humorous reaction to the vaccinations the Wailers had to get in preparation for a trip to Gabon. In the evening after the injections, the band members complained of side effects and begged off the sessions scheduled. But Carly Barrett, who'd skipped the shots, showed up and helped Bob cut the main parts of "Jump Nyabinghi"—Carly experimenting with innovative high-hat accents—plus basic tracks for "Jungle Fever."

"Mix Up, Mix Up" was on a two-track tape that Rita discovered in her own archives after Bob's death. She brought the tape to Neville Garrick and Tuff Gong engineer Errol Brown. What Neville called a "doorstep song," the recording had been made in the studio with just Bob, a guitar and a rhythm machine; it rambled on for twenty-five minutes, Marley singing to himself and changing lyrics as he went. Eight minutes of the song were initially isolated, with a tighter edit bringing the final track down to 3:43.

"Give Thanks," which closed Side One, was a late seventies effort that many of Bob's brethren considered an offshoot of "Redemption Song."

Side Two got under way with "Blackman Redemption," written by Bob in conjunction with producer Lee Perry and recorded in 1978 when Bob had returned to Jamaica for the Peace Concert. Side Two's final selection, "Rastaman Live Up," was also done with Lee Perry during the same period, Marley's stand against gang warfare being addressed from both practical and spiritual standpoints. In between these two songs were "Trench Town," a 1980 tribute to Bob's "deys inna yard"; "Stiff-Necked Fools," an update of a song Bob conceived in the Wailers' early reggae period, from which Peter Tosh had drawn the inspiration for "Fools Die" on his 1981 *Wanted: Dread & Alive* album; and "I Know," an outtake from the 1976 *Rastaman Vibration* sessions. At the time it was considered one of Bob's first "disco-style" efforts ("Exodus" being a later example), but he was never satisfied with the mix, particularly Family Man's rippling tambourine, which lent the track its crucial sense of velocity. During his treatment in Germany, Bob impulsively telephoned Family Man in Kingston and told him to remix "I Know" and see that Tuff Gong released it as a twelve-inch dance single. Family Man did so, and it found favor in Jamaica and England in both twelve-inch *and* seven-inch formats.

In Jamaica, when an honest but overworked tradesman agrees to accept a very difficult job, he asserts that he will "tek-a task *timely*" (resolve to work without lost time). For Neville Garrick, the artwork for *Confrontation* represented the first instance since Bob's passing when Garrick felt he could again apply himself timely and with whole spirit to the visual enhancement of his brethren's songs. To Neville, as he explained to Diane Jobson and Bob's other friends, "Bob has conquered death through his music. Rastaman live up." To celebrate that victory over death, Garrick put enormous effort, despite pressing deadlines, into an illustration in the gatefold inner jacket of *Confrontation*. It was an adaptation of a traditional Ethiopian painting commemorating Emperor Menelik II's triumph over Italian insurgents in 1896 at the Battle of Aduwa. This was the glorious battle that safeguarded Ethiopia's independence for the next forty years, the brave natives defeating the determined invaders (14,000 strong) by using tactics and arms they'd gained from the enemy.

Once King David had ruled the world with a psalm, the song-as-sword his enemies were never able to understand. With *Confrontation*'s "Chant Down Babylon," Marley demonstrated his conviction that Babylon could again be beaten with song, the sword it had unwittingly given him as a boy. Yet as Neville raced in May 1983 to complete his work in the Manhattan art department of Atlantic Records (which was then distributing Island Records), a curious occurrence made him realize—in a flood of memories—the terrible forces which had been arrayed against Bob Marley.

On the afternoon that Garrick dropped off the revised and final artwork for *Confrontation* at the Rockefeller Center offices of Atlantic, he returned to Room 722 at the Howard Johnson's Inn at 51st Street and Eighth Avenue to meet with a reggae associate. During the meeting he was shown a copy of a confidential CIA/State Department telegram, declassified on March 14, 1983, as per a request made under the U.S. Freedom of Information Act. Back in December 1976, the telegram had moved on secure government wires from the American embassy in Kingston to the office of the secretary of state in Washington, as well as to American embassies in the Bahamas, Barbados and other Caribbean locations. The communiqué's tag line was: SUBJECT: REGGAE STAR SHOT; MOTIVE PROBABLY POLITICAL.

Reading the four-paragraph wire about the assassination attempt on Marley, Garrick was flabbergasted by the implicit message that Marley had been wholly accepted in the intelligence community as a PNP pawn, his usefulness certified regardless of his fate:

> 1. VIOLENCE IN JAMAICA GAINED FRESH PROMINENCE ON FRIDAY, DECEMBER 3, WHEN BOB MARLEY, POPULAR JAMAICAN REGGAE STAR, WAS SHOT AND WOUNDED. THE INCIDENT, IN WHICH THREE ASSOCIATES OF MARLEY'S WERE ALSO WOUNDED, OCCURRED AT THE POP STAR'S HOME NEAR THE COMPOUND WHICH HOUSES THE RESIDENCES OF THE GOVERNOR GENERAL AND THE PRIME MINISTER. THE ASSAILANTS HAVE NOT YET BEEN IDENTIFIED, BUT CLEARLY HIT MARLEY AND HIS ASSOCIATES IN A PREMEDITATED ATTACK.
>
> 2. THE MARLEY SHOOTING HAS CAPTURED EVEN MORE ATTENTION THAN THE REGGAE ARTIST'S POPULARITY MIGHT SUGGEST WOULD HAVE BEEN THE CASE. IMMEDIATELY BEFORE THE SHOOTING, MARLEY AND MEMBERS OF HIS GROUP HAD BEEN REHEARSING FOR A FREE, PUBLIC CONCERT SCHEDULED FOR A PARK IN DOWNTOWN KINGSTON ON SUNDAY, DECEMBER 5. THE CONCERT, SPONSORED BY THE CULTURAL SECTION OF THE PRIME MINISTER'S OFFICE, WAS HELD DESPITE THE INCIDENT, WITH MARLEY PARTICIPATING—THOUGH FIVE HOURS LATE.
>
> 3. THE CONCERT WAS PART OF PEOPLE'S NATIONAL PARTY (PNP) ELECTION CAMPAIGN, AND WAS SCHEDULED TO COINCIDE WITH THE JAMAICA LABOUR PARTY'S (JLP) RELEASE OF ITS LONG-AWAITED MANIFESTO—TO THE DETRIMENT OF NEWS TIME AND PUBLIC ATTENTION FOR THE LATTER.
>
> 4. RUMORS ABOUND AS TO THE MOTIVATION FOR THE SHOOTING. SOME SEE THE INCIDENT AS AN ATTEMPT BY JLP GUNMEN TO HALT THE CONCERT WHICH WOULD FEATURE THE "POLITICALLY PROGRESSIVE" MUSIC OF MARLEY AND OTHER REGGAE STARS. OTHERS SEE IT AS A DEEP-LAID PLOT TO CREATE A PROGRESSIVE, YOUTHFUL JAMAICAN MARTYR—TO THE BENEFIT OF THE PNP. . . .

"It's alla lie, a blood-clot lie!" shouted Garrick, breaking off his reading in the midst of the fourth paragraph. "None-a this whole report is true. The concert was never political, it was never part of the PNP campaign!"

And then he paused as the realities woven into the communiqué's detached prose sank in. Despite the murderous antipathies arising from the Caymanas Park racetrack scam, Bob's presence at the Smile Jamaica concert was perceived primarily as a political statement. Plainly, the communiqué's text reflected the particulars as the prime minister's office had presented them to the political community inside and outside of Jamaica. Moreover, the timing of the Smile Jamaica concert had clearly been planned to intensify its political detriment to the JLP. Lastly, the rumors described in the wire's last paragraph were obviously those being circulated through diplomatic channels by mouthpieces for the PNP and the JLP. The conclusion was inescapable: whether Bob performed, perished, or both, the PNP had set him up from the start as a political target.

As he sat in his Manhattan hotel room, Garrick's thoughts sped back to the aftermath of the shooting. Following his awe-inspiring appearance at the concert, Bob had been returned posthaste to his secret encampment, which was at Strawberry Hill, the Blue Mountains retreat owned by Chris Blackwell. Chris had made arrangements for a private jet to pick up Bob and Neville in a remote corner of Norman Manley Airport at 5:30 Monday morning. Bob was to remain guarded by plainclothes government security officials until he was safely aboard the plane and en route to Blackwell's semiresidential Compass Point recording complex in Nassau.

However, Neville now recalled, when he and Bob awoke in the predawn hours on Monday, December 6, and began preparing to leave for the airport, there were *no* security police anywhere on Strawberry Hill. Four members of Bob's Rasta entourage were quickly enlisted as stalking-horses, taking a car to the airstrip to check on the flight. Eventually, Neville and Bob had no recourse but to drive down the mountain devoid of any police protection. They entered the closed Norman Manley Airport (it didn't open for business until approximately 7:00 A.M.) without any special clearance and found their own way to the waiting jet.

On the outskirts of the airfield, a few soldiers in jeeps watched the proceedings through binoculars but, curiously, kept their distance. Shaken and confused by the surreal setting, Bob and Neville gingerly crossed the tarmac, climbed aboard the aircraft, closed the door themselves and took off with the flight crew.

It was not until Marley and Garrick were safely in Nassau, and after several phone conversations had taken place between Nassau and Strawberry Hill, that the now-resurfaced plainclothesmen had any knowledge Bob was no longer in Jamaica. Moreover, the airport police in Nassau "freaked," as Garrick put it, when they saw Bob Marley emerge from the private plane, the cops oddly alarmed that the soul rebel was no longer on his native soil. Their attitudes were somewhat clarified when one of the highest-ranking Nassau policemen turned to Bob and asked, "Mr. Marley, is you asking for *political asylum*?"

Bob was stunned. "Nuh, mon," he answered flatly, "me jus' a tourist."

But the last straw, Garrick recollected, was the matter of the photographs he had taken in Kingston and Nassau immediately before and after the shooting. In addition to pictures snapped at Compass Point of the recuperating Bob's bullet wounds in the chest and arm, Garrick had also brought along film and negatives of Hope Road scenes, among them some exposures of suspicious characters who'd been hovering around the main house in the days just prior to the concert. On the very morning of the shooting, he had photographed Marley standing next to a VW parked in the deep shadows of a dense mango tree; Bob was talking to some unknown folk. Afterward, Marley had nervously told Garrick that the strangers had seemed to be "scouting" the place. When Neville developed the negatives of those pictures, the features of the unfamiliar callers were too obscured by the tree's shadows to make out.

Still, Garrick had taken all the photos, negatives and exposed rolls along to Nassau. It wasn't until the end of his and Bob's short stay in the Bahamas, when they were getting ready to catch a flight to London, that Neville realized all his photos—every contact sheet and scrap of film—had vanished.

"I never saw them again," he recalled to Bob's band and his Rasta brethren, rubbing a dark, peculiar-looking scar on his arm. Incidentally, some asked, what was the origin of the blemish? "Boy, I don't really know," he explained. "But it's weird, mon, because this spot, this mark on my arm, is *exactly* where Bob got the shot. And it's never gone away."

As those closest to Bob wrestled with the puzzles and burdens of his earthly bequest, the most prominent of his former collaborators were charting their own destinies. Between 1976 and 1981 Peter Tosh had released five solo albums, two of them for Columbia Records (*Legalize It, Equal Rights*) and three for Rolling Stones Records (*Bush Doctor, Mystic Man, Wanted: Dread & Alive*). On the whole, the Columbia albums were the superior artistic efforts due to the astringent arrangements of the songs and the contributions of numerous Wailers, including Bunny Wailer.

Of the Rolling Stones Records LPs, *Bush Doctor* had yielded a modest pop hit in November 1978 with Tosh's cover version (in duet with Mick Jagger) of the Temptations' 1965 R&B smash "(You Got to Walk and) Don't Look Back," but it was *Wanted: Dread & Alive*, the last of the LPs for the Stones label, that received the strongest overall commercial response. (The latter album was issued in the U.K. by the Stones, and in a joint arrangement with the Stones and EMI-America for the States; the U.K. release featured a different song selection.)

Wanted was Tosh's first album to crack the Top 100 of *Billboard*'s pop albums charts, rising as high as No. 91 during its thirteen-week run in the summer of 1981. The record also was the source of Tosh's inaugural American R&B hit, a rendition in tandem with singer Gwen Guthrie of Fred Harris and Ella Mitchell's "Nothing But Love," which reached No. 43 on *Billboard*'s soul music charts.

Wanted also coincided with the collapse of Peter's friendship with Keith Richards of the Rolling Stones, who had brought Tosh to the band's record company. Disgruntled with his limited commercial impact beyond Jamaica, Tosh had begun to blame the Stones, attacking them in the press (as he had Bob Marley) for allegedly thwarting his career. Keith Richards, who had allowed Tosh to use his longtime Jamaican residence for an extended period, ignored such public carping, apparently chalking it up to professional frustration. But the Rolling Stone lost his temper when, after landing on the island for a vacation trip, he discovered that Tosh had ignored all prior notification of his arrival and now refused to leave Keith's hillside villa in Ocho Rios, claiming it had become his property.

Reaching Tosh by phone, Richards engaged him in a brief swap of Kingston bark and coarse London bite:

KEITH: I'm coming down to the house. I need it for myself.
PETER: If yuh come anywhere near here, I'll shoot yuh.
KEITH: You'd better make sure you know how to use that gun, and

make sure you get the fucking magazine the right way 'round, 'cos I'm gonna be there in half an hour!

Peter left the premises. And he found himself no longer welcome at Rolling Stones Records.

Tosh was also the subject of continued harassment by Jamaican law enforcement officials for his outspoken support of the legalization of ganja. He claimed to be the victim of an increasingly aggressive array of "spiritual evil forces," particularly duppies. "Oh Bumbo Klaat," a 1981 Jamaican single on Tosh's Intel-Diplo label, resurfaced with a new mix on the British edition of *Wanted*; this song chronicled the evening he and four other brethren were attacked in his residence by three duppies.

According to Tosh, the ghostly assault commenced around 4:00 A.M., when one of his sleeping guests was roused and routed by a horrible giant who leapt feet-first into a bedroom from the veranda. As the fellow ran outside in terror, another of the guests was thrown to the floor by the rampaging poltergeists. Tosh himself awoke and glanced over his shoulder to see an unearthly beam of light shining through the roof and onto his bare back. Attempting to call out to the other two friends asleep in the room, Tosh found himself unable to speak, his tongue cleaving to the roof of his mouth. His limbs were paralyzed and felt as if they—like his tongue—were swollen to the point of exploding. Seeking an "inner communication to the Creator" he was suddenly inspired to shout out the word "Bumbaclot," and when he did, he found his speech returned, the word leaving his lips "like a bomb" and shattering the awful spell of the spectral aggressors.

Tosh's next album was *Mama Africa*, a 1983 release for EMI-America that included a cynical revamping of his "Peace Treaty," the singer lecturing with I-told-you-so pique all those who believed in 1978 that Jamaica's rival political gangs could bury the hatchet. A more appealing track was a reggae rewrite of Chuck Berry's "Johnny B. Goode," its tone magnificently incantatory as Tosh told of a rural guitar wizard from "deep down in Jamaica close to Mandeville." The powerful performance, which climbed to No. 84 on the *Billboard* pop singles survey, was rivaled only by "Where You Gonna Run," a re-casting of the Wailers' "Sinner Man" ska hit detailing the apocalypse. The updated reading on *Mama Africa* was one of despair, Tosh never sounding more authoritative than as he described the vain attempts of the world's miscreants to avoid the melting mountains and boiling seas of the Last Judgment. *Mama Africa* was a compelling document, climbing to No. 59 on the U.S. album charts to become Tosh's top-selling album thus far.

Bunny Wailer, always prolific, had changed his sound in the years immediately before Bob's passing, knocking out a number of albums (*Dub Disco Volume 1*, *Dub Disco Volume 2*, *Rock 'n' Groove*) that stressed the good-time dance music gaining ground in Jamaica's ballrooms. As Marley got worse, Bunny combined work on his 1981 *Rock 'n' Groove* album with a series of sessions at Harry J's and Dynamic Studios in which he cut some of Bob's classics, including "No Woman, No Cry," "Soul Rebel," "Redemption Song" and "Time Will Tell." Most of the Marley tracks featured the Taxi rhythm team (bassist Robbie Shakespeare and drummer Sly Dunbar) and elements of "dance hall," the treble-soaked "chat pon mike" (toasting) style familiar to the emerging reggae "stylee." This project was issued in 1981 on Bunny's Solomonic label as *Tribute to the Late Hon. Robert Nester* [sic] *Marley, O.M.* and instantly became the most popular album in Jamaica.

Apparently viewing the success on the island of the *Tribute* album as a mandate from a new generation of reggae fans, Bunny followed through with a skillful meld of old and new on his next LP, *Hook, Line & Sinker* (which contained a contemporary treatment of "Simmer Down") and *Bunny Wailer Live!* The live record, whose taut restorations included two songs from his 1976 *Blackheart Man* solo debut, had been recorded early in the morning of December 26, 1982, at Kingston's National Stadium, when Bunny took the stage at the Youth Consciousness Reggae Festival for his first JA concert appearance in some seven years. It marked the start of a slow but steady international comeback for Bunny, and word of mouth concerning his three-hour set greatly increased the U.S. audience for *Roots Radics Rockers Reggae*, a 1983 U.S. compilation of his best recent ballroom fare.

What was most significant about Bunny's foray into the dance-hall genre was his determination to advance the "ram" and "cork" (hot) aspects of dance hall's deafening "bottoms" and "toppers" (bass and treble sound mixing), while ignoring the "slackness" (vulgar to pornographic lyrics) and "lickshot/knockshot" (real or simulated pistol and rifle fire) that were characteristic of virtually all hip dance-hall releases. Old and new dance-hall DJs like U Roy, I Roy, Nicodemus, Dillinger, Brigadier Jerry, Yellowman, Josie Wales, Lovindeer, General Trees, Sister Carol and Lickshot Marsha had begun salting their own bawdy dance-hall toasting with "beat down de fence" salutes (gunfirelike noises made with pounded fists or bottles) in order to avoid being mocked as "dibi dibi" (dated) figures at the microphone stand. Bunny refused to add such sinister histrionics to his music, nor would he join in the catchphrase crazes that would come later. He was comfortable dispensing such frisky material as "Wirly Girly," whose saucy heat precipitated the "rub-a-dub partner" and "wine pon me" (close dancing) choreography of Kingston's modern ghetto dances. But when it came to responding to lickshot, his answer was the solemn "Cease Fire," "Trouble Is on the Road Again" and "Bodaration," all of which were hit singles in Jamaica in the early eighties. A true elder statesman, Bunny was shouldering the banner of socially responsible reggae while keeping abreast of the vanguard of dance hall's "roughneck" (hard-core) riddims.

As ever, the future of reggae was up to Jamaica's youth, but there were many veterans on the Kingston recording scene in the mid-eighties who openly wondered if reggae as they had known it could possibly survive. Granted, Jamaican popular music had been born in dance halls and Sound System jump-ups, and there had always been a slack side to the island music mill. Even the mento hits that fed many a rustic "brams" or "bruckins" (outdoor dance) during the forties and fifties were barred from Radio ZQI and RJR for their ribaldry: "Goosie Till a Morning," "Belly Lick," "Night Talk" and "Dr. Kinsey's Report" (the last a send-up of Dr. Alfred Charles Kinsey's 1948 best-seller *Sexual Behavior of the Human Male*).

From ska days onward, Jamaica's musical world was kept healthy by the youthful hope and spiritual conviction that it generated. To play music well took practice and commitment, and to sing it with commercial potency required a depth of feeling that could dispel the ghetto's most grinding pessimisms. But the death of Bob Marley, the post-Marley dive of Jamaica's economy and the rise of dance hall all conspired to weaken the Kingston Studio Systems, which had been the midwife of modern session-derived reggae.

When popularly priced compact keyboards and knock-off computerized recording technology began to trickle into Jamaica from Miami and New York, the hard- and software was snatched up by studio bosses who saw the possibilities of doing records with very few real musicians. A simple nonsense carol, tapped out on a tiny Casio console and then fattened by drum machines and phase-shifters could pass muster as luxuriant pop music in the current barren climate.

Vocals arrived via hungry teenage toasters—anxious inner-city spree boys who swarmed inside dance halls, lacking the funds or patience to hoist an instrument, but eager to snatch the microphone from the disc-spinning selector and his DJs. The final greed- and lassitude-spawned downstroke was the discovery that crowds were content to rub-a-dub along with vintage rhythm tracks seasoned with fresh toasting! Since most producers retained control of the riddims of bygone sessions, they raided their own archives and farmed the raw material out to the dance halls. As the new toaster-singers like Yellowman, Sugar Minott and Frankie Paul caught on, their half-live shows were recorded anew, producing an audacious reggae techno-hybrid that ate its young *and* old in one ghoulish gulp.

Joblessness among studio technicians was epidemic as their recycled labors lifted jabbering labrishers into the spotlight, and a musician's skill at bending notes, rattling off rimshots or blowing impeccable triplets became superfluous. If a producer or Sound System selector had the riddim tracks, then any toaster who could "nice it up" at the mike with a spew of "sass-mout' " was certain to move the gatekeeper to "peel off a mass" (pay cold cash) at the close of a well-attended show.

Once young musicians in the ghettos wanted to be able to play well enough to earn a bribe-subsidized seat next to the studio stalwarts. But the eighties approach to reggae was either closing most studios or shrinking their dance hall–directed needs to that of an occasional lone hornman spiking a "dub plate" with a few novelty notes. It was a producer's game, and the star performers were those who learned to play it as obscene emcees.

Meantime, rock, pop, funk and even cross-pollinated hip-hop poured into Jamaica from America and Britain, winning its fans, having its effect. But little of a comparable weight poured back out. Downtown Kingston became a consumerist carnival, boasting more TVs than flush toilets, more Michael Jackson impersonators per street corner than Stateside in Washington, D.C., and a slouching army of coked-out cabdrivers wearing Walkman-less headphones and "I Got Laid in JA" T-shirts. The best sources of full-band reggae became Britain, Sweden, West Africa and Japan, while JA itself was in danger of becoming a one-way street for even the U.S. and U.K. rap music it had been crucial in spawning. It was an accident of history, then, that at least one young, largely traditional reggae group called the Melody Makers was coming of age in Kingston. The fact that they were products of prep schools rather than the tenement-yard pecking order made it plain that the torch had been passed in more ways than one.

The group copped its name from *Melody Maker*, the British rock magazine, after seeing a poster-sized reprint of a cover story on their father. In their preteen innocence, the younger of Bob's children assumed the catchy words were a description of their dad, rather than the title of the publication. "If dem call Father dat, is a good name fe a group of us," reasoned twelve-year-old Ziggy. "Better den sayin' jus' 'de Marleys.' "

In the years after their father's death, the children and their mother Rita spent most of their time in an estate off Skyline Drive in Jack's Hill, the upland Kingston neighborhood perched near the Hope River Gorge on the promontories overlooking Kingston Harbor. The view—of the Blue Mountains in one direction, and the Caribbean Sea in the other—was a spectacle of lush, misty sensuality. And the suburban conventionality of the Marley residence, with its deep-hued couches and pin-neat dining room, was offset by the knowledge that aboriginal remains of the Arawak Indians had been excavated near its grounds.

The Melody Makers issued only one significant single in Jamaica in 1983: "Reggae Is Now" was credited to David "Ziggy" Marley. Authorship of the 45's B side of "Rock It Baby" was attributed simply to "Marley"; anyone on the island knew the difference, whether or not they owned the famous *Catch a Fire* album from which the venerable Wailers' song had been taken. Bob's children had not been idle, however, with eldest daughter Sharon taking time out from her college business courses during 1983 and '84 to help see her siblings through the recording of not one but two "debut" albums. One pass was an abortive undertaking piloted by Steve Levine, producer of the rock act Culture Club, whose bisexual leader, Boy George, became a favorite pop star in Jamaica after he vacationed there. The completed album, titled *Children Playing in the Streets*, was deemed too slick and pop-flavored by the people at EMI and was eventually shelved, but the trial singles "Met Her on a Rainy Day" backed by "Can't Be What You Want to Be" and "Rock It Baby" backed by "Feel Free" gained some attention in Britain in 1984.

The first Melody Makers album to reach the public intact was *Play the Game Right*, produced by Rita Marley's usual team of Grub Cooper and Ricky Walters, with both Ziggy Marley and the Wailers'

Tyrone Downie also credited for contributions in the control room. *Play the Game Right* arrived in stores early in 1985, several months after the release of *Valotte*, the debut by John Lennon's son Julian, and Ziggy's presence on *Game* prompted casual comparisons between the two male offspring of fallen superstars. Also noted were the eerie vocal similarities they shared with their respective fathers.

But besides Ziggy's obvious vocal roots, there were echoes of the spunky verve of Frankie Lymon. And the other Melody Makers' rich backing resembled a lively variant of the I-Threes. The sparse instrumental tack taken by the backing musicians—including the inevitable Wailers personnel—was particularly distinct on "Naah Leggo" and the title track, in which pithy, pealing ska/Stax horns parried with Aston Barrett's elastic bass, while Ziggy skatted using the dusky rasping technique he acquired from his parent. Despite some solemn themes, the Melody Makers' material displayed neither the cute conceits nor the overweening huff and puff of kids trying to sound like grown-ups.

Their album also coincided with the issue in JA of *Redemption Songs*, Cedella Booker's own LP, which was co-produced with "Family Man" Barrett for Tuff Gong Music's 56 Hope Road label. Mother B.'s throaty gospel crooning managed to seem intimate, reverent and informal in such traditional material as "You Gotta Move," and when she tackled Wailers' gems—particularly "Put It On (Lord I Thank You)"—she wisely shed her pose of surrogate reggae monarch, reserving her worship for the songs' messages, rather than the man who made them famous.

The high-and-mighty attitudes exhibited by members of the Marley clan had begun to change, a happy development unfortunately hastened by a slew of court actions against the Marley estate. The most threatening was filed in the Supreme Court of the State of New York in October 1984 by New Jersey–based music publisher Danny Sims, the entrepreneur who had once served as Bob's manager, song licensing agent and career guide. The civil action, drawn up against the representatives of the late Bob Marley's song publishing interests, was entered in the court records as *Cayman Music, Inc.*, v. *Rita Marley, as Administratrix of the Estate of Robert Nesta Marley, Tuff Gong Music, Bob Marley Music Ltd., Almo Music Corp., Rondor Music Corp., Island Records Inc., Atlantic Recording Corporation, etc. et al.*, with a counterclaim by the defendants against Danny Sims.

Sims alleged in his $6 million suit that between 1973 and 1976 Bob Marley avoided his contractual obligations by publishing his songs under pseudonyms and by withholding other songs from publication until after his contract with Sims's Cayman Music expired. Cayman further alleged that during this period Marley and the other defendants participated in a "conspiracy" to defraud Cayman.

In 1968, Bob Marley entered into a contract with Cayman's predecessor-in-interest (Johnny Nash Music, Inc.) in which he conveyed the exclusive publishing rights to all his past songs, as well as any songs he would compose in the following five years. At the same time, Marley entered into a contract with JAD Record Company (an affiliate of Johnny Nash Music) granting JAD exclusive production rights.

In 1973, Marley was released from his obligations under the production contract and, in a new contract with Cayman, agreed to extend his obligations under the publishing contract to October 1976.

Though the credits of songs on such albums as *Catch a Fire, Burnin'*, *Natty Dread* and *Rastaman Vibration* state otherwise, Sims claimed that Marley actually wrote "No Woman, No Cry," "Them Belly Full (But We Hungry)," "Natty Dread," "War," "Jah Live," "Rat Race" and "Roots Rock Reggae" under pseudonyms ascribed to Jamaican friends and associates such as Vincent Ford, Hugh Peart, Coghill Leghorn and Willy San Francisco. (However, various singles of some of these prominent songs did contain a Bob Marley writing credit.) Sims also claimed that Marley composed some twenty-six other songs that Bob supposedly saved until his agreements expired and he could release them under his own name.*

Cayman's first cause of action against the estate was for breach of contract; the second was for misrepresentation; the third was for intentional interference with contractual obligations; the fourth for conspiracy to defraud; and the fifth was for declaratory relief in con-

---

*Sims stated in his filing papers that he had no knowledge of these actions until he read Stephen Davis's book, *Bob Marley*, as well as Timothy White's *Catch a Fire: The Life of Bob Marley*, citing the first paragraph on page 23 of *Catch a Fire* as the ultimate impetus for his lawsuit:

> The network of restrictive confidences that Marley developed over the years was extensive, encompassing business arrangements, extramarital affairs, daily comings and goings, and songwriting collaborations. (In order to protect some of his publishing interests in later years, he reportedly made cunning arrangements to credit many of his songs to hangers-on and ghetto chums.)

The reader should be aware that sizeable portions of this book were entered as evidence in court, and that the author testified extensively during the trial about his journalism from 1975 to 1987 on Marley.

nection with the ownership of publishing rights to the songs in dispute.

Sims felt these alleged activities by Marley and the estate had resulted for Cayman Music in not less than $1 million in lost royalties, and maybe as much as $45 million. Hanging in the balance, then, was potentially the bulk of the inheritance due Ziggy Marley and the rest of Bob's legal offspring and rightful heirs.

The defendants in the estate, whose worth was then estimated at approximately $30 million, maintained that because this action was not begun until October 1984, eight to eleven years after the conduct complained of occurred, each clause of action was time-barred—i.e., the statute of limitations which governs contract actions had run out on any such claims. They also maintained that such actions on Marley's part were common knowledge, easily discoverable by the plaintiff during the period before the statute of limitations expired. They additionally alleged that Sims had mishandled his contracts with Marley and therefore had no rights to any of his songs.

Danny Sims's New York legal counsel for the case was Stewart Levy, a partner in the Fifth Avenue firm of Parcher Arisohn & Hayes (which also represented Bruce Springsteen, Mick Jagger, Keith Richards, Billy Joel and Paul Simon). Louis Byles, director of the Mutual Security Merchant Bank and Trust of Jamaica and a co-administrator of the estate, hired the New York–Miami firm of Sage Gray Todd & Sims to represent the estate outside of Jamaica. However, the estate's trial defense—and countersuit claim—was handled by Robert Brundige, a partner at the huge Wall Street firm of Hughes Hubbard & Reed, in conjunction with associate William M. Thomas Jr. Peter A. Herbert, another well-known Wall Street attorney, had also played a key role in researching that defense during the discovery/deposition stage.

The straitlaced litigators on both sides had their work cut out for them. Over the course of the three years (1984–87) it would take to prepare their respective cases for trial, they made numerous trips to Jamaica, sustaining buttoned-down discomfiture and cold sweats of a wholly unaccustomed variety as they searched the ghettos and the bush for witnesses, documentation and anything else that smacked of truth.

A pin-striped attorney might spend weeks scuffing his wing tips on goat paths and in cane fields as he tracked down an elusive Hope Road hanger-on of yore like aged cripple Vincent Ford. Once located, the infirm Ford's patois had to be painstakingly decoded with the help of a trained native stenographer. Finally, exultant at having extracted a sworn deposition from Ras Ford that buttressed Sims's position, the lawyer would return to his air-cooled boardroom in mid-Manhattan only to find that the other side had *also* obtained a signed Ford statement—and theirs said the exact opposite of the first attorney's.

Reggae, of course, waited for nuh mon, and Bunny Wailer, for one, kept his head down and his output high during this interval, releasing his dance-hall-savvy *Marketplace* album in autumn 1985. By this time, dance hall was experiencing stylistic sea changes in West Indian London enclaves like Clapham Junction, due largely to the innovative rapid-fire DJ rapping pioneered on Papa Levi's 1984 release of "Mi God, Mi King." Ironically, there were those in the British press who felt the dance-hall/DJ/rap genres were beneath Bunny's talents—and his public trust. "I know dat right now is de dance-hall stuff dat sells, dat's popular with de youth," he replied testily in one transatlantic phone interview. "So if dat's what dey want, it's my mission ta make great dance music for dem, ta fill dere ears. It's escapist, sure, but young people need ta release de tensions of tribulation. It's nuh bad t'ing."

But it was. Because the youth in JA and its colonial outposts were seeking hope, if not heroes, and there were none of either in sight. The average employed worker in Kingston was earning only J$60 a week, yet had to fork over a minimum of J$7 for a dozen eggs. When gasoline rose to J$10.99 a gallon in January 1985, poor people of both political parties had panicked and rioted, not just in Kingston but in sleepy villages island-wide, blocking every major road in Jamaica with flaming debris. Forty-nine days into the new year, the *Daily Gleaner* reported fifty-seven people shot, stabbed or lynched, twenty-nine of them by police. Despair roiled the sticky air as Seaga's economic "miracle" perished. The country had been stunned in 1984 when Reynolds Metals shut down and left Jamaica, but news of Alcoa's departure early in 1985 was sickening. By the summer of '85, Seaga was telling the nation he would no longer rule on the basis of public opinion, and Michael Manley begged for a return to power, his slate embarrassingly similar to his bankrupt ideas of the recent past.

Come 1986, there was tribulation without release, heralded, in the minds of all Rastas—whether Nyabingi Order, Twelve Tribes, Holy Theocratic, Ethiopian Salvation Union, Rastafarian Movement Association, Ethiopian National Congress, Rastafarian Melchizedek Orthodox Church, Rastafarian Repatriation Association of Jamaica or a dozen other public and secret sects—by numerous signs of the Last Days.

They believed the seven seals foretold in Revelation were now, in sequence, being split. The splendor of technology, as if the white horse and crowned rider of the first seal of the apocalypse, was "conquering its conquerors" in America, the most powerful nation extant, due to negligence, deception and bad faith. On January 28, 1986, the U.S. space shuttle *Challenger* exploded after its launch at Cape Canaveral, Florida, killing all seven aboard. And all around the States technological frailties multiplied as computers contracted viruses, metal grew fatigued, radar failed and circuits burned through.

Ghastly fighting raged in Lebanon, in Afghanistan, in Eritrea and Somalia, in Central America, and in racist South Africa. Terrorism proliferated on a global scale, as if the blood-red horse had burst forth from the second seal, its rider given "the power to take peace from the earth and make men slaughter one another."

And the planet's mighty were humbled or struck down, like unto the black horse from the third seal, whose "rider held in his hand a pair of scales." Deposed President Jean-Claude Duvalier of Haiti fled to France on February 7, the twenty-year rule of President Marcos of the Philippines was ended on February 26, Prime Minister Olof Palme of Sweden was shot dead by unknown assassins on February 28, Kurt Waldheim of Austria was revealed as a former Nazi officer on March 3, and Panama's Manuel Noriega was denounced as a drug thug.

As the AIDS virus continued its lethal advance, with other new maladies and sicknesses developing, and Ethiopia starved as never before, the Rastas could see the profile of the pale fourth horse from out of the fourth seal, its rider death—"And to him was given power over a quarter of the earth, with the right to kill . . . by famine and pestilence and wild beasts."

Looking heavenward for blessed alleviation in April '86, the dreads saw instead the ominous Halley's Comet as it roared through the heavens to proclaim a plague that started in the Soviet city of Chernobyl.

During a twenty-four-hour safety test at a massive nuclear reactor at Chernobyl in the Ukraine, two huge explosions tore open the reactor's superstructure on April 28 and blew the roof off the building housing it, igniting some thirty hyper-hot fires and unleasing the deadliest cloud of radiation in human history. The unofficial Soviet death toll immediately afterward was twenty-five, and two American physicists at the Lawrence Livermore National Laboratory said radiation from the Chernobyl disaster could cause tens of thousands of cancer cases, resulting in thousands of deaths in the next several decades. But Dr. John Gofman, professor emeritus of the University of California at Berkeley, who worked on the Manhattan Project to design the atomic bomb during World War II, estimated that the radiation from Chernobyl will cause a million cases of cancer, half of them fatal.

The European Community tentatively agreed to ban imports of fresh fruits and vegetables from the Soviet Union, Poland, Hungary, Czechoslovakia, Bulgaria, Rumania and Yugoslavia. In the ensuing weeks, radioactive rain so befouled northern Britain that three million lambs were prevented by its government from going to market. The Italian government forbade the sale of leafy vegetables and advised against giving children fresh milk, while dying Polish cows were photographed for the *London Times* as they were held at the Australian-Italian border. Minute amounts of radioactive waste from Chernobyl were detected in rainwater in Albany, New York.

Soviet officials insisted soon afterward that the disaster had been contained, yet a *New York Times* dispatch stated that on June 9, a Finnish monitoring station near the Soviet Union recorded a mysterious six-hour span of high atmospheric radiation levels whose ten-second peak was even higher than that recorded immediately after the Chernobyl accident. Interior Ministry official Esko Koskinen said Finland had no explanation for the alarming findings.

Finally, in the July 26 edition of the *Times* there appeared a report—duly photocopied by Rasta brethren and circulated from Negril to Morant Bay—that for dread believers made the greatest sense of all. Its headline was CHERNOBYL FALLOUT: APOCALYPTIC TALE AND FEAR. The article quoted a "prominent Russian writer," himself an "atheist," who was joining untold numbers of Russians in poring over Revelation 8:10–11.

"Listen, this is incredible," the writer told the *Times* correspondent as he opened a Bible to the pertinent passage and read aloud: " 'And the third angel sounded, and there fell a great star from heaven, burning as it were a lamp, and it fell upon the third part of the rivers, and upon the fountains of waters; and the name of the star is called Wormwood: and the third part of the waters became wormwood; and many men died of the waters.' "

What the Russian writer found incredible, the *Times* story continued, was that the Ukrainian word for wormwood was *chernobyl*. The

Soviet nuclear plant had gotten its name from the wormwood that once grew in abundance on the shores of the nearby Dnieper River.

This biblical conjecture was seeing print at the same time that numerous scholars, scientists and archaeologists at Washington's National Museum of Natural History and the University of Pennsylvania Museum were issuing announcements of dramatic historical findings lending credence to the existence of the Queen of Sheba and her biblical relationship with Solomon, as well as to the tale of the Israelites' exodus and the parting of the Red Sea that assisted their flight. Morever, an archaeological team composed of experts from two Israeli universities and the Texas-based Institute of Judaic-Christian Research discovered—in caves near the Dead Sea—a 2,000-year-old jug containing oil of the type used to anoint the kings of Judah.

This convergence of omens convinced Jamaica's Rasta communities that the slow tick of the Hour of Judgment had commenced. It was nearly too late to spread any warnings. But many dread elders attuned to reggae felt the notoriously travel-shy Bunny Wailer, embarking in the summer of '86 on what he termed his first world tour, made for a grand courier of urgent Rasta-wise admonishments to the multitudes. Indeed, Bunny's appearance before 14,000 fans in August at New York's Madison Square Garden was rightly trumpeted by observers as an amazing achievement for a "cult artist." When it was learned that Bunny was about to release yet another trite dance-hall LP, *Rootsman Skanking*, he was asked directly about his musical direction. His reply was that he had "a lot of conscious material," but that now was "not its right time."

And Bunny walked it like he talked it, as he subsequently kissed off interviews scheduled with the *Los Angeles Times*, *Good Morning America* and *The David Letterman Show*. When his capricious caravan hit his next major date, Oakland's Kaiser Convention Center, he missed without explanation or apology appearances set up with the local ABC, NBC, and CBS-TV affiliates, plus radio talks set up with NBC and ABC. Other honors that the singer did not show up to receive included a special ceremony in which Lionel Wilson, Oakland's black mayor, was to have presented Bunny with the key to the city. Because of the missed chances for promotion, the singer performed in Oakland to half the house needed to break even. Not surprisingly, his proposed global itinerary swiftly disintegrated. The Rastas back home shook their heads in dismay. Was there no stout arm left to carry the dreadlocks' standard?

Even greater shock waves were felt throughout the reggae community on July 16, 1986, when Don Taylor, Bob Marley's manager during the bulk of his Island Records years, sent a letter to the administrator general of Jamaica, stating that Rita Marley's 1978 documents authorizing transfer of Bob's chief assets to her were *frauds*, and that she had actually signed them with attorney David Steinberg in 1981. The scandal proved explosive. According to an estate official's affidavit, when Taylor's charges were brought before Rita, she confessed she had signed her name in '81 to papers backdated to 1978, saying she'd done so under the direction of David Steinberg and accountant Marvin Zolt.

Confronted with an order from Jamaica's Supreme Court that she be dismissed as an administrator of the estate—as well as demands that all estate property she acquired be accounted for or impounded—she sat down on September 11 at her desk in Tuff Gong's Kingston offices at 220 Marcus Garvey Drive and wrote the bank (with an attorney's help) a face-saving formal resignation from the estate:

Dear Mr. Byles:

Please accept my resignation as Co-administratrix of the estate of Robert Nesta Marley, deceased (the "Estate").

In the period following the death of my husband in May 1981, I was inexperienced in handling the complex business affairs relating to my husband's work in the entertainment industry. Because my only concern was to attempt to assure that my husband's affairs be continued in the manner in which they were conducted during Bob's lifetime and in accordance with his wishes, I turned to Bob's manager and close associate, Don Taylor, Bob's attorney, David Steinberg, and Bob's accountant, Marvin Zolt, for guidance and advice in the handling of these matters, and retained the services of Messrs. Steinberg and Zolt to represent my interests and the interests of the estate in the same manner as they had previously represented the interests of my late husband.

During the course of that representation and in reliance upon the advice which I received from Counsel Steinberg, I was instructed to sign my name and/or Bob's name to certain documents based upon the representation that this was necessary in order to effectuate a tax structure which had been approved by Bob with the advice of leading tax counsel in New York and to assure the orderly continuation of Bob's business affairs. In view of the advice which I received, together with the representation of my advisors that certain foreign assests were not assets of the estate, I did not feel my actions were improper.

I have since retained other counsel and, based upon their advice, conclude that I was previously mis-advised and mis-directed in this matter, and feel that, under the circumstances, I should immediately resign my position.

I would like to assure you, as I believe you are aware, that I have always done my utmost to administer the affairs of the estate in accordance with Bob's wishes and with the interests of the beneficiaries in mind, and will co-operate with you in every way to provide whatever information, documents and assistance you may require.

Yours very truly,
RITA MARLEY (MRS.)

On September 22, Louis Byles told the administrator general of Jamaica that the estate had retained Sage Gray Esqs. to represent its interests, and that the Mutual Security Merchant Bank and Trust's lawyers were moving to have the Supreme Court rescind its grant to her. Byles further announced that a royalty payment from Island Record Ltd. of US$154,000 had been received and held, pending investigations and audits of the estate's accounts. Island informed Byles that some US$2 million would likely be sent along during the period of inquiry. It was an indication that Bob's posthumous royalties had become quite substantial.

At the same time, considering the sizeable monies that would no longer be diverted to Rita, Byles sought approval from the Bank of Jamaica to send "greatly enhanced" benefits to Bob's children and infant beneficiaries.

The Jamaican government was scarcely more stable than the Marley estate, Prime Minister Edward Seaga announcing on October 13 that he would step down on August 12, 1987. Without elaborating, Seaga told a party conference in Kingston that he would not seek reelection as the JLP's leader. His term was due to end in 1989. By November 6, Seaga had reversed his decision, saying economic recovery and a new International Monetary Fund pact depended on his presence. Astute nonpartisan observers saw Seaga's tactics as designed to consolidate JLP support while his failed economic programs were under fire and the JLP was demoralized from heavy losses in July's municipal elections. Because Seaga lacked rivals even within his own ranks, his trick worked.

On December 16, the estate filed an $8 million lawsuit in New York against David Steinberg and Marvin Zolt, claiming they "developed and engaged in a pervasive and continuous conspiracy and scheme" to defraud the estate of $8 million, of which they retained $1 million in "fees."

The holiday season also saw the release of two more EMI-America albums by prominent reggae artists—"*Hey World!*" by Ziggy Marley and the Melody Makers (as they were now known) and *Beginning* by I-Three (itself a slight revision of their time-honored name). Pitched as the reggae equivalent of *Roots: The Next Generations*, these latest episodes in the two acts' recording sagas involved several intriguing plot twists. With this second Melody Makers LP, Ziggy made it clear he personally had no plans to either mime Yellowman and company's slack clowning or up the ante in the colloquial "sleng teng"/ "boops" babble-on sweepstakes that threatened to erase the righteous reggae gospel in his homeland. Instead, Ziggy looked to be thinking out loud about the artistic parameters of a moralistic path.

As on the preceding *Play the Game Right*, the best Ziggy-authored tracks on "*Hey World!*"—"666," "Police Brutality," "Lord We a Come," "Reggae Revolution"—showed his gift for topical parable without sacrificing any of his emotional verve. His siblings' backup singing was restrained but prismatic, their tart intonations subtly interwoven with lean strands of ringing percussion, keyboards, horns and brisk guitar, until what began as facile as a ring song ended up as nimbly meshed as a madrigal. The lyrics were more memorable for mood-building power than substantive punch, but there were enough pronounced outcrys ("Nuff youths a-get shot/In-a Brixton . . . in-a Washington . . . in-a Kingston!") to supply evidence of a developing conscience.

What Ziggy and kin really needed were peers to trade sparks with. This same lack of synergetic dimension forestalled I-Threes' *Beginning*. As the best female reggae singers of their era, Judy Mowatt, Marcia Griffiths and Rita Marley had excelled on their own and with the vintage Wailers. But instead of fashioning a fresh context for this trio, a huddle of producers (Thom Bell, Grub Cooper, Tyrone Downie, Ricky Walters) provided only familar shades of reggae, soca and supper-club soul. *Beginning* barely qualified as a backward glance, but as their frisky "That's How Strong" and "Jealousy" attested, there were buds yet to bloom on this branch of the family tree—provided the future brought a measure of sunshine.

The Jamaican Supreme Court officially dismissed Rita Marley as an estate administrator on February 3, 1987. The estate itself took no action whatsoever against her, citing her September 11 letter as elucidation of her trespass and simply saying that she was cooperating fully with the investigation.

Anonymous others outside the purview of the Marley clan lacked this spirit of cooperation. Just as details of the estate's difficulties were reaching downtown ears, a mysterious posse of kidnappers abducted Carly and Aston Barrett's father. Rumors in Trench Town had it that Rita Marley was approached for ransom money, and she had refused. Mr. Barrett's decapitated body was eventually found in the brush. It was also armless and legless.

The days of dying had returned. The next murder occurred on Good Friday, April 17, 1987. Carlton Barrett was driving home late that evening, another car trailing his. Barrett parked in front of his Kingston home and was ambling across his courtyard to the front door when an assailant slipped up behind him, pressing a pistol to the base of his squarish skull and squeezing off two rounds. Within days, Jamaican police had arrested his wife, Albertine, and her lover, a taxi driver named Lenroy, and charged them with the slaying.

The murder cast a pall over the rest of the Wailers band, which had recently returned from a successful overseas tour of such countries as Israel and New Zealand. After years of indecision and conflict over their future, the band members had recently united to renounce their individual 1982 agreements with David Steinberg and press a claim against the Marley estate for what they had determined to be a collective $5 million in unpaid royalties. The move coincided with renewed recording activity, including *Jerusalem*, a well-received joint album with Alpha Blondy, aka Seydou Kone, the Dimbokro, Ivory Coast–born reggae artist whose popularity in West Africa rivaled that of Bob Marley.

But the senseless killing of Carlton seemed to plunge the surviving Wailers into a new paralysis of depression and fear. At the urging of family members and management lawyers, they left Jamaica for their own safety and mental balance, booking concerts in the U.S., Europe, South America, Africa and various Arab countries in the Middle East, with the drumming handled by Cornell Marshall and later Mikey "Boo" Richards.

The legal assault on the Marley estate continued in the Supreme Court of New York, though its biggest adversary suffered a major setback. The Honorable Elliot Wilk ruled in a May 7, 1987, decision that the first and fifth causes of action (pertaining to breach and declaratory relief) in Sims's suit were barred by the six-year statute of limitations which governs contract actions, and he threw them out of court. Judge Wilk also ruled that the third cause of action in Sims's case, considered an "injury to property," was barred by an applicable three-year statute of limitations, and so it was also thrown out of court.

As for the acts constituting the fraud alleged in the second and fourth causes of action in Sims's suit, Judge Wilk noted that limitations period for fraud is six years from the commission of fraud or two years after the fraud was "discovered . . . or could with reasonable diligence" have been discovered. While the acts constituting the fraud in the second and fourth causes of action occurred eight to eleven years prior to Sims's commencement of civil proceedings, the court decided to give Sims every fair chance to pursue the remainder of his suit, with Justice Wilk stating, "It would appear that plaintiff will have some difficulty proving that it neither discovered, nor could, with reasonable diligence, have discovered the fraud less than two years prior to commencing this action. However, I am reluctant to resolve this issue, which represents mixed questions of law and fact, on motion papers which are not conclusive."

At a subsequent May conference, Justice Wilk set a November date for an expedited trial on the issue of whether the second and fourth causes (misrepresentation and conspiracy to defraud) of Sims's action against the estate were time-barred. If Sims prevailed, he would be the new owner of "No Woman, No Cry" and a slew of other Bob Marley classics.

While the media in the States seemed obsessed in August 1987 with a supposed New Age planetary wonderment termed the harmonic convergence, that month also marked more concrete occasions that were the talk of Jamaica. The island nation celebrated twenty-five years of independence from colonial rule. Also, Jamaica's first national hero, Right Excellent Marcus Mosiah Garvey, born a hundred years ago in St. Ann, was officially pardoned by his people of two 1929 JA convictions for sedition based on his writings—which had called for impeachment of abusive judges. In the States, Representative Charles B. Rangel (D–N.Y.) introduced a resolution in Congress to exonerate Garvey of his federal fraud convictions in the 1920s, calling them "unjust and unwarranted." Lastly, Reggae Sunsplash, Jamaica's most successful cultural enterprise, celebrated its tenth year with a show highlighted by an electrifying sunrise performance by Ziggy Marley and the Melody Makers.

After a long period of creative stagnation and business wrangles with his record label, Peter Tosh was busy improving his own reputation, his primary objective being a proposed concert tour, to commence at Madison Square Garden, in support of his EMI-America LP, *No Nuclear War*, which had been issued in July. However, discussions between the record label and Tosh business manager Joe Borzeki had not resulted in any advance funding for the concerts. With much of his income tied up due to numerous legal fights, Peter and Joe decided to try and borrow the necessary cash. As Peter and his common-law wife, Marlene Brown, caught a plane back to Kingston on September 6, 1987, he was telling close friends that the main reason for the tour was that he was broke.

He was also isolated. Tosh's last Jamaican concert had been in December 1983 in Kingston's National Arena; since then he had kept a low profile, his music seldom heard on the JBC, his fellow musicians keeping their distance. Many disliked Marlene Brown, Peter's woman, who had a reputation as a dabbler in obeah. Tosh had also broken ties with Bunny Wailer, who he accused of lowering the moral standards of reggae with his dance-hall records. Tosh denounced all singing toasters like Yellowman, as well as the newer dance-hall DJs, calling them "district John-Crows" (local scavenger birds; the John-Crow is a tropical turkey buzzard whose black plumage and red neck resemble the vestments of Reverend John Crow, the fabled Irish clergyman of slavery days who preached that blacks should not complain or revolt).

Lastly, Peter's former cohorts had tired of his constant bile, his incessant vituperative spiels, since his filing of lawsuits against EMI, Tuff Gong Records, an old manager, and a Brazilian record label. He'd also lost a long and ugly court battle for custody of the youngest of his eight children by various women, and his last house in Jamaica had been burned to the ground in 1986 by arsonists.

He was currently residing in an expansive two-story bungalow on Plymouth Avenue in Barbican, an upper-middle-class section of the Kingston suburb of St. Andrew. His retinue of late had dwindled to local craftsman Michael Robinson, "bush doctor" (occult herbalist) Wilton "Doc" Brown, JBC radio personality Jeff "Free-I" Dixon and his wife Joy, and famed drummer-percussionist Carlton "Santa" Davis.

There were other habitués at his home, however. These were the "buzzard higgler" and "bad beggarmon" (criminal mendicants) types who were the bane of every Jamaican music personality who had escaped—but not outdistanced—the West Kingston slums. These bad boys crept into even the nicest uptown precincts, knowing how to strike the balance between general nuisance, sycophancy and nagging reminder of an impoverished past. A smart bad boy on the beg would avoid disrupting suburban life, passing like a phantom through its tidy environs while never letting the former slum residents off the hook, subtly preserving the notion that the social-climbing reggae star and the ghetto sponger were *both* interlopers.

The maxim that "good reggae nevah quail de ghetto" endured among leading Jamaican musicians as both a slice of wisdom and a warning. From Bob Marley on down, no top-ranking artists from shantytown had ever entirely severed their ties with yard life, retaining a measure of acquaintance with its ways, and carrying an unresolved load of guilt about the brethren left lingering in its awful back lanes. Moreover, Jamaican reggae's triumphs as crossover music had always been tentative or conditional, its international potency still oddly dependent on roots savvy and cutting-edge status in downtown spheres. For better or worse, the ghetto remained the driving force of Jamaican rock, and nobody had ever found a way to keep his riddims tough without retapping the source. Tragically, that source knew how to tap back.

The morning after Peter Tosh and Marlene Brown had returned to Barbican, they were visited by Dennis "Leppo" Lobban, a higgler and self-styled dub poet whose criminal escapades in West Kingston had long paralleled Peter's gains as a performer. The thirty-two-year-old thug, whose smirking, screw-faced features bore a slight resemblance to the singer's, had been hitting on Tosh for cash and kindnesses since the early 1970s. Over the last two years Tosh, forty-two, had given him money to preserve his "cotch" at 2 Crescent Road in the ghetto, and to help feed a child by his woman.

On this muggy Monday morning in September, Lobban had come to complain that Marlene Brown's brother Dennis had not come through with promised favors. That the first caller since their return should be a cadger set the hot-tempered Marlene off, and she summed up her vexations with the grim crack that she didn't want Peter, herself or anyone else "ending up dead." This acrid jest was reference both to the recent murder by an associate of Leppo's of a couple the friend had been extorting money from, as well as to the police killing of the extortionists just one week ago. (Since August, just before their trip to New York, Tosh had also been griping in the presence of Marlene and others that the grounds of the house had begun to "smell like death," an anxiety she had never fully comprehended.)

Leppo let the matter drop, but he remained on the premises till late afternoon, smoking spliffs and lounging on the white wicker settees in the sunny living room dominated by photo portraits of Haile Selassie and Tosh. Leppo had been a rudeboy since his teens, earning his first three-month jail rap for vagrancy in 1971. In May 1974 he drew some serious time—fifteen years—for three separate counts of robbery with assault; two months later, the Kingston Home Circuit Court got around to convicting him for assault with intent to rob, robbery with aggravation, shooting with intent to kill, and wounding with intent to kill. The minimum aggregate sentence for his spree of larceny and attempted murder was twenty-five years at hard labor, but Leppo had served only twelve years and five months when he was paroled from prison on October 3, 1986. If all went well, Leppo's parole was to expire on June 6, 1991. On September 11, 1987, a Friday, at 7:30 P.M., Leppo paid his second call to Peter Tosh's residence.

Leppo approached the front gate, knocking and then hesitating in anticipation of someone calling off Peter's fifteen guard dogs. He had nothing to fear, for all the dogs but two were tethered, including those that were attack-trained. Tosh's friend Michael Robinson answered the knock. Robinson was surprised to see it was Leppo, who rarely came by after sundown, since the group inside (Peter, Marlene, Doc Brown, Santa Davis) had been expecting Free-I and Joy Dixon. While they'd been waiting for the couple, Santa had been entertaining Peter by describing an uncanny incident in Miami that day in which Pope John Paul II's outdoor mass had been aborted ("Jah lick him down!" Tosh exulted) when lightning struck the altar platform, one thunderbolt scorching a press photographer.

Robinson's curiosity at the sight of Leppo turned to anxiety when he saw two other strangers join the higgler as he made his way down the darkened path toward the house's front stoop. Michael led the trio into the foyer, whereupon the tallest stranger spun around, shutting and locking the door behind the group as he produced a 9mm Browning automatic pistol from the waist of his pants. In seconds, Robinson had three pistols trained on his temples, and he was hustled up the stairs to the living room as the tall man hissed at him not to make "any bumbaclot noise!"

"Everybody belly it!" shouted Lobban, stepping in front of the flickering television in the center of the dimly lit living room as Tosh and his friends gaped. "Everybody get flat!"

Nobody seated before the glowing TV moved, astonishment etched in cool blue-white on their faces. "Get flat!" Leppo repeated in a hysterical tone. "Dis is a holdup!"

Tosh, Wilton, Davis and Robinson sank to their knees and obediently stretched out on the cold floor. Marlene Brown, on her haunches beside the chair, refused to fall to her stomach.

"Where is the money?" Leppo bellowed to Peter, but only Marlene answered, explaining there was no money in the house. She reminded Leppo that his younger brother, who went by the alias of Handsome, had tried to borrow some money earlier in the day, and was told to return after the weekend, when a Monday morning bank trip would make a loan possible.

Leppo turned to her, rage in his bloodshot eyes, and hollered that it was her obeah that had brought this gunplay to pass—spells that stopped Peter from shelling out his customary alms to the bad men. "You dead for this tonight!" he vowed.

The tall gunman was impatient with these exchanges. He shouted for everyone to stand and divest their pockets and persons of any cash, jewelry, watches and so on. When he discovered Santa had J$200 on him, he exploded in fury, wondering what other valuables were being withheld. Tosh was approached, the tall man wresting the gold chain from the six-foot-six singer's neck as he raised his gun hand to pistol-whip him. Peter, being skilled in karate, automatically countered the blow, the tussle causing a nearby electric fan to topple to the floor.

Just then another knock was heard at the gate. As Leppo and his other gunman ordered Tosh to lie back down, the tall fellow spat that Tosh was "dead for that move tonight!" He stepped into the kitchen, taking up a machete kept beside the refrigerator for opening coconuts, and strode back to the sprawled Tosh, barking that he would chop Peter's head off if he didn't disclose where the money was.

Marlene was now exclaiming that it must be Free-I and Joy at the gate, pleading with the gunmen not to answer the knocks, to spare them.

Outside, the couple had grown quizzical with the lack of response, especially after hearing the fan crash to the floor within, and they pounded on the gate's metal mailbox to draw the attention of those inside the bungalow. The tall stranger appeared to escort them inside, and as soon as the nervous Joy and Free-I were across the threshold, the tall gunman ripped the gold chain from Free-I's neck and then jammed a hand into Free-I's trouser pocket, pulling out a J$400 wad of bills.

Leppo began wandering in and out of adjacent rooms, screaming, "*Where's the money?*" certain Tosh would not have returned from America without some. Peter and Marlene took turns reasoning with

Leppo, proposing various possibilities for when the bank opened on Monday. Hearing this, the tall, machete-toting gunman lost all composure, yelping to Leppo, "*Do* wha yuh come for!"

With that, Leppo wheeled around and fired a random shot at Marlene, who was huddled next to Joy. The bullet zipped across Marlene's scalp, ripping flesh as it sped, and then sliced into Joy's mouth, dislocating teeth, passing out through the side of her cheek. Both women went down in shock and horror, feigning death.

Badly agitated, Leppo's wild eyes darted from the women's blood-splattered brows to Peter's bowed head, and he stabbed his pistol into Tosh's forehead and fired twice, the bullets battering the outside of the singer's skull as they entered. Tosh's body snapped sharply from the force of the shots and then fell limp.

The sight seemed to drive all three gunmen over the brink of composure and they began firing in unison as they scampered about, eight or nine shots crisscrossing the room. A slug slammed into Michael Robinson's thigh as he crawled under a coffee table. There was a pause, and then more reports rang out. Doc Brown took a bullet in the head, dying instantly. Free-I received two shots behind his ear. Another shot was aimed at Michael Robinson, punching through his leather hat and slicing across his pate; he was lying there wondering how long it took a man to die when he felt another bullet burst into his back.

There was a last spray of chaotic gunfire, six or seven bullets bouncing and skittering in all directions. Santa flinched as one creased his shoulder. Joy froze as another pierced her right leg.

Then came an awful stillness. At length it was interrupted at some distance by scuffling feet, the muffled din of a racing VW bus engine and squealing tires.

Once all was again silent within and without, Marlene bolted up and lurched down to the street, screaming for help. Scattered neighbors, alerted by the two dozen booming pistol reports, stood stiffly about, stunned and speechless. All refused to move toward the house. An attorney whose home was directly opposite hastened past the tableau of onlookers and into the house. He bounded up the stairs, taking two at a time, but stalled at the top, jolted by the sight of the carnage, the tart stench of the gunpowder swirling his senses.

Hurrying back downward and out into the night air, the lawyer shouted to Marlene that he was going to bring his car around to take the wounded to the hospital. Joy and Marlene disappeared into the bungalow and quickly reemerged, bearing the semiconscious Tosh down the front walk and into the attorney's waiting automobile. Free-I was soon lifted inside after him. Lastly, Michael Robinson and Santa staggered into the sedan, which skidded off in the direction of University Hospital of the West Indies in Mona Heights.

Left behind inside Tosh's bungalow, Doc Brown's body lay in its own fluids before the TV.

Treatment at the hospital brought the massacre's brutal toll into perspective. Marlene Brown and Joy Dixon were treated for their flesh wounds and released. Santa Davis was admitted for his shoulder wound and was resting quietly. Michael Robinson was in critical but stable condition with three serious wounds. Free-I was in a coma, his doctors deciding he was too fragile to withstand emergency surgery for removal of the two bullets lodged in his cranium.

Peter Tosh was pronounced dead, and hospital authorities and police became anxious to locate a next of kin. They were told by friends and fans that, while his parents might still be alive, Peter had not seen either of them in more than two decades. Detective Sergeant Hugh Miller of the Halfway Tree Police Station was assigned to investigate the shooting melee, which had resulted in the slaying of Tosh and Wilton "Doc" Brown. Three days later, on Monday, September 14, Sergeant Miller's case became a triple murder, as Jeff "Free-I" Dixon expired while still in a coma in University Hospital's intensive care unit.

The following day Mrs. Alvira Coke, Peter's mother, arrived at his Barbican home, asking to discuss funeral arrangements with Marlene Brown. Marlene appeared at the front door and denounced Mrs. Coke with gutter slang, castigating her for abandoning Peter when he was an infant. Mrs. Coke attempted to press her proposal of burying Peter in his native parish of Westmoreland, but Marlene would hear none of it, ending the encounter with the words "I don't like you and Peter don't like you either."

On the 17th, Dennis "Leppo" Lobban surrendered to officials at the Kingston office of the Human Rights Council, claiming he saw his picture in local news telecasts concerning the warrants issued for his arrest. Police quickly arrived and took the street vendor—who professed innocence—into custody.

Marlene made arrangements to have Peter Tosh's remains

buried at Dovecot Memorial Park on Constant Spring Road in Kingston, but the prime minister's office phoned her at the Barbican house on Wednesday, September 23, to inform her that she had no right to custody of the body and must accede to Alvera Coke's wishes to have Peter laid to rest in Westmoreland in the village of Belmont.

Brown belittled the new burial site, claiming that it was beside Coke's pigsty, but Tosh's mother told the local press the grave and pen were separated by at least three "chains" (a common Jamaican linear measure for sixty-six feet or used to note distances of less than a mile).

On Friday, September 25, Peter Tosh's body was laid out in state at Kingston National Arena, with some 12,000 mourners filing past for a last viewing of "The Toughest." His body was dressed in a crisp khaki uniform, a white cape draped over it. His dreadlocked head was topped with a brimless African cap of white satin. Beside him in the bier was a walking staff on which was carved the inscription JAH LIVES. The public wake lasted four hours, Tosh's children frequently clustered on either side of the casket as the grieving and the curious streamed by.

The next day the national arena was the scene of a funeral ceremony attended by approximately a thousand friends, family members and the general public. Melody Cunningham, an old lover of Peter's, took part, but not Marlene Brown. The Amharic-English service, presided over by the Reverend Father Neville L. Manning Estifanos of the Ethiopian Orthodox Church of Jamaica, was twice disrupted. The first disturbance, occurring at the very start, was created by an anonymous man in a white outfit who approached the closed coffin and began to dance around it, chanting, "Rise, Peter. Rise, Peter." He was led off by police, as was the second agitator, an overexcited fellow waving a banner emblazoned with the words FREEDOM and GARVEYISM.

Once order was restored, Horace McIntosh, twenty, Peter's eldest son, offered a reading, and then his younger brother Andrew, nineteen, sang several of his parent's songs. After a eulogy by broadcaster Dermott Hussey, the coffin was lifted by the pallbearers, who were the McIntosh boys Horace, Andrew and Steve, plus musicians Sly Dunbar, Robbie Lyn and Carlton Smith. As saxophonist Dean Fraser played "Amazing Grace," the casket was carried to a white van for the 120-mile trip to Belmont, where it was installed in a makeshift crypt overlooking the Caribbean Sea.

Kingston remained ill at ease about the deaths, the edginess revived on Friday, October 2, when excited reports spread that Marlene Brown had escaped harm after being bushwhacked during the predawn hours while pulling her car into her driveway. She claimed the ambush came from four men in a car who brandished M-16s and fired at her as they sped past in the darkness.

On March 2, 1988, at the 30th Annual Grammy Awards ceremony at Radio City Music Hall in New York City, Peter Tosh was announced as a first-time winner in the Best Reggae Record category for his album *No Nuclear War*. One Pauline Burgess, who identified herself as a relative of Tosh's, picked up the award and said afterward that Tosh had more unreleased music she hoped a record label would issue.

Three weeks later, during an interview with the *Daily Gleaner* at his Solomonic Records office in the corporate area of St. Andrew, Bunny Wailer told Jamaica he did not care to be a reggae martyr. "Dat is what de people want all de time, somebody ta make a sacrifice, but the people dem don't want ta make none. Dey always want an individual ta come and go on the cross, but dem don't want ta make no sacrifice.

"Bob sing a song, say, 'How long will they kill da prophets/While we stand aside and look/Then some say dat's just a part of it/You have to fulfill da book.' Den dey go back to sleep.

"Me nuh inna nuh sacrifice business. Me have ta be here ta see de victory of good over evil and me not making nuh mistake. If Jah will dat I should go, I will go, and when I go, He will be with I, 'cause I not going because of nuh will of man."

It was the first time Bunny had made anything resembling a public appearance in Jamaica since he joined the bill of the Reggae Sunsplash '87 music festival. He continued to spend most of his time in seclusion on his 142-acre farm on the border of the parishes of Portland and St. Thomas, where he raised coffee, plantain, sugarcane, coconuts and soursop—all of which he sold locally, exported or gave away in the bush.

But he acknowledged to the *Gleaner* reporter that as a farmer he'd recently been experiencing problems with Jamaican banks. An outstanding loan that he'd expected to be paid from his royalty receipts abroad led to Bunny being cornered by agents of the bank in December '87 as he drove along Kingston's Lyndhurst Road. They seized his newly renovated Toyota Cressida, leaving him stranded on the sidewalk with what he described as the whiplash he suffered when the agents rammed his car. "I might have ta get a collar, as the X ray have shown a need fe it. Every time I get up me neck hurts.

"Dey have said dat dey are sorry, but dey should have known dey were going to be sorry," added Bunny, who assured the *Gleaner* that he planned to release a new album soon.

Following an unusual "Bunny Wailer Live" concert, held at the Llandilo Cultural Center on March 26 in Savanna-la-Mar to raise funds for his current projects and predicaments, the reclusive Wailer retreated once again to his remote farm.

The trial of Leppo began on Monday, June 13, 1988, in Kingston in the Gun Court Division of the Home Circuit Court, with Mr. Justice Patterson presiding. The crown, represented by Mr. Garth McBean, acting deputy director of public prosecutions, Mr. Paul Dennis, assistant director of public prosecutions, and Mrs. Lorna Errar-Gayle, crown counsel, called eleven witnesses during the five-day proceedings.

Leppo was charged jointly with Steve "Honey" Russell, twenty-six, a chauffeur and purchasing clerk with Hermes Ltd. who lived on Grosmond Avenue in Patrick City, St. Andrew. Russell testified that one of his co-workers at Hermes had asked him to take Leppo and two other men in a company van to Tosh's house, where he was told to wait. Upon hearing shooting, Russell said, he had started the engine to flee when the gunmen clambered into the van and directed him at gunpoint to drive. One witness confirmed that Russell had been in possession of the company van on the evening of the slayings, and another testified seeing Russell in the van as the men ran from the house and got inside the vehicle. Russell was subsequently freed when Judge Patterson upheld a no-case submission made by his two attorneys.

That left Leppo as the sole defendant, his two accomplices unaccounted for. Leppo testified that he was a "brethen" of Peter's and had last visited the singer's house on the Wednesday before he was killed, Tosh then loaning him J$1000. Leppo acknowledged having availed himself of Tosh's largess since their youth together in Trench Town: "Peter gave me assistance. Anything I wanted he gave me. He gave me a bed and money ta spend."

But Leppo denied murdering Tosh, and produced one witness to support an alibi that he was far from the scene on the evening of the killings: "Between six and eight P.M. on the night in question I was in a shop on Crook Street in Jones Town. I was dere having a drink wit' friends for about four hours. While dere I heard da news of my friend's death. I became astonished."

The jury of eight women and four men retired for six minutes on Friday, June 17, and returned to the court with the verdict: guilty on all three counts of murder. Glancing at Leppo, who stood under police escort wearing a gray-and-blue-striped shirt and blue corduroy slacks, Judge Patterson told the jury: "I would have arrived at the same verdict. I have no doubt in my mind that he went there that night and killed Tosh and the others. It was just by chance that the other four survived or we would have had seven people lying dead."

Leppo was sentenced to hang. "I am innocent, sir," he told the judge, but he was led away under tight security and consigned to St. Catherine District Prison, Spanish Town, where he joined 188 other condemned criminals on Death Row.

The trial of Cayman Music, Inc., against the Estate of Bob Marley et al. began on Monday, November 9, 1987, in the Supreme Court of the State of New York at 60 Centre Street in New York City. The Honorable Elliot Wilk continued to preside, and the case was heard before a jury of six and two alternates, which had been sworn in on November 6.

The proceedings were conducted in typically drab surroundings, the paneled upstairs courtroom wholly unremarkable except for the quaint figures assembled there in the long pewlike seats on either side of the bench. To the right sat Danny Sims, a bald, lantern-jawed black man whose sleepy eyes belied a careful, temperamental disposition. Poised over him was stocky Stewart Levy, a nervous, perspiration-prone partner in the law firm of Peter Parcher, the suave, silver-haired man who paced next to Levy.

To the left stood husky Bob Brundige from Hughes Hubbard & Reed, a courtly white man with a quick mind and an unkempt mien. His associate was William Thomas, a dapper, soft-spoken black who would share the trial chores. Gathered before them were the attorneys and officers of the Mutual Security Merchant Bank and Trust of Jamaica, the dominant figure in the prim caucus being coffee-complexioned Louis Byles, the stern-faced estate administrator and managing director of the bank.

These people were the constants during the two weeks of testimony, with other personalities—half of them casually dressed dreads—drifting in and out of the high-ceilinged chamber as witnesses were called to the dock. The only other relative constants during the trial were the involuntary expressions of consternation and horror on the faces of the integrated jury of men and women, and the icy rain that always seemed to be lashing the windows of the courtroom during particularly unsettling testimony.

Throughout the proceedings, attorneys for the estate characterized as transparently false Sims's claims that the "truth was revealed" concerning Bob Marley's use of songwriting pseudonyms through his reading of the two Bob Marley biographies published in 1983. Rather, the estate insisted, he could have discovered *any* facts that were not already known to him as late as November of 1978. Indeed, from 1968 through early 1973, Sims identified himself as Bob's "combined publisher/manager/executive producer," as confirmed by Sims himself in a press release issued in connection with the issue of a 1981 compilation album of Bob's tracks called *Chances Are*. Moreover, as the estate maintained, Sims was hired by Island Records in 1980 to provide special radio promotion for "Could You Be Loved" from *Uprising*, a song that appeared in Cayman's papers as one of the contested songs. It was hard to believe, said the estate, that after Sims worked closely together with Bob on the promotion of the song Sims knew nothing about the publishing status and authorship of "Could You Be Loved" until—as he alleged—1983.

Sims argued that only by his attorney's deposing of Bob's Rasta guru Mortimo Planno—actually a longtime associate of Sims since 1968—did he discover that "Could You Be Loved" was written by Bob prior to October 1976, during the period covered by the publishing agreements.

In fact, the estate insisted, "Could You Be Loved" had been *released* well before 1976. The song appeared on Wailers-produced record labels during the period of 1967–68 and 1970–71. Sims could easily have discovered what he needed to know in this case and dozens of others by *simply reading* the labels and album covers on the records issued before 1976.

Numerous inconsistencies in Sims's allegations were cited. For instance, the estate charged that Mr. Planno could not possibly have heard the song "Ambush in the Night" prior to October 1976, as he claimed in his deposition supporting Sims's case. The song "Ambush in the Night" was written about an assassination attempt on Bob Marley's life, an event that occurred in December of 1976. Thus the song could not have been written until well after the publishing agreement with Cayman had expired.

Beyond stating when he "first heard" certain other songs, Planno gave, according to the estate, only the most general statement that "Bob co-wrote virtually every song that he ever recorded." The statement was simply not true, in the eyes of the estate, and Mr. Planno had no such personal knowledge and said nothing to furnish any reliable basis for such a sweeping and obviously insupportable generalization.

Moreover, some of the Bob Marley songs in question in the trial had already been the subject of controversy and/or inquiries during the mid-1970s. As an example, in a letter dated December 3, 1975, from a German licensee of Marley's songs to Sims's then attorney and chief executive of the Copyright Services Bureau (which administered the copyrights for Cayman), the licensee inquired into the true authorship of "No Woman, No Cry" and "Them Belly Full." An attached article revealed that in an earlier album the two songs had been credited to Bob Marley *alone* and not to V. Ford, and the letter then questions, "Who the hell is V. Ford anyway?" Here again, the estate insisted, Sims was on notice of pseudonyms and chose not to do anything about it.

The estate also argued that the intrigue of Cayman's story dissolved quickly upon searching Cayman's papers for substance, evidence or proof. Vincent Ford, for instance, had made a new declaration for the defense that effectively undermined his prior declaration of September 19, 1984. In the new statement, Ford explained his earlier statements in the following manner:

> . . . I further declare that in early September of 1984, Danny Simms [*sic*] came to me and advised me that there was a vast sum of money that was being held by the Publishers regarding my songs "No Woman, No Cry," "Positive Vibration," "Roots Rock Reggae," and "Crazy Baldheads" and that these monies are really due to me and it would be paid over if I were to sign a statement saying that it was really myself and Bob who had written these songs and not myself alone and also that I have never received any monies for these songs. He further said that my signing this would in no way affect Bob Marley or his widow or estate.
>
> I was never advised that this statement was to be used in any sort

of court case and I was misled into signing an untrue statement and I did not realize the full extent of what I was signing and that I have been receiving regular sums of monies in respect of the publishing on these songs.

Further inconsistencies in Sims's position were repeatedly brought out when he took the stand in the case and was examined by the estate's counsel.

Q: . . . Isn't it a fact that during the late 1960s, early 1970s, you were experiencing a lot of double-contracting by Caribbean, Jamaican artists?

A: No, it's not true.

Q: Isn't it a fact that double-contracting in your mind means where an artist signs up with one publisher one day and next week signs up with somebody else and takes publishing advance money from each of them along the way?

A: Well, I found that out later on in my dealings with other people but that was much later on than the '60s and early '70s.

Q: I refer you to your deposition in the transcript, Mr. Sims. I refer you to p. 53. . . . You are asked a question: "What do you mean by double-contract? . . . You stated: "Artists that would sign a contract with me today and next week for an advance will sign with somebody else. I had that experience a lot. Especially with Caribbean artists . . . I think it is typical of the Caribbean artists to sign with as many people as they can. . . ." Do you recall that testimony?

A: Yes. . . .

Q: Isn't it also a fact that in early 1973 before your contract, Cayman Music and Marley, was signed, the one in October of 1973, that you were experiencing the same problem with Bob Marley?

A: Not double-contracting, no.

Q: Weren't you finding in fact that certain compositions written by Bob Marley subsequent to one of your publishing contracts had been claimed by Tuff Gong . . . and you claimed that constituted a breach of agreement between Bob Marley and Cayman Music?

A: What year are you speaking of?

Q: 1973?

A: Tuff Gong wasn't in existence in 1973.

To refute this answer, attorneys for the Marley estate moved to have a letter, dated March 19, 1973, and written on the letterhead of Copyright Service Bureau, marked as Defendant's Exhibit R. The letter, shown to and read in court for confirmation by Sims, was a notice to Bob Marley on Cayman's behalf charging him with a breach of agreement with Cayman over his Tuff Gong publishing.

Q: You stated yesterday under oath, did you not, that in London, in 1980, Bob Marley never admitted to you that he wrote "No Woman, No Cry."
A: He has never admitted that to me.
Q: I refer you to line 20, p. 147, of your deposition transcript, where you state, "I was made to understand from Bob Marley, this is when he came back to work for me as his manager in 1980, that Vincent Ford didn't write the song, he wrote it." Question: Bob Marley said that?
A: Yes.

And so it went, as the defense hammered away at Sims's position versus documentation or testimony to the contrary. It was also the contention of the prosecution, however, that Sims had been prevented from learning about or acting upon Bob Marley's use of pseudonyms in his song publishing because of the atmosphere of violence surrounding him. As witnesses Alan "Skilly" Cole (the Jamaican soccer star and close friend of Bob's) and Don Taylor (Bob's onetime manager) were called to the stand, the realities of ghetto life were fleshed out with bloodcurdling clarity.

The prosecution was aggressive in uncovering the details of the horse-race fixing and underworld wickedness that helped precipitate the assassination attempt on Bob Marley in 1976, pressing both Alan Cole and Don Taylor for particulars. The defense also joined in, usually to expose the character of the witnesses.

Q: Mr. Cole, are you familiar with the Stewards of the Jockey Club of Jamaica?
A: Yes, I am.
Q: Can you tell us just very briefly what is the Stewards of the Jockey Club?
A: That's the ruling body that run racing in Jamaica.
Q: Mr. Cole, are you aware that in March of 1976 the Stewards of the Jockey Club of Jamaica issued a proclamation warning off Alan Skill Cole from all courses in other places where the rules of racing are in force for a period of 20 years?
A: Yeah, I wasn't in the country at that time, but it happened.

Don Taylor was called to the docket to fill in the gray areas.

Q: Do you know who was behind the assassination attempt?
A: Yes.
Q: Who?
A: There was two guys—and it was a mixture of political, it was a thing that Cole had run a racketeering horse race and they thought that Bob was behind it because Alan was driving Bob's car. Alan, he fix horses at the track. He had fixed this big race and took off with the money. And Bob, oh, they must have felt that Bob was behind it, because Bob must have financed it, because Alan didn't have no way to get that kind of money away from Bob.

This mixed-up idea that he believed in the People's National Party, and so did I, and we had a lawsuit against Clement Dodd who was Bob's first recording company, that I started for not paying Bob, and tried to get back some of the copyrights, all those factors together caused the assassination . . .

Q: What happened to the alleged assassins?
THE COURT: Do you know what happened to them?
THE WITNESS: Yes.
THE COURT: What?
THE WITNESS: They were hanged. I saw one hung.
Q: The government of Jamaica hung them?
A: No, our friends down in the ghetto tried them and hung them.
Q: Who?
A: Guys we were raised with from Trenchtown.
Q: Where was the police?
A: They was not around.
THE COURT: Did you see them hung?
THE WITNESS: Yes, sir. I was 30 feet away when they tried them and hung them, the people in the neighborhood, in the gully. They tried them in the gully. They had me fly down. They had me say, "That's the one who shot me."
Q: Were any of the alleged assassins brought to trial?
A: No, none of the alleged assassins were brought to trial. None of them are alive.
Q: Did Bob Marley have anything to do with the alleged assassins not being alive?
A: The people. I don't know if Bob Marley did. Because of the love of Bob Marley by the people, the people took it upon themselves. They felt the government wasn't moving fast enough. They could move better than the government. They could investigate better than the police. . . .

The prosecution also grilled Don Taylor on the particulars of violence he experienced at Bob Marley's hands in Gabon in 1980.

Q: Can you describe the beating in Africa?

A: We had a situation where the promoter, we got to Africa. I dealt with this promoter who gave me deposits on two artists, on Bob Marley and Jimmy Cliff, and my office gave him separate receipts. When we got to Africa, promoter came here, he said he wanted to cancel Jimmy Cliff show. He would like his money back. I said, "You are crazy."

He find a way to tell Bob Marley that the money he gave me for Jimmy Cliff was really for Bob Marley, and I was trying to take that money for myself. Bob Marley is the kind of person who don't believe people. So he believe the guy, and he jumped up and started hitting me in front of the . . . that was in Gabon, Africa, Intercontinental Hotel.

That was our physical thing. That was the start of it in 1980.

Q: When was the second beating?

A: The second beating was OK. We started in 1980 from Gabon. I had told him I was never going to work for him again. So he was really angered because he knew that I was the only person who made all this money. I made all this money for him in six years. So he doesn't like to be defied. He said, "You are going to defy me."

He call me one day, say, "Taylor, come over to the house . . . . let's work out our problems, because I really want you to work with me."

So I went over there, because he lived right around the corner from me, and he was sitting by the pool. We were sitting by the pool, and he says, "I hear you say you are not going to work for me again." I said, "Yes, man, I can't be bothered working for you." He said, "Come into the bedroom with me. . . . I got something I want to show you."

I walked in the bedroom with him, and he says, "Yvette, bring that piece of paper."

Q: Yvette is who?

A: Yvette Morris was working for him as one of the secretaries, and he said, "Bring that piece of paper I asked you to type." He looked at the paper. I saw Alan Cole coming through the door with an Uzi submachine gun.

Q: That's the Israeli submachine gun. And the piece of paper had what on it?

A: He wanted for me to sign that I relinquish all commissions, all rights, anything I had claim to.

Q: Were you claiming that Bob Marley owed you commissions?

A: On the contract, because I had a lawyer write it.

Q: Did you sign the piece of paper?

A: He beat me up. Alan had the submachine gun. Every time he hit me, Alan had that gun. I couldn't believe Alan hold that gun at me. We were supposed to be all right. Finally his, Bob's kids, Ziggy and all of them, come through the door, and that's how it stopped. He [Ziggy] said: "Don is so good to you. He take six gunshots for you just a year ago [during the assassination attempt]. You do this to Don?"

I got real mad. I went to the police, reported it to Miami, bought . . . to the Tamiami Gun Shop and decided I was going to kill somebody. I couldn't believe he did that to me. That's the second time. All this time, in the next breath, "Don, you are a good man, I still want you to manage me." I said, "What's up to this man?" you know.

On the stand, Alan Cole was asked his side of this story.

Q: Turning your attention back to 1980, at Miami, Florida, was there an incident there relating to Don Taylor?

A: Yes.

Q: Would you tell Justice Wilk and the jury what happened?

A: Well, it was three weeks before we started the U.S. tour that ended prematurely [after Bob Marley became terminally ill]. And we invited Don to come over to Bob's mother's house for an argument, a little talk. Bob hadn't seen him in a couple of months. And he came, eventually he came after, took time for him to come. He was, he didn't really want to come at first when we spoke to him. But eventually he came. An argument developed inside of that room. And I closed the door. And it got rough. We got rough, and things like that.

Q: Got beaten up, right?

A: He got shaken up, beaten up. . . .

Q: Did you point an Uzi submachine gun at Mr. Taylor?

A: It wasn't an Uzi. . . .

Q: What was it?

A: It was an automatic .45, I think. . . . There was a rifle around, but I didn't point no rifle.

Alan Cole was also asked to testify about "rough" behavior on Bob Marley's behalf that he purportedly participated in during the early 1970s.

Q: So, let's talk for just a minute about monitoring or making sure that Mr. Marley's records get played on the air. What, if anything, did you do to see to it in the early '70s, and I'm talking now of the period

'72, '73, '74 through '76, to see to it that Bob Marley's records got played in Jamaica on the radio? Tell Justice Wilk and the jury, please.

A: Well, in those days, it was very difficult for Rastafarians to get airplay unless we were aligned to the big record companies. When I started working at that time as manager, we went independent. So we had a lot of problems in the record industry getting airplay and things like that. So it was my duty to see that we got proper airplays, see that our music was on the charts, and, you know, things like that.

Q: Well, let me be blunt now, Mr. Cole. You understand now you are under oath, do you not?

A: Yes, I understand.

Q: You understand it is your obligation to tell the truth?

A: Yes, I understand.

Q: Now, I'm asking you specifically to tell Justice Wilk and this jury what, if anything, you did or caused to be done in the '70s to get Bob Marley's records played on the air.

A: Well, as I said, it was a difficult period in that time. And for us to get airplay, we had to put a lot of strength, what you call muscle, to get played from the various disc jockeys, and things like that. So it was my duty to see that these things happened. . . . Well, sometimes we had to go there and, you know, beat disc jockeys and deal with program directors and things like that. . . . So in that sense, we had to use a little muscle, some force, to get airplay. . . . Occasionally we had to beat—we had to beat disc jockeys. We had to send guys to—smash their cars or things like that. Threaten them. . . . If you didn't play our records you have to leave the station. You have to leave. Things like that.

Q: Did any person leave the station as a result of threats or beatings?

A: Yeah, quite a few people left the station during that year. Disc jockeys, I believe, program directors, left their jobs. Some went out to leave the country.

Q: And during that period of '76, were you then successful in getting Bob Marley's records played on radio?

A: During that period of time. . . . Yes. Well, that was the period of time that we got most of his number-one songs in Jamaica. In that period.

Q: And that was your job, both before Don Taylor and when Don Taylor came aboard, right?

A: Before and when he came.

Q: Would you mind telling Justice Wilk and this jury who Ted Powder is?

A: Ted Powder was a subpublisher that worked for Federal Recording Studio or Federal Recording Company. . . .

Q: Wasn't he also the sublicensee for Jamaica for Danny Sims, Cayman Music?

A: Yes.

Q: So that, in fact, if royalties were owed to Bob Marley, and Cayman Music, for sales in Jamaica, it was Ted Powder that was responsible to pay Bob Marley?

A: That is correct.

Q: Now, did there come a time when you were passing either as manager or when Don Taylor came aboard as overseer, as you put that word, that you had differences with Ted Powder?

A: Yeah, we had differences with Ted Powder.

Q: Yes? Would you tell the court and jury, please, what happened?

A: Well, we had a conflict once—we had a conflict with Mr. Powder. About some money. And it got, what I would say, out of control. We had to beat Mr. Powder before we could get our money. . . .

Q: Ted Powder was Danny's man, Danny Sims's man in Jamaica, is that correct?

A: That is correct.

Q: How many people beat him?

A: About three guys. We had about three guys beat him about all of that time.

Q: And after that, is it a fact that Danny Sims came running down to Jamaica to pay Bob Marley some money?

A: Yes, Danny Sims came right after that. And we got some money.

Q: Was there any question in your mind whether Danny Sims knew about your beating or causing disc jockeys to be beaten to get records played on the air?

A: Everybody knew that.

Q: Including Danny Sims?

A: That's right.

Q: Was there a meeting in your room or suite, whatever it was, at the Essex House?

A: Yes. We had a meeting with Mr. Sims.

Q: This was in 1980, is that correct?

A: That's correct.

Q: Now, at that meeting, was there a confrontation or discussion about copyrights?

A: Yes, there was.

Q: In your presence?

A: Yes.

Q: OK. Tell Justice Wilk and this jury what happened.

A: OK. We were in my room and they were discussing about songs, you know. Copyright in general. And it got a little out of hand.

And we had some brothers—some Jamaican—you know, some Jamaican entourage. And it got real heated. And one of the brothers threatened to shoot Mr. Sims in the room. And he left.

Q: Mr. Sims left.

A: Yes, he left.

Q: How did he threaten Mr. Sims? What did he say? Tell the jury.

A: He tell him that he shoot him in his head.

Q: And that was because Danny Sims was questioning him about the fraud?

A: Yeah. He was questioning about his copyright, yeah. About the fraud in general.

Q: And what did Danny Sims do? Did he stay there and continue to demand his rights and ask somebody to admit that the fraud had taken place?

A: He left like a bird.

Q: Did he appear to be frightened?

A: He had to be frightened.

The estate argued that Marley threatened Sims only when Sims threatened him, maintaining that, significantly, Sims even waived his interest in the publishing rights to certain songs as part of the ongoing accommodations that both Bob and Sims made to each other as their business relationship developed over time.

Attorneys for both sides knew full well that nothing could possibly excuse the menacing and violent behavior Bob Marley and his associates had used in conducting certain of their affairs with individual music publishing figures and particular Jamaican disc jockeys. However, there had been reasons for this behavior. What was implicit in the revelations during trial testimony was that a ghetto-spawned and ghetto-fed sense of desperation and retribution influenced Marley's actions.

The rise in Jamaica of the musical culture of the sufferah had caused a welter of conflicts between the poor Rasta musician and the JA media establishment that bordered on outright class warfare. For even as Bob gained renown outside of Jamaica, the upper and middle classes controlling the JA airwaves had little but scorn for his "Dungle ditties." As he watched his music being repeatedly and systematically denied broadcast in his native land, and as he saw his publishing revenues inexplicably withheld, Marley sought recourse through tactics consistent with those of the politically tribalist bad men and street-minded sportboys who had been his friends or foes since youth. In his hurt and outrage, Marley felt these reprisals should come as no surprise to either savvy or elitist JA radio DJs or streetwise publisher-manager Danny Sims, who had maintained a residence in Jamaica since 1961 and had moved his entire record production company to Jamaica in the rock-steady era of 1967.

When Danny Sims and his counsel brought the tale of Alan Cole's beating of Ted Powder into open court in order to display the alleged violent atmosphere around Bob Marley, they made a serious tactical error, because Alan Cole told the jury too much about Ted Powder. Not only did Skilly explain who Ted Powder was—"Danny's man," the sublicensee in Jamaica for Sims's publishing interests—but the dread also went on to detail that, after Powder had been threatened, Sims appeared in Jamaica "right after that. And we got some money."

In short, according to Cole's uncontested testimony, Bob Marley truly *was* being denied money owed to him, money that was rightfully his through publishing agreements with Sims. Indeed, in the eyes of Marley and his brethren, Bob was being squeezed by a puppet master who could come and go on Air Jamaica as he pleased, while the Tuff Gong had to crouch over a pata stove in a slum plot, living hand to mouth as always even though his uncommon songs were becoming the talk of Britain and the States. To see his reggae being repressed locally, while having to beg for the mounting royalties he earned elsewhere, made him feel like the "penny ketcha," that pathetic fool who'll perform any toil for a pittance. And that was a humiliation which, as a youth, he'd promised himself he'd never permit.

As Cole himself corroborated on the witness stand, Marley's gripe was legitimate, his rage logical, his powerlessness real. And that's when the bullies in the Gong's camp stepped forward to offer their own surly solution.

As anyone (including its 1973 publisher, Danny Sims) who has ever heard and understood the song "Slave Driver" should have grasped, the hellfire you catch in the end is always the hellfire you stoked and toyed with from the start. So Jah seh.

It had been Alan Cole who had suggested—no, insisted—that direct retaliation was the only way to deal with derisive radio people and slippery subpublishers, largely because this had become the sole strategy that was getting Cole anywhere in Kingston since his soccer career had gone south. Cole still could become one of the greatest soccer coaches in the history of Jamaican football, but sadly, he liked the spree life better. And he had always wanted Bob to like it, too, although that never transpired.

Ghetto bonds run deep, but Marley had never trusted Skilly with anything of consequence after Cole had almost gotten Bob killed in the crossfire of his '76 Caymanas Park mix-up. Cole was never again involved in Bob's songwriting, either, and Bob didn't let him handle management chores. Henceforth Cole could tag along on tour, acting as an aide-de-camp while enjoying himself on Bob's tab, but that was it.

Don Taylor was another matter entirely. He was a West Kingston kid, sure, but never a back-alley footballer, never a slum bredred who passed the chillum or shared the rice pot, never Rasta. Taylor had told Marley that no straight record business type or baldheaded management executive would ever take a dread seriously, and Bob believed him for a spell. But when Bob caught Taylor acting "tricky" in Gabon, that was it for the fast talker from Franklyn Town.

On the witness stand, Taylor put his own verbal spin on the niceties of the Gabon incident. The fracas between Bob and Don in Gabon had centered on the fee that Don had told the Gong his band was getting paid: $40,000. When it was subsequently reported to Bob by Gabon officials that $60,000 had been paid out to Taylor—the manager allegedly setting $20,000 aside for himself—that was when the shouting, and the beating, had erupted. Neville Garrick had tape-recorded the three-hour fracas in Africa; and, according to Diane Jobson, who was also present, Taylor confessed to having skimmed money from Marley's concert advances for years. The consequent Miami contretemps with Taylor (which Alan Cole chose to heighten in his own inimitable fashion) occurred after Marley realized to his great distress that his estranged manager was, on paper, the only authorized officer besides himself for Bob Marley Music, Media Aids and Tuff Gong (his own publishing, his recording interests, and his record label).

For the *Uprising* album, Bob wrote a scathing song about Don Taylor called "Bad Card." The lyric ruminated on the intimate "propaganda" one cunning man can constantly feed a trusting companion until the elaborate nonsense becomes part of the environment the listener inhabits. But inevitably the moment of truth—the slipup in the game—comes as the high-stakes con man deals himself one ace too many. The bad card is revealed in the hand he shows.

As for Danny Sims, he had always claimed to be a wizard at

radio promotion; he was the man who would put Bob's unique sound on the airwaves. Yet he was always trying to dissuade Bob from actually recording reggae—and "message" reggae, at that. The chief way he saw Bob Marley being a money-maker was, in his own words, "in a rhythm-and-blues, Top Forty style." As Sims himself boasted to a reporter from the *Village Voice* just before the trial, "I discouraged Bob from doing the revolutionary stuff. I'm a commercial guy. I want to sell songs to thirteen-year-old girls, not to guys throwing spears"—in other words, not to savages in the jungle. Behind Bob's back, his reggae had often been derided as "jungle music." In time, Bob figured out where attitudes like that had come from. And he fought—until he grew too ill—to hold accountable or keep at bay those who gambled on his vulnerabilities.

All his professional life, since he cut "Judge Not" for Leslie Kong in 1961, Bob Marley had been consumed with the vision of his socially observant reggae. He looked at shantytown and saw the raw eloquence of its strivings; others drawn to him saw only the snake pit in which he created. In the ghetto, only dreamers and vipers flourished, and the life span of either was short. No step forward was won without new tensions and entanglements. No poker match was ever so perilous.

Now, with Bob Marley gone, and his survivors neutralized by their own mistakes and illusions, the chance to play the bad card seemed ripe for Sims. The Cayman Music owner had handled various recording talents over the last two decades—notably Johnny Nash, militant singer-songwriter Gil Scott-Heron, Miami soul vocalist Betty Wright, and the promising reggae-pop group Native—but his current pursuit of Bob Marley's posthumous commercial prospects could be interpreted as a grudging obsession with salvaging a monumental missed opportunity. And since Cole and Taylor had nothing left to lose, they joined the game.

In his summation before Judge Wilk and the jury on November 19, Cayman attorney Stewart Levy argued that "far from Cayman Music being tardy in bringing a suit, the fact of the matter is that it's almost miraculous that Cayman is here even today."

Estate counsel Robert Brundige concurred, although for different reasons. During Brundige's summation, he emphasized that Sims had lived long in Jamaica and run a production company there, had quickly learned of the double-dealing of Jamaican and Caribbean artists, had found from the start that Bob Marley was signing other contracts while with Sims's company, and had known that Marley was permitting other people to put songs Bob had written in their own names. Brundige noted for the jury that Taylor, Cole and Sims himself testified that Sims openly expressed knowledge of such practices "every time he saw" Bob from 1976 onward.

"You heard Mr. Sims say," Brundige added, "he always had a threat over Bob Marley's head."

Judge Wilk sent the jury to deliberate at 5:00 P.M. on November 19, 1987. At 6:07 P.M., the jury returned to announce they had not yet reached a verdict, so they were released until 9:30 A.M. on November 20.

The next morning, the jury requested a review of Sims's deposition concerning the 1980 meeting with Bob Marley in which Marley admitted writing "No Woman, No Cry." They also requested for further study copies of several pieces of evidence entered as exhibits: the *Kaya* and *Exodus* album sleeves, and a copy of a January 1976 cover story on Marley in *Crawdaddy* magazine, Bob's first such national exposure in the States, in which he volunteered authorship of several now-disputed songs. Lastly, they asked the judge for a clarification of where discovery of fraud lies between suspicion and proof, wondering if a probability of fraud is sufficient to constitute discovery.

The jury retired at 10:28 A.M. and returned at 11:27 A.M. to render verdicts on the two remaining actions in the lawsuit, finding in favor of the estate in both instances. On the question of whether Cayman had discovered the alleged fraud prior to October 24, 1982—when the statute of limitations expired—the jury answered yes. On the thus-moot question of whether Cayman, with the exercise of due diligence, could have discovered its claim of fraud prior to October 24, 1982, the jury voted five to one that, yes, Cayman could have.

Judge Wilk then moved to grant summary judgment in the case to the Marley estate. Cayman Music had lost every cause of action in the five-point lawsuit. The bitter three-year court battle was over (subject only to possible review at the appellate level), with each detail of the entire proceedings now logged forever in the public record.

"You think it's the end," sang Bob Marley in 1976 on *Rastaman Vibration*'s "Want More," "but it's just the beginning!" And in March 1988 Ziggy Marley and the Melody Makers released their third album, *Conscious Party,* on the new American subsidiary of Britain's Virgin Records. In a twinkling, an act that had been treated as a mere curiosity on a par with Musical Youth (five preteens from the U.K. who scored a Top Ten U.S. single in 1982 with "Pass the Dutchie," or cooking pot, a sanitized version of the Mighty Diamonds "Pass the Cutchie," or ganja pipe) was now being acclaimed as one of the most life-affirming new additions to either the reggae or rock landscapes.

Discontented with the poor sales of "*Hey World!*" Ziggy and his siblings had been eager to put their EMI contract to rest, and Rita Marley agreed. The parting was arranged, and the group shopped for a deal with a label that still had faith in the staying power of reggae. Virgin Records executive Jordan Harris, who tried to sign the Melody Makers during his tenure at A&M Records, induced them to come to the company, whose recent acquisitions (Steve Winwood, Keith Richards, Julia Fordham) were much admired in the record industry. Harris assured Ziggy that he would keep the Melody Makers as part of the package, and not try to spin him off as a solo attraction.

The producer slated to supervise the Melody Makers' Virgin LP had been Alex Sadkin, an Island Records veteran who had engineered or mixed such Bob Marley LPs as *Rastaman Vibration*, *Kaya* and *Survival*. But when the gifted Sadkin was killed in a grisly auto crash outside Kingston in July '87, Virgin proposed he be replaced with the Talking Heads' married duo of Chris Frantz and Tina Weymouth, who had worked with Sadkin on the Heads' *Speaking in Tongues* LP, and had woven reggae into their extracurricular recording as the Tom Tom Club. At first, innocence seeded with Rasta sexism spurred Ziggy to ask ire-raising questions like "Why-a Chris bring 'im *wife* inta de studio?" But eventually familiarity would breed contentment as Ziggy's zest for reggae's topical pow fused with Chris and Tina's pulsing vocabulary of grooves and tattoos.

Back on Jack's Hill, family discussions at the dinner table filled in any blanks in the Melody Makers' raw studio material as each of the group tossed aspects of their own adolescent ordeals into the hopper. Young Cedella, who had gone to a tony United Nations school, came home one afternoon with stories of how she didn't fit in with the rest of her classmates, her only companion being a girl named Molly. It was soulmate Molly's own identity crisis of being a black girl in love with a white guy named Lee that sparked her talks with Cedella and strengthened their sisterly bond. Lee came to school one day with a nasty black eye his racist father had given him for dating Molly, and when Cedella related the whole tale to Ziggy, he transformed it into a compelling biracial love parable, "Lee and Molly."

Serendipity intervened in other ways. Cutting portions of the album in New York during the second and third weeks of October, all parties were intent on a track called "Tumblin' Down," the foreboding in its lyrics a combination of Rasta-, Nostradamus- and Edgar Cayce's Great Pyramid–derived interpretations of civilization's impending collapse. As work on the song was winding up, the Dow Jones Industrial Average plunged 508 points, the worst stock market drop in history.

Halfway through the recording, Ziggy paused to do a duet with Sting in a new version of the Police's "One World" for an international TV special sponsored by a Third World booster organization, the Council of Europe. Musical ecumenicism was already the rule on *Conscious Party*. Throughout, the Melody Makers were backed by the Ethiopian band Dallol. Keith Richards, immersed in the township street music of South Africa as he cut his *Talk Is Cheap* album, heard about Ziggy's sessions and stopped in to lend some Soweto-tinged Chuck Berry riffs to "Lee and Molly." South African–born jazz great Hugh Masakela arranged the vocals on "Dreams of Home," the South African cast of the Broadway hit *Sarafina!* (based on the 1976 uprising of 200,000 children in Soweto) guested on that track, and Jerry Harrison of Talking Heads lent keyboards to *Conscious Party*'s send-off single, "Tomorrow People."

The Melody Makers embarked on a brief U.S. tour in April. An extensive road trip throughout Europe and Israel filled May and June (which included a meeting with Bruce Springsteen at the annual Paris "SOS Racism" concert). By July, *Conscious Party*, which had been listed in *Billboard*'s Top Thirty for the past eight weeks, was certified gold (500,000 copies sold) in the States by the Recording Industry Association of America, with Bob Marley and the Wailers receiving a platinum designation for *Legend*, a 1984 Island Records memorial compilation whose cover art was a photo portrait of Bob wearing Selassie's ring. Meanwhile, the Wailers band landed their own recording contract, signing with Atlantic Records for an album scheduled for release in spring, 1989 entitled *I.D.*

For August and September, the Melody Makers performed a schedule of arena dates co-billed with popular Australian rockers INXS in Canada and the States. Crowds were charmed to see how Bob's children had matured. The svelte and sophisticated Sharon was now twenty-three and married; Cedella, twenty, had a coed's smile and comely grace, and once-chubby Stephen was a slim and assured fifteen.

The most riveting transformation, though, was that of nineteen-year-old Ziggy. Once gangly and garrulous, his slight form and tapered oval face rendering him the spitting image of Nesta in his rudie phase, David "Ziggy" Marley now exuded the serene self-possession of an adult. The Marley features had deepened and broadened, his full lips and rounded nose shaping a profile that held Rita's vulnerability and will as well as Bob's fierce daring. Bob's intensity resided in Ziggy's sharp chin, high cheekbones, keen eyes. It was the face of a peace-maker: kind, focused, adamant.

Born October 17, 1968, in Trench Town, Ziggy entered Jamaica's strife-torn cosmology just forty-eight hours after pro–African studies demonstrations at the University of the West Indies had flared into one of Jamaica's worst campus disorders, leaving one person dead and $1 million worth of damage. At that time, Jamaica's worldly young students longed to play a vital part in post–civil rights race consciousness, and their activism was further focused weeks later when Mrs. Coretta King visited to accept the Marcus Garvey Prize for Human Rights on behalf of her late husband.

Ziggy came of age at a juncture in Jamaica's history when boosters of its heavily African heritage were bypassing postcolonial proprieties and reaching out to all who shared an interest in the urban culture of the Third World. At Melrose All-Age School, he got his first lessons in his country's historical sorrows, while at home he was exposed to his dad's Stevie Wonder albums. And if Boy George, Paul McCartney, Duran Duran and the Police somehow got stirred into the music mix, so much the better.

The boy's upbringing was markedly strict, most discipline applied in the post-toddler stage by a grandaunty who minded him while his mother and father were touring. Bob's idea of parental authoritarianism was usually shaded with a bit of ghetto levity; his scoldings included such cracks as "Hey, we gon' beat 'im ta see if 'e can sing!"

" 'Cause when you cry," as Ziggy later explained, "you exercise yar vocal chords, right?"

The first music Bob taught his son was the ancient digging song "Hold Him Joe," also called "Me Donkey Want Water." The phrase "Hold him Joe" was the ritual request for a tune as field hands' "pickers" (pickaxes or mattocks) fell with slashing strokes, the workers exclaiming, "Give us de song, Joe. Hold on ta de riddim, Joe. Give it to us, Joe!" And the stanzas built like so:

Hold 'im Joe, hold 'im Joe
Naah let him go
Don-key wan' wa-ter
Don-key wan' wa-ter

Me don-key like a peeny
Rub 'im down Joe
Rub 'im down Joe
Me jackass gone a pound
Bring 'im down Joe
Bring 'im down Joe!

"Peeny" is short for peeny-wally, a children's name for the Jamaican candle-fly, or firefly. This was a song Bob learned some thirty years before, when he rode his own pet donkey Nimble to Grandpa Omeriah's cultivation in Smith, toiling in the furrows with Grandma Yaya and Ciddy.

And if that was Ziggy's introduction into the African side of Jamaica, his initiation into the Jamaican side of Africa came when he stood backstage in April 1980 as his father's band performed at Zimbabwe's Independence Day concert. As tear gas used to quell disturbances began to burn Ziggy's eyes, his father covered the boy's face with a wet rag. Long after the sting from the pungent haze had subsided, Ziggy would remember the moment when his dad and he stood together while the Union Jack rippled down the flagpole and the Zimbabwe standard was raised in triumph.

The year 1988 saw Ziggy Marley and the Melody Makers establish new benchmarks for reggae, with "Tumblin' Down," the second single from *Conscious Party*, climbing to the No. 1 spot on both *Billboard*'s black singles and twelve-inch singles sales charts. The song was the first reggae hit ever to top the black chart, representing a breakthrough Bob had never achieved. (Months later, the album would win the award for Best Reggae Recording at the 31st Grammy Awards, while outtakes and comparable tracks from various Marley scions would surface on sound-track albums for such films as *Married to the Mob*, *The Mighty Quinn*, and *Slaves of New York*.) Also released in 1988 was an EMI-Manhattan LP, *"Time Has Come"—The Best of Ziggy Marley and the Melody Makers*, a collection of songs culled from the Melody Makers' two previous EMI albums, plus selections off the unreleased *Children Playing in the Streets* project. A notable track that heretofore hadn't been issued in the States was "Lyin' in Bed," a song written by Ziggy in his early teens in which he recounted a mystical experience he'd had in Jamaica one morning. Waking up in his bedroom, he'd found himself unable to rise from the mattress, as if held there, and then above his head Ziggy saw an apparition of his father, informing his son he'd spend his own life playing music. (Ziggy later conceded the "vision" was a photo on the wall.)

Ziggy's confidence in the rightness of his agenda had thereafter been plain to see. Just prior to *Conscious Party*'s release, he told Kingston reporters inquiring about the Marley estate's muddle that he for one was not overly concerned with the outcome of the financial warring. "Let dem 'ave it," he murmured, "me cyan go out an' mek me own money."

In the last few months of the year more grievous storms had buffeted Ziggy's world, with Hurricane Gilbert, the most powerful Caribbean tempest of the century, battering the island on September 12. (It was no coincidence, the Rastas warned, that the sinister whirlwind arrived on the anniversary of Peter Tosh's death.) Incubated as a low-pressure pocket off the coast of Africa, it grew into a 140-mile-per-hour maelstrom that ravaged Jamaica, especially Kingston and the southern coast. Seaga estimated that 500,000 people—nearly a fourth of the country's population—were left homeless, and property damage was put at $1 billion.

Two weeks before, the JLP and PNP had unofficially begun campaigning for an election in which Michael Manley, leading Seaga by twenty points in the opinion polls, hoped to regain the post he lost to him eight years past. But the PNP's fiftieth anniversary convention, set for September 16, was put off indefinitely as relief work got under way. Five days after the hurricane, the nation's first direct wallop by a killer wind in thirty-seven years, most of the island was still without electricity, telephones or running water. The raw materials needed for cleanup and reconstruction, such as lumber and nails, had already been in short supply. Few people had returned to their jobs, and food was bartered at "Gilbert prices" of double the already inflated costs. In the bush, entire villages had been wiped out. The official death toll reached forty-five, and scores of bodies piled up at the morgues.

But the sorriest news of all was the setback in Jamaica's already faltering economy. It became obvious that the gales that roared across the groves and pens of St. Thomas, Portland, St. Mary and St. Ann had nearly eradicated the country's foremost nontourist industries: bananas, coconuts, sugarcane, poultry—the last beset by $337.5 million in losses—with citrus, coffee and exotic fruits only a little better off.

Agricultural wounds were so deep, the *Gleaner* flatly reported, that with two months to go to harvest season, "Jamaica's ganja trade islandwide has been crippled. In many cases entire fields in western parishes of St. James, Hanover and Westmoreland have been lost. Farmers were sowing ganja seedlings in an effort to plant as much as they can, as quickly as they can, to get a crop by next spring." (Inconveniently, the hurricane aid package of approximately $25 million that Seaga squeezed out of Reagan included a proportional stipend for mandatory antidrug efforts.)

The only industry that leapt back into production was the ghetto record business. Although Harry J's studio suffered losses of $750,000 and Dynamic Sounds damages totaled $850,000, King Tubby's equipment was fine (although the famed producer would be mysteriously murdered within another five months), and neither Tuff Gong Records' studio nor its stamper plant were affected. At least ten songs about the hurricane were in the shops, with Lovindeer's "Wild Gilbert" and Gregory Issac's "What a Disaster" doing well. Moreover, JA promoters had noted an abrupt disinterest in dance-hall discs, with many predicting a return to the "consciousness and spiritual reggae of Bob Marley."

There had also been reports in Jamaica that once the country recovered from the hurricane, the broadcasting and musical publishing industries would be undergoing a restructuring. The government-owned JBC radio and television networks would continue to function as they were, although with likely management changes, while the creation of a new, privately owned commercial television channel was proposed. Regarding radio in the private sector, licenses were awarded to four new channels: the New Radio Company (AM/FM), and Radio Central, Radio East and Radio West (all FM). But legal snags stymied them.

There was also word of the government's willingness to finally enact an effective new copyright act to remove the intricate web of double-dealing, conflict of interest and outright larceny in which the Jamaican recording scene had been snared ever since World War II.

Politically, Seaga proved the loser during the months of reconstruction after the storm, with charges of JLP favoritism in relief efforts and attacks from all quarters over humiliating bureaucratic bottlenecks. JLP national security minister Errol Anderson had a warehouse crammed with supplies that he was personally dealing out to cronies, and JLP candidate Joan Gordon-Webley was caught meting out American-donated flour in sacks emblazoned with her likeness.

But when Manley matched his two terms of centralized socialism against Seaga's eight years of penurious budgets and free enterprise, the results were the same: economic stagnancy propagated by a cult of personality. So very distant was either leader from the goals they'd hawked that Manley dared seek retroluster through the publication of his 575-page *A History of West Indies Cricket*. On the surface, the text touted the cutthroat competitiveness of modern Caribbean cricketers, which forced authorities to pay higher salaries and enforce a less genteel professionalism.

Taken as a whole, however, the much-hyped book was a tacit endorsement of cricket as a colonial policy of the British raj in *these* Indies. Manley pined for the wicket meritocracy that produced J. K. Holt, Sr. and Jr., and the Babe Ruth of JA batsmen, George Alphonso Headley. It is royalty of this colonial ilk who kept young bowlers sweating in the pitches of ivy-covered Jamaica College on Old Hope Road—instead of strumming rabble-rousing gully sonnets like that dangerous dread who once owned Island House.

Someday talented new politicians from downtown or uptown would be allowed to emerge from the Jamaican Senate to lead the people, but for now the nation was cowed by two sets of discredited policies—and the gunmen who enforced them. It was a tired and lonely tug-of-war, and the candidates were isolated in their personal lives as well, with Seaga separated from his wife, Mitsy, and Manley estranged from his fourth spouse, Beverley.

Seaga, fifty-eight, would eventually call for national elections to be held on February 9, 1989. Manley, sixty-five, crowed that they were "long overdue." The biggest problem, however, was that the electorate knew both sides were out of ideas, so the incidents of campaign street violence reflected not tribalism so much as despair. Much of this violence has traditionally stemmed from the fact that victors in the island's two-party system have always openly shunned the defeated, ruthlessly monopolizing all jobs, housing and subsidy programs. JLP supporters expected to be cut off without a crumb under a new regime, while PNP members knew how piddling government benefits for them would likely be.

Seaga and Manley had signed a peace agreement prior to the start of active campaigning on January 15, both sides vowing to refrain from armed attacks and intimidation, but it wasn't long before gunfire began to punctuate the proceedings. In the aftermath of the brutal 1980 campaign, the official death toll had eventually reached 750. This time, even with 10,000 soldiers and police deployed around the island in helicopters, jeeps and armored transports to prevent disorders, violent skirmishes proved widespread. Troops had to fire shots and tear gas in order to accomplish early closing of many melee-engulfed polling stations.

George Ramocan, a spokesman for Seaga, charged incidents of ballot-stuffing in eight of the sixty parliamentary districts. Manley's representatives made their own charges of voter fraud and hooliganism. Seaga himself seemed to crack under the tension on February 9 while trying to quell a midmorning argument between two officials at a local polling depot. The frustrated prime minister suddenly exploded in fury, shoving a nearby cameraman from Cable News Network and allowing an aide to seize the cameraman's videotape. (Seaga later stated he "very much regretted" the outburst, maintaining there had been "nothing in malice.")

When the dust settled on Friday, February 10, Manley's People's National Party had won a clear majority in the Jamaican Parliament, and he was taking credit for keeping street turbulence to a minimum. Two days after the election, the official death toll for the three-week campaign was given as 12. Considering that the 1980 elections had been preceded by nine months of vote-wangling, the average seven-day political murder rate had still been high—and harrowing. One of the last fatalities attributed to election strife was Mrs. Glenna Williams, a twenty-five-year-old pregnant housewife.

In his first news conferences and interviews after regaining power, the lank, silver-maned Manley pledged greater compassion for Jamaica's poor and said he would try to strengthen good relations with the United States, while quietly noting he would resume diplomatic ties with Cuba. But Jamaica's foreign debt of $4 billion, plus the pressure-cooker restrictions imposed on its economy by the International Monetary Fund, ensured that it had little room for reform programs or political improvisation of any sort. So the social time bomb continued to tick. Meanwhile, the very island itself was coming unhinged.

At 10:35 P.M. on November 11, 1988, Jamaica was rocked by an earthquake that sent citizens tumblin' down from their beds and nightclub stools. It was the third and worst quake in the preceding six months, and it emboldened the Rastas of the Ethiopian Africa Black International Congress Church of Salvation in Bull Bay to assure JLP deputy prime minister Right Honorable Hugh Shearer that in the last days he would be treated harshly. These Rastas had been suing the government since the summer, symbolically seeking $20 million in repatriation funds. Shearer called their kind "frivolous and vexatious."

But the Rastas of all Jamaica believed such words were more accurately applied to the kind of "poli-trick-al" existence the Seagas and Manleys had created. A world in which the Armenians, as close to Job's people as the dreads themselves, had suffered an earthquake-triggered tragedy whose massive death toll was actually tied to inadequate government construction codes. A world in which the ozone was being depleted by aerosol cans and fossil fuels, causing global warming. A world in which the Aral Sea, the fourth largest inland body of water, is being reduced to desert by corrupt irrigation practices.

And as the Brazilian and American national forests burned, and acid rain fell, and skin cancer became rife, and arsenals of poison gas multiplied, and rivers and oceans turned crimson from chemicals and renegade algae, and the death of birth halted nature, and Ronald Wilson Reagan retired to his Bel Air villa on 666 St. Cloud Street, Rastas pointed once more to Revelation 8:6–9: "Then the seven angels that held the seven trumpets prepared to blow them. The first blew his trumpet; and there came hail and fire mingled with blood, and this was hurled upon the earth. A third of the earth was burnt, a third of the trees were burnt, all the green grass was burnt. The second angel blew his trumpet; and what looked like a great blazing mountain was hurled into the sea. A third of the sea was turned to blood, a third of the living creatures in it died, and a third of the ships on it foundered. . . ." And Earth was in the path of an asteroid due in 2015. Yet men mocked these omens, and morality became a masquerade. The JA courts released those charged with Carlton Barrett's murder (pending re-trial)* when no witnesses would testify, and Leppo bided his time in Spanish Town Prison.

Just as 1988 had ended, Danny Sims issued on the Urban-Tek/Slam Records label what he referred to as "the first new Bob Marley album in almost six years." It was a collection of "rough" tracks from the rock-steady era with "up-to-the-second" nonreggae arrangements grafted onto them. The song titles were familiar to anyone purchasing Cayman Music's Marley reissues for the last two decades: "Lonesome Feeling," "Duppy Conqueror," "Rock My Boat," "Caution," "Soul Shakedown Party." In the press notice that accompanied the album,

*Barrett's wife and two accomplices were finally convicted in 1991.

it was explained that "Sims has spent the last several years making sure that he had the complete legal rights to the Marley product. 'This is a completely legitimate release and we have the contract rights to prove it,' says Sims." An odd concerts-oriented agreement the cancer-stricken Marley had signed with Sims and Cole in the last months of his life was cited as additional justification. The notice added that "also involved in the Slam Records Bob Marley project is Don Taylor, who was Marley's manager and personal advisor from 1974 to 1980, which was the height of Marley's international and U.S. reputation." This was the same Don Taylor whom jurors in the Marley estate trial had heard Sims describe, in a taped interview labeled Defendant Exhibit T, as "a total fucking amateur for this business. And a discredit to this business."

Meantime, Andrew Tosh, born June 19, 1967, took to the road to perform his father's music and his own, releasing an album on Trojan Records Attack subsidiary called *The Original Man*. It featured tracks with titles like "My Enemies," "Poverty Is a Crime," and "I'm the Youngest." His promising shows across the States were often benefits to raise money for the Freedom College in Tanzania, which housed and educated South African refugees. One night before he ascended the stage, Andrew was blunt: "I always t'ink I might be a target. I keep a watch on my 'ead, you know."

On another battle front, control of the Marley estate was sought by both Chris Blackwell's Island Logic, Inc., and Bob's family,* while estate administrators sued Rita Marley and Cedella Booker for alleged illegal withdrawals of $16 million and $500,000, respectively.

Calm, collected Bunny Wailer negotiated his own passage through the 1988–89 firestorms by quietly unveiling *Liberation*, the finest album he had ever composed. On its red, green and gold cover was superimposed the Universal Declaration of Human Rights. It made stirring reading for listeners as Wailer sang, with a non-dancehall gentleness he'd never before shared, of the "Serious Thing" that our rape of the earth has become, and the inhuman pest that "Botha the Mosquito" represented. The degradations of crack and other drugs were spelled out on "Dash Wey the Vial." The cruelty of disenfranchisement was considered on "Liberation." And all those he'd known in this life who had hurt or transgressed against him were forgiven on "Rise and Shine" and "Want to Come Home."

With no fanfare or bluster, Bunny had decided to open his heart

*An $11.5 million joint purchase took place in December 1991.

to the possibilities of his higher self, uplifting his brethren with the sound of the better person he humbly aimed to become—while there was time left to try.

There was hardly a soul among devout Rastas who was not profoundly moved by these gestures, and yet they too continued to look for portents—ones that favored the pariah. Sitting in limbo, overwhelmed by ruination from the hurricane, frightened by the prospect of another improvident Manley regime, the sufferahs searched for solace.

On Sunday evening, October 23, 1988, a cable TV concert program first proposed by Chris Blackwell had been beamed from the Dominion Theater in London, England, to subscribers and satellite dish owners throughout the Americas and the Caribbean. It was carried and supported by MTV, Britain's Channel 4, Initial Television, MGMM and ITV. And in the following days, weeks and months, little pieces of that concert recurred in the bleak lives of the sufferah. They turned up in photocopied newspaper clippings pinned to the wattle walls of remote huts. They rattled out of beat boxes in slum record shops. They flashed and shimmered in the shop windows on Halfway Tree Road. They eddied out of dashboard speakers in taxicabs, and sprang from CD players in the parlors of fine villas in St. Andrew. And each time it happened, whether to a street vendor or a chambermaid, it helped the people of the ghetto feel a little bit better, because they knew they had not been forgotten.

With each fleeting fragment of that certain concert—the Smile Jamaica Benefit for Jamaican Hurricane Relief—the sufferahs were reminded that for a few moments in this fading century, big stars and Caribbean favorites like U2, Keith Richards, Eddy Grant, Boy George, Robert Palmer and the Tom Tom Club took notice of their increasingly pitiable lot. But what they treasured most of all from that program was the sight of the spindly dread of nineteen years, who stood beside Bono to sing the song the Irish rock star co-wrote with Bob Dylan, the show's emotional climax.

And as Bono gave Ziggy Marley a verse, no one anywhere could miss the ancestral echoes in the young dread's vibrant voice, or the phantom behind those features, and yet none could doubt he was an original spirit, a new beginning of the kind within all men's grasp. And the sufferahs rejoiced when they saw the spark of the peacemaker in the teenager's eyes as he threw his lengthening locks back and sang:

We've conquered the past
Da future's 'ere at last
We stand at de entrance to a new
world we cyan see
De ruins to my right
Will soon lose sight of me
I said, "Love rescue me!"

In rum bars, sportboys still boasted of knowing the Gong. Session men from the Coxsone days swore there would never be an equal. Lowly Rasta disciples of the Twelve Tribes, frustrated in their earthly schemes, shouted that only the locksman who wore the emblemed band of the Royal House of His Imperial Majesty Haile Selassie I on his finger was the Mighty Messenger for all children of the ghetto.

But the wisest of Rasta brethren knew that Jah alone can measure the true worth of a man's deeds, and that signs and their power are not a matter of either jewelry or material possessions but rather of the faith in Him that they unlock.

These most prudent Rastas turned to that portion of the Scriptures that reaffirms the continuity of all things under Heaven. In Ecclesiasticus 17:17–22 they found the passage which assured that love shall indeed rescue the righteous, and that prophecy will finally be fulfilled:

For every nation He appointed a ruler,
But chose Israel to be His own possession.
So whatever they do is clear to Him as daylight;
He keeps constant watch over their lives.
Their wrongdoing is not hidden from the Lord;
He observes all their sins.
A man's good deeds He treasures like a signet-ring,
And his kindness like the apple of His eye.

As the 1990s dawned and the citizens of Jamaica assessed the rulers of their nation, it was plain that democratic leadership had taken a backseat to sinister back-room wrongdoing, empowered by the same illicit flood of guns that had once driven Bob Marley from his homeland.

Back in 1976, upon his arrival in Nassau after the attempt on his life, Bob had begun writing a never-recorded two-stanza song about the "Devil's disciples" who gave "the order to shoot us," announcing to "all the wicked people" who wanted to destroy Rasta: "Goodbye."

"They will make war against the Lamb," he predicted, "but the Lamb will overcome."

Although Michael Manley was back in power, his health was poor, his battle with prostate cancer intensifying and cutting into his official duties and his sense of political passion. In a stunning reversal, he disavowed any persistent sympathies for communism, abandoned "all thoughts of nationalization" of island industries and promised "to release the spirit of entrepreneurship"; that is, Caribbean capitalism, in deference to the United States' wishes.

"The world has changed, Jamaica has changed, and I think I have changed," Manley said of his politics. "My goals are the same, but there is no easy path for the Third World today."

And there was no easy road to prosperity, either. The Jamaican Defense Force (JDF), with the backing of the U.S. Drug Enforcement Agency, raided Ginger Ridge in the parish of St. Catherine in late 1989 to destroy the local ganja harvest. Peasant growers protested to the Parliament that it was their principal cash crop, the only thing keeping whole families from destitution, because government maintenance of the roads was so pitiful that farmers couldn't even truck their fruits and vegetables to market—which is why the JDF soldiers had bypassed the impassable land routes and staged their raid as paratroopers.

"To learn from and admit mistakes is a signpost of wisdom," Manley noted, tacitly acknowledging that the course he'd charted had reached a dead end. His own former policies completely disregarded, he was actually trying to sound like Seaga! But nobody really cared anymore—not the populace, not the politicians and certainly not the United States, which flew a drowsy Vice President Dan Quayle into Kingston in 1990 for a fifteen-minute news conference in which he told Manley, "In recent years, we have worked together in the war against illegal drugs, and on behalf of President Bush, I want to congratulate you on your leadership in fighting this courageous battle."

Quayle plainly hadn't been reading the last two years of investigative reports and columns in the *Daily Gleaner* saying that Jamaican drug posses currently rampaging across America had been traced directly back to their PNP and JLP tribalist origins in Kingston.

U.S. law enforcement experts concluded that the homicidal gangs that Manley and Seaga had created, trained and fostered were now beyond their control. As Carl Stone, Jamaica's top nonpartisan columnist, wrote in the *Gleaner* in July 1990:

> The situation of the street gangs has changed fundamentally since the 1970s. Politics is a minor source of income for the gangs and they are no longer dependent on the politician. They have been replaced by a new

> generation of younger, tougher and more ruthless leaders who have less loyalty to politicians. Drugs have emerged as the main income source for the street gangs in the 1980s and 1990s, replacing politically connected income sources. Additionally, the newly emergent drug don is challenging the politician for control of political territory in some areas of the city where ten years ago, the politicians' word was law.

Kingston posses were now menacing the entire political hierarchy of the country, the death toll often reaching 100 in a given month as unaffiliated drug gangs stormed police stations to free drug dons who had renounced their old party ties. Manley and Seaga had unleashed the political shootists, and now their amoral monsters were literally coming to get *them.*

The JLP ranks had lately been torn apart by scandals that included a vicious anti-Seaga "Gang of Five" party revolt led by former Minister of Public Utilities and Transport Pearnel Charles—the faction refusing to support Seaga as opposition leader—and an intramural JLP blackmail and espionage ring linked to the JLP gun-smuggling enterprise that had precipitated the 1976 state of emergency, the attempt on Bob Marley's life, the bloody aftermath of the star-crossed 1978 Peace Concert and the street carnage that characterized the 1980 elections.

The PNP was simultaneously gripped by a wave of cabinet-level corruption in which seven top officials (including the cancer-beset Manley) had been ordered to pay back millions in taxpayers' money that they had allegedly spent on their private homes. Six *other* members of Manley's government stood accused of gross incompetence, negligence and bad faith in the execution of their duties: all of which had the *Gleaner*'s headlines screaming, GOVERNMENT SHOULD RESIGN—STENCH RISES AS MORAL AUTHORITY LOST.

"Political leadership in Jamaica, dominated for the past 20 years by two men, is facing the prospect of change," stated the *Financial Times* in July 1990. "For the island of 2.3 million people, where politics has traditionally been vibrant to the point of violence, any change in leadership would mark the end of an era—begun in the late 1930s by people who brought up the present political mainstays—in which all matters political have been built around the personalities of party leaders."

Manley's political successor was plainly Percival James Patterson, the current deputy prime minister, who had filled in when Manley was rushed off-island for drastic prostate treatment or emergency care from a life-threatening bout of pneumonia.

Musically, the inheritors of the Marley-Wailers legacy were also in a transitional phase. The Melody Makers were pursuing an admirably activist Pan-African path, giving benefit shows in 1989 in support of the twenty-three-year guerilla war for independence in Namibia, the diamonds- and uranium-rich African country bordered by Angola, Zambia, Zimbabwe, Botswana and South Africa. The Melody Makers then appeared at a March 1990 gala concert in Namibia's capital city of Windhoek to observe the new nation's liberation from seventy-five years of South African rule.

These activities took place amidst the release of the *One Bright Day* set of 1989, which saw modest R&B chart success with its "Look Who's Dancing" single but also boasted the eloquent "Black My Story (Not History)" chant. *One Bright Day* also showed the sobering impact of parenthood on Ziggy, the twenty-year-old thrilled with the birth on July 12, 1990, of Daniel, Bob Marley's grandson. Produced at Compass Point Studios, with the help of the *Conscious Party* team of Chris Frantz and Tina Weymouth, *One Bright Day* displayed a skilled integration of the Melody Makers' own growing pop/rock–minded body of work and the sociospiritual assets of its family ties, plus a unique aura of brother-and-sister solidarity, with Ziggy leading the way. Other highlights included the up-tempo ballad "One Bright Day" and "Justice," inspired by murdered South African activist Stephen Biko, a song Ziggy thought his dad would appreciate: "My father was carrying on Our Father's work, and we are all part of something greater than any of us individuals."

Ziggy and the Melody Makers released their *Jahmekya* album on Virgin in 1991, which included a rendition of Bob Marley's obscure sound-system favorite, "Rainbow Country," and "Good Time," which became a Top 30 hit on *Billboard*'s Hot R&B Singles chart.

By December 1991, when the Jamaican Supreme Court finally awarded the rights to Bob Marley's music to the singer's widow and children, Ziggy had added a daughter on to his own brood with companion Lorraine Bogel. Born on December 9, she was named Justice in honor of the court verdict.

Ziggy had been writing his own songs since age ten, his first original effort being "Brown Eyed Baby," a love tune with the refrain: "Brown-eyed baby / I love you in my heart / I never want to part," and he learned to keep reggae time on a Mickey Mouse drum kit. Later his increasingly conscious lyrics reflected academic instruction at the exclusive Vaz Preparatory School on Dunoon Road near the Bournemouth Gardens section of Kingston. When his parents' mounting success led to extended overseas tours, Ziggy and his sisters were sent to outlying Bull Bay to live with their Auntie Viola, Ziggy attending Bull Bay All-Age Primary.

As for the other Melody Makers, eldest child Sharon Marley Prendergast (now a mother herself) had been eight months old when Rita first met Bob. One of the chief reasons Bob insisted on marrying Rita before he went to Delaware to visit his mother was so the infant Sharon, "his favorite," in Rita's words, would officially be part of the family.

Studying for a career in business administration even as she continued touring and recording with the Melody Makers, Sharon also tried her hand at acting, appearing alongside half-sister Cedella in the 1989 Denzel Washington/Robert Townshend film *The Mighty Quinn*.

The confident and outspoken Cedella, now twenty-four, had been Bob and Rita's firstborn, entering the world in Kingston in August 1967. Bob had nicknamed her "Nice Time," a cross-reference to the 1967 Wailers single celebrating her birth at Kingston Public Hospital, yet she was anything but easygoing. Taking voice lessons from a Miss Enever in Jamaica during preparations for the Melody Makers' "*Hey World!*" album in 1986, she quit because the vocal coach was "trying to make us sing opera." Cedella also would regularly remark how odd it seemed that her Rasta parents had her educated in Catholic schools, but she ultimately conceded that Father Williams, an instructor at Alpha Academy on South Camp Road, had been one of her most important mentors.

A decade after his "Nice Time" tribute to his daughter, Bob Marley did a 1977 session, coproduced by Lee Perry at Island Studios in London, for a new rendition of "Keep On Moving" (subtitled "London Version") in which he sang, "Tell Ziggy I'm fine, and to keep Cedella in line!" Cedella repaid the gesture in the 1990s, christening her first child Soul Rebel in honor of her late father.

The most promising member of the group, however, was Stephen Marley, who handled the vocals on *One Bright Day*'s high-powered "Who Will Be There" and took an increasingly pronounced role overall in *Jahmekya*. Stephen was born on April 20, 1972, in Wilmington, Delaware, while Rita was living with Bob's mother. At the time, Rita had been toiling full-time as a nurse's aide in a local hospital and moonlighting as a housemaid. Her second son became a father himself in 1991 with the birth of Joseph Robert Nesta Marley.

Family pride and unity of purpose took on new meaning once the way was cleared for the Marley estate to be sold to the Marley family and

Chris Blackwell's Island Logic company for a reported $11.5 million (up from an initial offer of $8.2 million). The estate's marketable luster was further enhanced by international acclaim for *Talkin' Blues*, a mini-anthology from Island Records/Tuff Gong of invigorating mid-1970s rarities and live broadcasts—including a KSAN radio concert in San Francisco during the Wailers' pathfinding 1973 tour—intercut with 1975 interview extracts from Bob and obscure treats such as the previously unreleased R&B romp "Am-A-Do."

But the behind-the-scenes moves that ensured the Marley family's control of Bob's back pages were highly unusual and never fully grasped by the media. At the time of the sale, the Mutual Security Merchant Bank and Trust Company of Jamaica (which had served as the administrator of the estate after Rita resigned) could only keep cash in trust for beneficiaries and was not permitted to run a business. Thus the bank was anxious to avoid mountains of clerical paperwork by selling off the musical assets of the holdings Marley left when he died intestate—including the steady stream of royalties disbursements. MCA had bid $12.8 million for the estate, but the administrators had lately elected to sell to the more experienced, Blackwell-led Island Logic organization.

Learning this, the Marleys appealed to the Privy Council for reconsideration of the agreement, because they had no enduring role to play in such a wholesale transaction. The Privy Council sided with the family and requested that the administrators advertise and assess the Marley catalog's assets more thoroughly before a final sale agreement.

During the Marley estate's own ongoing litigation against defendants Marvin Zolt of the accounting firm of Zolt & Loomis, P.C., and attorney David Steinberg et al. for prior mishandling of the estate—a court case that ultimately resulted in a judgment of fraud against Zolt and Steinberg—Rita Marley had revealed under oath on September 22, 1992, in U.S. District Court in New York precisely how the unusual 1991 Island Logic deal with the Marley family beneficiaries had been accomplished:

"At that point I met with [bank/Marley Estate administrator Louis] Byles and I met with Mr. Blackwell," she detailed, "and I said, well, why not let's go into a joint agreement where the beneficiaries would still have some shares of these assets. We would not want it to be sold, but if so . . . let us, the beneficiaries, be the purchaser.

"Blackwell," Rita continued, "insisted that he had already made an agreement with the administrators to purchase. . . . They had his money and there was a written agreement. . . . And we said no, you don't own the assets, Mr. Byles had no right to sell the assets, the Privy Council ruled that out, it was not approved by us. . . . So at that point Mr. Blackwell agreed that he would go back and make another agreement with us, the beneficiaries, wherein it would be between himself and us."

However, Rita explained, "at that point, we did not have the cash" to make the purchase. Incredibly, Blackwell agreed to lend the money to the family so they could buy Bob's catalog. Moreover, the family agreed to a concession to make up the difference between the best offer from MCA and Island Logic's top bid, by which they had to relinquish as individual beneficiaries any income from the sale—including the right to receive royalties—until Blackwell recouped his loan to the Marleys.

Under the arrangement, the then-current adult beneficiaries among Bob's children—namely Cedella, David (aka Ziggy), Stephen, Rohan, Robert and Stephanie—were each given an equal share in the newly formed Bob Marley Foundation, as was Rita, who surrendered all prior assets in order to assume the same equal-share parity with the children. The rest of the so-called infant beneficiaries among Bob's offspring were likewise allowed to apply to the Foundation when they reached the age of eighteen—"meaning," as Rita put it, "that they would put the proceeds from their shares of entitlement to the Foundation."

Therefore, once all debts were paid and loans recouped, with interest, by Blackwell, the proceeds from sales of Marley's catalog would flow unimpeded to the Marley Foundation, Marley's wife and children sharing in a joint asset that showed the potential for incalculable growth in value. Meanwhile, Blackwell made a distribution deal with PolyGram Records to handle projects like the 1992 *Songs of Freedom* box set as well as remix albums such as the *Dreams of Freedom: Ambient Translations of Bob Marley in Dub* collection that producer Bill Laswell oversaw in 1997. Merchandizing operations were brought under the Foundation, as was the Tuff Gong label, the Bob Marley Museum and the Addis Ab record manufacturing wing. All in all, it was a strikingly equitable arrangement and bespoke Blackwell's cooperative goodwill toward the principals. It also showed a unique attitude on the part of Rita Marley toward what the U.S. District Court of New York called "the maintenance of the children."

Grilled at various points during 1992 court proceedings as to whether she was jealous of the mothers of Bob's other kids or hostile to the children themselves, Rita Marley offered a moving account of Rasta bonds in the face of the otherwise frail state of modern Caribbean family structure.

"In Jamaica," she testified on September 17, "I would want to say it's a custom, but normally what happens where in a family there is children outside of the marriage—and some of the wives refuse this—but wives like myself who have a faith in a religion that's called Rastafari, we believe that all children are ours.

"We believe that as a woman, we are the mothers of all children. So within that faith, it was always understood that whatever children my husband will have or would have, they will be mine as long as they are called by his name, and that that was always how it was treated.

"When the kids were born, he would say to me, 'Well, Rita, this woman has a child for me. I'm going to bring the child for you to see, and you feel this child is mine?' And I would say yes, or I would say no. So that was our life, that was the life that we establish to love all children."

Such assertions seemed easier to make than to execute, so the court probed deeply into Rita's life as a Rasta mother to discern the mechanisms of this arrangement.

Rita disclosed that the second reason Bob insisted Rita and he be married on the day before he migrated to Delaware was so he could sponsor her to migrate there, but "it didn't work out," she explained, "because the law said that he was a minor at the time that his mother brought him in and he was not able to sponsor a wife at that time.

"He was very disturbed," she said of Bob, "and his mother wrote me to say she had no peace in the house. At that point he was working in Dupont Hotel in Delaware, as a bellboy. He wrote me one day to say he was vacuuming and the vacuum burst in his face. That was the end of it; he walked out of the job."

After Bob's string of equally frustrating gigs in Delaware in auto plants, restaurants, chemical labs and warehouses, he returned to Trench Town to start the Wail 'n Soul/Wail 'N' Soul 'M enterprise with Bunny, Peter and Rita, Bob's JA base until the early Tuff Gong label.

Bob and Rita would sleep in the tiny stall (lent by her Aunt Viola) that was home by night, record shop by day.

"I would go and take a box of record [*sic*], because we had no transportation," Rita recounted, "so I had to transport the records on my head . . . to various record shops downtown, and in the country parts for distribution to various jukebox. It was a pleasure for me, because we felt independent and this was the beginning of our business. So I would go out with the records while Bunny, Peter and Bob would stay and write songs and make recordings"—with Rita often singing backup. As Bob's far-flung offspring began to turn up, Rita found she had to be as flexible in motherhood as she had been in the family's record firm.

Rohan Marley was born in May 1972, the son of Janet Hunt. "His mother was a dancer in a club," Rita testified, "and she left him with her mother, and her mother wasn't able to take the proper care that was needed for Rohan. One morning when Rohan was around four years old, and we were living at Washington Drive, Bob brought him to say that he needs some health care, he had a lot of bad cavities in his mouth and he was asking me to take him to the doctor, have him checked up, which I did. And from there Rohan stayed with us on and off.

"Rohan was very energetic and he was, like, the bully of the boys," Rita continued. "So he would fight a lot in school, unlike Ziggy and Stephen, who went to the same school. So the teacher said she was unable to keep him. . . . I spoke to his mother and I told her that I would love to send Rohan to his grandmother. She was happy with that, and Rohan was sent to Miami to live with Mrs. Booker"—who adopted him.

In manhood, Rohan would remain a formidable presence with a short fuse, serving as an informal Rita-appointed "bodyguard," in her words, for the Melody Makers. He later excelled as a starting linebacker for the University of Miami's Hurricanes football team. His tough exterior belied a nagging streak of insecurity as well as a genuinely tender and caring side he did not always know how to express. But Rohan's hair-trigger temper would continue to pose a regrettable handicap, as illustrated by his arrest by Miami Beach police in the early 1990s on the charge of trying to run over a cop with his pickup truck. The officer had allegedly told Rohan he couldn't make a left-hand turn. The surprisingly high tension in such a mundane encounter may have stemmed in part from a previous Marley family incident involving the Miami police.

At 3:30 P.M. on February 18, 1990, Anthony Elmer Booker, Cedella Marley Booker's nineteen-year-old son by Edward Booker, had appeared at South Dade's Cutler Ridge Mall dressed entirely in white, his immaculate outfit topped with a bulletproof vest. Resting on his shoulder was a 12-gauge shotgun.

Anthony began asking dumbfounded shoppers, Did they "feel like dying" that day? "I'm twice the man my brother was," witnesses said he barked at passersby. "I'm twice as big and bad as Bob Marley."

However, Bob Marley was neither very big, nor belligerent nor known to have possessed or even held a firearm in his entire life.

"There had to be a personal problem there," Miami Metro police sergeant Frank Wesolowski told the *Daily Gleaner*.

Earlier in the month, after a trip to Jamaica during which he backed his mother on bass guitar during a Bob Marley Birthday Celebration held at 56 Hope Road, the normally sedate Booker had returned a changed man. Family members first noticed his shift in mood after a white cow—frequently perceived as a harbinger of obeah—had crossed the path of the car Anthony rode in along a narrow stretch between Nine Miles and Linstead. Anthony grew nervous, irritable and erratic, insisting to his mother he was "a big man" now. When he later stalked off the plane for home just before it was to take off, he was taken to a Kingston doctor and diagnosed with anxiety.

Back home on Vista Lane in Miami, Anthony became obsessive about cleanliness and emptied the house's music room and adjacent office of all their furnishings, locking himself in that section of the ranch-style dwelling with several bottles of water and refusing to come out. At one point he blew out one of the windows with a shotgun. Where the loaded weapon came from, no one could ever explain. Stalking out of the house on the afternoon of Sunday, February 18, he yelled for his nephew, Rohan, then sixteen, to get him the keys to the Bookers' yellow Jeep. Sizing up his armed and raging relative, Rohan complied and then watched as Anthony sped off in the vehicle.

Arriving at the Mall, Booker was menacing everyone in sight in a fitful, unfocused ten-minute sweep—until he spied Metro-Dade officer Gus Gort. Anthony immediately fired off an unprovoked round that missed the cop. Officer Gort instinctively shot back once and ducked for cover as the safety catch on his service revolver accidentally snapped back into a locked position.

Gort was crouched behind a vehicle, grappling with his jammed gun, just as off-duty detective George Cadavid happened onto the scene. Cadavid had been browsing in clothing stores with his wife and six-year-old son, seeking a gift for a friend's child, when he heard the weapons' volleys. He grabbed his family and lay flat on the pavement as people around him screamed. Hastily scanning the parking lot, he glimpsed Booker, poised with his shotgun, as he peered around a van seventy-five feet from the frantic Gort, and saw that Anthony was about to close in on the patrolman. The off-duty Cadavid could also see that Gort didn't know where Booker was lurking and that Booker was likewise oblivious to Cadavid himself.

Having never before used his own gun in the line of duty, Cadavid leaned across the hood of his Toyota 4-Runner to steady his aim. He fired, the bullet finding Booker's chest just above his armored vest.

Stunned, Anthony took two steps, kneeled, and fell headfirst onto the tarmac. He was dead.

An autopsy of Booker revealed no evidence of drugs in his bloodstream. And although Cedella Booker noted the incident had occurred amid the contention over the Marley estate, she could neither adequately account for Anthony's precipitous despair or the envious rage he expressed regarding his late half-brother Bob, nor clarify how Anthony was able to remain armed and sequestered for three days in a secured wing of her suburban home—ranting from behind a locked door, shattering a window with his shotgun fire and yelling oaths at her and other family members—without anyone on the premises summoning some sort of professional aid, psychiatric counsel or law enforcement intervention in an effort to save the young man before it was too late.

Also born in 1972 like Rohan, and likewise in need of the understanding that somehow eluded Anthony Booker, was Robert "Robbie" Marley, son of Trench Town–based mother Lucille Williams. "I had a good relationship with his mother, Pat, as we call her," said Rita. When Robert was plagued with liver spots, Rita took him to a physician, monitored the treatment (given her training as a nurse) and soon took over his care, with Grandmother Booker helping out, as Robbie moved between Florida and Jamaica. After he fell in with a bad crowd in New York, Robbie returned to Rita, was enrolled at the University College of the West Indies and soon contemplated a career in computer graphics.

Karen was born "around 1973 in England," Rita said. "Her mother was Janet Bowen. Bob told me about Karen while she was still in England and that her mother was bringing her to Jamaica to live with her great-grandmother," in the greater Kingston community of Harbour View, St. Andrew, where she was to attend school. Bob wanted to get to know her, added Rita, but "she didn't know who Daddy was and she was scared of Bob at the first time. And gradually she would come every weekend."

Because Bob was near death in Germany at Dr. Issels's clinic, he asked Rita to take care of Karen permanently, enrolling her in Wolmer's Girls' School along with daughter Stephanie, who was born in 1974. Both girls later got scholarships to Wolmer's Prep School.

On June 4, 1975, Julian was born in England to Barbados native Lucy Pounder. Although he would be raised in London, both Julian and Lucy often came to Jamaica or Miami to stay with Bob and Rita. Kymani (later spelled Ky-mani), son of Anita Belnavis, was born "around 1976, in Jamaica," according to Rita, and began spending summers and

Christmas vacations with Bob and Rita as part of a rapidly accelerating custom for *all* the kids. He moved to Jamaica in 1992.

Damian Marley, aka Jr. Gong, was the son of Cindy Breakspeare and entered the world on July 21, 1975, in Jamaica (his first name often publicly spelled with an *e*). One of Bob's last requests in Germany, Rita explained, was to have Damian's name changed, based on a discussion they'd once had about the 1978 movie *Damien: Omen II*, about the coming of the Antichrist and "Damien being a devil. . . . It was inappropriate for him as a Rastafarian to have a child with that name.

"It was a pressure for me to do," Rita stated. "I felt sorry he asked at that point, because he was very sick. In the Ethiopian Orthodox faith, when he is baptized, we are given [an] Ethiopian name, like you are given a new name. . . . I took Damian to church that Sunday and I told the priest that Bob had asked for him to be baptized, and that was done and he got a new name." Damian also became a frequent visitor—"almost permanent," as Rita put it—to her home in Jamaica.

Last, Makeda Jahnesta, daughter of Yvette Crichton, was born in 1981. Cedella Booker signed the papers admitting Bob's paternity of the infant because Rita hesitated, but by 1992 Makeda Jahnesta was spending summers at Rita's house and had become a beneficiary like the rest of the flock.

The consequences of embracing these children would be significant, however, bringing Rita comfort in the midst of travail as well as sorrow and hostility from unexpected quarters.

Long after Bob's death, Rita's relationship with Bob's mother would be a tense and oddly recriminatory one, at least on Cedella Booker's end. In 1996, Mrs. Booker decided inexplicably to publicly announce that Stephanie Marley, whom Bob had quietly raised as his daughter, was possibly the offspring of another man. Even if Mrs. Booker simply wanted to embarrass Rita for an incident the mother-in-law conceded had been admitted to while Bob was still alive, it seemed a gratuitous humiliation of young Stephanie by her titular grandmother. To add insult to injury, Booker further asserted that Bob had told her in Germany that he somehow believed Rita's infidelity had been the actual source of his cancer. Bob supposedly confided, "Mamma, is Rita give me cancer. Imagine, me left Rita and gone go work in England fe her, and when me gone Rita breed fe me friend."

Assuming that the deathly ill and dysphoric Marley ever said such an irrational thing, and even if infidelity could possibly cause cancer, it would only be fair to note that Rita's capacity to inflict either hurt or even disease in such a manner would have long since been surpassed by Bob's own abundant culpability on that score.

On a far more credible note, it was plain that Rita Marley (while often assisted, to be sure, by her mercurial mother-in-law) had vowed before Jah Rastafari to love and befriend all of her husband's children, and she would keep her promise.

While Bob had lain ill in Germany, with the cumulative, materialistic facets of his short life swirling in disarray around him, Bunny Wailer and Peter Tosh also confronted Rita. Through their attorneys they claimed they held shares in the original Tuff Gong label. As Rita later testified in U.S. District Court, Louis Byles informed Bunny and Peter's counsel that the original Tuff Gong entity's only liable asset was some property called Alterry bought in the Tuff Gong name, and the company was shown "to be owing Mr. Marley a large sum of money that he invested in the company." Undeterred, Peter and Bunny came, said Rita, "to the operating compound at 56 Hope Road and told me I should shut the business down."

For a time, according to Rita, a Mr. Kurt Holt was employed by the company as a manager: "He came in and made a new [umbrella] structure for the companies to operate under that was formed as the Rita Marley [Music] group of companies, and Tuff Gong Records was at that point stricken off by the administrators" from the registrar of companies.

This new enterprise began manufacturing records at 220 Marcus Garvey Drive after buying Federal Recording from the Kourie family. All equipment was taken from Tuff Gong Studios, and 56 Hope Road was "stagnant for a while," Rita testified, adding, "The administrators, Mr. Byles and Mr. Desnoes, decided that this property should be sold." It was bought by the Marley family as the site of the Bob Marley Museum, with Sharon Marley Prendergast as curator.

All of the children pulled together creatively to forge a new future and fresh assets for the Bob Marley Foundation, such as *The Marley Family Album*, issued on February 6, 1995, to honor Bob's fiftieth birthday. In 1996 came the *Mr. Marley* album by Damian "Jr. Gong" Marley, and Julian Marley and the Uprising's *Lion in the Morning* project, both executive-produced for the WEA-distributed Lightyear label by Stephen Marley on behalf of Tuff Gong International/Ghetto Youths International. Member of the Melody Makers pitched in on the albums, as did Rohan and Ky-mani, plus veteran Wailers musicians like Family Man Barrett, Tyrone Downie and Earl "Chinna" Smith. In 1997 *Marley Magic: Live in Central Park at Summerstage* arrived, the album and video featuring Ziggy and the Melody Makers, Damian, Julian, Rita and new Tuff Gong artist Yvad in an entertaining concert event.

Meanwhile, after the poorly received 1993 *Joy and Blues* record, the Melody Makers had quietly departed Virgin Records and signed with Elektra, issuing in 1995 the critically praised album *Free Like We Want 2 B*. That album yielded their first Top 10 Jamaican hit in years, "Hand to Mouth," a soaring dancehall stomp whose proceeds benefitted Ziggy's alma mater, the Melrose All-Age School.

Ziggy and the Melody Makers went on to be a dominant presence on the *Billboard* Top Reggae Albums chart in 1997 because of both their *Fallen Is Babylon* album on Elektra, with its rhythmic, dub-laden single remake of Curtis Mayfield's "People Get Ready," and Virgin's *The Best of Ziggy Marley and the Melody Makers (1988–1993)*.

These gains coincided with Rasta rejoicing that Aramaic inscriptions found at Tell Dan in northern Israel in 1993 offered the first archaeological proof of the ancient Israelites' House of David. But other news seemed to bode ill. Just as the Bible had foretold of false prophets and stray lambs in the Last Days, so it became known that among the seventy-two victims of cult leader David Koresh's fiery mass death during a 1993 standoff with FBI agents in Waco, Texas, was Livingstone Malcolm, Cedella Booker's nephew.

On February 21, 1994, Bunny Wailer enlisted the late Peter Tosh's elderly mother, Alvira Coke, in filing a writ in the High Court of Justice, Chancery Division, in England, against Island Records, Ltd.; Tuff Gong International; PolyGram and the Bob Marley Foundation et al. "I am the only living founder of Tuff Gong," Bunny told the press. "I am getting an injunction against the box set," meaning *Songs of Freedom*.

For all the anguish the Marleys had been through in creating the Bob Marley Foundation, this latest action was the most upsetting, because the family felt it was under siege from within, Bunny being related through Cedella Booker's past relationship with his father, Thaddius, which produced the daughter Mrs. Booker raised, Pearl.

Bob's beleaguered widow Rita seemed most irate, announcing to the press that Bunny was "crazy." No less upsetting was an armed robbery at young Cedella's Jamaica home in August 1994 after the Melody Makers' intoxicating performance at Reggae Sunsplash. A five-man armed militia in a vehicle with government license plates materialized at her gate, with supposed orders to search the premises for drugs. Once inside, they acted too brazen for police on official business, and Cedella said she was calling her attorney to report them to their superiors.

A gun barrel was placed to Cedella's temple as Sharon stood by with a four-month-old baby, her fourth child. "Shut up your pussy-hole mouth," the gunman barked, demanding, "Where's the Sunsplash money?" After stealing the funds, the men vanished, the real police later rebuking Cedella for being deceived by the ruse. "*Cho*—Jamaica fucked up sometimes," she fumed, bewildered and astonished.

First accosted in court by Bunny, then held up by goons masquerading as cops, Cedella was finding it difficult to tell the good guys from the bad. She also commiserated with her mother's protracted suffering from assorted Wailers fallout, whether from Bunny or Bob's former manager, Don Taylor, who had sought revenge after Rita refused to end the lawsuit with Cayman Music by means of the cash settlement Taylor proposed.

As Rita stated under oath during cross-examination in the 1992 Zolt/Steinberg trial, Taylor "pursued [*sic*] me that Bob was owing Cayman Music and there was an existing lawsuit so it would be best to pay off Mr. Sims and get that over with."

Q: And, in fact, had you done so, had you paid out this money to Cayman Music, Mr. Taylor was going to get a piece of it at the other end, wasn't he?

A: Yes sir.

Q: And he was angry about that?

A: Yes. He was very angry, along with Mr. Sims. They were both very angry because Mr. Sims said Don Taylor had promised him that the settlement will [*sic*] have taken place. So they were both very upset at that point.

Q: And as a result of that trial, Mr. Sims and Cayman Music got nothing, right?

A: They got nothing, sir.

"Watching her go through all these struggles," Cedella mused of her mom in 1995, "if I was a different kind of woman, I would hate men."

The schemes against Rita and the family seemed unrelenting, and Bunny's attack on the clan was a bitter pill, because he had often conceded that Rita was a vital part—from the earliest sessions—of the artistic and commercial alliance that became Tuff Gong Records: "Yeah, well, she's on some of the tracks, but she's always been on some of the tracks," Bunny affirmed in a 1986 interview. "That was from when we had our own Wail 'N' Soul label."

In 1993 Bunny began issuing outré projects under a bizarre

Ras/Solomonic/Tuff Gong banner like *The Never Ending Wailers*, a crude recasting of abysmal two-track 1968–1971 tapes from Bunny, Peter and Bob (and Rita), grafted onto what was billed as "newly recorded, strengthened harmonies" by Bunny, Junior Braithwaite and Vision Walker, cut in 1984, plus Andrew Tosh's overdubs. The result sounded like haunted-house effects for a cut-rate carnival attraction. Bunny compounded the ghoulish grudge match by issuing *Bunny Wailer: Hall of Fame—A Tribute to Bob Marley's 50th Anniversary*. Made up of fifty-two slipshod tracks of Marley-Wailers covers introduced with addled, pseudosolemn commentary devoid of any vulnerability or warmth, this umpteenth "tribute" to Bob sadly exposed a simmering resentment toward the man Bunny claimed to honor.

The fact that cynical projects of Bunny's like *Hall of Fame* and *Time Will Tell: A Tribute to Bob Marley* (a 1990 record recycled from the 1981 *Tribute* on Solomonic), as well as his 1994 *Crucial!* odds-and-sods release, were getting recognition from gullible Grammy voters (while Bob himself had never won a Grammy, and Bunny's own superb *Blackheart Man* and *Liberation* albums had been ignored) was ample evidence that opportunism, vanity and myopia were tainting the thrust of Jah music. Regrettably, Babylon had invaded the psyche of the Wailers community, conquering from within for the sake of a trademark that Bunny himself had forfeited to Bob and Rita in the mid-1970s when he began his own Solomonic label, much as Peter had broken away to found the Intel-Diplo imprint. (The trademarks lawsuit was settled in May, 1999 with Bunny and parties granted $2 million and use of the old "three fists" Tuff Gong logo.)

But any sense of fairness, professional propriety or custodial responsibility was long open to question, dating back to the Wailers' earliest days with Coxsone Dodd. After years of silence on the subject, Coxsone suddenly claimed in 1994 that he was never paid by hoodlum Nate McCalla of Calla Records for U.S. distribution of the Wailers' ska sides that McCalla had licensed and then sold to CBS Records circa 1976 for its *Birth of a Legend* anthology.

(McCalla vanished after a 1977 shootout at a Maryland concert in which police suspected the Genovese crime family had a financial interest. He was finally located in 1980 in a rented home in Fort Lauderdale, Florida, leaning forward in a lounge chair with the TV on, the back of his head shot away, his badly decomposed body apparently suspended in that position for at least a week.)

Coxsone boasted during a 1994 *Billboard* interview that the word "Scorcher," familiarly set in parentheses below the titles of many of the

Wailers singles later appearing on *Birth of a Legend*, was his "writing name. I'm registered with the Performing Rights Society as Scorcher." This was illuminating news, particularly for those previously told by Dodd, with a laugh, that Scorcher "just describe the beat." Even a source at the Mechanical Copyright Protection Society (MCPS) in London told *Billboard* that he believed Scorcher was "a term used by Sound Systems owners in Jamaica, meaning a good record."

The MCPS source was correct, insofar as the long-popular term had been misperceived and duly recirculated. But an investigative report by *Billboard* published in July 1994 revealed the truth: "Scorcher" was Dodd's self-described nom de plume, under which he held the copyrights to numerous ska songs generally believed to have been written by leading Jamaican recording artists, including Bob Marley and Bunny Wailer.

"I was scorching at the time," added Dodd without irony, "so I figured I was the Scorcher."

Until new copyright laws were finally passed in Jamaica in 1993, it was not uncommon for producers to claim songwriting credit as well as recording rights for songs cut in their studios—and sometimes they did so without the songwriter-performer's knowledge. Dodd insisted that a song he produced, such as "Simmer Down," would be developed as he listened to the catchphrases and concerns of dancers at his mobile sound-system dances. He said he brought the concept back to the Wailers and, along with them, devised the lyrics to the immortal ska classic.

Yet Bob Marley claimed he wrote the "Simmer Down" lyrics to calm his mother's anxieties about his rude boy companions and won the Ward Theater's Opportunity Knocks talent contest (see chapter 1) with his solo performance of the song—two years prior to Dodd's Studio One recording session with the Wailers.

A spokesman for the U.K.'s Performing Rights Society (PRS) said that it had seven different versions of "Simmer Down" in its international files (some of them registered with different agencies). One, dated 1978, was credited to Marley; another, dated 1981, designated the writer as Clement Dodd, whom PRS confirmed was Scorcher.

Dodd later withdrew his songs from PRS and registered them with BMI, which informed *Billboard* that, as Scorcher, Dodd was listed as the writer of 141 compositions, including "Simmer Down." One version of the song, dated 1968, lists Dodd as the sole author; the other, filed 1991, has Dodd sharing credit with Marley. (Songs attributed to Marley alone are registered with ASCAP. Bob departed the PRS and joined ASCAP after his label established operations in the United States.)

Bunny Wailer told *Billboard*, "The Wailers are known to be songwriters. Coxsone don't have any reputation to be a songwriter. People put their names on other people's works." Commenting on the Scorcher writing credit for such Wailers songs as "One Love," Bunny added, "That's bullshit. Coxsone Dodd is not a writer. All these guys claim they had something to do with the Wailers. What are these guys doing now? Coxsone is claiming he's writing songs? Why isn't he writing still?"

Rita Marley's reaction was blunter: "Who the hell is Scorcher?" She said she was aware Dodd had claimed authorship of some of Bob's ska songs and seethed that "Bob had a problem with it."

So did Danny Sims, who insisted to *Billboard*, "I acquired the rights to all those songs. I became the publisher of all Bob Marley's material. They were unpublished songs when I took over Bob Marley." Sims said of Dodd, "He had no publishing agreement with Marley. What I did see from him in the early days was a recording agreement; he owned the masters."

Dodd countered by saying, "I refused to sign papers from Danny trying to release the rights," adding that he had a valid contract with Bob until 1969. (Dodd also told reporters he was negotiating with Sony Records to settle the old licensing issues with its CBS label that Nate McCalla's murder left unresolved.)

Sims advised *Billboard* that he himself had collected "millions" in royalties from 1967 to 1992, when he sold the catalog for $3.5 million to Island Logic, the entity Blackwell set up to manage the Marley assets for the Bob Marley Foundation.

"All those songs," Sims concluded, "are now owned by Rita and the kids." But Sims disputed Rita's claim that, except for certain of Dodd's licensing deals, disputes over publishing and masters have prevented her and Bob's eight adult children and beneficiaries from receiving royalties from the ska reissues.

As for Blackwell, he told *Billboard* he had a partnership with the family for publishing rights, with 75 percent owned by Marley's adult beneficiaries and 25 percent by an Island entity, with overall revenues at an annual level circa 1994 of $5 to 6 million.

Chris Blackwell would have his own poignant confrontations in the 1990s with an unalterable past and its consequences in the present. In August 1996, he journeyed to Newport, County Mayo, Ireland, for the funeral of his beloved Anglo-Irish father, Joseph Blackwell, who had died at the age of eighty. Chris's wing of the celebrated Blackwell dynasty was maturing, with Chris himself turning sixty ten months later.

The year before, on Saturday, February 18, 1995, in St. Vincent's

Ward of Dublin's Mater Hospital, Blackwell had lost, to lymphoma, another Irishman dear to him. Fifty-one-year-old Denny Cordell had produced the Moody Blues' "Go Now" and founded Deram Records, serving as producer on Procol Harum's "A Whiter Shade of Pale" and discovering both Joe Cocker and Marc Bolan. He also founded Shelter Records, releasing Bob Marley's first U.S. single in 1972, called "Doppy [*sic*] Conqueror" on the label copy, and signed the band Mudcrutch, which became Tom Petty and the Heartbreakers (Denny produced their 1976 debut album). Cordell later launched Mango Records in a joint venture with Blackwell and coordinated the release of the first Mango album in 1975, the soundtrack to *The Harder They Come*. In 1991, as Island's creative director, he signed the Cranberries.

In March 1997, Michael Manley died at seventy-two of prostate cancer, bringing to a close a sociopolitical cult of personality first conceived on the famed Drumblair estate in uptown Kingston, where his father, Norman Manley, and his sculptor mother, Edna, hosted an artistic and political salon during colonial rule in the 1930s.

Michael Manley left his worldly goods, including two homes—one in Kingston on the subdivided Dumblair grounds (carved up during lean times in the 1960s), the other in the east Kingston mountains at Mavis Bank—to his fifth wife, Glynne Ewert, and his five children: Rachel, Joseph, Sarah, Natasha and David. The prime minister's post, as anticipated, passed to P. J. Patterson.

But Manley's greatest legacy was nothing so genteel: the swarms of ungovernable drug posses he had set in motion to intimidate or eliminate the citizens he claimed to champion.

Blackwell had watched as the old plantocracy crumbled amid the uncertain new Jamaican hierarchies of reggae aristocracy, rising drug dons and assorted record business operatives still eager, greedy or naive enough to want to bridge the gaps between them.

The most notorious figure in Blackwell's own background was Grace O'Malley (1530–1603), a famed female pirate who preyed on the English vessels that plied the Irish Sea. Captain Joseph Blackwell, Chris's father, was the son of well-to-do Gordon Blackwell, a member of the London Stock Exchange, who was killed in the First World War; afterward Joe moved with his socially prominent pianist mother to the south of France, growing up between Irish horse country and the beaches of Nice.

Joe Blackwell met the attractive and magnetic Blanche Lindo in the 1930s through her planter brother Roy, an Army friend. She was one of four children descended from anglicized Sephardic Jews who arrived in Jamaica from France in the mid-sixteenth century, the Lindos serving as licensed privateers with letters of marque from the English Crown. The Lindo pirate motto was, "No prey, no pay."

By 1693, a member of the Lindo family was the first Jew admitted to the London Stock Exchange. A century later, as British statesman William Wilberforce pleaded in Parliament to abolish slavery, a Lindo went to London to argue for caution, claiming the economy of the Caribbean would be ruined without slow withdrawal of the odious institution.

In the 1790s Alexander Lindo funded Napoleon's wars against the British, losing his investment when France lost the campaign. But the Lindo name became firmly entrenched in Jamaica: the Seaga-controlled section of Kingston called Tivoli Gardens was first known as Lindo Town, back in 1815 when freed blacks were allowed to settle there.

Patriarch Cecil Vernor Lindo had strengthed the Lindo Brothers trading firms after lucrative forays to Costa Rica to sell dry goods to railway workers. They acquired the Jamaican Ward Estate in 1915, which encompassed J. Wray & Nephew, and Appleton Central Limited, the heady fiscal fountain from which Appleton Rum cascaded. Cecil Lindo also sold his holdings in St. Catherine and Clarendon to the United Fruit Company in 1928 in the biggest land transaction in Jamaican history up to that point: $2 million in cash.

Blanche's father, Percival, bought the rum business from his brother Cecil in 1940 and then sold out the bulk of his interest to the Henriques family in 1957 (who joined the D'Costas and Lindos as the leading Sephardic Jewish faction of Jamaica's Twenty-one Families).

Blanche and Joe owned the finest stable of racehorses in Jamaica, dominating annual meetings at the old course on the land that later became Goldeneye, the Caribbean hideaway where Ian Fleming wrote his James Bond novels. After her divorce from Blackwell in 1945, Blanche moved to England for a spell and joined the Berkshire horse set, but she resumed life in Jamaica for good after son Christopher had finished his schooling at Harrow.

Among Blanche's admirers back in Port Maria, where she built her seaside Bolt House manse, were actor Errol Flynn, who longed to wed her, and Fleming, who longed to bed her. Fleming and Blanche met while he was writing *From Russia with Love* at Goldeneye, and despite her initial dislike of his forward, haughty style, they became lovers and lifelong friends.

All these connections, all this wealth and influence, were stretched out before Chris Blackwell in 1997 as if they were a carpet: luxuriant and flowing, but frayed in spots, with a section of it suddenly to be jerked out from under him.

Island had been immersed in planning for its fortieth anniversary in 1999, having already issued an initial series of commemorative ska and British R&B compilation albums, when long-smoldering disagreements flared with Alain Levy, president/CEO of PolyGram, the corporate conglomerate to which Blackwell had sold Island in 1989 for some $300 million.

Caught in a battle of wills with Blackwell over the right of director Robert Altman to edit his upcoming PolyGram film, *The Ginger Man*, Levy resolved the tiff with Altman but wrote Blackwell a letter questioning his loyalty and his position on the board of directors.

"When I renewed my contract a few years ago with PolyGram," Blackwell informed the *Los Angeles Times*, mindful that his current contract only extended to 1999, "I was under the impression that I was going to be able to build an entertainment business with an independent feeling within PolyGram, but it isn't going to happen."

Steadily chafing under an alleged corporate strategy in the 1990s to drive up stock prices with quick pop hits at the perceived expense of developing grassroots artists for the long term, Blackwell felt his independent instincts were being devoured by the corporation that had gobbled up Island, and he resigned from the PolyGram board.

Suddenly, in the first week of November 1997, the lifetime achievement that was Island Records, which Blackwell had expanded to include rock, jazz, reggae and world music labels; hotels; cinemas; films and digital media for DVD audio and video, was slipping out of his hands—at least insofar as the music end of it was concerned.

Blackwell was and would always remain a maverick, a gambler and a rule-breaking visionary. While still a sixteen-year-old schoolboy at Harrow, he was found smuggling liquor and cigarettes onto the grounds for sale. As a result of the infraction, he became the first student in a century to be caned before the student body. "I didn't flinch a muscle; I was just like Clint Eastwood," he recalled. As a young man in Jamaica, he was photographed leading his father's champion horses to collect their cups; one of the most renowned steeds in Jamaica's modern history was Brown Bomber, cited in the 1943 *Race Year in Jamaica* for copping the Jockey Club Stakes, Derby, Eclipse Stakes, Lonsdale Cup, and Sir Arthur Richards Cup. When young Chris later found a job selling air-conditioning units, his superior Richard Todd remembered Blackwell as his top vendor, landing a certain account called Marley & Plant, a construction and civil engineering firm on Riverton Road in Kingston, owned by a family with a ne'er-do-well son who fathered a child with a black woman out in St. Ann.

The next step toward Blackwell's destiny in 1997 was the decision in December to move his separate and still-independent Island Trading Company businesses out of the PolyGram building in Worldwide Plaza on New York City's 8th Avenue and into new headquarters at Columbus Circle, announcing that future projects would be launched under a new standard called Islandlife.

Exactly thirty-four years earlier, in December 1963, Island Records' top-selling release was a single just played on the Ready Steady Go program, Kentrick Patrick's "Don't Stay Out Late" (WI-079). Now Blackwell was counting on current public tastes for keeping late hours far from home, as he staked his future success on such Islandlife holdings as his Island Outpost resorts and nightclubbing inns including Jake's Village, Strawberry Hill, The Caves and the rentable Goldeneye and Bolt House properties in Jamaica; plus Compass Point and Pink Sands in the Bahamas; and the Marlin, Cavalier, Leslie, Tides, Kent and Casa Grande hotels in Miami Beach. Blackwell also announced the expansion of his Manga Entertainment video firm and Blue Mountain Music Publishing, as well as the formation of a new record label and the Palm Pictures low-budget film company. The long-term viability of all these enterprises was highly promising, but it seemed likely that Blackwell—who wed fiancée Mary Vinson in Jamaica in May 1998, and who'd seen Island Records as a "nurtured" label, as opposed to the large companies performing a merely "useful" service as "bankers and distributors, not creators"—would run his latest ventures with a typically Jamaican sense of judgment and intuitive deference to power.

To illustrate: Back in 1961, while still serving as Assistant District Commissioner to Socialist Governor-General Sir Hugh Foot, Blackwell was in the Kingston offices of the High Commission one day when a peculiar peasant woman appeared bearing a breadfruit tree as a kind of state gift. Blackwell quickly moved past the smug, bemused general staff and greeted the woman with great respect. He thanked her graciously for the bestowal and then made certain—despite the perplexed whisperings of his coworkers—that the sapling was planted with care and ceremony. Blackwell knew the woman's offering of the plant was a sincere expression from the peasantry who dominated Jamaica in every meaningful sense, and that, like the rest of the nation, the tree owed its vitality to the calloused hands that actually nurtured it. And Chris knew one thing more: the gift-giver was an obeah woman, with clout the High Commission could never hope to comprehend or countermand.

As 1998 neared, Bob Marley's posthumous *Legend* compilation of classic singles had spent an unsurpassed sixty-four cumulative weeks and counting atop *Billboard*'s Top Pop Catalogue Albums chart, its closest competitor being *Time Pieces: The Best of Eric Clapton* at thirty-seven weeks. It had been well over a decade since the U.S. release, on April 4, 1984, of *Legend*—which has sold more than 12 million units worldwide (with terrific sales volume in locales as unlikely as Turkey).

A North American sales perennial on a par with the Beatles' *Sgt. Pepper's Lonely Hearts Club Band*, Pink Floyd's *Dark Side of the Moon* and the Eagles' *Greatest Hits 1971–75*, Marley's *Legend* had consistently soared higher in weekly unit purchases than those other storied rock records, even when the reconstituted Floyd and reunited Eagles were in the midst of sold-out reunion tours.

Legend's appeal would not slacken even with the issue in 1992 of the extensive four-CD, seventy-eight-track *Songs of Freedom* retrospective. The *Freedom* box set enjoyed an incredible 87-week stay on *Billboard*'s Top Reggae Albums chart, while the subsequent *Natural Mystic* anthology of Marley music earned a 103-week run on the reggae chart, with twenty weeks in the No. 1 spot.

Songs of Freedom also yielded two international hit singles with "Iron Lion Zion," which peaked in the U.K. at number 5, and "Why Should I"/"Exodus," which climbed to number 42 on the British surveys. Meanwhile, Marley hasn't been absent from the U.K. Top 75 albums chart since 1984.

There was a remarkable tale here, of exodus and survival and uprising and confrontation—as presaged in Marley's marvelous, thematically linked 1977–1983 album series of the same nomenclature—but it was much more than a story of careerism or statecraft or charts or record sales. The triumphant and yet-expanding outreach of Bob Marley's rebel music was a lesson in the merits of pursuing one's personal fulfillment to its greatest spiritual ripple effect.

The progressive spirit of sociomusical goodwill that Marley and the Wailers encouraged had quickly found expression in the astounding growth of so-called world music. In 1979, when Bob scheduled a concert tour in Australia, his shows had a transforming effect on the contemporary aboriginal music scene, prompting a dramatic blending of socially conscious reggae sensibilities into the didgeridoo-steeped *corroboree* that is the native equivalent of a Rasta Grounation ceremony. Such aboriginal bands as Us Mob and Bart Willoughby's No Fixed Address wrote Marley-fueled songs, like "Address's We Have Survived." When No Fixed Address evolved into the Mixed Relations, the ecumenical Marley influence coalesced down under with hip-hop as Public Enemy's Chuck D guested on the hit "Take It or Leave It."

Mandawuy Yunupingu, founder of Yothu Yindi, Australia's foremost exponent of aboriginal rock, has repeatedly acknowledged Marley as "a big influence on my songwriting, with his freedom themes. . . . Some of the things I feel about my life, our country, are the same as Marley would have felt."

In South America, that feeling was mutual. In Brazil in 1974, two young Bahians known as Vovo and Apolonio were stirred by the Pan-African pride of Bob Marley and decided to create a more activist brand of *bloco afro* Carnaval group in Salvador, which they christened Ile-Aiye (Yoruban for "House of Life"). Debuting at Carnaval the following year, Ile-Aiye was a sensation that blossomed into an organization of 2,000 members, as well as spurring other musicians to found comparable blocos afro like Muzenza, Araketu and Olodum. Next, samba-reggae caught on as a hectic new hybrid, and the re-Africanization of Bahian music had begun, leading in the 1990s to phenomena like Gilberto Gil jamming with the Wailers band.

Mexican-born Carlos Santana "almost toured with Bob in 1979," in the guitarist's wistful words, and it was a sorely missed epiphany for the progenitor of Latin rock, who became a convert to Marley in 1974 when he heard Eric Clapton perform "I Shot the Sheriff" live in Tampa, Florida, while the two guitarists were on tour together. "I said, 'That's a *bad* tune!'" Santana recounted years later, "and Eric later explained he was a huge fan of Bob's, and so I decided to check out the man himself. The first album I bought was *Catch a Fire,* and from then on I was hooked." Ever since, Santana has been playing and proselytizing on behalf of Marley's legacy.

Ubongo originator Remmy Ongala was born in Zaire in 1947 when it was still the Belgian Congo. Some thirty years later, he was a top guitarist in the Tanzanian capital of Dar-es-Salaam who still felt ashamed of the shaggy locks he promised his superstitious mother he'd never shear. But circa 1976, "when records by Bob Marley came out [i.e., were widely imported to Central Africa], I saw that he had hair like mine," said Ongala. "So after that, I felt all right. I became proud of my locks."

Thomas Mapfumo, gifted popularizer of the *m'bira* thumb piano and pioneer of Zimbabwe's distinctive *chimurenga* or "struggle music" dance style, was merely a local star on the modern Harare scene until he was invited to share the bill with Marley in the Zimbabwe independence show, whereupon he was catapulted to international fame virtually overnight. Journalists reviewing Mapfumo's 1984–85 European tours duly noted his adoption of many of Marley's stage moves and mannerisms, as well as the marked reggae undertow in his *shangara* rhythms.

In 1982, when Island Records first issued Nigerian prince King Sunny Ade's *Juju Music* album, the wildly kinetic guitarist/vocalist/bandleader was cast as a kindred spirit of the late reggae superstar. "In terms of popularity," noted Ade's French producer-manager Martin Meissonier, "it is probably true that Sunny is the second Third World star after Marley. But he is not like the *new* Bob Marley." Ade's spokesman got it right. Ade's reputation benefited from a brief alignment with that of his predecessor, but time would show that although Marley would not be succeeded or eclipsed in the planet-rock pantheon, his pathfinding influence was beyond estimation.

Seydou Kone, aka Alpha Blondy, of the Ivory Coast, shaped his entire approach to reggae utilizing the Marley template, stretching from Blondy's 1982 hit in the capital city of Abidjan with his *Jah Glory* album, on through his international breakthrough in 1986 with the *Jerusalem* record, cut in Tuff Gong Studios with drummer Carlton Barrett and other members of the Wailers band.

The same is true of South African singer Lucky Dube. After four gold albums made in the *mbaqanga* township mode, Dube began to shift his sound to reggae circa 1985 in homage to principal influence Bob Marley. Lucky's initial reggae record, banned by local radio stations, was titled *Rastas Never Die*.

In 1988, when *New York Times* reporter James Brooke called on firebrand saxophonist-singer Fela Anikolapu-Kuti at his renowned nightclub in Lagos, Fela announced he was intent on returning to the ancestral worship traditions of his people, the Yoruba. Fela then indicated a shrine containing images of his mother; an Egyptian god named Khuti; Ghanian pioneer of Pan-Africanism Kwame Nkrumah; and Bob Marley.

Nigerian reggae also adopted Marley as an apostle, his sound-shaping presence manifest from 1988 onward in the music of Majek Fashek, Ras Kimono, and Natty 'B' and the Root Rastas.

By the late 1980s in Surinam, Marley's reggae had infiltrated the popular dance rhythms of *kawina*, *kaseko*, and *aleke* in the former Dutch colony off the coast of South America. The results surfaced in the music of bands like Sukrasani and the Holland-based Draver Boys.

In Japan, Marley-driven reggae had enjoyed solid roots in Tokyo since an early 1980s club scene that yielded the seminal dub band Mute Beat. By the early '90s, twenty-five-year-old Japanese reggae star P.J. (son of a black American dad and a Japanese mom) had developed a big fan base thanks to English/Japanese vocals that any saki-soaked passerby might mistake for the Gong himself. And one can only wonder what Bob would have made of Okinawan female chorus group the Nenes, who covered "No Woman, No Cry" on their 1993 album, *Ashibi*.

Back in the States, one of the more prodigious nominees for the Best Reggae Album Grammy at the thirty-seventh annual award ceremonies in 1995 had been *Stir It Up*, a twelve-track dancehall/hip-hop/acid jazz treatise. Its cover version of the Marley-authored title track was handled by nineteen-year-old Diana King, who was raised in Marley's Hope Road neighborhood and sometimes played with his kids. King did a stunning job with the song, but voters looking for more exotic fare could check out *Stir It Up*'s wryly licentious interpretation of "I Shot the Sheriff," which Jamaican singer Annette Brissett said she conceived while "just buggin'" in her pad in Fort Lauderdale, Florida.

One of the hottest acts of 1996 was the Haitian-American hip-hop group, the Fugees, based partially on the strength of their fine cover version of the indefatigable "No Woman, No Cry," while Warren G earned a gold single in the United States in 1997 with his own undistinguished take on "I Shot the Sheriff."

But of all the roots and branches of Bob Marley and his influence, the most persuasive ones promised to be the ongoing efforts of his children. Noting in 1995 that the Marley family had "lots of kids" within the immediate clan to provide companionship and mutual support, Melody Maker Sharon Marley Prendergast reminded the public that "Bob always said, 'You guys won't need friends because I have so much of you.'"

Fed up with over a decade of infighting among the adult factions around Bob—who were supposedly committed to spreading his spirit of "oneness"—and feeling that the grasping fight over the Tuff Gong trademark seemed to promise an empty victory for either side, the Marley children had begun by 1998 to distance themselves from all the old logos, enterprises and faded commercial symbols associated with their father's work.

Although Tuff Gong International's U.S. division pacted in February 1998 with Atlantic Records' Mesa imprint to market and promote the reggae releases of such acts as Steel Pulse, Aswad, and Mystic Revealers, Stephen Marley demonstrated the new agenda of his brothers and sisters by devising the Ghetto Youths label and production company for many of their new collaborative efforts.

"The Ghetto Youths label is for *this* Marley generation," he emphasized, having launched the debut solo album and singles for both Julian and Damian "Jr. Gong" Marley from this imprint. The chart success of Damian's debut made him one of the Top 10 Reggae Artists of 1997 in *Billboard*. Stephen vowed that, besides hosting the solo work of the various Marley children, Ghetto Youths would also be the home for a slew of high-quality projects that would overshadow (as well as shame) numerous spiteful releases currently cluttering the Marley sections in the record stores.

One of the most visible proposed projects under the new Ghetto Youths banner was to be a 1998–99 collaborative album Stephen tentatively titled *Black Survivors*. Inspired by what had been the original working title (*Black Survival*) of his late father's 1979 *Survival* album, *Black Survivors* (twice retitled as *A Rebel's Dream* and then *Chant Down Babylon*) was designed to further that prior record's intentions to reach a black R&B–hip-hop audience, in this case by involving contemporary artists from those reggae-friendly genres.

And as a signal to rival parties who'd long been peddling grossly inferior demos and outtakes of his father's earliest work, Stephen and production cohorts Damian and Julian Marley intended to use the excellent family library of Bob's modern, unissued studio sessions as the basis for the specially arranged new tracks.

The artists integrating these exceptional, never-released alternative recordings of latter-day Marley anthems into their own interpretations of the songs would include Steve Tyler and Joe Perry ("Roots, Rock, Reggae"), Fugee's star (and helpmate of Rohan Marley) Lauryn Hill ("Turn Your Lights Down Low") and Cheeks of the Lost Boyz ("Guiltiness").

The move was also seen as a chance to counteract the self-hating poses and cynical commercial demonization of black youth long perpetuated by gangsta rap, communicating "not just that Bob Marley was a great writer and a prophet," in Stephen's words, "but to really penetrate that audience, especially the gang youths that really need the message from someone as strong as our father."

Stephen Marley was taking the lead in guesting on other politically progressive rap artists' records celebrating his father's music, such as the

1997 *Chocolate Supa Highway* album for Capitol Records by Spearhead, for which Stephen and the group's Michael Franti cut a redrafted rendition of "Rebel Music." Similarly, Stephen had invited Wyclef Jean of the Fugees to join him on Stephen's own "Everybody Wants to Be" track on the Melody Makers' *Fallen Is Babylon* album—a galvanizing tune that merited considerable airplay in Jamaica in 1997.

The women in the Melody Makers conceived an offshoot act called the Marley Girls, which included Makers' harmony singer Erica Newell. In 1997 they recorded the song "Unbelievable" for the Island Jamaica soundtrack to the film *Dancehall Queen*, and a full-length Marley Girls album was envisioned for the future.

Meanwhile, Stephen, Ziggy, Julian, Damian and Ky-mani Marley (who also hit the Hot 100 in 1998 with "Gotta Be . . . Movin' On Up" by Prince Be Featuring Ky-mani) had begun wood shedding as a separate, all-male Marley combo with an eye toward a series of Ghetto Youths singles and albums. Moreover, Stephen decided to return to 56 Hope Road for many of these ventures, supervising the installment of new recording facilities on the former Tuff Gong Studios site under a more appropriate name: Marley Music.

Still more Marley family labels, groups and releases were on the drawing board for the first generation of Marley's children, most of whom were now adults and eager to bring their own fast-growing toddlers into the artistic fold. Never again, they pledged, would they permit familial squabbles, hurtful sniping by envious associates, or legacy-oriented avarice and backbiting to undermine the family name.

"Overall, it's love and unity," said Stephen of the message the Marley children looked to transmit both inside and outside the fold, recognizing the need for suitable role models on the threshold of the next millennium while adding that "everyone is equal."

And, he might have noted, heroes were getting harder and harder to find. Everybody in the tottering new world order seemed desperate in the fading 1990s for a potent role model, mythic exemplar, or pop culture polestar to help pull them through. In Lagos, local kids imagined themselves in the green body suit and solar-powered cape of comic book superhero Captain Africa, whose avowed mission as depicted by Ghanaian artist Andy Akman was to "fight evil and dark forces that threaten Africa and the whole world." In Britain and America, we were apparently willing to settle for the Mighty Morphin Power Rangers, Snoop Doggy Dog, or the Spice Girls.

Yet if these actually were the Last Days, as Rastas believed with unswerving fervor—glancing heavenward as warnings of global warming resumed, its surge linked to the disastrous Asia-Pacific pollution levels cited in Yale University studies as the worst in the world, with the earth's weather patterns meanwhile growing increasingly freakish—many surmised that it couldn't hurt to at least *try* to turn them into the best days still possible.

Meanwhile, Jah continued at the millennium's close to beckon the best of men to depart from their earthly plane, Joe Higgs succumbing in Los Angeles in December 1999 after a long bout with cancer. He was 59, and left behind a dozen children. (Don Taylor also died of heart disease in 1999.)

Faith in Jah got Marley in touch with his conscience, and faith in himself set him on a course so unlikely and so edifying that no soul around the man remained unmoved by the dimensions and lessons of Bob's self-realization.

For example, consider Englishman Julian Maitland-Walker, an expert in European law whose Somerset home could scarcely be farther from the Trench Town goat paths out of which the Tuff Gong emerged. However, because Maitland-Walker was the great-grandson of Robert Marley, white brother of Bob's father, Norval Sinclair Marley, he had his own unique perspective on one ghetto-bred reggae singer's uncommon strides in the twentieth century. As Maitland-Walker saw Bob: "In an oddly aristocratic manner, he dignified black music in a way no other black man has." And in a wonderfully humble manner, Robert Nesta Marley, O.M., dignified belief in humanity in a way no other Everyman could.

Yet in the end, as in the beginning, it is the Scriptures that put it best—according to Bob's Rasta brethren, who saw him as the modern equivalent of the biblical Joseph, the favored eleventh of the elderly Jacob's twelve sons who was betrayed as a youth by his jealous brothers and sent into bondage in Pharaoh's Egypt.

Thus the Rastas looked to Genesis 45:5–8, wherein the returned Joseph revealed his identity to his confused and forlorn siblings. Consoling his brothers as they trembled in shock and shame, weeping with them, forgiving their terrible follies, Joseph gathered each near and spoke of the powerful mysteries of personal destiny. And finally, in a voice as soft and daunting as distant thunder, he told them: "Be not grieved. For it was not you that sent me hither, but God."

Appendix 1

DUPPY CONQUEROR

What follows is the original, previously unpublished preface to this book, written as a result of the information, testimony and local evidence I acquired regarding belief in the supernatural in Jamaica (i.e., obeah), particularly among those closest to Bob Marley.

Brer Duppy is a familiar character in Afro-Caribbean stories about the fabled mischievous spider, Anancy. As defined by *The Dictionary of Jamaican English*, edited by F. G. Cassidy and B. B. LePage (Cambridge University Press), a "duppy" is "the spirit of the dead, believed to be capable of returning to aid or (more often) harm living beings, directly or indirectly; they are also believed subject to the power of obeah and its practitioners, who can 'set' or 'put' a duppy upon a victim and 'take off' their influences."

"Duppy Conqueror," a term used in the lyrics of the song of the same name by Bob Marley and the Wailers as heard on their 1973 *Burnin'* album, is defined as "A belligerent or bullying person; a derisive epithet often coupled with bull-bucker"—a man who thinks he is strong enough to buck a bull. In Rasta terms, a duppy conqueror was someone tough and courageous to a truly mystical extent; that is, a person who could defeat evil in all its daunting supernatural forms, from malevolent ghost to the devil himself.

In order to demonstrate the degree to which such belief systems are enmeshed in the fabric of Jamaican culture, I prepared this early preface. Later, when Holt, Rinehart and Winston senior editor Paul Bresnick persuaded me to make the title of this book *Catch a Fire*—which literally means to "catch Hell," and which spoke more to the torment between faith and hard fact, damnation and redemption—I turned my attention to expanding my work on an explanatory section that evolved into the comprehensive introduction titled "Riddim Track."

Nonetheless, this early preface is still instructive about the mystical manner in which day-to-day struggles for earthly and spiritual survival are frequently and rather soberly interlaced in Jamaican life. It also helps explain why I once described this book-in-progress to *USA Today* as a sort of "ghost story," the saga of a man's pitched battles against forces seen and unseen en route to fulfilling his temporal and spiritual destiny; in short, Bob Marley's often frightening fight to save his own soul.

Preface

It is a relatively mundane occurrence for ghost stories and accounts of weird and uncanny phenomena to find their way onto the front pages of the *Daily Gleaner*, Jamaica's 149-year-old newspaper (nearly twenty years older than the *New York Times*). Occult phenomena of one form or another seem to be common in Jamaica, and although no one is exactly sure why this is so (some point to the island's proximity to the Bermuda Triangle, some blame poltergeists or evil spirits dispatched through magic spells cast by natives, others simply shrug and say it has always been that way), the practice of dispassionately reporting these events is accepted as a part of everyday life. Witness a front-page article in the February 10, 1965, *Daily Gleaner*, headlined MYSTERY STONING, WETTING OF STONY HILL GIRL:

> Mysterious stonings of people and places have reached Stony Hill. But the latest victim is also being doused and spat upon. Nine-year-old Eunie Richard of Norbrook has been plagued since December 13, her father, cultivator Mr. James Richard, told the Gleaner yesterday. None of the other members of the family—Mrs. Icylin Richard, 41, and 15-year-old Valrie—have been menaced.
>
> "'It happens at all hours of the day," Mr. Richard said. "Stones shoot past Eunie's head and some have fallen near her feet. Mysteriously saliva falls on her face and water wets her all over the body." Only once has she been hit—with a "fist-size rock" on the head.
>
> The missiles also come through windows, smashing furniture and mirrors. There is no stoning when Eunie leaves the house. On January 14 she went to live with an aunt two miles from Norbrook. The stones followed her. Eunie visited her parents periodically and was stoned on the way.
>
> Distressed, Mr. Richard took his daughter to a St. Mary "healer man" two weeks ago. "The healer examined her and said nothing was wrong with my child, but things have worsened since," he said. "Now, I don't know what to do."
>
> Eunie now lives with a relative in a nearby district. There is no change.
>
> This is the year's first report of the phenomenon for which no explanation has yet been found. Mrs. Humie Dalling, 29, left Kinloss, Trelawny, with her family in terror last December. Pans, bottles, and stones showered her house.
>
> Tenants of a rambling old Buff Bay house heard stones drop on the roof, saw them fall in the yard and appear in a bucket of drinking water in November.

Some would argue that anyone who attempts to chronicle events taking place in Jamaica will inevitably be faced with a wealth of the kind of inexplicabilities reported routinely in the *Gleaner*. For example, the Jamaican Telephone Company goes on strike for a week, with interisland and transcontinental phone service completely cut off, yet all commerce continues at its same curious "soon come" pace, and the rumor mill that is the island's largest cottage industry (next to the ganja trade) never misses a beat. A murderous criminal the police have been tracking for months suddenly turns up, a neatly dressed corpse, lying on the station house stoop. Another good example: incumbent Jamaican Prime Minister Edward Seaga chooses as his chief bodyguard a baby-faced, thirty-year-old detective sergeant named Keith Gardiner. From outward appearances Gardiner seems an unlikely choice. But then it is revealed that the ghetto people call him "Trinity" and believe that he cannot die; he had confiscated more illegal guns (private possession being, without exception, forbidden), has been through more shootouts and has cut down more adversaries than colleagues twenty years his senior; he has survived battles in which bullets knocked out four of his teeth and half-severed his tongue; he has walked away from stakeouts in which hostile fire broke his leg in three places but failed to slacken his predatory pace; he has single-handedly foiled bold daytime robberies, canceling one such attempt in Kingston by summarily wasting all three armed culprits.

Such stories are the grist for myths, superstitions and legends on which many Jamaicans thrive. They fill the daily papers published in Kingston and Montego Bay. The questions arise: Are the reporters being hoodwinked or hoodooed? Or are facts and phantasms indeed impossibly intermingled on this particular island?

When you ask Keith "Trinity" Gardiner, one of six children born destitute in the appalling Kingston slum of Trench Town, if he really is immortal, he grins like an Eagle Scout who has just earned another merit badge and proceeds to deftly reload his trusty Browning 9mm.

There is a unique culture of supernaturally validated violence in the society, but also a more generous amount of kindly, hopeful and variegated religiosity, encompassing African animism and shamanism; French-Haitian creole rites that melded African and indigenous Iwa spirits into forms of Voodoo; the messianic "cargo cults" of Caribbean slavery days, which saw deliverance in the mainsail of a ship popping up on the horizon; dyed-in-the-wool doctrinaire Baptistism, transplanted from the American South; devout Spanish Catholicism; Anglicanism and Episcopalianism; Buddhism and Taoism from transplanted Chinese workers and servants; Moslem doctrines practiced by the Lebanese merchant class; Judaism brought by traders; sects who combine something from much of the above with certain regional creeds owed to local traits and predicaments, and more. A few have nearly faded out; most have not.

All such influences contributed in some manner to the environment in which Bob Marley grew up. Many had a profound personal effect on him, and a few, if you believe the believers, were embodied by him or were within his powers to manifest and direct to his own ends.

Appendix 2

SONGBIRD OF "SIMMER DOWN": THE BEVERLY KELSO STORY

The following piece is an example from the range of deep-background interviews I did while researching this book, much of the material informing aspects of the text without being specifically quoted or used in previous editions. This background piece was first published in a slightly different form in 1991 in the annual Bob Marley Collector's Edition of *The Beat* reggae and world music magazine and is a rare interview with the bubbly and sweet-natured singer whose keening vocals, in tandem with Cherry Green's, served as ska-era precursors to the I-Threes' reggae choir.

"I'll never forget how I started with Bob Marley and the other Wailers!" exclaims Beverly Kelso, her flutelike repartee reminiscent of effervescent 1940s film star Butterfly McQueen. "I was about sixteen at the time," she recalls with a giggle. "At that time, my father was in England, and I was looking to do something exciting for myself, to learn to get along in the world too, so I was singin' and performin' in one of what we used to call 'fun clubs.' This one club was a place on Wellington Street that teenage people could go to in the early evenin' to dance and show their talent.

"It was about three o'clock in the evening, and I was singin' down the aisle of the club and Bob came in and saw me. After my song he came right over and asked if I wanted to sing with his group. I started laughin' and he said, 'Nuh, I'm serious!' So I told him, 'Okay, any time that you're ready.' This was in 1963. It was early in the year.

"The next Wednesday he come over to my house on Columbus Road, and told me to be at the studio Thursday, the next day, to record!" That studio, of course, was the 13 Brentford Road headquarters of producer Coxsone Dodd's Jamaica Recording and Publishing Studio, Ltd.—or Studio One, for short. And Beverly's inaugural session was for "Simmer Down," a Marley composition that would prove to be the Wailers' first hit. Spiced with the tart tenor sax of Roland Alphonso, it was a ska-paced piece of advice from Marley for Jamaica's rampaging rude boys (slum hooligans).

"When I got there," Kelso continues, "we had ten minutes' rehearsal, and Bob just had me doin' this chorus of 'Simmer down, simmer down,' over and over behind him. It was done so fast, but the next thing I know, our recordin' is a success, and we must do stage shows everywhere, at theaters like the Palace, and travelin' between Kingston and Montego Bay. My sister made this gold dress for me, to match these gold jacket outfits that Mr. Dodd had given the Wailers the money for. And Mr. Dodd had a picture taken of us for publicity. I couldn't believe it was all happenin'!"

Neither could Jamaica's downtrodden. "Simmer Down," which hit number 1 in February 1964, was something quite new.

"I knew from the minute I heard 'Simmer Down' at their audition that the Wailers had that *intelligent* teenage sound that was needed in Jamaica, telling the youth, 'Don't slip up or else,'" reflects Coxsone Dodd. "People don't realize that when the Wailers first come to me, it was Junior Braithwaite who was behaving as the leader of the group. Junior would do the lead singing on another early Wailers tune, 'It Hurts to Be Alone,' but Bob was the natural leader, and his singing on 'Simmer Down' showed that. When Junior left to go to the United States, Bob took over.

"Before the Wailers hit," says Coxsone Dodd, "the most popular group was the Techniques with Slim Smith, but the Wailers just took over completely, and then everybody got on the ska bandwagon. My basic arrangement with Bob, to be frank, was like an adoption thing, because his mother was soon out of the country [having emigrated to Delaware], and Bob had been staying with Toddy [Livingston], Bunny's father, who couldn't afford to carry him fully. I had an extra room in a separate part of my recording building that was next to the studio, and Bob was living there on my okay for about two years. He wanted to be right by the studio around the clock for rehearsal work, and he seemed quite comfortable there. So I also made him the rehearsal manager for new talent."

Bob's promotion to a formal position of authority at Studio One inadvertently accelerated the departure of the Wailers' female backup support. Cherry Green (whose last name was formerly believed to be Smith), a girlfriend of Kelso's who provided the vocal counterpoint for Beverly's backing harmonics, was ultimately dismissed. But the more talented Kelso resigned.

"I was with the group about three years," says Kelso. "I stopped singin' because of Bob's attitude about the music. He was a very nice guy, but I didn't like certain things. We would be practicing a song like 'Lonesome Feelings,' or 'It Hurts to Be Alone,' 'There She Goes'—so many songs I don't remember them all—and if you make a mistake he would jump down on you and be very tough, because that's the way he was taught. But I was too quiet, somber and shy, and I'd start crying and say, 'Oh, I'm gonna leave.'

"Sometimes I would cry, and he would apologize and say, 'Oh, Beverly, you know how I am,' and I'd go back in Mr. Dodd's studio and start singin' again. But the attitude was hard to take, and I left by 1965."

Bunny Wailer (as Livingston has called himself since 1976) confirms Kelso's account. "Things were getting strictly professional," he explains, "an' Beverly an' Cherry couldn't cope. At the same time, the rest of the Wailers had people who *we* must learn to keep up with, like our musicians, the Skatalites, who backed us up on most of the ska recordings."

There was another factor influencing Kelso's parting with the Wailers: their frequent use of ganja in the studio. If Beverly felt stifled by the rude boy air of the Wailers' control room, she nearly suffocated from the billowing spiffs that often surrounded her at the studio microphones.

"I didn't like them smoking when we'd go into the studio!" she confesses sheepishly. "It's air-tight there in the studio, and with all that smoke you'd take a deep breath and choke and start coughing. And they'd get mad and say, 'Oh, it's just because *you* don't smoke! This is the thing to do!' So I couldn't support it—and I couldn't quarrel about it."

Although Kelso bowed out of the Wailers, she remained an avid fan, haunting the Kingston shops for their latest releases, while marveling at their pioneering skill and popular outreach as they evolved from a ska vocal attraction, to a top rock steady band, and finally into *the* global reggae force. In 1979, just as Bob and company were unveiling the *Survival* album, Beverly migrated from Jamaica to the States, initially settling, appropriately enough, in the Jamaica section of Queens in New York City.

In time, she was drawn to a circle of Brooklyn-based friends (including a relocated Cherry Green) who were active in the urban reggae scene, and she did occasional vocal sessions. "But *just* backup singing," she emphasizes, laughing. "For a while, I was thinking about going back to school to get some music and voice training, but I went back to school and did something else more practical for me instead of that."

Nonetheless, Kelso says she "still thinks of Trench Town and Bob and those days—I loved them," and she doesn't want to convey the idea that her qualms about the Wailers studio *modus* ever diminished either her own professionalism or her deep respect for Bob Marley's artistic aims.

"These things we've been discussing here might just happen on a certain day," she summarizes with a chuckle. "But then whenever Bob would come to work next in the studio, he would say sweetly, 'Beverly, I need help from you on this verse and song and things!' And he could *always* depend on me to help the goal."

Appendix 3

"RASTA DON'T WORK FE NUH CIA!": DECLASSIFIED CIA AND STATE DEPARTMENT COMMUNIQUÉS

What follows are complete copies of two Central Intelligence Agency/State Department communiqués cited in chapter 17 ("Time Will Tell"). First requested from the CIA via registered mail received on September 13, 1982, these cables were declassified (or excised) as per my written requests to the CIA during 1982–83 under the Freedom of Information Act (5 U.S.C. 52). The documents were among the materials (telegrams, articles, etc.) mailed to me by the CIA for the expressed use of research for *Catch a Fire: The Life of Bob Marley*.

The first document, a two-page Department of State telex, is readable in its entirety. The second document, a three-page U.S. government cable from the American Embassy in Kingston to the State Department in Washington, D.C., was only partially declassified, with the censored portions blacked out and remaining confidential.

Former Jamaican Prime Minister Michael Manley repeatedly charged that the CIA had sought to destabilize Jamaican society during his left-wing regimes in the 1970s and late 1980s to early 1990s. Manley focused in particular on 1976, the year of the assassination attempt on Bob Marley, as well as three attempts on Manley's own life (July 14, September 23, December 15), plus incidents in which shots were fired at PNP activists D. K. Duncan and Hugh Small. In June 1976, in an address before Jamaica's House of Representatives, Manley had released documents and tapes seized during an investigation of an opposition (Jamaican Labor Party) candidate who had been a Security Forces officer; the tapes were secretly monitored copies of Security Forces transmissions, and the documents described a proposed counterinsurgence plan based in the parish of St. Ann (Bob Marley's birthplace) involving several hundred men and arms, code-named "Werewolf." As Manley later noted pointedly, despite heated refutations in 1976 from the U.S. government and the Edward Seaga–led JLP—which was alleged to have been in league with the CIA—neither the existence of the "Werewolf" documents nor the tapes has "ever been explained."

In his 1982 memoirs, *Jamaica: Struggle in the Periphery*, with regard to what he'd termed a "reign of terror" in 1976, Manley asserted, "They deny it to this day but I prefer the judgments of the heads of the Jamaica Security Forces at the time. Police, army, and Special Branch [internal security police] concurred that the CIA was actively behind the events. My common sense left me with no option but to agree." In July 1980, the editors of *Covert Action Information Bulletin* held a press conference in Jamaica at which they released the names of fifteen alleged CIA employees in the Kingston U.S. Embassy.

Department of State

DECLASSIFIED

CONFIDENTIAL

AN: D760451-1141

CONFIDENTIAL

PAGE 01 KINGST 05317 071423Z
50 46
ACTION ARA-10

INFO OCT-01 ISO-00 CIAE-00 DODE-00 PM-04 H-01 INR-07 L-03
NSAE-00 NSC-05 PA-01 PRS-01 SP-02 SS-15 USIA-06 CU-02
CHA-02 /060 W
------------------ 027957
R 071316Z DEC 76
FM AMEMBASSY KINGSTON
TO SECSTATE WASHDC 3323
INFO AMEMBASSY BRIDGETOWN
AMEMBASSY GEORGETOWN
AMEMBASSY NASSAU
AMEMBASSY PORT

DEPARTMENT OF STATE
REVIEWED BY EC 3/14/83
RDS/ OR XDS
TS AUTH.
ENDORSE
DECLASSIFIED
RELEASABLE
FOI EXEMPTIONS

C O N F I D E N T I A L KINGSTON 5317

E.O. 11652: GDS
TAGS: PINT, JM
SUBJECT: REGGAE STAR SHOT: MOTIVE PROBABLY POLITICAL

1. VIOLENCE IN JAMAICA GAINED FRESH PROMINENCE ON FRIDAY, DECEMBER 3 WHEN BOB MARLEY, POPULAR JAMAICAN REGGAE STAR, WAS SHOT AND WOUNDED. THE INCIDENT, IN WHICH THREE ASSOCIATES OF MARLEY'S WERE ALSO WOUNDED, OCCURRED AT THE POP STAR'S HOME NEAR THE COMPOUND WHICH HOUSES THE RESIDENCES OF THE GOVERNOR GENERAL AND THE PRIME MINISTER. THE ASSAILANTS HAVE NOT YET BEEN IDENTIFIED, BUT CLEARLY HIT MARLEY AND HIS ASSOCIATES IN A PRE-MEDITATED ATTACK.

2. THE MARLEY SHOOTING HAS CAPTURED EVEN MORE ATTENTION THAN THE EGGAE ARTIST'S POPULARITY MIGHT SUGGEST WOULD HAVE BEEN THE CASE. IMMEDIATELY BEFOE THE SHOOTING, MARLEY AND MEMBERS OF HIS GROUP HAD BEEN REHEARSING FOR A FREE, PUBLIC CONCERT SCHEDULED FOR A PARK IN DOWNTOWN KINGSTON ON SUNDAY, DECEMBER 5. THE CONCERT, SPONSORED BY THE CULTURAL SECTION OF THE PRIME MINISTER'S OFFICE, WAS HELD DESPITE THE INCIDENT, WITH MARLEY PARTICIPATING -- THOUGH FIVE HOURS LATE.

3. THE CONCERT WAS PART OF PEOPLES NATIONAL PARTY
CONFIDENTIAL

DECLASSIFIED

CONFIDENTIAL

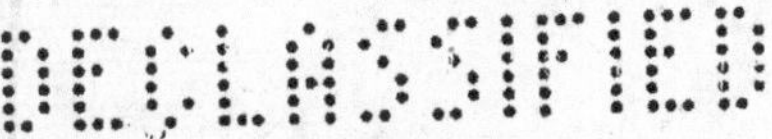

CONFIDENTIAL

CONFIDENTIAL

PAGE 02 KINGST 05317 071423Z

(PNP) ELECTION CAMPAIGN, AND WAS SCHEDULED TO COINCICE WITH THE JAMAICA LABOUR PARTY'S (JLP) RELEASE OF ITS LONG-AWAITED MANIFESTO -- TO THE DETRIMENT OF NEWS TIME AND PUBLIC ATTENTION FOR THE LATTER.

4. RUMORS ABOUND AS TO THE MOTIVATION FOR THE SHOOTING. SOME SEE THE INCIDENT AS AN ATTEMPT BY JLP GUNMEN TO HALT THE CONCERT WHICH WOULD FEATURE THE "POLITICALLY PROGRESSIVE" MUSIC OF MARLEY AND OTHER REGGAE STARS. OTHERS SEE IT AS A DEEP-LAID PLOT TO CREATE A PROGRESSIVE, YOUTHFUL JAMAICAN MARTYR -- TO THE BENEFIT OF THE PNP. THOSE HOLDING THE LATTER VIEW NOTE THAT OF THE FOUR PERSONS SHOT, THREE OF THEM -- INCLUDING MARLEY -- SUFFERED ONLY MINOR WOUNDS. TOO, THE ASSAILANTS MAY SIMPLY BE ENEMIES OF MARLEY OR ONE OF HIS ASSOCIATES. WHATEVER THE CAUSE, THE INCIDENT WILL E WITH US FOR SOME TIME, GIVEN MARLEY'S POPULARITY. CONTRIBUTING TO THIS VIEW IS THE FACT THAT, WHILE THE NEWSPAPERS HAVE GIVEN THE SHOOTING PROMINENT COVERAGE, THE REPORTING HAS BEEN CURIOUSLY UNINFORMATIVE.
GERARD

CONFIDENTIAL

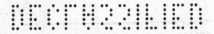

CONFIDENTIAL

EXCISE

DECLASSIFIED

AIRGRAM 36

CONFIDENTIAL 22

TO: DEPARTMENT OF STATE

INFO: AMEMBASSIES BRIDGETOWN, GEORGETOWN, LONDON, NASSAU, OTTAWA, PORT OF SPAIN

FROM: AMEMBASSY KINGSTON DATE: 2/28/81

E.O. 11652: GDS 4/28/87 (FORBES, J) OR-P
TAGS: PDIP, PINT, PLPR, JM
SUBJECT: Jamaican Governor General Knighted

REF:

1. (U) Jamaica's Governor General, Florizel Glasspole, was knighted by Queen Elizabeth II on April 17, four weeks after Prime Minister Edward Seaga had announced the Government of Jamaica's decision to allow Jamaicans to accept foreign honors.

2. (U) Seaga's announcement touched off a wave of speculation in the media that the Governor General would be knighted, and local reaction indicates that most Jamaicans are pleased with the honor. (The Governor General received 150 congratulatory messages and cables on the first day after the announcement and many more on subsequent days.) Government members in the House of Representatives paid tribute to and congratulated the Governor General when the House met on April 22.

3. (U) At the same time that Jamaica House released the news of the Governor General's knighthood, it announced that Jamaican reggae superstar Bob Marley who is being treated for cancer in the Federal Republic of Germany, had been awarded the Order of

CONFIDENTIAL

POL:CSkinner/JDForbes 4/24/81 POL:JDForbes

DCM:RTHaverkamp

MARLEY, Bob

= JAMAICA

DEPARTMENT OF STATE A/CDC/MR
REVIEWED BY T. BROWN DATE 4/11/83
RDS or XDS EXT. DATE
TS AUTH. REASON(S)
ENDORSE EXISTING MARKINGS
DECLASSIFIED RELEASABLE
RELEASE DENIED in part
PA or FOI EXEMPTIONS B1, A5

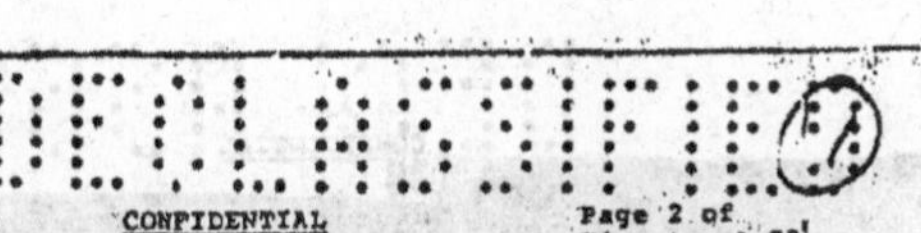

E
B1, A

CONFIDENTIAL

Page 2 of
Kingston A-22

Merit, Jamaica's third highest honor. In responding to the government's tribute to the Governor General, the Opposition moved to congratulate Marley at the same time and allowed itself to be maneuvered into a position of not paying tribute to the popular Governor General.

4. (U) Glasspole was named Governor General, or representative of the Queen as Head of State, in 1973 by the previous People's National Party (PNP) government led by former Prime Minister Michael Manley. He was reconfirmed in that position last November after the Jamaica Labour Party's (JLP) victory in the October 1980 general election. Glasspole has a long career as a trade union leader, prominent member of parliament, and minister of education and labor for the PNP, and his reconfirmation by the JLP was a tribute not only to his popularity but also to the fairness with which he executed the office of Governor General, especially during the 1980 election campaign.

BF

5. (U) Queen Elizabeth conferred the honor of Knight, Grand Cross of the Order of St. Michael and St. George (G.C.M.G.), on the Governor General. He already holds Jamaica's highest honor, the Order of the Nation (O.N.), which is conferred only upon governors general, and he is the Commander of the Order of Distinction (C.D.). In January of 1973, he was awarded the Order of Andres Bello (first class) by the President of Venezuela. According to a 1968 parliamentary decision, Jamaican orders take precedence over the comparable United Kingdom Imperial and Commonwealth Orders and other foreign orders. Thus, according to Jamaican protocol, the correct manner of styling the Governor General is now "The Most Honorable Sir Florizel Glasspole, O.N., G.C.M.G., C.D." His wife, the former Ina Josephine Kinlock, now is called "Lady Glasspole."

6. (U) Seaga's decision to allow Jamaicans to accept foreign honors reverses a trend away from imperial and commonwealth practice begun in 1968 when a bipartisan parliamentary committee under JLP Prime Minister Hugh Shearer recommended that only the governor general be eligible for UK honors. In June 1973 the new PNP government acted on another bipartisan parliamentary recommendation and instituted the Order of the Nation for the governor general, and subsequently it followed a policy of allowing only awards of Jamaican honors. In making his announcement of a reversal of this policy at the March 20 <u>Daily Gleaner</u> awards banquet, Prime Minister Seaga justified his decision by stating that Jamaican awards had now acquired so much prestige that they no longer needed to be protected from competition.

B1, A5

CONFIDENTIAL

12

DECLASSIFIED

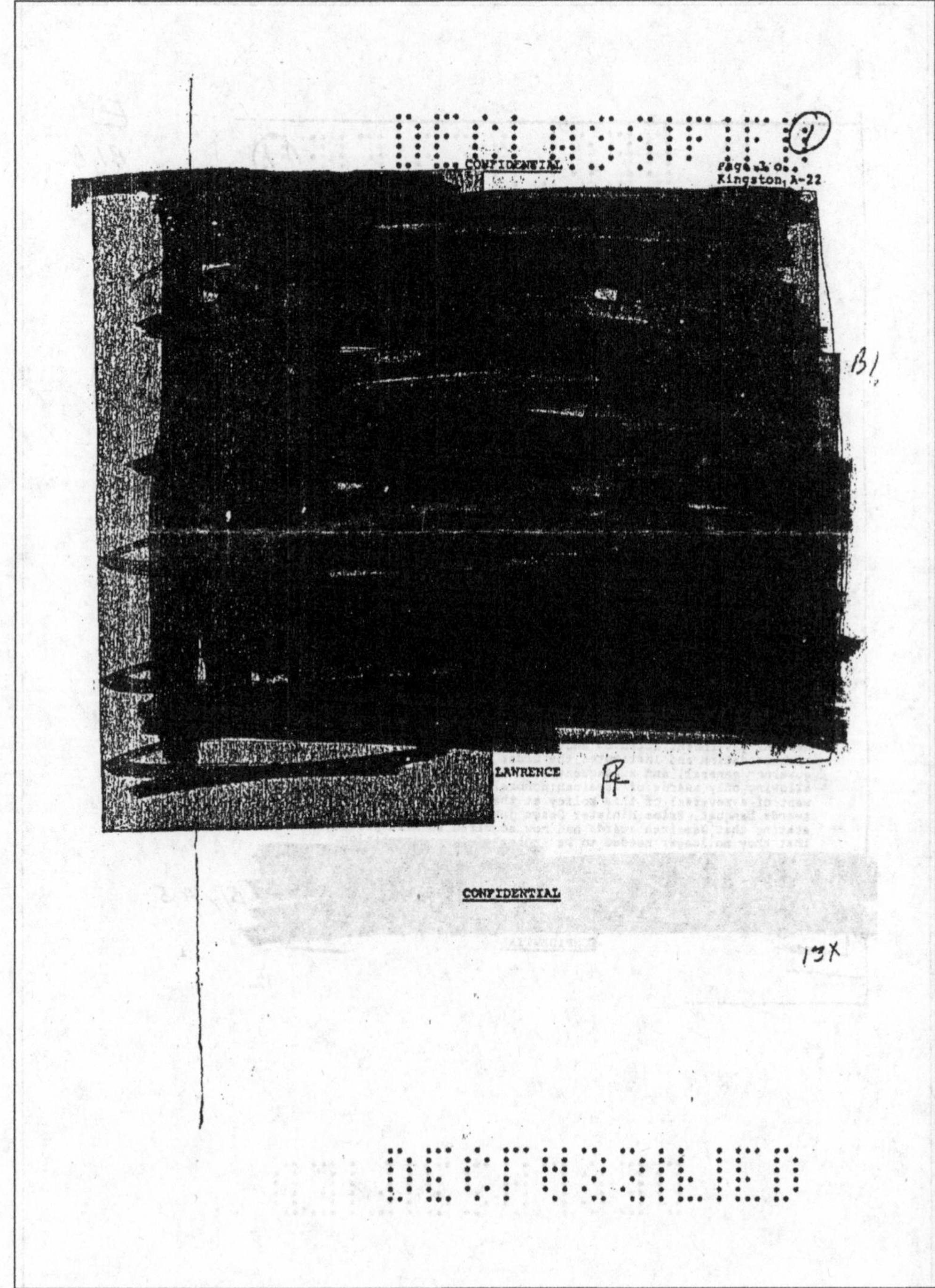

CONFIDENTIAL

Page 10
Kingston, A-22

LAWRENCE

CONFIDENTIAL

Appendix 4

JUDGE NOT (BEFORE YOU JUDGE YOURSELF): *CAYMAN MUSIC, INC. V. THE BOB MARLEY ESTATE*

Excerpts from the author's testimony in the 1987 trial proceedings of *Cayman Music, Inc.*, v. *Rita Marley, as Administatrix of the Estate of Robert Nesta Marley, Tuff Gong Music, Bob Marley Music Ltd., Almo Music Corp., Rondor Music Corp., Island Records, Inc., Atlantic Recording Corporation, etc. et al.*

As indicated in footnotes to chapter 17 of this book, the author was asked to testify in this court action filed in 1984 by Bob Marley's onetime manager and publisher, Danny Sims, who claimed that Marley had concealed the authorship of dozens of his songs from 1973 to 1976 in order to avoid his contractual obligations to Sims. The defendants argued that Sims had waited until Marley was dead to file his suit, that Marley's actions were common knowledge, easily discoverable by the plaintiff during the period before the statute of limitations on such claims expired and that Sims had mishandled his contracts with Bob during this period and had no rights to any of the songs in question.

Sims asserted in his filing documents that he had no knowledge of Marley's actions regarding this body of songwriting until he read Stephen Davis's book *Bob Marley*, as well as Timothy White's *Catch a Fire: The Life of Bob Marley*, citing material in the latter book as the ultimate motivation for his legal action.

The statute of limitations issue was at the core of the court battle; that is, what did Sims know and when did he know it? Many readers of *Catch a Fire* have wondered what my testimony was on this subject during the trial and how I learned of or helped publicize the "common knowledge" of these practices by Marley, because this information has not heretofore been published in editions of this book.

Danny Sims's New York legal counsel, Stewart Levy (a partner in the Fifth Avenue law firm of Parcher Arisohn & Hayes), was most aggressive in pursuing me for a deposition for the case. I was voluntarily deposed on June 25, 1986, at the firm's offices, with

Marley Estate counsel Peter Herbert on hand. During the lengthy deposition, portions of *Catch a Fire* were read aloud, as well as portions of my January 1976 *Crawdaddy* magazine article; portions of my verbatim September 1975 interview with Marley—now contained in the book *Rock Lives: Profiles & Interviews* (Henry Holt/Owl Books, New York)—and portions of my review of the album *Chances Are* in the March 18, 1982, issue of *Rolling Stone*.

Levy strenuously followed a line of questioning to prove that Sims could not possibly have learned of Marley's use of pseudonyms until reading my book, despite his long association with Bob Marley, his knowledge of Jamaican culture and the fact that he spent the majority of his time there from 1961 to 1984.

At one point, in referring to my four-day 1975 trip to Kingston to interview Bob—as well as the passage in the "Riddim Track" chapter of *Catch a Fire* that states, "in order to protect some of his publishing interests in later years, [Marley] reportedly made cunning arrangements to credit any of his songs to hangers-on and ghetto chums"—Levy posed three extremely pointed questions to me:

> Q: Did any of the people you spoke to about the reportedly "cunning arrangement" ever say that they had informed, or Bob Marley had informed, Danny Sims all about it?
>
> A: It was described as . . . it was my perception, in those first two days, that it was common knowledge and a kind of ghetto game.
>
> Q: But you are talking to me, Stewart Levy, a thirty-three-year-old chubby New York Jewish lawyer. OK? Now, if someone like myself were down there, and to the best of your opinion, would these people, if they knew I was representing Danny Sims, have given me absolute details about this cunning arrangement so I could report it to the proper authorities?
>
> A: Yes. On the record, you are talking to a skinny Irish Catholic kid from Paterson, New Jersey, who wore white bucks for the better part of those [four] days down in Kingston and people were saying to me, "My, you look like Prince Charles," and at first I thought it was a joke, but it was their perception. At the time I think Prince Charles may have been in the Navy. People in the ghettos of Kingston take you as they find you. I was a stranger to those people. . . .
>
> Q: If Bob Marley had put together this reportedly cunning arrangement to protect his publishing interest, was it your opinion that he was shrewd enough and tough enough to implement the arrangement?
>
> A: It was an ongoing thing. It was not necessarily the "arrangement" type of publishing. It was the way those around him were living their lives. . . . I would say you couldn't get to Bob Marley unless you understood the nature of him to begin with. Bob Marley was not an inaccessible personality. So to go and get him to have any arrangement of any kind, business or personal, you had to learn through that labyrinth his nature to begin with. . . . Because you couldn't have gone into the bush or the ghettos of Kingston or even up to Hope Road and secured his time without first learning the process of getting to him. Everybody around him knew how to get to Bob Marley because they had learned how to get to Bob Marley. I never met a naive person connected with Bob Marley.

Following further review of my files after the deposition, on March 15, 1987, I voluntarily submitted to counsel for both sides a copy of my deposition combining a small number of amendments, plus supporting documents—the most important ones detailing or underscoring a telephone exchange and subsequent in-person encounter I had with Danny Sims in 1976 in his New York offices. As I wrote in my cover letter to the attorneys:

It was a brief telephone conversation in the late summer of 1976 to arrange an interview about his relationship with Bob Marley, while I was Managing Editor of *Crawdaddy*. Indeed I introduced myself on the phone as the person who had written the recent *Crawdaddy* cover story about Bob Marley, of which he said he was well aware. As I now recall, Mr. Sims also noted that an artist with whom he had dealings, Gil Scott-Heron, was a sometime writer for *Crawdaddy*, which of course he was. Mr. Sims asked me to come to the midtown offices of Cayman Music for an afternoon appointment, which I did.

After sitting in Mr. Sims' waiting room with his secretary for approximately 90 minutes (I recall there were Gil-Scott Heron Arista Records posters on the wall), with her periodically buzzing in to inform him of my presence, he left the office, addressing me as he departed only to say he changed his mind about speaking to me about Bob Marley. At the time of that scheduled but aborted interview, I was aware of Marley's general writing habits and apparent use of pseudonyms.

That was the sole personal contact I can ever remember having with Danny Sims.

With these and other depositions and discovery materials from such witnesses as Sims; soccer champion and longtime Bob Marley friend, manager and associate Alan "Skilly" Cole; Ira B. Selsky, vice president of business affairs for Almo Music and Rondor Music; prominent Rastafarian leader and former Bob Marley manager Mortimer Planno, aka Planner; Jamaican former manager Don Taylor, and Jeri Spencer, former executive vice president of administration for Copyright Services Bureau, a private publishing and licensing agency associated with Cayman Music, the protracted lawsuit proceeded to trial.

The Hon. Elliot Wilk of the Supreme Court of New York threw out most of the causes of action in the suit because of the statute of limitations on such actions but set a trial date of November 1987 to determine if the causes of action regarding misrepresentation and conspiracy to defraud against the Marley Estate were time-barred.

On November 10, 1987, I voluntarily appeared—that is, without subpoena—before Judge Wilk and a jury of six and two alternates in the Supreme Court of the State of New York at 60 Centre Street, Manhattan, to testify in the case of Cayman Music, Inc. against Rita Marley et al. Present were Sims, Marley Estate administrator Louis Byles of the Jamaica Mutual Security Bank and Trust Co., Ltd., Jamaican attorney George Desnoes, Taylor, Cole and others, including plaintiff trial counsel Levy and defendants' trial attorney William M. Thomas, Jr.

What follows are excerpts from the official court records of my lengthy testimony on the stand. Attorneys for the plaintiff and defendants are not identified in the questioning to avoid prejudicing the reader.

Examination of Timothy White

[Mr. Thomas has the aforementioned page 23 of *Catch A Fire—The Life of Bob Marley* admitted for evidence as Defendant's Exhibit H-1.]

Q: Why were you in Jamaica in 1975?

A: I was a reporter for the Associated Press at the time. I was assigned by *Crawdaddy* magazine to do a cover story on Bob Marley and the other reggae personalities.

Q: What was the subject matter or purpose of the article at you went down there to write?

A: The purpose of the article was really to introduce Bob Marley and his music and his culture to an American audience.

Q: Now you stated that the statement that was quoted in Mr. Sims' affidavit was based upon information that you got while you were in Jamaica on this three to four day trip. What was the specific nature of that information that you gained while you were down in Jamaica in 1975?

A: I should explain, in going down there to interview Bob Marley, he lived in a kind of a compound, you'd call it. It was a mansion, an old Jamaican great house, a mansion, and there was a social scene around it. And so when I went over to meet Bob, you know, it was a common thing, as I realized immediately, now and then, as time went on, to sort of talk with other people.

I mean, it was a very festive kind of social scene. And in talking with Bob, I talked with him for a while, and I would go and talk with other people, you know. At one point later on, I did a formal interview, but I was introduced to the other people that he worked with, his musicians, his friends, and aides-de-camp, his managerial kind of people and also to people, in particular—I'm answering your question—one man, his name was Jeff Walker, he was a head of publicity for Island Records, and the other was Dickie Jobson.

He was described by Bob as one of his sort of long-time friends, kind of a managerial person too and a liaison between himself and Island Records and other record companies and things.

In a car ride Jeff Walker and I took on those first days in Kingston, we went to Hellshire Beach, which is a beach outside of Kingston, and on the way Jeff Walker asked Dickie Jobson, you know, to "explain all sorts of things to Tim. Explain Bob and what he'd be up to lately."

And I had a lot of questions too. Who is that person I just met? Who else is in the band, you know, for this record that Bob is working on now?

This kind of thing. And in the course of that, Dickie explained in greater detail something that was sort of manifest from the time I first started to ask Bob about songs and other people around him, and that was the fact that a number of the songs that he had written, you know, in the last few years, though they weren't under his name, were written by him, and it was described then and afterwards, as a kind of game.

It was an open thing, you know, and—it was spoken of by Jeff Walker and by Dickie Jobson, it was spoken of by other people, you know, in the days to come when I was down there, that were in that Hope Road kind of complex.

So, in other words, I learned—it was just a kind of a wrinkle in Bob's career that this was something that he had done.

Q: I gather from what you said, that you did not ask about whether Bob was writing this or that song, but it was something that Jeff asked Dickie Jobson to tell you about?

A: It came up in an organic way. We were just, you know, talking about this and that, and things that Bob was working on at the time. He was recording the song I believe called—I mean, he was recording a song called "Jah Live" at the time, I think, and so it didn't come about based upon, you know, any intense questioning by me.

It was all just discussed, you know, in terms of a general understanding of what Bob was up to these days, what he had been up to, you know, and I pressed it a little further and just asked a bit more to understand what was going on, because there were names being bandied about, and I didn't know who they were, you know. I didn't know who Ford was, V. Ford, you know.

Different people were being mentioned, so in the process of just trying to get a footing as a reporter it was explained to me very openly, very casually, you know, with actually a laugh and a smile.

Q: Now, was this whole issue of song ownership by Bob something that you went down to do some research on?

A: No. Actually at the time I had no particular interest in it. I mean, there was so much to find out about Bob Marley. What I was mostly interested in was finding out about his background, where he came from, where he was born.

You see, because I had West Indian friends as a kid, I knew all about Rastafarianism, Bob's religion, which was the thing most written about. His religion felt Haile Selassie, the Ethiopian ruler, was a living God, but I had all that background, so I was interested in interviewing Bob Marley the same way I would interview Elton John for *Crawdaddy* or Eric Clapton, someone like that.

I wanted to establish his background for historical purposes, because I felt strongly that this was something that hadn't been done, and it bothered me. You know, I felt that people weren't interviewing Bob Marley the way he should be interviewed, you know. So it was in my interest to start to document the history of his recording career and who he was as a person, where did he come from, you know, his family background, you know, Jamaican culture as impacted upon him, as he was influenced by it, history of the Jamaican recording industry, that kind of thing.

Q: Was this information a closely guarded secret?

A: I learned about it the first day was there. You know, the sun hadn't set on the first day, and this was spoken of and bandied about.

THE COURT: Sorry, which information?

THE WITNESS: Oh, about Bob's songwriting credits being shared with his ghetto chums and hangers-on and things.

Q: Now, Mr. White, did you ever try to confirm the information that you received down there with respect to Bob's songwriting practices?

A: I never spoke to him directly about it, but I would speak to him about, you know, particular songs. I'd say, when did you come to write this song? And how did you come to write that song? On that particular trip, he played me a song that he was working on called "Children Playing in the Streets." He sat under a tree on the front lawn of his home and played a lyric fragment for me, you know, a verse or so of it. . . .

I wasn't—I was more interested in the nuts and bolts of how these songs were written, the experience, organic background to them, that kind of thing.

I didn't get into the publishing aspects of it, and, indeed, I've never gone into the publishing aspects of anybody that I've ever interviewed. . . . I'm not a business writer.

Q: Now, when you returned [from] Jamaica in September of 1975, did you make any further inquiry about Bob's practices or authorship?

A: . . . Around the summer of 1976, I called Cayman Music which, you know, was the publishing—one of the publishing companies that Bob had an affiliation with previous to Island Records, and I had heard Danny Sims, his name mentioned, and so I called their offices, which I believe were on West 57th Street, and called to see if I could come over and talk to him, interview him, you know, and just find out what all this was all about, what Bob's career had been like prior to Island Records.

[At this juncture, Mr. Thomas moved to have the *Crawdaddy* article "Bob Marley and the Reggae Rebellion" admitted to the Court as Defendant's Exhibit 1.]

Q: What did Mr. Sims say?

A: As I said, "Hi," in essence, "Hello, my name is Timothy White, *Crawdaddy*." He said he was familiar with the magazine, and "I know about your writing about Bob." . . . I remember distinctly that he said, "So you want to talk about Bob Marley." That's one quote I remember. Then he said, "Come on up." We set a date for the near future.

Q: And so what happened next after you set a date?

A: I went up to the office . . . and there was a receptionist there, and I sat and waited for quite a while, for about an hour and a half. . . . So I sat there and waited and there was a receptionist there, a black woman, and from time to time, I would get up and ask, "Is this going to take much longer," or whatever. . . . And then, at one point, Mr. Sims came out of the office and walked past me and sort of left the reception area and went out to the elevators and things, and on the way he just said, "I changed my mind, I changed my mind."

I almost didn't realize who it was or whatever. It was an instantaneous thing, him leaving and just going past me. He just said, "I changed my mind, I changed my mind." That was it. Like his hand was in the air, like a quick dismissal thing. The whole thing didn't take but a few seconds and that was it.

Q: Didn't there reach a time when you became the token Caucasian journalist who could get at Bob Marley and get stories that no one else could?

A: No. There were a lot of white writers who had good relationships with Bob Marley. . . .

Q: Is it your contention that in 1976, when you tried to meet with Danny Sims, you were going to tell Mr. Sims that Bob Marley was defrauding him out of all his publishing? Were you going to tell him that?

A: I had no direct knowledge of anything. . . . I have never seen a contract of Bob Marley's of any kind. I was there to interview him about his role in Bob's career.

Q: So if there ever came a time when you learned and had knowledge of Bob Marley's fraud, wouldn't you have gone to my client, or at least written him a letter. . . .

A: It's not my role as a reporter, but it would have made a good article.

Q: But you never wrote that article, did you? . . .

A: I might have, if I had gotten an interview with Danny Sims.

Examination of Danny Sims

Q: You just stated that you had not read prior to this trial the article by Timothy White in the magazine named *Crawdaddy*; is that accurate?

A: By Tim White in *Crawdaddy*? No, I didn't read that article.

Q: So when Timothy said when he spoke to you and you told him you had read it, Timothy White was telling a lie?

A: I never spoke to Timothy White to my knowledge.

Q: Timothy White was never in your office waiting for an interview with you?

A: I think he was. But I never spoke to him. . . .

Q: Mr. Sims, also in your affidavit, you stated that the thing that came to light that led you to know that this fraud had been committed were the two books by Mr. [Stephen] Davis and Mr. White, did you not?

A: Yes, somebody said that. . . .

Q: Mr. Sims, paragraph 27 of that affidavit. Do you not quote from Mr. Davis' book: *Bob Marley: The Definitive Biography of Reggae's Greatest Star*. . . . While almost all the songs are undoubtedly Bob's, he was still signed by Danny Sims as a songwriter, and he wanted to avoid paying Cayman Music the major portion of his composer's royalty." You quoted from that book, did you not?

A: Yeah.

Q: And also in paragraph 29 [of your affidavit from Mr. White's book, *Catch a Fire—The Life of Bob Marley* . . . you also quoted from that book that this brought to light to you where Mr. White stated:

"In order to protect some of his publishing interests in later years, . . . reportedly made cunning arrangements to credit many of his songs to hangers-on and ghetto chums." You quoted that passage too, did you not?

A: Yes.

Q: You also stated in here that these books were published, first published abroad in 1983, did you not?

A: I might have said that . . .

Q: Isn't it a fact that with respect to Mr. Davis, that in March of 1982, you had a lengthy interview with him, did you not?

A: Yes.

Q: And isn't it a fact that during that interview you gave Mr. Davis the information that led him to write those pages in the book you quoted, did you not?

A: I don't—don't think so. To use some of the things that I said in his book, that is his right as a journalist.

Q: Isn't it a fact, Mr. Sims, that a tape was made of that conversation that you had, that interview with Mr. Davis?

A: He might have taped the conversation. I don't remember.

Q: Isn't it a fact that you also asked him to send you a copy of the tape so you can confirm the accuracy of the statements if in case it was going to be in print?

A: I don't remember.

Q: Isn't it a fact that he sent you a copy of the tape?

A: I don't remember . . .

Q: And didn't you tell Mr. Davis: "But let me tell you something. We just found out we're going to get ready to go to court. We're going to take all the songs back that they wrote under pseudonyms"; didn't you tell Mr. Davis that in March of 1982?

A: I don't remember telling him that. But certainly that's my intention if I could have found an irregularity.

[On November 19, 1987, a tape subpoenaed from Stephen Davis was played for the exclusive courtroom scrutiny of Judge Wilk. Mr. Sims, also present, was furnished with a transcript in order to read along with the tape.]

Q: Mr. Sims, did you recognize the voices that you just heard on that tape?

A: Yes . . . One voice sounded like me.

Q: And do you recognize the other voice?

A: No.

Q: Would it help if we played some additional portions of the tape?

A: No. I met this gentleman one time. I would never recognize his voice again, and there is nothing you could do to make me recognize his voice.

Q: Mr. Sims, you said you only met Mr. Davis once?

A: I don't remember.

Q: You just said you only met once?

A: I said I don't recall how many times I met him. I remember meeting him once . . .

Q: Mr. Sims, that was your voice, correct?

A: I think so.

[It was established through repeated playings of the tape that the voice Sims identified as his own is making or replying to statements he had earlier testified he'd made to Davis in Davis's March 1982 interview with him. Sims's counsel, Mr. Levy, also concedes the voice is Sims's own. Therefore, the Court allows the tape to be admitted over Levy's objections as Defendants' Evidence U, with the transcript of the tape admitted as Defendants' Evidence V. The tape dated March 31, 1982, whose quotations and context were not previously disclosed in the text of Davis's book, is played in open court:

DAVIS: In all these years afterward, he would try to hide his provenance of his songs. In other words, he would give songs on his album that were obviously his to, say, Rita Marley or Alan Cole or Leghorn Cogill.

SIMS: Or Bob Marley wrote under pseudonyms. They did that "No Woman No Cry," he put Vincent Ford on that. . . . But let me tell you something. We just found out, we're just ready to go to court. We're going to take all the songs back that they wrote under pseudonyms.

DAVIS: In other words, all this stuff that's credited to Rita, all this stuff that's credited to Vincent Ford, all this stuff that's credited to Leghorn Coghill and Alan Cole and R. Marley, that's in reality . . .

SIMS: Bob Marley.

After the tape has been played, the court resumes its questioning of Sims.]

Q: At the time you gave the interview did you know Bob Marley's fraud against you?
A: No . . .
Q: But at that time did you have any knowledge about being defrauded?
A: None at all.
Q: At that time or approximately at that time did you speak to any of your lawyers about bringing a lawsuit?
A: Yes.
Q: Did you have any evidence sufficient to bring a lawsuit?
A: No, no more than I had all along, and I was investigating all along.

The Verdict

In his summation before Judge Wilk and the jury, Cayman attorney Stewart Levy stated that "far from Cayman Music being tardy in bringing a suit, the fact of the matter is that it's almost miraculous that Cayman is here even today." Levy also stated, "You heard Timothy White, an author of the Bob Marley biography, say that in his view Bob Marley's songs were endemic to the culture he grew up in, and it would not surprise him at all that other people in the ghetto wrote those songs."

(The actual testimony, in answer to Levy's direct question on Bob's songs—"They came out of Marley's life experience?"—was: "They are derived from ghetto colloquialisms and many things, from the folklore-isms and things like that, sayings he grew up with, and also he wrote about the experiences of his friends, getting to know his friends and the kind of social milieu that they moved in both in the ghetto and elsewhere.")

Levy argued, "Bob Marley's songs are not the type of songs that Andrew Lloyd Webber would write. . . . Basically, it's a reggae beat with simple lyrics."

Continuing his summation, Levy stated, "Who is the neutral witness? Timothy White. He's very neutral. He presents himself as a Bob Marley expert. He built his career on Bob Marley. He has written numerous articles on Bob Marley. You heard me ask him, 'You are never afraid down there?' He said, 'Well, I got afraid in '76 when there was martial law in Jamaica and in the '80s.' Did he ever confront anyone about [fraud]? No. Did he ever tell Mr. Sims about it? No. 'Do you have any hard evidence of it?' 'No.'

"Mr. White," Levy continued, "was invited down there by the record company, wined and dined. He wanted to do a big national media thing on it, the national media. Big break for him. One thing for White to have access and another thing for Mr. Sims.

"Now," said Levy, "the judge will instruct you on what reasonable diligence means. But consider, is it reasonable to expect that someone is going to read a ten-page article in an obscure rock and roll magazine called *Crawdaddy*?"

Regarding Stephen Davis's information from Sims, Levy concluded, "Why did [Sims] wait for him to publish it? One thing for Mr. Sims to shoot the breeze with Mr. Davis. But what about Mr. Davis publishing—undoubtedly there was some hanky-panky going on? Well . . . if Mr. Sims read it in the book, don't you think it's logical for Sims to say, 'Gee, maybe there's more than suspicion? Maybe Davis found something. Maybe I ought to check it out again.'"

After weighing these arguments and the questions concerning what Levy himself

SUPREME COURT OF THE STATE OF NEW YORK
COUNTY OF NEW YORK

---------------------------------------x

CAYMAN MUSIC, INC.,
Plaintiff, :
-against- : 24020/84
RITA MARLEY, as Administratrix of the :
Estate of Robert Nesta Marley, et al.,
:
Defendant,
:
-against-
DANNY SIMS,
:
Additional Defendant
on Counterclaim. :
---------------------------------------x

Deposition of TIMOTHY WHITE, held at the offices of Parcher Arisohn & Hayes, Esqs., 500 Fifth Avenue, New York, New York, on the 25th day of June, 1986, at 10:35 o'clock a.m., pursuant to Subpoena, before Andrew L. Pustay, a Notary Public of the State of New York.

chose to characterize as "hanky-panky" involving his client, the jury rendered its final verdicts on the remaining actions of the Cayman lawsuit, finding in favor of the Marley estate and against Danny Sims.

Cayman and Sims also lost every subsequent appeal in the case, and the Marley estate, including Bob's children and their heirs, retained control of "No Woman, No Cry" and the rest of the late reggae superstar's disputed songs.

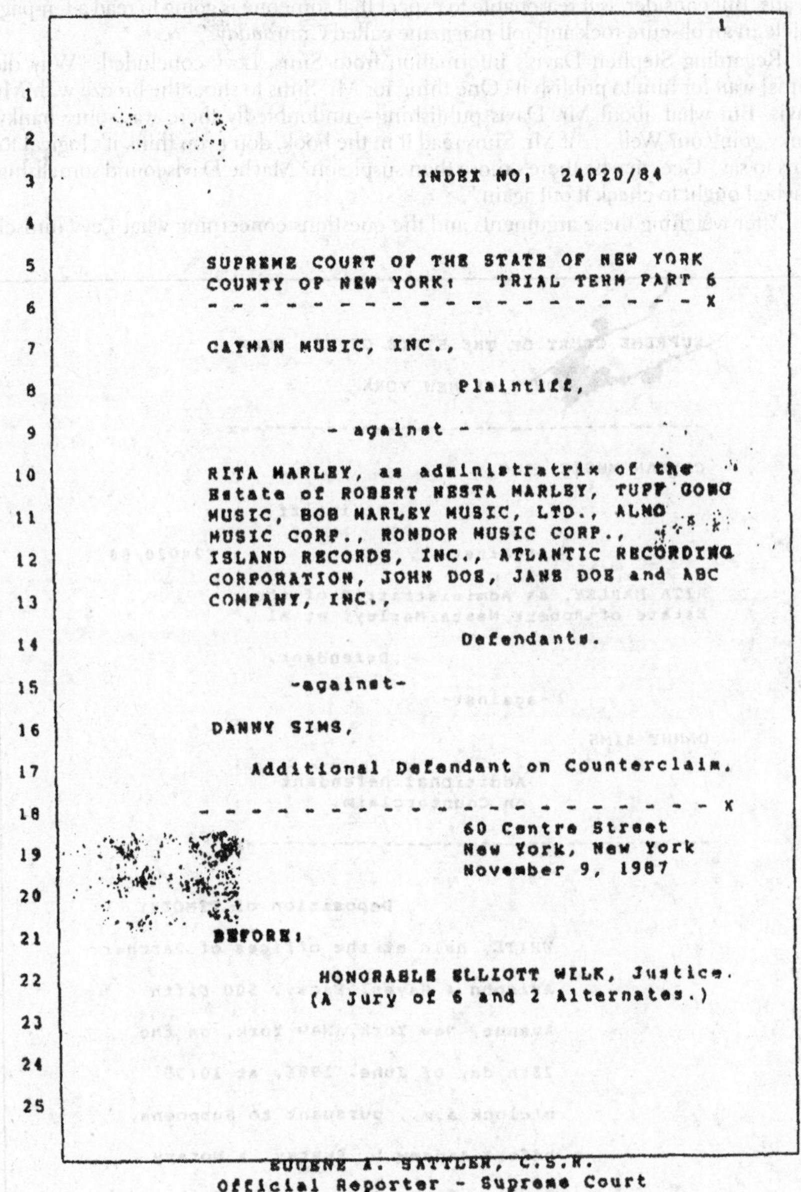

1

INDEX NO: 24020/84

SUPREME COURT OF THE STATE OF NEW YORK
COUNTY OF NEW YORK: TRIAL TERM PART 6
- X

CAYMAN MUSIC, INC.,

Plaintiff,

- against -

RITA MARLEY, as administratrix of the Estate of ROBERT NESTA MARLEY, TUFF GONG MUSIC, BOB MARLEY MUSIC, LTD., ALMO MUSIC CORP., RONDOR MUSIC CORP., ISLAND RECORDS, INC., ATLANTIC RECORDING CORPORATION, JOHN DOE, JANE DOE and ABC COMPANY, INC.,

Defendants.

-against-

DANNY SIMS,

Additional Defendant on Counterclaim.

- X

60 Centre Street
New York, New York
November 9, 1987

BEFORE:

HONORABLE ELLIOTT WILK, Justice.
(A Jury of 6 and 2 Alternates.)

EUGENE A. SATTLER, C.S.R.
Official Reporter - Supreme Court

Iron, Lion, Zion

AUTHOR'S NOTES ON SOURCES, DOCUMENTS AND APPENDIXES

The process of reporting and writing this still-expanding book on Bob Marley and his milieu has never ceased to be an absorbing, often bedeviling and consistently surprising one. Humility is the best policy when inquiring into the intricacies of reggae, West Indian culture and especially accounts of Marley's personal life and professional ascent, because much is open to interpretation and there is seldom agreement or concord among most of the central figures in the highly emotional and subjective saga.

Even names are subject to variant spellings, with Omeriah Malcolm's first name occasionally cited by relatives as "Omariah." The first name of Peter Tosh's mother appears on documents as both "Alvera" and "Alvira," and Captain Marley's middle name is recorded and cited as both "Sinclair" and, less frequently, the un-Anglicized "St. Clair." Spellings of the names of Bob Marley's children are equally inconsistent, with the kids themselves (like Kymani aka Ky-mani) offering different versions at different times.

Indeed, most of what is known about Bob Marley—from his coming-of-age experiences and composing credits to his Rasta creed and the advocacy of the supernatural that bolsters it—is controversial and often strains credulity. Marley and many people around him claimed to have had "visions" that directed and often validated their actions. On a more mundane level, there are basic disagreements over fundamental events in Bob's background and life experience. Bob himself firmly told me more than once that his formal name was always Robert Nesta Marley (*not* Nesta Robert Marley, as some now assert) and that he "never really know" his father, their only memorable—and distressing—encounter occurring when Bob was taken on the bus into Kingston as a child to be met by an aging, ailing and angry Norval Marley, who was said to be too sick to make the trip to fetch him.

As Bob recalled in an interview with me in 1979, "I look up and see a mon, old, with white hair—and I don' wanna deal wit' him. Him tek me by the arm, and I cry . . . and when I wake up he is gone."

The fact of his black son had become discomfiting to Bob's father, and the senior Marley apparently intended to hide the child until Bob's whereabouts could no longer be traced. Strangely, Norval found the kidnapping to be amazingly easy, with more than a year passing afterward without any substantial inquiry or questioning beyond a series of quizzical letters from Cedella. Far more expeditious means of communication were available even in rural Jamaica. Omeriah Malcolm and his family, for example, had promptly telegrammed Norval Marley back in 1945 to inform him of Bob's birth and, later, of Bob's childhood illnesses. Yet a great deal of time passed with no one journeying to Kingston to investigate, to visit the little boy, to send him seasonal gifts or scrutinize firsthand his health or progress. That no one insisted on documentation (photos, school records, etc.) to certify his well-being, and no one contacted the civil authorities after his whereabouts became a matter of inexplicable mystery.

In sum, there has never been adequate explanation for these curious matters, just as there has never been a logical reason for allowing the mentally unstable Anthony Booker to linger for days behind a locked door in his mother's Miami house with no food and a loaded gun.

Oddly, there has also been a tendency since Marley's death to overlook or conveniently discount his own conflicting assertions and descriptions of his past, giving greater credence to the equally inconsistent accounts of survivors whose dates, details and descriptions of key characters and activities have changed from one published anecdote to another. In one account, a Maggie James may be the higgler who found Bob after he was lost or abandoned in Kingston. In the next recounting by the same source, it's Maggie Simpson who found the misbegotten toddler.

Fair enough. In matters great and small, the memory can prove faulty. But memories can also be selective when retrieving traumatic incidents, sometimes in a manner that portrays the subject in the best possible light. It's important to bear in mind that many stories about Marley's life have taken on greater significance as his posthumous reputation has soared, and sources who formerly took an unguarded approach to their respective tales of Bob's past are now increasingly concerned about how *they* come off.

Faced with these tactical postures and philosophical dilemmas, the informing premise of *Catch a Fire: The Life of Bob Marley* was to allow everyone to have his or her say; that is, unlike many articles and book-length reminiscences about Marley, this text does not take any particular side or favor one personal perspective over another. It is not the gospel according to a manager or a wife or an entrepreneur or a mother or a band member or an offspring or a neighbor or a record producer or an aide-de-camp or a politician. On the contrary, this text is informed by all testimonies, outlooks, opinions convictions, orthodoxies, assertions and "visions"—notwithstanding even the personal vendettas, vicious accusations and wildly shifting alliances that transpired between many of the story's principals before and since Marley's passing.

In the many editions of this book and its extensive discography, this writer has likewise tried to tell the story from everyone's often passionate, prejudiced or self-protective point of view, while striving to avoid easy solutions and remain open to new questions. Ultimately, there may prove to be little if any consensus on the life of Bob Marley, but I hope that readers of this text will at least feel close to the many intersecting paths of thought and clashes of memory and belief that compose the uniquely atmospheric whole.

Meanwhile, the majority of the primary players in Bob Marley's life and legacy have continually engaged each other in court battles based on long-simmering jealousies, rivalries and questions of ownership and inheritance. This latest, fully revised edition of *Catch a Fire* delves into more such legal bouts. Contrary to popular belief, however, these fights did not stem merely from Marley's refusal to draft a will or otherwise settle his financial affairs in his final days. Rather, they are rooted in the lifelong tensions of complex relationships with his family; fellow musicians and confidants.

It has become popular or personally advantageous for disgruntled former Island

Records employees and frustrated or openly racist adversaries to assert, for instance, that Chris Blackwell (aka "Whiteworst") broke up the original Wailers by electing to promote the group as Bob Marley *and* the Wailers. Two decades of investigation into this question only confirm what I learned back in 1975 from Marley himself: Bob broke up the original Wailers by pursuing his own ambitions as the most effective singer, songwriter and showman in the group. He worked hard all his life for the right to run his career on his own terms, and when the chance came with Blackwell, Marley took it, enthusiastically reemphasizing his own name in the presentation of his music, much as he had once done solo back in the early 1960s.

Even the Wailers' ska and early rock steady eras saw a host of singles on Clement Dodd–owned labels on which Bob was billed as a solo act or lead singer, including a 45 of "One Love" on Studio One (CD 1036A) credited to "Bob Marley"; assorted singles on either Dodd's Tabernacle label or blank sound-system pressings such as "Just in Time" (WIRL CS1069-1), credited to Bob Marley and the Spiritual Sisters; and the similarly attributed "Have Faith" (CS DODD 35). Also, "Rocksteady Part 2," the B-side of "Rock Steady," on Studio One (SO 0084B) was credited to "Bob Marley & the Wailers Studio One." Peter Tosh's own aspirations were obvious in the credit for his "Hoot Nanny Hoot" single on Dodd's label Muzik City (FC6425), which read "Peter Tosh and the Wailers"; later reissued in 1965 by Island in the U.K., the single's credit was "Peter Touch [*sic*] & the Wailers," its B-side being "Do You Remember" by "Bob Marley & the Wailers."

As Bob's Rasta friend and sometime cook, Bird, said in a 1982 interview in New York, "Bob wanted to make it internationally, Peter compromise, Bunny—no compromise."

Moreover, although it was Marley who made himself a multimillionaire through extraordinary struggle and effort, it was Blackwell in his honesty and fair dealing who made it possible. Indeed, the list of millionaire reggae artists is a rather short one, given the shady and high-handed business practices of the overwhelming majority of producers and record executives who handled the best-known performers since the music's inception in Jamaica.

Interviewing or chatting with Marley himself on a regular basis in the years between our first face-to-face meeting, at his 56 Hope Road home in September 1975, and our last talk, in his Essex House hotel room two days before he collapsed in Central Park in September 1980, this journalist found that Bob was quite happy to be on his own, making music that wove American rock, funk and modern folk forms into his unique new hybrid. Marley expressed no desire to reunite the core trio of himself, Bunny Wailer and Peter Tosh, calmly but repeatedly referring to that ska-to-early reggae alliance as "over." Marley looked back on their past together as an exciting, fruitful but increasingly difficult span in which the three musicians found their boyhood triumverate ultimately diverging into separate outlooks, exacerbated by their initial European touring.

As Marley once remarked to British journalist Ray Coleman, "The pressure of the way we had to work was why the Wailers didn't agree, because we didn't get any help, we were out on tour under some steep conditions that first time. . . . It's just pressure from all sides, we're born to get pressure, we come upon the earth to get pressure. You get pressure from your family, pressure from strangers, pressure from *all* over."

Coleman and this writer discussed those and other statements by Marley, much as we pooled information over the years about Marley admirer Eric Clapton, the latter musician being the subject of a distinguished biography by Ray. Bob's comments about dissension in the original Wailers ranks echoed remarks he made in 1979 when inviting me to sit in on a daylong series of promotional interviews at his Manhattan hotel to promote the *Survival* album. Marley was entering an uncertain period in which his presence in the African American market was widening while his mainstream appeal was wavering (with even *Rolling Stone* reluctant to devote more space to chronicling Marley). Meanwhile, Bob himself made it plain he would remain the leader of his band, sidestepping any inferences of re-forming the seminal trio for promotional, touring or recording purposes. He was committed to the independent course he had charted from *Natty Dread* onward.

At my first meeting with Marley in Kingston in 1975, I brought along a box of assorted Jamaican Ska Beat, Coxsone, Upsetter, Black Heart and Tuff Gong singles I had collected since my teens, most of them purchased in Brooklyn or in small shops near Yankee Stadium in the Bronx. My awareness of the Wailers and West Indian music stemmed from boyhood acquaintances with classmates of Caribbean descent while attending Public School No. 25 in Paterson, New Jersey, which, like many industrial cities on the eastern seaboard (Wilmington, Trenton, Boston, Toronto) had a significant West Indian population.

Marley was taken aback that a young American reporter would be apprised of his back catalogue of Caribbean releases or have a strong interest in Caribbean history, folklore and music. (Apart from the Wailers, I was actually a bigger calypso buff than a ska, rock steady or reggae fan.) In the ensuing years, I visited Marley at Harry J's studio in Jamaica while he was cutting the *Rastaman Vibration* album and locally released singles like "Jah Live," as well as at Island's Basing Street Studios and so-called "Bomb Shelter" back-alley studios in St. Peter's Square during the making of *Exodus* and *Kaya*. (I also tagged along with Chris Blackwell on trips to Sterling Sound in Manhattan for mastering work on aspects of *Rastaman Vibration* and Toots and the Maytals' *Reggae Got Soul*.)

As chance would have it, I usually wound up hearing the finished tracks and seeing the final, prerelease album artwork for the *Live!*, *Rastaman Vibration*, *Exodus*, and *Survival* albums with Bob in Kingston or in Island Records' New York, Los Angeles or London offices, with artist Neville Garrick often on hand to explain the designs and imagery. (Bob and Neville giggled in Island's old Carnegie Hall offices at 7th Avenue and 57th Street as they showed me the truth of the notation on the original, burlap-like embossing on the *Rastaman* LP jacket that its surface was "great for cleaning herb.")

Poignantly, I also accompanied Neville Garrick to Island's offices in the Warner Communications building in Rockefeller Center in 1983 as he delivered the original illustration for Marley's posthumous *Confrontation* album (its cover dragon wearing a later-deleted papal miter).

Besides Blackwell and company soliciting my suggestions for the songs to be included on *Legend* in 1985, I worked with Island press chief Rob Partridge on the liner notes and track-by-track description and donated a carton of my own accumulated memorabilia to the array depicted in *Legend*'s centerfold. In 1992, I was invited by Blackwell to work on the *Songs of Freedom* project, likewise suggesting tracks for inclusion and assisting Partridge and journalist colleague Chris Salewicz on liner notes.

Nonetheless, despite all the cordial interviews, talks and behind-the-scenes encounters I was privy to over the years, it would not be fair to describe myself as a close friend of Bob Marley's. Rather, I was a working journalist, and my press credentials and affiliations were always the primary basis of my entrée. To be a close friend to someone is to have them freely devote significant portions of their private life to you and vice versa. For Marley and me, as well as his family, friends and associates, when the work was done all of us returned to our own separate existences. This also includes Al Anderson, Marley's lead guitarist in the mid-1970s, who I knew as a teenager when we played in kindred rock bands in Montclair, New Jersey. In short, most of my contact with Marley and company came within the bounds of my job as journalist.

Even Marley's later requests that I sit in on the interviews of others were to serve a professional purpose: Bob wanted me to see how little had changed since he was first widely called upon in 1973–74 to explain his dreadlocks and his Rasta creed, when naive or racist reporters treated him like a novelty figure or a noble savage, surprised he could read, write or express himself beyond expounding on biblical tracts.

Some who write or expound on reggae have lately sought to characterize themselves as preeminent authorities on Marley, his recordings and his every move, turning such efforts into an increasingly haughty, grasping or heated contest. This author claims no such ambitions, credentials or capability in this area; this text has been repeatedly revised and expanded out of simple necessity as well as enthusiasm. I encourage any readers with suggestions or information they might deem useful for future editions of this book to write to me in care of the publisher.

For each reggae camp follower or archivist dispensing individual interpretations and anecdotes on the lecture circuit or at reggae festivals, there remain a number of reggae reporters from the 1970s and early '80s who actually spent a great deal of time with Bob but are modest about this fact. Writers Penny Reel, Isaac Fergusson, Neil Spencer, Chris Salewicz, Helene Lee, photographers Adrian Boot and Dennis Morris, broadcaster-reporters Dermott Hussey and Neville Willoughby, and documentarian Don Letts all got to know Bob very well during their years of chronicling his activities. The most self-effacing journalist of all in this respect is probably veteran British writer Vivien Goldman (coauthor with Adrian Boot of *Bob Marley: Soul Rebel—Natural Mystic* [Bellow & Higton/St. Martin's Press, London/New York] and author of *The Book of Exodus* [Three Rivers Press]), who reported extensively on Bob and his rise to prominence, toured widely with him (including during his *Babylon by Bus* trek), often watched him at work in the studio and even stayed at Hope Road for an extended period as his guest—without ever touting or overplaying her extraordinary contact with the man.

Still, because Marley was an underdog in the mainstream marketplace during much of the 1970s, coverage of him required a certain resolve that fed an inclination to champion his uncommon output. Although I certainly revered most of Marley's work and greatly appreciated the recordings of Peter Tosh (who'd visit my *Crawdaddy* office in 1976 with friend Lee Jaffe to fire up his herb pipe and play his latest tracks) and to a lesser extent those of Bunny Wailer (whose international 1976 Island Records ad campaign for *Blackheart Man* was centered around the text of my prerelease rave in *Crawdaddy*), I must point out that I was critical of many of their recordings. I gave Marley's "Punky Reggae Party" a negative review in *Crawdaddy* and sharply criticized Tosh's *Bush Doctor* and *Mama Africa* albums in, respectively, *Rolling Stone* and *Musician*.

I openly admired later albums of Bunny's such as *Liberation* and praised in *Rolling Stone* the first of Bunny's record projects revisiting vintage Wailers and Marley material, namely 1980's *Bunny Wailer Sings the Wailers*. But after Bunny followed that album with his 1981 *Tribute to the Late Hon. Robert Nester* [sic] *Marley, O.M.* album, as well as the 1990 record *Time Will Tell: A Tribute to Bob Marley*, and *then* the tepid two-CD 1995 *Hall of Fame: A Tribute to Bob Marley's 50th Anniversary* (pointedly issued, in the last instance, as Bunny was engaged in an acrimonious fight to wrest Tuff Gong records away from the Marley family), I felt it necessary to reprove him in *Billboard* for what appeared to be an unseemly exploitation of Bob to bolster his own waning commercial outreach.

Which brings us to the essential nature and scope of this book's reporting. Besides my numerous interviews and encounters with Bob Marley himself, the text is informed by talks with his family and friends, beginning with the material gathered for my January 1976 cover story on Marley in *Crawdaddy*, the first such exposure Marley received in a national magazine.

In the winter of 1977, after a year of detective work, I located via phone Cedella Marley Booker, Bob's mother, who told me she'd have to check with her son before speaking further. Marley later recalled as much to me in 1979 at the Essex House during a relaxed talk that showed his playful side: "True, true. She call me and she seh, 'Can

I talk to this boy what call me? Him say him name Timothy White.' And I laugh a bit, and I say, 'Timothy White?' And she say, 'Yes, that is the one him just call.' And I say, 'If Timothy White try that hard to find ya, ya must talk wit' him!'" I enlisted the assistance of photojournalist Peter Simon for the visit with Bob's mother, and in the spring of 1977 we drove down from New York to Wilmington, Delaware, where I conducted the first in-depth interview Mrs. Booker had ever granted, small portions of which were combined with a review of *Exodus* and Tosh's *Equal Rights* in the August 1977 issue of *Crawdaddy* under the headline, RASTÁMOM VIBE.

I made a series of trips to Jamaica and England between 1975 and 1977 to link up with Bob, view him in the studio, investigate his old stomping grounds in Kingston and the greater London area and to explore rural Jamaica while researching an extensive historical essay for a hoped-for photo book–cum–discography slated to be one of a (rescinded) series edited by longtime colleague Ken Barnes.

During these trips I circumnavigated the entire island, meeting and interviewing friends and associates of Bob's, including Seeco, Family Man, Bunny Wailer, Peter Tosh, Joe Higgs, Countryman, Dickie Jobson, Tommy Cowan, Al Anderson, Jimmy Cliff, Toots Hibbert, Earl "Chinna" Smith and Carly Barrett, as well as producers and promoters around Bob, Peter and Bunny, including Coxsone Dodd, Harry Johnson and Alex Sadkin.

Sometimes I was with film director and close Marley associate Dickie Jobson, and other times with Island Records' Jeff Walker or a reggae artist. Often I went off on my own. One sleepless 1975 morning at sunrise I paid a cab driver outside the Kingston Sheraton a flat fee of $50 U.S. to introduce me to the city's uptown and downtown precincts. We steered our way through Barbican and Hope Pastures and descended to Concrete Jungle, Trench Town and its Rema sector, Jones Town, Denham Town, then wound around National Heroes Park through Allman Town and through Cross Roads and up Halfway Tree Road to New Kingston.

I rode up front with the driver or we walked along eating fruit I had purchased—as Marley had often done—at Papine Market near the juncture of Hope Road and Gordon Town Road, and we got back to the Sheraton at 9:30 A.M. Strangely enough, it was one of the most placid and instructive times I ever spent in Jamaica. The people were friendly and unsuspicious, happy to point out Bob Marley's old neighborhood landmarks and haunts, such as his former yard and dwelling on 19 Second Street.

While staying at the Chela Bay Hotel in Ocho Rios in 1976, I investigated rural St. Ann in depth and talked with producer Jack Ruby, aka Lawrence Lindo, at his home and studio (he boasted he'd premiered Bob's "Rainbow Country" as a dub plate for his itinerant sound system), as well as Rasta elder Ras Morris, aka Fabian Clark, and Justin Hinds of the Dominoes.

Unpredictable Lee Perry (born Rainford Hugh Perry in 1936 in Kendal, Hanover Parish) was interviewed at length in his Black Ark studio before he destroyed it in 1979. I twice visited Perry's outwardly tidy, fenced-in cottage and studio stronghold at 5 Cardigan Crescent in the Washington Gardens section of Kingston, once finding him in an acute state of agitation and intoxication, smashing crockery, swilling Tia Maria and swearing oaths while his woman and their children cowered in the back bedroom, the door wedged shut behind a chest of drawers. After Perry had passed out in his studio behind the house, his lady, Pauline, crept out, made some tea and played remixes of Perry's *Super Ape* album while he snored on the floor before the console. On the next visit, Lee was subdued, self-possessed and gave me a more cogent assessment of his years of "collaboration"—a key description in his mind—with Bob Marley. The scenes and descriptions of Perry's demeanor in the text are drawn from these firsthand interactions with Perry.

I visited Coxsone's record store and dropped by Studio One, Dynamic, Federal, Joe Gibbs's studio and dub pioneer King Tubby's Dromilly Ave. laboratory (ironically Tubby was murdered on February 6, Marley's birthday, in 1989), and a number of nightclubs Bob and company frequented. Also visited were Countryman's Hellshire beach encampment and shoreline sites such as Gunboat Beach, where Perry and his sound system competitors had often hosted dances. Likewise the Dungle, the indescribably destitute garbage dump peopled by scavengers.

I met Claudie Massop in the yard at 56 Hope Road in 1977 after he returned from self-imposed exile in England, talked with Bucky Marshall in a Kingston restaurant and watched as Bob and Alan Cole and their cohorts played soccer on the front lawn at Hope Road.

I learned about political strife in Jamaica by traversing Kingston and the rest of the country while it was under martial law, negotiating my way through roadblocks as both uniformed and plainclothes PNP Security Forces roamed the parishes, enforcing the curfews that then–Prime Minister Manley decreed as part of his "Heavy Manners" campaign to crack down on civil unrest and the alleged CIA-orchestrated destabilization of his left-wing regime.

More than once I found myself fending off accusations on Halfway Tree Road that my sunglasses and neat attire somehow indicated I was a CIA agent. And one memorable afternoon in Tommy Cowan's yard it was abruptly demanded that I explain my presence in the company of ghetto musicians when jeeps mounted with machine guns rolled onto the premises, a half-dozen sweating young troops leaping out to intimidate those assembled.

On another occasion in 1982, a Jamaican official and I turned a corner in a car she was driving one evening at 9:00 P.M. and found ourselves in the middle of a shootout in Denham Town, members of tribalist factions trading small weapons fire in the middle of the street, while flames from a burning car created wavy shadows in which the gunmen crouched. We backed up and sped off in the direction from whence we came.

Even during the depths of Heavy Manners, however, the north coast remained an appealing lure for the Caribbean wayfarer, and because it was the birthplace of Bob Marley, I spent a fair amount of time between 1976 and 1982 in the Garden Parish of St. Ann's. Both Runaway Bay and St. Ann's Bay are small but picturesque coastal villages, the latter dominated by a statue of Marcus Garvey, with a number of tidy rum bars that welcome the thirsty traveler. There are good hotels in the region of Dunn's River Falls, and it proved fairly easy to find one's way to most interior villages with resort-supplied directions or the afternoon assistance of an off-duty hotel staffer. Over the years, I explored St. Ann's terrain from Discovery Bay to Steer Town, Bamboo to Claremont, and the entire Stepney–Rhoden Hall–Nine Miles district.

The parish of St. Ann's as it was in the late 1970s and the region as it became after Marley's death were two entirely different places, the former seeming sleepy, lush and less defined in terms of its focal points and pace. By the early '80s it was a more tense, protective and off-kilter enclave, the unhurried ways of its farming and pen-keeping life noticeably ruptured by its new status as the burial site of Bob Marley. And the countryside felt markedly more unhappy under the sinister, goon squad–infested rule of Prime Minister Seaga.

During a trip to Nine Miles in April 1982, the small car carrying photographer Peter Simon and me was halted at a roadblock two miles before the gas station in Brown's Town by a gun-toting militia. Dressed in work clothes and soiled Jamaican army shirts, they searched our foreign compact and frisked a youth from Ocho Rios who had helped show the way, relieving him of a concealed switchblade. One gunman ordered me to look away from his confederates' surly interrogation of the youth by sharply poking the side of my head with the tip of an M-16.

The winding, dusty road into the heart of the village had been partially resurfaced in 1982 with homemade gravel, there were a smattering of salt fish and Red Stripe vendors in a vicinity where there had been none before, and a platform stage had been built on the hillside opposite the half-finished stucco crypt where Bob's coffin was kept.

Because we were the only callers, the villagers were wary but accommodating, and I sat on a row of boulders under a tree next to the tiny hut in which Bob was born. A trickle of people strolled over to say hello and extend their hands in the gentle upward clasp that is the common country greeting. I asked about their backgrounds and was informed they were in-laws and cousins of families who had dominated the area for decades, their surnames being Wilby, Lewis, Lemonious, Alexander, Willoughby, Davis. All claimed to be related or acquainted with the Malcolms and, by extension, Bob Marley.

Early scenes in the book pertaining to Bob's childhood, journeys to Kingston, beliefs and superstitions regarding his unsettling "wolf eyes" stare and fortune-telling are derived from extensive interviews with Cedella Booker, brother David Malcolm and Lurline Brown Malcolm but also with residents of Nine Miles, Rhoden Hall and Alva.

Whenever thoughts of certain figures in this book are quoted from distant historical points, readers should be aware that this material was derived from the reminiscences of the subjects themselves or obtained from their associates, contemporaries or family members who shared their inherited information and recollections on what took place or what the principals involved had told them had taken place. During primary and deep-background interviews, people were continually asked what they recalled or heard from the principals regarding their stated impressions, opinions, mindsets, and reflective expressions concerning past occurrences.

For instance, the scene in which Omeriah Malcolm looks out over the village of Nine Miles from the veranda of Yaya's house was derived in part from the memories of villagers as two of them walked me over to Big House and asked permission within to allow me to step onto the porch as they described Omeriah, his family maxims and his personal habits. Many local people maintained that Bob Marley's maternal grandfather was easygoing, but son David Malcolm later noted he had "a bad temper." Some say he preferred rum, others noting that native gin was his alcoholic beverage of choice. But none disagreed about Omeriah's power in the district in his dual role as custos and herbalist/bush doctor.

The front door and windows of Cedella's little hut, normally locked and shuttered, were opened for me during a visit so I could survey the modest interior. I was shown inside other homes in the village as I asked about domestic customs, farming methods and harvest activities in the district and the attendant night picnics and shelling matches (also called "katreels" from *quadrille* and the Scotch *reel*) after crops were reaped. These were events alluded to by Cedella Booker, and they were recalled by Bob himself in greater detail during an interview with Neville Garrick at the Island Records of offices in the Carnegie Hall building in 1976 on the eve of the release of the *Rastaman Vibration* album.

Bob also spoke at length in Essex House interviews in 1978 and '79 about the folkoric figure of fear that the "blackheart man" had been in rural culture. My own questions were initially prompted by a comment he'd made in a November 1976 interview in *Chic* magazine after being asked if he'd been aware of Rastafarians as a kid: "Me remembah me mutha come down de street an' tell me, say, is a black art man. Me run go hide unna de bed, an' is no black art man, yuh know."

As Bob elaborated to me in 1979, "Well, me mother and me auntie and people would warn, saying, 'Be good, or the blackheart man gon' get you.' . . . And I would be afraid, and sometime have a bad dream. One time I get up in the morning, and it is misty, an' I tek a little peek out the shack an' I think I see a blackheart mon. And then I run and jump into my mother's bed an' hide me face [*laughter*]!"

His details of these and other stories became scenes early in the book—often fleshed out further by villagers' insights, vivid remembrances and superstitious gossip about the preadolescent Bob's otherworldly traits or Cedella's girlhood indiscretions. (Some neighbors maintained, for instance, that she hadn't sought to "consecrate" herself to the local church until she'd been caught consorting with Captain Marley.) Basically, these local observers were in awe, a bit afraid of or resentful toward the Malcolms and Marleys and their sway over the area, but also proud of them, too.

Given the prominence of the Malcolms, the villagers were eager to substantiate their impact on Nine Miles, and during one trip I was steered through the large, two-story stucco and cinder-block house down the path from Big House that had once been the home of Omeriah's sister, Rittie Lemonious, or "Aunt Rittie," as Bob knew her. Looming beside Rittie's home was a skeleton of tall staffs erected to preserve the original dimensions and floor plans of Omeriah's former five-room house.

Details of Omeriah's "Nine Night" funeral, etc., came from his cousins, among them the Lewises, Alexanders and Lemoniouses, who also explained that Omeriah's brother Nemiah had once run a little store in Nine Miles—"everything in one cupboard"—and helped coordinate important ceremonies such as funerals or seasonal shelling matches.

Residents were acquainted with many of the medicinal plants Omeriah used in his bush medicine, picking a few sprigs to illustrate or naming a number of them—such as cotton leaves, baby gripe, black joint, garden bitters, sweet cup (also called kangsknot)—and complaints that correlated with their utilization. But they confessed they didn't know all the contents of his various remedies and "physics," or the "secrets" of how to administer them. Payment for his services was said to be handled through some form of country barter.

I saw the cultivation ground at Smith and vicinity, discussed the farming cycles with local growers and field hands and heard stories of the speeches and tales offered at shelling matches. Their subject matter reflected the influence of Freemasonry in the region, the time-honored beliefs of the Malcolms that their family tree had Egyptian blood—David Malcolm maintaining in May 1982 that "my grandfather on my mother's side was from Egypt"—plus the highly politicized Pan-African pride prevalent in the parish that was the birthplace of Marcus Garvey.

One of the better speakers at evening harvest picnics during Bob's childhood was said to be Jacob Malcolm, variously described by villagers as "Omeriah's uncle" and "Yaya's second cousin," who regaled those clustered around bonfires with the saga of Prester John as related in the text. (I had not heard of this mythic king nor been previously acquainted with the mystical Coptic fables freely told in St. Ann, a parish well-known for its orators, storytelling and fervent acceptance of mysticism.)

There was *labrish*-like chatter from the locals as they recounted the startled impressions Bob made on local passengers when he was sent on his initial bus trip to Kingston to rendezvous with Captain Marley. Described in a similar vein was Cedella's hurried reconnaissance and retrieval of Bob via those same buses—the young mother reportedly being hastened on the errand by an agitated Omeriah—and then Bob's final solo trip at the age of ten to join his relocated mother, Omeriah himself putting Bob on the bus for Kingston and his new Trench Town home.

Surprised that such commercial conveyances would have circulated so far beyond the A1 coastal highway in the late 1940s and early 1950s, I sought out the various depots in the region to learn where one reportedly could have caught "country buses" into Kingston. I also did extensive research on the subject through the University of the West Indies and the Research Institute for the Study of Man in Manhattan, poring through numerous back issues of the UWI's *Social and Economic Studies* journal for material on the development of internal transport in Jamaica, such as W. F. Maunder's 1954 treatise, "The Significance of Transport in the Jamaican Economy: An Estimate of Gross Expenditure on Internal Transport."

These studies made it clear that from the late 1940s onward independently operated buses commonly ran between the southern hill country of St. Ann, or more remote parishes like St. Elizabeth, and downtown Kingston. Archival data show that these buses were managed by small firms (of as few as two secondhand vehicles) bearing names such as Treasure Girl, Mayflower, Ambassador and May Reach (the last firm being the source of a popular jest and unofficial motto of the era throughout St. Ann: "We May Reach Kingston today, or We May Not!").

By car, I eventually retraced what would have been the bus route from the Rhoden Hall region. Next I researched the same route as it would have appeared during that juncture, examining a wide range of scholarly, municipal, social agency and national planning–related field study photographs depicting the exact periods in question, because they pertained to road conditions, settlement patterns, architecture and economic planning issues in the towns, stretches of highway and neighborhoods that led all the way from Stepney to the bus depot in downtown Kingston. The resources and publications of the Institute of Social Research were helpful in this respect.

Retracing people's precise feelings and notions about a human factor in the life of Bob Marley like "Captain" Norval Sinclair Marley proved far more problematic. Norval was known to be hostile to Christianity, attributable by some to the unmarried Cedella Malcolm's belated decision to embrace the local church's dictate against illicit love after being discovered with him. A rumor in the region, however, holds that Norval's antipathy toward the church actually stemmed from his links to, or sympathy for, Freemasonry.

"He was a kind man," said David Malcolm of Norval, "and he would give us money if we was going anywhere, to buy something for ourselves."

"A beautiful man, a wonderful person in his way," is how Cedella Booker summarized him to one journalist. Yet in Mrs. Booker's own Movement of Jah People/Bob Marley Festival concert program in 1997, a writer she'd enlisted to coauthor her memoirs bluntly decried Norval as a "lecherous old codger," a "bleating old goat," "a gamy old whiteman," and "a potential child molester," adding that "Mother [Booker] says that on visits to her father, this 50-year-old busha [Norval] would pinch her 9-year-old nubs of breasts and say, 'You feathering yet?'"

Bob Marley usually referred to Norval as an "English guy, a Captain in the Army," as he once told writer Karl Dallas. David Malcolm said, "He had a British accent, and he had a British background; he was living in England before Jamaica." One of the Lewises in Nine Miles recalled him as a "short, red-skinned English man." Strangely, Cedella would evolve from calling him an Englishman in the 1980s to referring to Norval as "a white Jamaican" by the '90s. To this day, much of her knowledge of her furtive husband's background and movements appears to be conjecture.

Nine Miles villagers' memories of Captain Marley's son were largely fond ones, several people asserting that Bob's first musical instrument was a banjo and that he showed talent as a boxer. Much later, his hobbies were said to include horse racing, one of the Lemonious family describing Bob as "a tough bettor." The last time anyone remembered Bob being in Nine Miles was in April 1978, when he stayed for a few days and gathered a small crowd inside Auntie Rittie's house as he played songs on an acoustic guitar, among them "Rat Race."

The most prominent thread in my research for this book was spiritual belief, but regardless of the current faith or religious affiliation of those Jamaicans interviewed, no doctrines were given greater credence than those underlying the heterodoxy of obeah. Villagers spoke often but usually obliquely of the intense activity of "angels, good and bad" in the area.

Cedella has told stories of how a Jamaican "science man" named Hubert Hall repented on his deathbed for his evil spell casting, including an instance of dark conjury in which he caused Omeriah's car to flip over on an embankment in Nine Miles. The accident caused bodily injury to most of the auto's occupants (including a relative who had her hair scorched off), but Omeriah was able to stymie the spell with his own countervailing powers, suffering nothing more than a facial scratch. Moreover, it seems that Hall had been suborned into performing his nefarious sorcery for the mere payment of a dish of goat's-head stew—a traditional "devil's dish." In rural Jamaica, "Mr. Goat Mouth" is the personification of one threatening evil.

The spooky story in this book about Marley and his ill-fated standoff with a nettlesome nanny goat was told to me by Bob himself in the mid-1970s after I'd reached Kingston on an evening flight and arrived at my hotel to find the kitchen closed. The only food a steward on the night shift could offer was a warmed-over plate of curried goat he fixed for me in the kitchen, complete with a piece of vertebrae laid across the middle of the morasslike mound of gamy meat. Still feeling squeamish the next day, I explained the cause of my nausea to Bob and he offered his queer tale as a kind of cautionary parable, the inference being that goats in any form are devilish and that confrontations with them should be avoided or openly defied.

Bob's ability to "read the vibe" around him supposedly dated from his childhood, when his uncanny skill at palmistry was attested to by no less a local personage than District Constable Solla Black; many of the rural citizens in Black's jurisdiction in nearby Stern Hill had similar experiences with the eerie boy, then known as Nester.

The most electrifying interviews Bob or Rita Marley have ever given concern the duppy that attacked them both in the 1960s, back when they billeted in a back room of Coxsone's studio compound in Kingston. And anyone who has seen the 1992 film documentary *Stepping Razor—Red X*, on the life of Peter Tosh, can't help but be struck by the fact that, regardless of his childhood grounding in Christianity or his outspoken adult embrace of Rasta, Tosh was obsessed with and tormented by the presence of malignant magic in the world. An accidental mutilation by barbed wire of his eyelid in his youth convinced him he could peer through the torn skin tissue and veil of blood into a normally unseen world of spectral evil and its battle against the forces of good.

The bitter dissension that erupted among those friends and family accompanying Marley during his last desperate days of treatment in the Bavarian clinic of Dr. Issels reportedly had less to do with the customary tensions and jealousies around the courtiers of the reggae superstar than frightful disagreements over unorthodox last-ditch attempts to cure him. According to an interview in Manhattan in the spring of 1982 with the ghetto confrere of Bob's called Bird, Cedella was fixing some bush medicine in Germany for Bob when Issels's treatment wasn't working. "Some kind of potions and magic she said she learned from her father . . . light candles and things and fix potions. Freaked everybody out completely."

For Cedella's part, she admits Bird did come to her accusingly after seeing her burning incense around Bob's hospital room ("because I knew Nesta liked the smell," she later stated), Bird asking her, "You a obeah woman?"

"He was as serious as a judge," Marley's mother stated, adding, "I just looked at him like he was a madman and went about my business." Such contretemps in Bavaria speak volumes about the almost unresolvable fear and mistrust that obeah, or even the suspected hint of it, harbors in Jamaican culture, where even the avowed desire to use the supernatural solely for the purpose of good is regarded with alarm. Cedella later noted with bitter irony that Bird, a reputed gunman, was killed in a gun battle in Kingston, adding icily that "he would meet this violent death on Marley Road." It was, in a sense, her version of Bob's goat story of causal retribution.

In my experience of more than twenty years of inquiry about and dialogue with the personalities closest to Marley, all scoffed at others' suggestions that obeah was afoot in a given scenario—and yet each and every one who did so later volunteered their own tales attesting to obeah as a forceful and odious reality.

Once described as the pirate-designed burg that obeah built, the hellish city of

Kingston is still viewed by Rastas as the Caribbean headquarters of wickedness. What's certain is that Kingston is a latter-day amalgam of drowsy postcolonial borough and broiling open sore, a place where people high and low live by a sometimes cruelly practical and often pernicious sense of improvisation. Many opine that the Caymanas Park Race Track scam in which Bob became embroiled is an apocryphal story. It is not. The identities of the prominent jockey and his confederates who helped throw the race, and all the other collateral details of the matter, are well-known to Jamaican racing authorities (such as the Stewards of the Jockey Club, the administrative body that barred the participants from continued involvement in the sport) as well as JA and U.S. police officials, who have kept tabs on Jamaican ghetto crime and its overlap with other Caribbean underworld activities and posse movements in the United States.

One of the last men slain in revenge for the assassination attempt on Marley was Carl "Byah" Mitchell, a JLP goon active in the burgeoning new West Kingston cocaine trade (Byah was purportedly force-fed the drug until it stopped his heart).

According to in-depth confidential discussions this writer has had over the last decade with key members of the JLP and PNP, former U.S. Information Service agents stationed in Jamaica in 1976 and New York law-enforcement officials currently active in U.S. prosecution of Jamaican drug posses under the Federal Racketeer Influenced and Corrupt Organizations Act (RICO), Byah Mitchell was generally believed to have been contracted by the CIA to plant and instruct some of the gunmen who staged the murderous assault on Marley's house. Byah's involvement was seen to be a facet of the CIA-JLP destabilization campaign that Michael Manley had long been railing against in the press.

Byah's accomplice in the Marley shooting, the enforcer who actually helped lead the charge on Hope Road, was a Seaga-loyal lieutenant named Lester "Jim Brown" Coke, one of the founders of the Shower Posse. In Kingston in 1992, Brown burned to death in prison under unexplained circumstances—on the very same morning that his gunman son, Jah-T, was interred in a solemn funeral after being blown off his motorcycle from automatic weapons fire. As with the credo that there are no facts in Jamaica, it's also said there are no accidents or coincidences.

What's always been most puzzling in Kingston circles is the fact that some members of the assault squad came from Marley's own PNP neighborhood of Concrete Jungle. One-third of the reason for this vengeful breach of neighborhood kinship is that the jilted members of the race-fixing cartel had been friends of Marley's own ghetto chums. The second piece of the puzzle is that these toughs were eager to prove their mettle by gunning down a reggae hero—particularly someone who seemed to be trying to play it both ways politically in case Manley didn't get past Seaga in the latest election. Shortly before the shooting, Marley had been seen hanging out on alternate nights with PNP kingpin Bucky Marshall and key JLP hood Mitchell. If Marley didn't respect tribalism, it was argued, why should these young assassins?

The third piece of the puzzle is that as far back as 1976, political badmen who had customarily been in the exclusive employ of one or another political party were just starting to go "independent"—using what they had learned about money laundering and racketeering to work scams (big-ticket ganja smuggling, cocaine production and export) that actually cut across neighborhood lines. Both the JLP and PNP vigorously fought this trend, even purging renegades by setting them up for the other side to butcher, but "freelance stylee" still flourished.

Recruitment for independent gang activities was intense among homeless slum boys in their teens. In fact, even Marley and his band had been astounded at the youthfulness of some of the Hope Road assailants, several of the hit team appearing to be sixteen years old or younger. (To bolster their courage before the attack, each of the green young gunmen had allegedly been compelled to snort and eat large doses of cocaine.)

Only years after the assassination attempt did savvy Caribbean analysts realize that

Marley's would-be slayers were in the vanguard of an ugly new brand of adolescent ghetto "ninja" who killed solely for money and personal reputation rather than for politics. Yet even these outlaws were being used by both political parties to carry out an untraceable crime: the near-slaying of the Tuff Gong. And the crime remained untraceable because Rasta vigilantes were tipped off as to the whereabouts of each gunman; as noted in the book's text, not a single one ever lived to face charges.

I'm grateful to sources in the Homicide division of Manhattan District Attorney Robert M. Morgenthau's office—one of whom is an expert on Jamaican crime and its symbiosis with reggae culture in the U.S. and overseas—for invaluable advice and added insight into much of what I learned about the backgrounds of those involved in the Marley shooting incident, the murder of Peter Tosh and other Kingston-based underworld activities surrounding associates of the Wailers.

Indeed, officials in the Manhattan's D.A.'s office have had many notorious badmen from Jamaica in custody over the years as police investigated the spread to the United States of the PNP-loyal Spangler and Towerhill posses, and the JLP-aligned Shower posse. Some of these badmen also reconfirmed for authorities the accuracy of details in this book, while, in at least one instance, actually citing this author as a professional reference. (Knowing he'd appreciate the gesture, an official in the D.A.'s office requested that an autographed copy of this book be sent to one of these criminals after his imprisonment.)

As for politicians instrumental in propagating ska, rock steady and reggae as sociopolitical tools, I was introduced to Michael Manley at a fund-raising dinner in Manhattan while an editor at *Rolling Stone* and interviewed Edward Seaga for the first time at a meeting in the Grand Hyatt Hotel in Manhattan on December 5, 1982 (the day after an American Friends of Jamaica dinner cochaired by David Rockefeller). I was also given a private tour of Jamaica House and its grounds in Kingston back in March 1982.

Babsy Grange, director of culture during the Seaga regime in the 1980s, was quite helpful to me while I researched this book and was also kind enough to drive me from Kingston over the mountains to Oracabessa on the north coast in March 1982 for a small, daylong private party hosted by Chris Blackwell at Goldeneye, Ian Fleming's former estate and the initial setting of his mother Blanche's lifelong friendship with Fleming. Chris gave me a tour of the property, explained how Fleming acquired it and how ailing British Prime Minister Anthony Eden convalesced there after the political nightmare of the Suez incident. Afterward, a group of us swam in the hideaway's private cove.

In need of propane gas for the evening barbecue, Chris later invited me to ride with him to Blanche's Bolt House estate in Port Maria to fetch a tank of fuel. Once there, he showed me around the lovely hillside manse and its grounds overlooking the sea, sharing family pictures and mementos. He had a maid serve us cold drinks at the coffee table in the living room where Blanche Blackwell said that Fleming once sat bent over the galleys of his James Bond novel, *Dr. No*, the British author mumbling, "What mush! This is bloody *mush!*" as he made his final corrections.

Other residences I repeatedly visited were Blackwell's Compass Point house and adjacent studios in Nassau, The Bahamas; his country house outside Reading in Berkshire, England; and his Strawberry Hill estate above Kingston, Jamaica, where I spent one entire evening talking with Countryman, and another one listening to tales of obeah from associates of Bob's. On another trip to Strawberry Hill, a rather hyper Don Taylor told me his version of his life story, and then Jon Bradshaw, an old friend of Chris Blackwell's, told me aspects of Chris's own saga over dinner as Chris looked on bemusedly. Blackwell would later drop me off at the Terra Nova, explaining what it was like to grow up there in the era before it became a hotel. (I booked guest rooms there during subsequent research trips.)

I visited 56 Hope Road a dozen times before, during and after Bob's active residence there, interviewing him in his upstairs bedroom and private back-room office on the grounds, playing with his children and talking at length with Rita. I returned to the Hope Road compound months after the assassination attempt on Marley, a still-hobbling Don Taylor acting out scenes from the armed assault while I put my fingers through the bullet holes in the rear pantry and at other points on the premises.

Judy Mowatt and Marcia Griffiths were interviewed about their role in the Wailers at Harry J's on the day Marley and the band were recording "Jah Live." After Bob's death, Mowatt was interviewed in 1982 at her home in Kingston.

Besides our chats during the 1970s, Rita Marley was interviewed in depth at the Gramercy Park Hotel in 1982 and backstage after a Marley family concert in honor of Bob on Tuesday, May 11, 1982, at Gusman Hall in Miami, Florida.

After our first face-to-face meeting in Delaware, Cedella Booker spoke with me dozens of times between 1977 and 1983, whether on the phone, in Manhattan during visit there (including after the Bob Marley Memorial Service on Sunday, May 31, 1981, at the Community Church of New York at 40 East 35th Street in Manhattan) and in her home on Vista Lane in Miami.

Constantine "Dream" Walker was interviewed at the author's apartment on East 60h Street early in 1983, and Alan Cole was spoken with by phone from his Kingston home in the spring of 1983. Others interviewed for the book included Ernest Ranglin, who sat for a joint interview with Roland Alphonso in a Manhattan rehearsal studio in the late 1970s, with Alphonso being interviewed in a follow-up talk on April 6, 1983. Wayne Perkins, the "white Wailer," was interviewed by phone in Los Angeles in the midst of demo sessions on April 7, 1983.

More interviews in April 1983 during final work on the first edition: artist Tony Wright was interviewed by phone on April 7, talking from his home in Woodstock, New York; Glen Adams was interviewed by phone from his home on East 41st Street in Brooklyn on April 7 as a follow-up to my joint interview with him and Clement Dodd in the 1980s while Glen was convalescing in a Brooklyn hospital; Errol Brown, Bob's longtime engineer and producer, was interviewed by phone on April 7 while staying at the Howard Johnson's on 51st Street and 8th Avenue in Manhattan; Beverly Kelso was interviewed by phone on April 8 from her home on Woodhull Avenue in Brooklyn; Cindy Breakspeare Tavares was interviewed by phone on April 15 from her home on Constant Spring Road in Kingston; engineer Karl Pitterson was interviewed by phone on April 15 from his home on Summit Drive in Laguna Beach, California; Clement Dodd was interviewed again, by phone, on April 26 from his record shop on Fulton Street in Brooklyn.

The extreme sadness that accompanied Bob Marley's death in 1981 also paralleled a certain measure of regret among those who had been aware of the downward spiral of his immediate sphere in the months before the graveness of his illness was disclosed. I saw with my own eyes at the Essex House during Bob's concert stand with the Commodores at Madison Square Garden in September 1980 that, as Bob grew weaker from his illness, a decidedly unspiritual, unscrupulous element began to crowd out the old ital-minded Rasta road crew who used to prepare meals for him and the band in a healthful, low-key family atmosphere.

Instead, his large, apartment-sized suite was filled with sharp-dressed nondreads in tailored suits and open-collared shirts: Brooklyn hustler types, some carrying guns, who gulped expensive wine, huddled in anterooms for raucous chatter, or slipped into lavatories in small groups for suspect conferences, locking the doors behind them.

Most upsetting, almost no one but the precious few band members occasionally in evidence paid any attention to Bob, who lay stretched out, exhausted, in the back bedroom, repeatedly asking that his door be closed against the loutish din. Material near the close of chapter 16 ("Exodus") was drawn from scenes I witnessed.

In the decade after Bob's death, band members and longtime confidants volunteered details about the drastic decline in the scene surrounding him during his last weeks on the road. Word was that members of Bob's new "non-Rasta" entourage would rent rooms far away from the main hotel of Marley and his band, securing suites in the Wellington Hotel on 7th Avenue instead of the customary Essex House base on Central Park South, and use these satellite digs for parties filled with known West Indian thugs—with an absent, afflicted Bob expected to pick up the tab.

In time, these stories expanded to include word that the terribly drained reggae star had been urged to at least consider stimulants such as the amphetamines found in diet pills to restore his sapped strength. The whispered advice he was allegedly given by one confidant was that drugs, prescription or otherwise, were the only way he could hope to get through the tour—which he was being intimidated by some non–Island Records hustlers into completing due to dodgy promotional deals those hustlers had cut on the side.

One night just before Marley reached New York City, an old crony had told him that, because he had no choice but to finish the road trip, he really ought to consider some drastic steps to make certain he didn't "collapse onstage." Bob reportedly became horrified at the mere dignity-robbing notion of such an idea, the image of it plunging him into a state of near panic.

Recountings of such developments mounted in the 1980s after Marley's death, but it wasn't until an unlikely encounter with singer-songwriter Marshall Crenshaw backstage after an autumn 1989 show at the Paradise club in Boston that such sporadic but always consistently disturbing testimony took on a woeful clarity. Crenshaw introduced himself and told me his wife, Ione, had formerly worked as a medical assistant to a pediatrician in the same two-suite Manhattan office at 983 Park Avenue that contained the private practice of oncologist Yashar Hirshaut—the physician who she said treated Bob Marley immediately after his 1980 collapse in Central Park. Crenshaw said his wife, a fan of Marley's, had always been upset at what transpired in the doctors' offices that day.

In an interview that eventually took place on October 16, 1990, Ione explained why, telling me that Dr. Hirshaut, who had seen her reading a copy of an early edition of this book, began to talk about his prior examination of Marley.

"He said it was a real strange situation in that he could never examine Bob Marley alone," she explained. "He always had these, like, they were Mafia guys around him. He said that they were very domineering.

"Bob was brought to his office after this [collapse] happened. He was just taken out to the regular patient information area, where he was asked his mother's name and his father's name. Marley said he didn't know anything about his father. . . .

"So the doctor was asking him what happened, and why he had collapsed. . . . And the doctor said he just felt this horrible vibration in the room with Bob, and he had all these hoods with him, and it was very frustrating to try and give him medical help."

Marley was terror stricken, and felt increasingly alone in his suffering. According to Ione, a shaky, disconsolate Bob told Hirshaut he planned to leave for Bavaria to seek help from Dr. Issels. "Hirshaut knew about that guy," she explained, "and said, 'No, he's a quack. There's no way you should go to him; you're wasting your time. I can help you here.' He was trying to convince him not to take that trip.

"And this physician," says Ione of Hirshaut, "he had such a high rate of success with whatever treatment he came up with, the treatment of his own patients with cancer. I'd see a lot of them come in and out of the office, and many of these people were just like Marley. But ultimately he didn't take his advice.

"He'd say, 'Bob, I believe I can help you live longer.' And I thought, 'Oh my God,'" she recalled, now near tears. "But [Bob] said those hoodlums around him wouldn't let him, talked him out of it."

Thus, Bob Marley would approach his ending much as he approached his beginning: bewildered and isolated, an orphan of circumstance.

"As [Hirshaut] was telling me," Ione concluded, "you could see it in his eyes, how frustrated he was that he lost a patient. So the last Dr. Hirshaut had any contact with [Marley], he was on the way to that other [doctor] in Europe."

After Bob Marley was gone and the void created by his loss was grasped, the depth of his contributions became more comprehensible. His albums proved far more popular after the *Legend* retrospective was issued in 1984. By the 1990s, Bob had become something of a cottage industry, with a number of fans hustling to corner the market on Marley memorabilia and any supposed authority that might stem from it. Sadly, at least one collection that many fellow journalists and devotees contributed to, with the ongoing understanding and assurance that it was to be donated to a university or library for nonprofit scholarly use, instead became its accumulator's private hoard and self-promotional source of income.

It's worthwhile to remember that Bob Marley was a remarkably generous man who spent amazingly little on himself, yet gave freely to anyone around him who was in need. Blackwell, Rita Marley, Neville Garrick and others have estimated that Bob supported hundreds if not a thousand or more people and beleaguered Kingston petitioners.

With this in mind, this writer has either written gratis since 1984 or donated to charity the fees from freelance articles, album liner notes pertaining to Bob Marley and Caribbean or world music and published excerpts of this text as they appeared in *Spin* or *Mojo* magazines, or special projects such as the 10th anniversary liner notes for the 1996 remastered, enhanced-CD edition of Paul Simon's *Graceland* album, an essay in the 1997 concert program for the fourth annual Bob Marley Festival in Miami, Florida, sponsored by Cedella Marley Booker's Movement of Jah People organization, or the preface written for the 1994 book by photographer Bruce W. Talamon, with text by Roger Steffens, *Bob Marley: Spirit Dancer* (W. W. Norton & Company, New York).

Among the many organizations receiving donations from this author in Bob Marley's memory that readers might want to consider for similar gestures of their own are Amnesty International, 322 8th Avenue, New York, NY 10001; Memorial Sloan-Kettering Cancer Center/Kristen Ann Carr Fund, 1275 York Avenue, New York, NY 10021; The United Negro College Fund, 500 East 52nd Street, New York, NY 10021; The American Civil Liberties Union, 125 Broad Street, 18th Floor, New York, NY 10004; Isis Fund/The Walden Woods Project, 44 Baker Farm, Lincoln, MA 01773-3004; the Boys' Town Industrial Training Centre, 6 Collie Smith Drive, Kingston 12, Jamaica, West Indies; Alpha Boys' Home, 26 South Camp Road, Kingston 4, Jamaica, West Indies.

And if, like many of Marley enthusiasts, you are an avid but unselfish hobbyist when it comes to collectables (posters, rare recordings, news clippings, bumper stickers, backstage passes, and promotional materials pertaining to Marley), you may want to consider bestowing something from your trove of keepsakes on the Bob Marley Museum, 56 Hope Road, Kingston, Jamaica, in care of its curation department so that it might be shared with kindred fans from around the planet who now frequent that site. (The museum recently announced in *Billboard* that it will send donors a special certificate of thanks signed by Rita Marley.)

In 1990, on the forty-fifth anniversary of Bob Marley's birth, Island Records and Amnesty International launched a commemorative funding program for support of Amnesty's human rights efforts in Third World countries, with an annual contribution of $75,000 from Island, supported by PolyGram, the label's new owner.

Of the many books written about Marley and reggae culture, this writer recommends that interested readers seek out the aforementioned *Bob Marley: Soul Rebel—Natural Mystic,* as well as *The Complete Guide to the Music of Bob Marley,* by Ian McCann (Omnibus Press, London); *The Guinness Who's Who of Reggae,* edited by Colin Larkin (Guinness Publishing Ltd./Square One Books, London); *Marcus Garvey: Life and Lessons* and *The Marcus Garvey and Universal Negro Improvement Association*

Papers, edited by Robert A. Hill and Barbara Bair (University of California Press, Berkeley); *The Other Side of Paradise: Foreign Control in the Caribbean*, by Tom Barry, Beth Wood and Deb Preusch (Grove Press, New York); *Jamaica Handbook*, by Karl Luntta (Moon Publications Inc., Chica, California); *Bob Marley, Reggae King of the World*, by Malika Lee Whitney and Dermott Hussey (Kingston Publishers, Ltd./E. P. Dutton, New York); *Born Fi' Dead: A Journey through the Jamaican Posse Underworld*, by Laurie Gunst (Henry Holt/Owl Books, New York); *The Kebra Nagast: The Lost Bible of Rastafarian Wisdom and Faith from Ethiopia and Jamaica*, edited by Gerald Hausman, with an introduction by Ziggy Marley (St. Martin's Press, New York); and most especially *Bob Marley: Songs of Freedom*, by Adrian Boot and Chris Salewicz (Viking/Penguin Books, New York), which is a handsome and heartfelt tribute to the man and his milieu.

This book and all the texts cited above are efforts to bring both the hard-core fan and the novice closer to the experience of Bob Marley, his arresting gifts and undeniable flaws, his fears and forbearance, his courage to act on hope and the amazing arc of his artistic and spiritual destiny. Yet all of us labor in the massive shadows of the music itself.

The next time you play a recording by Bob Marley, or catch his music on the radio or see it depicted in a video, focus for an instant on the contemplative feeling it engenders, its penetration to the innermost place at which the riddim and the message might touch your heart. In that moment, you will surely be as close to the best intentions of Marley's creative inspiration as any other medium could ever seek to bring you.

Bob Marley had a simple, eloquent, timeless phrase for that sweet spot he wants all of us to find, together, within ourselves: One Love.

Permissions Acknowledgments

Grateful acknowledgment is made for use of portions of the following:

"Dancing Shoes" by Neville Livingston, copyright © 1976, April Music, Inc., and Shakat Music. Rights administered by April Music, Inc. Used by permission. All rights reserved.

"Jail House" by Bob Marley, copyright © 1976, April Music, Inc. and Shakat Music. Rights administered by April Music, Inc. Used by permission. All rights reserved.

"Shame & Scandal," by Joseph Robinson, copyright © 1958, Ben Ghazi Music, Inc. Used by permission.

"Jah Live," Bob Marley Music, Ltd. B.V., administered by Almo Music Corp. (ASCAP) for the world excluding the Caribbean. All rights reserved. International copyright secured. Used by permission.

"Johnny Was (Woman Hold Her Head and Cry)," by R. Marley Music, copyright © 1976, Bob Marley Music, Ltd. B.V., administered by Almo Music Corp. (ASCAP) for the world excluding the Caribbean. All rights reserved. International copyright secured. Used by permission.

"Exodus," by Bob Marley, copyright © 1977, Bob Marley Music, Ltd. B.V., administered by Almo Music Corp. (ASCAP) for the world excluding the Caribbean. All rights reserved. International copyright secured. Used by permission.

"Punky Reggae Party," by Bob Marley and Lee Perry, copyright © 1977, Bob Marley Music, Ltd. B.V. (ASCAP), Island Music (BMI). All rights administered by Almo Music Corp. (ASCAP) for the world excluding the Caribbean, on behalf of Bob Marley, Music, Ltd. B.V. All rights reserved. Used by permission.

"Zimbabwe," by Bob Marley, copyright © 1979, Bob Marley Music, Ltd. B.V., administered by Almo Music Corp. (ASCAP) for the world excluding the Caribbean. All rights reserved. International copyright secured. Used by permission.

"Children Playing in the Streets," by Bob Marley and Rita Marley, copyright © 1979, Bob Marley Music, Ltd. B.V., and Rita Marley Music, Ltd., administered by Almo Music Corp. (ASCAP) for the world excluding the Caribbean. All rights reserved. International copyright secured. Used by permission.

"Them Belly Full, But We Hungry," by Bob Marley, copyright © 1974, Bob Marley Music, Ltd. B.V., administered by Almo Music Corp. (ASCAP) for the world excluding the Caribbean. All rights reserved. International copyright secured. Used by permission.

"Redemption Song," by Bob Marley, copyright © 1980, Bob Marley Music, Ltd. B.V., administered by Almo Music Corp. (ASCAP) for the world excluding the Caribbean. All rights reserved. International copyright secured. Used by permission.

"Ambush in the Night," by Bob Marley, copyright © 1979, Bob Marley Music, Ltd. B.V., administered by Almo Music Corp (ASCAP) for the world excluding the Caribbean. All rights reserved. International copyright secured. Used by permission.

"War," by Alan Cole and Carlton Barrett, copyright © 1976, Bob Marley Music, Ltd. B.V., administered by Almo Music Corp (ASCAP) for the world excluding the Caribbean. All rights reserved. International copyright secured. Used by permission.

"Want More," by A. Barrett, copyright © 1976, Tuff Gong Music (ASCAP). All rights reserved. Used by permission.

"Love Rescue Me," by Adam Clayton, Laurence Mullen, David Evans, Paul Hewson, and Bob Dylan, © 1988 U2 (N/A), administered by Chappell & Co. (ASCAP) / Special Rider Music (ASCAP). All rights reserved. Used by permission.

Discography

The preparation of a discography on any Jamaican group with a history as varied as that of the Wailers is an undertaking that would try the patience of anyone but Jah Rastafari Himself. I compiled this list over the last fifteen years, consulting sources in New York, London, Kingston, Brooklyn and Los Angeles. Along the way, I had the invaluable advice and assistance of noted collector-archivists Hank Holmes, Leroy Pierson and Roger Steffens, who corresponded with me during the 1980s and 1990s, sending suggestions—"pure guesses," to use Pierson's phrase—or emendations (discographical and otherwise) for revised editions of what Steffens kindly described in one letter to me, following this book's last extensive update, as a "brilliant, tireless, inclusive, revelatory piece of work." If so, this would not have been possible without all the help and encouragement; thus I've kept and treasure these supportive epistles. (I would also like to thank the record producers, the Wailers, Vivien Goldman, Penny Reel, Ken Braun, Douglas J. C. Thomson, Charlie Morgan, Lars Fyledal and Lowell "Bigga" Hill.) Even so, this discography should not be assumed to be complete by any means: the Wailers have appeared on hundreds of singles, whether prerelease, bootleg, rerelease, normal release, etc. To further complicate matters, a single song could be redone an indeterminate number of times (examples being "One Love" and "Bend Down Low" from the ska to reggae eras). Singles could also be mislabeled (there are Studio One singles pressings of "Jail House" and "Ruddie" that have the labels mixed up, and Studio One LPs on which they are miscredited; similarly, sides titled "Sinner Man" and "Zimmerman" are the same record).

Moreover, many ska, rock steady and reggae 45s bear no catalogue numbers or release dates. But even this might not be so maddening if the Wailers'

Jamaican producers kept accurate release ledgers—most kept none to speak of and still don't. In some cases, the fact that a song appears on a label founded by a prominent producer does not always mean it was his personal production; a record like "Lick Samba," while produced by Bob Marley, appeared on the Beverley's Music label because that was the publishing company it happened to be assigned to.

The single most important point to bear in mind when going through this discography is that *it represents a release schedule for a body of work, not a recording history*. It is only concerned with the dates when discs were manufactured and issued—*not* when the songs were composed or recorded.

A Jamaican producer might play an acetate dub plate or a prerelease pressing of a "hit" record at Sound System dances for as much as a year before issuing the record commercially. The single might then enjoy "hit" status on the Jamaican radio charts for another year before being picked up for British release. By the time "Simmer Down," for example, was deemed a "hit" in the London roots community (late 1964), it had been popular in Jamaica for almost two years. Yet if you ask the producer or the artists when they actually recorded the song, they'll tell you it was the winter of 1963. At the Wailers' first Studio One audition in December 1963, they performed "I'm Going Home," "Do You Remember," "Straight and Narrow Way," "I Don't Need Your Love," and, lastly, Bob's song "Simmer Down." Cut the next day with the Skatalites, "Simmer Down" debuted at Coxsone's sound system that night, and soon sold 70,000 units.

Think of this discography as a Wailers Recording Catalogue Primer.

WAILERS TRACKS

Early Leslie Kong Productions

Bob Marley cut some ska sides for Leslie Kong's Beverley's label between late 1961 and 1963 (labeled as Bob Morley, Bobby Martell, and then as Robert Marley and the Beverley's All-Stars) before working with Clement Dodd of Studio One. Bob recorded his first record for Leslie Kong, "Judge Not," at the end of 1961, followed by other sides that included "Terror" and "One Cup of Coffee," a remake of a 1961 Claude Gray country hit that bore no resemblance (contrary to popular belief) to Brook Benton's "Another Cup of Coffee," which was released in May 1964 on the U.S. Mercury label.

Early Solo Leslie Kong Productions on U.K. Singles Credited to Robert Marley

ISLAND		
Judge Not/Do You Still Love Me	WI 088	1963
Exodus [Ernest Ranglin]/One Cup of Coffee	WI 128	1963

Clement Dodd Productions

Clement Dodd–Produced Sides on JA Singles

These are among the ska tracks recorded by the Wailers for Dodd during 1963–66, which appeared back-to-back or with various artists on Dodd's World Disc, Studio One and Coxsone labels, among others, the sides credited to either the Wailing Wailers, the Wailers, or Peter Touch [*sic*] and the Wailers, with Constantine "Dream" Walker subbing for Bob Marley on such songs as "Let Him Go." Rita Anderson/Marley also sang backup on tracks like "Wages of Love." Beneath many of the song titles, set in parentheses, was the word "Scorcher"; "that just describe the beat" for Sound Systems, Dodd claims, but concedes it's his Performance Rights Society alias.

Simmer Down / It Hurts to Be Alone / I Don't Need Your Love / Mr. Talkative (later redone as "Mr. Chatterbox") / Play Boy / Your Love / Lonesome Feelings / There She Goes / Love and Affection (aka "Love & Affection," "Love or Affection") / Teenager in Love / Where Will I Find / What's New Pussycat / Maga Dog / And I Love Her (the Beatles song) / I Am the Toughest / Donna / I Made a Mistake / Jerk in Time / Wings of a Dove / Hoot Nanny Hoot / Do You Remember (aka "How Many Times") / Where Is My Mother / Jumbie Jamboree / I'm Gonna Put It On (aka "Put It On," cut with The Sharks backing band) / Cry to Me / Destiny / Ten Commandments of Love / Dancing Shoes / Ska Jerk / The Jerk (a different song) / Without You / Shame and Scandal / Rolling Stone (a recast rendition of Bob Dylan's "Like a Rolling Stone") / One Love / Nobody Knows / Love Won't Be Mine (aka "Love Won't Be Mine This Way") / Another Dance / Don't Ever Leave Me / Lonesome Track / Tell Them Lord / True Confession / Rocking Steady / Lemon Tree / Do It Right / Hooligan (aka "Holligan") / Let Him Go (aka "Rude Boy Get Ball") / I'm Going Home (aka "I Am Going Home") / Don't Look Back / Sound the Trumpet / When the Well Runs Dry / Habits / Can't You See / Dance with Me / I Want Somewhere (aka "Somewhere to Lay My Head") / Sinner Man (aka "Zimmerman") / Rude Boy (aka "Rule them Rudie," "Rude Boy Ska") / Jail House (aka "Jailhouse," "Rudie Boy" and "Good Good Rudie") / Who Feels It (aka "He Who Feels It Know [*sic*] It" and "Linger You Linger") / Get Ready / Do You Feel the Same Way (aka "Do You

Feel the Same Way Too") / I'm Still Waiting (a song influenced by Billy Stewart's "Sitting in the Park") / Climb the Ladder / Amen / I Left My Sins / What Am I Supposed to Do / Treat Me Good / Let the Lord Be Seen in You / White Christmas / Straight and Narrow Way (aka "Straight & Narrow") / Wages of Love / Go Jimmy Go / I Need You (a different song with the same title was cut circa 1966 with Bunny on lead and Dream Walker on backup) / Freedom Time (aka "Children Get Ready") / Dreamland (aka "Dream Land") / Sunday Morning / Tell Them Lord / I Stand Predominant / Just in Time / Diamond Baby (a song influenced by Curtis Mayfield's "Talking 'Bout My Baby") / Where's the Girl for Me

Clement Dodd–Produced Sides on U.K. Singles

SKA BEAT

Simmer Down/I Don't Need Your Love	JB 186	1964
Lonesome Feelings/There She Goes (both with the Mighty Vikings backup band)	JB 211	1965
Train to Skaville (the Soul Brothers)/I Made a Mistake	JB 226	1965
Love & Affection/Teenager in Love	JB 228	1966
And I Love Her/Do It Right	JB 230	1966
Zimmerman/Lonesome Track	JB 249	1966

ISLAND

It Hurts to Be Alone/Mr. Talkative	WI 188	1965
Play Boy/Your Love	WI 206	1965
Hoot Nanny Hoot (Peter Touch & the Wailers)/Do You Remember (Bob Marley & the Wailers)	WI 211	1965
Hooligan/Maga Dog	WI 212	1965
Shame and Scandal (Peter Touch & the Wailers)/The Jerk	WI 215	1965
Don't Ever Leave Me/Donna	WI 216	1965
What's New Pussycat/Where Will I Find	WI 254	1965
Independent Anniversary Ska (I Should Have Known Better; the Skatalites)/Jumbie Jamboree	WI 260	1966
Put It On/Love Won't Be Mine	WI 268	1966
He Who Feels It Know [*sic*] It/Sunday Morning	WI 3001	1966
Let Him Go (Rude Boy Get Bail)/Sinner Man	WI 3009	1966
I Am the Toughest (Peter Touch & the Wailers)/No Faith (Marcia Griffiths)	WI 3042	1966
Bend Down Low/Freedom Time	WI 3043	1966

RIO

Dancing Shoes/Don't Look Back	R 116	1966

DOCTOR BIRD

Rude Boy/Ringo's Theme—This Boy (Rolando Al & the Soul Brothers)	DB 1013	1966
Good Good Rudie/Oceans 11 (the City Slickers)	DB 1021	1966
Rasta Put It On (Peter Touch & the Wailers)/Ska with Ringo (Rolando Al & the Soul Brothers)	DB 1039	1966

SUPREME (U.K. IMPORT)

Let the Lord Be Seen in You (Bob Marley & the Spiritual Sisters)/White Christmas (Bob Marley & The Wailers)		1966

STUDIO ONE (U.K.)

Pussy Galore (credited to Lee Perry, but Wailers sing the harmonies)/Provocation (Roland Alphonso)		1966
Come By Here (Norma Frazier)/I Stand Predominant	SO 2024	1966

BAMBOO

Stranger in Love (John Holt)/Jailhouse	BAM 55	1970

Clement Dodd–Produced JA Albums

Note: Not included in this list of LPs is an entire album of such gospel songs as "Just in Time" that Jackie Mittoo (who played on the sessions) says Marley cut with Coxsone. The Wailers also reportedly cut an album's worth of Christmas songs for Dodd ("Sound the Trumpet" among them) that may or may not have been released in Jamaica in the mid-1960s.

The Wailing Wailers—Jamaica's Top-Rated Singing Sensation, Accompanied by the Soul Brothers	Studio One	

Put It On / I Need You / Lonesome Feeling / What's New Pussycat / One Love / When the Well Runs Dry / Ten Commandments of Love / Rude Boy / It Hurts to Be Alone / Love or Affection / I'm Still Waiting / Simmer Down

Marley, Tosh, Livingston & Associates	*Studio One*	

Another Dance / Lonesome Track / Rolling Stone / Can't You See / Let Him Go / Dance with Me / Maga Dog / I Want Somewhere / Hoot Nanny Hoot / Dreamland

The Best of Bob Marley & the Wailers	Studio One/ Coxsone GW 0002	1974

I Am Going Home / Bend Down Low / Mr. Talkative / Ruddie / Cry to Me / Wings of a Dove / Small Axe / Love Won't Be Mine / Dancing Shoes / Sunday Morning / He Who Feels It Knows It / Straight and Narrow Way

Clement Dodd–Produced U.K./U.S. Albums

STUDIO ONE/BUDDAH

The Best of Bob Marley & The Wailers SO 1106 1976

Destiny / Ruddie Boy / Cry to Me / Love Won't Be Mine / Play Boy / Sunday Morning / Put It On / I Need You / What's New Pussycat / Where Is My Mother / Wages of Love / Jailhouse (this track is actually "Ruddie Boy"—i.e., the same song, mislabeled, appears twice on the record)

CALLA

The Birth of a Legend, Bob Marley & the Wailers CAS 1240 1976
(The liner notes on this two-record set list, often erroneously, the lead vocalist on each track.)

I Made a Mistake / One Love / Let Him Go / Love and Affection / Simmer Down / Maga Dog / I Am Going Home / Donna / Nobody Knows / Lonesome Feeling / Wings of a Dove / It Hurts to Be Alone / I'm Still Waiting / Who Feels It / Do You Remember / Dancing Shoes / I Don't Need Your Love / Lonesome Track / Do You Feel the Same Way / The Ten Commandments of Love

CBS

The Birth of a Legend, Bob Marley & the Wailers, Featuring Peter Tosh XZ 34759 1977
(Half of the Calla album, from "I Made a Mistake" through "Lonesome Feeling.")

Early Music, Bob Marley and the Wailers, Featuring Peter Tosh XZ ZX 34760 1977
(Second half of the Calla album, from "Wings of a Dove" through "The Ten Commandments of Love.")

EPIC

Birth of a Legend 1963–66 ZGT 46769 1990
First CD release of this ska material. The original master tapes were restored for this project via Stephen St. Croix's remarkable Revectoring distortion-removal process, and

then digitally remastered, rendering each track clearer and crisper than the day they were released in Kingston! Liner notes by Timothy White include interview material with Coxsone Dodd, Beverly Kelso, Bob, Peter and Bunny.

Bob Marley & the Wailers with Peter Tosh
"Maga Dog," "Simmer Down," and ten other ska standards.

HEARTBEAT

Bob Marley & the Wailers: One Love at Studio One CD HB111/112 1991
A compilation of forty Wailers ska favorites, made notable by the inclusion of the previously unreleased "This Train," "True Confession" and "Wages of Love Rehearsal," as well as alternate takes of "It Hurts to Be Alone," "Playboy," "And I Love Her," "I'm Gonna Put It On," "Sinner Man" and "Rocking Steady." Liner notes by Leroy Pierson and Roger Steffens.
Destiny: Rare Ska Sides from Studio One 11661-7691-2 1999
"Destiny," "Rock Sweet Rock," an acoustic "Where Is My Mother," "White Christmas," plus fifteen less noteworthy sides. Liner copy by Leroy Pierson and Roger Steffens.

Wailers and Friends 11661-7701-2 1999
"Oh My Darling" by Bob Marley and Marcia Griffiths, "One More Chance," "Friends and Lovers," and "A Deh Pon Dem," by Rita Marley and the Soulettes and the Wailers, and "Bless You" by Bunny Livingston and Rita Marley are highpoints in this quirky eighteen-track Coxsone miscellany.

Climb The Ladder HB 251 2000

Dancing Shoes / (I'm Gonna) Put It On / Lonesome Track / Climb The Ladder / Love Won't Be Mine This Way / Dreamland / Lemon Tree / Nobody Knows / Wings Of A Dove / Sinner Man / Ten Commandments Of Love / Sunday Morning / I Made A Mistake / I Don't Need Your Love / Donna / The Jerk / Just In Time

Greatest Hits at Studio One HB 257 2003

One Love / (I'm Gonna) Put It On / Simmer Down / Treat Me Good / Who Feels It Knows It / Cry To Me / It Hurts To Be Alone / Dreamland / Let Him Go / Sinner Man / Jailhouse / Love and Affection / Maga Dog / I Am Going Home / I Need You So / I'm Still Waiting / And I Love Her / Sunday Morning

Later Leslie Kong Productions

Leslie Kong–Produced JA Sides

These tracks were among those cut for Leslie Kong's Beverley's label during late 1969 and 1970; while it was the tail end of the rock steady era and the Wailers were attempting to get in synch with the popular beat, they wound up with a sound much closer to the emerging reggae beat than that of rock steady. For this reason, it is mistakenly assumed that these tracks were cut years later than they were. Because they were unpopular at Sound Systems, very few eventually saw commercial release on singles in Jamaica. They later (1969–74) appeared in Britain on the Summit and Trojan labels, either back-to-back or with other artists on the flip sides:

Soul Captives / Caution / Do It Twice / Go Tell It on the Mountain / Stop the Train / Soul Shakedown Party (aka "Soul Shake Down Party") / Soon Come / Can't You See / Cheer Up / Back Out / Freedom Train

Leslie Kong–Produced Sides on JA Singles

BEVERLEY'S

Soon Come/Version	S.R. 133	1969

Leslie Kong–Produced Sides on U.K. Singles

TROJAN

Soul Shake Down Party/Shake Down Version (Beverley All-Stars)	TR 7759	1970
Soul Shakedown Party/Caution	TR 7911 (reissue)	1974

SUMMIT

Stop the Train/Caution	SUM 8526	1971
Freedom Train/Version	SUM 8530	1971

Leslie Kong–Produced JA Albums

BEVERLEY'S

The Best of the Wailers	BLP 001

Soul Shake Down Party / Stop the Train / Caution / Soul Captives / Go Tell It on the Mountain / Can't You See / Soon Come / Cheer Up / Back Out / Do It Twice

Leslie Kong–Produced U.K./U.S. Albums

ALA

Shakedown	ALA 1982 (serial no., not release date)	
Tracks are the same as on *The Best of the Wailers*.		
Soul Captives	ALA 1986	
Tracks are same as above.		

HAMMER

Bob Marley & The Wailers	HMR 9006	
Tracks are the same as above, but in different sequence.		

TROJAN/BEVERLEY'S

The Wailers: The Best Of The Wailers	TJPBX245	2005
Released as part of Trojan's "Soul Revolutionaries" Box Set		

Leslie Kong–Produced Sides on U.K. Albums

TROJAN

Hit Me with Music, Various Artists	TRLS 82	
Soul Shakedown Party		

Lee Perry Productions

Lee Perry–Produced JA Sides

These are some of the early reggae titles the Wailers released with Lee Perry between 1969 and 1972, which appeared on his Black Heart, Justice League, Maroon and Upsetter labels:

> Small Axe / Keep on Skanking (the Upsetters with Bob Marley on lead vocals) / Cross the Nation / Second Hand (aka "Brand New Second Hand," "Secondhand") / My Cup / Duppy Conqueror (numerous versions) / Kaya (aka "Kayah") / African Herbsman / Dreamland (aka "Dream Land") / Mr. Brown / Picture on the Wall / Soul Rebel / Try Me / 400 Years / No Sympathy (aka "My Sympathy," an instrumental version of preceding track) / Corner

Stone / No Water / Reaction / Soul Almighty / It's Alright (aka "Night Shift") / Stand Alone / All in One (medley) / Sun Is Shining (aka "To the Rescue") / Don't Rock My Boat (aka "Don't Rock the Boat," "I Like It Like This," "Satisfy My Soul") / Put It On / Riding High / Brain Washing / Run for Cover / Down Presser / Fussing and Fighting / Keep On Moving / Reaction / Memphis (instrumental)

Lee Perry–Produced Sides on JA/U.K. Singles

UPSETTER

My Cup/Son of Thunder (Lee Perry & the Upsetters)	US 340	1970
Dreamland/Version of Cup (Upsetters)	US 342	1970
Duppy Conqueror/Justice (Upsetters)	US 348	1970
Duppy Conqueror/Zig Zag		
Duppy Conqueror/Duppy Version		
Mr. Brown/Dracula (the Upsetters)	US 354	1970
Kayah/Version (the Upsetters)	US 356	1971
Small Axe/All in One	US 357	1971
Picture on the Wall (Rass Dawkins & the Wailers)/ Picture Version (the Upsetters)	US 368	1971
More Axe/The Axe Man	US 369	1971
Dreamland/Dream Version	US 371	1971
More Axe/The Axe Man (same as above)	US 372	1971
Keep On Moving/African Herbsman	US 392	1972

PUNCH

What a Confusion (Dave Barker)/Small Axe	PH 69	1971
Down Presser/Got the Tip (Junior Byles)	PH 77	1971

UNITY

Duppy Conqueror/Justice (the Upsetters)	UN 562	1970

TROJAN

Mr. Brown/Trench Town Rock (produced by Bob Marley)	TR 7979	1976

Lee Perry–Produced Sides on U.S. Singles

UPSETTER (NYC)

Don't Cross the Nation/ Version (the Upsetters)	LP 007	1970
Don't Cross the Nation/All in One	LP 007	1970

"Don't Cross the Nation" is by Earl "Little Roy" Lowe

Small Axe/Version (the Upsetters)	LP 009	1971
Secondhand/Secondhand Pt. 2	UP 9001	1971
More Axe/Axe Man		1971

SHELTER (DISTRIBUTED BY CAPITOL)

Doppy Conquer [*sic*]/Justice (the Upsetters)	7309	1971
Doppy Conquer/Doppy Conquer (a promotional copy, with a stereo A side and a mono B side)	7309	1971

CLOCKTOWER

Duppy Conqueror/Duppy Version	CT 505	1971

BLACK HEART

African Herbsman/Stand Alone	45 8042	1974

Lee Perry–Produced JA Albums

MAROON

Soul Rebels, Bob Marley & the Wailers 1970

Soul Rebel / Try Me / It's Alright / No Sympathy / My Cup / Soul Almighty / Rebels Hop / Corner Stone / 400 Years / No Water / Reaction / My Sympathy

UPSETTER

Soul Revolution, Bob Marley & the Wailers 1970

Keep On Moving / Don't Rock My Boat / Put It On / Fussing and Fighting / Duppy Conqueror v/4 / Memphis / Riding High / Kaya / African Herbsman / Stand Alone / Sun Is Shining / Brain Washing

Soul Revolution II, Bob Marley & the Wailers 1971

Dub versions of the above tracks. The record came out in a limited Jamaican edition and is extremely rare. Collectors should be aware that *Soul Revolution* is now widely available in a *Soul Revolution II* jacket that has color photos on a blue background. The original dub jacket was pale green with black-and-white photos.

Lee Perry–Produced U.K. Albums

TROJAN

Soul Rebels, Bob Marley & the Wailers TBL 126 1970
(Contents identical to Jamaican LP of same name.)
Released on Upsetter and Trojan labels
Re-released as part of Trojan's "Soul Revolutionaries" Box Set TJPBX245 2005

African Herbsman, Bob Marley & the Wailers TRLS 62 1973

Lively Up Yourself (produced by Bob Marley, Tuff Gong) / Small Axe / Duppy Conqueror / Trench Town Rock (produced by Bob Marley, Tuff Gong) / African Herbsman / Keep On Moving / Fussing and Fighting / Stand Alone / All in One / Don't Rock the Boat / Put It On / Sun Is Shining / Kaya / Riding High / Brain Washing / 400 Years

Rasta Revolution TRL 89 1974/ CDTRL 89 1988

The "Soul Rebels" album in a different running order minus "My Sympathy," and adding two tracks: "Mr Brown" and "Duppy Conqueror." The album also forms part of Trojan's "The Early Years 1969–73" box set.

TRLS 89 1974

Mr. Brown / Soul Rebel / Try Me / It's Alright / No Sympathy / My Cup / Duppy Conqueror / Rebel's Hop / Corner Stone / 400 Years / No Water / Reaction / Soul Almighty

Soul Revolution I & II TRLD 406 1988
(The famous original and rhythm/dub LPs in one set, including unreleased "Memphis" and "Soul Rebel Version 4." Notes by Steve Barrow.)

The Complete Upsetter Collection TBOXCD 013 2000
An extremely comprehensive six CD set that collects all known Upsetter tracks (and a few Tuff Gong tracks too) including alternate takes. Sleeve notes by Laurence Cane-Honeysett.

Soul Rebel / Soul Rebel Version Four (The Upsetters) / Soul Rebel Alternate / Soul Rebel Dub (The Upsetters) / Try Me / Try Me Version (The Upsetters) / It's Alright / It's Alright Version (The Upsetters) / It's Alright Alternate / No Sympathy / No Sympathy Version (The Upsetters) / My Cup / Version of Cup (The Upsetters) / Rebels Hop / Rebels Hop Version (The Upsetters) / Corner Stone / Corner Stone Version (The Upsetters) / Jah is Mighty / Four Hundred

Years / Four Hundred Years Version (The Upsetters) / No Water / No Water Version (The Upsetters) / Reaction / Reaction Version (The Upsetters) / Soul Almighty / Soul Almighty Version (The Upsetters) / Shocks of Mighty Part One (with Lee Perry) / Shocks of Mighty Part Two / Shocks of Mighty Version (The Upsetters) / True Love (Carl "Rass" Dawkins and Bob Marley & The Wailers) / Cloud Nine (Carl "Rass" Dawkins and Bob Marley & The Wailers) / Don't Let the Sun Catch You Crying (Dave Barker and Bob Marley & The Wailers) / Don't Let the Sun Catch You Crying Version (The Upsetters) / Duppy Conqueror / Duppy Conqueror Version Four (The Upsetters) / Upsetting Station (Dave Barker & The Upsetters) / Duppy Conqueror Alternate / Mr. Brown / Mr. Brown Version (Dracula) (The Upsetters) / Small Axe / More Axe / Battle Axe (The Upsetters) / Shocks '71 (Dave Barker, Charlie Ace & The Upsetters) / More More Axe / The Axe Man (The Upsetters) / Picture on the Wall (Carl "Rass" Dawkins and Bob Marley & The Wailers) / Picture on the Wall Version Three (The Upsetters) / Dreamland / Dreamland Instrumental (Winston Wright & The Upsetters) / Dreamland (U Roy & The Upsetters) / Dreamland Version Two / All in One / All in One Part Two / Copasetic (The Upsetters) / Down Presser / Down Presser Version (The Upsetters) / Long Long Winter / Long Long Winter Version (The Upsetters) / Love Light / Love Light Version (The Upsetters) / Love Light Alternate / Send Me That Love / What a Confusion (Dave Barker & Bunny Wailer) / Man to Man / Man to Man Version (The Upsetters) / Keep On Moving / Keep On Moving Version (The Upsetters) / Moving Version (Big Youth & The Upsetters) / Keep On Moving Alternate / Don't Rock My Boat / Don't Rock My Boat Version (The Upsetters) / Don't Rock My Boat Alternate*** / I Like It Like This (Johnny Lover)*** / Don't Rock My Boat Alternate*** / Put It On / Put It On Version (The Upsetters) / Fussing and Fighting / Fussing and Fighting Version (The Upsetters) / Memphis (Peter Tosh & The Upsetters) / Memphis Version (The Upsetters) / Riding High / Riding High Version (The Upsetters) / Kaya / Kaya Version (The Upsetters) / Turn Me Loose / African Herbsman / African Herbsman Version (The Upsetters) / Stand Alone / Stand Alone Version (The Upsetters) / Sun Is Shining / Sun Is Shining Version / Brain Washing / Brain Washing Version / Brand New Second Hand / Brand New Second Hand Version (The Upsetters) / Brand New Second Hand Alternate / Concrete Jungle*** / Concrete Jungle Version*** (Wailers All Star Band) / Rainbow Country / Rainbow Country Version (The Upsetters) / Satisfy My Soul Babe*** / Satisfy My Soul Babe Version*** (Wailers All Star Band) / Keep On Skanking / Natural Mystic / Natural Mystic Version (The Upsetters) / I Know A Place / I Know A Place Version (The Upsetters) / Who Colt the Game / Who Colt the Game Version (The Upsetters) ***Tuff Gong Production

Lee Perry–Produced U.S. Albums

PRESSURE DISC

Soul Revolution Part II, Bob Marley & the Wailers LPS 507 1981
(Contents identical to Jamaican *Soul Revolution* on Upsetter label.)

Reggae Revolution Vol. 2, Bob Marley & the Wailers 50028
(Contents identical to Jamaican *Soul Revolution* on Upsetter label.)

Reggae Revolution Vol. 3, Bob Marley & the Wailers 50029

Mr. Brown / Duppy Conqueror / Rebel's Hop / 400 Years / Soul Almighty / Lively Up Yourself / Small Axe / Trench Town Rock / All in One / Keep On Moving

PHOENIX

Marley Phoenix 10 1982

Kaya / Mr. Brown / Rebel's Hop / 400 Years / Soul Almighty / My Cup / Cornerstone / No Water / Reaction / Try Me

Danny Sims, Johnny Nash, Arthur Jenkins–Supervised Sessions

These tracks reportedly are among what Danny Sims describes as "in the neighborhood of seventy-two" tracks supposedly cut on his own between 1968 and 1972 while working with Johnny Nash and Arthur Jenkins. According to Bunny Waller, they are largely demo tracks the Wailers cut at Dynamic Studios in Kingston and in London studios under the direction of Sims, Nash and Jenkins for Cayman Music and JAD Music (the latter company named for Johnny, Arthur and Danny). Bunny maintains that key personnel on most of the tracks were Bob Marley, Peter Tosh, Bunny Waller and Rita Marley; with Hux Brown on guitar, Jackie Jackson on bass and Hugh Masakela adding trumpet in some instances. Bunny notes that "Reggae on Broadway" was cut in CBS Studios in London with Johnny Nash's backup band, Rabbit and the Jungles, led by keyboardist John "Rabbit" Bundrick. "Them should nevar release da songs 'pon nuh album," Bunny charges, "because we only do dem as demos fe other companies ta listen."

Danny Sims denies that the sessions were demo sessions, and adds that in addition to his own material (forty songs, by Bunny's estimate), Bob also recorded a series of songs by the R&B writing team of Jimmy Norman and Al Pyfrom. The idea, says Sims, was "to cut Bob Marley in a rhythm-and-blues, Top 40 style so we could try to gain acceptance for him in America." When a number of the tracks were compiled for the 1982 *Chances Are* LP, Chris Blackwell of Island Records charged Warner-Elektra Atlantic Records with "cynical exploitation," and alleged that the tracks had been overdubbed.

Put It On / How Many Times / I'm Hurting Inside (aka "Hurting Inside") / Oh Lord, I Got to Get There / It Hurts to Be Alone / The World Is Changing / Gonna Get You / Lonely Girl / Lonesome Feeling / Stay with Me / Milk Shake and Potato Chips / Reggae on Broadway / Dance to the Reggae (aka "Dance Do [*sic*] the Reggae") / There She Goes / Mellow Mood / Treat You Right / Chances Are (aka "Changes Are") / Soul Rebel / Hammer / You Can't Do That to Me / Touch Me / Thank You Lord / Wisdom / Bend Down Low

Sims, Nash, Jenkins–Produced Sides on JA/U.K. Singles

WIRL

Mellow Mood/Bend Down Low (by Bob Marley Plus Two)

CBS

Reggae on Broadway/Oh Lord I Got to Get There	CBS (UK) 8114	1972

COTILLION

Reggae on Broadway/Gonna Get You (12" disco)	79250	

Sims, Nash, Jenkins–Produced Sides on U.S. Singles

COTILLION

Reggae on Broadway/Reggae on Broadway (long and short versions; 12" disco)	DMD 291	1981
Reggae on Broadway/Gonna Get You	46023	

Sims, Nash, Jenkins–Produced Sides on U.S./U.K. Albums

NEW CROSS

Soul Rebel, Bob Marley & the Wailers	NC 001

There She Goes / Put It On / How Many Times / Mellow Mood / Changes [*sic*] Are / Hammer / Tell Me (aka "You Can't Do That to Me") / Touch Me / Treat You Right / Soul Rebel

COTILLION

Chances Are SD 5228 1981

Reggae on Broadway / Gonna Get You / Chances Are / Soul Rebel / Dance Do [*sic*] the Reggae / Mellow Mood / Stay with Me / (I'm) Hurting Inside

ACCORD

Jamaican Storm, Bob Marley & the Wailers SN 7211 1982
(Contents identical to *Soul Rebel* LP on New Cross label.)

JAMAICA

Bob Marley and the Wailers/Bob, Peter, Bunny & Rita JR 10002 1985
JAD sides with new music tracks added.

Oh Lord / It Hurts to Be Alone / Lonesome Feelings / Milkshake & Potato Chips / Touch Me / Lonely Girl / The World Is Changing / Treat You Right / Soul Shake Down Party

JAD RECORDS

Soul Almighty: The Formative Years, Vol. I JAD 1001-2 1996
Touted as music from "the JAD vaults" but sounding like it came from someone's sock drawer, this "restoration" of the Wailers' most obscure 1967–72 tape meanderings, which *Dub Missive* magazine denounced in 1996 as "a cruel hoax," finds a mediocre host of modern Stateside pop studio musicians unable to shore up hack R&B scribblings like "Splish for My Splash," "Fallin' In and Out Of Love" and "What Goes Around Comes Around." The enhanced CD aspects of the effort fail to eclipse its central worthlessness. As the *Dub Missive* deduced, this stroke of exploitation is "quite possibly the worst reggae CD ever."

Note: After protracted legal wrangling, Universal finally secured the rights in 2004 to release the entire Bob Marley & the Wailers catalogue from the time they left Studio One in 1967 to the time they signed with Chris Blackwell in 1972. Though Timothy White described Volumes I–III of JAD's *"Complete Wailers 1967–1972"* series as "inferior reissues" in an earlier edition of this work, they have at least tied up all the loose ends. Universal has now re-released the entire JAD series with the occasional additional "bonus" track. The vast majority of these tracks first appeared as seven-inch Jamaican, U.K., or U.S. singles, as listed in this discography.

The Complete Wailers 1967 to 1972 Part One	JAD 474326 PM 599/ABO689 1	1997
The Complete Wailers 1967 to 1972 Part Two	JAD 823267 2 PM 599/ABO698 1	1997
The Complete Wailers 1967 to 1972 Part Three	JAD 495250 2 PM 596/AB 07521	1998
The Complete Wailers 1967 to 1972 Part Four	JAD AB 1233 1PM 580/53724 2 PM 580	2002
The Complete Wailers 1967 to 1972 Part Five	JAD AB 1234 1PM 580	2002
The Complete Wailers 1967 to 1972 Part Six	JAD 542 222 1PM 262	2002
The Complete Wailers 1967 to 1972 Jungle Dub	JAD LP AB 0759 1	1998
The Complete Wailers 1967 to 1972 Jungle Dub Part Two	JAD LP AB 1075	2001

Universal/JAD "The Complete Story 1967 to 1972"
(Credited to Bob Marley & the Wailers unless otherwise stated.)

Soul Rebels	0602498 66 7446	2004
Soul Revolution Part II	0602498 66 7514	2004
The Best of the Wailers (Beverley's)	0602498 66 8054	2004
Upsetter Revolution Rhythm (Instrumental)	0602498 66 8061	2004
Play Play (Rita Marley)	0602498 67 1023	2004
Can't Blame the Youth (Peter Tosh)	0602498 67 1030	2004
Original Cuts	0602498 67 1092	2004
127 King Street	0602498 67 7612	2004
Ammunition Dub Collection	0602498 67 7629	2004
Black Dignity (Peter Tosh)	0602498 67 7636	2004
Fy-ah, Fy-ah (3-CD Box Set)	0602498 67 9654	2004
Wail 'N' Soul 'M Singles Selecta	0602498 72 6822	2005
Classic (The Universal Masters Collection)	0602498 820 1541	2004
Feel Alright	0602498 13 4276	2004
Grooving Kingston 12 (3-CD Box Set)	0602498 16 4723	2004
The JAD Years (An Introduction To)	981 875 0	2004
The Essential Collection (Bob Marley)	982 033 2	2004

Odd and Obscure Productions JA/U.K./U.S.

Clancy Eccles–Produced Sides on U.K. Singles

DOCTOR BIRD

Nice Time/Hypocrite	1091	1967

TROJAN

Thank You Lord/Wisdom TRO 9065 1981

Bunny Lee–Produced Sides on U.K. Singles

JACKPOT

Mr. Chatterbox/Walk Through the World JP 730 1970

SIRE

Escape from Babylon, Martha Velez SASD 7515 1976

A singular Bob Marley project: the production (with the help of Lee Perry in Jamaica and Craig Leon and Richard Gottehrer in New York) of an entire LP by a white female non-Jamaican singer. An unjustly overlooked early reggae crossover record, it features backup by the I-Threes, the (post-Bunny and Peter) Wailers, the Zap Pow Horns and some recast writing by Bob ("There You Are" [aka "Stand Alone"], "Happiness" [aka "Hurting Inside"], "Disco Night," the last in collaboration with Velez).

Money Man / There You Are / Wild Bird / Disco Night / Bend Down Low / Happiness / Come On In / Get Up, Stand Up

TUFF GONG

Bob Marley Interviews . . . 1982

Interviews from 1973 conducted with Bob Marley by journalist Neville Willoughby that segue into portions of the appropriate Wailers tracks, with "Natural Mystic" as the recurring theme song.

Natural Mystic (live) / Trenchtown Rock (with dub section) / Redemption Song / Babylon System / Time Will Tell / Natural Mystic / Revolution (live) / Survival / One Drop / Roots, Rock, Reggae (live) / Guava Jelly (instrumental) / Rat Race

WIRL

Nice Time/It Hurts to Be Alone WLS 1044/1045

Since the A side is produced by Clancy Eccles and the B side by Coxsone Dodd, and the label is a photocopy of the older JA WIRL label, this is a likely pirate.

EDEL/HYPNOTIC

Sun Is Shining (remix by Funkstar De Luxe) 1999

PALM PICTURES

Sun Is Shining (remix by Ibiza All Stars & Messy Boys) 1999

(JULIAN MARLEY)

Me Name Jr. Gong (Alamo Remix featuring Grand Puba/Album Version/Inna Dub Style) 54240–2 1998

Unusual Multi-Producer Compilation LPs

TROJAN

In the Beginning, Bob Marley & the Wailers TRLS 221 1983
Thirteen assorted Lee Perry, Leslie Kong, JAD, and Bunny Lee sides, including the obscure "Adam and Eve," "Jah Is Mighty," and "Turn Me Loose."

Bob Marley & Friends: Roots of a Legend CDTAL901 1997
A two-CD, 46-track satchel of crude rare tracks, out-of-tune putterings, halting demos and half-realized dub-outs, often from Lee Perry's cutting room floor—as fleshed out with random throat-clearing bosh from Big Youth or Dave Barker. Included on the early 1970s-era disc are "Shocks of Mighty," a variant of "Soul Almighty"; "Run for Cover," which sounds like a work tape for "Soul Rebel"; the primitive "Send Me That Love" and "Love Light," plus the formerly unreleased "Rainbow Country," a slight but breezy riff. Also surfacing is a so-so cover of "Long Long Winter" from the Impressions' classic 1964 ABC-Paramount album *Keep on Pushing*. On the second disc are random sides of Bunny Lee and Joe Gibbs studio vintage, like Bunny Livingston's "Dreamland," Peter Tosh's "Arise Blackman," plus silly penny arcade-style organ instrumentals by Peter. Don't let the handsome package fool you: this ultrapregnant EP is more puny stems than pure roots.

MILAN

True Roots 53399-2 1997
A briefer mutation of the above, salted with some familiar Leslie Kong stuff ("Back Out," "400 Years"), and a dumb instrumental ("Happy People"). Buyers beware: one day soon some rascal will sweep all such scraps into one pile and pronounce it the Rema equivalent of the Sistine Chapel.

Wailers Productions

Wailers-Produced Sides for Wail 'N' Soul 'M, Tuff Gong

Tired of being ripped off by local producers, Bob sank his savings and whatever other money he could scrounge up into several record labels and shops, the first being the Wail 'N' Soul 'M label, headquartered at 18A Greenwich Park Road in Kingston in 1967–68, then 14 Crescent Road. In 1970–71 he started Tuff Gong records and had record stores at Orange Street and then at 127 King Street, the latter being the chief local outlet until Tuff Gong International, Ltd., at 56 Hope Road. These sides appear on the Wail 'N' Soul 'M (aka Wail 'N' Soul) and Tuff Gong labels, which also issued 45s by the I-Threes, the Wailers All-Stars and Family Man Barrett. When not distributed by his own company, Sonic Sounds, Ltd., Peter Tosh's Intel-Diplo label was often distributed by Tuff Gong. Some of the Wailers' finest songs have appeared on these labels, raw, uncompromising music that was usually remixed or rerecorded if released outside of Jamaica. The producers include Bob Marley (customarily) and Alan Cole, Lee Perry and Peter Tosh. Clement Dodd did distribution in 1967–68.

Among the well-nigh innumerable sides between 1967 and 1982:

Lick Samba / Selassie Is the Chapel / Midnight Ravers (aka "Midnite Ravers") / Screw Face / Craven Choke Puppy / Stir It Up / Bus Dem Shut / Hurting Inside / Send Me That Love / This Train / Trench Town Rock (aka "Trenchtown Rock") / Ammunition (instrumental) / Pound Get a Blow / Hypocrites (aka "Hipocrites") / Don't Rock My Boat (aka "Don't Rock the Boat Satisfy My Soul," "I Like It Like This") / Satisfy My Soul Jah Jah (different song) / Steppin' Razor (aka "Stepping Razor," "Walking Razor") / Comma Comma / Hold On to This Feeling / Nice Time / Ticket for an Eroplane (aka "The Letter") / Fire Fire / Guava Jelly (two different local versions) / Concrete Jungle / Once Bitten (Peter Tosh & the Wailers) / Redder Than Red / Knotty Dread [*sic*] / Lively Up Yourself / Belly Full (aka "Them Belly Full") / Road Block (aka "Rebel Music," "Three o'Clock Roadblock") / Talkin' Blues (aka "Talking Blues") / Bend Down Low / No Woman, No Cry / Rat Race / Lion (Peter Tosh & the Wailers) / Chant I (aka "Rastaman Chant") / Sun Is Shining / Run for Cover / Tread Oh (aka "Tread Along") / All in One / Rock It Babe / Get Ready (aka "Freedom Time") / Selassie Is the Chapel / This Man Is Back / Pyaka / Jah Live (produced by Lee Perry) / Smile Jamaica / Roots, Rock, Reggae / War / Exodus / Rastaman Live Up / Work / Guided Missile / Blackman Redemption / Punky Reggae Party / Downpressor / Ambush / One Drop / Bad Card / Comin' In from the Cold (aka "Coming In from the Cold") / Trouble on the Road Again / Could You Be Loved / I Know / Soultown / Let the Sun Shine In (aka "Let the Sun Shine on Me") / Lyrical Satyrical I [*sic*] / You Should Have Known Better (aka "Back Biter") / Funeral / The Lord Will Make a Way

Wailers–Produced (aka R. Marley, B. Marley, Wailers, Tuff Gong, A. Cole; Except as Noted) Wail 'N' Soul 'M and Tuff Gong JA Singles

EARLY (1967–70) SINGLES, A SAMPLING

Bend Down Low/Mellow Mood (first Wail 'N' Soul 'M 45, with a red, green and gold label) 1967
Thank You Lord/Nice Time 1967
Hypocrites/Pound Get a Blow 1967
Nice Time/Rock It 1968
Pound Get a Blow/Burial 1968
Satisfy My Soul Jah Jah/Craven
Satisfy My Soul Jah Jah/Satisfy Version (by Bob Marley; actually, this is "Craven" again)
Hurting Inside/This Train 1968
Rock My Boat/I Like It Like This (Johnny Lover)
Redder Than Red/Red (Version)
All in One/Version
Rock It Baby/Version
Guava Jelly/Guava (Version)
Get Ready (aka "Freedom Time")/Play, Play (Rita Marley) 1968
Back Biter/Version
Tread Oh/Instrumental (aka "Tread Along") 1969
Run for Cover/Sun Is Shining (first Tuff Gong single) 1970

LATER TUFF GONG AND 56 HOPE ROAD SINGLES, A SAMPLING

Trenchtown Rock/Trenchtown Version 1971
Kingston 12 Shuffle (U Roy & Bob Marley)/Ammunition (The Wailers All-Star Band) 1971
Ammunition (The Wailers All-Star Band)/Backbiter (You Should Have Known Better) 1971
Bellyful/Version 1971
Lick Samba/Samba 1971
Midnite Ravers/Ravers Version 1972
Craven Choke Puppy/Choke (The Wailers Group) 1972
Road Black/Rebel Music (Version) 1972
Craven Version (Big Youth)/Thank You Lord 1972
Knotty Dread/Version 1974
Talking Blues/Version (with I Roy) 1975
Jah Live/Concrete (produced by Lee Perry) 1975
Smile Jamaica, Part One/Part Two (two different tempos) 1976
Work/Guided Missile (produced by A. Barrett) 1976
Roots Rock Reggae/War 1976
Exodus/Instrumental 1977

Punky Reggae Party/Punky Reggae Version (7" and 12" disco; coproduced by Bob Marley and LeePerry)		1977
Rastaman Live Up/Don't Give Up (coproduced by Bob Marley and Lee Perry)		1978
Blackman Redemption/Version		1978
Hypocrites/Nice Time (reissue of 1967 Eccles tracks)		1979
One Drop/One Dub		1979
Bad Card/Rub-a-Dub Style		1980
Ambush/In Dub		1980
Comin' In from the Cold/Dubbin' In		1980
Redemption Song/Redemption Song (band version)		1980
I Know/I Know Dub (7" and 12" disco)		1981
Zion Express/Redemption Song (7" and 12" disco)		1981
Trenchtown/Version (7" and 12" disco)		1982

Wailers-Produced Wail 'N' Soul 'M and Tuff Gong Sides on U.K. Labels

WIRL (UK)

Bend Down Low/Mellow Mood

MUSIK CITY

Habits/Amen

TROJAN

Stir It Up/This Train	TR 617	1968

ESCORT

To the Rescue/Run for Cover	ERT 842	1970

SUPREME

Let the Lord Be Seen in You (Bob Marley & the Spiritual Sisters)/White Christmas		1971
I Like It Like This/I Am Sorry (Bunny Gale)	SUP 216	1971

BULLET

Soultown/Let the Sun Shine on Me	BU 464	1971
Lick Samba/Samba (Version)	BU 493	1971

GREEN DOOR

Lively Up Yourself/Live (Tommy McCook)	GD 4002	1971
Trenchtown Rock/Grooving Kgn. 12 (Version)	GD 4005	1971
Guava Jelly/Redder Than Red	GD 4025	1972

PUNCH

Screw Face/Face Man (Version)	PH 101	1972
You Should Have Known Better (aka "Back Biter"; by Tuff Gong All-Stars)/Instrumental	PH 114	1972

Wailers-Produced U.S. Tuff Gong Sides

G&C

Trenchtown Rock/Version (A side has an extra verse)	C&G 5000	

TUFF GONG

Kingston 12 Shuffle (U Roy)/Ammunition (instrumental; the A side is a U Roy dub of the Jamaican version)	TG 5002	
Lively Up Yourself/Guava Jelly (different lyrics)	TG 5005	
Craven Choke Puppy/Version	TG 5007	
Steppin' (Walking) Razor/The Letter	TG 5009	
Midnight Ravers/Version	TG 5014	

TUFF GONG/SHANACHIE

Music Lesson/Nice Time (12") (old tracks containing Bob reworked with Bunny, Peter, Junior Braithwaite and Vision as the Original Wailers)	12-001	1985

Island Records Productions

*Bob Marley or *Bob Marley and Chris Blackwell–Produced U.S. and U.K. Blue Mountain/Island/Tuff Gong Intl. Singles (Except as Noted)*

Baby Baby [*sic*] We've Got a Date/Stop That Train	BM 1021	1973
Concrete Jungle/Reincarnated Souls	WIP 6164	1973
Rock It Baby/Stop That Train*	1211	1973
Concrete Jungle (Mono)/No More Trouble (Stereo)*	1215	1973
Get Up, Stand Up/Slave Driver*	WIP 6167	1973
Get Up, Stand Up/Slave Driver	P 1218	1973
I Shot the Sheriff/Pass It On/Duppy Conqueror (3-song promo EP)	IDJ	1973

So Jah Seh/Natty Dread	WIP 6262	1974
Lively Up Yourself/So Jah Seh	IS027	1974
No Woman, No Cry/Kinky Reggae (both tracks live; 7" and 12" disco; produced by Steve Smith and Chris Blackwell)	WIP 6244	1974
No Woman, No Cry/Kinky Reggae (both tracks live; produced by Steve Smith and Chris Blackwell)	IS 037	1975
Jah Live/Concrete	WIP 6265	1976
Roots, Rock, Reggae/Cry to Me	IS 060	1976
Johnny Was (Woman Hold Her Head and Cry)/Cry to Me	WIP 6296	1976
Positive Vibration/Roots, Rock, Reggae	WIP 26348	1976
Who the Cap Fit/Roots, Rock, Reggae	IS 072	1976
Roots, Rock, Reggae/Stir It Up	WIP 6309	1976
Exodus/Stir It Up	IS 089	1977
Exodus/Instrumental (7" and 12" disco)	WIP 6390	1977
Exodus/Instrumental (7" and 12" disco)	IXP-7	1977
Waiting in Vain/Roots	IS092	1977
Waiting in Vain/Roots	WIP 6402	1977
Jamming/Punky Reggae Party (7" and 12" disco; produced by Bob Marley and Lee Perry)	WIP 6410	1977
Is This Love/Crisis (Version)	IS099	1978
Is This Love/Crisis	WIP 6420	1978
Satisfy My Soul/Smile Jamaica	WIP 6440	1978
War/No More Trouble/Exodus (live; produced by Chris Blackwell and Jack Nuber)	IPR 2026	1978
Stir It Up (live; produced by Chris Blackwell and Jack Nuber)/Rat Race	WIP 6478	1979
So Much Trouble in the World/Instrumental	WIP 6501	1979
Survival/Wake Up and Live	WIP 6553	1979
Survival/Wake Up and Live	IS 49080	1979
One Drop/Kaya	IS 49156	1979
Could You Be Loved/One Drop/Ride Natty Ride (3-song 12" EP)	WIP 6610	1979
Zimbabwe/Survival	WIP 6597	1979
Zimbabwe/Africa Unite/Wake Up and Live (3-song 12" EP; same catalogue number as preceding)	WIP 6597	1980
Could You Be Love/One Drop	WIP 6610	1980
Three Little Birds/Every Need Got an Ego to Feed	WIP 6641	1980
Redemption Song/Redemption Song (with band; 7" and 12" disco)	WIP 6653	1980
Coming In from the Cold/Redemption Song	IS 49636	1980
Jammin'/No Woman No Cry	IS 49755	1981
Jamming/No Woman, No Cry (12")	12WIP6246	1981
Buffalo Soldier/Buffalo Dub (also 12")	DMD 628	1983

One Love/People Get Ready/So Much Trouble/Keep On Moving (regular and dub 12" EP)	121S(X) 169	1984
Could You Be Loved/Africa Unite	422–875 676–4	1990
Get Up, Stand Up (live 12" from *Talkin' Blues*)	PR12 6651-1	1991
Iron Lion Zion/Smile Jamaica/Three Little Birds/Iron Lion Zion (12" Mix)	864405–2	1992
Why Should I/Exodus/Why Should I (Bone Remix)/ Exodus (Kindred Spirit Remix)		1992
Keep on Moving (from *Natural Mystic* album)		1995
Easy Skanking/Redemption Song (Band Version)/Punky Reggae Party (Long Version)/ All Day All Night (previously unissued) (on CD, cassette, 12" vinyl)	TGX5	1995

Bob Marley–Produced Albums on Tuff Gong

A Tuff Gong counterpart of all Island albums was released in Jamaica, all of them with different mixes and slightly different cover art. *Survival* (1979) was perhaps the most physically exotic Tuff Gong release from the "Island Era," having been pressed on red, yellow, green and translucent vinyl in Jamaica for collectors.

Island Albums in the U.S./U.K. (Produced as Noted)

Catch a Fire, produced by Bob Marley and Chris Blackwell — ILPS 9241 — 1973

Concrete Jungle / Slave Driver / 400 Years / Stop That Train / Baby We've Got a Date (Rock It Baby) / Stir It Up / Kinky Reggae / No More Trouble / Midnight Ravers

Burnin', produced by Chris Blackwell and Bob Marley — ILPS 9256 — 1973

Get Up, Stand Up / Hallelujah Time / I Shot the Sheriff / Burnin' and Lootin' / Put It On / Small Axe / Pass It On / Duppy Conqueror / One Foundation / Rasta Man Chant

Natty Dread, produced by Chris Blackwell and the Wailers — ILPS 9281 — 1974

Lively Up Yourself / No Woman, No Cry / Them Belly Full (But We Hungry) / Rebel Music (Three o'Clock Roadblock) / So Jah Seh / Natty Dread / Bend Down Low, Talkin' Blues / Revolution

Live! Bob Marley & the Wailers, produced by Steve Smith and Chris Blackwell	ILPS 9376	1975

Trenchtown Rock / Burnin' & Lootin' / Them Belly Full / Lively Up Yourself / No Woman, No Cry / I Shot the Sheriff / Get Up, Stand Up

Rastaman Vibration, produced by Bob Marley & the Wailers	ILPS 9383	1976

Positive Vibration / Roots, Rock, Reggae / Johnny Was / Cry to Me / Want More / Crazy Baldhead / Who the Cap Fit / Night Shift / War / Rat Race

Exodus, produced by Bob Marley & the Wailers	ILPS 9498	1977

Natural Mystic / So Much Things to Say / Guiltiness / The Heathen / Exodus / Jamming / Waiting in Vain / Turn Your Lights Down Low / Three Little Birds / One Love/ People Get Ready

Kaya, produced by Bob Marley & the Wailers	ILPS 9517	1978

Easy Skanking / Kaya / Sun Is Shining / Is This Love / Satisfy My Soul / She's Gone / Misty Morning / Crisis / Running Away / Time Will Tell

Babylon by Bus, produced by Bob Marley & the Wailers	ISLD 11 1298	1978

Positive Vibration / Punky Reggae Party / Exodus / Stir It Up / Rat Race / Concrete Jungle / Kinky Reggae / Lively Up Yourself / Rebel Music / War / No More Trouble / Is This Love / Heathen / Jamming

Survival, produced by Bob Marley & the Wailers and Alex Sadkin	ILPS 9542	1979

Wake Up and Live / Africa Unite / One Drop / Ride Natty Ride / Ambush in the Night / So Much Trouble in the World / Zimbabwe / Top Rankin' / Babylon System / Survival

Uprising, produced by Bob Marley & the Wailers	ILPS 9596	1980

Coming In from the Cold / Real Situation / Bad Card / We and Dem / Work / Zion Train / Pimper's Paradise / Could You Be Loved / Forever Loving Jah / Redemption Song

Confrontation, produced by Chris Blackwell and the Wailers — 7 90085-1 — 1983

(Album was also released in the U.K. as a picture disc.)

Mix Up, Mix Up / Buffalo Soldier / Chant Down Babylon / I Know / Stiff-Necked Fools / Jump/Nyabinghi / Trench Town / Give Thanks and Praises / Blackman Redemption / Rastaman Live Up

Legend — 7 90169-1 — 1984

A comprehensive greatest-hits collection, including a fold-out memorabilia display and liner notes by Timothy White, in association with Rob Partridge of Island Records, Ltd.; production credits as on the original tracks, with five sides given contemporary dance remixes by Eric Thorngren for the U.S. release (see asterisks).

Is This Love / No Woman No Cry* / Could You Be Loved / Three Little Birds / Buffalo Soldier* / Get Up Stand Up / Stir It Up / One Love/People Get Ready / I Shot the Sheriff / Waiting in Vain* / Redemption Song / Satisfy My Soul / Exodus* / Jamming*

Rebel Music — 90520 — 1986

"War" and other rabble-rousers; liner notes by Neil Spencer.

ISLAND/TUFF GONG

Talkin' Blues — 422-848 243 — 1991

Unissued live and studio performances interspersed with interview clips. Includes the title track, "Walk the Proud Land," and the previously unreleased "Am-A-Do." Liner notes by Rob Partridge.

Natural Mystic (The Legend Lives On) — 314-524103 — 1995

An anthology of Marley's tuneful social commentary.

Natural Mystic / Easy Skanking / Iron Lion Zion / Crazy Baldheads / So Much Trouble in the World / War / Africa Unite / Trenchtown Rock (live) / Keep On Moving (special remix) / Sun Is Shining / Who the Cap Fit / One Drop / Roots, Rock, Reggae / Pimper's Paradise / Time Will Tell

AXIOM/ISLAND

Dreams of Freedom: Ambient Translations of Bob Marley in Dub, Remix production by Bill Laswell — 314-524 419-2 — 1997

Rebel Music (3 O'Clock Roadblock) / No Woman No Cry / The Heathen, Them Belly Full (But We Hungry) / Waiting in Vain / So Much Trouble in the World / Exodus / Burnin' and Lootin' / Is This Love / One Love (People Get Ready) / Midnight Ravers

TUFF GONG/ISLAND/DEF JAM

Chant Down Babylon 314 549404-2 1999

Commemorative project executive-produced by Stephen Marley, featuring guest artists on modern-era archival Bob Marley tracks. A track of Lenny Kravitz doing "Roots, Rock, Reggae" was shelved.

No More Trouble—with Erykah Badu
Rebel Music—with Krayzie Bone
Johnny Was—with Guru
Concrete Jungle—with Rakim
Rastaman Chant—with Busta Rhymes & Flipmode Squad
Guiltiness—with Lost BoyZ featuring Mr. Cheeks
Turn Your Lights Down Low—with Lauryn Hill
Jammin'—with MC Lyte
Kinky Reggae—with the Marley Brothers and the Ghetto Youths Crew
Roots, Rock, Reggae—with Steven Tyler and Joe Perry
Survival . . . Black Survivors—with Chuck D
Burnin' and Lootin'—with The Roots featuring Black Thought

UNIVERSAL/TUFF GONG

One Love: The Very Best of Bob Marley & The Wailers B00005J9UI 2001

Stir It Up / Get Up, Stand Up / I Shot the Sheriff / Lively Up Yourself / No Woman, No Cry / Roots, Rock, Reggae / Exodus / Jamming / Waiting in Vain / Three Little Birds / Turn Your Lights Down Low / One Love/People Get Ready / Is This Love / Sun Is Shining / So Much Trouble in the World / Could You Be Loved / Redemption Song / Buffalo Soldier / Iron Lion Zion / I Know a Place

TUFF GONG/ISLAND

Live at the Roxy 0602498010419 2003

Introduction / Trench Town Rock / Burnin' and Lootin' / Them Belly Full (But We Hungry) / Rebel Music (3 O'Clock Road Block) / I Shot the Sheriff / Want More / No Woman No Cry / Lively Up Yourself / Roots, Rock, Reggae / Rat Race / Encore / Positive Vibration / Get Up, Stand Up/No More Trouble/War

Note: Between 2001 and 2004 Tuff Gong/Island reissued many of the classic Bob Marley albums listed above, most with bonus tracks. They also released deluxe editions of many of those albums, including *Catch a Fire, Burnin'*, *Rastaman Vibration*, and *Exodus.*

JA/U.K./U.S. Compilation Albums Featuring Wailers Tracks

STUDIO ONE

History of Ska, Vol. I: The Golden Years 60–65, Various Artists
Love & Affection

Christmas in Jamaica, Various Artists
Sound the Trumpet

Oldies but Goodies, Vol. I, Various Artists
It Hurts to Be Alone
Put It On

Ska Strictly for You, Various Artists C66
Love and Affection
Shame and Scandal

MELODISC

Honeys, Various Artists (all Wailers tracks credited to Bob Morley [*sic*] & the Wailers)
Simmer Down / How Many Times / Go, Jimmy, Go

STEADY

Solid Gold Series: Reggae's Greatest Hits, Vol. I, Various Artists S132
It Hurts to Be Alone

TROJAN

Foolish Fools, Cynthia Richards & Friends TBL 123 1970
Nice Time / Mellow Mood

TOTAL SOUNDS

Bunny Lee Then, Various Artists
Mr. Chatter Box

ISLAND

Soul of Jamaica	HELP 15	1973

Concrete Jungle
Guava Jelly, by Owen Grey (written by Bob Marley)

This is Reggae Music, Vol. I	ILPS 9251	1974

I Shot the Sheriff / Concrete Jungle / Guava Jelly, by Owen Grey

Catch This Beat—The Rock Steady Years 66/68	ILPS 7	1980

Rasta Put It On (Peter Touch [*sic*] & the Wailers)

One Big Happy Family	IRSP 1	1980

Exodus

TIME-WIND

Crying for Freedom	F/3 80014	1981

A German-pressed 3-record boxed set of LPs, consisting of *Soul Revolution, Rasta Revolution* and *The Best of the Wailers* (the Leslie Kong album).

MANGO

Countryman, the Original Soundtrack from the Film	MSTDA 1	1982

Natural Mystic / Rastaman Chant / Rat Race / Jah Live / Three o'Clock Road Block / Small Axe / Time Will Tell / Pass It On

Bob Marley & the Wailers—The Box Set	BMSP 100	1982

An unusually lavish collector's edition of 9 Bob Marley and the Wailers Island LPs—*Catch a Fire, Burnin', Natty Dread, Live! Rastaman Vibration, Exodus, Kaya, Survival, Uprising*—in a special limited-edition premium pressing of 10,000 sets. The collection comes in a heavy, hinged cardboard case, each record in a different commemorative sleeve, with lyrics for all tracks printed on the back. An absolutely priceless possession for the connoisseur.

Reggae Greats—Wailers	MLPS 9795	1984

Concrete Jungle and 9 other classic Island tracks.

ISLAND/TUFF GONG

Bob Marley: Songs of Freedom	314-512 280–2	1992/ 1999

A revelatory 4-cassette/CD boxed set of 78 impeccably presented tracks. Rarities include the unissued songs "Iron Lion Zion," "High Tide or Low Tide" and "Why Should

I." Full-color 64-page booklet features a foreword by Rita Marley, reminiscences from Eric Clapton, John "Rabbit" Bundrick and Derrick Morgan, plus liner notes by Rob Partridge and Timothy White—and a track-by-track annotation. Reissued by Island/Tuff Gong/Def Jam as 314–514-432 on Nov. 16, 1999.

TROJAN

The Early Years 1969–1973 CDTAL600 1993
Limited edition, 4-picture-CD set of *Rasta Revolution, African Herbsman, In The Beginning* and *Soul Revolution II* albums.

RELATIVITY

A *Tribute to Bob Marley: The Riddim of a Legend* 88561 1995
Covers of Marley/Wailers classics by group members (Peter Tosh, Judy Mowatt), immediate family (Ziggy Marley & The Melody Makers), friends and admirers. Well-executed project by producer Alan Becker with WUSB reggae deejay Kibret Neguse, who also did the liner notes.
Stir It Up—Diana King
African Herbsman—Ziggy Marley & The Melody Makers
Jah Live—Judy Mowatt
Slave Driver—Taj Mahal
I'm a Rastaman (Rastaman Chant)—Inner Circle
Natural Mystic—Dennis Brown
Jammin'—Grover Washington, Jr.
Rainbow Country—Ziggy Marley & The Melody Makers
Get Up, Stand Up—Peter Tosh
One Love—Anthony Malvo & Flourgon
Natty Dread—Freddie McGregor
Comma Comma—Johnny Nash

ISLAND JAMAICA

Dancehall Queen: Original Motion Picture Soundtrack 314-524 1997
Includes "Unbelievable," by the Marley Girls (Sharon Marley Prendergast, Cedella Marley and Melody Makers backup singer Erica Newell).

Unreleased Sides (A Sampling)

Rescue Me / I Love Music / Turn Over / I'm Like a Wounded Lion in a Jungle / Jingling Keys / Shoot Up the Town / Back Against the Wall / Mango Coconut Sugar / They Set You Up My Son / Gimme Just Another Try / A Toast to the People / I'm a Rastaman / Black and White / Dancin' on the One / We're All Alike / Reggae the Night Away / Shout Afrik / (Why Do My People Keep Spreading) Rumors / Can't Take Your Slogans No More / Every Day's Such a Lonely Day / I'm Having a Real Good Time / Jungle Fever / Shakeup / Feel All Right / Babylon Feel This One / Who Colt the Game / Call Me Dada / I'll Come Back in a Song / Sophisticated Psychedelication / Don't Draft Me / Jailbreaker (writing demo) / Place of Peace (writing demo) / Record a New Song(writing demo) / Vexation (writing demo) / Jump Them Out of Babylon/Jump Them Inna Babylon (writing demo) / Pray for Me (writing demo)

PETER TOSH SOLO TRACKS

Peter Tosh Solo Sides on JA Singles

Peter Tosh (aka Touch, McIntosh, Mackingtosh) said that he began his solo recording career with Clement Dodd around 1966, testing his solo aspirations with a blank label rendition for Coxsone of "Can't You See" (CC DODD64), afterward cutting his first rendition of "I Am the Toughest" bearing his name for the Studio One label (CD 1033-A).

Other Clement Dodd–Produced Sides on JA Singles

STUDIO ONE

It's Only Time (Peter and Rita)/Tall in the Saddle (Roland Alphonso)

MUZIK CITY

Amen (Peter Touch [*sic*] & the Wailers)/Habits 1964

COXSONE

Rasta Shook Them Up (Peter Tosh; aka "Rasta Put It On")/Ringo Ska 1965

Making Love (Peter Touch [*sic*] & The Chorus/Voo Doo Moon (the Soul Brothers)

I Am the Toughest/Toughest Version

Joe Gibbs–Produced Sides on JA Singles

JOE GIBBS

Maingy [*sic*] Dog (credited to Joe Gibbs 3rd & 4th Generation, but is actually Tosh with backup group)/Hot Dog
Rudies Medley (Joe Gibbs 3rd & 4th Generation)/Rude Boy Version (Joe Gibbs & the Soulmates)
Arise Black Man/Man Dub
Maga Dog/Bull Dog (The Now Generation)

Joe Gibbs–Produced Sides on U.K. Singles

BULLET

Selassie Serenade/Cat Woman (Glen Adams)	BU 414	1969

UNITY

The Return of Al Capone/O Club (Lenox Brown)	UN 525	1969
Sun Valley/Drums of Fu Manchu (Headley Bennett)	UN 529	1969

SHOCK

Here Comes the Judge/Rebeloution [*sic*] (Winston Wright)		1971

PUNCH

Rudies Medley (3rd & 4th Generation)/Rude Boy Version (Joe Gibbs & the Soulmates)	PH 91	1972

PRESSURE BEAT

Them a Fe Get a Beatin'/Get a Beatin'	PB 5509	1972
Maga Dog/Version		

Peter Tosh–Produced Sides on JA Singles

Peter Tosh did a number of solo sides between 1969 and 1971, largely at Randy's Studio 17 or Joe Gibbs's Studio, for the Randy's, Joe Gibbs, Shock, Justice League, Upsetter, Trans Am, and Tuff Gong labels, among others, including "You Can't Fool Me Again," "Rightful Ruler" (with U Roy), "Black Dignity," "Here Comes the Sun" (the George Harrison song), "Here Comes the Judge," "Oppressor Man" (aka "Downpresser," "Downpressor Man"), "Leave My Business," "Arise Blackman," "What Would the People Say," "Rasta Jamboree," "400 Years" and "Once Bitten." Around 1971 Peter Tosh started his own solo label, Intel-Diplo HIM (Intelligent Diplomat for His Imperial Majesty).

INTEL-DIPLO HIM

Maga Dog/Version	1971
Dog Teeth/Version	1971
Lion/Version	1971
Can't Blame the Youth/Version	1972
No Mercy/Version	1972
One Foundation/Version	1973
What You Gonna Do/Version	1973
Burial/Version	1973
Ketchy Shuby/Version	1974
Brand New Secondhand/Version	1974
Hammer/Version	1975
Mark of the Beast/Version	1975
Legalize/Rasta Smoke It	1975
Igziabeher/Version	1975
Dracula/Vampire Version	1976
Babylon Queendom/Iration	1976
Equal Rights/Version	1977
Downpressor Man/Version	1977
African/Version	1977
Stepping Razor/Version	1977
I'm the Toughest/Version	1978
Bush Doctor/Version	1978
Bumbo Klaat/Version	1980

SOLOMONIC

Anti-Apartheid/Solidarity	1978

Peter Tosh–Produced Sides on U.K./U.S. Singles

ISLAND

I Am the Toughest/No Faith (Marcia Griffiths)	WI 3042	1967

VIRGIN

Legalize It/Brand New Second Hand	VS 150	1976
Stepping Razor/Version		1977
Stepping Kazor/Legalize It		1979

EMI

(You Gotta Walk) Don't Look Back/Soon Come (coproduced by Robbie Shakespeare)	EMI 2829	1978
Oh Bumbo Klaat/Nothing But Love	EMI 8083	1981
Reggae Mylitis/Coming in Hot	A-8094	1981

CBS

Legalize It, Why I Must Cry/Till Your Well Runs Dry (demo-EP)	AE7 1109	1976

ROLLING STONES

Soon Come/(You Got to Walk and) Don' Look Back/ Don't Look Back (Don't Space Out; with Mick Jagger, coproduced by Robbie Shakespeare)	DSKO 130	1978
Recruiting Soldiers/Buck-in-Hamm Palace	RS 20000	1979
I'm the Toughest/Toughest Version (Word, Sound & Power, 12" disco)	MRSR 103	1979
Buk-in-Hamm Palace/The Day the Dollar Died/ Dubbing in Buk-in-Hamm (12" disco)	MRSR 104	1979
Crystal Ball/Dubbing in Buk-in-Hamm/Buk-in-Hamm (12" disco)	DSKO 193	1979
Nothing But Love/Cold Blood/Oh Bumbo Klaat (with Gwen Guthrie; 12" disco)	12RSR 107	1981

Peter Tosh JA/U.K./U.S. Solo Albums

COLUMBIA

Legalize It	X698	1976

Legalize It / Burial / Whatcha Gonna Do / No Sympathy / Why Must I Cry / Igziabeher (Let Jah Be Praised) / Ketchy Shuby / Till Your Well Runs Dry / Brand New Second Hand

Equal Rights	PC 34670	1977

Get Up, Stand Up / Downpressor Man / I Am That I Am / Stepping Razor / Equal Rights / African / Jah Guide / Apartheid

ROLLING STONES

Bush Doctor	COG 39109	1978

(You've Got to Walk and) Don't Look Back / Pick Myself Up / I'm the Toughest / Soon Come / "Moses"—the Prophets / Bush Doctor / Stand Firm / Dem Ha Fe Get a Beaten / Creation

Mystic Man	COC 39111	1979

Mystic Man / Recruiting Soldiers / Can't You See / Jah Seh No / Fight On / Buk-in-Hamm Palace / The Day the Dollar Die [*sic*] / Crystal Ball / Rumours of War

Wanted: Dread & Alive SO 17055 1981

Coming In Hot / Nothing But Love / Reggae-Mylitis / The Poor Man Feel It / Cold Blood / Wanted Dread & Alive / Rastafari Is / That's What They Will Do / Fools Die

Wanted: Dread & Alive (U.K. Edition) CUN39113 1981

Coming In Hot / Nothing But Love / Reggae-Mylitis / Rok [*sic*] with Me / Oh Bumbo Klaat / Wanted Dread and Alive / Rastafari Is / Guide Me from My Friends / Fools Die

EMI-AMERICA & RADIC

Mama Africa RDC 2005 1983

Mama Africa / Glasshouse / Not Gonna Give It Up / Stop That Train / Johnny B. Goode / Where You Gonna Run / Peace Treaty / Feel No Way / Maga Dog

EMI

Captured Live EG 2401671 1984
(Recorded at the Greek Theater in Los Angeles)

Coming In Hot / Bush Doctor / Africa / Get Up Stand Up / Johnny B. Goode / Equal Rights / Downpressor Man

EMI-AMERICA

No Nuclear War ELT 46700 1987

No Nuclear War / Nah Goa Jail / Fight Apartheid / Vampire / In My Song / Lesson in My Life / Testify / Come Together

CAPITOL/PARLOPHONE/EMI

The Toughest (The Selection 1978–1987) CI 90201 1988
(Compiled by Neil Spencer, with his liner notes)

Coming In Hot / Don't Look Back / Pick Myself Up / Crystal Ball / Mystic Man / Reggaemylitis [*sic*] / Bush Doctor / Maga Dog / Johnny B. Goode / Equal Rights/Downpressor Man / In My Song

HEARTBEAT

The Toughest featuring The Wailers, Skatalites, Upsetters HB 150 1996
Studio One Productions:

Hoot Nanny Hoot / Maga Dog / Amen / Jumbie Jamboree / Shame and Scandal / Sinner Man / Rasta Shook Them Up / The Toughest / Don't Look Back / When the Well Runs Dry / Making Love / Can't You See / Treat Me Good

Upsetter Productions:

Rightful Ruler (with U Roy) / Four Hundred Years / No Sympathy / Secondhand (Brand New Secondhand) (Versions One & Two) / Downpresser

COLUMBIA LEGACY

Peter Tosh: Honorary Citizen C3K 65064 1997

A mostly marvelous 3-CD box set that features a disc of some of Tosh's best JA singles ("Rightful Ruler," "Black Dignity," "Leave My Business," "Mark of the Beast" and the rare "Here Comes the Sun"); a disc of live material in Detroit, Chicago, Boulder, Calgary, Reseda, CA, and L.A.'s Roxy club including "Coming In Hot," "Mystic Man" and full-bore and acoustic treatments of "Get Up, Stand Up"; plus a CD of top album cuts like "Stepping Razor." Liner notes by Leroy Jody Pierson and Roger Steffens enhance the fitting tribute—which is marred only by the intrusive title cut, a clumsy work sung by a cousin of Tosh's who now controls his Intel-Diplo company.

Scrolls of the Prophet: The Best of Peter Tosh CK 65921 1999

Superior in its elegant simplicity to the "Citizen" collection, this set features excellent liner notes by noted KROQ deejay Wayne Jobson, who was truly a close personal and professional associate of Peter's and who also produced the definitive *Stepping Razor-Red* X documentary.

Get Up, Stand Up / Stepping Razor / Downpressor Man / Equal Rights / (You Gotta Walk and) Don't Look Back / African / Legalize It / Bush Doctor / Igziabeher (Let Jah Be Praised) / Fools Die / Mystery Babylon (previously unreleased) / Ketchy Shuby / Till Your Well Runs Dry / One Love / Get Up, Stand Up (acoustic, live)

Legalize It CK 65922 1999

Reissue remastered by Bruce Dickinson. Features bonus track "Ketchy Shuby (Instrumental)."

Equal Rights CK 65923 1999

Reissue remastered by Bruce Dickinson. Features bonus tracks "Pick Myself Up (Live)" and "African (Live)."

PRESSURE SOUNDS

Talking Revolution PSCD 48 2005

CD One "Live At the One Love Peace Concert 1978":

Igziabeher (Let Jah Be Praised) / Four Hundred Years / Stepping Razor / Speech / Funeral (Burial)/Speech / Equal Rights / Speech / Legalize It/Get Up Stand Up

CD Two "Acoustic Set":

Fools Die (Wisdom) / Jah Guide / I Am That I Am / Fire Fire (Babylon Burning) / Pick Myself Up / Stop That Train / Handsome Johnny / Don't Wanna Get Busted / Peter Speaks About the Half Way Tree Incident / Legalize It / Get Up, Stand Up

Peter Tosh Sides on JA/U.K./U.S. Compilation Albums

JOGIB

The Heptones Meet the Now Generation JG 003
Maga Dog

TROJAN

The Trojan Story, Part II TRLD 402 1976
Them A Fe Get a Beatin'

20 Explosion Hits TRS 81 1976
Maga Dog

ISLAND

This Is Reggae Music, Vol. 3 ILPS 9391 1976
No Sympathy

MANGO

Rockers, the Original Soundtrack from the Film MLPS 9587 1979
Stepping Razor

DELICIOUS VINYL

Marked for Death—Music from the Motion Picture 443 002-2 1990
Steppin' Razor

ANDREW TOSH TRACKS

Andrew Tosh is the son of Peter, and his mother is the sister of Bunny Wailer.

Andrew Tosh U.K. Albums

ATTACK/TROJAN

The Original Man ATLP 102 1988

Same Dog Bite / Too Much Rat / Heathen Rage / My Enemies / My Enemies/Dub Version / Magga [*sic*] Dog / I'm the Youngest / Poverty Is a Crime / Poverty Is a Crime/Dub Version / The Original Man / The Original Man/Dub Version

TOMATO

Make [sic] Place for the Youth 2696722 1989

Stop What You Doin' / Things I Used to Do / What [*sic*] Did You Do It / Come Together / Time Is Longer Than Rope / Message from Jah / One Step to Happiness / Small Axe / Evil Ones / Make Place for the Youth / Stop What You Doin' (Instrumental)

HEARTBEAT

Original Man CDHB 140 1994
(Material heard on 1988 album, plus 8 dub mixes.)

BUNNY WAILER SOLO TRACKS

Around 1972, Bunny Livingston, aka Bunny Wailer, formed his own solo record label, Solomonic Records, headquartered at 14 Old Retirement Road in Kingston. Wailer's real but inconsistent gifts took many dispiriting turns in the 1980s and 1990s, from warring with the Marley family over the Tuff Gong brand name to trading on his association with Bob to gain attention via multiple "tribute" records. Other saddening missteps included his songs circa 1991 ("Dance Ha Fi Gwan," "Dance Massive," "Don Dadda") after a denuncatory shower of bottles drove him from a Kingston stage at a December 1990 Reggae Sting concert, Wailer chiding his audience on record (for "disrespecting dem own reggae king") with the same self-importance that sparked their original ire. By 1993, even the supportive *Beat* magazine dismissed his "Woman" Solomonic single with a one-word review: "Awful." Still, Bunny can be superb when he stops the wire-pulling and shows some self-effacing sincerity. Below is a digest of his better singles efforts.

Bunny Wailer–Produced Solo Sides on JA Singles, a Sampling

SOLOMONIC

Life Line/Version
Bide Up/No Love (with the Wailers)
Bide Up/Search for Love
Pass It On/Trod On (both sides credited to the Wailers)
Life Line/Dream Land (actually a Trench Town Rock Version)
Arab's Oil Weapon/Version (both sides credited to the Wailers)
Rasta Man/Dreamland 1976
Rastaman/Istan: Vision Land 1976
Battering Down Sentence/Version 1976
Bright Soul/Fallen Angel (12" disco) 1977
Rockers/Theme from Rockers (Version; 12" disco) 1978
Let Him Go/Version 1978
Love Fire/Love's Version (7" and 12" disco) 1978
Roots, Radics, Rockers & Reggae/Peace Talk (7" and 12" disco) 1978
Bright Soul/Falling Angel (Version) 1979
Free Jah Children/Dubwise (Solomonic Stars) 1979
Rock in Time/Rock 1979
Power Struggle/Version 1979
Gamblings/Version 1980
Togawar Game/Crucial 1980
Crucial/Version 1980
Innocent Blood/Version 1980
Cease Fire/Version 1980
Unity/Version (7" and 12" disco) 1981
Rise and Shine/Solomonic Dub (7" and 12" disco) 1981
Cool Runnings/Version 1981
Collic Man/Version 1981
Galong So/Version 1981
Ballroom Floor/Version 1981
Riding/Version (7" and 12" disco) 1981
Rock and Groove/Ga Long So (12" disco) 1982
Back to School/Schooldays (7" and 12" disco) 1982
Trouble Is on the Road Again/Version 1982
Bodaration/Version (12") 1983
Jump Jump/Version (12") 1985
Bald Head Jesus/Version 1988

Bunny Wailer–Produced Solo Sides on U.K./U.S. Singles

ISLAND

Amagideon [*sic*, "Armageddon"]/Blackheart Man	BUNNY 1	1976
Dreamland/Dreamland Dub	WIP 6347	1976
Follow Fashion Monkey/Instrumental	IS 062	1976
Dreamland/Dreamland Dub	IS 076	1976
Get Up, Stand Up/This Train (12" disco)	IPR 2003	1977
Love Fire/Loves Version	IOR 2015	1978
Roots, Radics, Rockers & Reggae/Fig Tree/ Armagideon (3-song EP)	PR 2025	1978
Dancing Shoes/Walk the Proud Land (7" and 12" disco)	WIP 6685	1981

SOLOMONIC (U.K.)

Riding/Rise and Shine	SMA1	1981

NIGHTHAWK

Arab Oil Weapon/Life Line (there are two different versions of this 12" disco)	1001	1981

SHANACHIE

Peace Talks/Rockers	Shanachie 5009	1983

Bunny Wailer–Produced JA and/or U.S./U.K. Solo Albums

SOLOMONIC

Blackheart Man (different mix and cover art from Island LP) 1976

Blackheart Man / Fighting Against Conviction / (The) Oppressed Song / Fig Tree / Dreamland / Rastaman / Reincarnated Souls / Bide-Up / This Train

Protest (different arrangements and cover art from the Island LP) 1977

Moses Children / Get Up, Stand Up / Scheme of Things / Quit Trying / Follow Fashion Monkey / Wanted Children / Who Feels It / Johnny Too Bad

Dub Disco Volume 1 1978

Roots Radics / Battering Down / Amagedon [*sic*] / Fig Tree / Love Fire / Rasta Man / Dreamland

Struggle 012 1979

The Old Dragon / Bright Soul / Got to Move / Power Strugglers / Let the Children Dance / Free Jah Children / Struggle

In I Father's House 1980

Roots Raddics / Rock in Time / Rockers / Wirly Girly / Let Him Go / Love Fire

Bunny Wailer Sings the Wailers 1980

Dancing Shoes / Mellow Mood / Dreamland / Keep On Moving / Hipocrite [*sic*] / Rule This Land / Burial / I Stand Predominate [*sic*] / Walk the Proud Land / I'm the Toughest

Dub Disco Volume 2 1980

Dancing Shoes / Mellow Mood / Keep on Moving / Hypocrite / Worly Girly [*sic*] / Burial / I Stand Predominate [*sic*] / Walk the Proud Land / Toughest [*sic*]

Rock 'n' Groove 1981

Rock and Groove / Another Dance / Dance Rock / Cool Runnings / Roots Man Skanking / Jammins / Ballroom Floor

Tribute to the late Hon. Robert Nester [sic] *Marley, O.M.* 1981

Soul Rebel / I Shot the Sherriff [*sic*] / Crazy Baldhead / Time Will Tell / War / Slave Driver / Redemption Song / No Woman No Cry

Hook, Line & Sinker 1982

Riding / Hook, Line 'n' Sinker / Soul Rocking Party / The Monkey / Swap Shop / Simmer Down / Back to School

Bunny Wailer Live! SM009 1983

Blackheart Man / Armagedon [*sic*] / Crucial / Dance Rock / Rock 'n' Groove / Ballroom Floor / Toughest

Just Be Nice 1990

Quasi-hip-hop editions of such songs as "Electric Boogie," the title track, "Ridin'," "Hook, Line and Sinker," "Back to School," "Ballroom Floor" (a revamping of the Wailers' rendition of "Rolling Stone"), "Soul Shakedown Party," "Hit Back the Crack," "Bad Dub" and a cover of Sly and the Family Stone's "Family Affair," all mixed by New York deejay "DJ Doe" Rodriguez.

SHANACHIE

Roots Radics Rockers Reggae Shanachie 43013 1983

Roots Radics Rockers Reggae / Cease Fire / Let Him Go / The Conqueror / Rockers / Wirly Girly / Rockin' Time / Love Fire

Marketplace Shanachie/ SM LP 010 1985

Stay with the Reggae / Jump Jump / Dance Hall Music / Cool and Deadly / Ally Worker / Dance the Night Away / Electric City / Tear in Your Eyes / Home Sweet Home / Together

Rootsman Skanking Shanachie 43043 1986

Ballroom Floor / Collyman / Dance Rock / Gamblings / Rootsman Skanking / Cool Runnings / Cry to Me / Rock 'n' Groove / Another Dance / Jammins

Rule Dance Hall Shanachie 43050 1987

Rule Dance Hall / Jolly Session / Saturday Night / Trash ina We Bes [*sic*] / Put It On / Reggae in the U.S.A. / Haughty Tempo / Camouflage / Hot Foot Head / Stir It Up / Old Time Sinting [*sic*] / Reasons

Liberation Shanachie 43059 1988/89

Rise and Shine / Liberation / Botha the Mosquito / Want to Come Home / Ready When You Ready / Didn't You Know / Dash Wey the Vial / Bald Head Jesus / Food / Serious Thing

Time Will Tell: A Tribute to Bob Marley Shanachie 1990

U.S. release of 1981 *Tribute* Solomonic LP, plus renditions of "Bellyfull" and "Rebel Music."

Gumption Shanachie 43079 1990/91

Sounds Clash / Pieka "Bus Dem Shut" / Dog War / See and Blind / Warrior / Never Grow Old / Gumption / Wheel Yo Belly / Don Man / Reggae Burden

Dance Massive 43095 1992
("Ram Dance," "Girls" and eight other dancehall sides.)

Crucial! 45014 1993
(Collects "Innocent Blood," "Baldhead Woman," "Unity" and other JA-only sides. Liner notes by Roger Steffens.)

Retrospective 45021 1995
A cross-section of Bunny's solo songs from the 1970s to the early 1990s as licensed by Shanachie, including "Roots, Radics, Rockers, Reggae," "Liberation" and "Dance Hall Music."

RAS

The Never Ending Wailers RASCD 3501 1993
A Bunny Wailer set intended to spite the Marley Foundation. Inferior two-track 1968–1971 Wailers tapes, spliced onto 1984 overdubs by Bunny, Peter Tosh, Junior Braithwaite—plus an *over*-overdubbed Andrew Tosh. The project pointedly obscured the presence of Rita Marley on the original performances.

Hall of Fame: A Tribute to Bob Marley's 50th Anniversary RASCD 3502 1995
Bunny hurries through fifty-two slipshod Marley/Wailers covers.

Bunny Wailer–Produced Sides on U.S. Compilation Albums

NIGHTHAWK

Wiser Dread 301 1981
Life Line
Arab Oil Weapon

RAS

Reggae for Kids RAS 3095 1992
Back to School

More Reggae for Kids RAS 3232 1997
Didn't You Know

RITA MARLEY TRACKS

Rita Anderson Marley began her recording career in 1964 as a member of the Soulettes, a vocal trio whose other members were Marlene "Precious" Gifford and Rita's first cousin, Constantine "Dream" Walker. The Soulettes cut their first records with Clement Dodd.

Clement Dodd–Produced Soulettes JA Sides

COXSONE

I Love You Baby	1965
Opportunity	1965
Pied Piper	1965
A Time to Turn	1966
La La Lover	
Tighten Up	1968
Don't Care What You Say (aka "Don't Care What the People Say")	

TUFF GONG

Bring It Up/My Desire	1972
I Do/Version	1973

Rita Marley has recorded a number of solo singles, some of them released under the names Esete and Ganette. Her earliest records were remakes of Soulettes songs.

Rita Marley Solo Sides on JA Singles, a Sampling

WAIL 'N' SOUL 'M

Gee Whiz (credited to Esete)/Version

TUFF GONG

I've Been Lonely/Version	
Man to Man/Version	1977
A Jah Jah/Version	1978
Thank You Lord/Version	1978
That's the Way Jah Planned It/Jah Plan	1979
The Beauty of God's Plan/Version	1979
One Draw/So High	1981

One Draw/The Beauty of God's Plan (12" disco)		1981
Play Play/Play Dub		1981
There Will Always Be Music/Always Be Dub Music: Limited Edition, Dedicated to Bro. Nesta Marley		1982
There Will Always Be Music/Who Feels It (12" disco)		1982

RITA MARLEY MUSIC

Good Girls Culture/Version		1985
Who Colt the Game/Version		1990
To Love Somebody (with Charlie Chaplin)		1992

Rita Marley Solo Sides on U.K. Singles

RIO

Pied Piper/It's Alright (produced by C. S. Dodd)	R108	1966
Crawfish (The Soul Brothers)/You Lied (produced by C. S. Dodd)	R118	1966
Blood Pressure (The Soul Boys)/Come to Me (produced by C. S. Dodd)		1966

LONDON

Put Your Hand in the Hand/Version (Rita Marley & Ernie Smith)

ATTACK

This World/Same Thing	ATT 8044	

Rita Marley Solo Sides on U.S. Singles

SHANACHIE

One Draw/That's the Way (12" disco)	SH 5003	1981
Harambe/There Will Always Be Music (12" disco)	SH 5004	1982
The Beauty of God's Plan/My Kind of War (12" disco)	SH 5005	1982
Good Girls Culture/Good Girls Rap/Good Girls (Instrumental) (12" EP/45 rpm)	SH 5013	1985
Earth Runnings/Hurt Runnings (Version) (12" disco)	SH 5015	1987

Rita Marley JA Solo Albums

TUFF GONG

Who Feels It Knows It		1980

(There are two versions of this LP; approximately 1,000 copies of a pressing were mistakenly released in which

"Good Morning Jah" on Side Two was omitted, "I'm Still Waiting" was included twice and "The Beauty of God's Plan," later to appear on *Harambe,* was added.)

A Jah Jah / That's the Way / Who Feels It Knows It / One Draw / Thank You Jah / Good Morning Jah / I'm Still Waiting / Play Play / Jah Jah Don't Want / Easy Sailing

RITA MARLEY MUSIC

Harambe 1982

The Beauty of God's Plan / Fussin' and Fighting / Harambe / King Street / There'll Always Be Music / My Kind of War / Who Is Your Neighbor / Love Iyah / Retribution / Who Can Be Against Us

Rita Marley U.S. Solo Albums

SHANACHIE

Who Feels It Knows It SH 43003 1981
(Same tracks as the Tuff Gong LP.)

Harambe SH 43010 1982
(Same tracks as the Rita Marley Music LP.)

We Must Carry On SH 43082 1991

I Know a Place / Serious Time / Who Colt the Game / So Much Things to Say / To Love Somebody / Earth Runnings / Bust Them Shut / Dem a Fight / Just One More Morning / Special Rhythm

Rita Marley Solo Tracks on JA/U.K./U.S. Compilation Albums

MANGO

Club Ska '67 MLPS 9598 1980
Pied Piper

Rita Marley Solo Albums on European Labels

TABATA MUSICA Y LETRA

Spectacles for Tribuffalos TB CD 202 1995
An experimental collaboration between Rita Marley and Spanish vocalists/composers Ignacio Scola and Gregorio

Paniagua, recorded principally at the Monasterio de Camorritos in Cercedilla, Spain. The ambitious, impressionistic music is an often lovely, sometimes overwrought but always intriguing avant-garde meld of Caribbean and European jazz, theater, reggae and semiclassical song forms.

Lady Bellows / Behaving Like Two Fools / Navigation / Miracle Baby / The Sunshine Song / If You Are Afraid / Buby's Charles / Like So Many Years Before / Equis Pototia / Yellow Cab / Fish Blues / What Are You Dreaming Of?

Rita Marley Solo Tracks on European Labels

TABATA

Miracle Baby/What Are You Dreaming Of?	TB CDS-202	1995
Lady Bellows	TB CDS-212	1995

JUDY MOWATT TRACKS

Judy Mowatt started her career in 1965 as lead singer with the Gaylets (aka the Gaytones), a beloved female vocal trio in Jamaica that also included Beryl Lawson and Merle Clemenson. The group stayed together until 1970 (when Lawson and Clemenson moved to the States) and had hits in Jamaica with such singles as "I Like Your World" and "Son of a Preacher Man," the Dusty Springfield hit. Her first solo single was "I Shall Sing," the Miriam Makeba song, released by Tip Top Records in 1970, During this period she also released the hit singles "I Love You," "I'm Alone" and "Cry to Me" on the High Note label. In the mid-1970s, Judy started her own label, Ashandan.

Judy Mowatt Solo Sides on JA Singles, a Sampling

TUFF GONG

We've Got to Leave the West/Leave the West	1976

ASHANDAN

Mr. Big Man/Version	
You Pour Sugar On Me/Version (Judy Mowatt & the I Threes)	1975
Only A Woman/Orthodox Revelation	1975
Black Woman/Black Beauty (with Joy Tulloch)	1977

Change Is Gonna Come/Version		1978
Many Are Called/Version		1978
Joseph/Version		1979
Put It On/Put It Jah		1979
Slave Queen/Slave Woman Version		1979
You're My People/Peoples Version		1980
Big Woman/Big Bird		1982
Didn't I Do It/Version		1982
You Don't Care/Version		1982
GAY FEET		
Way over Yonder/Version (Julianne and the Gaytones)		1971
SONIC SOUNDS		
Love on a Two-Way Street/Instrumental (Franklyn "Bubbler" Waul)		1981

Judy Mowatt Solo Sides on U.K./U.S. Singles

GAY FEET		
Emergency Call/Version	GS 207	
EMI		
Pour Sugar on Me/What an Experience (produced by Bob Marley & Alan Cole)	EMI 2469	1976
GROVE		
Black Woman/Black Beauty (with Joy Tulloch)	GM 8	1976
ISLAND		
Joseph/Down in the Valley	WIP 6792	1980
My My People/Black Woman	PR 2041	1981
HORSE		
Mellow Mood/Version	HOSS 40	1973
I Shall Sing/Version (Judy Mowatt and the Gaytones)	HOSS 42-A	1974
TROJAN		
Way over Yonder/Version	TR-7900	1973
Emergency Call/Version	TR-7912	1973

SIRE

Pour Some Sugar/What an Experience	(mono) SAA 729	

SHANACHIE

I Am Not Mechanical/You're My People	SH 703	1982

Judy Mowatt Solo JA and/or U.S./U.K. Albums

TUFF GONG

Mellow Mood 1977

Black Woman (released one year later on U.S. Mercury) 1979

Strength to Go Through / Concrete Jungle / Slave Queen / Put It On / Zion Chant / Black Woman / Down in the Valley / Joseph / Many Are Called / Sisters' Chant

Mr. Dee-J 1981

Mr. Dee Jay / Glad Song / I Am Not Mechanical / Big Woman / Trade Winds / On Your Mark / Think / Get Happy / Only a Woman / King of Kings

SHANACHIE

Only a Woman 43007 1982

You're My People / Only a Woman / Trade Winds / Think / Got to Leave the West / I Am Not Mechanical / On Your Mark / Big Woman / You Don't Care / King of Kings

Working Wonders 43028 1985

Black Man, Brown Man / Working Wonders / Lovemaking / Let's Dance / So Many Eyes / Mother Africa / Ethiopia Salaam / Hush Baby Mother / Traveling Woman / King's Highway

Love Is Overdue 43044 1986

Sing Your Own Song / Love Is Overdue / Try a Little Tenderness / Long Long Time / Rock Me / Get Up Chant / Screwface / Hold Dem Jah / One More Minute / Who Is He

Look at Love	43087	1991

Fly African Eagle / Watchdogs / Groovin' / Guilty / Candle in the Window / Jah Live / Tomorrow Nation / Skin of My Skin / Look at Love / Lioness in the Jungle / Day by Day / Warrior Queen / Never Get Weary

POW WOW

Rock Me	PWD 7442	1993

Simmer Down / Rock Me / Guava Jelly / Zion Chant / Bubbling / Lean on Me (with Jack Radics) / Life / Mad, Mad World / I Shall Be Released / House on Fire / Victory Is Near / God Bless the Children / Life (Hard Bass Mix)

MARCIA GRIFFITHS TRACKS

One of Jamaica's leading female vocalists, Marcia Griffiths has had hits on the island since the mid-1960s. In 1969, she teamed up with Bob Andy, formerly of the Paragons, and for several years they were the Caribbean version of Peaches and Herb. Their recording of "Young, Gifted and Black" was a Top 10 hit in Britain in 1970, with "Pied Piper" climbing to the No. 11 spot the following year.

Marcia Griffiths Solo Sides on JA Singles, a Sampling

HIGHNOTE

Peaceful Woman/Version	SP 123	
Stepping Out of Babylon/Version		
Dreamland/Dub (Revol's)	SP 0065	

TUFF GONG

Naturally/Version		1977
Steppin'/Version		

SOLOMONIC

Tribulation/Version (12" disco)		1979
Woman a Come/Version		1981

COXSONE

Truly/Version
Tell Me Now/Version
Melody Life/Version
Mark My Word/Version

MANGO

Carousel Mango 91350-2 1990

Electric Boogie / Do Unto Others / Groovin' / All Over the World / Carousel / Sugar Shack / The One Who Really Loves You / Money in the Bank / Electric Boogie (dub mix)

HEARTBEAT

Truly 7639-2 1999

I Need Love / Shimmering Star / Truly / Try a Little Smile / I Shall Sing / Stepping Stones / Baby Oh Baby / Tonight / No No No / My Ambition / I Cried / Sea Of Love / Sha La La I Love You / You Mean the World to Me

VP RECORDS

Certified VPCD 1526 1999

Then Came You / Feel So Real / Tell Me Now / Everlasting / I Got to Cry / Certified / I Want to Be with You / Born to Be / Just Try Me / This World / Partner for Life / Why Me? / Ready for the Good Life / Amour Love / Today's Song / Problems

TROJAN

Pied Piper: The Best of Bob & Marcia TJACD044 2002
Includes the following Marcia Griffiths solo tracks:

Don't Let Me Down / Band of Gold / I Just Don't Want To Be Lonely / Put A Little Love in Your Heart / Sweet Bitter Love / Play Me

MARLEY FAMILY TRACKS

Marley Family Collaborative Albums on U.S. Labels

HEARTBEAT

The Marley Family Album CDHB 160 1995
I Know—Bob Marley and the Wailers
Many Are Called—I-Threes
Keep On Pushing—Rita Marley
Pushing (Vibes Mix)—Rita Marley & Wickerman
Lion in the Jungle—Julian Marley

True Love—Maccabee (Wanooto)
One Draw (1990s Style)—Rita Marley
(Looking for) New Ways of Loving—Dhaima
Spend the Night (Murder Mix)—Richie B, Steven Marley
Look through the Window—Rita Marley, Freddie MacGregor
Trodding (Original 12" Mix)—Melody Makers
Genesis (Remix)—Dallol
Sugar Pie—Melody Makers
Lion in the Morning (Version)

LIGHTYEAR/WEA/GHETTO YOUTHS INTL.

Marley Magic: Live in Central Park at Summerstage 54182-2 1996
Far superior to the above concept, this is a 2-CD set (also on home video) of a live New York concert on July 7, 1996.
Opening Remarks—Pat McKay
Lion in the Morning—Julian Marley
Me Name Jr. Gong/Crazy Bald Heads—Damian Marley
Same Old Story—Julian Marley
Searching—Damian Marley
Babylon Cookie Jar—Julian Marley
Love and Unity—Damian Marley
Exodus—Julian Marley
We Need Love—Yvad
Music Is the Food of Love—Yvad
No Peace—Yvad
Freedom—Yvad
So Much Things to Say—Rita Marley
Good Girls Culture—Rita Marley
That's the Way—Rita Marley
Harambe—Rita Marley
To Love Somebody—Rita Marley
Guava Jelly/No Woman, No Cry—Rita Marley
Jammin'/Lively Up Yourself—Rita Marley
Natty Dread—Ziggy Marley & The Melody Makers
Positive Vibration—Ziggy Marley & The Melody Makers
Stir It Up—Ziggy Marley & The Melody Makers
Get Up, Stand Up—Ziggy Marley & The Melody Makers
Water & Oil—Ziggy Marley & The Melody Makers
Sun Is Shining—Ziggy Marley & The Melody Makers
Free Like We Want 2 Be—Ziggy Marley & The Melody Makers
Could You Be Loved—Ziggy Marley & The Melody Makers

TUFF GONG/WEA/LIGHTYEAR

Tuff Tracks 54242-2 1998
Kpangolo—Majek Fashek

Trop De Sanf—Kreyol Syndikat
Girls Night Out—Marley Girls
Me Name Jr. Gong—Damian Marley
Arm Your Soul—Julian Marley
Hotel California—Majek Fashek
Natty Dread—Ziggy Marley and the Melody Makers
You're for Real—Floyd Lloyd
Easy—Kreyol Syndikat
Attack Back—Julian Marley
So Much Things to Say—Rita Marley
One Cup of Coffee—Damian Marley
Big City—Floyd Lloyd
Me Name Jr. Gong—Damian Marley Remix Featuring Grand Puba

MELODY MAKERS TRACKS

Melody Makers Sides on JA Singles

TUFF GONG

Children Playing in the Streets/Dubbing in the Streets	1979
Sugar Pie/Version	1980
Trodding/Trod In	1980
Jah Is the Healing/Nah [*sic*] Leggo	1985

RITA MARLEY MUSIC

What a Plot/Version	1982
Reggae Is Now/Rock It Baby	1983

Melody Makers Sides on U.S./U.K. Singles (A Sampling)

SHANACHIE

What a Plot/Children Playing in the Street [*sic*]	SH 5006	1983

EMI

Met Her on a Rainy Day/Can't Be What You Want to Be	1984
Rock It Baby/Feel Free	1984

VIRGIN

Tomorrow People/We a Guh Some Weh	7-99347	1988
Tumblin' Down/Tumblin' Down (remix)/Tumblin' Down (dub)	0-96603 (12" dance)	1988
Reggae This Mix: Tomorrow People/Dub This: Tomorrow People/Dub a Pella: We a Gun Some Weh/Edit This: Tomorrow (12" dance)	7-96703-0	1988
"One World" (Sting/Ziggy Marley)	(Air date)	May 1988

(Just prior to the release of Ziggy & the Melody Makers' *Conscious Party* LP, Ziggy Met with Sting in New York City to cut a new version of Sting's old Police song for use as music to open a worldwide television special for the Council of Europe's North/South Campaign to aid underdeveloped nations.)

All Love (KRS-One mix)/All Love (edit)/Lee & Molly (live at Philadelphia Spectrum 8–21-88)	2-96439	1989
Look Who's Dancing (club mix)/Look Who's Dancing (7" edit)/Look Who's Dancing (12" dub)/Rat Race (live at Palladium; Hollywood, California, 5-10-89)/ Pains of Life (special CD single with liner note: "This Record is Livicated to the Year of the Rasta Child")	2-96541	1989
Black My Story (Not History)(CD promo single for Black History Month)	PRCD3245	1989
One Bright Day/Love Is the Only Law	4-99132	1989

ISLAND

Angel of Harlem/A Room at the Heartbreak Hotel/ Love Rescue Me* (CD3 Single by U2; *live guest vocal by Ziggy Marley)		1988

VIRGIN

Kozmik (Edit 2)/Rainbow Country		1991
Kozmik (KRS-One Mix)/Rainbow Country		1991

ELEKTRA

Power to Move Ya/Hand to Mouth	PRCD 9223-2	1995
People Get Ready (R.H. Factor Reggae Vocal Mix)/ Album Edit	64164-2	1997

Melody Makers Sides on JA/U.K./U.S. Compilation Albums

Reggae Sunsplash '81—A Tribute to Bob Marley	El 60035 G	1982
Sugar Pie		

A&M

Free to Be . . . A Family	SP5196	1988
Free to Be . . . A Family		

REPRISE

Music from the Film "Married to the Mob"	25763-4	1988
Time Burns		

CAPITOL

Original Motion Picture Soundtrack "Tequila Sunrise"	CI-91185	1988
Give a Little Love		

DISNEY

For Our Children	60616-2	1991
Give a Little Love		

KIDS ROUNDER

Arthur and Friends	11661-8084-2A	1998
Theme Song		

Melody Makers JA/U.K./U.S. Albums

EMI-AMERICA/TUFF GONG

Children Playing in the Streets (Unreleased LP)	ST-17129	1984

Met Her on a Rainy Day / Reggae Is Now / Children Playing in the Streets / Rock It Baby / What a Plot / Our Way / Feel Free / Jah Is the Healing / Can't Be What You Want to Be / Lying in Bed

Play the Game Right	ST-17165	1984

Naah Leggo / What a Plot / Play the Game Right / Aiding and Abetting / Revelation / Children Playing in the Streets / Reggae Is Now / Unuh Nuh Listen Yet / Rising Sun / Natty Dread Rampage

"Hey World!"	ST-17234	1986

Give a Little Love / Get Up Jah Children / Hey World / Fight to Survive / Freedom Road / Say People / 666 / Police Brutality / Lord We a Come / Reggae Revolution

EMI-MANHATTAN

"Time Has Come"—The Best of Ziggy Marley and the Melody Makers (A collection of the first two EMI LPs, plus the unreleased "Lying in Bed" and "Met Her on a Rainy Day" from the *Children Playing* LP.)	EL90952	1988
Reggae Revolution (Unreleased retrospective CD)		1997

Met Her on a Rainy Day / Rock It Baby / What a Plot / Children Playing / Feel Free / Jah Is the Healing / Can't Be What . . . / Lying in Bed / Give a Little Love / Get Up Jah Jah Children / Hey World / Fight to Survive / Play the Game Right / Lord We a Come / Reggae Revolution / Aiding and Abetting / Natty Dread Rampage

VIRGIN AMERICA

Conscious Party	Virgin 790878-1	1988

Tumblin' Down / New Love / A Who a Say / Have You Ever Been to Hell / Lee and Molly / Tomorrow People / We Propose / What's True / Dreams of Home

One Bright Day (Available in a handsome, limited-edition silk-screened brown cardboard CD case.)	PROCD-ZIGGY	1989

Black My Story (Not History) / One Bright Day / Who Will Be There / When the Lights Go Out / All Love / Look Who's Dancing / Justice / Love Is the Only Law / Pains of Life / Urb-an Music / Problems / All You Got / When the Lights Go Out (Jamaican Style)

Jahmekya	91626	1991

Raw Riddim / Kozmik / Rainbow Country / Drastic / Good Time / What Conquers Defeat / First Night / Wrong Right Wrong / Herbs an' Spices / Problem with My Woman / Jah Is True and Perfect / Small People / So Good So Right / Namibia / New Time & Age / Generation

Joy and Blues	87961	1993

Joy and Blues / Brothers & Sisters / There She Goes / Talk / Rebel in Disguise / X Marks the Spot / Head Top / African Herbsman / World So Corrupt / Garden / Mama / This One

The Best of (1981–1993)	44098-2	1997

Kozmic / Look Who's Dancin' / One Bright Day / Goodtime / Joy and Blues / Justice / Black My Story (Not History) / Lee & Molly (featuring Keith

Richards) / New Love / Tomorrow People / Brothers & Sisters / Rainbow Country / Tumblin' Down / Small People / When the Lights Go Out / Who Will Be There / Conscious Party

ELEKTRA

Free Like We Want 2 B	61702-2	1995

Power to Move Ya / Free to Be Like We Want 2 B / Today / Water and Oil / Live It Up / Tipsy Daisy / Bygones / Hand to Mouth / In the Flow / Don't Go Nowhere / G7 / Keep On / Beautiful Mother Nature

Fallen Is Babylon	62032-2	1997

Fallen Is Babylon / Everyone Wants to Be / People Get Ready / Postman / Brotherly Sisterly Love / Born to Be Lively / Long Winter / I Remember / Day by Day / Five Days a Year / Notice / Diamond City / Jah Bless / People Get Ready (R.H. Factor Reggae Vocal Mix)

Spirit of Music	62396-2	1999

Keep My Faith / We Are One / Beautiful / Gone Away / All Day All Night / Higher Vibration / All I Need Is You / One Good Spliff / Let It Go / Months of Sunshine / Many Waters / High Tide Or Low Tide / Won't Let You Down / Jah Will Be Done

Live Volume One	Elektra	2000

Power to Move Ya / Conscious Party / Beautiful Day / Jah Bless / One Good Spliff / Free Like We Want 2 B / Jammin' / Postman / Stir It Up / Higher Vibration / People Get Ready / Could You Be Loved / I Know You Don't Care About Me

I-THREES TRACKS

I-Threes Sides on JA U.S. Singles, a Sampling

WAIL 'N' SOUL 'M

Medley/Version (the Wailers All-Stars)

TUFF GONG

Many Are Called/Chosen
No Woman No Cry/Version

56 HOPE ROAD

Precious World/Precious Dub

SHANACHIE

Music for the World/Many Are Called (12")	5007	1983

RITA MARLEY MUSIC

To Love Somebody/Version (by Rita & the I-Threes)		1991

I-Threes Sides on JA/U.S./U.K. Compilation Albums

ELEKTRA

Reggae Sunsplash '81—A Tribute to Bob Marley	El 60035 G	1982

Them Belly Full (Rita Marley & The I-Threes)

I-Threes Albums on U.S./U.K./JA Labels

EMI-AMERICA/EMI/RITA MARLEY MUSIC

Beginning	ST-17222	1986

(Credited to I-Three [*sic*])

Come to Me Tonight / Now That We Are Standing / Mamma Can't Buy You Love / Neighbour / Baby Be True / Calling Out / That's How Strong / Jealousy / Sing Joy / He Is a Legend

SHANACHIE

Holding Up Half the Sky: Women in Reggae/ Roots Daughters	45027	1996

The I-Threes are represented by "Many Are Called," while Marcia Griffiths ("Steppin' Out of Babylon"), Judy Mowatt ("Black Woman") and Rita Marley ("One Draw") also appear separately on this well-chosen anthology. Liner notes by Roger Steffens.

CEDELLA MARLEY BOOKER TRACKS

Encouraged by her son, Cedella Marley Booker first began cutting demos of gospel-reggae tracks in 1977, during the period when Bob was writing material for the *Exodus*

LP. After Bob's death, she wrote a number of songs, among them "Mother, Don't Cry"—the song's refrain is: "Mother, don't cry/ I'll be all right." Those were Bob Marley's last words. Pearl Livingston is the featured backup singer on the tracks listed below.

Cedella Booker Sides on JA Singles

TUFF GONG

Stay Alive/Redemption Song (not the Bob Marley song) — 1982

Cedella Booker JA/U.S. Albums

56 HOPE ROAD

Redemption Songs — Rita Marley Music — 1984
(Ten tracks, including "Mother, Don't Cry")

ROIR

Awake Zion — ROIR A-184 — 1990
Slightly revised cassette-only rerelease of *Redemption Songs*. Liner notes by Stephen Davis. (Issued on CD by Rykodisc)

MUSIC FOR LITTLE PEOPLE

Smiling Island of Song — 42521 — 1992
A delightful collection of Carribean folksongs for children, including Bob Marley's "Three Little Birds." Co-produced by Leib Ostrow & Taj Mahal.

Cedella Booker Sides on U.S. Albums

MUSIC FOR LITTLE PEOPLE

A *Child's Celebration of Folk Music* — 942585-2 — 1996
Colon Man

JULIAN MARLEY TRACKS

Julian Marley Albums on U.S. Labels

LIGHTYEAR/WEA/TUFF GONG/GHETTO YOUTHS INTL.

Lion in the Morning, Executive Producer: Stephen Marley 54178-2 1996

Loving Clear / Blossoming and Blooming / Lion in the Morning / Now You Know / Babylon Cookie Jar / Same Old Story / Attack Back / Arm Your Soul / Ease These Pains / When the Sun Comes Up / Got to Be

A *Time and a Place* Ghetto Youths 2003

Father's Place / Where She Lay / Harder Dayz / Build Together / Summer Daisies / One Way Train / Systems / I'll Never / Sitting In the Dark / Rock with Me / Sunshine / Couldn't Be the Place / Time

Julian Marley Sides on U.S. Singles

LIGHTYEAR/WEA/TUFF GONG/GHETTO YOUTHS INTL.

Loving Clear/Lion in the Morning 54182-2 1996

DAMIAN "JR. GONG" MARLEY TRACKS

Damian "Jr. Gong" Marley Albums on U.S./JA Labels

LIGHTYEAR/WEA/TUFF GONG/GHETTO YOUTHS INTL.

Mr. Marley, Executive Producer: Steven Marley 54177-2 1996

Trouble / Love and Inity / 10,000 Chariots / Old War Chant / Party Time / Kingston 12 / Keep on Grooving / Searching (So Much Bubble) / One More Cup of Coffee / Julie / Me Name Jr. Gong / Mr. Marley

Half Way Tree Motown 2001

Educated Fools (with Bounty Killer) / More Justice / It Was Written (with Capleton) / Catch a Fire / Still Searchin' (Yami Bolo) / She Needs My Love (Yami Bolo) / Mi Blenda / Where Is the Love / Harder (Interlude) / Born To

Be Wild / Give Dem Some Way / Half Way Tree (Interlude) / Paradise Child / Stuck In Between / Half Way Tree / Stand a Chance (Yami Bolo)

Educated Fools Ghetto Youths 2002

Educated Fools Remix (Damian Marley & Bounty Killer) / Love Haffi Request (Buju Banton) / No Time to Grudge (Determine) / Put On Da Pressure (Mr Mojo & Lasa) / No Pardon (Bounty Killer) / Love Can Save the Human Race (Yami Bolo) / Have to Be Strong (El Pancho) / Yuh Nah Hear (Capleton) / Babylon A Gwaan So (Daddington) / Set It Off (Kymani Marley & Spragga Benz) / You in Trouble (Sli) / Instrumental

Welcome To Jamrock Ghetto Youths/Universal 2005

Confrontation / There for You / Welcome to Jamrock / The Master Has Come Back / All Night (featuring Stephen Marley) / Beautiful (featuring Bobby Brown) / Pimpa's Paradise (featuring Stephen Marley & Black Thought) / Move! / For the Babies (featuring Stephen Marley) / Hey Girl (featuring Stephen Marley & Rovleta Fraser) / Road to Zion (featuring Nas) / We're Gonna Make It / In 2 Deep / Khaki Suit (featuring Bounty Killer & Eek A Mouse) / Carnal Mind

Damian "Jr Gong" Marley Sides on U.S. Singles

LIGHTYEAR/WEA/TUFF GONG/GHETTO YOUTHS INTL.

Searching (So Much Bubble)/Dance Hall Mix/ Club Mix 1996

KY-MANI (MARLEY) TRACKS

Ky-mani (Marley) Albums on U.S. Labels

GEE STREET/V2

The Journey 63881-32527-2 1999

Rude Boy / Fell in Love / Country Journey / Dear Dad / Return of a King / Emperor / Party's On / Hi-Way / Tom Drunk / No Faith / Your Love / Fire Fire / Warriors / Lord Is My Shepherd

ASTON "FAMILY MAN" BARRETT TRACKS

Family Man Sides on JA Singles, a Sampling

CORPORATIVE SOUND

Traitor/Version (Family Man All Stars)
Slaving in Babylion [*sic*]/Version (Winston Jarrett) L0002 1975

FAMS

Trouble Dub (with the Wailers)/Dub Feeling
Distant Drums/Version (Family Man & Knotty Roots)
Eastern Memphis (the Wailers)/Rebel Am I (Family Man & the Rebel Arms)

Family Man Sides on U.K. Singles

ESCORT

Bandit (Errol Wallace)/Family Man Mood (Aston Borrot [*sic*]) ES 817 1969

DUKE

Get Together (Carl Dawkins)/Installment Plan (Family Man) DU 93 1970

TROJAN

Deep River/Under Grass
You Can Do It Too/Instrumental

DOWNTOWN

Herb Tree (Family Man)/Holy Holy (Studio Sound) DT 491 1972

Family Man U.S. Albums

HEARTBEAT

Cobra Style: Productions from the Wailers' Musical Director 11661-7657-2 1999

Cobra Style—Familyman and the Rebel Arms
Back Web—Brimstone
We're Gonna Make It—Jimmy Riley

Eastern Memphis—Familyman and the Rebel Arms
Guided Missile—Familyman and the Rebel Arms
Babylon—Brimstone
Elegant Shape—Ashantiwah
Distant Drums—The Wailers Band
Children of the Ghetto (Disco Mix)—Senya
My Girl—New Wave and the Rebel Arms
Well Pleased—Familyman and the Rebel Arms
Woman in Love—Maria Anderson and the Wailers Band
Work—Familyman and the Rebel Arms
Natural Woman (Disco Mix)—Senya
Cobra Style (Disco Mix)
Well Pleased (Disco Mix)

Familyman in Dub	11661-7659-2	1999

Cobra Style Dub / Steppers Rock / Familyman Skank / Rebel Am I / E.T. Special / Pleasing Dub / Dubbing Naturally / Dub Combination / Pickney Dub / A Distant Dub / Tribute to Y Mas Gan / Elegant Dub / Iron Rock / Dub Maker

JOE HIGGS TRACKS

Joe Higgs Sides on JA/U.K./U.S. Singles (With and Without Roy Wilson), a Sampling

CAMEL

Hit Me Back Baby/Version		1969

CLANDISC

Herbsman (King Stiff & Andy)/Don't Mind Me (Higgs & Wilson)	CLA 207	1970
Mademoiselle/Version	CLA 208A	1970

BLUE MOUNTAIN

Lay a Foundation /Version	BM 1019	1972

ELEVATION

Journey to Freedom/Freedom Journey (with Karl Masters)		1972
Invitation to Jamaica/Version		1972

MICRON

More Slavery/Version

ROOSEVELT

The World Is Upside Down/Version

SOLOMONIC

Brimston & Fire (Atarra—Joe Higgs & Wailing Souls)/Version 1974
Sincerely/Version 1976
Talk to That Man/Version (7" and 12" disco) 1980

ISLAND

I Am the Song (The Prophet)/Worry No More WI 3026

MCA

The World Is Upside Down/Version MCA 40090 1973

Joe Higgs Sides on JA/U.K. Albums

GROUNATION

Life of Contradiction GROL 508 1974

Come on Home / Got to Make a Way / Wake Up and Live / Life of Contradiction / Who Brought Down the Curtains / There's a Reward / Hard Times Don't Bother Me / My Baby Still Loves Me / She Was the One / Song My Enemy Sings

I STOP

Unity Is Power Stop 1002 1979

Devotion / One-Man Kutchie (Pipe) / Unity Is Power / Gold or Silver / Love Can't Be Wrong / Vineyard / Small World / Think of the Moment / Sadness Is a Part of My Heart / Sons of Garvey

ALLIGATOR

Triumph! Alligator 8313 1985

Come a Little Closer / So It Go / Hurt My Soul / Satisfy My Heart and Soul / It's Goodbye / Step by Step / Sound of the City / Creation / I'm Right There / Young and Wild

SHANACHIE

Family 43053 1988

Family / African-Can / You Didn't Know / There's a Reward / Day O / Upside Down / Hurry Home / Mother Radio / Free Africa

Blackman Know Yourself Shanachie 1990
Blackman Know Yourself 43077

Oh Carol / Small Axe / Sons of Garvey / She Was the One / Steppin' Razor / Saturday Morning / Wave of War / Let Us Do Something / Sun Is Shining

First Family of Reggae 9100 1991
Features "Family" by Joe Higgs, plus "Joseph" by Judy Mowatt and "Boderation" by Bunny Wailer.

ISLAND RECORDS HISTORIC REGGAE TRACKS

U.S./U.K. Collections Devoted Only to Island Reggae

MANGO

Pressure Drop—Island Celebrates 25 Years of Jamaican Music MBOX 25 1988
Truly and utterly in a class by itself, this breathtakingly splendid seven-LP, 96-track boxed set of music tracing the history of the Island label from its founding on May 8, 1962, is the most remarkable reggae collection ever released anywhere, anytime. Complete with a full-color nineteen-page insert of photos, vintage album art and superb liner notes by Steve Barrow, it's a possession that ranks with the road map to Mount Zion. The two Bob Marley and the Waders tracks included are "Jah Live" and "Smile Jamaica" (issued not in 1978, as stated here, but rather in 1976), but it's the context that makes this an adventure in paradise. The seven LPs, each in an annotated, color-coded sleeve of durable textured paperboard, are as follows:

Volume One: "R&B-JA Style" • "Ska"
Volume Two: "Ska" • "Rock Steady"
Volume Three: "Leslie Kong—Beverley's Productions"
Volume Four: "Rasta"
Volume Five: "Lee 'Scratch' Perry—Upsetter Productions"
Volume Six: "Sly & Robbie—Taxi Productions"
Volume Seven: "Reggae Girls" • "Dance Hall"

Tougher Than Tough: The Story of Jamaican Music	518 399-2	1993

A 4-CD, 95-track anthology, nicely packaged but not as crisply envisioned and boldly executed as *Pressure Drop*, its categories too prosaic to convey much beyond the obvious chronology:

Forward March 1958–1967
Reggae Hit the Town 1968–1974
Natty Sing Hit Songs 1975–1981
Dance Hall Good to We 1982–1993

U.S./U.K. Albums by "The Wailers Band"

In a quirky subcategory, but not a class by itself, The Wailers Band is the stage name adopted by those members of Bob's last group that elected to stay together and create another career for themselves after his death. The Wailers Band is led by guitarist/vocalist and chief songwriter Junior Marvin, with veterans Aston Barrett on bass, Al Anderson on lead guitar and Earl Lindo on keyboards. New members are percussionist Irvin "Carrot" Jarrett, pianist Martin Batista and drummer Michael "Boo" Richards. The band's sound is essentially pop-party music with a reggae flavor.

ATLANTIC

I.D.	781960-4	1989

Solution / Children of the World / Reggae Love / Irie / Love Is Forever / Chasing Tomorrow / Rice and Peas / Life Goes On / Have Faith in Jah / One One CoCo / P's & Q's

A&M RECORDS

Majestic Warriors	28965 4002 4/2	1991

Liberty / Trip / Dancing Boys / Sweet Cry Freedom / My Friend / Out of Exile / Showdown / Bad Mind People / Nothing for Nothing / Live & Love / Rock On Be Strong / Could You Be Loved

RAS

Jah Message	RASCD 3169	1996

Where Is Love / Know Thyself / Rasta / My Redemption / Miracle (The Message) / Jah Love (Believers) / Wrong Tree / Rastaman Sound / Many Roads to Zion / Heroes (Marcus Garvey) / All Day All Night / Some Say (Let It Grow) / Kick the Habit

Bibliography

BOOKS

Annual Abstract of Statistics, No. 24. Kingston: Department of Statistics, 1965.

Auger, Roy, Rex Nettleford, and M. G. Smith. *The Rastafarian Movement in Kingston, Jamaica*. Kingston: The University of the West Indies, 1960.

Banbury, R. Thomas. *Jamaican Superstition, or the Obeah Book*. Kingston, 1894.

Barrett, Leonard. *The Rastafarians, Sounds of Cultural Dissonance*. Boston: Beacon Press, 1977.

———. *Soul-Force: African Heritage in Afro-American Religion*. New York: Doubleday, 1974.

———. *The Sun and the Drum*. Kingston: Sangsters, 1976.

Beckwith, Martha. *Black Roadways: A Study of Jamaica Folklife*. Chapel Hill, N.C.: University of North Carolina Press, 1929.

———. *Jamaican Anansi Stories*. New York: American Folklore Society, 1924.

Brathwaite, Edward. *The Development of Creole Society in Jamaica, 1770–1820*. London: Oxford University Press, 1971.

Brodber, Erna. *Abandonment of Children in Jamaica*. Kingston: Institute of Social and Economic Research, University of the West Indies, 1974.

———. A *Study of Yards in the City of Kingston*. Kingston: Institute of Social and Economic Research, University of the West Indies, 1975.

Buissert, David. *Historic Architecture of the Caribbean*. London: Heinemann Educational Books, 1980.

——— and Michael Pawson. *Port Royal, Jamaica*. London: Oxford University Press, 1975.

Carey, Robinson. *The Fighting Maroons of Jamaica*. London: William Collins and Sangster, 1969.

Cartey, Wilfred, and Martin Kilson. *The African Reader: Colonial Africa*. New York: Vintage Books, 1970.

Cassidy, Frederick C. *Jamaica Talk*. London: Macmillan, 1971.

Clarke, John Henrik, with Amy Jacques Garvey. *Marcus Garvey and the Vision of Africa*. New York: Random House, 1973.

Clerk, Asley. *Music and Musical Instruments of Jamaica*. Kingston, 1916.

Crahan, Margaret E., and Franklin Knight. *Africa and the Caribbean—The Legacies of a Link*. Baltimore: The Johns Hopkins University Press, 1979.

Cronon, E. D. *Black Moses*. Madison, Wis.: University of Wisconsin Press, 1966.

Curtin, P. D. *Two Jamaicas: The Role of Ideas in a Tropical Colony*. Cambridge: Harvard University Press, 1955.

Davis, Stephen, and Peter Simon. *Reggae Bloodlines*. New York: Anchor Press/Doubleday, 1977.

Diop, Cheikh Anta. *The African Origin of Civilization—Myth and Reality*. Translated and edited by Mercer Cook. New York: Lawrence Hill & Co., 1974.

Eaton, George E. *Alexander Bustamante and Modern Jamaica*. Kingston: Kingston Publishers, Ltd., 1975.

Economic and Social Survey: Jamaica. 1976, 1977, 1978, 1979, 1980. Kingston: National Planning Agency, 1977, 1978, 1979, 1980, 1981.

Elkins, W. F. *Street Preachers, Faith Healers and Herb Doctors in Jamaica, 1890–1925*. Brooklyn: Revisionist Press, 1977.

Emerick, Abraham. *Obeah and Duppyism in Jamaica*. Woodstock, Mass.: self-published, 1915.

Ethiopian World Federation, Local 33. *The Ethiopian Orthodox Church*. Kingston: 1975.

Frankfort, Henri. *Ancient Egyptian Religion*. New York: Harper Torchbooks, 1961.

Gardiner, Sir Alan. *Egypt of the Pharaohs, an Introduction*. New York: Oxford University Press, 1972.

Halliday, Fred, and Maxine Molyneux. *The Ethiopian Revolution*. New York: Schocken Books, 1981.

Hansberry, William Leo. *Pillars in Ethiopian History*. Washington, D.C.: Howard University Press, 1981.

Hyatt, Harry M. *The Church of Abyssinia*. London: Luzac & Co., 1928.

Isaac, Ephraim. *The Ethiopian Church*. Boston: Henry N. Sawyer Company, 1968.

Jekyll, Walter. *Jamaican Song and Story*. New York: Dover, 1966.

Kerr, Madeline. *Personality and Conflict in Jamaica*. London: Collins, 1961.

Knight, Franklin W. *The Caribbean—The Genesis of a Fragmented Nationalism*. New York: Oxford University Press, 1978.

Lacey, Terry. *Violence and Politics in Jamaica*. Manchester: Manchester University Press, 1977.

Lemesurier, Peter. *The Great Pyramid Decoded*. New York: Avon, 1979.

Livingston, Jones T. *Caribbean Rhythms—The Emerging English Literature of the West Indies*. New York: Washington Square Press, 1974.

Lowenthal, David. *West Indian Societies*. London: Oxford University Press, 1972.

Manley, Michael. *The Politics of Change*. Washington, D.C.: Howard University Press, 1975.

Mosley, Leonard. *Haile Selassie: The Conquering Lion*. London: Weidenfeld and Nicolson, 1964.

Naipaul, V. S. *The Middle Passage*. New York: Vintage Books, 1981.

Nettleford, Rex. *Mirror, Mirror—Identity, Race and Protest in Jamaica*. London: Collins, 1974.

Osae, T. A., S. N. Nwabara, and A. T. O. Odunsi. *A Short History of West Africa, A.D. 1000 to the Present*. New York: Hill and Wang, 1973.
Owens, Joseph. *Dread—The Rastafarians of Jamaica*. Kingston: Sangster Books, 1976.
Patterson, Orlando. *The Children of Sisyphus*. Boston: Houghton Mifflin, 1965.
Phillippo, J. M. *Jamaica: Its Past and Present State*. London: J. Snow, 1843.
Phillips, A. S. *Adolescence in Jamaica*. Kingston: Jamaica Publishing Company, 1976.
Roberts, George W. *The Population of Jamaica*. London: Cambridge University Press, 1957.
Rubin, Vera, and Lambros Comitas. *Ganja in Jamaica*. New York: Anchor Press/Doubleday, 1976.
Schwab, Peter. *Haile Selassie I—Ethiopia's Lion of Judah*. Chicago: Nelson-Hall, 1979.
Smyth, Piazzi. *The Great Pyramid—Its Secrets and Mysteries Revealed*. New York: Bell Publishing Company, 1978.
Staff, Frank. *Glossolalia—Tongue Speaking in Biblical, Historical and Psychological Perspective*. Nashville: Abingdon, 1967.
Stitchin, Zecharia. *The Stairway to Heaven*. New York: St. Martin's, 1980.
Sundkler, Bengt. *Bantu Prophets in South Africa*. London: Oxford University Press, 1961.
Thelwell, Michael. *The Harder They Come*. New York: Grove Press, 1980.
Thomas, Michael, and Adrian Boot. *Babylon on a Thin Wire*. London: Thames and Hudson, 1976.
Tompkins, Peter. *Secrets of the Great Pyramid*. New York: Harper Colophon Books, 1978.
Ullendorff, Edward. *Ethiopia and the Bible*. London: Oxford University Press, 1968.
———. *The Ethiopians—An Introduction to Country and People*. London: Oxford University Press, 1973.
Ullendorff, Edward (trans.). *The Autobiography of Emperor Haile Selassie I: My Life and Ethiopia's Progress, 1892–1937*. London: Oxford University Press, 1976.
Van Sertima, Ivan. *They Came Before Columbus—The African Presence in Ancient America*. New York: Random House, 1976.
Vivo, Raul Valdez. *Ethiopia's Revolution*. New York: International Publishers, 1978.
Webb, James Morris. *The Black Man: The Father of Civilization Proven by Biblical History*. Chicago: Fraternal Press, 1924.
Williams, Joseph J. *Psychic Phenomena of Jamaica*. New York: Dial, 1934.
———. *Voodoos and Obeahs: Phases of West India Witchcraft*. New York: Dial, 1932.
Williams, K. M. *The Rastafarians*. London: Ward Lock Educational Books, 1981.

ARTICLES AND PAMPHLETS

I have also culled information from countless issues of the *Amsterdam News*, *Black Books Bulletin*, *Black Echoes*, *Black Music* and *Jazz Review*, *Black Music*, *The Boston Globe*, the *Boston Phoenix*, *Caribbean Review*, *Crawdaddy*, *Everybody's*, the *Face*, *Jahugliman*, the *Jamaican Daily News*, *The Jamaica Journal*, the *Jamaican Star*, *Judgement Times*, *Melody Maker*, *Musician*, *National Geographic*, the *New Musical Ex-*

press, *The New York Times*, *People* (the Caribbean magazine, not the Time-Life publication), *Pressure Drop*, the *Reggae Beat Newsletter*, the *Reggae News*, *Reggae Roots*, *Rolling Stone*, *Sounds*, *Skywritings*, *Survival* (the Tuff Gong Records circular), *The Village Voice*, the *West India Medical Journal*.

In order to gain an understanding of daily life in Jamaica during Bob Marley's lifetime, and to check facts and acquire material used in this book to provide an accurate historical background for the events described, I read through hundreds of issues of the Jamaican *Daily Gleaner* at the library of the Institute of Jamaica, 12 East Street, Kingston, and I read through an equal number of issues of the *Weekly Gleaner* at the Research Institute for the Study of Man, 162 East 78th Street, New York, N.Y. 10021.

Among the magazine articles and pamphlets that proved helpful were the following:

Agency for Public Information, Kingston, Jamaica. "Our National Heroes." *API* (September 1981).

American Cancer Society Staff. "Issels Combination Therapy." *ACS Circular Letter* (December 13, 1974).

Anderson, Jervis. "Home to Jamaica." *The New Yorker* (January 19, 1976).

Asprey, G. F., and Phyllis Thorton. "Medicinal Plants of Jamaica." *West India Medical Journal* (December 1954).

Bilby, Kenneth M. "Bongo, Backra & Coolie Jamaican Roots." *Notes to Folkways Record Album No. FE 4231* (1975).

Bradshaw, Jon. "Blackwell's Island." *Rolling Stone* (May 27, 1982).

Brown, Samuel E. "Treatise on the Rastafarian Movement." *The Journal of Caribbean Studies* 6 (1966).

Carr, Patrick. "Bob Marley Is the Jagger of Reggae." *Village Voice* (June 30, 1975).

Clark, Sebastian. "The Burning Reggae Years." *Black Echoes* (February 1976).

Coleman, Ray. "Root Strong in Funky Kingston." *Melody Maker* (June 12, 1976).

Cooper, Carol. "Tuff Gong: Bob Marley's Unsung Story." *Village Voice* (September 10, 1980).

Cromelin, Richard. "An Herbal Meditation with Bob Marley." *Rolling Stone* (September 11, 1975).

Crowe, Cameron. "Bob Marley: The Shooting of a Wailer." *Rolling Stone* (January 11, 1977).

Farrell, Barry. "Bob Marley—The Visionary as Sex Symbol." *Chic* (November 1976).

Fergusson, Isaac. "'So Much Things to Say'—The Journey of Bob Marley." *Village Voice* (May 18, 1982).

Fisher, Michael M. J. "Value Assertion and Stratification: Religion and Marriage in Rural Jamaica." *The Journal of Caribbean Studies* 14 (1969).

Goldman, Vivien. "Bob Marley in His Own Backyard." *Melody Maker* (August 11, 1979).

Goodison, A. "Dietary Survey and Eating Habits of the Rastafarians." *Caribbean Food and Nutrition Institute Report* (1976).

Goodwin, Michael. "Marley, the Maytals and the Reggae Armageddon." *Rolling Stone* (September 11, 1975).

Griffith, Pat. "The Drum in Reggae." *Black Echoes* (January 1978).

———. "Skanker with Action." *Black Echoes* (August 1976).

Gritter, Headley. "The Magic of Bob Marley." *Record Review* (April 1980).

Hill, Robert. "Dread History: Leonard P. Howell and Millenarian Visions in Early Rastafarian Religions in Jamaica." *Epoche* (December 1981).

Huey, John. "Hypnotic Sound of Reggae Floats Far from the Slums of Jamaica." *Wall Street Journal* (August 10, 1981).

Independent Citizens Research Foundation for the Study of Degenerative Diseases. "The Doctor Who Dared to Be Free: Josef Issels." *ICRF Newsletter* (Winter 1974).
Kallyndyr, Rolston, and Henderson Dalrymple. "Reggae: A People's Music." London: Carib-Arawak Publications, 1973.
Lechenperg, Harald P. "With the Italians in Eritrea." *National Geographic* (September 1935).
McCormack, Ed. "Bob Marley with a Bullet." *Rolling Stone* (August 12, 1976).
Moore, W. Robert. "Coronation Days in Addis Ababa." *National Geographic* (June 1931).
Noel, Peter. "Marley: 'Mama Don't Cry for Me.'" *Amsterdam News* (May 16, 1981).
Null, Gary, and Leonard Steinman. "The Politics of Cancer, Part Six-Suppression of Alternative Cancer Therapies: Dr. Josef Issels." *Penthouse* (August 1980).
Roberts, Leo B. "Traveling in the Highlands of Ethiopia." *National Geographic* (September 1935).
Rudis, Al. "Rasta in the Material World." *Sounds* (June 12, 1976).
Shapiro, Steve. "Knockdown Calypsos by the Growling Tiger." *Notes to the Rounder Records Album 5006* (1979).
Simpson, George E. "Political Cultism in West Kingston, Jamaica." *Institute of Social and Economic Research 4* (1955).
Southard, Addison E. "Modern Ethiopia." *National Geographic* (June 1931).
Spencer, Neil. "Me Just Wanna Live, Y'Unnerstan?" *New Musical Express* (July 19, 1975).
——. "'Me No Political Man'—Inside Bob Marley's U.K. Hideaway." *New Musical Express* (April 23, 1977).
Steffens, Roger. "Dreadlocks Forever—The Life and Death of Bob Marley." *Los Angeles Reader* (May 22, 1981).
Taylor, Steve. "The Fortune Teller." *Face* (1982).
Thomas, Michael. "Jamaica at War." *Rolling Stone* (August 12, 1976).
——. "The Wild Side of Paradise." *Rolling Stone* (July 19, 1973).
Weekend Star Staff Investigators. "Did Massop Die the Way the Cops Say?" *Jamaican Weekend Star* (February 9, 1979).
White, Garth. "Rudie Oh Rudie." *Caribbean Quarterly* (1967).
Whitman, Alden. "Haile Selassie of Ethiopia Dies at 83." *The New York Times* (August 28, 1975).
Williams, Richard. "The Facts of Reggae." *Melody Maker* (February 19, 1972).

SELECTED SOURCES FOR REVISED AND EXPANDED 1989–2006 EDITIONS

Besides many dozens of issues of *Caribbean Contact*, the *Daily* and *Sunday Gleaner*, the *Daily* and *Weekend Star*, *The New York Times*, *New Musical Express*, *Melody Maker*, *Q*, *The Reggae and African Beat*, *The Reggae Report*, *The Dub Missive*, *Billboard*, *Musician*, *Maclean's* and *Everybody's*, I note the following:

Atkinson, Steve. "Dead Brit Was Marley Cousin." *Daily Mirror* (April 21, 1993).
Ambursely, Fitzroy, and Robin Cohen, eds. *Crisis in the Caribbean*. New York: Monthly Review Press, 1983.
Barker, Rodney. *And the Waters Turned to Blood: The Ultimate Biological Threat*. New York: Simon & Schuster, 1997.
Barrow, Steve, and Peter Dalton. *The Rough Guide to Reggae*. London: Rough Guides, 2004 (third edition).
Beckford, George, and Michael Witter. *Small Garden . . . Bitter Weed: Struggle and Change in Jamaica*. London: Zed Press, 1980.

Beruff, Jorge Rodriguez. "Militarization and the Caribbean Basin Initiative." *Puerto Rico Libre!*, 6, no. 4.

"Birth of a Legend: Genealogists Have Located Bob Marley's Ancestral English Home." *Pulse!* (April 1993).

Booker, Cedella. Letter to Timothy White. "Thank you and keep up the good work . . ." (October 19, 1992).

——. Letter to Timothy White. "I pray this letter finds you and your family well . . ." (April 27, 1993).

——. Letter to Timothy White. "The Movement of Jah People wish to . . ." (April, 1995).

——. With Anthony Winkler. *Bob Marley, an Intimate Portrait by His Mother.* London: Penguin Books, Ltd., 1996.

Boot, Adrian, and Chris Salewicz. *Bob Marley: Songs of Freedom.* London: Penguin Books, 1995, pp. 28, 34, 38.

Boyle, Chris. "Reggae's Favorite Son—Ziggy Marley." *Reggae and African Beat* 7, no. 3 (1988).

Caruso, Michael. "Burnin' and Lootin'—The Gutting of the Bob Marley Estate." *Village Voice* (April 14, 1987).

Cayman Music, Inc., v. Rita Marley, as Administratix of the Estate of Robert Nesta Marley et al., Supreme Court of the State of New York, County of New York, Trial Term Part 6, Index No. 24020/84.

Cayman Music, Inc. v. Rita Marley et al. v. Danny Sims. "Order so appealed dismissed as moot, March 2, 1989. Appellate Division of the Supreme Court of New York (Case No. 362239).

Chambers, Anne. *Granuaile: The Life and Times of Grace O'Malley, c. 1530–1603.* Dublin: Wolfhound Press, 1983.

Chapman, Rob. *Downbeat Special Studio One Album Discography.* Devon: Rob Chapman, 1996.

Cheyney, Tom. "Carlton Barrett: Reggae's Master of Time." *Music Connection* (June 15–June 28, 1987).

Cullen, Robert B. "The Initiative That Wasn't." *Time* (December 1, 1986).

Dalke, Roger. *Ska to Reggae U.K. Label Discographies (Various Volumes).* Woking: Top Sounds International, 1979 to 2001.

Dannen, Fred. "The Godfather of Rock & Roll." *Rolling Stone* (November 17, 1988).

Davis, Stephen. *Bob Marley.* New York: Doubleday, 1985, pp. 222–223.

DeCurtis, Anthony. "Ziggy Marley, Reggae's Heir Apparent." *Rolling Stone* (March 24, 1988).

De Koningh, Michael, and Laurence Cane-Honeysett. *Young, Gifted and Black: The Story of Trojan Records.* London: Sanctuary Publishing, 2003.

Fyledal, Lars. Letter to Timothy White. "As you can see, I'm a serious collector of Bob and Wailers . . ." (August 2, 1983).

Gayle, Carl: "The Upsetter." *Black Music* (February 1975).

Goldman, Vivien, and Chris Salewicz. Unpublished history of Island Records (1987).

Grant, Michael. *The History of Ancient Israel.* New York: Charles Scribner's Sons, 1984.

Henry, Balford. "I Will Not Be a Reggae Martyr, Says Bunny, Last of the Wailers." *Sunday Gleaner* (March 20, 1988).

ICA. "Peter Tosh—Victim of the Shitstem." *Reggae Report* 6, no. 6 (1988).

Jeffrey, Don. "Copyrights 'Scorch' Jamaican Artists." *Billboard* (July 16, 1994).

Katz, David. *People Funny Boy: The Genius of Lee 'Scratch' Perry.* Edinburgh: Canongate/Payback Press, 2000.

Kenner, Rob. "The Family Stand." *Vibe* (October, 1995).

King, Francis X. *Witchcraft and Demonology.* Exeter Books, 1987.

Kristof, Nicholas D. "Across Asia, A Pollution Disaster Hovers." *The New York Times* (November 28, 1997).

Kurlansky, Mark. "Showdown in Jamaica." *The New York Times Magazine* (November 27,1988).

Landis, Fred. "The CIA and the Media: IAPA and the Jamaica *Daily Gleaner.*" *Covert Action Information Bulletin* no. 7 (December 1979–January 1980).

——. "CIA Media Operations in Chile, Jamaica and Nicaragua." *Covert Action Information Bulletin,* no. 16 (December 1981).

Lane, Chris. "Bob Marley Live at the Lyceum." *Blues & Soul* (August 19 to September 1, 1975).

Lemonick, Michael D. "Report on Asteroid 1989FC." *Time* (May 1, 1989).

Livingston, Neville O'Riley, Alvira Coke et al., plaintiffs; and Island Records Ltd., Tuff Gong Intl. Ltd., defendants. Writ of Summons. Supreme Court of Judicature, Chancery Chambers, England, 1994 (CH 1194 L No. 1076).

McCann, Ian and Harry Hawke. *Bob Marley: The Complete Guide to His Music.* London: Omnibus Press, 2004.

McDarrah, Timothy, and Frank DiGiacomo. "Former Law Partners Duel Over a Song." *New York Post* (October 26, 1990).

McKenzie, Rear Admiral Robert P., press conference, August 9, 1981, Vieques, Puerto Rico.

Markowitz, Alan, and Ian Katz. "Gunman Related to Marley." *Miami Herald* (February 20,1990).

Marley, Rita. "Cross-examination, September 16, 17, 18, and 22, 1992, J. Reid Bingham as Ancillary Administrator of the Estate of Robert Nesta Marley, v. Marvin Zolt; David Steinberg; Greenstein, Gorelick, Price, Silverman & Laveson; Coudert Brothers, et al." United States District Court Southern District of New York (Case No. 86 Civ. 9477 [KC]).

May, Patrick. "Sudden Terror at the Mall." *Miami Herald* (May 25, 1990).

Morgan, Charlie. *Coxsone's Music: A Discography.* Lakeba, Wash.: Outernational (1997).

The New York Times. "Chernobyl Fallout: Apocalyptic Tale and Fear" (July 26, 1986).

Observer Station. *Bob Marley: The Illustrated Disco/Biography.* London: Omnibus Press, 1985.

Oumano, Elena. "R&B Stars Sing with Marley on Ghetto Youth Set." *Billboard* (December 13, 1997).

Partridge, Rob. Unpublished letter to the editor of *The Beat:* "In His 'The Last Word on the Marley Box Set' cover story in the Volume 11 Number 6 issue of *The Beat . . .*" (January 15, 1993).

Pierson, Leroy. Letter to Timothy White. "I'll just list the Wailers titles & labels of some of the rarer discs . . ." (1983).

——. "The Truth About Johnny Too Bad." *Reggae 6 African Beat* 7, no. 5 (1998).

Reagan, President Ronald, address before the Organization of American States, February 24, 1982.

Russell, George, and Wilton Wynn. "A Grand Master's Conspiracy." *Time* (June 8, 1981).

Sheler, Jeffrey L. "Mysteries of the Bible." *U.S. News & World Report* (April 17, 1995).

Sheridan, Maureen. "Peter Tosh, The Last Words and Violent Death of a Reggae Hero." *Musician,* no. 110 (December 1987).

Snowden, Don. "Andrew Tosh Shoulders Reggae Legacy." *Los Angeles Times* (April 7,1988).

Steffens, Roger. "Peter Tosh, Rebel with a Cause." *Reggae and African Beat* 5, no. 1 (1986).

——. "Bunny Comes to Babylon." *Reggae & African Beat* 7, no. 3 (1986).

——. Telephone conversation with Timothy White, offering information on murder of Carly Barrett (April 18, 1987).

——. Foreword. *Reggae & African Beat* 7, no. 3 (1988).

——. Letter to Timothy White. "This is a transcript of the lyrics to the songs . . ." (May 1989).

——. Letter to Timothy White. "Here are a couple of notes for use in refining the next edition . . ." (October 28, 1989).

——. Telephone conversation with Timothy White, offering information on the Wailers in 1968 (June 15, 1990).
——. Telephone conversation with Timothy White, offering background on "Simmer Down" (February 11, 1991).
——. Telephone conversation with Timothy White regarding Peter Tosh discography (April 21, 1991).
——. Letter to Timothy White. "Latest Island-Marley estate update, Chris seems on verge of giving up . . ." (September 1991).
Steffens, Roger, and Leroy Jodie Pierson. *Bob Marley and the Wailers: The Definitive Discography*. Cambridge: Rounder Books, 2005.
——. "The Last Word on the Marley Box Set." *The Beat 11*, no. 6 (1992).
——. Fax to Timothy White regarding reggae discography information (June 25, 1992).
Stone, Carl. "Continuing Crisis of Jamaica's Economy." *Caribbean Contact* (December 1984).
Thomson, Douglas J. C. Letter to Timothy White. "The Wailers music has long been a great interest of mine . . ." (August 10, 1983).
Turner, Michael and Robert Schoenfeld. *Roots Knotty Roots: The Collector's Guide to Jamaican Music (Volume One: 78 and 45rpm Singles)*. Maryland Heights: Nighthawk Records, 2001.
Vlautin, John. Island Records press release of unpublished letter to *The Beat* by Rob Partridge regarding "The Last Word on the Box Set": "It is generally considered to be good professional and ethical journalistic practice to allow responsible replies . . ." (May 24, 1993).
Wendt, Doug. "Reggae In Crisis." *Reggae and African Beat* 6, no. 4 (1987).
White, Timothy. "Bob Marley's Jamaica." *Crawdaddy* (January 1976).
——. "Bush Doctor—Peter Tosh." *Rolling Stone* (April 19, 1978).
——. "Jump Up!" *Rolling Stone* (April 16, 1981).
——. "Bob Marley Finds His Zion." *Rolling Stone* (March 3, 1982).
——. "Who Feels It Knows It—Rita Marley." *Rolling Stone* (April 29, 1982).
——. Request via Certified Mail No. P274-979264, Freedom of Information Officer, Central Intelligence Agency, Washington, D.C. 20505 (September 13, 1982).
——. Deposition of Timothy White. "Held at the offices of Parcher, Arisohn & Hayes, Esqs, 500 Fifth Avenue, N.Y., N.Y., on the 25th day of June, 1986, at 10:35 o'clock a.m., re: Cayman Music, Inc. Plaintiff, Against Rita Marley, As Administratrix of the Estate of Bob Marley, et al., Defendant, Against Danny Sims, Additional Defendant on Counterclaim; revised March 15, 1987." Superior Court of the State of New York (Case No. 24020/84).
——. "The Passing of Peter Tosh/I Am That I Am." *Reggae and African Beat* 6, no. 5 (1987).
——. "Time Will Tell: The Surveillance of a Soul Rebel." *Island Life 1962–1987/25 Years* (1987).
——. "Judge Not (Before You Judge Yourself). Cayman Music Inc. v. the Bob Marley Estate: The Dread Verdict on the Soul Rebel's Legacy." *Reggae and African Beat* 7, no. 3 (1988).
——. "Bob Marley, Reggae's Soul Rebel, Strived to Share the Best of Shantytown with the World, but the Worst of Shantytown Wanted Him Silenced." *Spin* (June 1991).
——. "Walkin' and Talkin'." *The Beat 10*, no. 2 (1991).
——. "Chris Blackwell: An Interview with the Founding Father of the Reggae Music Industry." *Billboard* (July 13, 1991).
——. "The World Party." *Mojo* (March 1995).
——. "Bob Marley: Roots Rock Reggae." *Bob Marley Festival '97 Program* (February 8, 1997).

Index